SELLING DESTINATIONS

DESTINATIONS

Geography for the Travel Professional

Fifth Edition

Marc Mancini, Ph.D.

Department of Travel
West Los Angeles College

DELMAR
CENGAGE Learning™

Australia • Brazil • Japan • Korea • Mexico • Singapore • Spain • United Kingdom • United States

DELMAR
CENGAGE Learning™

**Selling Destinations:
Geography for the Travel
Professional, 5th edition
Marc Mancini**

Vice President, Career and
Professional Editorial: Dave Garza

Director of Learning Solutions:
Sandy Clark

Acquisitions Editor: James Gish

Managing Editor: Larry Main

Product Manager: Anne Orgren

Editorial Assistant: Sarah Timm

Vice President, Career
and Professional Marketing:
Jennifer McAvey

Marketing Director: Wendy Mapstone

Marketing Manager: Kristin McNary

Marketing Coordinator: Scott Chrysler

Production Director: Wendy Troeger

Senior Content Project Manager:
Kathryn B. Kucharek

Art Director: Bethany Casey

For product information and technology assistance, contact us at
Professional & Career Group Customer Support, 1-800-648-7450

For permission to use material from this text or product,
submit all requests online at **cengage.com/permissions.**
Further permissions questions can be e-mailed to
permissionrequest@cengage.com.

Library of Congress Control Number: 2008931911

ISBN-13: 978-1-4354-8581-5
ISBN-10: 1-4354-8581-5

Delmar
5 Maxwell Drive
Clifton Park, NY 12065-2919
USA

Cengage Learning products are represented in Canada by Nelson Education, Ltd.

For your lifelong learning solutions, visit **delmar.cengage.com**
Visit our corporate website at **cengage.com.**

NOTICE TO THE READER

Printed in Canada
3 4 5 6 7 12 11 10

Contents

Preface

Does the sheer volume of things the travel industry expects you to know about the world overwhelm you? Do you ever wonder how that knowledge can be translated to real, everyday career experience? Then *Selling Destinations*—whether you're a student, trainee, or working professional—is written with you in mind.

Who Should Use This Text

Selling Destinations is a geography book for those who sell, or who plan to sell, places. At first glance, it may seem to be primarily a study or reference work for travel counselors, and it is certainly that. *But it will prove equally useful to you even if you're in another segment of the travel industry,* for two reasons. First, you need to know how travel agents deal with geography, because you depend on their ability to sell. Second, everyone in the travel industry, in one way or another, sells places. The insights and strategies that this book gives can be used by anyone who deals with the traveling public: travel supplier reservationists, travel agents, tour guides, sales representatives, cruise directors, corporate travel managers, and more.

    Selling Destinations can be a quick way of bringing yourself up to speed on most major tourist destinations. It can be a powerful and rapid reference tool. And it can become a springboard to other, more specialized treatments of destination geography.

What Makes This Book Unique

As you'll discover, *Selling Destinations* is a very different kind of geography book:

- **It approaches geography from a travel industry perspective.** Important tourist destinations receive detailed treatment in chapters of their own. Secondary destinations merit several pages or paragraphs in special "Potpourri" chapters. Facts and places that travel industry personnel rarely deal with are given only a passing reference (though the appendices direct you to other reference sources that contain the information you'll need).

- **It treats geography as something the travel industry sells.** To be able to match visitors to destinations and services is the key to travel industry success. *Selling Destinations* underscores precisely how you can do this in your day-to-day work.

- **It makes reading about destinations fun.** Some say a geography book needs to be serious. That's nonsense. Your study of destinations can be academically rigorous *and* fun. That's why this textbook uses a breezy, magazine-style prose to make learning about places an enjoyable yet educational experience.

- **It uses many educational devices to make sure you remember what you read.** The biggest problem with most books is that you remember only about 30 percent of what you read. *Selling Destinations* addresses this problem in two ways. First, it limits itself to what you need to know to be a travel professional; it won't clutter your mind with obscure details. Second, its two-color highlighting, lists, headings, subheadings, graphs, tables, photos, and application activities serve to clarify and reinforce information. The result: You absorb a far greater percentage of what you read.

How This Book Is Organized

Selling Destinations' part-and-chapter structure is dictated by travel and touristic concerns.

- **The book is divided into six major parts.** Part I lays a sturdy geographic and sales foundation for all information to come. Parts II through VI cover the world's principal geographic areas: North America; Latin America; Europe; Africa and the Middle East; Asia, Australia, and the South Pacific.

- **A short introductory overview** opens each of Parts II through VI. Each overview is followed by several **in-depth chapters** on major touristic centers. (There are 24 such chapters in the book, each focusing on those destinations most visited by North American tourists.) Each part finishes with a **potpourri chapter** that gathers together those remaining destinations not covered in an in-depth chapter.

- **Three useful appendices** list typical lengths of time spent by tourists in major cities, research resources, and destination-related feature films. A detailed **index** follows.

- **Pronunciation guides** follow place names that are especially difficult. They're set off in brackets and spelled phonetically.

How Each Chapter Is Organized

The organizational subheadings of *Selling Destinations* are critical to the book's sales-geography philosophy:

- An **introduction** gives a historical, cultural, or visitor perspective on the destination. It also lists major geographic features, patterns of tourism, and languages spoken.

- **How Travelers Get There** discusses modes of transportation, national airlines (with airline codes), major airports (also with codes), and traveling times from the United States, if relevant.

- **Weather Patterns** analyzes seasonal weather and touristic patterns.

- **Getting Around** focuses on internal modes of transportation, both in broad subregions and within major cities.

- **Important Places** discusses touristic highlights and day-trip possibilities from central hub cities.

- **Possible Itineraries** lays out typical visitor travel patterns within the destination area.

- **Lodging Options** enumerates the lodging choices of a destination, including principal hotel chains and landmark hotels.

- **Allied Destinations** suggests the typical places that are easily combined with a primary destination as part of a larger itinerary.

- **Cultural Patterns** (where applicable) examines the local cultural behaviors of which travelers should be aware.

- **Factors That Motivate Visitors** analyzes why a person typically travels to the destination covered.

- **Possible Misgivings** enumerates those psychological barriers to a destination—perhaps valid, perhaps not—that a person may have, and how or if they should be countered. While the ability to get beyond objections is essential to travel agents, it's equally valuable to tourist bureau, cruise, and tour personnel.

- **Sales Strategies** lists the extra services that a person may wish to arrange—the kinds that yield extra profits to almost all sellers of travel.

- **Activities** close each chapter. A **Map Activity** tests your knowledge of geographic places and their attractions. A **Case Study** permits you to apply your knowledge to hypothetical travelers. A **Creative Activity** challenges you to take a hypothetical situation in the travel industry and turn it into an innovative solution. Some describe actual scenarios you'd face in various segments of the travel industry. Others are more whimsical; these serve as springboards to deeper creativity. In all cases, the goal is to help you marshal all you know, to tap into your creativity—and to have *fun*. These Creative Activities also lend themselves readily to in-class group solutions.

What Major Visual Elements Are Used

Selling Destinations features nearly 300 visual elements to enliven the information that it presents:

- You'll find more than 100 area, city, state, and country **maps**. As you read the text, you'll be able to follow along on the map; that way you'll instantly know where the place talked about is situated. The maps are simplified to give special attention to cities and areas that tourists frequent.

  Some chapter maps contain symbols. Following is a key to the symbols you will encounter.

  MAP LEGEND:

  ⊛ capital city   ▲ attraction

  ✈ major air gateway   ⛰ mountains

- In many chapters you'll be able to consult a **For Your Information** box that summarizes geographic facts about a major destination, such as population, area, currency, languages spoken, history, and even on which side of the road you should drive.
- **Climate at a Glance** charts will enable you to rapidly determine the typical temperature, rainfall, and tourist season patterns of major world destinations.
- **Qualifying the Traveler** grid boxes will help you identify the types of people who are attracted to the major destinations.
- **Travel Trivia** boxes give you unusual, entertaining, surprising, or even weird bits of information that help round out your understanding of the industry and of the world.
- **Margin Notes** provide intriguing and/or offbeat tangents to the place being covered. These tips for travelers and bits of information will help you better understand each destination.

Trivia comes from the Latin phrase for "three roads." Where three roads met, the Ancient Romans would erect bulletin boards, where they would post little bits of information.

What Isn't Included

It would have been nice to include *everything* that the world has to offer to tourists, but that would have meant a publication bigger than a telephone book. That's why we've concentrated on the *essentials*. For the rest, a number of fine resources—electronic or paper-based—can fill out your knowledge on something we may have chosen to leave out. Those sources are listed in Appendix B.

Selling Destinations deliberately avoids information that can become rapidly outdated or should more appropriately be looked up in standard, frequently revised sources (most of which are listed for you in the appendixes). Such information includes money conversion rates, visa requirements, and the like. This book also gives minimal attention to destinations that regularly suffer from political turmoil, terrorism, epidemics, and similar factors that make a place difficult or inadvisable to sell. Because a destination's touristic climate can change abruptly, we suggest that you consult the U.S. Department of State website at http://travel.state.gov.

How To

Learn as Much as You Possibly Can

Learning about travel destinations is fun! But all those names . . .

Here are a few clues on how you can do your best when studying from *Selling Destinations*. One reminder: If your textbook is owned by your school, *you must not write in it*. If you yourself bought it, however, feel free to use all of the study strategies you're about to learn. Then keep your book for future reference. Consider it an investment. It'll be an extremely valuable resource in your work and, certainly, when you're planning your own future travels.

1 **Use the margins** to write comments, insights, reminders, and extra things your instructor tells you about.

2 **Fill out all the activities**. They're designed to help you reinforce and remember what you're learning.

3 **Use colored highlighters** to underscore what you have trouble remembering. Key concepts are already boldfaced or italicized, so you have a head start. But using, say, yellow to highlight difficult concepts and blue to indicate things you're really having trouble with is a great way to study.

4 **Use index cards** to review. Imagine a question that could appear on a test and put it on one side of the card. Put the answer on the other side. Then shuffle the cards and use them to review. Put aside the cards you have trouble with and come back to them later.

What You'll Be Able To Do

Of course, learning is not just about facts and ideas. It's about what you can *do* with that information. So here's a list of behavioral objectives; that is, how you will apply what you study in this book:

- Explain the relationship between sales and geographic knowledge
- Relate the impact of general geographic principles and facts on travel and tourism
- Explain how most career paths in the travel and tourism industry require familiarity with destination information
- Arrange transportation to the world's great tourism centers
- Describe the likely weather patterns at most tourist destinations, at any time of the year
- Predict the likely volume of tourists visiting most major destinations at various seasons
- Delineate the internal transportation options of most major countries and cities
- Describe the lodging options at most major destinations
- Lay out typical visitor itineraries in major countries
- Suggest destinations that are often combined with visits to major destinations
- Give special travel tips that can enhance a trip

- Interpret the cultural patterns unique to major foreign destinations
- List the factors that motivate a traveler to visit major destinations
- Describe the kinds of people who are drawn to a certain destination
- Enumerate the principal misgivings a traveler might have about a visit to most of the world's major destinations
- Cite opportunities to upsell and cross-sell major destinations
- Locate major destinations on general and specific maps
- Look up information that is of a more specific nature on a destination
- Apply all of the above to hypothetical situations

To the Instructor or Trainer

If you're new to *Selling Destinations*, welcome! You're now part of a family of over 400 educators who rely on our textbook to bring students and trainees up to speed on travel geography. If you've taught from *Selling Destinations'* first four editions, you'll notice some changes. We've retained what you've told us are the strongest features of our book while reshaping its voice to speak to the needs of all future travel professionals—not just travel agents. In this way, we can help you to better adjust to the swiftly changing landscape of travel education.

Selling Destinations—a combined textbook–workbook—was created with your pragmatic needs in mind. It can serve as your primary textbook; the many features listed above make it extremely effective when you're dealing with students or trainees who must round out their checkered knowledge of world geography. Or it may be used as a sales application supplement to more conventional texts. It's well suited to compressed, one-semester geography programs, yet it lends itself easily to programs with multiple geography courses. As we mentioned, *Selling Destinations* works equally well for those of you who teach travel generically (for *all* travel career segments) and those who focus mostly on travel agent skills. Its format lends itself especially well to online courses.

To further encourage your flexibility in using this book, each chapter is independent from the others. You can present chapters in whatever order you prefer. Note that "Part" sections, however, set the stage for what's to come and are, therefore, less adaptable to shifting.

A feature that will be especially useful to you is the *Instructional Resource Manual*, which amplifies the book and makes your teaching much easier. Among its contents: a set of behavioral objectives, teaching tips, answers to all textbook activities, supplementary research activities, blank maps for reproducing and for quizzing students, and an extensive test bank. In this edition, for the first time, the blank maps are also available online as PowerPoint slides.

Information given in this textbook has been cross-checked against multiple sources, all of which are cited in the appendices. Whenever possible, firsthand experience—that of the author or of various destination experts—has been used to buttress content. If you spot any changes or additions you feel should be made—an important new attraction, a changed hotel name, and so on—please send your comment to Dr. Marc Mancini at West Los Angeles College, 9000 Overland Ave., Culver City, CA 90230, USA. If we use it, we'll be pleased to credit you in our next edition.

To Our Canadian Educators

A special Canadian version of *Selling Destinations*, with extra chapters on Canada and other Canada-specific content, can be ordered from Nelson Canada.

Acknowledgments

The author wishes to acknowledge Betsy Crockett and her class for their careful reading of this text; they helped ensure the book's accuracy and completeness. The author also would like to thank the following reviewers:

Rosalie Fernandez, Kapi'olani Community College, Honolulu, HI

Amy Hart, Columbus State Community College, Columbus, OH

John Lindsay, Highline Community College, Des Moines, WA

Ezat Moradi, Houston Community College, Houston, TX

Patricia A. Schwenk, Mohawk College of Applied Arts and Technology, Hamilton, Ontario, Canada

And a special thanks to my research assistants, Robert J. Elisberg (first edition), Charlene Ambrose (third edition), and Karen Fukushima (second through fifth editions), for their efficient, thorough, and enthusiastic support throughout this project, as well as to Justus Ghormley for his wonderful photographs.

Marc Mancini

Travel Trivia

Real North American Places with "Weathered" Names

Cool, California	Cyclone, Pennsylvania	Sprinkle, Texas
Floods, British Columbia	Rains, South Carolina	Rainy River, Ontario
Hurricane, Utah	Mist, Oregon	Sunshine, Maine
El Niño, Mexico	Thunder Bay, Ontario	Snow, Oklahoma
Tropic, Utah	Seabreeze, North Carolina	Thunder Butte, South Dakota
Tradewinds, Texas	Sunshine, Wyoming	Stormville, Pennsylvania
Windy, Kentucky	Cold Lake, Alberta	Arctic, Indiana

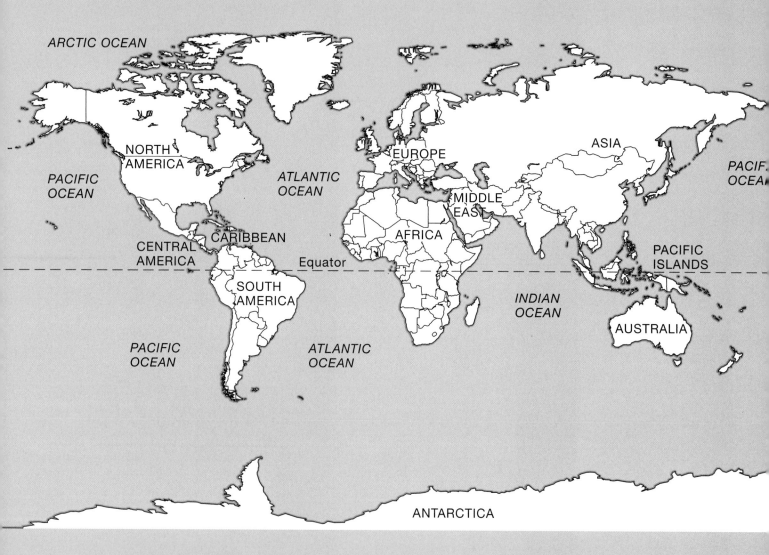

PART I

BASIC INGREDIENTS
Geography and How to Sell It

Here's a surprise: If you're in the travel business, you don't really sell travel. What you sell is *geography*. For example, if someone flies on a specific flight at a certain time and price, yes, they've bought *travel. They're going from one place to another.* But the act of traveling in an aircraft holds little pleasure. No, the reason that person is traveling is to get to a place, and places are what geography is all about.

To perform any travel-related sales job in a professional manner, you must be aware of at least some aspects of the places that travelers favor. Corporate travel managers; incentive operators; convention and meeting planners; tourist bureau representatives; hotel sales, marketing, and reservation staff; tour planners; cruise personnel; and airline employees—they all have to know their geography much better than the average person to do their jobs right.

The most obvious sellers of destinations are travel agents. That's why this book often examines the world through their eyes. But even if you're not a travel agent, you still need to know how they deal with geography, for virtually every person who serves the travel industry—including hospitality professionals—are somehow affected by how travel agents sell.

No matter which segment of the industry you're in, though, you'll profit enormously from a deep and lasting familiarity with the world you sell, the kind that the following chapters will give you. And don't forget that word *sell*. The object is not simply to inform people about a destination, which is worthwhile in itself, but to motivate them to *buy* that destination—with their hearts as well as with their wallets.

The typical North American vacations with three other people for three days and three nights.

Basic Concepts of Destination

Selling a place is an art. It requires knowledge of the destination *and* of the traveler. The following five strategies will help you maximize your ability to sell a place.

1. You Must Know All the Relevant Facts about a Destination

Travel geography differs from all other forms of geography in this way: It concentrates on those features about a destination that affect travel and tourism. To know that people in Burundi speak Kirundi, that one of Burkina Faso's principal crops is groundnuts, and that Montana is America's leading producer of tin may make you more culturally literate and certainly a winner at Trivial Pursuit. But will this knowledge help you in the travel industry?

Agawam, Massachusetts, has the lowest zip code in the United States: 01001.

Probably not. The likelihood is very low that anyone will ever ask you about Kirundi, groundnuts, or tin. (For that matter, it's improbable that you'll ever encounter anyone going to Burundi or to Burkina Faso.)

On the other hand, to know that many Swedes speak English, that a good place to lodge New York City–bound travelers is just south of Central Park, and that opals are a good buy in Sydney *are* useful geography-related facts. Climate, transportation options, itinerary routings, hotel locations, and key attractions—these are things you need to know to motivate people's interests, to help shape their travel experience, and to sell and serve them effectively and well.

2. You Must Know What Kind of Traveler Favors a Destination

What's the biggest mistake that travel professionals make? To believe that what they like everyone else will like. Maybe you're the type of person who adores classical music, but hates lying on the beach. So you favor such destinations as Vienna and Milan, but not Hawaii or the Caribbean. After all, doesn't everyone enjoy a concert by the Vienna Boys' Choir or an opera at Milan's La Scala? No. Each place attracts its own type of visitor. Matching destination with traveler type is the key to sensitive, efficient, and profitable marketing and selling.

How many "types" of travelers are there? What motivates them to travel? There are countless ways to slice the tourist "pie." One way is to separate them into **leisure** travelers (those who travel for pleasure) and **business** travelers. You can further subdivide each of these broad categories. Business travelers, for example, may go somewhere to attend a convention or to conduct business and may add a vacation component to their trip.

Tourists whose primary motivation is leisure, in turn, can be subdivided into many types. One approach categorizes leisure travelers into 12 groups:

- **History buffs** primarily want to learn about a destination's past. They see travel as a way to experience what they've studied and read about.
- **Culture seekers** are fascinated by different ways of life. They're intrigued by how other people express their culture via distinctive customs, food, art, and so on.
- **Ethnic travelers** are like culture seekers, but they wish, above all, to explore the culture from which their ancestors came.
- **Religious pilgrims** seek an experience tied to their spiritual beliefs.
- **Environmental travelers** are drawn to scenery and the beauty of places and include two important subsets: ecotourists, who wish to see places such as the Brazilian rainforest, where flora and fauna are endangered; and campers, who like to experience a natural place (though it might be from a well-insulated RV).
- **Recreational travelers** wish to participate in such "mass-appeal" sports as golf, tennis, snorkeling, or skiing.
- **Adventure seekers** prefer more demanding and hardy sports or activities, such as white-water rafting, surfing, mountain hiking, or diving—frequently in off-the-beaten-path locations. Their tastes can even run to true physical challenges, such as mountain climbing or skydiving. This is called hard adventure travel, in contrast to more mainstream "soft" adventure tourism.
- **Entertainment seekers** are drawn to activities such as dancing, partying, gambling, and nightclub shows. Their tastes can also run to more "serious" entertainment, such as theater and concert performances.
- **Shoppers** love to buy things on trips, and are perhaps a subset of the previous categories, because they view purchasing as entertainment or adventure.
- **Sensual travelers** wish to indulge their senses via, say, gourmet dining, sunbathing, or a stay at a spa.

■ **Status seekers** travel to trendy, often expensive destinations, and sometimes bring back significant purchases. They define themselves—both to themselves and to others—by the places they visit.

■ **Interpersonal travelers** voyage primarily to socialize and meet people. An important subcategory is people who travel to visit family and friends—and often stay with them. This motivation accounts for the largest number of personal trips.

As you read this listing, did you think of a place that fits each kind of traveler? Did you think of someone you know who is the type described? Good, you're already thinking like a true travel professional. And did you imagine individuals who combine the traits of several or many categories? Great, because most people do travel for multiple reasons, even though one primary motivator may control their destination choices.

To try your hand at matching traveler types to destinations, turn to the end of this chapter and do Activity 1.

3. You Must Know the Individual Client You Are Serving

Now imagine that you are, say, a travel agent. You do understand what kind of client favors a place. But are you able to identify that type of client when he or she comes to you for advice? In sales, the act of analyzing a client's needs and wants is called **qualifying** or **interviewing**. This is usually achieved by asking open-ended questions, called **probes**. Asking the right questions and listening carefully to the client's answer is the key to effective qualifying.

What kind of questions will you ask? At first, of course, you must determine the basics, such as traveler name, possible destinations, dates, budget restrictions, and so on. But then you can probe, for example, to find out what the person does for a living. That might provide a clue. A university history professor might really enjoy the idea of going to Europe, but an Orlando vacation might leave the traveler cold.

Other possible probes: "Is your trip for business or pleasure?" (Business clients usually have much more focused travel plans.) "Are you an active outdoor person?" "Do you like adventurous places?" "Is this a family vacation?" "What was your favorite vacation and why?" A good way to probe is via contrasting questions: "Do you want to rest on your vacation or be active?" "Do you want to visit someplace exotic or a more familiar kind of culture?"

Note that such questions help you determine what traveler type you're dealing with—an essential step to match the person's needs with your recommendations. Failing to do so can lead to a mismatch—something sure to lead to dissatisfaction, complaints, or worse.

Qualifying isn't a skill used only by travel agents. Cruise, air, and tour reservationists often must clarify a caller's destination needs. Tourist bureau personnel are constantly assessing which offerings will appeal to potential visitors to the destinations they represent. Hotel concierges must recommend all sorts of destination-related experiences; the best ones ask hotel guests plenty of questions before "selling" their recommendation.

Several other points bear discussion:

■ Don't expect people who are thinking about a vacation to know exactly where they want to go. One study concluded that half of all travelers start out with only the vaguest idea of where to spend their vacation. The others do have a rather specific destination in mind, but they hope that you'll bring efficiency, quality, and insight to their trip.

■ A person's primary motivation can change from one trip to the next. On one vacation, Mr. Jones may want to visit every major museum in Europe, but on the next, he'll want to kick back at an isolated beach resort.

■ Always review travelers' needs with them before going on to make your recommendations. This tests whether you understand their needs and permits them to add to their list.

Nearly 1.6 billion people will travel outside of their own country by 2020, according to the World Tourism Organization.

- When you recommend a particular destination, explicitly describe how it satisfies the person's wishes. It's not enough to say, "The Cayman Islands is where I think you should go." Put it this way: "You wanted to do some diving, not travel too far, and go in April. The Caymans have great diving, are only a two-hour flight away, and usually have great weather in April."

- Your recommendations should also convey a sense that you know the place intimately. Travelers realize that a travel professional can't have visited every place on the globe. But they do hope that in the absence of actual experience, you still "know your stuff" and have the equivalent of firsthand experience.

- Sprinkling little "insider tips" into your recommendations will help establish you as the professional that you are.

4. You Must Be Ready to Respond to a Person's Misgivings

Your descriptions of a place may be so powerful that closing the sale will be easy. But sometimes matching a person to a place isn't enough. Fears, either rational or emotional, may stand in the way: "A trip to Tokyo sounds great, but how will I be able to communicate with the Japanese?" "I'd like to go to New York City, but isn't it awfully expensive?" "An African wildlife safari sounds wonderful, but isn't it dangerous?"

Faced with such objections, a travel professional, when appropriate, provides sales-building responses, or **counters**. You should tell someone who worries about communicating in Japan that many of Tokyo's tourist industry personnel speak some English. You can recommend less expensive hotels or weekend hotel packages to New York-bound travelers. An African wildlife safari is less intimidating if you counsel someone to travel as part of a tour offered by a reputable tour operator.

To allay misgivings isn't always the proper approach. Sometimes the objections a person brings up are so valid—say, the country really is too dangerous or is totally inappropriate in some other way—that you must say so and counter with a completely different destination. To simply dismiss an objection without thought is unprofessional and unethical, and could even trigger a lawsuit later on.

5. You Must Search for Enhancement Opportunities

Three general strategies permit you to enhance your company's profits from someone's trip, as well as enhance the traveler's experience. They're especially used in travel agency, car rental, lodging, and cruise sales environments:

- **Upselling** allows you to improve the quality of the traveler's vacation while generally increasing your profits. Some examples: superior-category hotel rooms, first-class seats on a flight, a full-size car rental instead of a compact one, a more extensive **FIT** for a client. (FIT stands for foreign independent travel, but it often refers to any itinerary created from scratch, not just foreign ones.) Always start by recommending the best product that is reasonably appropriate to a person's needs, then work down. To start with budget recommendations and work up is a poor sales-and-service approach. Effective upselling also is very much tied to geographic factors. For example, a hotel's appeal may come from its proximity to prime attractions, or to the ocean views its rooms afford (both geographic factors). Also, a person is far more likely to be tempted by a convertible car rental if the destination's weather is warm and inviting.

- **Cross-selling** requires you to offer "extra" products or services. For example, people often contact a travel agent only to book a flight. They haven't thought about anything else; they may even wait until they get to their destination to set up other services. This deprives the agent and the agency of potential income and the client of possible savings or convenience. Good travel agents offer to book hotels, car rentals, train trips, theater tickets, city tours, meal plans, boat charters, travel insurance, airport-to-hotel transfers, and whatever else seems appropriate. They underscore the benefits of these services to their client's vacation plans. And they point out the advantage of booking these things in advance.

Cross-selling is much simpler than it used to be: Computers now allow access to all sorts of services. Further, **all-inclusive packages**—combinations of services that can be booked with one call—have made cross-selling easy. Independent tour packages, escorted tours, all-inclusive resorts, and cruises enable agencies to draw profits from virtually everything their clients do—including eat and drink.

- **Follow-up** conversations with customers enable companies and their employees to find out how a trip went. This follow-up often yields geographically relevant insights. Follow-up surveys and client feedback enable cruise lines to rethink their itineraries, tour operators to identify hot new destinations, and airlines to apply for new routes.

Let's say you're a travel agent. Follow-up will help you deepen your own destination knowledge. For example, a client could return from St. Martin and tell you that he couldn't get around the island without renting a car. In the future, you'll know to recommend a car rental to a St. Martin-bound tourist. Follow-up also cements the client–seller relationship, offers an opportunity to make amends for problems experienced during the trip, and opens the door to selling future trips to the client.

Are cross-selling, upselling, and a follow-up sale manipulative? They can be, but only when you pressure someone into buying something that person doesn't want or shouldn't have. Travelers often have vague, low, or unrealistic limits on what they want. Your job is to focus on their plans, suggest ways to genuinely improve their vacation, and perhaps even save them a few dollars (since services arranged in advance, or as part of a package, are often less costly).

How Other Travel Professionals Sell Places

We used the example of a travel agent to explain each of the five sales and service tactics above. But if you're contemplating some other career in the industry, these sales techniques very much apply to you, too:

- A cruise activities director may recommend and sell shore excursion tours.
- Airline reservationists can upsell a caller to the comfort of business class on a long overseas flight.
- A car rental representative can suggest a convertible for the client's tropical vacation.
- A hotel clerk or concierge can make shopping, restaurant, and nightlife arrangements for the hotel guest.
- Flight attendants often answer questions about that flight's destination or explain the many places where their airline flies (a key consideration for members of frequent-flyer programs).
- A tour conductor relates all sorts of facts about the destinations that the tour group will visit.
- An incentive-trip planner can show corporate clients how certain add-on activities will enhance their employees' experience.
- A representative from a convention and tourist bureau can show an audience how the destination fulfills their expectations.
- A hotel's sales and marketing director must promote the geographic benefits of staying at the property, for example, ocean-view rooms, proximity to attractions or businesses, easy access to public transportation, closeness to trails at a ski resort, and so on.
- Even professionals in the food-services industry must think about geography. Location is one of the key elements of whether a theme restaurant (e.g., Planet Hollywood) will succeed or fail.

About 50 percent of travelers pick the restaurants they will eat in before arriving at their destination.

So the ultimate purpose of both sales and service in the travel field is this: to create the perfect match between the desires of a traveler and the assets of a place. But to do this, you must not only love places but also know them.

Geography—The Great Unknown

Gil Grosvenor, chairman of the National Geographic Society, tells of a couple who once told him that they might be taking a cruise to Las Vegas (a desert-bound city). Writer S. J. Perelman relates that he once told a student that, on graduating from college, she should travel around the world. Her response was, "I know, but there are so many places I'd rather see first!" Travel agents make embarrassing mistakes, too. A traveler was once found wandering around the airport in Oakland, California, asking where the New Zealand immigration officials were. His travel agent had mistakenly booked him on a flight to Oakland, instead of Auckland, his intended destination.

A *USA Today* poll discovered that one in seven Americans can't find the United States on a world map. One in five is unable to identify a single country on a map of Europe. One in four can't find the Pacific Ocean, even though it covers one-third of the surface of the earth.

You might wear clothing made in Indonesia, drive a Japanese car fueled by Saudi Arabian oil, watch a British program on a South Korean television set, and eat Mexican food while being served by a Salvadoran. But do you know precisely where any of these places are?

To be living in this century and to not know the world is a shameful indictment of our education system. But to be a travel professional and not to know geography is something else. Would you trust a physician who didn't know anatomy, a builder who didn't know how to read blueprints, or a bank teller who didn't understand math? Should the general public trust travel professionals who can't read maps, who don't know that summer comes to Australia in December, or who book clients bound for the nation of Colombia to the city of Columbia, South Carolina? That has happened, too.

But you can make a difference. You can decide to know the world you sell. And it starts right now with a commitment to understand the underpinnings of travel geography itself.

The Kinds of Maps

Maps are the blueprints of travel. Dozens of types of maps exist; these are the ones travel professionals work with the most:

Flat Maps. Standard flat maps are those we're most familiar with. They come in many varieties, with the "Mercator projection" (see Figure I–1) the most commonly used.

Because you can't flatten out the curved earth, flat maps are somewhat distorted, especially when the whole world is displayed; extreme northern and southern areas may become grossly magnified. In Figure I–1, a typical map, Greenland appears larger than the United States. In reality, the United States is more than four times larger than Greenland. A way to remember: Maps that can lie flat, lie (i.e., they're inaccurate).

Flat maps mislead in a second way. If you draw a trip on such a map as a straight line—which seems logical—you'll be making a big mistake. On most flat maps, the shortest distance between two geographic points should be traced out as a *curved* line (often called a great circle route and always arcing toward polar regions). For example, the shortest route from Los Angeles to Cairo might appear, on a flat map, to be on Alitalia Airlines via Rome or Paris. But if you look at a polar projection map (see Figure I–2) or trace the route on a globe, you'll see that going on Finnair via Helsinki will be a bit shorter. There is another surprise: From New York, the shortest way to Bangkok, Singapore, and Beijing is via Helsinki. So when looking at world maps, remember that curved routes are usually the most direct.

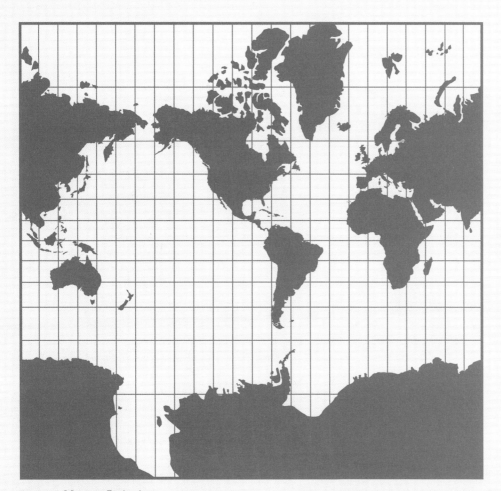

Figure I–1 Mercator Projection

Route Maps. These are useful reference tools. Each airline often distributes a map that shows all the routes that it flies. This can be a handy visual aid if you're trying to keep a traveler on one airline for a trip, either for fare reasons or to help build up frequent-flyer miles. AAA also produces superb route maps, including some that give driving times between major cities.

Globes. Even though globes are awkward to use and lack detail, they're the most accurate maps around. Keep one handy. They're fun to play with and often help you plot out itineraries.

Locator Maps. These are often found in travel industry reference sources. Usually representing a small area, such as a city, they help you find the locations of attractions and hotels. Locator maps indicate places through a grid of numbers and letters rather than with the degrees of a conventional map (see Figure I–3).

Mental Maps. A mental map represents the way you picture geography in your mind. Mental maps can be deceiving: The farther away a destination is, the more simple, closer together, and error prone the mental map becomes. For instance, people who have never been to Europe may think they can drive around to see most of its major cities in a week or two, that Paris is a day's drive from Rome, that a cruise on the Danube takes only a few days. In reality, Europe is bigger than the entire United States, Rome is nearly a thousand-mile trip from Paris, and the Danube is so long that most cruises last more than a week. For a well-known, amusing illustration of what a distant place seems like mentally, see Figure I–4.

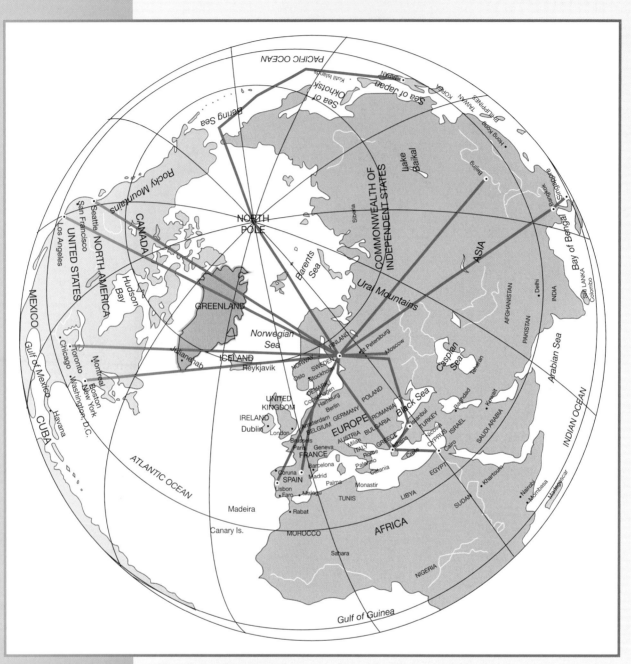

Figure I–2 Polar Routes
Source: Courtesy of Finnair

Photographing the World

Satellite photos of the earth as seen from space were once accessible only to military analysts, scientists, and spies. Now you can see just about any important place in the world via Google Earth, Yahoo! Maps, or Microsoft's Live Search Maps, right there on your home computer.

Such photos have many applications to travel. Is that hotel right on the beach? Is there a massive remodel going on at that resort? Is the lodge really that close to the ski lifts? 3-D technologies even permit you to "test drive" the streets of, say, Manhattan before you actually get there, and from a ground-level, lifelike perspective.

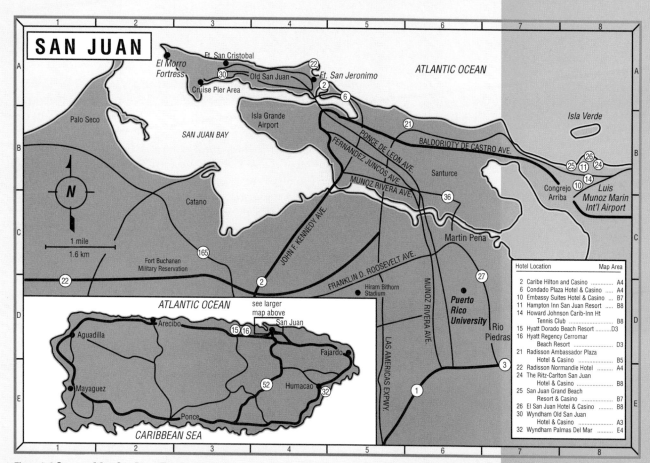

Figure I–3 Locator Map San Juan, Puerto Rico
Source: Hotel and Travel Index/Reed Travel Group

The map includes the following labels and hotel locations:

SAN JUAN

El Morro Fortress, Ft. San Cristobal, Old San Juan, Ft. San Jeronimo, ATLANTIC OCEAN, Cruise Pier Area, Isla Grande Airport, Isla Verde, Palo Seco, SAN JUAN BAY, PONCE DE LEON AVE., BALDORIOTY DE CASTRO AVE., FERNANDEZ JUNCOS AVE., Santurce, MUNOZ RIVERA AVE., Congrejo Arriba, Luis Munoz Marin Int'l Airport, Catano, JOHN F. KENNEDY AVE., Martin Pena, 1 mile 1.6 km, Fort Buchanan Military Reservation, FRANKLIN D. ROOSEVELT AVE., Hiram Bithorn Stadium, Puerto Rico University, Rio Piedras, MUNOZ RIVERA AVE., LAS AMERICAS EXPWY.

Inset map: ATLANTIC OCEAN, see larger map above, San Juan, Arecibo, Aguadilla, Fajardo, Mayaguez, Humacao, Ponce, CARIBBEAN SEA

Hotel Location	Map Area
2 Caribe Hilton and Casino	A4
6 Condado Plaza Hotel & Casino	A4
10 Embassy Suites Hotel & Casino	B7
11 Hampton Inn San Juan Resort	B8
14 Howard Johnson Carib-Inn Ht Tennis Club	B8
15 Hyatt Dorado Beach Resort	D3
16 Hyatt Regency Cerromar Beach Resort	D3
21 Radisson Ambassador Plaza Hotel & Casino	B5
22 Radisson Normandie Hotel	A4
24 The Ritz-Carlton San Juan Hotel & Casino	B8
25 San Juan Grand Beach Resort & Casino	B7
26 El San Juan Hotel & Casino	B8
30 Wyndham Old San Juan Hotel & Casino	A3
32 Wyndham Palmas Del Mar	E4

Figure I–4 A Perspective

Other Map Considerations

Several other map-related components have an impact on a travel professional's sales experience.

Hemispheres. Everything north of the equator is called the Northern Hemisphere, and everything south, the Southern Hemisphere (see Figure I–5). Seasons in the **Northern Hemisphere** are familiar to us: January comes in winter, and July in summer. But in the **Southern Hemisphere**, January has summer weather, July, winter weather. When selling travelers a Southern Hemisphere destination, keep these reversed seasons in mind. Remember, too, that the world is also often divided into a **Western Hemisphere** (North and South America) and an **Eastern Hemisphere** (everything else).

Latitude. Latitude is the distance measured north and south of the equator (expressed in standard geography as *degrees*). The farther away from the equator your destination, the greater the variations will be between seasonal temperatures and between hours of night and day.

For example, **Point Barrow**, a north-shore Alaska town at a **polar latitude**, might be an intriguing destination for some in June and July. Why? Because that's when temperatures there are warmest and daylight is longest. Indeed, the summer midnight sun is a unique experience. But December and January would be a terrible time for such a visit, for darkness and bitter cold prevail. Remember that these seasonal days are exactly the opposite in the Southern Hemisphere: A trip to Antarctica, an exotic and increasingly popular journey, would be best in December or January, worst in June or July.

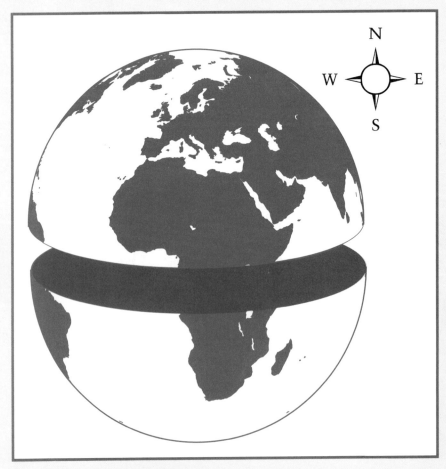

Figure I–5 Hemispheres

Death Valley, 250 miles east of Los Angeles, recorded a temperature of 134°F on July 10, 1913.

The earth's magnetic north pole (where compass needles point) is in Canada, almost 600 miles away from the actual North Pole. It also drifts constantly, moving about 6 to 25 miles per year.

As one gets closer to the equator, seasonal and daylight differences become less pronounced. For instance, Nairobi, Kenya (in Africa), sits just south of the equator. Unlike Point Barrow, where the average temperatures fluctuate more than 70°F between summer and winter, Nairobi—at a **tropical latitude**—sees a yearly fluctuation of only about 8 degrees and minimal variation of daylight. Areas between tropical and polar latitudes are called **temperate latitudes** and have neither pronounced nor minimal variations. Because of the absence of extremes, most major industrialized nations lie within this temperate zone.

By the way, most maps represent latitude lines (also known as parallels) as horizontal lines, measured in degrees. A good memory trick: LATitude lines are FLAT.

Longitude. Longitude is the distance east and west of an arbitrary line, called the **prime meridian**, which passes through the Old Royal Observatory in Greenwich, England. Represented as vertical lines on most maps, longitude lines (like latitudes) are measured in degrees. Longitude will have less of an impact on your selling destinations, except in one respect: Time zones tend to parallel longitude lines (also known as meridians).

Before the late 1800s, each city had its own time, determined by the sun-caused shadows on a sundial. Railroads found it next to impossible to create accurate schedules or timetables. So, in 1884, the world's major nations agreed to create 24 standard time zones, each extending over about 15 degrees of longitude (see Figure I–6). Because the prime meridian is located there, Greenwich became the reference point (called Greenwich Mean Time, or GMT). If it's 1 P.M. in Greenwich, it's five hours earlier, that is, 8 A.M. in Washington, D.C. (expressed as –5); conversely, in Tokyo, it's 10 P.M. (expressed as +9).

Time zones aren't all that regular. For example, China—even though it extends through four theoretical time zones—observes only one time, that closest to Beijing, the capital. In other places, the zone's boundaries zigzag around cities, islands, lakes, or mountains. India should have two time zones, but has averaged the two together. Instead of being, say, two o'clock in the west and three o'clock in the east, it's *two-thirty*

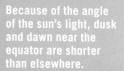

Because of the angle of the sun's light, dusk and dawn near the equator are shorter than elsewhere.

Russia is the world's largest country. It spans 11 time zones.

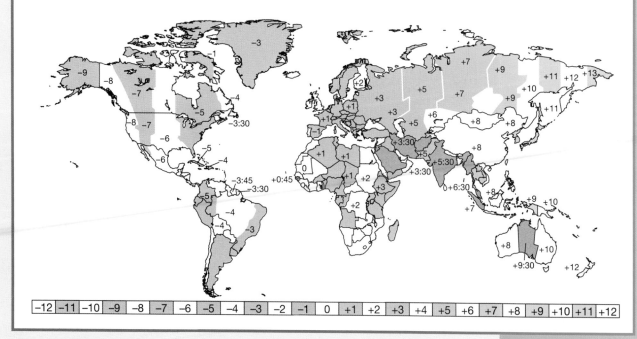

Figure I–6 Time Zones

across the entire country. Daylight savings time, when clocks are set forward to extend daylight into evening hours, complicates things even more. (Arizona, Hawaii, and parts of Indiana don't even observe daylight savings time.)

A trip that crosses many time zones creates that tired feeling called **jet lag** and could affect the traveler in many other ways. A flight from Los Angeles to Miami takes about five hours, but the passenger, because of the time zones, arrives at a time that's about eight hours later. For example, a passenger leaving Los Angeles at noon flies five hours and arrives at 8 P.M., Miami time. That's why business travelers often book a morning departure for an eastward transcontinental flight; otherwise, they'd arrive at their destination late in the evening. For westbound travel, the problem is less severe: Someone leaving Miami for Los Angeles could depart at 1:30 P.M., fly for about five hours, and yet arrive at 3:30 P.M., Los Angeles time. Because it stretches out their workday, many business travelers count on this.

The International Date Line. A rather challenging bit of time zone figuring involves the international date line, a vertical zigzagging line that bisects the Pacific Ocean (see Figure I–7). Crossing it requires a bit of complicated thinking, often expressed as "gaining a day" or "losing a day." Remember the following and you won't be bewildered: (1) When you cross the date line traveling westward, the day changes to the next day—for example, Tuesday, say, at 2 P.M. immediately becomes Wednesday at 2 P.M.; and (2) when you cross the line traveling eastward, the day changes to the previous day—Thursday becomes Wednesday, for example. The time of the day (except at midnight) means nothing. A traveler could cross at 2 P.M., 7 A.M., or 10 A.M. It's all the same. The day changes (but the hour remains the same).

> The international date line is on the opposite side of the earth from the prime meridian.

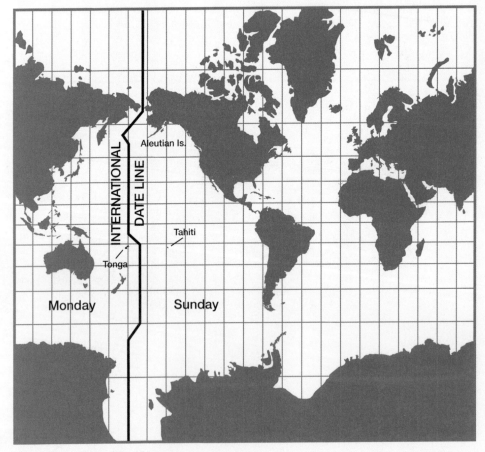

Figure I–7 International Date Line

Let's look at an example. Passengers flying from Honolulu westward to Tokyo on a Monday morning departure would arrive after about a nine-hour flight. But it would be Tuesday, because they crossed the date line. In turn, if they flew from Tokyo on a Saturday morning, they would arrive in Honolulu on Friday, again because they crossed the date line, this time west to east.

Because the flight is long and many time zones are crossed, the complications can be even greater. If you were to leave Honolulu for Tokyo at 11 P.M. on Wednesday, it would become Thursday an hour after departure, and you haven't even crossed the date line yet. A little later, you would cross the date line (on Thursday), at which point it would become Friday! So, you left on Wednesday and arrived on Friday, even though you flew only nine hours.

Confused? Don't worry. Airline schedules give arrival times that are already adjusted for time-zone crossings and for lost or gained days (indicated by some sort of symbol next to the time). If you're an airline reservationist or a travel agent, you won't have to do the complicated equations. But *do* make sure that you know which day the passenger will be arriving, or you may book the hotel stay for the wrong day.

Elapsed Flying Time and the 24-Hour Clock. One thing people often ask and isn't always given in airline timetables: How long will a flight take? First, you must understand that time in the travel business is often expressed as a four-digit number: 7:00 A.M. is 0700, 11:25 A.M. is 1125, noon is 1200. Afternoon and evening continue up to the digit 24: 1:00 P.M. is 1300, 7:30 P.M. is 1930, midnight is 2400 (or 0000, to represent the beginning of the day).

To figure out elapsed flying time within one time zone, simply subtract the departure time of a flight from the arrival time. If a flight leaves Paris at 0800 and arrives in Lyon at 0900, the flight took one hour. If a plane leaves San Diego at 1520 and lands in San Francisco at 1645, the flight took one hour, 25 minutes.

What happens when time zones are crossed? Then it gets a bit more difficult, adding or subtracting the number of time zones. Many travel reference resources give charts that enable you to figure out complex elapsed flying-time problems. Fortunately, airline reservation systems compute elapsed flying time automatically.

Landforms

All destinations relate, in some way, to a landform. Let's now look at the principal landforms and how they're linked to the destinations you may deal with.

Continents. Continents are the major landmasses of the earth (see Figure I–8). There are seven continents. (Some people argue that there are only six; they think of Europe and Asia as one continent, *Eurasia*.) You'll likely deal most with **North America** and **Europe**, but **Asia, Australia, South America,** and **Africa** all boast destinations you may someday sell. Even **Antarctica** has become a destination for tourists via cruises from Chile, Argentina, and New Zealand.

Islands. Because of their natural, isolated beauty, islands are often major destinations. Thousands of them cover the earth, but the most popular groupings are found in the **Caribbean,** in the **Mediterranean** (especially south and east of the Greek mainland), and throughout the Pacific (see Figure I–8).

Cays. Also called *keys,* cays are sandy coral islands that are low and small, examples: the **Cayman Islands** and the **Florida Keys. Atolls** are also small coral islands, but they're usually ringlike and partially or totally enclose a lagoon.

Peninsulas and Capes. Both of these are projections of land into the water. Generally, peninsulas are longer than capes. Among the peninsulas that are popular destinations are **Gaspe,** Quebec; **Baja,** Mexico; **Iberia** (which contains Spain and Portugal); and **Florida.** Some touristically important capes are **Cape Cod,** Massachusetts, and **Cape Canaveral,** Florida (see Figure I–8).

At the moment it sets over the ocean, especially in tropical places, the sun often seems, for a split second, to flash green.

Antarctica has the highest average altitude of any continent.

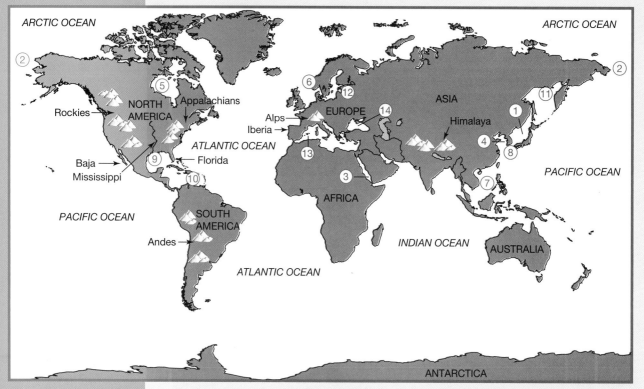

Figure I–8 Landforms and Waterways of the World: 1—Sea of Japan; 2—Bering Sea; 3—Red Sea; 4—Yellow Sea; 5—Hudson Bay; 6—North Sea; 7—South China Sea; 8—East China Sea; 9—Gulf of Mexico; 10—Caribbean; 11—Sea of Okhotsk; 12—Baltic Sea; 13—Mediterranean Sea; 14—Black Sea

Panhandles. The term *panhandle* is often applied to a narrow portion of a country or state that "sticks out" into another. For example, Alaska's panhandle extends southward into Canada and Florida's panhandle protrudes westward into Alabama.

Reefs. Reefs are ridges of land that rise to or near the surface of water. They're often found just offshore. Composed of sand, rock, and coral, reefs can offer superb diving opportunities. Major reef diving and snorkeling areas lie off Australia's northeast coast; off the east coasts of Africa and Brazil; and throughout the Caribbean, the South Pacific, Indonesia, and the Philippines.

Mountains

Mountains profoundly affect travel. Their dramatic beauty impresses virtually every kind of visitor. Their snow-covered slopes attract skiers. Their forbidding heights can make travel slow and indirect. And volcanic mountains often put on quite a show (and pose an ever-present danger).

Mountains also affect climate. When moisture-bearing winds strike a mountain, precipitation often results at its peak and on its **windward** side. On the opposite side of the mountain, the **leeward** side, it's often much drier (see Figure I–9). For example, the winds that strike the Hawaiian Islands, and their volcanic peaks, generally come from the east and northeast. As a result, they create clouds, rain, and strong waves on the windward shores. On the other hand, most Hawaiian beach resorts are along the islands' western and southwestern shores, where it's most likely to be sunny. Another example: The westerly winds that flow into the Pacific Northwest often bring clouds and rain to Seattle and Vancouver—both of which are on the windward side of the Cascade Mountain Range. The area just east of these mountains (the leeward side) is more dry and sunny.

At any time, 20 volcanoes are erupting somewhere on earth.

Foam from breaking waves covers 3 to 4 percent of the earth's surface.

Figure I–9 Tropical Island Wind Patterns

There are all kinds of mountains: rugged ones, like North America's **Rockies**, Europe's **Alps**, South America's **Andes**, and Asia's **Himalaya**; old, worn-down ones, like the East Coast's **Appalachians** in the United States; and volcanic ones, like those of Hawaii, the Caribbean, Iceland, Central Africa, Japan, and the most volcanic nation of all: Indonesia.

Closely allied to a mountain is a **plateau**. A plateau is a broad, flat area that rises above the surrounding land and, because of its elevation, typically has cooler weather. (Mexico City is a prime example.) **Mesas** are smaller, steeper-sided versions of plateaus; **buttes** are even smaller, towerlike versions. The dramatic mesas and buttes of the American Southwest attract many tourists to that region's national parks.

Bodies of Water

Stop and think: Can you name one popular destination that's *not* near water? Not easy, is it? The majority of the places you'll sell are near bodies of water. It goes even beyond that. One example: Lodging's relationship with bodies of water usually affects pricing. A hotel right on Waikiki's beach sands can get much more money for its rooms than a hotel several blocks inland.

Gulfs. Gulfs are large areas of ocean that penetrate into land. A good example is the **Gulf of Mexico**. **Bays** are similar to gulfs, but are generally smaller and less enclosed by land; **Chesapeake Bay**, in Virginia and Maryland, is an example. **Fjords** [FEE-YORDZ] are also inlets from the ocean or the sea; they are usually long, narrow, and lined with steep cliffs. The most dramatic ones notch into the coastlines of Norway, New Zealand, Chile, and Argentina.

Tourist sites are often associated with gulfs, bays, and fjords; beach resorts line the Gulf of Mexico's shores, and ships commonly cruise through the fjords of Norway.

Rivers. Rivers provide significant cruise opportunities for you to sell. Currently, the most popular are North America's **Mississippi**, Europe's **Rhine** and **Danube**, Africa's **Nile**, and for the more adventurous, South America's **Amazon**. A **glacier** is a sort of "river" of near-solid ice and compacted snow that flows very slowly down from high, cold places.

Ninety-seven percent of the earth's water is salt water.

Many glaciers are bluish. The reason: Refraction causes blue shades of light to be reflected off the ice, while all other colors are absorbed.

In polar regions, a glacier may eventually tumble into the water, creating icebergs. Glaciers are often imposing tourist attractions, most notably in Alaska, Canada, Switzerland, Peru, and New Zealand. When a mass of ice sits, like a lake, over a broad area, it's called an **ice field**. The biggest ice fields (like those in Antarctica) are called **ice sheets**.

Waterfalls. These dramatic cascades of water are magnets for tourists. Both **Niagara Falls** and Germany's **Rhine Falls** have been major attractions for centuries, while more remote ones—such as South America's **Iguazu Falls** and Africa's **Victoria Falls**—are becoming increasingly popular destinations.

Seas. Seas are large bodies of water, usually salty, but sometimes fresh. They can be a region of water within an ocean, but usually some sort of land boundaries, such as islands or continental shoreline, partly or almost fully enclose a sea. Like gulfs, seas are often the site of resorts, cruises, and water-sport activities. Geographers count more than 50 seas. Among those most associated with tourism are the **Caribbean** and the **Mediterranean**.

Lakes. Lakes are smaller than seas, are usually fresh, and are mostly or fully encircled by land. They, too, often feature resort and recreation facilities. A few large saltwater lakes have been labeled seas, like the **Caspian Sea** and the **Dead Sea**.

Lagoons. Lagoons are shallow bodies of water, generally separated from the ocean by reefs or barrier islands. Those in tropical areas often provide easy snorkeling opportunities.

Bayous. Bayous [BYE-yooz] are marshy or swampy areas. Those in Louisiana have become tourist attractions.

Deltas. Deltas are the low, V-shaped areas at the mouths of rivers. Many important port cities, such as New Orleans (Louisiana) and Alexandria (Egypt) are located at deltas.

Geysers. Geysers are jets of steaming water that shoot high into the air. New Zealand, Iceland, and (in the United States) Yellowstone National Park have geysers that are tourist attractions.

Springs. Springs occur where water flows naturally to the earth's surface. Spa resorts are often located near springs. One of the world's most famous spa resorts is Brenner's Park-Hotel & Spa in Baden-Baden, Germany.

The Great Lakes contain one-fifth of the world's fresh water.

People who intend to swim in the Dead Sea are warned not to shave. The sea's 33 percent salinity (ocean water is 3 percent) would cause stinging.

The world's oceans contain enough salt to build a wall along the equator 180 miles high and 1 mile thick.

The Maid of the Mist sightseeing vessel sails toward Niagara's Canadian Falls
Image copyright Alexander Iotzov, 2008. Used under license from Shutterstock.com

Oceans. Oceans are the greatest bodies of water. There are four oceans: the **Atlantic**, the **Pacific**, the **Indian**, and the **Arctic** (refer back to Figure I–8). (It could be argued that there's only *one ocean*: All four oceans are connected and the boundaries among them are not clearly defined.) Ocean water sports, whether off a continental area (such as Florida) or around an island (such as Tahiti), attract many tourists.

One thing that's useful to those who sell travel is how to predict ocean water temperatures. This information isn't found in popular reference books or websites, yet tourists who look forward to swimming ask about it all the time. Three factors determine ocean water temperature: *season*, *latitude* (the nearer the equator, the warmer the ocean is likely to be), and *ocean currents*. This last factor is one of the hardest to predict. Yet knowing something about the Coriolis effect will help you make that prediction with greater confidence.

The **Coriolis effect**, among other things, makes oceans circulate in a clockwise fashion in the Northern Hemisphere and a counterclockwise manner in the Southern Hemisphere. The resulting currents enable water to pick up heat at the equator and carry it along; conversely, in the polar regions, the currents chill down and carry cold water away for some distance. If you look at Figure I–10, you'll see why ocean water off California is surprisingly cool, yet along the southeastern U.S. coast, it's comparatively warm. A significant variation: The shape of the North Atlantic permits warm water to flow along a **Gulf Stream** from near the equator all the way to Great Britain. (That's one reason why London in the winter only occasionally gets really cold, while parts of Alaska and Canada, at the same latitude, are frozen.)

Generally, ocean water on the east coast of a continent tends to be warmer than ocean water on the west coast of that same continent. The water off, say, Australia's eastern Gold Coast resort area is much warmer than that off Perth, on Australia's western coast, though the two are only a few degrees different in latitude. That also explains why the water off the Galapagos Islands (which sit on the equator) is cooler than you'd expect. The northern-flowing currents carry water from the frigid Antarctic region.

Does the Coriolis effect determine temperatures in smaller bodies of water? Not really. The water temperatures of, say, the Mediterranean, are governed largely by the seasons. Its water is chilly in the winter, but sunlight heats it up rapidly as summer approaches.

Two facts also worth knowing: (1) Seacoast locations have fewer extremes of temperature than those farther inland; and (2) regions that border cool ocean currents (e.g., California) tend to have a drier climate than those along warmer ocean waters (e.g., Florida's east coast).

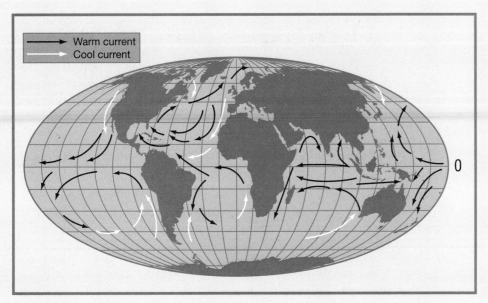

Figure I–10 Ocean Currents

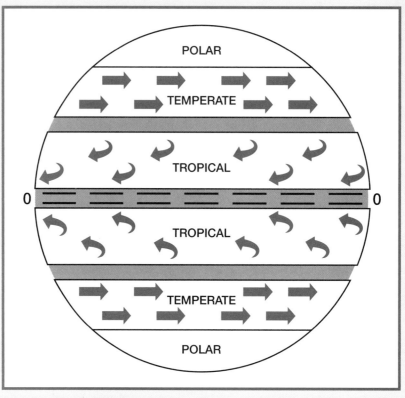

Figure I-11 Wind Patterns

Winds

Winds are among the most unpredictable of the geographically related events. If you've ever sailed a boat, you know that firsthand. But there are general earth-wide patterns, especially for the prevailing winds that stream above the capricious surface breezes (see Figure I-11). Following are some of the major wind flows that affect the destinations a travel professional deals with.

The Westerlies. The westerlies are winds that tend to blow around the globe from west to east in temperate areas between 30 and 60 degrees latitude, both in the Northern and Southern Hemispheres. The United States, Canada, and Europe lie within this belt. Now you know why weather maps on the evening news display weather flowing from west to east.

If you have cable TV, watch the *Weather Channel* for 30 minutes. You'll be surprised at how many of the concepts you've just read about are referred to. How do the westerlies affect travel? First, the high-altitude, high-velocity core of these westerlies, the **jet stream**, is responsible for making east-to-west flights take longer. (A flight from New York to San Francisco, for example, takes at least 30 minutes longer than one from San Francisco to New York.) Second, western coastal regions, mostly within a 40- to 60-degree belt, tend to be rainier than eastern coastal regions, especially where mountains are involved. Some examples of regions with rainy west coasts: Oregon, Washington State, British Columbia, the Alaskan panhandle, southern Chile, Ireland, Portugal, Croatia, and New Zealand.

Terrain, ocean temperatures, seasons, and many other factors conspire to create many exceptions to the above. To determine the rainfall patterns for key destinations, consult the "Climate at a Glance" charts sprinkled throughout the book.

The Trade Winds. The trade winds are humid breezes that tend to flow from east to west. These winds are most pronounced in the tropical band between about 25 degrees north and 25 degrees south. North of the equator, trade winds often come from the northeast instead of the east, and south of the equator, they frequently come from the southeast. For complicated reasons, much of Africa and some tropical parts of Asia (especially India) don't always follow the east-to-west trade wind pattern. But it does hold for Central and South America, for a good part of Australia, and especially for tropical islands.

When a tropical island is mountainous, the western coast is almost always leeward and therefore drier. This is where you should lodge visitors (refer back to Figure I–9). Because there are no mountains to squeeze the rain from the trade winds, flat islands are usually breezy and relatively dry. (A good example is Aruba, a flat coral island in the Caribbean.)

Storms

Storms often disrupt travel plans. Sometimes you can know when they're more likely to occur and thus recommend the best time to visit certain destinations.

Hurricanes. Hurricanes are among the earth's most violent storms. Usually born near the equator, hurricanes migrate in rather unpredictable patterns (see Figure I–12). They can cover hundreds of square miles with high winds (74 mph or above) and heavy rains for a day or two in one place before moving on. When they're born near the Caribbean or Mexico, they're called hurricanes; when they originate in the western Pacific, they're called **typhoons.** The southward-heading ones around Australia and in the Indian Ocean are called **cyclones,** the official generic name for all such storms.

Hurricanes generally occur from June to November in the Northern Hemisphere, with about 80 percent of them coming in August, September, and October. (Of course, hurricane season brings not only the chance of vacation-damaging storms, but also bargain rates.) Cyclones almost never affect Europe, South America (except occasionally on its Caribbean shoreline), Africa (except for the region around Madagascar and Mozambique), or the western coast of the United States and Canada. Hurricanes also rarely maintain strength if they move far inland over a continent; instead, they degenerate into large rainstorms.

Monsoons. Each year around summertime in certain parts of the world, winds reverse in such a way as to cause a lengthy, distinct, and heavy rainy season. This monsoon condition can dampen anybody's trip. India has torrential monsoon rains from June to September; China's less intense season comes from May to September; and Korea sees quite a bit of rain in July and August. Northern Australia, Indonesia, and Singapore have monsoon-like conditions from December through March, whereas the south-facing parts of West Africa have a monsoon weather pattern from May to October.

The word *monsoon* is also used in the U.S. Southwest—especially in Arizona—to describe the usually brief, intense rainstorms that occur during periods of hot weather.

Cloudbursts. Cloudbursts are heavy showers that occur suddenly. They're a major factor in the tropics. A typical pattern is for the morning to be sunny, the afternoon to be

On average, 1.6 hurricanes reach the United States each year.

Antarctica receives about the same amount of precipitation as the Sahara Desert (less than 2 inches yearly).

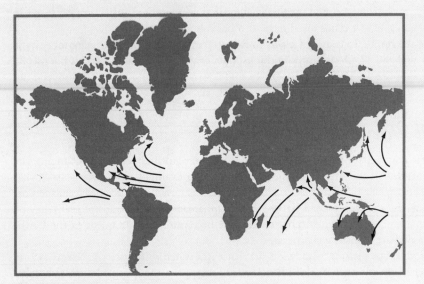

Figure I–12 Hurricane Areas

partly cloudy, and a heavy downpour to occur in the late afternoon or early evening. Visitors to tropical destinations should be warned to start the day as early as possible if they want to avoid the possibility of getting wet.

Other Aspects of Climate

There's a saying among meteorologists: "Climate is what you expect, weather is what you get." This does point out an important distinction: *Weather* refers to what's going on in the atmosphere at a given time and place; *climate* refers to the weather that prevails typically in a region at a certain time of the year. When you tell people that Acapulco is usually warm, dry, and sunny in January, you're talking about climate. When they return to tell you that it rained and was chilly for three of the seven days they were there, they're talking about the weather.

Travel professionals can't be expected to predict the weather. But they should know what climate will prevail. Climate is a critical traveler concern; knowledge of it can help to clinch a satisfying sale. Here are three facts you should keep in mind:

■ **The higher a destination is, the cooler it will be.** Mexico City, which sits on a plateau, reaches an average high of only 73 degrees in July, whereas Manzanillo, a Mexican beach resort at virtually the same latitude (but at sea level) is typically in the high 80s in the same month. In a more extreme example, it can be snowing at Lake Arrowhead, a California mountain resort at a high altitude, while 20 miles away in Palm Springs, at a much lower altitude, vacationers are baking by their hotel pools.

■ **The windier it is, the colder it will feel.** It could be 20°F in Moscow, but if it's not windy, the weather won't feel too uncomfortable. But if it's 40°F and the wind is whipping, it'll seem much colder. On the other hand, windy days can also be helpful. The trade winds in Hawaii can make an 85-degree day feel absolutely wonderful.

■ **When arranging a flight in which a stop or connection is involved, consider what the climate at the stopover city will be.** For example, for a January itinerary, it might, if practical, be advisable to connect via a warm-weather city, such as Phoenix, Dallas, or Atlanta, rather than via Denver, Minneapolis, or Chicago, where winter weather could interfere with air travel. Conversely, in August, Northern cities may make better stopovers than Southern ones, where thunderstorms are more common.

Two other important points about determining the climate bear mentioning. First, carefully study the climate tables or graphs you use. Do they give rainfall in inches, as do those in this book? Do they list days with rain or days with no rain? Are temperatures given as average highs and lows, as record highs and lows, or as the average of the entire day? Second, make sure you find out if temperatures are measured in Fahrenheit (used in the United States) or in Celsius (used in most other countries).

Just for the record, to convert Celsius to Fahrenheit, multiply the Celsius number by 9, divide by 5, and add 32. Or, to simplify things, memorize the following: 30°C is hot (86°F), 22°C is pleasant (72°F), 15°C is chilly (59°F), and 0°C is freezing (32°F). That way you can gauge most other Celsius temperatures by comparison.

Global Warming and Tourism

Most experts now believe that human industrial and agricultural activity is changing the world's climate. Will this affect tourism? Absolutely. For example, earlier you learned that glaciers are attractions in many places. However, glaciers have begun to shrink and recede. The snow and ice that has topped Africa's Mt. Kilimanjaro for thousands of years may be gone within a few decades. Hurricanes seem to be becoming more frequent in the Caribbean. Ski resorts are reporting shorter seasons.

And if ice keeps melting worldwide, all that extra water will cause the oceans to rise. If that happens, the sands of Waikiki Beach would disappear, the Everglades could become

Old Faithful Geyser draws visitors to Yellowstone National Park
Photo by Justus Ghormley

a lake, the canals of Venice, Italy, might overflow daily, and low-lying island-nations, like the Maldives, would vanish beneath the sea.

Manmade climate change could affect travel and tourism more than any other industry. That's why travel professionals, future and present, should vigorously support measures to stem a trend that could impact them deeply.

Human Geography

Most of what you've read in this chapter has to do with **physical geography**, the study of the earth's land, air, and water. But studying the peoples of the earth, an equally noble discipline, is usually called **human** or **cultural geography**. Religion, food, politics, language, national boundaries, art, agriculture, economics, and even history, all in some way affect geography. In the chapters that follow, we often bring up one or more of these considerations, for tourism is, after all, an activity of people, not of ocean currents or rocks.

The people of the earth speak about 3,000 distinct languages.

On the U.S. Atlantic Coast, Saturdays are 22 percent rainier than Mondays. One theory: It's a result of weekday car emissions.

One part of human geography that may bear some scrutiny right now is touristic patterns. People want to go to places for many reasons; climate, vacation time, and school holidays seem to be the most important factors. When tourism is buzzing in a place, it is called **high** or **peak season**. (It's also the most expensive season.) When tourists are fewest, it's called **low** or **off-season**. (Real vacation bargains can also be had.) And times in between, when neither a great many people nor a very few people are visiting, are called **shoulder seasons**.

In most places, fall and spring are shoulder seasons; some of the most satisfying vacations take place during shoulder season because the weather may be pretty good, rates aren't at their highest, and crowds are seldom seen. In temperate or arctic regions, high season usually takes place in summer, but tropical resorts peak in winter (with all those travelers wanting to get away from the cold). Conversely, for temperate and arctic areas, winter is the low season. One exception: ski resorts, which thrive at this time.

Holidays also profoundly affect travel patterns. In most countries, **people don't like to take regular vacations during family holidays,** such as Thanksgiving, Passover, or Christmas. They do like to fly to stay with family around these times, meaning that airfares are high, but hotels in most destinations are usually empty and offering bargains. One other interesting pattern: Travel falls sharply a few days after New Year's Day; January is bargain month in many places. But other holidays, such as the U.S. Fourth of July or Japan's Golden Week (April 29 to May 5), set off massive peaks of tourism. Most French and Italians leave their cities en masse in August for Riviera or Alpine vacations; thus, a sort of shoulder season exists in Paris and Rome at summer's end—when most business travel halts and when mostly foreign tourists are left to stay in these cities' hotels.

Make sure to consult each chapter's "Climate at a Glance" chart. In addition to climate, these charts show the destination's tourism patterns.

One odd factor that affects tourism profoundly: the **"event" effect**. An event—either positive or negative—can create a strong, often disproportionate impact over a wide geographic area, and for a long time. Negative events produce the most dramatic (and often irrational) effects. The 1991 Gulf War wiped out tourism in Egypt, Morocco, and even Europe, though these places were hundreds, even a thousand miles away. And the 1989 San Francisco earthquake reduced tourism for months across all of California. It's all about the public's misunderstanding of geography. Fortunately, the event effect can also be positive: The Olympics, a world's fair, or the Super Bowl can enhance tourism for years, not only at the venue city but also for the entire region or country.

A tsunami is a massive wave, usually triggered by an earthquake, which can cross thousands of miles of ocean before devastating shorelines. The 2004 tsunami in the Indian Ocean was a prime example.

Similar to the event effect is the power of imagery to affect destination choice. The tragic sight of jets flying into the World Trade Center towers in 2001 made New York City, in one poll, the city that travelers would most want to avoid. Indeed, those polled ranked it more dangerous than the Middle East. This sort of reaction, of course, is utterly irrational and eventually fades away, as positive images and experiences replace negative ones. For example, within about two years, tourism and business travel to New York City reached, then surpassed, pre-9/11 levels.

Reference Tools

The 30 chapters that follow focus more precisely on the most popular places travelers want to visit. But even if you memorize every word in this book, there will be times when someone asks a question that you can't answer. For the most useful reference tools that may contain the information you seek, be sure to consult Appendix B of this book.

One Last Point

If you're thinking about a career in travel, you're about to embark on a great journey of discovery, not just through this book but in real life. Most people in the travel business go into it, in part, to experience their world. In essence, you'll fill in your mind's geographic blanks, put names to places, and experience destinations you couldn't even pronounce before you visited them.

In other words, they'll become part of you. And the chapters that follow will prepare you for that rich, glorious experience.

Summary

Here's a summary of the most important sales-enhancing geographic facts in this chapter:

- Think "curved line" when you're deciding what route or airline to recommend for a long flight.
- Seasons in the Southern Hemisphere are the reverse of those in the Northern Hemisphere.
- When crossing the international date line from east to west, it becomes the following day; from west to east, it becomes the previous day.
- Winds called the westerlies flow west to east in most temperate parts of the globe, affecting weather and jet travel time.
- The trade winds flow more or less from east to west in the tropics.
- Mountainous tropical islands are usually drier on the western, leeward coast.
- Ocean water on the east side of a continent tends to be warmer than ocean water at the same latitude on the west side.
- Hurricane (cyclone) season in most places peaks in August, September, and October.
- Areas with monsoon conditions usually get rain during their summer season.
- The higher (in altitude) a destination is, the cooler it will be.

Someone once said, "Without geography you're nowhere." Well, you now know the underpinnings of geography. This is a great starting point. You're now ready to learn about those many "somewheres" that are essential to travelers. That's what the rest of this book is all about.

In 1970, women represented 1 percent of all business travelers. They now account for about half.

In the late eighteenth century, England's Captain Cook became the first European to "discover" Hawaii. Yet a seventeenth-century Spanish map shows volcanic islands in the Pacific, just about where Hawaii lies. There's no record of any Spanish ship ever visiting there before Cook. The map remains a mystery.

Travel Trivia

Things Geographers Don't Agree On

- Which is the world's longest river, the Nile or the Amazon.
- Whether Australia is an island or a continent.
- Whether the world's highest mountain should be measured from sea level (it would be Mt. Everest) or from the ocean bottom (it would be Mauna Kea, Hawaii).
- What exactly is the difference among a lake, a sea, and a gulf.
- Whether Europe and Asia form one continent or two.
- What distinguishes a cape from a peninsula.

NAME _____   **DATE** _____

ACTIVITY 1

Qualifying the Traveler

Based on your current knowledge of geography, name one place, anywhere in the world, which you think might appeal to the traveler type named below:

Type	Place	Type	Place
1 History buff	_____	**7** Adventure seeker	_____
2 Culture seeker	_____	**8** Entertainment seeker	_____
3 Ethnic traveler	_____	**9** Shopper	_____
4 Religious pilgrim	_____	**10** Sensual traveler	_____
5 Environmental traveler	_____	**11** Status seeker	_____
6 Recreational traveler	_____	**12** Business traveler in the garment industry	_____

Turn back to page 3 to continue with the sales portion of the text.

NAME _____   **DATE** _____

ACTIVITY 2

Reading a Hotel Locator Map

Study the locator map of downtown Chicago, then answer the following questions:

1 Which museum is at I-6 on the map?

2 A person has business at the Sears Tower. Which hotel is closest to it, the Sheraton Plaza Chicago or Allegro Hotel?

3 It seems easier to lodge people near which of the following: the University of Illinois or Northwestern University?

4 A visitor to Chicago will be driving from the Hyatt Regency to Milwaukee, a city to the north. Which street and highways will the visitor has to take?

5 A person wants to see the famous Water Tower. At which map coordinates is it?

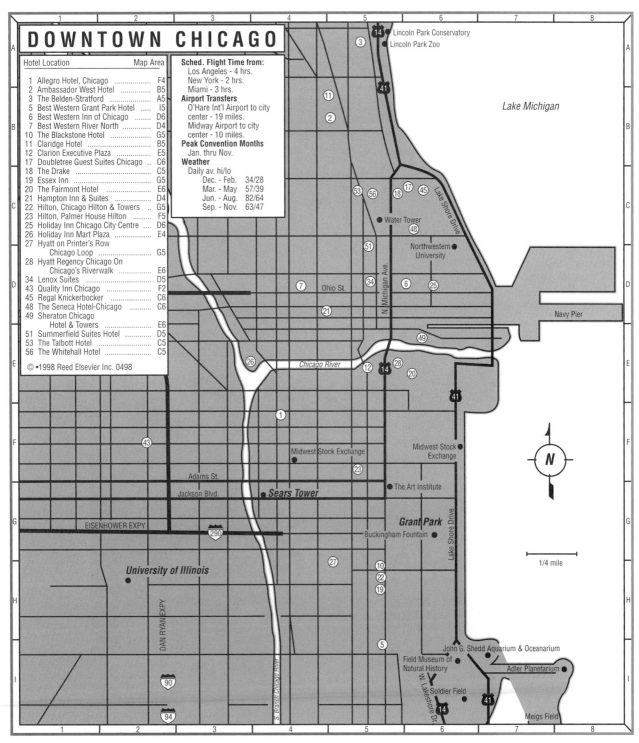

DOWNTOWN CHICAGO

Hotel Location	Map Area
1 Allegro Hotel, Chicago	F4
2 Ambassador West Hotel	B5
3 The Belden-Stratford	A5
5 Best Western Grant Park Hotel	I5
6 Best Western Inn of Chicago	D6
7 Best Western River North	D4
10 The Blackstone Hotel	G5
11 Claridge Hotel	B5
12 Clarion Executive Plaza	E5
17 Doubletree Guest Suites Chicago	C6
18 The Drake	C5
19 Essex Inn	G5
20 The Fairmont Hotel	E6
21 Hampton Inn & Suites	D4
22 Hilton, Chicago Hilton & Towers	G5
23 Hilton, Palmer House Hilton	F5
25 Holiday Inn Chicago City Centre	D6
26 Holiday Inn Mart Plaza	E4
27 Hyatt on Printer's Row Chicago Loop	G5
28 Hyatt Regency Chicago On Chicago's Riverwalk	E6
34 Lenox Suites	D5
43 Quality Inn Chicago	F2
45 Regal Knickerbocker	C6
48 The Seneca Hotel-Chicago	C6
49 Sheraton Chicago Hotel & Towers	E6
51 Summerfield Suites Hotel	D5
53 The Talbott Hotel	C5
56 The Whitehall Hotel	C5

© •1998 Reed Elsevier Inc. 0498

Sched. Flight Time from:
Los Angeles - 4 hrs.
New York - 2 hrs.
Miami - 3 hrs.
Airport Transfers
O'Hare Int'l Airport to city center - 19 miles.
Midway Airport to city center - 10 miles.
Peak Convention Months
Jan. thru Nov.
Weather
Daily av. hi/lo
Dec. - Feb. 34/28
Mar. - May 57/39
Jun. - Aug. 82/64
Sep. - Nov. 63/47

NAME _____   **DATE** _____

ACTIVITY 3

Identifying Geographic Features

Below is a rendition of an imaginary tropical island in the Pacific. Letters identify the various geographic features. Match the features with the letter.

1. A peninsula _____
2. The coolest area _____
3. A bay _____
4. A rainier, windward area _____
5. A cape _____
6. A dry, leeward area _____
7. A lake _____
8. A coral reef _____
9. A river _____
10. A fjord-like feature _____

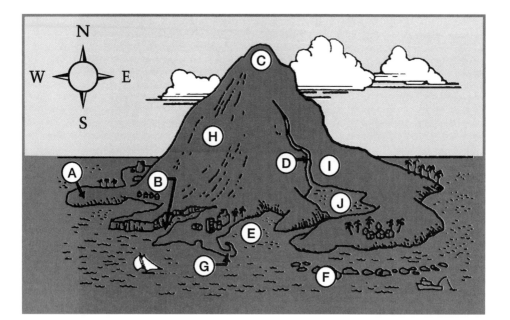

NAME _____   **DATE** _____

ACTIVITY 4

Reading Climate at a Glance Charts

Examine the four charts on the next two pages, then answer the following questions:

① Which season would probably provide the best overall weather for a business traveler to visit Kolkata?

② Which of the four cities has the widest range between summer and winter temperatures?

③ Without looking at a map, determine which of the cities is clearly a Southern Hemisphere destination.

④ Which of the cities has the least monthly variation in rainfall?

⑤ Without looking at a map, which of these four cities would probably be closest to the equator?

⑥ In which month does Melbourne have its coolest temperatures?

⑦ Which city is the most likely to have snow in the winter?

⑧ Which two cities seem to have the greatest variation between daytime and nighttime temperatures?

⑨ What factor probably accounts for Quito's relatively low temperatures?

⑩ In one of these cities, it goes down to around 15°C at night in February. Which city is it?

⑪ What probably accounts for Kolkata's off-season for tourists?

⑫ Which month in Chicago will probably provide the best weather and temperatures, without hordes of tourists?

Climate at a Glance
KOLKATA, INDIA

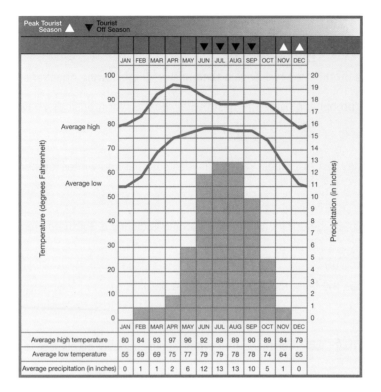

	JAN	FEB	MAR	APR	MAY	JUN	JUL	AUG	SEP	OCT	NOV	DEC
Average high temperature	80	84	93	97	96	92	89	89	90	89	84	79
Average low temperature	55	59	69	75	77	79	79	78	78	74	64	55
Average precipitation (in inches)	0	1	1	2	6	12	13	13	10	5	1	0

Climate at a Glance
QUITO, ECUADOR

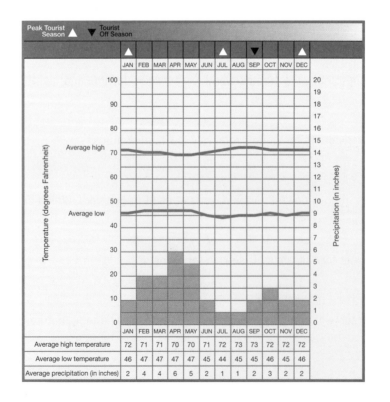

	JAN	FEB	MAR	APR	MAY	JUN	JUL	AUG	SEP	OCT	NOV	DEC
Average high temperature	72	71	71	70	70	71	72	73	73	72	72	72
Average low temperature	46	47	47	47	47	45	44	45	45	46	45	46
Average precipitation (in inches)	2	4	4	6	5	2	1	1	2	3	2	2

Climate at a Glance
MELBOURNE, AUSTRALIA

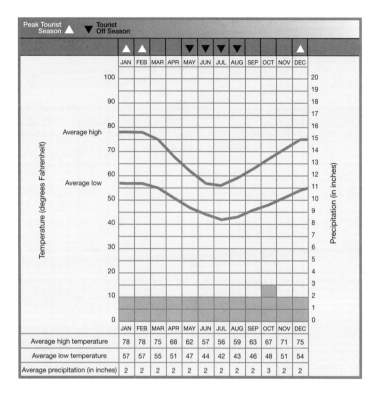

	JAN	FEB	MAR	APR	MAY	JUN	JUL	AUG	SEP	OCT	NOV	DEC
Average high temperature	78	78	75	68	62	57	56	59	63	67	71	75
Average low temperature	57	57	55	51	47	44	42	43	46	48	51	54
Average precipitation (in inches)	2	2	2	2	2	2	2	2	2	3	2	2

Climate at a Glance
CHICAGO, ILLINOIS

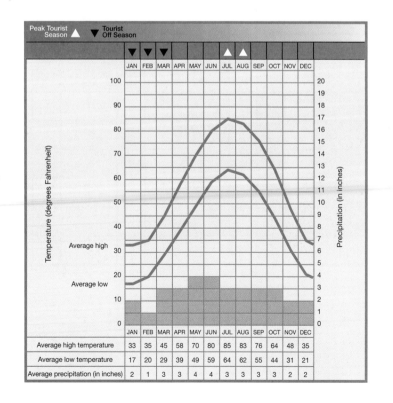

	JAN	FEB	MAR	APR	MAY	JUN	JUL	AUG	SEP	OCT	NOV	DEC
Average high temperature	33	35	45	58	70	80	85	83	76	64	48	35
Average low temperature	17	20	29	39	49	59	64	62	55	44	31	21
Average precipitation (in inches)	2	1	3	3	4	4	3	3	3	3	2	2

NAME _____ DATE _____

ACTIVITY 5

A Geographic Crossword Puzzle

Across

3. The most accurate map.

4. Monday becomes Sunday if you cross the date line traveling . . .

6. A month of hurricanes.

7. What Cod is.

8. The side of a continent with cooler ocean temperatures.

9. People cruise down this river.

11. The longitude line that passes near London.

15. A place with lots of volcanic activity.

18. The dry side of a mountain.

19. In the Caribbean it's a hurricane; in the western Pacific it's a . . .

20. The direction the north Pacific's currents turn.

Down

1. A map with an A, B, C, 1, 2, 3 grid.

2. A state without daylight savings time.

5. The least-visited continent.

10. Tropical winds.

12. A European mountain range.

13. Thirty-two degrees Fahrenheit equals ___ degrees Celsius.

14. In the travel industry, time is often expressed according to the 24- ___ clock.

16. There are four of these in the world.

17. The Gulf Stream is in the . . .

NAME _____ **DATE** _____

ACTIVITY 6

Putting It All Together

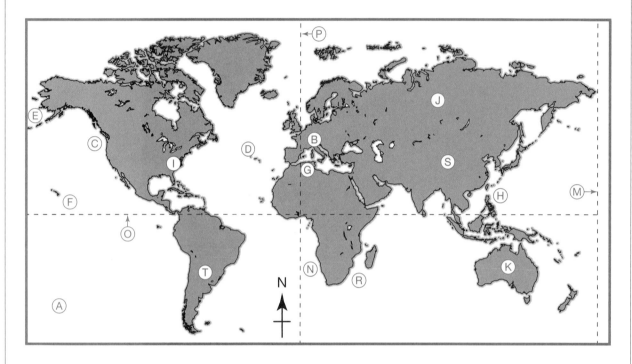

Examine the world map above, then answer the questions by giving the letter or location on the map. You may use each letter only once; there will be some letters you won't use.

_____ ❶ An area that, because of prevailing winds, has high rainfall.

_____ ❷ An ocean where currents flow counterclockwise.

_____ ❸ An area with many typhoons in the summer.

_____ ❹ Cross it and the day changes.

_____ ❺ The most popular overseas continent for American travelers.

_____ ❻ An African coast that has cool ocean water temperatures.

_____ ❼ The country with the most time zones.

_____ ❽ An area a jet would cross if flying from Seattle, Washington, to Japan.

_____ ❾ A continent that has winter in July and has a cyclone season.

_____ ❿ A place where prevailing winds typically come from the east.

NAME _____   **DATE** _____

ACTIVITY 7

Geography on the Web

Find at least one website that provides good information on each subject listed below. Each website must be different—no repeats.

For example, health issues/concerns for a specific country to be visited.

wwwn.cdc.gov/travel/

① Distances and routes between one place in the United States and another

② Predicted weather conditions for any place in the world

③ How to get an international driver's permit

④ Which cruise lines visit a certain port

⑤ Where a certain event will take place

Now, using only Google's image and/or mapping functions, answer the following:

⑥ Describe what the Royal Pavilion in Brighton, England, looks like.

⑦ What is the London Eye?

⑧ What is just north of the Rock and Roll Hall of Fame and Museum?

⑨ Can you walk out of Miami Beach's Fontainebleau Hotel right out onto the beach?

⑩ Tourists can safely observe polar bears in the wild near Churchill, Manitoba. What keeps the tourists safe?

⑪ In which country is the Copper Canyon and what form of transportation is it famous for?

⑫ What's so special about the house at 92 Second Street in Fall River, Massachusetts?

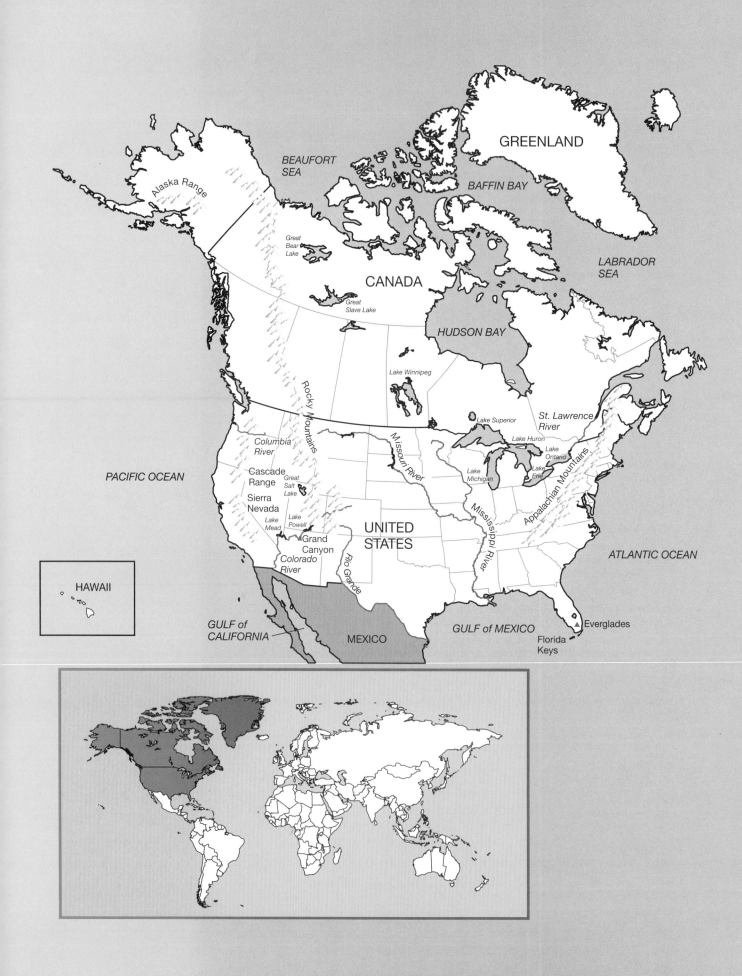

GREENLAND

BEAUFORT
SEA

Alaska Range

BAFFIN BAY

*Great
Bear
Lake*

CANADA

LABRADOR
SEA

*Great
Slave Lake*

HUDSON BAY

Lake Winnipeg

Rocky Mountains

Lake Superior

St. Lawrence
River

*Columbia
River*

Missouri River

*Lake
Huron*

*Lake
Ontario*

Cascade
Range

*Great
Salt
Lake*

*Lake
Michigan*

*Lake
Erie*

PACIFIC OCEAN

Sierra
Nevada

*Lake
Mead*

*Lake
Powell*

Grand
Canyon
Colorado
River

UNITED
STATES

Mississippi River

Appalachian Mountains

Rio Grande

ATLANTIC OCEAN

HAWAII

GULF of
CALIFORNIA

MEXICO

GULF of MEXICO

Everglades

Florida
Keys

PART II

NORTH AMERICA

Charm of the Familiar

Think you know North America? Then where in Canada do cars appear to roll uphill backward? In what city is Disneyland located? Which North American region has the most thunderstorms yearly?

Maybe you knew the answers, maybe not. (The answers, in order: Magnetic Hill in Moncton, New Brunswick; Anaheim, California; central Florida.) The important point is this: Many people have only the haziest of images about any destination beyond a few hundred miles of their hometown. To serve travelers, you'll have to bring those distant images into focus. And you, yourself, will need to know North America just about as well as you know your own backyard.

That yard probably extends farther than you think. Geographers usually define North America as everything from Canada to the Panama–Colombia border. That includes rarely visited Greenland, the island nations of the Caribbean, and many of the south-of-the-border countries, such as Mexico, Guatemala, El Salvador, Honduras, Costa Rica, and Panama. (We'll address these Caribbean and Latin American countries later, in Part III.) All you need to know about Greenland is that it's a self-governing territory of Denmark, its 839,999 square miles are mostly ice-covered, it supports only 56,000 people, and it draws few tourists.

So, in this Part II, we'll limit ourselves to the United States and Canada and save all North American countries between the United States and Colombia for later.

Where the Regions Are

Take a look at a map of North America. By far the broadest area is taken up by Canada, the world's second-largest country. **Eastern Canada** is composed of the **Atlantic provinces** (**New Brunswick, Nova Scotia, Prince Edward Island**, and **Newfoundland and Labrador**) and Canada's two largest provinces, **Quebec** and **Ontario**, which together form **Central Canada**. **Western Canada** includes **British Columbia, Alberta, Saskatchewan**, and **Manitoba**. (The latter three provinces are sometimes called the **Prairie provinces** or the **Prairies**.) Three northern territories cap off the country: **Yukon, the Northwest Territories**, and **Nunavut**.

Two U.S. states, both south of British Columbia, make up the **Pacific Northwest**: **Washington** and **Oregon**. Above them, and separated from them by British Columbia and Yukon, is **Alaska**. Below them are **California, Nevada, Utah, Arizona**, and **New Mexico**—often labeled the **Southwest**. (Occasionally, you'll hear of **California, Nevada, Oregon**, and **Washington** grouped as the **Far West**.) Over 2,000 miles to the southwest of the North American continent is the U.S. state of **Hawaii**.

In most towns in Greenland, there are more dogs than people.

The United States spans six time zones.

35

The **Rocky Mountain** region is a buffer between the Pacific region and the middle of Canada and the United States. Which states make up the U.S. Rocky Mountain area is somewhat debatable—several of them qualify for inclusion in the Southwest, while others are considered part of the Great Plains area. For our purposes, let's say the Rocky Mountain states include, from north to south, **Montana, Idaho, Wyoming**, and **Colorado. Texas**, the second-largest U.S. state after Alaska, almost needs a category for itself, though it's often mentioned in the same breath with **Oklahoma**, which is just north of it. The flat agricultural area that stretches above Oklahoma is generally called the **Great Plains**. It's made up of, from north to south, **North Dakota, South Dakota, Nebraska**, and **Kansas**.

The **Midwest** encompasses many states, including **Minnesota, Wisconsin, Michigan, Iowa, Illinois, Indiana, Missouri**, and **Ohio**. (Yes, many of these states are in the eastern half of the United States, but they still call themselves Midwestern.) The **South** also covers a vast area. Its states are **Kentucky, Tennessee, North Carolina, Arkansas, Mississippi, Alabama, Georgia, South Carolina, Louisiana**, and **Florida**.

West Virginia and **Virginia** are occasionally labeled southern or can be classified with the **Mid-Atlantic** states: **New York, New Jersey, Pennsylvania, Maryland**, and **Delaware**. And between Maryland and Virginia is the **District of Columbia**, a "neutral" federal district that marks the U.S. capital, **Washington, D.C.** Finally, **New England** nestles in the northeast corner of the United States. Its members are **Maine, Vermont, New Hampshire, Massachusetts, Connecticut**, and **Rhode Island**.

A Satellite View

Imagine you're in the space shuttle. You look down on North America. What do you see? A continent of sharp contrasts: the flat plains of the continent's center, the worn peaks of the Appalachian Mountains, the permanent icecaps of the far north, or the barren deserts of the U.S. Southwest. Because these natural features (and other ones, like lakes, rivers, and oceans) have such a strong impact on travel plans, it's important to understand where and what they are.

Bodies of Water

Looking down from the space shuttle, you notice that the North American continent is flanked by three oceans: the **Atlantic Ocean** that lines the eastern shores, the **Arctic Ocean** that caps our continent, and the **Pacific Ocean** that laps against its western coast. Curving into Mexico and the U.S. Southeastern border is the **Gulf of Mexico**; winds blowing over the Gulf help create the warm and often humid climate of that area. To the northeast, separating the United States from Canada, are the **Great Lakes: Superior, Michigan, Huron, Erie**, and **Ontario**. These lakes—and their shores—are important both to tourism and commerce. Toward the western side of the continent is another noticeable body of water, the **Great Salt Lake**, and to the north are several huge lakes: **Great Bear, Great Slave**, and **Lake Winnipeg**. Dominating this northern region is a very big body of water: **Hudson Bay**.

Look more closely and you'll spot several major rivers. The **St. Lawrence** slices into the continent's northeastern region. To the west, the **Columbia River** forms part of the border between Oregon and Washington. The **Mississippi River** divides the United States almost in half, starting up in Minnesota and traveling down through the Midwest and South to Louisiana, where it empties into the Gulf of Mexico. Even today, tourists can take a riverboat trip past its historic riverfront towns. The **Missouri River** starts in Montana and passes through the Great Plains states, finally merging with the Mississippi River in Missouri.

In the Southwest, the **Colorado River** winds from Colorado through Utah and forms part of the borders of Arizona, Nevada, and California; along the way, you'll see that it's been dammed, creating two lakes that are major recreation areas: **Lake Mead** in Nevada, and **Lake Powell** in Utah. The Colorado is also a popular rafting site for tourists. The **Rio Grande** marks off a large part of the country's southern border between Texas and Mexico.

Throughout North America, many smaller rivers and lakes help shape landscape. In the New England and Atlantic provinces, numerous inlets dig into the coastline and are

A paddle wheel steamboat churns its way up the Mississippi
Image copyright KennStilger47, 2008. Used under license from Shutterstock.com

popular recreation centers. Swampy bayous cover much of Louisiana, as do those of the **Everglades** in Florida. And Florida's collection of islands off its southwest coast, the **Florida Keys**, is a major tourist destination.

Mountains

Three mountain ranges loom over the North American landscape. They have a major effect on climate, travel conditions, and skiing. The impressive scenery they offer is a major factor for tourists. The weathered **Appalachian Mountains**—prime camping and hiking areas— rise in Pennsylvania, continue southwesterly down through Maryland, West Virginia, Virginia, Tennessee, North Carolina, and Kentucky, and end in northern Georgia. Other mountain ranges farther north, in New York, New England, Quebec, New Brunswick, and Newfoundland and Labrador, are popular summer tourist and winter skiing resorts. (Some geographers consider those northerly mountains an extension of the Appalachians.)

The **Rocky Mountains** run down the entire western length of North America, from Alaska to New Mexico, through Yukon, British Columbia, Alberta's western edge, Montana, Idaho, Wyoming, Colorado, Utah, and Arizona. One depression near the Rockies would be very noticeable from above: the cavernous **Grand Canyon** in Arizona. Along the west coast are two ranges (some consider them tributaries of the Rockies): the **Cascade Mountains**, stretching from northern California through Oregon and Washington to British Columbia, and the **Sierra Nevadas**, running most of the length of California. Like the Rockies, they both present great skiing and hiking opportunities. The Cascades continue northward from British Columbia into Alaska, where they become the **Alaska Range**. Between the Rocky and Appalachian Mountains are the flat lands of the U.S. Great Plains and Midwest, and Canada's Saskatchewan and Manitoba.

Four state capitals carry the names of United States presidents: Lincoln, Madison, Jackson, and Jefferson City.

The only place on North American soil where you drive on the left is the U.S. Virgin Islands.

Climate

As a rule (and there are many exceptions), the southern portion of Canada and the northern portion of the contiguous United States have warm or hot summers, but cold snowy winters, whereas the southern region of the United States is mild to hot year-round. Because of this, southern portions of the continent tend to be all-year destinations, whereas tourism in the north is largely limited to the summer. Of course, skiers do head north in the winter, and October is prime foliage season there.

Winter in Alaska and Canada can be cold and harsh. However, late spring, summer, and early fall are surprisingly mild; and in southern Canadian cities, like Toronto and especially Vancouver, winter isn't as bitter as people might imagine.

Rainfall and humidity patterns vary widely across the continent. Rain is frequent in the Pacific Northwest and, often in the form of thundershowers, in the U.S. South and Southeast. The U.S. Southwest is dry and desert-like, with rain coming mostly in the winter months. Hurricanes are most likely along the Gulf and Atlantic coasts in the summer and fall.

Tourism Patterns

North American tourism patterns are probably familiar to you. In brief, summer is high season for most of Canada and the United States. (This high season extends from the last weekend of May to the first weekend of September.) One exception is the desert resorts in California, Arizona, and Nevada. These areas, where summer temperatures can be scorching, have their low season during June, July, and August.

Fall and spring are shoulder seasons for tourism in most places. Many travelers with flexible schedules (e.g., retirees) profit from the lower rates and the cool (but not yet cold) temperatures that prevail. So, too, do conventions, which seem to flourish during this time. Easter, however, is a springtime high period, especially in Washington, D.C., Florida, and to some extent, California; students and families often travel during the week before or after this holiday. October's fall foliage season is also a high period in many forested areas. And during spring, certain beach resorts are packed—the reason: It's spring vacation break at many colleges.

Winter is a low period for Canadian and U.S. tourism, except at ski resorts and at certain warm-weather places (e.g., desert resorts). Special winter events, too, can draw crowds to cold-weather locations. For instance, Quebec City's Winter Carnival, the Festival of Lights in Niagara Falls, and New York City's pre-Christmas shopping opportunities serve as magnets for tourists.

The Grand Canyon is one of North America's most dramatic natural attractions
Image copyright Bryant Jayme, 2008. Used under license from Shutterstock.com

North American Distances

What is most striking to Europeans visiting North America? How big it really is. Even North Americans underestimate their continent's size. Why? The answers are many: The places are so familiar, air travel has compressed journey times greatly, and states and provinces are commonly seen as being parts of large blocks (e.g., Ohio and Minnesota seem close to each other because they're both in the Midwest).

There's a flip side to this. Because cities like **New York, Boston, Philadelphia, Baltimore,** and **Washington, D.C.,** have strong identities, some people are surprised to find how close these cities are to one another. (Theoretically, you could drive through them all in one day.) In fact, though the Northeast is populous, many of its states are tiny and the area is actually quite compact. On the other hand, the Western states are so vast and uncrowded that distances between major cities are considerable. (For instance, even though **Los Angeles** and **Portland** are in adjacent states, they're more than 1,000 miles apart; conversely, **Providence** and **Boston**, also in adjacent states, are only 50 miles from each other.)

For all the continent's size, however, air service is so good among urban centers that distances seem short to travelers. And within regions, commuter airlines shrink those distances even more. On busy routes, fares can be very reasonable—even cross-country. However, if a route isn't greatly traveled, even if it's a short distance, prices can be high. Keep in mind that air travel isn't a cure-all for distance: Service between small towns can be limited or nonexistent.

America's love of cars is well known, and many travelers will want to drive to their destination, especially in the compact U.S. Northeast. The network of highways is generally excellent, and so, too, are most state, provincial, and rural roads. Out West, though, the wide-open spaces truly are wide; direct major routes between secondary destinations aren't always possible to find.

Getting around *within* a city is another matter. Urban transportation in Canada is generally excellent, but in the United States it often leaves something to be desired. Your recommendations will vary according to the situation: a car rental for Los Angeles, taxis for New York City, streetcars and subways for Toronto.

Although **Amtrak** offers some major routes in the United States (with high-speed service between Washington, D.C., and Boston), the train system there is geared more to commerce than to commuters. Trains aren't nearly as fast, nor the routes as diversified, as those in Europe. That's one reason why motorcoach tours and intercity buses (usually operated by **Greyhound**) are the ground transportation of choice for many travelers in

Memphis, Tennessee's, airport handles more cargo than any other in the world. The reason: It's FedEx's hub.

Because the earth spins, if you're in North America you're traveling right now at about 600 to 900 mph.

A number of "private" train experiences are offered across North America, especially in Alaska and Canada.

The Chateau Frontenac looms over historic Quebec City
Image copyright Andre Nantel, 2008. Used under license from Shutterstock.com

the United States. Still, there *are* good rail routes throughout the country; special fares are commonplace; and train travel remains one of the great, romantic, scenic means of travel. Amtrak Vacations, a division of Amtrak, offers complete lodging-transportation packages that feature rail travel as one component. In Canada, **VIA Rail Canada** provides solid and dependable service, but its routes are somewhat limited.

Cruises have become a very common means of seeing North America. Among the most popular itineraries: New England and the St. Lawrence River, the Inside Passage in British Columbia and Alaska, and the Mississippi, along with its many tributaries.

Some Miscellaneous Considerations

Here are a few items that may prove useful when dealing with people traveling within North America:

- The "hub-and-spoke" concept is important to North American air travel. Each airline has one or two cities where it has an especially large number of flights connecting. North America's busiest domestic hub cities, with the airlines that rely on them the most:

Atlanta (Delta)	Dallas (American)	Philadelphia (U.S. Airways)
Calgary (Air Canada)	Denver (United)	Phoenix (U.S. Airways)
Charlotte, NC (U.S. Airways)	Detroit (Delta)	Salt Lake City (Delta)
Chicago (American, United)	Houston (Continental)	Toronto (Air Canada)
Cincinnati (Delta)	Minneapolis (Delta)	Vancouver (Air Canada)
Cleveland (Continental)	Montreal (Air Canada)	

- For international departures, North American carriers concentrate on Los Angeles, San Francisco, Miami, New York City, Toronto, and Vancouver as hubs, though many other cities can serve as departure points for travelers heading to foreign places. These cities serve as hubs to domestic coastal and near-coastal cities, as well.

- Hotels in North America often have special reduced-rate packages with easy requirements, such as age, business, or membership in organizations.

- AAA makes available to its members free or low-cost maps and travel kits. In fact, AAA is the world's largest publisher of maps and destination-related materials.

- The costs of staying in any North American city can vary enormously. Big cities (e.g., New York) tend to be expensive; smaller cities (especially in the U.S. South and Midwest) tend to be less so.

- Most hotels in North America belong to chains, and each chain tries to maintain a certain quality level among all its properties. Though there can be *great* variation within a chain (especially Hilton, Sheraton, Hyatt, and Holiday Inn), here is what level each chain generally represents:

Luxury	High End	Mid-Range	Budget
Four Seasons	Crowne Plaza	Clarion	Baymont
Peninsula	Fairmont	Delta	Best Western
Regent	Hyatt Regency	Doubletree	Comfort Inns
Ritz-Carlton	Inter-Continental	Embassy Suites	Days Inn
	JW Marriott	Hilton	Econo Lodge
	Le Meridien	Holiday Inn	Fairfield Inn
	Omni	Hyatt	Hampton Inns
	Renaissance	Marriott	Howard Johnson
	Sheraton Resorts	Radisson	La Quinta
	Sofitel	Ramada	Quality Inn
	Westin	Sheraton	Red Roof
			Rodeway Inn
			Travelodge

New York City's 660-acre La Guardia Airport could fit inside the 880-acre terminal building at JFK Airport.

Montreal, on the St. Lawrence River, is the world's largest inland port.

NAME _____   DATE _____

CREATIVE ACTIVITY

Listed below are seven possible vacation trips throughout North America. Try to think of one or more persons you know who might enjoy taking each trip. Write down their names for each vacation and give several reasons why you think it would appeal to them. If necessary, browse through upcoming Chapters 1 through 9 for additional information to guide you.

1. A seven-day riverboat cruise up the Mississippi River

2. A visit to Winter Carnival in Quebec City

3. A four-day stay in the Florida Keys

4. A week's stay in July at a New England hotel that faces the Atlantic

5. A nine-day escorted motorcoach tour of Boston, New York, Philadelphia, and Washington, D.C.

6. A raft trip down the Colorado River

7. A weekend in Utah's Rocky Mountains

Travel Trivia

North America's Distinctive Foods and Drinks

- Tourtiere in Quebec
- Espresso in Seattle
- Beignets in New Orleans
- Chili on spaghetti in Cincinnati
- Key lime pie in Florida
- Cheese steak sandwiches in Philadelphia
- Stone crabs and black beans in Miami
- Hot-smoked salmon in British Columbia
- Sourdough in San Francisco
- Sausages in Milwaukee
- Deep dish pizza in Chicago
- Beaver tails in Ottawa
- Quahogs, scrod, clam cakes, coffee cabs, chow mein, and chourico in southeastern Massachusetts

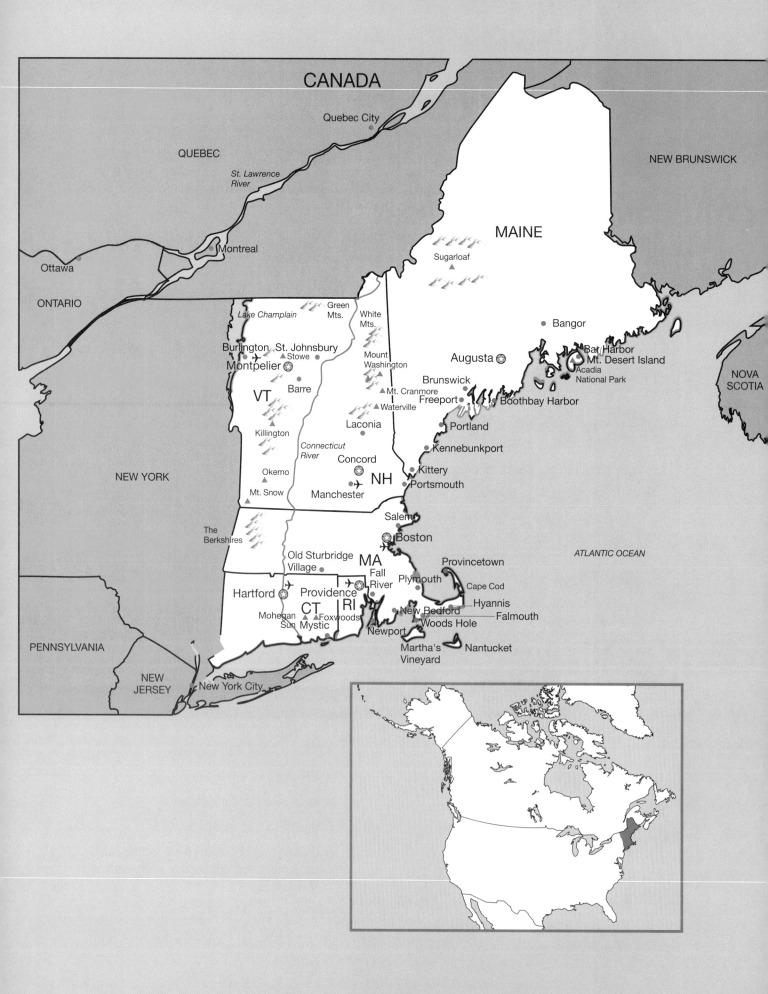

Chapter 1

New England
The Cradle of Liberty

If you grew up in the United States, you almost surely heard stories of the Pilgrims stepping on Plymouth Rock, of the first Thanksgiving meal, and of Paul Revere's midnight ride. So it's not surprising that if you mention New England to someone, a swirl of strong, clear images will come to mind: whaling ships, monuments, museums, white clapboard houses, and clambakes by the sea. No wonder it's such a popular destination.

There's a wealth of cities, states, and attractions in the compact northeast corner of the United States. Northernmost is **Maine**, a sparsely settled state of wild, stark beauty. To the southwest of Maine are **Vermont** and **New Hampshire**. (To keep these two straight, remember that Vermont is shaped like a *V*.) Both states are mountainous and wooded, with many charming towns dotting the landscape. South of Vermont and New Hampshire is **Massachusetts**, the most visited of the New England states. Finally, in New England's south are **Connecticut** and **Rhode Island**, the smallest U.S. state.

How Travelers Get There

Travelers have many ways to get to New England. If it's by car, they'll enter through New York State or Canada. If it's by air, they'll fly in on one of a half-dozen carriers that service the area. Cruise ships stop at New England cities on their way between New York City and Montreal. Rail service to New England is from Washington, D.C., and from New York City, it is via **Amtrak's** Metroliner or high-speed Acela train. Bus service is a good option for budget-minded visitors.

Most travelers bound for New England fly into **Boston's Logan Airport** (BOS), but **Providence**, Rhode Island (PVD); **Burlington**, Vermont (BTV); **Manchester**, New Hampshire (MHT); or **Hartford**, Connecticut (BDL), are good alternatives. Why? Because Logan is a very congested airport. Moreover, Boston itself would be a difficult city to navigate on arrival day. Flying time to New England is about five to six hours from the West Coast and one hour from New York.

Weather Patterns

"If you don't like New England's weather, wait a minute." That's an old saying locals use to describe their wildly changeable climate (see Figure 1–1). Winters are cold and snowy, especially in the mountain areas and away from the coast. Crisp, blue-skied winter days can be glorious. Early spring can be dreary, but May is usually a beautiful month. Summer temperatures are generally around 70 or 80 degrees, though very hot, humid spells occur more than New Englanders would like. Fall is especially beautiful; the fall foliage in October is justly famous.

Massachusetts has no cities named for saints. The reason: The founding Pilgrims and Puritans thought saints were too Catholic.

Boston cream pie is the official dessert of Massachusetts.

Rhode Island is only 37 miles wide and 48 miles long, but it has 400 miles of shoreline.

In what may have been the most expensive public works project in history, Boston channeled much of its highways underground. Its nickname: The Big Dig.

Climate at a Glance
BOSTON, MASSACHUSETTS

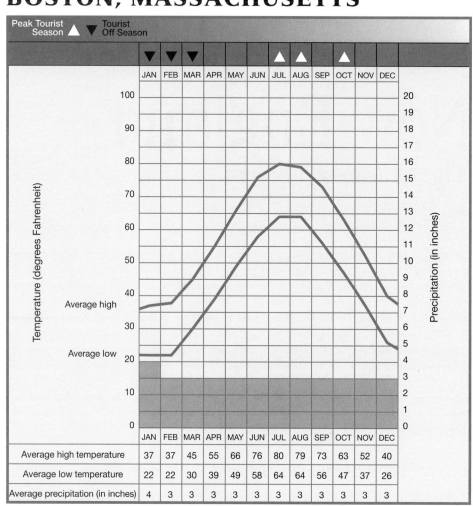

Figure 1–1

Overall, New England's precipitation is about the same year round. Multiday storms are possible most of the year, except in summer, when rainfall tends to occur in short, intense downpours. Tourist season peaks in the summer months and again during fall foliage time, with a sharp drop-off, except for skiers, in the winter.

Getting Around

Boston's city transportation system—especially the "T" subway-train network—is extensive. To visit all New England, however, visitors would do best to use a car. The highway network is superb, and quaint rural roads are numerous. Traffic jams are uncommon, except in and around Boston, where they can be monumental, or during summer weekends and holidays, when certain roads that access popular vacation places (e.g., Cape Cod and New Hampshire) get congested.

For people who don't want to drive, a New England motorcoach tour is an appealing option. Budget vacationers like the region's excellent bus system. Amtrak connects Boston with several key New England cities. Distances are so short that brief commuter flights are useful only for those in a real hurry and willing to pay for it. Ferry service to the offshore islands of **Martha's Vineyard** and **Nantucket** can make for a pleasant day's outing.

Two gables of the legendary House of the Seven Gables
Image copyright Laura Stone, 2008. Used under license from Shutterstock.com

Important Places

Which places in New England are must-sees? It's a hard choice—there are so many. What follows are New England's most popular cities and attractions.

Boston

Boston is a graceful and historic city. Because its attractions are clustered in a compact area, visitors can walk the well-marked, 5-mile **Freedom Trail** and see most of the historical sites in a day. City tours and boat tours are also an excellent way for people to orient themselves to Boston. Cultural opportunities and fine dining experiences abound.

Among the sights that are "musts":

- **Boston Common**, the oldest park in the nation, and the adjoining **Public Garden**, with its unique "swan boats."
- **The Old State House**, the seat of Massachusetts's government.
- **The Boston Tea Party Ship**, a full-sized replica of one of the ships involved in the well-known protest. A museum next door documents its history.
- **Many museums**, especially the **Museum of Fine Arts**, the **Museum of Science**, the **New England Aquarium**, and **JFK Library & Museum** (south of the city on Columbia Point).
- **Faneuil** [FAN-yule] **Hall Marketplace** (including **Quincy Market**), a restored complex of shops, dining facilities, and historic buildings.

The longest place name in the United States belongs to a Massachusetts lake: Chargogagmanchauga-ugaugaugaugcharbun-agungamaugg, which means, "You fish on your side of the lake, I'll fish on my side, and nobody fishes in the middle."

Boston's subway system, constructed in 1897, was the first in the United States

The Italian food in Boston's North End is superb.

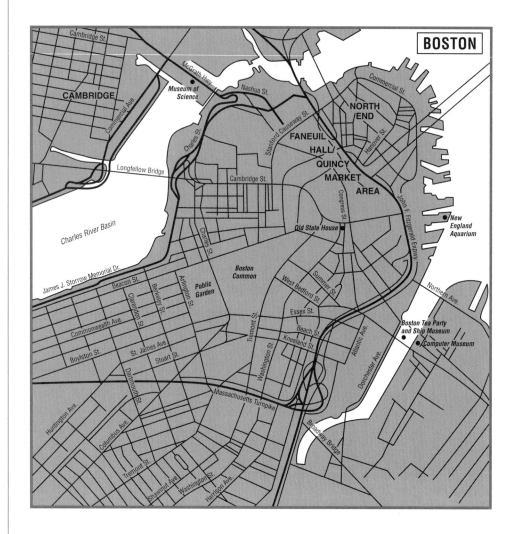

- **The U.S.S. *Constitution*,** nicknamed *Old Ironsides*, a 200-year-old frigate used in the War of 1812.

The Fig Newton is named after Newton, Massachusetts.

- **Cambridge,** home to **Harvard University** and its own fine museums.

    Among the **day trips** from Boston are:

- **Salem,** the infamous seat of the Massachusetts witchcraft trials and the location of Hawthorne's *The House of the Seven Gables.*
- **Plymouth,** with its universally known rock (it's a bit of a disappointment), replica of the *Mayflower*, and fascinating recreated settlement, **Plimoth Plantation.**
- **The Berkshires,** Massachusetts's western mountain range, with its breathtaking vistas, especially in fall foliage season, and its **Old Sturbridge Village,** a living history museum that captures New England as it was centuries ago.
- **Cape Cod,** potentially a stay-over option in itself, which boasts superb beaches, and **Provincetown,** at the Cape's tip.

Vermont, New Hampshire, and Maine

These three Northern states have much in common: forested hills, country inns, small towns, and dramatic scenery. Many of New Hampshire's attractions are only a little more than an hour's drive from Boston and could be made into a day trip. Most of this state's sites lie in the **White Mountains,** along old Route 3. **Mt. Washington,** whose summit can

Ben & Jerry's, in Waterbury, Vermont, offers tours of its ice-cream factory.

be reached by a cog railway, is New England's highest mountain, and **Laconia** is every visitor's idea of a New England town. **Portsmouth**, New Hampshire's former capital and its only seaport, is filled with many quaint homes, shops, and taverns.

Vermont is even more picturesque than New Hampshire, perhaps because it's less industrialized than its neighbor. It's a state of pristine lakes, covered bridges, and excellent ski trails. Many cute little towns dot two major highways; **Barre** [BARE-ree] (once the source of most of the nation's granite), **Montpelier** (the capital), and **Burlington** are along Interstate 89, and **St. Johnsbury** (noted for maple syrup) is on Interstate 91.

Maine is more than three times larger than any of its neighbor states, yet most of its area is dense forest and uncultivated brush. Maine's rocky coastline is breathtaking. This is best seen at **Bar Harbor**, the gateway to **Acadia National Park** and to cruises into Canada. **Boothbay Harbor** is a major boating center. **Kennebunkport** is a charming summer resort that has attracted the likes of Booth Tarkington, Rachel Carson, and George Bush. **Kittery** is a well-visited shipbuilding center, and **Brunswick** has many historic buildings.

As for skiing, **Killington** and **Stowe**, Vermont; **Sugarloaf**, Maine; and **Waterville**, New Hampshire, are highly praised. Other well-known ski resorts are **Mt. Snow** and **Okemo**, Vermont; and **Mt. Cranmore**, New Hampshire.

The Southern Coast

Many travelers make the mistake of treating this region as simply something to cross on the way from New York to Cape Cod or Boston. Yet some of New England's finest attractions lie along its southern coast. From west to east, they are:

- **Mohegan Sun Casino** in Uncasville, Connecticut, and **Foxwoods Resort and Casino** in Ledyard, Connecticut, Native American–owned casino-hotels that bring Las Vegas–like glitz to New England.

- **Mystic**, Connecticut, a seaport that looks much the same as it did in its whaling heyday.

There are more islands in the Maine archipelago than in either the Caribbean or Polynesia.

Connecticut's official state insect is the praying mantis.

A stark, windswept vista of Maine's Acadia National Park
Image copyright 2265524729, 2008. Used under license from Shutterstock.com

Marble House is one of Newport's famous mansions
Photo by Marc Mancini

Stroll the Cliff Walk, a path that skirts the ocean and mansion lawns of Newport.

- **Providence**, Rhode Island's rejuvenated capital, with many restaurants, nightspots, and stately old houses near **Brown University**. On selected nights, a remarkable display, **Waterfire**, illuminates the city's riverfront area.
- **Newport**, Rhode Island, a gem of an attraction that features nearly a dozen great cliffside mansions open to the public. (Two of the most impressive: **The Breakers** and **Marble House**.) Here, too, are the **Tennis Hall of Fame** and **Touro Synagogue**, founded in 1763. It's about 90 minutes from Boston.
- **New Bedford**, Massachusetts, where Melville's *Moby Dick* is set, with its restored downtown area and remnants of a once-booming whaling industry.
- **Martha's Vineyard** and **Nantucket**, Massachusetts, charming islands accessed by ferry from several southern Massachusetts ports.

Possible Itineraries

The name *Connecticut* means "long river place" in the Mohican language.

Visitors who plan to hub out of Boston or another city will need at least a week to fully sample New England. Tourists may also decide to stay over in several towns and cities, with their whole itinerary taking as much as two weeks. An appropriate itinerary would start in Boston, travel up into New Hampshire, Maine, and Vermont for a few days, and then head down through the Berkshires and continue south to Connecticut. The trip could continue along the south coast to Cape Cod, then back to Plymouth and Boston.

Lodging Options

The Borden House in Fall River, Massachusetts, where Lizzie Borden (may have) murdered her parents, is now a tourist attraction; bed-and-breakfasts are available.

Hotels and motels are plentiful in New England. Boston's luxury properties are expensive, as are those on Cape Cod; lodging in the summer outside Boston, though, can be reasonable. In fact, for those who intend to stay in only one or two cities and hub their way out to various attractions, a good option would be to lodge in and around Providence, Fall River (Massachusetts), or any one of Boston's outlying towns. Each of these is at a major juncture of highways. A well-developed network of inns and bed-and-breakfasts exists throughout New England.

Allied Destinations

A trip to New England can be easily combined with a trip to the Mid-Atlantic region, especially to New York State and New York City (a little more than four hours driving time from Boston). One option is to combine the trip with eastern Canada: Montreal is only about 300 miles from Boston, and Halifax, Nova Scotia, is but a short cruise from Bar Harbor, Maine.

Factors That Motivate Visitors

Among the factors that will pique interest in New England are:

- It has a historic heritage and plenty of cultural and educational opportunities.
- Travel outside Boston, especially during the off-season, is quite affordable.
- Scenery—both seaside and mountain—is impressive.
- Driving around is very easy, especially outside Boston.
- The region is very close to New York and Canada.
- Cruises afford an efficient way to see the coastal towns.
- The fine food of the area (especially the seafood) has a renowned reputation and is reasonable.
- Excellent skiing facilities exist in Vermont, Massachusetts, and New Hampshire.
- The summer beaches and water-sport opportunities are quite good, especially along the southern coast and Cape Cod.
- The fall foliage season is beautiful. (Make sure to book early!)

Qualifying the Traveler
New England

For People Who Want	High	Medium	Low	Remarks
Historical and Cultural Attractions	▲			Especially Boston area
Beaches and Water Sports		▲		Mostly summers
Skiing Opportunities	▲			Very good, but not alpine
Lots of Nightlife			▲	Boston mostly
Family Activities		▲		Experience history
Familiar Cultural Experience	▲			Well-known landmarks
Exotic Cultural Experience			▲	Some ethnic neighborhoods
Safety and Low Crime		▲		Some crime in Boston
Bargain Travel		▲		Outside Boston and off-season
Impressive Scenery	▲			In mountains, along ocean
Peace and Quiet		▲		Especially northern areas
Shopping Opportunities	▲			Mill outlets for clothing
Adventure		▲		Mountain-related
To Do Business		▲		Especially in and around Boston, Providence

An offbeat attraction in Dedham, Massachusetts: the Museum of Bad Art.

The waters off New England used to have so many lobsters that the colonists would feed them to their chickens.

The Trapp Family, of *Sound of Music* fame, owns a ski lodge in Stowe, Vermont.

Possible Misgivings

Even the most appealing destinations provoke a few misgivings. Here are some you're likely to encounter:

- "All that history and scenery will be boring." Suggest New England's beaches, ski trails, and the nightlife in Boston.
- "It's too expensive." Only Boston and a few other areas are costly. Lodge off-season or in off-the-beaten-path cities, such as Providence, Fall River, New Bedford, or Boston's outlying towns. Bargains can also be easily had in New Hampshire, Vermont, and Maine (except during fall foliage season).
- "I don't like to drive." Concentrate the visitor's plans in Boston so that public transit can be used. Suggest an escorted tour or a cruise.
- "I once flew into Boston and the place was frantic!" Suggest flying into Providence or other cities as an alternative.

Sales Strategies

The best way to upsell New England is to suggest an expansion of the planned itinerary or to bring up the idea of a motorcoach tour or a New England–Canada cruise. Some of Boston's lower-cost hotels leave something to be desired; a top-class hotel is advisable. A city or boat tour of Boston and, especially, a car rental are obvious cross-sell opportunities. If an upscale traveler has limited time, and especially if the traveler doesn't want to drive, commuter flights between New England's points of interest could be an attractive option. Winter ski packages and fall foliage tours of New England are perennial bestsellers.

Travel Trivia: Unusual North American Place Names

Bald Head, Maine	Moose Jaw, Saskatchewan
Happy Jack, Arizona	Walla Walla, Washington
Bat Cave, North Carolina	Black Gnat, Kentucky
Lollipop, Texas	Colon, Missouri
Medicine Hat, Alberta	Cut and Shoot, Texas
Broken Arrow, Oklahoma	Elbow, Saskatchewan
Clam, Michigan	Porkee, Pennsylvania
Noodle, Texas	Droop, West Virginia
Couch, Missouri	Salvage, Newfoundland and Labrador
Five Fingers, New Brunswick	Funk, Nebraska
Okay, Oklahoma	Tuna, Pennsylvania
Toad Suck, Arkansas	Lithium, Missouri
Truth or Consequences, New Mexico	Zzyzx, California
Asphalt, Kentucky	Moose Factory, Ontario
Hygiene, Colorado	Egg Harbor City, New Jersey

NAME _____   **DATE** _____

MAP ACTIVITY

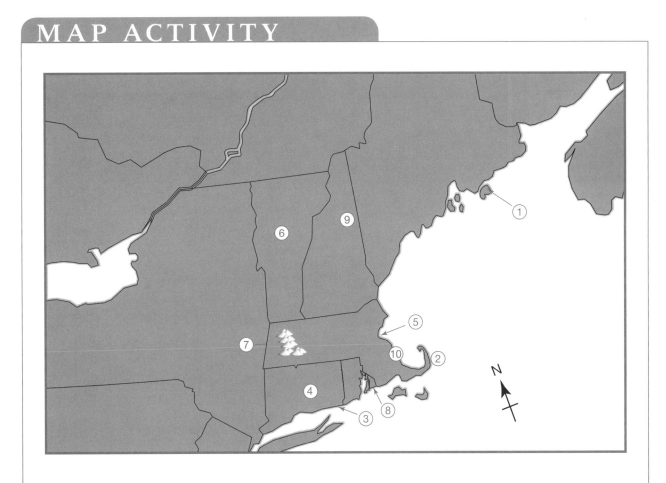

A traveler wants to visit the places listed below. Which number represents each on the map?

Place/Attraction	In Which State?	Number on Map
A. Bar Harbor	A. _____	A. _____
B. Mystic	B. _____	B. _____
C. The Freedom Trail	C. _____	C. _____
D. The Berkshires	D. _____	D. _____
E. Mt. Washington	E. _____	E. _____
F. Cape Cod	F. _____	F. _____
G. Foxwoods	G. _____	G. _____
H. Montpelier	H. _____	H. _____
I. Newport	I. _____	I. _____
J. Plymouth	J. _____	J. _____

NAME _____   **DATE** _____

CASE STUDY

Mary and Jane Pepperidge grew up in Boston and now, after 20 years, want to return to New England during fall foliage season. They intend to fly to Boston and then drive around the countryside in a rental car. They're willing to spend extra money for the trip, though they also like value for their dollar. The length of the trip is not a consideration for them.

Circle the answer that best suits their needs.

1 When should they go?

    Late summer   September

    May   October

    Why?

2 In which of the following areas would they see great fall foliage scenery?

    Mystic   The Berkshires

    Cape Cod   Walpole Prison

    Why?

3 Which of the following cities would *not* have an airport that could serve as an alternative to Logan Airport?

    Providence   Burlington

    Hartford   Salem

    Why?

4 Which of the following would be *least* likely to appeal to these people?

    A stay at a seaside lodge on Cape Cod

    A fine hotel in Boston

    A side trip up Route 89

    Something better than a subcompact car

    Why?

NAME _____   **DATE** _____

CREATIVE ACTIVITY

You're a travel counselor at an agency that sells many trips to New England. Recently you saw a chart in an industry magazine that lists all the possible cross-sell items that could be offered to travelers. You want to create a list that you can consult whenever you send someone to New England. Check all the cross-sell items that you think could apply to a New England holiday. Then, go on the Internet. Find five New England companies that actually offer five of the activities you checked. Write each company's name next to the checked item.

__ air sightseeing excursion

__ attraction admission

__ balloon ride

__ barge cruise

__ bicycling tour

__ boat cruise (limited)

__ bon voyage party

__ campground reservation

__ car rental

__ car rental insurance

__ city tour

__ concert

__ convention arrangements

__ culinary classes

__ cultural event

__ dine-around package

__ dinner theater

__ diving package

__ ferry transport

__ fishing package

__ gambling package

__ glass-bottom boat tour

__ golf package

__ helicopter tour

__ hiking package

__ honeymoon package

__ horseback-riding package

__ hunting package

__ insurance

__ interpreter service

__ jeep rental

__ kennel service

__ limo service

__ luau

__ meal plan

__ meet-and-greet service

__ meeting arrangements

__ motorhome rental

__ nightclub show

__ nightlife tour

__ passport photo service

__ postcruise land package

__ precruise land package

__ private car

__ private guide

__ pub-hopping tour

__ raft adventure

__ rail excursion

__ rail pass

__ resort package

__ safari outing

__ sailing package

__ shopping tour

__ shore excursion

__ ski package

__ snorkel package

__ spa enrollment

__ sporting event ticket

__ submarine ride

__ tennis package

__ theater ticket

__ theme park admission

__ tramway ride

__ transfer service

__ travel accessories

__ traveler's cheques

__ video rental/sale

__ walking tour

__ wedding package

__ welcome party

__ yacht charter

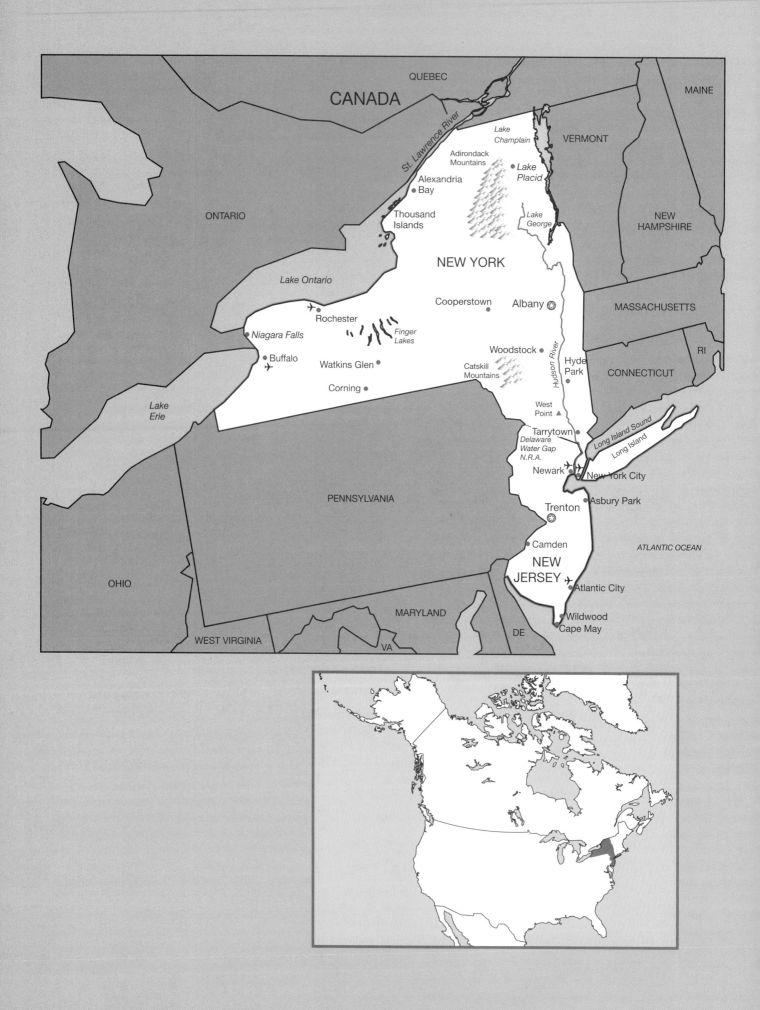

Chapter 2

New York and New Jersey
Broadway and Boardwalk

What does a person imagine when thinking of **New York City**? Great museums? Nightlife until dawn? Crowding? Broadway theater? It'll be a complex vision, for sure.

There's plenty beyond "The Big Apple," too: **upstate New York**, the upscale beaches of **Long Island**, and the huge gaming casino-hotels along **Atlantic City**'s Boardwalk.

First, a little geography: New York City is just off the Atlantic Ocean, between New England and the Mid-Atlantic States. America's most populous city, New York comprises five divisions, or boroughs; when travelers say, "New York," though, they usually mean not the entire city, but the borough-island of **Manhattan**, where the business and tourist action are. The other four boroughs are largely residential and industrial.

New York, of course, also refers to the entire state New York City is in. New York State, which stretches several hundred miles northward and westward from New York City, has many attractions of its own, including **West Point**, the **Catskill** and **Adirondack Mountains**, the **Finger Lakes**, and **Niagara Falls**. **Albany**, not New York City, is the state capital.

To New York City's south is the state of New Jersey. The 50-mile-long Jersey shore is famous for its beaches. **Atlantic City**, the best known of its beach cities and famous for its gambling, is about a two-hour drive from Manhattan.

New Jersey was named for England's Duke of Jersey; New York for the English Duke of York.

How Travelers Get There

A vast network of highways, rail lines (including the high-speed Acela train), and air routes converge on New York City. Getting there won't be a problem. Choosing which airport to fly into might be a more difficult decision. **La Guardia** (LGA) is only 8 miles from downtown Manhattan, but the route between them can be slow moving, especially around rush hour. **Kennedy International Airport** (JFK) is farther out (15 miles), as is **Newark Liberty International** (EWR), in nearby New Jersey. Flying time from West Coast cities is about five hours.

How to transfer from any of these airports to the city is even more complicated. Cabs and limousines (usually cars, not actual limos) are the favored means of transportation, but they're expensive, especially from Newark. Rail lines now link Newark and JFK with transfer stations where passengers can catch trains to Manhattan's Penn Station. Share-a-ride cabs operate from La Guardia. Buses and minibuses also provide transfers from all three airports, and car rentals are an option as well.

What should you recommend? People in a hurry or on a budget should, if possible, fly into La Guardia, especially if they aren't arriving during rush hour. Newark is perhaps the

Ausable Chasm, in upstate New York, is one of America's oldest private attractions.

best choice for travelers who can use the train, who won't be shocked by a hefty taxi fare, or who want to avoid stop-and-go traffic. Because of traffic and distance, JFK is rarely the best choice, yet it receives more flights (especially from a long distance) than the other two; visitors may have no choice but to fly into this airport. (Fortunately the train service makes JFK somewhat less arduous.) For those who want to drive into and around New York City, a warning: City traffic is intense and parking fees astronomical.

Several smaller airports service New York City and the overall region. Atlantic City (ACY) has a modest airport; **Rochester** (ROC) serves the northern part of New York; and **Buffalo Niagara** (BUF) is often used by visitors to western New York State and Ontario, Canada. Many other New York cities have medium-sized airports. Rail lines and highways enter New York State and New Jersey from every direction. They are heavily used. For example, more than 90 percent of all visitors to Atlantic City arrive by car or bus.

A reminder: New York City is a major cruise port, with ships leaving for (and coming from) Canada, New England, Bermuda, and, occasionally, Europe and more southerly United States and Caribbean ports.

Weather Patterns

New York State and New Jersey have typical Northeastern U.S. weather: warm to hot summers and cold winters. Late spring and fall are extremely pleasant. Humidity can be a factor

The Statue of Liberty was, in part, inspired by the Colossus of Rhodes, a huge statue that stood at the harbor entrance of Rhodes, a Greek island.

Climate at a Glance
NEW YORK, NEW YORK

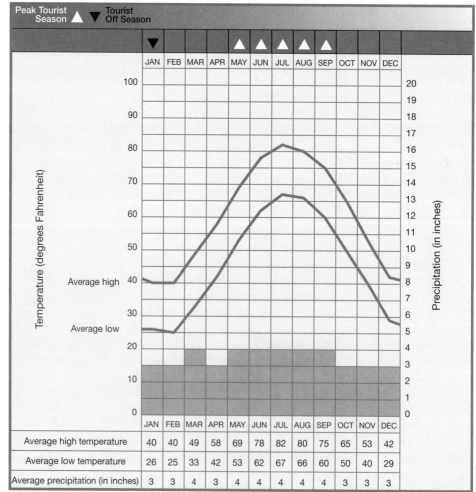

	JAN	FEB	MAR	APR	MAY	JUN	JUL	AUG	SEP	OCT	NOV	DEC
Average high temperature	40	40	49	58	69	78	82	80	75	65	53	42
Average low temperature	26	25	33	42	53	62	67	66	60	50	40	29
Average precipitation (in inches)	3	3	4	3	4	4	4	4	4	3	3	3

Figure 2–1

at any time of the year, with rainstorms or snowstorms in the winter and sudden thundershowers in the summer. Upstate New York has colder winters than New York City, often with considerable snow. New York City tends to be warmer than most cities, perhaps because all that concrete retains the heat. Precipitation can also wreak havoc in the city, causing traffic jams and making an available taxi almost impossible to find (see Figure 2–1).

As for tourist patterns, upstate New York and most of New Jersey peak in summer, with tourism dropping off as the cold sets in. Atlantic City is packed on weekends. New York City has virtually no off-season, except perhaps in January and, to some extent, on weekends.

Getting Around

New York State and New Jersey have well-developed highway systems, but with many tolls. The train and bus systems are also quite convenient and are popular with New York commuters. One of the most popular short cruises out of New York City: a trip up the Hudson River.

The best way to get around New York City is by taxi; they're plentiful, relatively inexpensive, and fast. The subway and bus system is extensive and convenient. Contrary to what you may have heard, New York subways are relatively safe, especially during the day. A multitude of cars for hire and limos swarm through the city; they're a good choice for upscale visitors. New York is also a very walkable city, though only in certain areas and at certain times. Travelers should check with hotel staff before setting out on foot for a destination within the city.

Visitors to New York City can also get around by tour. Motorcoach tours are usually excellent (guides are licensed by the city) and the Circle Line boat tour that circles Manhattan is famous. The ferry rides to the **Statue of Liberty**, **Ellis Island**, and **Staten Island** afford wonderful, inexpensive views.

Important Places

This area's destinations can be divided into two categories: New York City itself, and New York State and New Jersey. Some of the latter category's attractions may be done as day trips from New York City, though most visitors who stay in Manhattan rarely take such day trips, except perhaps the Hudson River cruise.

New York City

New York City is astonishingly rich in attractions. Many, like **Chinatown** or the huge **St. John the Divine Cathedral**, are best visited as part of a city tour. Among the most popular attractions people visit on their own are:

- **The Statue of Liberty**, perhaps the world's most famous statue, and Ellis Island, both accessed by a ferry from Battery Park (or from Liberty State Park in Jersey City, New Jersey). Due to security and safety issues, visitors can no longer climb up inside the statue.
- **The Empire State Building**, whose higher levels afford the best views of Manhattan.
- **The United Nations**, one of New York's most graceful structures and an important world forum.
- **Rockefeller Center**, a "city of tomorrow" designed in the 1930s, with its famous skating rink (a cafe in the summer), the NBC Studio Tour, Radio City Music Hall (one of America's largest theaters), and nearby St. Patrick's Cathedral.
- **Superb museums**, most notably the **Metropolitan Museum of Art**, the **Museum of Modern Art** (MoMA), the **Guggenheim Museum**, and the **Museum of Natural History**.
- **Well-known neighborhoods**, including **Greenwich Village**, **Chinatown**, **Little Italy**, **South Street Seaport** (a renovated riverside restaurant and shopping area),

Of major U.S. cities, New York has the highest percentage of people who walk to work.

The world's largest cathedral (St. John the Divine) and largest synagogue (Temple Emanuel) are both in New York City.

The Statue of Liberty wears 24.9-feet-long sandals, the equivalent of a women's shoe size 879.

Lightning strikes the Empire State Building about 25 times per year.

Central Park is larger than the nation of Monaco.

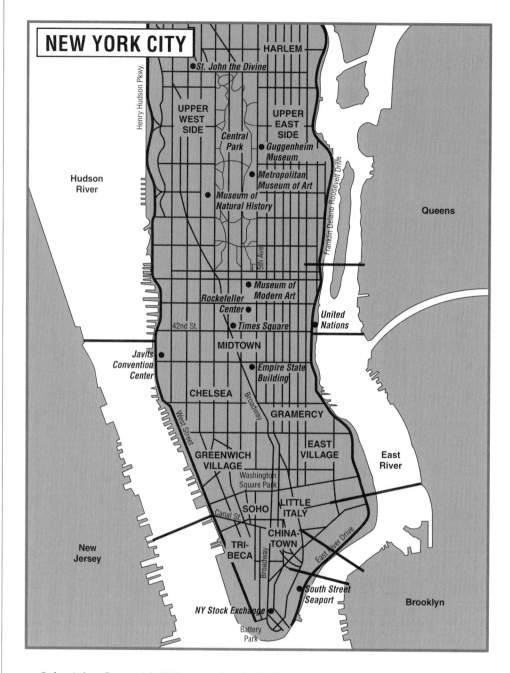

Soho (what Greenwich Village used to look like), neon-lit **Times Square**, and **Central Park** (superb during the day, *not* advisable at night).

- **Ground Zero**, where the Twin Towers of the World Trade Center were destroyed by terrorists, has become an often-visited memorial site.

- **Abundant nightlife opportunities**, most notably the wealth of Broadway and off-Broadway plays and musicals, and major sporting events.

New York State

The rest of the state of New York is equally interesting. The following are the most popular with leisure travelers:

- **The Hudson River Valley.** Often called "America's Rhine," this picturesque route just north of New York City features many points of interest. Among them: **Tarrytown**, which captures the world of Washington Irving's *The Legend of Sleepy Hollow*;

New York City's St. Patrick's Cathedral soars above Fifth Ave
Image copyright Christina Richards, 2008. Used under license from Shutterstock.com

West Point, the U.S. military academy; and **Hyde Park**, best known for its Vanderbilt Mansion and the home of Franklin Roosevelt.

- **Long Island**. Stretching eastward from New York City and paralleling the southern New England coast, Long Island features excellent beaches, superb boating and fishing, many rental cottages, and mansion-dotted towns. It's more of a destination for New Yorkers, though, than for tourists from other regions.

- **The Catskills**. Northwest of Hyde Park is the Catskill Mountain area, long known for its old-time entertainment. Nearby is **Woodstock**, now an artists' community, which was the site of the legendary '60s rock-music festival. Northeast of the Catskills is the state's capital, Albany, with its huge, stark complex of government buildings.

- **The upstate Lakes District**. Both **Lake Champlain** and **Lake George** are lined with resorts, hotels, old forts, and all manner of tourist attractions. In fact, things can get a little too touristy in both places. Here also are the Adirondack Mountains, which offer six million acres of campsites, chasms, fishing, unspoiled hiking trails, and fall foliage. **Lake Placid**, within the Adirondacks, is a noted ski resort area that hosted the 1980 Winter Olympics. The very northwest part of the state borders Lake Ontario and the St. Lawrence River. Here are the **Thousand Islands** with many pleasing vistas, homes, and mansions—most often visited via half-day cruises out of the town of **Alexandria Bay**.

- **The Finger Lakes**. This region in the west-central part of the state delights photographers with its waterfalls, wineries, scenic vistas, imposing gorges, and 600 miles of shoreline. Also nearby are **Corning**, with its well-known glass factory and museum; **Watkins Glen**, famous for its gorge and auto racing; and the **Baseball Hall of Fame**, in **Cooperstown**.

There are nearly 2,000 islands in the Thousand Islands.

The New York Stock Exchange has a fascinating exhibition tour on weekdays.

■ **Niagara Falls**. Although near Buffalo, New York, Niagara Falls is covered in greater detail in Chapter 6 (Canada and Alaska). The New York side of the falls is not as dramatically beautiful as the Canadian side, nor is it where the best lodging is located. (Canada has all the Falls-view properties.)

Atlantic City

The first thing to strike visitors to Atlantic City is the familiar street names: Atlantic City inspired the board game Monopoly. The second thing to grab their attention is the intense strip of hotels, casinos, restaurants, amusements, shopping centers, and nightspots that line the Boardwalk. Beyond that, there's not much else to see; the beach is impressive and the convention center vast, but the area away from the Boardwalk is run-down. Those who have spent time in Las Vegas may be a bit disappointed: Atlantic City isn't quite the attraction for high rollers and themed resorts that Las Vegas is. Indeed, most people who go to Atlantic City do so as a brief getaway from East Coast cities, to perhaps win a few dollars and to take in some first-rate entertainment.

The Jersey Shore boasts broad beaches, popular nightclubs, and much family entertainment, though it's not the beach resort area it was 100 years ago. **Wildwood** is probably the best-known town along the shore, with a half-dozen amusement areas and lively after-dark entertainment. **Asbury Park** is also well known as the place where many rock performers became famous. And a visit to **Cape May**, an astonishing collection of well-preserved Victorian buildings and houses, would be a delightful recommendation. Two other New Jersey options are **Camden**, with its impressive aquarium, and the ruggedly scenic **Delaware Water Gap National Recreation Area**, with its camping, hiking, and other outdoor activities.

Possible Itineraries

It takes five to seven days to experience New York City, though the city's high cost may make such a stay quite expensive. A three- or four-day stay could enable visitors to see New York's principal highlights at a somewhat more reasonable cost. Atlantic City probably warrants no more than two days. A motoring tour of upstate New York could be done in about a week, with one or two days at such attractions as Niagara Falls, Lake Champlain, the Finger Lakes, or Lake George.

Atlantic City's historic Boardwalk
Photo by Marc Mancini

Lodging Options

One thing visitors must know: They'll pay about twice as much for lodging in New York City as they would for the same level of value in most other U.S. cities (though very good weekend "bargain" packages are often available). Rooms also tend to be small. The most popular, convenient, and safe lodging area in New York City is south and east of Central Park, though fine hotels are scattered throughout the midtown area. Hotels in the Times Square–Broadway theater district are plentiful; many new properties have been built there and many older ones renovated. New York's downtown district—where the **Wall Street** stock exchanges, numerous corporate headquarters, and quite a number of tourist attractions are located—offers a few lodging choices.

Atlantic City is a comparative bargain. The glitzy, hulking properties along the Boardwalk can be pricey, but special three-day, two-night tour packages (especially on weekdays) are plentiful and may be a genuine bargain.

Accommodations across the rest of New Jersey and New York are generally reasonable, with the usual spectrum of hotels, motels, bed-and-breakfasts, and camping facilities.

Allied Destinations

All the following are within a day by land or an hour or two by air from the New York–New Jersey area: New England, southeastern Ontario, southern Quebec, Pennsylvania, Delaware, Maryland, Washington, D.C.; and parts of Virginia, West Virginia, and Ohio. Destinations in any of these areas are a logical extension of a New York–New Jersey stay. Remember, too, that New York City is a hub for cruises (especially to Bermuda and Quebec) and for flights to Europe, Africa, and, in some cases, South America. Travelers bound for these places often like the notion of a day or two in New York City as a way to break up a long trip.

Factors That Motivate Visitors

Those who wish to visit New York City will probably want to do so for the following reasons:

- There's a remarkable wealth of tourist attractions.
- There are numerous transportation options into and out of the city.

An urban legend: If you were to stay in Times Square, within a few days you'd see someone you know.

Three original stores—Macy's, Bloomingdale's, and FAO Schwarz—are worth a special visit.

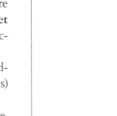

Gananoque is one of several points of departure for Thousand Islands cruises
Image copyright LesPalenik, 2008. Used under license from Shutterstock.com

- The shopping is extraordinary; as one brochure puts it, "If you can't find it in New York, it doesn't exist."
- New York City is home to more corporations and hosts more conventions than any other U.S. city.
- No city has a greater variety of choices for fine dining and nightlife.
- The city's museums are among the world's greatest.
- Christmas time is festive.
- There's a constant stream of major sporting events.
- The cultural, artistic, and entertainment opportunities are seemingly endless.

People have a separate set of expectations for the rest of the area. Among the features that may attract them are:

- camping and skiing opportunities, especially in the Adirondacks, and the great natural beauty of upstate New York and parts of New Jersey;
- the convenient system of highways, making driving easy;
- the beaches and water sports, especially on Long Island, the Jersey Shore, and in the upstate Lakes District; and
- gambling in Atlantic City and Native American–run casinos.

Half-price theater tickets are available on the day of performance at Times Square.

Qualifying the Traveler
New York City

For People Who Want	High	Medium	Low	Remarks
Historical and Cultural Attractions	▲			Superb museums
Beaches and Water Sports			▲	Mostly for locals, Long Island is good
Skiing Opportunities			▲	Catskills and Adirondacks
Lots of Nightlife	▲			Superb theater
Family Activities	▲			Famous tourist sites
Familiar Cultural Experience		▲		New York City *is* different
Exotic Cultural Experience		▲		New York City *is* different
Safety and Low Crime		▲		Not as bad as reputation
Bargain Travel			▲	Extremely expensive
Impressive Scenery			▲	Must go north of city
Peace and Quiet			▲	A noisy city
Shopping Opportunities	▲			For luxury items
Adventure			▲	
To Do Business	▲			More corporate headquarters than any other city

Possible Misgivings

New York and New Jersey are wonderful destinations. However, uninformed travelers often have reservations about going there, especially to New York City. Here are a few examples of misgivings and how to handle them:

- "New York City is too expensive." There are ways to reduce the cost of a New York City holiday. Recommend a shorter stay than they may have intended, thus cutting lodging cost; seek out weekend bargain rates at moderately priced hotels; emphasize the low cost of transportation to, around, and from Manhattan; mention discount theater ticket prices; advise them to eat at coffee shops and delis rather than at full-blown (and full-priced) restaurants.
- "New York City is dangerous." New York City is a much safer place than it used to be. Emphasize that your lodging recommendation is in a safe area. Advise them to check with hotel personnel about when and where it's safe to walk around.
- "Upstate New York sounds boring." The wealth of natural and manmade attractions is striking; even the most jaded can't help being impressed. If mentioning this doesn't work, maybe this is the kind of person who will flourish in New York City.
- "Atlantic City is only for gambling." The beach here and all along the coast is wonderful, the entertainment is excellent, and nearby Cape May is an architectural wonder.

Sales Strategies

Upselling hotels in New York City and Atlantic City is an attractive strategy, because budget properties in both places can provoke complaints. Outside these cities, car rentals and bus or train travel are appropriate services to offer to those not driving their own cars.

New York City offers many cross-sell opportunities. Airport transfers via limousine services are very popular. Theater tickets, city tours, and boat cruises can be booked in advance. Suggest FIT extensions into allied destinations if the traveler's vacation time permits. Remember that business travelers may wish to extend their stay in New York City for leisure, perhaps with their families joining them. Also, cruisers are often open to a pre- or post-cruise package in New York City.

Major tour operators offer a gamut of tours to Atlantic City, New York City, and upstate New York. Ski packages to upstate resorts are popular as well.

New York City has eight times more taxis than Los Angeles.

New York City has about 25,000 acres of parkland.

Travel Trivia

Where Fast Foods Were Invented

Hot dog: New York City
Sandwich: England
Submarine sandwich: Groton, Connecticut
Big Mac: Pittsburgh, Pennsylvania
Pizza: Greece, Italy
Fortune cookie: Los Angeles, California
Chop suey: San Francisco, California
Ice cream: China
Ice-cream cone: St. Louis, Missouri
Ice-cream soda: Philadelphia, Pennsylvania

SOURCE: The History Channel

NAME _____   **DATE** _____

MAP ACTIVITY

A traveler wants to visit the places listed below. Which number represents each on the map?

Place/Attraction	In/Near Which City?	Number on Map
A. An enormous waterfall	A. _____	A. _____
B. The Metropolitan Museum of Art	B. _____	B. _____
C. The Boardwalk	C. _____	C. _____
D. Hundreds of Victorian houses	D. _____	D. _____
E. South Street Seaport	E. _____	E. _____
F. St. John the Divine Cathedral	F. _____	F. _____
G. A glass factory	G. _____	G. _____
H. A noted ski resort	H. _____	H. _____
I. A Thousand Islands cruise	I. _____	I. _____
J. Radio City Music Hall	J. _____	J. _____

NAME _____   DATE _____

CASE STUDY

Abe Farkas is a lawyer and his wife, Susan, is a stock analyst. They live in Cincinnati and want a three-day weekend getaway to Manhattan. They can leave late Friday afternoon and must return by Sunday night. They love theater, fine dining, and museums. They have been to New York City at least a half-dozen times before.

Circle the answer that best suits their needs.

1 In which area should they probably stay?

    Downtown   The Broadway district

    Brooklyn   The Boardwalk

Why?

2 Which would probably appeal to them the most?

    Theater tickets   A cruise up the Hudson

    A car rental   A full-day tour

Why?

3 Which recommendation would be correct?

    You should have breakfast at Tiffany's

    It'll be just a short walk from your hotel to Radio City Music Hall

    Visit Hyde Park, Manhattan's largest park

    While you're in Soho, you should go see MoMA

Why?

4 Which New York City attraction should you suggest that they visit?

    A Stock Exchange tour   A tour of the United Nations

    A Rockefeller Center tour   The Museum of Modern Art

Why?

NAME _____   **DATE** _____

CREATIVE ACTIVITY

You're an executive with ACME Hotels, a chain of mid-priced lodging properties headquartered in Boston. The company, which targets families with children, has decided to expand into New York State and New Jersey. The corporation has asked you to propose five cities in which to locate these hotels. What would your five recommendations be, and why?

Location	Reasons
① New York City	① Key American tourist city. New York City has a need for more hotels that are family affordable. Large population within driving distance.
②	②
③	③
④	④
⑤	⑤

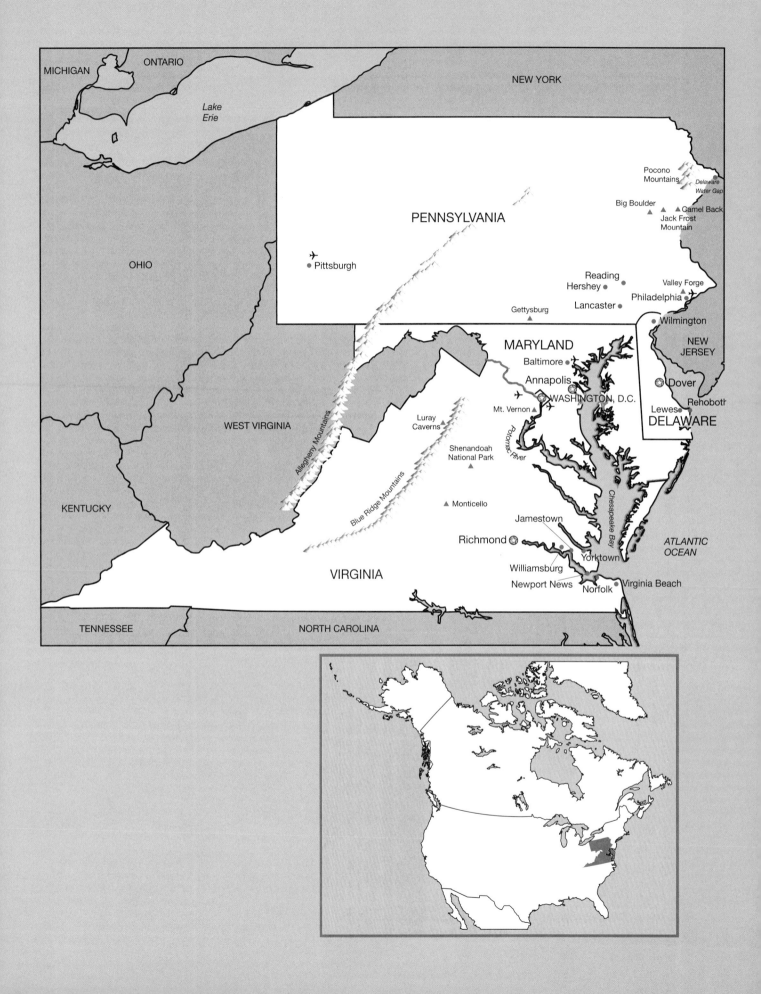

MICHIGAN

ONTARIO

NEW YORK

Lake Erie

OHIO

PENNSYLVANIA

Pocono Mountains

Delaware Water Gap

Big Boulder ▲   ▲ Camel Back
Jack Frost
Mountain

✈ Pittsburgh

Reading
Hershey ●   Valley Forge ▲
Lancaster ●   Philadelphia ✈

Gettysburg ▲

Wilmington ●

MARYLAND

NEW JERSEY

WEST VIRGINIA

Baltimore ●
Annapolis

WASHINGTON, D.C. ✈
Mt. Vernon ▲

Dover ⊛

Rehoboth

Lewes ●

DELAWARE

Luray
Caverns

Shenandoah
National Park ▲

Allegheny Mountains

Potomac River

Chesapeake Bay

KENTUCKY

▲ Monticello

Blue Ridge Mountains

Jamestown

ATLANTIC
OCEAN

Richmond ⊛
Yorktown

VIRGINIA

Williamsburg
Newport News   Norfolk   ● Virginia Beach

TENNESSEE

NORTH CAROLINA

Chapter 3

Pennsylvania, Maryland, Virginia, and Washington, D.C.

The Mid-Atlantic Medley

The Mid-Atlantic is a symphony of sounds: the mute ringing of the Liberty Bell in **Philadelphia**, Pennsylvania; the emotional strains of "The Star Spangled Banner" written outside Fort McHenry near **Baltimore**, Maryland; wheels rolling along the cobblestones of the first American settlement in **Jamestown**, Virginia; or the old echoes of debate in **Washington, D.C.** The Mid-Atlantic region also embraces both New York and New Jersey (each covered in the previous chapter) and Delaware. So it's no wonder that this is one of the most popular tourist areas for Americans. (It attracts a significant percentage of visitors from other countries, too.)

Pennsylvania is the northernmost of the states to be covered in this chapter. Stacked south of it are **Delaware, Maryland, Washington, D.C.,** and **Virginia.** In Pennsylvania, the **Pocono Mountains** resorts are in the northeast part of the state; in the very southeastern corner, on the eastern border, is Philadelphia; and west of this major city are the Amish of the **Pennsylvania Dutch country. Pittsburgh**, in the state's southwest, also has some interesting sights.

South of Pennsylvania Dutch country is Baltimore, Maryland, located on the west coast of **Chesapeake Bay**, just across from the eastern peninsula where the rest of Maryland and Delaware are. A short drive south of Baltimore, on the **Potomac River**, is the nation's capital, Washington, D.C. Most of the attractions that interest visitors to Virginia are found in the **Tidewater Virginia** region, the southeastern portion of that state: the colonial villages of **Williamsburg, Yorktown,** and **Jamestown**; **Virginia Beach**; and harbor communities such as **Newport News** and **Norfolk**. The beautiful **Shenandoah National Park** begins in northern Virginia and runs southwesterly through the state.

How Travelers Get There

Access to this busy, highly populated region is diversified and convenient. For air travelers, the major gateway into Philadelphia and much of Pennsylvania is **Philadelphia**

The Liberty Bell is probably smaller than you expect it to be.

Soft-shell crabs and crab cakes are Maryland delicacies.

International Airport (PHL). Western Pennsylvania's gateway is **Pittsburgh International Airport** (PIT). Flights to Baltimore land at **Baltimore–Washington International Airport** (BWI), which can also serve as a gateway to Washington, D.C. The nation's capital is also directly serviced by both **Ronald Reagan National Airport** (DCA), which is almost downtown, and **Dulles Airport** (IAD), which is about 45 minutes away in Virginia. Most of these cities are, by air, about five hours from the West Coast and an hour from New York City.

There's also an extensive network of highways into the region for travelers who'll be either driving themselves or taking the bus, a good option for the budget minded. Train service to Philadelphia, Baltimore, and Washington, D.C., is very good, too (especially Amtrak's high-speed train, Acela), though it's limited for the rest of the area.

Weather Patterns

The climates of Philadelphia and Baltimore are similar: hot and humid summers, with average high temperatures of around 80 or 90 degrees, and cold, snowy winters, with average low temperatures of around 30 degrees. Spring and fall are very pleasant. The Poconos are a little cooler, with cold and snowy winters. Summer is the main tourist season.

Washington, D.C., is renowned for its beautiful, temperate springs, when the cherry blossoms bloom (and student tours are everywhere). Summers are also well known, but for

Some "short-stop" D.C. attractions: the National Archives (with the Declaration of Independence and the Constitution), Ford's Theater (where Abraham Lincoln was shot), and, just across the street, Peterson House (where Lincoln died).

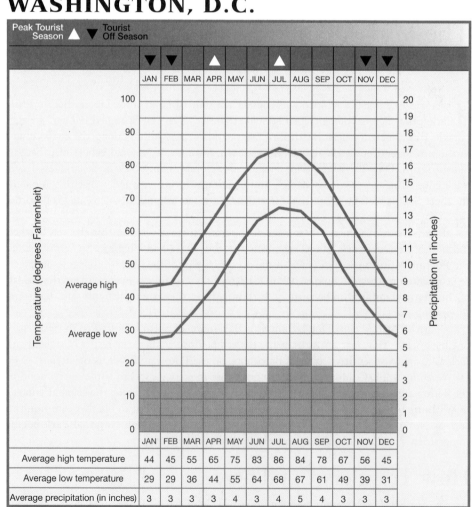

Climate at a Glance
WASHINGTON, D.C.

	JAN	FEB	MAR	APR	MAY	JUN	JUL	AUG	SEP	OCT	NOV	DEC
Average high temperature	44	45	55	65	75	83	86	84	78	67	56	45
Average low temperature	29	29	36	44	55	64	68	67	61	49	39	31
Average precipitation (in inches)	3	3	3	3	4	3	4	5	4	3	3	3

Figure 3–1

being humid and hot. These are by far Washington's two busiest tourist seasons (though tourism begins to drop off as early as August). Falls are pleasant, with some rain, and winters get chilly and a bit snowy (see Figure 3–1). Southeast Virginia has mild summers and fairly mild winters. September to May is the best time to visit here; summers are the most crowded. Fall is a particularly spectacular time to see the changing foliage of Shenandoah National Park.

Getting Around

Most of the region's major cities are so close to one another that it's not usually necessary to fly between them. But for those who do fly, there are many airports, as well as major carriers and commuter airlines serving them. Train and bus connections are good. However, driving is probably the best way to get around. Traffic is heavy in the congested Mid-Atlantic corridor.

Once within a tourist center, though, it's another story. The cities are large, and hectic urban driving conditions almost always prevail. Philadelphia is crowded, with limited parking and expensive taxis; however, Philadelphia does have a good subway and bus system. Washington, D.C., has limited parking and streets become one-way during rush hour. Taxis are inexpensive; the city has an excellent subway system and very good buses. Most major sights are fairly close to one another. As in Philadelphia, city tours are an excellent way for visitors to get around. Escorted tours through the Pennsylvania Dutch country are very popular. Cars aren't allowed in Colonial Williamsburg.

Important Places

The historic sites of Philadelphia, Washington, D.C., the Williamsburg area, and Baltimore are this region's most popular. In addition, there are the lovely natural attractions of the Pennsylvania Dutch country, the Poconos, and Shenandoah National Park.

Philadelphia

Philadelphia was the first capital of the United States. It's where Benjamin Franklin, George Washington, Thomas Jefferson, and many other notable figures lived, worked, and founded a nation. Among its many attractions are:

- **Independence National Historical Park**, which comprises most of the city's famous sights. These include **Independence Hall**, where the Declaration of Independence was signed and the Constitution drafted; **Congress Hall**, where the first U.S. Congress met; and the **Liberty Bell**, which is housed in a glass pavilion near Independence Hall. Other park attractions: the **Betsy Ross House** (where legend says she made the first U.S. flag); **Christ Church** (the house of worship for Benjamin Franklin and George Washington); and **Franklin Court** (the grounds of Franklin's home).

- **Great museums**, including the **Franklin Institute Science Museum**, with its hands-on exhibits, a planetarium, and Franklin artifacts; the **Rodin Museum**, with the largest collection of Rodin's artwork outside France; the excellent collection of the **Philadelphia Museum of Art**; and one of the most unusual, rich, and eccentrically displayed collections in the nation, the **Barnes Foundation**, housed in a mansion-like structure on the outskirts of Philadelphia. (There are plans to move it to a downtown location.)

- **Philadelphia Zoo**, the nation's oldest zoo.

- **Valley Forge State Park**, just outside town, the famous site of George Washington and his troop's encampment.

- North of Philadelphia is **Reading** [RED-ing], which many consider the discount outlet shopping center of North America.

An almost exact reproduction of Independence Hall is at Knott's Berry Farm, in Buena Park, California.

The tradition in Philadelphia is to throw a penny on Benjamin Franklin's grave in the Christ Church graveyard.

If you're in Philadelphia during the Christmas season, visit Wanamaker's (now a Macy's department store) for the traditional light show and booming organ music under its famous bronze eagle.

Perhaps the most famous flawed artifact in the world: Philadelphia's Liberty Bell
Image copyright pmphoto, 2008. Used under license from Shutterstock.com

Pennsylvania Dutch Country

The beautiful farmland of this area—about 50 miles west of Philadelphia—is home to the Amish and Mennonites, descendants of a strict German religious sect. (They weren't Dutch at all, but *Deutsch*.) The region's center is **Lancaster**, which features several farmers' markets with banquets of justly renowned homemade food. Among the other interesting towns is **Hershey**, famous for its chocolate world exhibit, eccentric streetlight posts (they're shaped like Hershey kisses!), and an enjoyable theme park.

A half-day trip from this area is **Gettysburg National Battlefield**, where Abraham Lincoln delivered his famous address in 1863, commemorating the decisive U.S. Civil War battle that took place here.

The Pocono Mountains

Only two hours north of Philadelphia, this mountain resort area is popular in the summer (especially among honeymooners) and also in winter for skiing. The best of its ski resorts are

Big Boulder, Camel Back, and Jack Frost Mountain. Nearby is the Delaware Water Gap National Recreation Area (which extends in from New Jersey).

Pittsburgh

This city, majestically located at the confluence of three rivers, was once picked as the United States' most "livable" city. Pittsburgh boasts several major museums, including the Frick Art Museum and the Carnegie, a world-renowned center for culture. (A number of museums in Pittsburgh have the name Carnegie attached to them.) Not far from Pittsburgh is Fallingwater, arguably the most famous structure ever designed by the great architect Frank Lloyd Wright.

Pittsburgh lost the "h" in its spelling in 1891, but after 20 years of protest, had it put back in 1911.

Baltimore

Baltimore has many treasures of its own: a symphony, fine museums (like the Museum of Art, with its post-Impressionist collection), the huge National Aquarium, and many renovated historical buildings. Among the other points of interest here are:

- Fort McHenry National Monument, where Francis Scott Key watched the battle that inspired him to write "The Star Spangled Banner."
- The U.S.S. *Constellation*, an all-sail vessel that's the only U.S. Civil War–era military vessel still afloat.
- Harborplace, erected over Baltimore's old dock area, with nearly 200 restaurants, cafes, and shops.

Maryland's capital, Annapolis, is just 30 miles away. It boasts many restored eighteenth-century buildings, among them the colonial State House. The U.S. Naval Academy is here, too.

Maryland is the only U.S. state to have an official sport: jousting.

Delaware

The small state of Delaware contains several noteworthy attractions. Winterthur Mansion and Country Estate in Wilmington is quite beautiful and worthy of a visit. Also of interest are the historical town of Lewes, the beach town of Rehoboth, and the restored sections of the state capital, Dover.

Wilmington, Delaware, was once a Swedish colony. Fort Christina marks the site.

Washington, D.C.

The sights of the nation's capital are numerous and well known. But the city isn't always what everyone expects. Washington is a company town, and the business of the town is, of course, government. Among the many wonderful attractions are:

- The White House, home of the president. The White House Visitors Center has a video and exhibits.
- The Mall, a long, park-like rectangle where many of the city's famous monuments are located, including the inspirational Vietnam Veterans Memorial and the obelisk-like Washington Monument, the tallest structure in the city. Nearby are the stately Lincoln Memorial (where Martin Luther King, Jr., made his "I have a dream" speech) and the graceful Jefferson Memorial.
- The Smithsonian Institution, the granddaddy of museums. Actually, the Smithsonian is a fascinating collection of separate museum buildings, many of them on the Mall. They include the huge National Air and Space Museum (which displays such gems as the Wright Brothers' airplane), the Museum of Natural History, the Museum of American History, and the U.S. Holocaust Memorial Museum. The red sandstone "Castle" houses the Smithsonian Information Center, which gives an overview of the Institution.

Under the Lincoln Memorial is a rarely seen area where stalactites and stalagmites have formed.

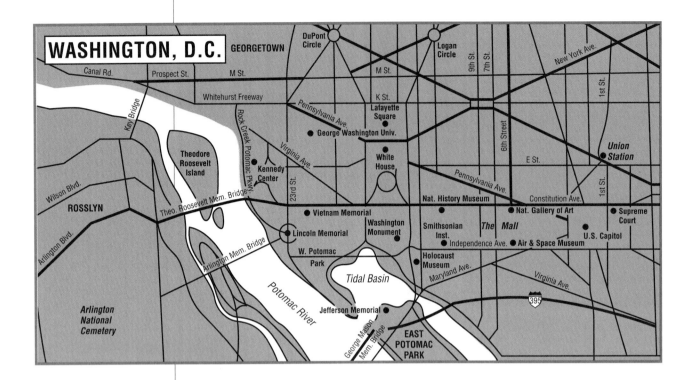

- **The National Gallery of Art**, on the Mall as well, with a vast collection of artwork from around the world.
- **The International Spy Museum**, which gives an overview of espionage and its historical applications.
- **Washington National Cathedral**, the sixth-largest cathedral in the world. One of its stained-glass windows commemorates the *Apollo 11* flight and contains a piece of moon rock.
- **Arlington National Cemetery**, just outside town (in Virginia), the resting place of some of the most famous names in U.S. history, and the location of a memorial to the crew of the Space Shuttle *Challenger* and of the **Tomb of the Unknowns**.
- **Capitol Hill**, where the seats of government are found. Visitors can tour the Capitol itself, where the Senate and House of Representatives meet; there's artwork throughout the halls, and the galleries are open to watch the legislative sessions. Visitors can also watch the proceedings in the nearby **Supreme Court Building** from October through June.

Capital refers to a city. *Capitol* refers to a building.

Not far from the city, and a popular half-day trip, is Virginia's **Mt. Vernon**, the plantation home of George Washington. **The National Air and Space Museum's Center**, near Dulles International Airport, has a huge collection of remarkable aircraft and spacecraft—most of which are here because there was no room for them at the museum's primary location on the Mall. And **Wolf Trap Farm Park**, the location of an internationally famous summer festival, is the first national park devoted to the performing arts.

Tidewater Virginia

Located in a triangular area along Chesapeake Bay, Tidewater is one of the most historic regions in the United States. The scenic **Colonial Parkway Drive** takes visitors through this beautiful area of colonial villages and plantations.

Williamsburg is the most popular Tidewater site, a lovingly restored eighteenth-century town with period craftsmen, taverns, horse-drawn carts, and a standing militia. Its preserved structures include the second-oldest college in the country, the **College of William and Mary**, with a building designed by famed architect Christopher Wren.

Jamestown was the first permanent settlement in America; the **Jamestown Festival Park** harbors the three ships that brought John Smith's retinue across the ocean in 1607. Yorktown was where the final battle of the American Revolutionary War took place. **Yorktown Battlefield** has tours and a museum.

The most impressive and best-known plantations in the region are located west of Williamsburg and along the James River's north shore. A day trip just south of the Tidewater area is to the harbor towns of **Newport News**, with its Mariner's Museum, and **Norfolk**, where NASA's Langley Research Center offers fascinating aeronautical artifacts. Just south is the popular summer resort of **Virginia Beach**, which could merit a longer stay.

Another day trip is to **Richmond**, the historic state capital. Its attractions range from the Revolution—**St. John's Church** is where Patrick Henry cried out, "Give me liberty, or give me death"—to the U.S. Civil War, as the city was the capital of the Confederacy.

Shenandoah National Park

This park—in Virginia but only 75 miles from Washington, D.C.—lies between the Blue Ridge Mountains to the east and the Shenandoah River to the west. The **Appalachian Trail** runs through the park, as does the beautiful 105-mile **Skyline Drive**. It's most crowded in the fall, when the forest colors are stunning. The famed **Luray Caverns**, with their remarkable stalactites and stalagmites, are nearby.

Possible Itineraries

For first-time tourists, nine days through historic Philadelphia, Washington, D.C., and Tidewater Virginia would permit a sampling of the area's attractions. For return visitors, several side trips would be worthwhile, including excursions into Pennsylvania Dutch Country, Baltimore, or the Virginia harbor towns. Short trips to the resorts of the Poconos or Virginia Beach would also be good suggestions. For those who just want to see Washington, D.C., five days or so would be enough to visit most of the major sights.

Thomas Jefferson's mansion home, Monticello, is nearby.

Nearly one-third of the land in the United States is owned by the U.S. Federal Government.

A view of the Washington Monument and the Mall
Image copyright VanHart, 2008. Used under license from Shutterstock.com

Lodging Options

Every possible type of accommodation is available, from grand luxury hotels to budget motels. In Philadelphia, most hotels are around Rittenhouse Square and Logan Circle. In Baltimore, they're between the Civic Center and Center Plaza. In Washington, D.C., hotels are clustered north of the Kennedy Center and Lafayette Square; around Union Station; and along the Potomac, south of Reagan National Airport. For political buffs, two hotels stand out: The **Willard Inter-Continental** is where, legend has it, the art of lobbying began, and, of course, there's the **Watergate**. The **Hay-Adams Hotel** offers views of the White House across Lafayette Square. From Capitol Hill to the White House are many older, less expensive hotels. Many hotels and campgrounds are just outside the Tidewater Virginia area. In Williamsburg, the **Williamsburg Inn** is elegant and beautifully restored. Most hotels in Virginia Beach are along the Boardwalk. Shenandoah National Park has a few lodges and many campgrounds.

This area also offers a wide selection of alternative lodging. Washington, D.C. contains some bed-and-breakfasts. Visitors to the Pennsylvania Dutch Country might enjoy staying in a Mennonite farmhouse. And guesthouses in the Tidewater Virginia area are also popular.

Allied Destinations

The Mid-Atlantic States are strategically located for those wishing to extend their trip to other areas. Pennsylvania borders Ohio to the west and New York to the north, which in turn leads to New England through Connecticut and Massachusetts. Keep in mind also that New York and Washington are jumping-off points for flights to Europe, so the area could be a side trip before such a long flight. Ontario is separated from Pennsylvania only by Lake Erie. Virginia borders West Virginia, Kentucky, North Carolina, and Tennessee, opening a gateway to the South.

Factors That Motivate Visitors

Although U.S. history colors every corner of the Mid-Atlantic States, it's important to understand all the reasons that draw vacationers to the region. These include:

- Historical buildings, monuments, and sites are everywhere.
- Low airfares, convenient ground transportation, and reasonable lodging make the area a good bargain.
- The area brims with superb cultural attractions: great museums, symphonies, arts festivals, and the unique lifestyle of the Pennsylvania Dutch.
- The scenery is impressive, especially in Shenandoah National Park.
- There are very good winter and summer resorts.
- Skiing opportunities abound, especially at the Virginia resorts of Homestead and Wintergreen, or the Pocono ski areas of Jack Frost and Big Boulder.
- The area is accessible: Cities and attractions are fairly close together and are near many other parts of the United States.

Possible Misgivings

As strong as the appeal of this area is, some visitors will have concerns that you may have to address:

- "Washington, D.C., is so hot and humid." It is, but only in the summer, and all buildings are air-conditioned. Spring and fall are particularly beautiful.
- "Except for its historic buildings, Philadelphia is dull." In fact, the city has a world-class orchestra, great museums, and a lively nightlife. This objection might also be raised

English King Charles II originally wanted to call Pennsylvania "Sylvania," then added the name "Penn" to honor Admiral William Penn.

Sir Walter Raleigh named Virginia in honor of Queen Elizabeth I, the "Virgin Queen" of England.

About 60 percent of tourists in Washington, D.C., say they go for "cultural reasons."

When John Adams moved into the White House in 1800, it was America's biggest home.

Qualifying the Traveler
Washington, D.C.

For People Who Want	Appeal			Remarks
	High	Medium	Low	
Historical and Cultural Attractions	▲			Extremely high appeal
Beaches and Water Sports			▲	Must leave city
Skiing Opportunities			▲	Must leave city
Lots of Nightlife		▲		Good restaurants
Family Activities	▲			A must for students
Familiar Cultural Experience	▲			Well-known sites
Exotic Cultural Experience			▲	
Safety and Low Crime		▲		Crime mostly outside tourist areas
Bargain Travel		▲		
Impressive Scenery		▲		Impressive parks
Peace and Quiet		▲		Quiet at night
Shopping Opportunities			▲	
Adventure			▲	
To Do Business	▲			U.S. government related

about Washington, D.C., and more justifiably: The capital's nightlife is largely limited to dining, museums, and concerts.

■ "There's not much to see in Baltimore." Besides being home to some important historical sites, the city is a great jumping-off point to Washington, D.C., and Philadelphia.

■ "Tidewater Virginia is restored buildings and nothing more." Nearby are the harbor communities, Virginia Beach resorts, an amusement park, and the state capital of Richmond.

■ "There's a lot of crime in Washington, D.C." The city is safer than it used to be, but, as in any large city, visitors should use caution. The tourist areas are very safe during the day and relatively so at night.

Sales Strategies

The region presents many opportunities to up-sell and cross-sell. City tours of Washington, D.C., and Philadelphia are popular and excellent ways to see those cities. Don't forget car rentals for those who prefer to drive. Booking an escorted tour of the Pennsylvania Dutch Country facilitates visiting the area; for a special tour of this part of the country, you might even suggest setting up a personalized guide. Coach tours of the Tidewater Virginia area can help tie those communities together. And keep in mind that many of the cities covered in this chapter are extremely close to one another; a vacation can be easily expanded by adding an additional destination to the already-planned trip.

Travel Trivia

U.S. Cities with Dubious Names

Panic, Pennsylvania	Eek, Alaska	Hell, Michigan
Odd, West Virginia	Belcher, New York	Bad Axe, Michigan
Hemlock, Ohio	Looneyville, West Virginia	Hooker, Oklahoma
Pitts, Georgia	Needles, California	War, West Virginia
Boring, Maryland	Last Chance, Colorado	Roachtown, Illinois
Crummies, Kentucky	Terror Bay, Alaska	Muck City, Alabama
Tightwad, Missouri	Gross, Kansas	Girdle Tree, Maryland

NAME _____   **DATE** _____

MAP ACTIVITY

A traveler wants to visit the places listed below. Which number represents each on the map?

Place/Attraction	In/Near Which City/State?	Number on Map
A. The Smithsonian Institution	A. _____	A. _____
B. A chocolate factory	B. _____	B. _____
C. The U.S. Naval Academy	C. _____	C. _____
D. Where "The Star Spangled Banner" was written	D. _____	D. _____
E. The International Spy Museum	E. _____	E. _____
F. A restored colonial village	F. _____	F. _____
G. The Liberty Bell	G. _____	G. _____
H. The Jefferson Memorial	H. _____	H. _____
I. Where Patrick Henry made his "Give me liberty" speech	I. _____	I. _____
J. Betsy Ross House	J. _____	J. _____

NAME _____ **DATE** _____

CASE STUDY

Robert Townsend, a 34-year-old aerospace engineer from El Segundo, California, is attending a November convention in Washington, D.C. The convention ends on Thursday. On Friday morning Mr. Townsend will meet with business clients, but after lunch he is free. He has already seen the standard historical D.C. sights on a previous trip, but he'd like to stay over, see more of the region, and fly back to El Segundo late Sunday.

Circle the answer that best suits his needs.

1 Which would probably be the most appropriate service to set up in advance?

A car rental   Tickets to Wolf Trap Farm Park festival

A ski package   An escorted tour of the Pennsylvania Dutch area

Why?

2 Which place to visit would probably be out of his geographic range?

Richmond   Hershey

Gettysburg   Pittsburgh

Why?

3 Which attraction would probably be least appealing to Mr. Townsend?

The Franklin Institute   The National Air and Space Museum

Annapolis   Virginia Beach

Why?

4 Though Mr. Townsend flew into DCA, he could probably fly back out of any of the following airports, except one. Which one?

PHL   IAD

BWI   LGA

Why?

NAME _____   DATE _____

CREATIVE ACTIVITY

You're about to participate in an unusual scavenger hunt. The object: to take your photo next to seven attractions (described in clues) that are scattered throughout the Mid-Atlantic region. The clues will be given to all contestants at noon on the steps of the U.S. Capitol. The first person back to the steps with all seven photos will be declared the winner. (Their outing must be by car.) Using the following clues, try to name the attractions. You may have to consult other chapters or other reference tools to arrive at the answers.

Your Photo Next To	What Is It?	Where Is It?
A bright kiss		
A famous thinker		
Old pointy things		
Discounted Levi's		
A cluster of stars		
Midshipmen		
The building that sank Nixon		

How long do you think it would take to win the contest? Consult an atlas or a road map, if you need to, and plot out a route for the most efficient path from place to place.

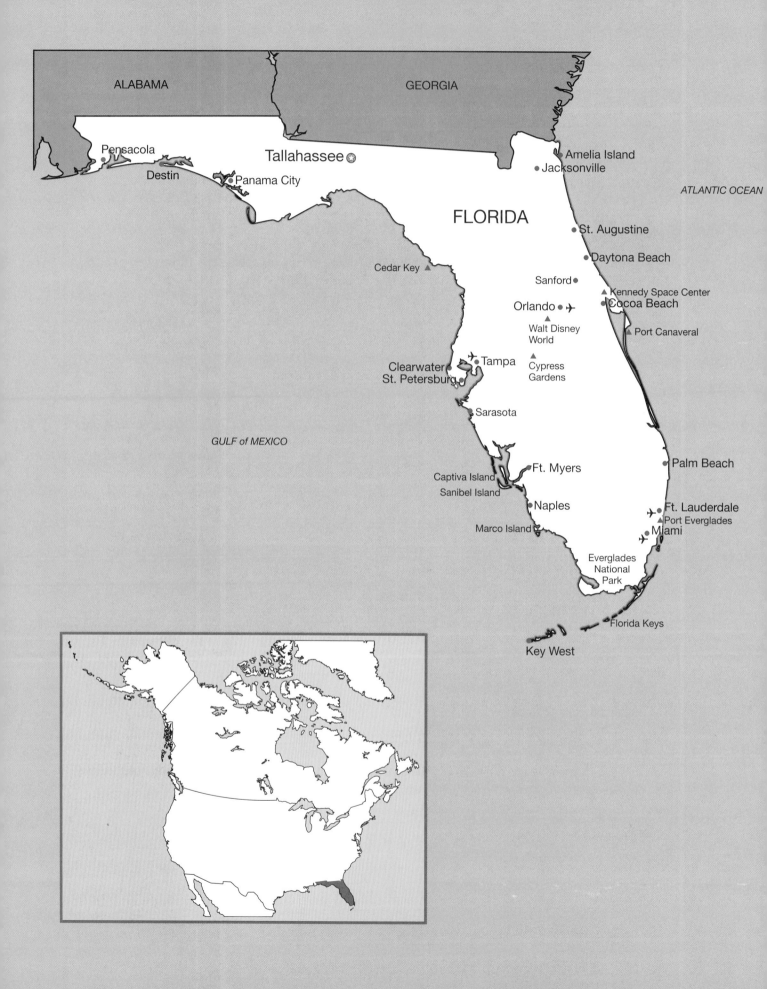

ALABAMA

GEORGIA

Pensacola

Tallahassee ☆

ATLANTIC OCEAN

Destin

Panama City

Amelia Island

Jacksonville

FLORIDA

St. Augustine

Daytona Beach

Cedar Key ▲

Sanford ●

Kennedy Space Center

Orlando ● ✈

Cocoa Beach

Walt Disney
World ▲

Port Canaveral ▲

Cypress
Gardens ▲

Clearwater ✈ ● Tampa

St. Petersburg

Sarasota

GULF of MEXICO

Ft. Myers

Palm Beach

Captiva Island

Sanibel Island

Naples

Ft. Lauderdale

Port Everglades ▲

Marco Island

Miami

Everglades
National
Park

Florida Keys

Key West

Chapter 4

Florida
Where the Mouse Roars

Orlando wasn't much more than a sleepy little citrus town until a mouse showed up. *The* Mouse. Mickey himself. Walt Disney, creator of Mickey and much, much more, had long regretted not having bought up more land in Anaheim, California. Though Disneyland prospered there, its expansion was limited by the other entrepreneurs who surrounded the Magic Kingdom with hotels, motels, restaurants, and minor attractions. This time it would be different, Disney decided. His corporation bought up vast swaths of land, planned out extensive services, even envisioned an entire "city of tomorrow" where employees would live in futuristic happiness.

Most of Disney's dream—somewhat altered, but just as grandiose—has come true. Many other major attractions also have sprung up around the Disney property. The result: The Orlando area has become one of the most popular vacation spots in the United States. And Florida, long a magnet for vacationers, has become the most visited state of all.

Florida is a flat peninsula, stretching southward into tropical waters: The Gulf of Mexico is on the west, the Atlantic Ocean on the east. Florida's east coast has been a resort destination for over a century. From north to south are the cities of **Jacksonville, St. Augustine, Daytona Beach, Cocoa Beach, Palm Beach, Ft. Lauderdale**, and **Miami**, to name a few. Extending southwestward are the **Florida Keys**, a string of bridge-connected, water-flanked islands that ends at **Key West**.

Florida's west coast, more recently developed as a destination, boasts several first-rate beach resorts, most especially around the tri-city area of **St. Petersburg, Clearwater**, and **Tampa**. The **Pensacola** area, in Florida's northwestern "panhandle" corner, is also a major resort destination, especially for those driving from Louisiana, Mississippi, or Alabama. It boasts some of the most beautiful beaches in North America. And of course, almost dead center in the Florida peninsula: **Orlando**.

How Travelers Get There

Florida—especially Orlando—is a family destination, and loading up the car with kids and baggage is an efficient way to get there. Many packages (usually including air, hotel, admissions, and car rental) to Orlando are available; this is the preferred choice of most who live a good distance from Florida. Several airlines fly to Florida's other major cities, too. The state's busiest airports are Miami (MIA), Orlando (MCO), Tampa (TPA), and Ft. Lauderdale (FLL), which is just north of Miami and is a less congested alternative to MIA. Flying time to Florida is about three hours from New York City, four from Chicago, and five from California. Florida's airports (except perhaps Miami) are models of efficiency.

The most visited Disney theme park in the world is the Magic Kingdom at Walt Disney World.

The highest mountain in Florida is Walt Disney World's Mt. Everest.

Florida has the second-longest state coastline in the United States. (Alaska has the longest.)

Florida is the number-one family destination in North America. (California is number two.)

Several convenient train and bus routes lead into scenic Florida as well. An offbeat choice: **Amtrak** auto trains that carry the family car—and family—from Lorten, Virginia (just south of Washington, D.C.), to Sanford, Florida (north of Orlando).

Weather Patterns

Florida has extraordinary weather, especially in the winter, when daytime temperatures hover around 70 or 80 degrees, with only occasional rain. Days and certainly nights can be chilly; humidity can also make things uncomfortable, even at this cooler time of the year (see Figure 4–1). Summers are very hot and humid, with frequent brief but intense thunderstorms (and an occasional hurricane) from June through September. Fortunately for summer visitors, breezes temper the heat, especially along the coast.

Because people who live in colder climates visit Florida in the winter and families visit in the out-of-school summer period, there's no real tourist off-season in Florida, though the number of vacationers does drop off a bit in June, and September through November. Anyone going to Florida should avoid holiday periods, if at all possible, because of the crowds. Spring break, when students swarm to Florida, is especially frantic in beach cities.

The original Ripley's Believe It Or Not Museum is in St. Augustine. Among its displays: a London Tower Bridge model made out of 264,345 matchsticks, a clock made out of clothespins, and a painting made out of 63 pieces of toast.

Climate at a Glance
ORLANDO, FLORIDA

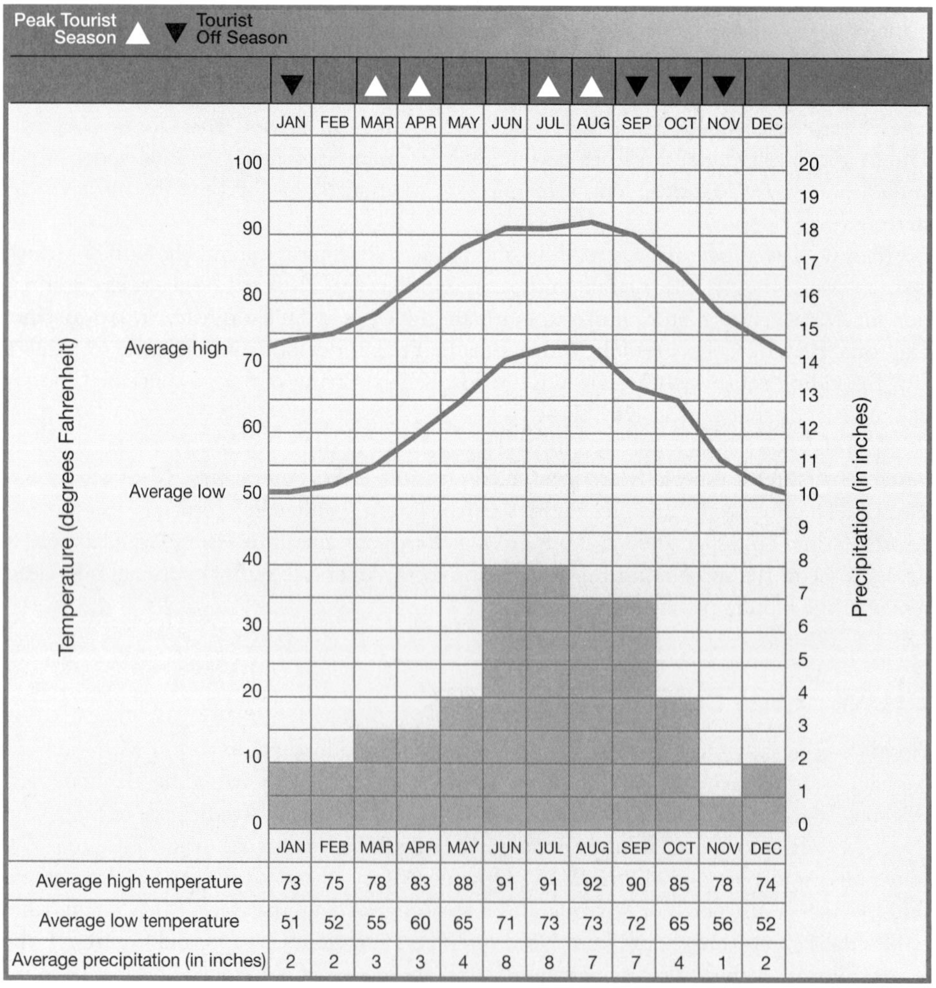

	JAN	FEB	MAR	APR	MAY	JUN	JUL	AUG	SEP	OCT	NOV	DEC
Average high temperature	73	75	78	83	88	91	91	92	90	85	78	74
Average low temperature	51	52	55	60	65	71	73	73	72	65	56	52
Average precipitation (in inches)	2	2	3	3	4	8	8	7	7	4	1	2

Figure 4–1

Getting Around

In most places in Florida, a car rental is almost a must. Car rental prices here are extremely affordable. Bus travel is an option for those on a budget. One conceivable way to avoid a car rental or bus travel would be to stay in **Walt Disney World** (where monorails, boats, and shuttles take people from place to place) or in a single resort city and never leave, which can be an attractive option for some.

It's possible to fly between Orlando and Miami, or between several Florida cities and Key West. Several cruise lines call on Key West as part of a Caribbean cruise. The **Conch Train** in Key West takes visitors on an interesting 1.5-hour trip around this quaint island town.

Important Places

Florida is best understood when divided into four principal tourist areas: Orlando, the Atlantic Coast cities, the Miami–Florida Keys area, and the west coast. Each appeals to a somewhat different kind of person, as we'll see later.

Castillo de San Marcos guards St. Augustine
Image copyright Michelle Marsan, 2008. Used under license from Shutterstock.com

On many of Florida's Atlantic beaches, you're permitted to drive on the beach itself.

Orlando

The Orlando area attracts more family vacationers than any other place in the world. But it also appeals to couples, young people, older travelers, and even honeymooners. There are three distinct clusters of attractions in the Orlando area: Walt Disney World, non-Disney attractions in the Orlando region, and attractions that can be visited as day trips from Orlando.

Walt Disney World clearly dominates Orlando's tourism. Within its enormous boundaries—it's about the same size as San Francisco—are hotel clusters, shopping and entertainment centers (especially **Downtown Disney**), campgrounds, animal sanctuaries, sports complexes, and water parks. Four Disney theme parks, though, monopolize most visitors' attention:

- **The Magic Kingdom**, the ultimate theme park, usually tops any visitor's list. It's very similar to California's Disneyland, though it covers a much larger area.
- **Epcot** is, in effect, a permanent world's fair, with both national and corporate pavilions— all of them providing spellbinding entertainment. This is one of the most adult of Orlando's attractions and, during busy times, requires two days to fully experience.
- **Disney's Hollywood Studios** is a diverting look at how movies are made; it includes numerous attraction rides and many buildings that are reproductions of Hollywood landmarks.
- **Disney's Animal Kingdom** is a 500-acre cross between a zoo and a theme park. It stresses what we must do to preserve endangered species, but also boasts some exciting rides.

Outside Disney's vast empire are several other independent attractions, both major and minor. **Sea World** is the world's largest marine park. The **Universal Orlando Resort** requires two days to see. It's divided into two parks: **Islands of Adventure** (with thrill rides) and **Universal Studios Florida** (which has a character very distinct from Disney's Hollywood Studios). Connecting the two is **CityWalk**, a vibrant strip of stores, restaurants, and entertainment venues.

Other major attractions lie within about a two-hour drive of Orlando. To the east, near Cocoa Beach, is the **Kennedy Space Center**, the home of America's space program. Buses take visitors on a tour of the facility (and, on space shuttle launch days, to viewing sites); its excellent museum traces the history of man's exploration of the cosmos. To Orlando's south is the 233-acre Cypress Gardens, one of North America's oldest theme parks, reopened in 2005 as **Cypress Gardens Adventure Park**. And to Orlando's west in Tampa is **Busch Gardens Africa**, an extensive attraction that melds a zoo-like wild-animal preserve with an amusement park.

The Atlantic Coast Cities

In the late 1800s, several entrepreneurs decided to run railroad lines down from the U.S. Northeast and develop Florida into a resort vacation and retirement destination. Their plan worked. A sun-bleached string of towns and cities sprang up along the coastal routes; they still draw millions of visitors each year. Among the most important destinations, from north to south, are

- **Jacksonville**, with its many cultural activities, sports events, nearby beaches, and, to the north, the offshore resort of **Amelia Island**, with its unspoiled beaches, golfing, and relaxed ambience.
- **St. Augustine**, the oldest city in the United States, with its old Spanish fort (the Castillo), historical restored streets, shops, and restaurants.
- **Daytona Beach**, the home of Daytona International Speedway, and one of the college vacation crowds' favorite haunts.

Florida is bigger than England.

Over 90 percent of visitors to Florida have visited the state before.

Amelia Island is the only U.S. territory to have served under eight flags. What are they? France, Spain, England, the Patriots of Amelia Island, Florida, Mexico, the Confederacy, and the United States.

A Saturn V rocket at Kennedy Space Center
Photo by H. Fukushima

- **Cocoa Beach**, a smallish city with reasonable seaside lodging just a few miles from Kennedy Space Center. Close by is **Port Canaveral**, from which some cruises depart.
- **Palm Beach**, an upscale beach city with outstanding architecture, especially the old mansions along Ocean Boulevard.
- **Ft. Lauderdale**, with its long stretches of prime sand, 3,000 eating establishments, and 40,000 registered boats. Nearby **Port Everglades** is a major departure point for cruises.

The Miami–Florida Keys Area

Miami—one of America's most exciting cities—has fabulous restaurants, fascinating architecture, rich cultural diversity, cruise opportunities, and picture-perfect beaches of **Key Biscayne** and **Miami Beach** (a separate city from Miami). The city has also undergone an intriguing renaissance, becoming, among other things, one of the most visited cities for Latin Americans. You should counsel visitors to Miami to see the following:

- **Vizcaya Museum and Gardens**, a baronial home near **Coconut Grove** (Miami's famous artistic community) and upscale **Coral Gables**.
- **The South Beach Art Deco District**, a vibrant strip of renovated old buildings that features trendy seaside eateries.
- **Little Havana**, a colorful and festive enclave of Cuban restaurants and shops.
- **Everglades National Park**, the swampy habitat of alligators, weird birds, and tourist air-boats, about an hour from Miami.
- **The Florida Keys**, a destination unto itself, with its 180-mile-long string of 32 islands, 42 bridges, and awesome seascapes that stretch out to the magical town of Key West. A drive from Miami to Key West, with stops, can easily take a half-day, so you should perhaps suggest lodging in Key West.

A rather unusual attraction near Miami: Monkey Jungle, where the visitors are in cages and the monkeys are outside.

An interesting activity in Key West: a guided tour of the Key West City Cemetery.

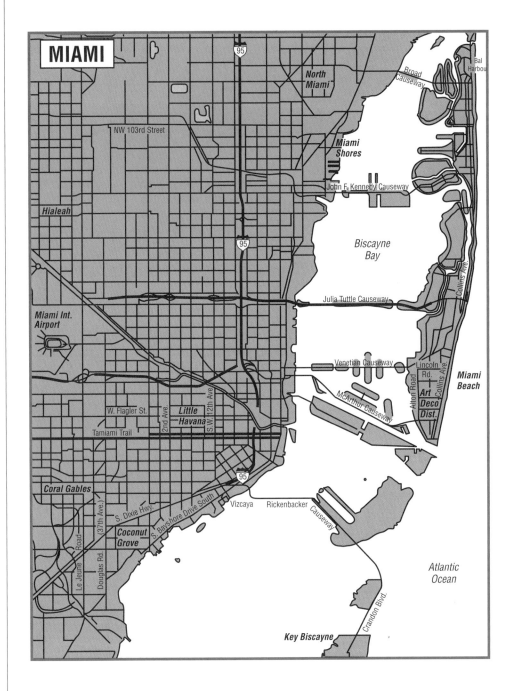

Florida's West Coast

Many interesting beach cities dot the Gulf of Mexico rim of Florida, yet Florida's west coast remains less known than its Atlantic side:

- **Ft. Myers**, a major port of sailing for those who love to fish.
- **The Resort Islands—Sanibel** and **Captiva** (off Ft. Myers) and **Marco** (off **Naples**)— with their fine fishing, seashell-laden beaches, and many upscale hotels and condos.
- **Sarasota**, home of the **Ringling Circus Museum**.
- **Clearwater**, the west coast's prime beach community, only a short distance from the progressive metropolises of **St. Petersburg** (with several interesting museums) and **Tampa** (with its Busch Gardens).
- **Cedar Key**, a quintessential fishing village that's now also an artists' colony.

■ **The Florida panhandle**, which faces south onto the Gulf and is in Florida's northwest corner. Here can be found numerous beaches (some noisy and crowded, others pristine and preserved), fishing resorts, old Spanish-themed **Pensacola**, and Florida's capital, **Tallahassee** (which is inland). Among the popular beach resorts: **Panama City** and **Destin**.

Possible Itineraries

Probably the most popular itinerary for vacationers (especially families) requires about six or seven full days in Orlando, with three or four days in Walt Disney World and the rest spent visiting nearby attractions. Many people lodge at Walt Disney World and limit themselves to its attractions, especially on shorter trips. They would, however, miss the fascinations that lie outside Disney World's perimeter. For tourists who want to see everything in and around Orlando and have the time to do it, about ten days should suffice.

An Atlantic-coast itinerary would require about a week, with travelers driving from Jacksonville to Miami and stopping along the way. Miami and the Keys merit six or seven days, as would a trip along Florida's west coast.

Some people will want to see all of Florida in a week. Explain to them that it's almost impossible. Suggest that they stay in Orlando or Miami and hub out. If they want to see the highlights of Florida, it might be possible to stay in Orlando for three days, then drive

According to one estimate, it would take 41 days to see all of the Orlando area's attractions.

Among U.S. cities, Miami has the greatest number of people who speak a language other than English at home.

Tourists test the physics of centrifugal force at Universal Orlando
Image copyright Tom Hirtreiter, 2008. Used under license from Shutterstock.com

up to St. Augustine and down to Cocoa Beach for two days. From there, they could drive down to Miami and the Keys for four days, and up to the Clearwater–Tampa area for two. This results in an 11- to 12-day trip, but a very hectic one.

Remember that Miami and Ft. Lauderdale are major jump-off points for cruises and flights to South America and the Caribbean. Indeed, a short stay in Miami can be a welcomed add-on to someone's Caribbean plans. Packages that combine an Orlando vacation with a Bahamas or Caribbean cruise (usually out of Port Canaveral and some on Disney-owned ships) are also very popular with families.

Lodging Options

Lodging in Florida is comparatively inexpensive, especially in the Orlando area. Visitors can stay right on the Walt Disney World Resort property; there's everything from expensive to budget-priced accommodations. Guests staying at Disney-owned hotels are allowed extra time at the Disney theme parks. These hotels are themed; a unique example is **Disney's Animal Kingdom Lodge**, where guests in savannah-view rooms can watch animals, including zebras, gazelles, and giraffes, from their balconies.

Many fine hotels (usually part of well-known chains)—and a few awful ones—are located a few miles away. Some of the best are in the **Main Gate** area, and many are along **International Drive**. The Universal Orlando Resort also has interesting themed hotels (including the **Portofino Bay Hotel** and a **Hard Rock Hotel**) that adjoin its parks.

Miami has many downtown hotels (frequented by business travelers, people on pre- or post-cruise stays, and conventioneers), but most people will want to stay on the long island of seaside property that is Miami Beach. For the upscale, recommend the superdeluxe properties in the Key Biscayne, Coral Gables, central Miami Beach, and **Bal Harbour** areas. The **Biltmore Hotel** in Coral Gables is a National Historic Landmark.

The central Miami Beach district features one of the country's most famous properties: the **Fontainebleau**. Those seeking moderate lodging should consider the "art deco district" and North Miami Beach "Motel Row." Be careful: The quality of lodging in both these budget areas varies enormously. Ritz-Carlton has many luxurious properties in Florida (in fact, it has more hotels here than in any other U.S. state). Throughout Florida are also many condominiums, several spas, and resorts. One of the most famous: the **Breakers**, in Palm Beach, is considered by some to be the most striking hotel in Florida.

Allied Destinations

The most obvious add-on to a trip to Florida is a voyage into the Caribbean by either ship or plane. A stay in Florida's panhandle and, for that matter, all of Florida, is easily combined with a New Orleans vacation. So, too, are any vacations spent in the Southern states, especially in the Savannah, Georgia, area. Remember that there's considerable air service from Miami to South America. A short stay in Miami might be a way to break up a trip to this major tourist area.

Factors That Motivate Visitors

Florida boasts a wealth of tourist-motivating factors:

- It has a year-round tropical climate.
- A low-cost vacation is feasible.
- It's easily accessible by car, train, or plane.
- Many bargain air–hotel–car packages are available.
- There's an astonishing concentration of family attractions in the Orlando area.
- Deep-sea fishing and other sport opportunities abound.

Palm Beach has an unusual ordinance: No fast-food restaurants, movie theaters, neon signs, or car dealerships are allowed within city limits.

Baseball fans can root for their favorite teams in Florida during spring training.

Qualifying the Traveler
Florida

For People Who Want	Appeal			Remarks
	High	Medium	Low	
Historical and Cultural Attractions		▲		Mostly Miami and St. Augustine
Beaches and Water Sports	▲			Along coast
Skiing Opportunities			▲	None
Lots of Nightlife		▲		Especially Miami
Family Activities	▲			Especially Orlando
Familiar Cultural Experience	▲			
Exotic Cultural Experience		▲		Mostly Miami
Safety and Low Crime		▲		Miami has some crime
Bargain Travel		▲		Especially Orlando
Impressive Scenery		▲		Seascapes and Everglades
Peace and Quiet			▲	Small towns only
Shopping Opportunities		▲		Mostly Miami and Palm Beach
Adventure			▲	Everglades
To Do Business		▲		Especially Miami

- Florida is an air and cruise gateway to Latin America and the Caribbean. Its principal cruise ports are Miami, Port Everglades (Ft. Lauderdale), Port Canaveral, and Tampa.
- It's a major destination for students on Spring Break.
- Miami has great cultural diversity.
- A well-developed highway system crisscrosses Florida.
- Superior beach resorts are found along both the Atlantic and Gulf coasts.

Possible Misgivings

As popular as Florida is, it also elicits certain predictable objections:

- "Florida is only for families with kids." Recommend any Florida destination outside Orlando. Even in Orlando, Disney's Animal Kingdom and Epcot can be very entertaining for adult visitors.
- "It's too hot and humid." Recommend a late fall, winter, or early spring visit.
- "There aren't many cultural opportunities." Miami appeals to culture seekers and Key West has many historical assets. Orlando's Epcot is a pop-cultural experience. But it is true that Florida, as a cultural destination, clearly is not on par with, say, Europe.
- "What about hurricanes?" Avoid late summer and fall. Remember: Florida isn't under a constant barrage of hurricanes. One or maybe two a year is the norm. Some years there aren't any. And a hurricane usually affects only a portion of the state.

An unexpected treat in St. Petersburg: The Salvador Dali Museum.

Sales Strategies

Comprehensive packages are probably the best way to draw maximum profitability from an Orlando vacation: Typical packages include air, hotel, ground transportation, admissions, and maybe some meals. You should always try to upsell lodging almost anywhere in Florida; even deluxe properties can be reasonable. Always offer to book car rentals, which are generally very reasonable and often quite necessary to get around Florida. Offer a full-size or luxury car rental to a family. You can also book boat charters in advance for those who fish; the commissions can be considerable. You can suggest expansions of vacation plans with extensions into the Bahamas and the Caribbean, usually via cruises.

Travel Trivia

The Author's 10 Favorite U.S. Amusement Parks

1. Disney's Animal Kingdom, Disney World, Florida

2. Islands of Adventure, Universal Orlando, Florida

3. Disneyland, California

4. Universal Studios Florida, Universal Orlando, Florida

5. Magic Kingdom, Disney World, Florida

6. Disney's Hollywood Studios, Disney World, Florida

7. Epcot, Disney World, Florida

8. Kings Island, Ohio

9. Universal Studios Hollywood, California

10. Sea World Orlando, Florida

SOURCE: Marc Mancini

NAME _____   **DATE** _____

MAP ACTIVITY

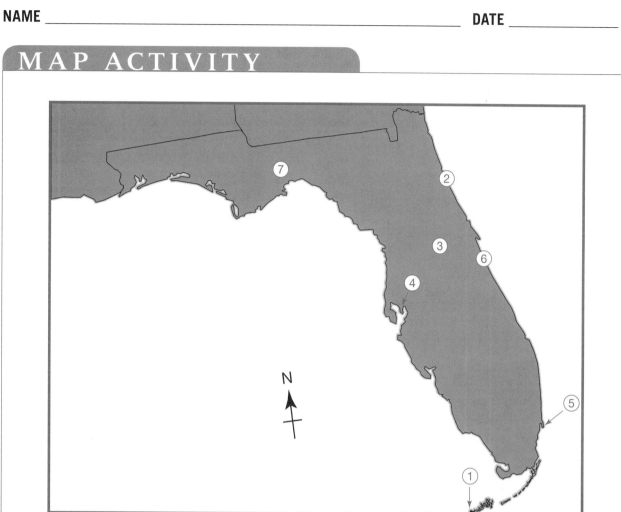

A traveler wants to visit the places listed below. Which number represents each on the map?

Place/Attraction	In/Near Which City?	Number on Map
A. Epcot	A. _____	A. _____
B. Sea World	B. _____	B. _____
C. The Conch Train	C. _____	C. _____
D. The oldest city in the United States	D. _____	D. _____
E. Kennedy Space Center	E. _____	E. _____
F. Vizcaya Museum and Gardens	F. _____	F. _____
G. The Fontainebleau	G. _____	G. _____
H. Busch Gardens	H. _____	H. _____
I. Florida's Panhandle capital	I. _____	I. _____
J. Walt Disney World	J. _____	J. _____

NAME _____   **DATE** _____

CASE STUDY

Bart Beavis, 50-years-old and recently divorced, is an outgoing individual who lives in Anaheim, California. He wants to get away for his two-week vacation and is interested in Florida. He loves fishing, water sports, and sightseeing; a few of his buddies who live in Florida may join him for these activities. He's not a fan of idling on the beach, though, and he hates hot, humid, or stormy weather. He's prepared to spend a good sum of money on his trip.

Circle the answer that best suits his needs.

1 When would you suggest that he go?

September   June

Early May   Late August

Why?

2 What would Bart *not* be able to easily do on his journey?

Make a side trip to Nashville   Make a stopover in New Orleans

Take a cruise   Take a side trip to Jamaica

Why?

3 What would most appeal to Bart?

A yacht charter   A train tour of Florida

A Magic Kingdom package   An alligator hunt

Why?

4 Which of the following cities should *not* be considered as a lodging spot?

Ft. Lauderdale   Key West

Ft. Myers   Orlando

Why?

NAME _____ **DATE** _____

CREATIVE ACTIVITY

Travel and Leisure magazine once conducted an online poll to determine which cities, places, and attractions were "worth revisiting." The winner: Washington, D.C. (i.e., 40 percent said that Washington, D.C., merited a second trip). Why do you think those polled felt the way they did? Write your answer below.

Now, consider the following places. Do you think they merit a second visit? Again, write your reason in the space provided.

Place	Yes or No?	Why or Why Not?
❶ The Florida Keys		
❷ Orlando		
❸ The Kennedy Space Center		
❹ Miami		

What three places in the United States and/or Canada, other than the ones above, do you think most merit a return visit? (Try to select at least one place in Florida.) Again, explain why.

Place

❶

❷

❸

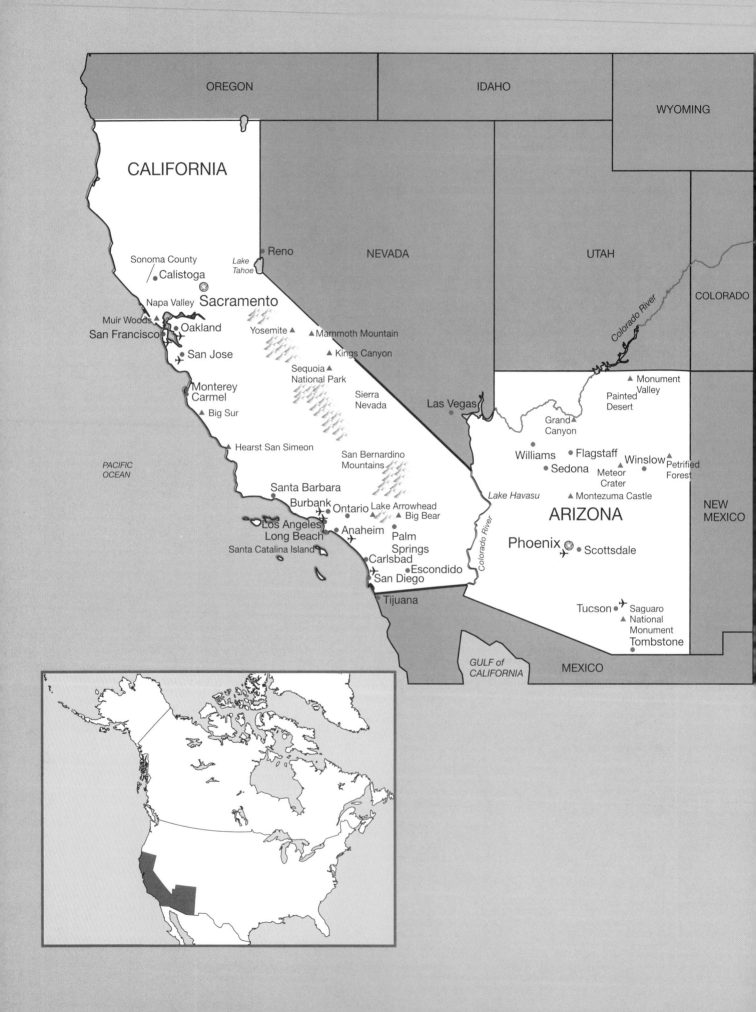

Chapter 5

California and Arizona
Glamour and Grandeur

It all depends on whom you're talking to. Say the name "California" and the first thing some will think of is the glitz of **Hollywood** or the free-spirited sophistication of **San Francisco**. Others will conjure up the images of magnificent natural wonders like awesome **Yosemite** [yo-SEM-mih-tee] **National Park**, the rolling **Wine Country**, or the majestic redwoods.

California is often divided geographically into two areas, North and South, each with a distinct character. Southern California is largely desert and industrial, with **Los Angeles**, bordering the Pacific Ocean off its west coast, as its heart. The L.A. metropolitan area sprawls far south, through **Anaheim** (and the **Disneyland Resort**), and north, past the San Fernando Valley, home of **Burbank**, where many of the movie studios are found. In the very south is lovely **San Diego**.

Northern California is more forested. Its centerpiece is the port city of San Francisco. To the south are the beautiful towns of **Monterey** and **Carmel**, and to the north is the Wine Country of the **Napa Valley** and **Sonoma County**. Yosemite National Park is east of San Francisco, near the Nevada border. Northeast of San Francisco, incidentally, is the state capital, **Sacramento**; it's not, however, much of a tourist center.

California is connected on the southeast to Arizona. Largely desert (though there are mountains throughout its northern portion), Arizona has stunning scenery, notably in the areas around the **Grand Canyon** and **Sedona**. A bit south of Arizona's center is **Phoenix**, the state's capital and cultural center. Off in the southeast corner is **Tucson** [TOO-sahn], a city heavily influenced by Native American culture.

In Arizona, you can drive past a place called Nowhere, a village named Eden, and a town called Why.

How Travelers Get There

Los Angeles is one of the country's easiest cities to reach by air. Most flights land at **Los Angeles International Airport** (LAX); however, **Burbank Airport** (BUR) is convenient for travelers who are staying in the San Fernando Valley or who prefer less crowded terminals. There's also **John Wayne Airport (SNA)** in **Orange County** (for those visiting Disneyland and other attractions in that area), and **Ontario Airport (ONT)**, east of L.A. **San Diego International Airport (SAN)** serves the most southerly part of California.

Flights to northern California are also numerous. The major gateway is **San Francisco International Airport (SFO)**. However, many flights land at **Oakland (OAK)** and **San Jose (SJC)** as well.

Meteor Crater, outside Winslow, Arizona, is where a giant meteor crashed into the ground 22,000 years ago.

Most Arizona-bound travelers will fly into **Sky Harbor International Airport** (PHX) in Phoenix, though there's also a busy airport at Tucson (TUS). Flying time to all these destinations from the East Coast is about five to six hours.

A leisurely and scenic way of reaching the area is by train. **Amtrak** has lines to both Los Angeles and San Francisco that can be accessed from many cities across the United States. One of the L.A. routes goes through **Flagstaff**, Arizona. Cruises access San Diego and Los Angeles on repositioning cruises from the Caribbean, Acapulco, Vancouver, and Hawaii. A rich complex of highways flows into Arizona and California from neighboring states.

Weather Patterns

To describe the climates of California and Arizona is no easy task. The reason: Totally different climate conditions can exist within miles of each other. For example, a visitor to southern California can drive from the beach in Santa Monica to inland San Bernardino and into the nearby mountains, passing from pleasant, breezy beach temperatures through hot desert air, and into snow—all in less than two hours.

It snows in Los Angeles two or three times per century.

Four general climate patterns exist in California and Arizona. **Coastal California**, which includes the beach areas, tends to have warm but dry summers and pleasantly comfortable winters, with occasional rainstorms between November and March (see Figures 5–1

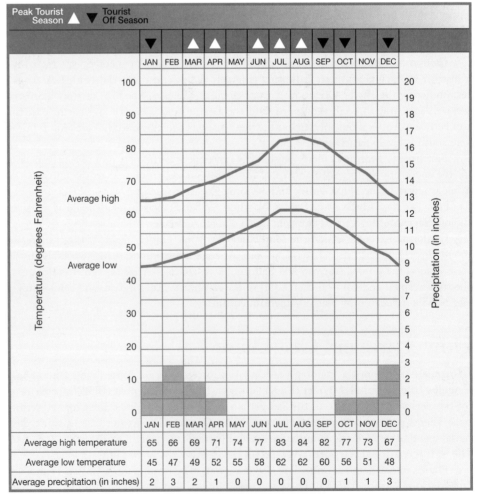

Climate at a Glance ————————————
LOS ANGELES, CALIFORNIA

	JAN	FEB	MAR	APR	MAY	JUN	JUL	AUG	SEP	OCT	NOV	DEC
Average high temperature	65	66	69	71	74	77	83	84	82	77	73	67
Average low temperature	45	47	49	52	55	58	62	62	60	56	51	48
Average precipitation (in inches)	2	3	2	1	0	0	0	0	0	1	1	3

Figure 5–1

Climate at a Glance
SAN FRANCISCO, CALIFORNIA

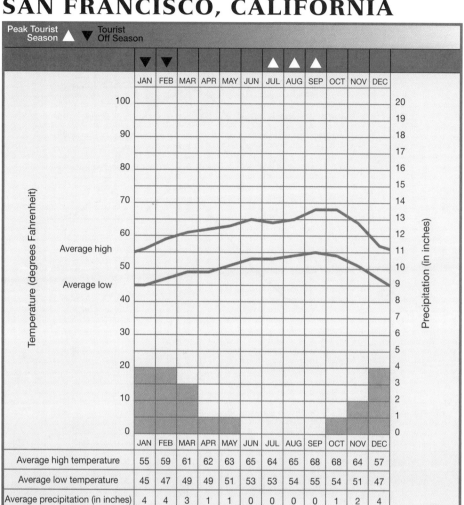

	JAN	FEB	MAR	APR	MAY	JUN	JUL	AUG	SEP	OCT	NOV	DEC
Average high temperature	55	59	61	62	63	65	64	65	68	68	64	57
Average low temperature	45	47	49	49	51	53	53	54	55	54	51	47
Average precipitation (in inches)	4	4	3	1	1	0	0	0	0	1	2	4

Figure 5–2

and 5–2). Fog along the immediate coast can occur anytime, though it happens less frequently in the fall (which may be California's most pleasant season). Nights are surprisingly cool. Of course, the farther north a traveler goes up the coast toward San Francisco and beyond, the chillier the year-round temperatures become (and the greater the likelihood of fog). As Mark Twain put it, "The coldest winter I ever spent was a summer in San Francisco."

The second pattern occurs in California's **valleys and near-coastal areas** (e.g., Anaheim). The climate is somewhat like coastal California, but with temperatures that run 10 to 15 degrees warmer and with fog only rarely. The third pattern marks the vast, flat **deserts** of California and Arizona. Summer, early fall, and late spring feature extremely sunny, torridly hot, and bone-dry weather. Daytime temperatures of over 100 degrees are typical. Winter is much more pleasant, with warmth, sunshine, and only occasional rain (see Figure 5–3). **High-elevation areas** (e.g., the Grand Canyon and California's mountain resorts) represent the last pattern: cold, snowy winters with warm daytime sun (even if there's snow on the ground) and pleasantly cool to warm summers.

Remember: California's ocean temperatures are chilly, even in the summer. As for tourist patterns, California enjoys major tourism year-round, with a slight thinning of crowds in the fall. The Grand Canyon's peak season is summer. The desert and ski resorts have their high seasons in the winter; rates plunge during the summer.

Climate at a Glance
PHOENIX, ARIZONA

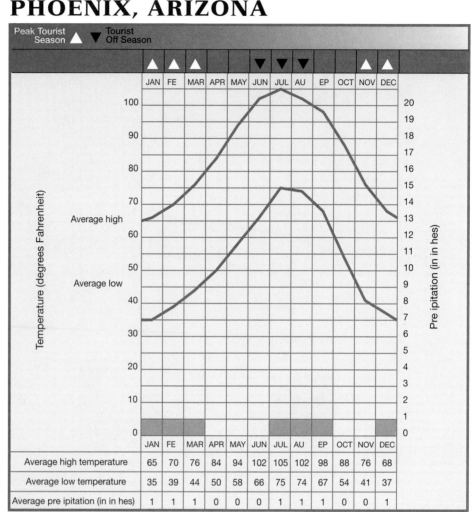

	JAN	FE	MAR	APR	MAY	JUN	JUL	AU	EP	OCT	NOV	DEC
Average high temperature	65	70	76	84	94	102	105	102	98	88	76	68
Average low temperature	35	39	44	50	58	66	75	74	67	54	41	37
Average pre ipitation (in in hes)	1	1	1	0	0	0	1	1	1	0	0	1

Figure 5–3

Getting Around

Both California and Arizona have excellent freeway systems (though in both states, distances can be great). And yes, California's massive freeway system in urban areas suffers awesome congestion. Many air connections tie the major cities together, especially along the Los Angeles–San Francisco corridor. For those who enjoy train travel, several Amtrak routes are convenient and scenic, especially the **Coast Starlight** (Los Angeles to San Francisco and beyond) and the **Pacific Surfliner** (from San Luis Obispo to San Diego). There are also train rides and cruises through California Wine Country.

Public transportation in Los Angeles leaves a bit to be desired, although a fairly new rail-subway system is impressive. Because the city is so spread out, taxis can be expensive. City tours (especially past the homes of the stars) are popular. For most visitors, however, car rentals are by far the preferred way to get around. The highways are well laid out and the streets are wide. Rush hours (7 A.M. to 10 A.M. and 3 P.M. to 7 P.M.) can be truly awful.

San Francisco is much easier to get around, though the hilly streets can be difficult for cars and pedestrians. The excellent BART subway gets travelers around the Bay Area. And of course, there are the famous and fun cable cars.

To get to the Grand Canyon from Flagstaff, visitors can either drive themselves on a beautiful (but slow) route or take a bus from the city's bus depot. In the summer season, the Grand Canyon Railway operates a vintage steam train from Williams, Arizona, 60 miles north to the Grand Canyon. (Vintage diesel trains are used the rest of the year.) One-day air excursions to the Grand Canyon from Las Vegas, Nevada, are popular. Phoenix, like Los Angeles., is spread out; car rentals or the adequate bus system are the preferred options for getting around.

Important Places

California and Arizona have a wealth of attractions. Here are the principal ones.

Los Angeles

Los Angeles is the heart of any trip to southern California and a magnet for millions of visitors yearly. A sprawling city of extremes, Los Angeles. is the kind of place people either love or avoid like the plague. As befits the second-largest city in the United States, the Los Angeles area brims with first-rate attractions: theme parks, museums, beaches, nightlife, restaurants, theater, and its own brand of glitz. Among the most popular attractions are:

- **The Disneyland Resort**, which is actually in Anaheim, about a half-hour from Los Angeles itself. It encompasses **Disneyland** (the granddaddy of theme parks), **Disney's California Adventure** (which celebrates the Golden State), and **Downtown Disney** (an entertainment, dining, and shopping district). Visitors could easily spend two days here.

- **Other theme parks**, like **Universal Studios Hollywood** (another must), **Knott's Berry Farm** (plenty of rides and famous foods), and **Six Flags Magic Mountain** (a more conventional theme park with a huge collection of thrill rides).

- **Grauman's Chinese Theater**, where movie stars' footprints are enshrined in cement. Nearby are the **Hollywood & Highland** shopping and entertainment center (the home of the Academy Awards ceremonies) and the **Walk of Fame** (where star-shaped plaques honoring the famous are embedded in the sidewalk).

"Real" studio tours at Warner Bros., Sony, and Paramount are available.

Two of the most recognizable rides at Disney's California Adventure
Photo by Marc Mancini

- **Beverly Hills**, with its posh Rodeo [roh-DAY-oh] Drive and mansions (which can be experienced via a "stars' homes" tour).
- **Excellent museums**, like the **L.A. County Museum of Art**, the offbeat **Museum of Contemporary Art**, and the **Getty Center**, perhaps the world's wealthiest museum.
- **The Queen Mary**, in nearby **Long Beach**, the former ocean liner now permanently docked as a hotel and tourist attraction. Some cruises depart from a terminal nearby. Long Beach boasts a good number of waterfront restaurants, hotels, shops, secondary attractions, and the world-class **Aquarium of the Pacific**.
- **The Venice Boardwalk**, with its assortment of beachside eccentrics (and those who come to see them). Three more trendy places to look, shop, and stroll: **Santa Monica's Third Street Promenade**, **The Grove** (next to Farmer's Market), and **CityWalk** (which adjoins Universal Studios).

L.A.'s Farmer's Market is a favorite among locals for food and shopping.

Various **day trips** can be taken from Los Angeles, many of which can be extended into longer stays:

- **Catalina Island**, "26 miles across the sea from L.A.," exactly as an old song said. There are beautiful coves, mountains, hiking, buffalo herds, and boat and bus tours. (Officially it's Santa Catalina Island, but few people call it that.)
- **Big Bear** and **Lake Arrowhead**, popular and pretty water-and-ski resorts, in the nearby **San Bernardino Mountains**.

The Spanish named California after an imaginary island, Califina, cited in a then-popular romance novel.

A little farther out from Los Angeles and within an easy day's drive are some places that could make nice, short overnight stops of their own:

- **Palm Springs**, a fashionable desert resort. It's not quite as posh as it once was, but the resort complexes in nearby **Palm Desert** and **Rancho Mirage** are luxurious. During college spring break, it's a wild place indeed. A nearby attraction is an aerial tramway that takes visitors to the top of lofty **Mt. San Jacinto**.
- **Santa Barbara**, with its mission, boutiques, great ocean views, good small museums, and lovely gardens.
- **Sequoia** and **Kings Canyon National Parks**, with their famed towering redwood trees. These parks are about equidistant from San Francisco and Los Angeles.

San Diego

Only a couple of hours south of Los Angeles is San Diego. Though close enough for a long, tiring day trip from Los Angeles, this beautiful city—with its revitalized downtown core—should be seen on its own. Among its popular attractions are:

There's an exact reproduction of Shakespeare's Globe Theatre in San Diego's Balboa Park.

- **San Diego Zoo**, one of the world's greatest zoos. Most of the animals are kept in natural habitat surroundings, not cages. The zoo is actually just one part of **Balboa Park**, the city's centerpiece, with lakes, gardens, and many museums.
- **Sea World**, one of the world's great marine life amusement parks.

Close to San Diego are:

- **San Diego Wild Animal Park**, a large animal preserve with tours.
- **Tijuana**, the Mexican city about 20 minutes away, across the border from San Diego. It's rather dirty and impoverished, but bargain hunters still go there. Most day visitors park their cars on the U.S. side and walk across the border to Tijuana.

San Francisco

The Palace of the Legion of Honor in San Francisco is an exact reproduction of the one in Paris.

As Los Angeles is to southern California, so, too, is San Francisco the hub of central and northern California. San Francisco has wonderful restaurants, cutting-edge nightlife, and excellent symphony and opera. Among the attractions are:

- **Fisherman's Wharf,** a lively waterfront open-air market, with stalls selling that day's catch and the smells of sourdough bread permeating the air. This crowded district has excellent restaurants and interesting shops.

- **Ghirardelli Square,** a busy, fun shopping center right near the Wharf that was once a chocolate factory. Several similar shopping complexes are also in the area.

- **Golden Gate Park,** a wonderful, huge recreation area with many lakes, several museums, and the beautiful **Japanese Tea Garden.**

- **Alcatraz,** the famed old prison in San Francisco Bay that the National Parks Service maintains as a tourist attraction.

- **Chinatown,** with the largest number of Chinese in any area outside of China. It gets crowded, but tourists enjoy walking among the pagoda-like buildings, checking out the import shops, and eating.

- **A few other attractions:** the oddly shaped **Coit Tower** on **Telegraph Hill,** crooked **Lombard Street,** and the Italian **North Beach** restaurant area.

Several areas outside San Francisco make for great **day trips:**

- **Monterey** and **Carmel,** to the south. These gorgeous towns have beautiful scenery, famous golf courses, and a lovely old mission. Monterey's aquarium is outstanding. The renowned **17 Mile Drive** is a must-see.

- **Muir Woods National Monument,** just to the north of San Francisco. This stunning park features walks among spectacular redwoods. On the way, a visitor could stop at **Sausalito,** a quaint waterfront town across the bay from San Francisco. Getting there offers a good opportunity to cross the **Golden Gate Bridge,** a world-famous landmark.

San Francisco's Lombard Street is the world's crookedest.

- **Hearst San Simeon State Historical Monument**, with its famous ornate castle. It's a long day trip from San Francisco, at the southerly end of the scenic **Big Sur** Coastal Road. (It's actually closer to Santa Barbara.)

Most skiers know about **Lake Tahoe**, a popular resort on the Nevada border, just across from Reno, Nevada. It's about a four-hour drive from San Francisco. The Tahoe area contains a number of world-class ski resorts, including **Heavenly Valley, Alpine Meadows,** and **Squaw Valley.** To the south of the lake (nearer Yosemite) is the **Mammoth Mountain–June Mountain** ski area.

The Wine Country

Only an hour's drive north of San Francisco, Napa Valley and Sonoma County—the two biggest wine-producing regions in the United States—are commonly visited for several days on their own. The wineries have fascinating architecture; redwood forests and lovely little shops are all along the way. The Wine Country can be visited by car, train, or boat.

These cars are not in a garden. They're descending Lombard Street, the "crookedest street in the world"

Image copyright Albo, 2008. Used under license from Shutterstock.com

Fairfield, California, is the home of Jelly Bellies. Factory tours are available.

The town of **Calistoga** is famous for its mineral springs and spas, which have attracted visitors since the nineteenth century.

Yosemite National Park

Yosemite is one of the most beautiful locales in the world, with numerous waterfalls and such justly renowned spectacles as **Half Dome** and **El Capitan**. This is a must visit for anyone near the area.

Yosemite's El Capitan cliff is three times higher than the Empire State Building.

Phoenix

This desert city (Arizona's capital) and its neighbor, **Scottsdale**, are surrounded by hulking mountains and are steeped in Native American history. The city has several mega resorts and all manner of dude ranches. Phoenix is also a baseball mecca from late February to early April, when major league teams train here.

Its most popular attractions include:

- **The adjoining town of Scottsdale**, with impressive upscale art galleries, resort hotels, golf courses, and shops specializing in Native American crafts.
- **Architectural landmarks**, notably **Taliesin West** (the fascinating school created by Frank Lloyd Wright) and the **Cosanti Foundation** (the strangely wonderful, futuristic workshop of Paolo Soleri). Tours of both are available.

An attractive day trip is to Sedona, famed for its astonishing red cliffs; Sedona can be accessed by driving along the scenic Verde River valley or from Flagstaff, as part of a shorter, half-day trip through spectacular **Oak Creek Canyon**. Not far from Sedona is **Montezuma Castle**, the 800-year-old ruins of an ancient North American civilization, situated in the side of a cliff. To the west is **Lake Havasu**, most famous as the site of the relocated **London Bridge**. (There's nothing weirder than seeing this structure in the middle of the desert.)

Eat in one of the several country-and-western restaurants on the outskirts of Phoenix. A western delicacy: rattlesnake (which tastes like chicken).

Grand Canyon National Park

This is possibly the most famous natural landmark in the United States. It's breathtaking. The **South Rim**, which offers the best views, is the most popular area to visit and is jam-packed in the summer. The canyon's depths can be seen by hiking, riding on a mule, flying in a helicopter or plane, or rafting on the Colorado River. Hotel accommodations in the park are somewhat limited; most lodging is in Flagstaff (about 90 miles away).

Far to the northeast are the **Painted Desert** and **Petrified Forest National Park** (east of Flagstaff) and **Monument Valley** (northeast) with its ancient Native American ruins and familiar vistas. (Monument Valley appeared repeatedly in Western movies.)

Tucson

This city is extremely popular in the winter for its dude ranches, resorts, and the controversial, ecologically sealed community, **Biosphere 2**. **Old Tucson Studios**, where many Westerns were shot, is just west of town. Several Tucson museums showcase Native American art. The city is also near **Saguaro National Park**, with its giant cacti. About 100 miles southeast of Tucson is **Tombstone**. Here's the Old West as it must have been, complete with the legendary **OK Corral, Boot Hill**, and the **Bird Cage Theater**.

Possible Itineraries

Where should first-time tourists to California go? Probably to either Los Angeles or San Francisco and their surrounding areas. There's enough to do close by Los Angeles and San Francisco to warrant a stay of five to seven days at each. Tourists often want to drive the coastal road between the two cities, but it's a long distance that's better done in two days,

This ancient Native American dwelling, Montezuma's Castle, is one of Arizona's more notable attractions

Image copyright Bryan Busovicki, 2008. Used under license from Shutterstock.com

with a stop perhaps at Hearst Castle. Return visitors may prefer to get out of the urban centers and discover the riches of the state, exploring the southern California coastal communities or the desert for a week, or driving through the Wine Country and forestland of the north. Five-day excursions to Yosemite or the Grand Canyon and their surrounding areas are worthwhile trips of their own. A relaxing three to five days stay in Phoenix allows visitors to get away from it all.

What about an Arizona-only trip? Two itineraries are common. In the first, travelers fly into Phoenix and, taking a northerly route, visit the Petrified Forest, the Painted Desert and/or Monument Valley, the Grand Canyon, and Sedona. They might also detour to Lake Havasu, returning to Phoenix. This itinerary would take about a week. In the second, travelers stay in Phoenix for two or three days, then head south to Tucson, Tombstone, and Saguaro National Monument. This could be done in about six days.

Lodging Options

California offers an abundance of lodging choices. Because it's so spread out, Los Angeles has no real lodging center; there are, however, hotel clusters around the L.A. airport, Beverly Hills, Universal Studios, Marina del Rey, Santa Monica, Century City, West Hollywood, downtown (more appropriate for some business travelers), and the Disneyland Resort in Anaheim. The **Beverly Hills Hotel**, with its famous bungalows, is where legendary movie stars have resided. The San Diego area also boasts some excellent hotels, especially the **Hotel Del Coronado**, an astonishing bit of wooden Victorian whimsy. Santa Barbara's **Four Seasons Biltmore** is a landmark.

In San Francisco, hotels tend to be based at Nob Hill, Union Square, Fisherman's Wharf, and on either side of Market Street. There are at least a half-dozen world-class hotels here, as well as many lesser known gems. Yosemite has a wide range of accommodations, from hotels to tents and cabins; the **Ahwahnee Hotel** is rustic yet elegant, and a national landmark. For a change of pace, bed-and-breakfasts are popular in California, especially in the Wine Country.

Some Arizona resorts in the north close in the winter, whereas those in the south may close during summer months. Most hotels are open year-round, though, and may drastically

In Arizona, more boats are owned per capita than in any other U.S. state.

In San Luis Obispo—between Santa Barbara and Hearst San Simeon—is the Madonna Inn, where each room has a different theme. (The Cave Man room is the most popular.)

lower their rates off-season. Lodging in the Phoenix area is clustered downtown and north of the city near the Metrocenter, as well as throughout Scottsdale. Frank Lloyd Wright designed the luxurious **Arizona Biltmore** resort. In Scottsdale is the **Phoenician**, a glitzy resort carved out of the side of a mountain. These and other Arizona hotel resorts attract conferences and conventions. Dude ranches offer an intriguing lodging option, especially for horse lovers. **Grand Canyon National Park Lodges** include all the lodging properties within the park itself. Tucson has a surprisingly rich collection of upscale resorts (such as the **Canyon Ranch**) and ranches.

Allied Destinations

California is a good jumping-off point for the Pacific Northwest states of Oregon and Washington. It also borders Nevada and is a short flight to Las Vegas. California is a common stop for long flights to Hawaii and Asia. Both California and Arizona border Mexico, with cruise ships heading southward from Los Angeles, Long Beach, and San Diego to Mexico's Baja Peninsula, and beyond. Remember, too, that Arizona adjoins Colorado, New Mexico, and Utah (with its many national parks).

Factors That Motivate Visitors

Among the diverse reasons that motivate travelers to southern California are:

- It has superb weather year-round.
- They want to see the "movie capital," Hollywood. (They also hope to bump into a movie star; good luck to them.)
- There's wonderful outdoor recreation available all year.
- Los Angeles, Long Beach, and San Diego are departure points for cruises to Mexico and, occasionally, the Panama Canal.
- The area brims with natural wonders.
- Los Angeles is a convenient way to break up a trip to trans-Pacific destinations.
- There's plenty to do at night in the major cities.
- Some of the finest theme parks are here.

Northern California appeals to people for altogether different reasons. They might prefer visiting here because:

- San Francisco is sophisticated yet has a small-town, European feel.
- There's the natural splendor of mountains and redwood forests.
- The Monterey–Carmel area has renowned golf courses.
- The climate is temperate.
- San Francisco has exciting nightlife and great restaurants.
- The Wine Country is a unique, almost European attraction.
- Northern California has world-class skiing; there are several less extensive ski resorts northeast of Los Angeles, too.

Arizona, too, has its own appeal:

- The Grand Canyon is a unique spectacle.
- There are several interesting resorts and ranches.
- Many Northerners head to Arizona in the winter, staying in retirement trailer parks, condos, and timeshares.
- Arizona hosts many conventions, especially in the Phoenix/Scottsdale area.
- It boasts an Old West and Native American ambience.

The Golden Gate Bridge isn't golden. It's painted burnt orange.

Qualifying the Traveler
Southern California

For People Who Want	Appeal			Remarks
	High	Medium	Low	
Historical and Cultural Attractions		▲		Los Angeles and San Diego museums
Beaches and Water Sports	▲			Water is cool
Skiing Opportunities			▲	Some in San Bernardino mountains.
Lots of Nightlife		▲		Mostly Los Angeles.
Family Activities	▲			Especially theme parks
Familiar Cultural Experience	▲			A little different yet still U.S.
Exotic Cultural Experience		▲		Offbeat lifestyles and Latino influence
Safety and Low Crime		▲		Tourist areas are safe
Bargain Travel		▲		
Impressive Scenery	▲			Mountains, desert, and ocean
Peace and Quiet			▲	Only in desert and mountain towns
Shopping Opportunities		▲		Just about everything
Adventure			▲	Hiking, biking
To Do Business	▲			Key to the Pacific Rim

Possible Misgivings

Some parts of California will set off warning bells for a few potential visitors. Arizona might raise some questions for others. Among concerns to address are:

- "The thought of driving in Los Angeles frightens me and there's no public transportation." Driving at times other than rush hour is usually easy. And there are buses, a subway, a growing rail system, and all sorts of city tours.
- "People in Los Angeles are weird." Mention that the city is a melting pot of people and cultures. It's diverse, open, free-spirited, and friendly.
- "Los Angeles is so smoggy." Late fall to early spring is much better than summertime. Coastal areas are also far less smoggy. There's 50 percent less smog in Los Angeles than there was two decades ago.
- "All there is to see in southern California is Los Angeles" A short drive out of the city, and you can be in the desert, mountains, San Diego, or Santa Barbara—just for starters.
- "San Francisco has a lot of strange people." Like all stereotypes, this one holds little water. Yes, San Francisco is a somewhat counterculture city, but the diversity actually helps make it a more interesting place.
- "Arizona's too hot." Suggest the winter, when it's more pleasant in the south. In the summer, Arizona's northern regions are cooler than the southern ones.

One of the most bizarre attractions in the United States: Winchester Mystery House in San Jose, California. This rambling Victorian mansion has—among other things—stairs leading nowhere and windows that open onto other rooms.

- "There's nothing to do in Arizona." Phoenix is a very interesting city, but its appeal is subtle and takes awhile to appreciate. Tucson and Tombstone are unique attractions.

- "The Grand Canyon is crowded." Suggest touring the North Rim rather than the South Rim, or going off-season.

Sales Strategies

California and Arizona offer many ways to upsell or cross-sell. A car rental is an obvious recommendation. Los Angeles city tours are very popular, because the city is so spread out. City tours are also a good idea in San Francisco. You might suggest that visitors extend their trip in southern California to include the Grand Canyon, Las Vegas, or Mexico (perhaps on a cruise). A popular winter activity is a whale-watching cruise; they most commonly depart from San Diego and Monterey. And around the Christmas holiday, the lavish, glorious **Bracebridge Dinner** is a long-standing pageant at the Ahwahnee Hotel in Yosemite.

For those going to Arizona, a river-rafting trip down the Colorado River through the Grand Canyon is spectacular. Helicopter or plane trips over the canyon are famous. Arizona is a popular resort state, and upselling to a resort hotel could make this quiet state a great deal of fun.

Cruises to Mexico or repositioning cruises along California's coast are quite popular. Year-round three- or four-day cruises to Ensenada, Mexico, and seasonal seven-day cruises farther south to other Mexican port cities mostly leave from San Pedro (Los Angeles's port), Long Beach, and San Diego. Small-ship cruises and railway excursions can be sold to visitors wanting to tour the Wine Country in a unique way.

A movie crew filming a 1912 Western brought buffalos to Catalina Island. When the shoot was finished, the buffalos were left to fend for themselves. Some of their descendants are still there.

Travel Trivia

The Author's 10 Favorite Odd Attractions in North America

1. Winchester Mystery House, San Jose, California

2. The Museum of Bad Art, Dedham, Massachusetts

3. The Museum of Jurassic Technology, Culver City, California

4. Mutter Museum, Philadelphia, Pennsylvania

5. The Madonna Inn, San Luis Obispo, California

6. London Bridge, Lake Havasu, Arizona

7. Magnetic Hill, Moncton, New Brunswick

8. Lizzie Borden's House, Fall River, Massachusetts

9. Kansas Barbed Wire Museum, La Crosse, Kansas

10. Any wax museum

SOURCE: Marc Mancini

NAME _____   **DATE** _____

MAP ACTIVITY

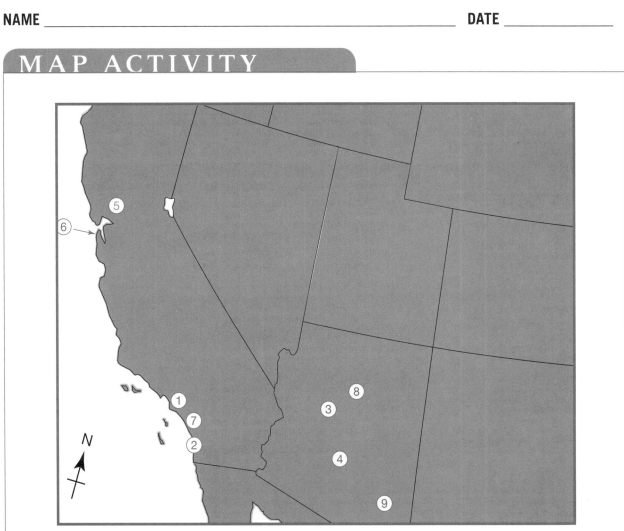

A traveler wants to visit the places listed below. Which number represents each on the map?

Place/Attraction	In/Near Which City/State?	Number on Map
A. The OK Corral	A. _____	A. _____
B. Astonishing red cliffs	B. _____	B. _____
C. The Arizona Biltmore	C. _____	C. _____
D. Grauman's Chinese Theater	D. _____	D. _____
E. A mineral spring centered in the Wine Country	E. _____	E. _____
F. Lombard Street	F. _____	F. _____
G. Disneyland	G. _____	G. _____
H. A city near the Grand Canyon	H. _____	H. _____
I. Sea World	I. _____	I. _____
J. Alcatraz	J. _____	J. _____

NAME _____   **DATE** _____

CASE STUDY

Judi and Gordon Hayford of Toronto Canada, are taking their three teenage children on their first long-distance family trip—in this case, to Los Angeles. Their children have five days off during the winter school break. They're especially looking forward to Disneyland.

Circle the answer that best suits their needs.

1 What other attraction would you suggest for the family?

    Fisherman's Wharf   Montezuma Castle

    Universal Studios   Hearst Castle

    Why?

2 What area should the Hayfords probably lodge in?

    Hollywood   Anaheim

    Monterey   Palm Springs

    Why?

3 If they decided to leave Los Angeles and drive off on a one- to two-day trip, what place would you recommend?

    Yosemite   Sonoma

    Wally World   San Diego

    Why?

4 Which of the following would *not* be a good enhancement to their trip?

    A whale-watching cruise   The Bracebridge Dinner

    A car rental   A tour of the stars' homes

    Why?

NAME _____   **DATE** _____

CREATIVE ACTIVITY

You're driving down a lonely desert road outside of Palm Springs. Your car inexplicably stalls. Suddenly, a flying saucer lands next to you. A four-foot-tall green alien exits the craft and, in perfect English, says, "Human being! I wish to visit five interesting things in California and Arizona. No more, no less! What must I see? They must please me, or I will disintegrate you!" List your five responses below, along with the reason for your choice.

Your Suggestion

1

2

3

4

5

Your Reason

1

2

3

4

5

ARCTIC
OCEAN

Point
Barrow

Nome

Alaska

UNITED
STATES

BEAUFORT
SEA

Queen Elizabeth
Islands

GREENLAND

BAFFIN
BAY

BERING
SEA

Alaska
Range

Fairbanks

● Denali Nat. Park

Anchorage

GULF of
ALASKA

Dawson
City

Yukon

Great
Bear
Lake

Whitehorse

GLACIER
BAY

Skagway

Sitka

Juneau

Ketchikan

British
Columbia

Northwest
Territories

Great
Slave
Lake

CANADA

Nunavut

Hudson Strait

LABRADOR
SEA

Labrador

Alberta

Lake Athabasca

Churchill

HUDSON
BAY

Quebec

L'Anse Aux Meadows

Newfoundland

Vancouver
Island

Jasper
Nat. Park

Saskatchewan

Reindeer Lake

Manitoba

New
Brunswick

Gaspé

Prince
Edward
Island

Vancouver

Banff
Nat. Park

Lake
Louise

Calgary

Lake
Winnipeg

Ontario

Laurentian
Mountains

Moncton
St. John

Port Angeles

Victoria

Winnipeg

Lake
Superior

Quebec City
Montreal

ME

Halifax

Yarmouth

Nova
Scotia

Seattle

WA

Montana

North
Dakota

Minnesota

Wisconsin

Michigan

Ottawa

Kingston
Toronto

Niagara Falls

VT/NH

NY

Buffalo

Fredericton

BAY of
FUNDY

Gananoque

MA
CT RI

PACIFIC
OCEAN

Oregon

Idaho

Wyoming

South
Dakota

Iowa

IN

OH

PA

MD

NJ

DE

Nevada

Utah

Nebraska

Illinois

WV

VA

California

Colorado

Kansas

Missouri

KY

NC

Arizona

New Mexico

Oklahoma

Arkansas

TN

SC

ATLANTIC
OCEAN

MS

AL

GA

Texas

LA

FL

MEXICO

Rocky Mountains

Edmonton

Chapter 6

Canada and Alaska
The Great White North

The French philosopher Voltaire once called Canada "20 million acres of snow." Americans once labeled the United States purchase of Alaska, at 2.5 cents an acre, a "folly." Follies, indeed. These two areas are keys to the wealth of the North American continent and popular destinations for tourists from everywhere.

Why does this chapter lump a U.S. state and an entire country together? The reason is geographic. Alaska and Canada form a physical cap to North America. The entire area has a certain similarity of climate, topography, and history. Tourists also often get to Alaska via Canada. Don't conclude, though, that the whole region is a simple extension of U.S. culture: Canada has its own cultural identity, and Alaskans pride themselves on their distinct way of thinking.

In the far northwest of the continent (and only a few miles from Russia, to which it once belonged) is Alaska, the largest U.S. state. Its total population, though, is only about 677,000; **Anchorage**, its largest city, has about 284,000 residents.

Toronto is as far south as the French Riviera.

FYI
FOR YOUR INFORMATION   CANADA

CAPITAL: Ottawa	**RELIGIONS:** Roman Catholic and Protestant
AREA (SQUARE MILES): 3,852,000	**LANGUAGES:** English and French
TIME ZONES: GMT: −8 to −3:30	**CURRENCY:** 1 Canadian dollar = 100 cents
DRIVE ON: Right	**ELECTRICITY:** 110 volts, 60 cycles AC
POPULATION: 33,200,000	

CAPSULE HISTORY: Cabot arrives, 1497; Cartier claims it for France, 1534; British defeat French, 1763; confederation, 1867; railroad spans Canada, 1885; St. Lawrence Seaway begun, 1954; first constitution enacted, 1981–1982.

For reference sources, tourist bureaus, and suggested lengths of stay, see the Appendices.

115

Canada is the world's second biggest nation in size (slightly less than four million square miles), with 10 provinces and 3 territories. But like Alaska, Canada is sparsely settled; its population is about 33 million, a little less than that of the state of California (which is one-twenty-fourth the area). Most Canadians, for reasons of climate and commerce, live along their country's southern border; almost 9 million reside in the metropolitan areas of only two cities, **Toronto** and **Montreal**. Canada can be divided into six principal regions of tourism, from west to east: **Yukon, British Columbia,** the **Canadian Rockies, Ontario, Quebec,** and the **Atlantic Provinces.** Canada's vast Nunavut [NOO-nah-vut] and North-west Territories, and extensive Plains provinces (Saskatchewan and Manitoba) are places of great natural beauty (including Churchill, famous for its polar bears) and a few significant cities (such as Winnipeg), but they're not prime tourist destinations.

How Travelers Get There

To drive into Canada is relatively simple: Much of eastern Canada is within a day's drive of New England and New York; western Canada is similarly close to Washington, Oregon, Idaho, and Montana. Travelers can drive into Alaska via the Alaskan Highway, which ties into roads in British Columbia and the Yukon Territory, which borders eastern Alaska. Ferries and cruise ships are also a prime way of accessing Alaska: On the west coast, boats sail from Washington to several spots in British Columbia and Alaska; on the east coast, there's ferry service from Bar Harbor, Maine, to **Yarmouth, Nova Scotia.**

Air service is extremely convenient. **Air Canada** (AC) offers connections from U.S. cities into Canada, as do several U.S. carriers. The four main Canadian gateways are **Vancouver** (YVR), **Edmonton** (YEG), Toronto (YYZ), and Montreal (YUL). As for Alaska, convenient service exists from many points in the lower 48 states to Anchorage (ANC) and **Juneau** [JOO-no] (JNU), the state capital. **Alaska Airlines** (AS) is the state's well-known carrier. Train service into Canada is quite good, especially in the east: Niagara Falls, Toronto, and Montreal are served by trains that depart from Washington, D.C., New York City, Chicago, and Boston.

Weather Patterns

Canada and Alaska have cold climates. Winters are snowy and freezing, especially in the interior. But there are a few surprises. Coastal British Columbia, though wet, has very little snow or real cold in the winter. People may encounter hot days in July and August in Toronto, Montreal, and even in **Fairbanks,** in Alaska's interior (see Figures 6–1 to 6–3). Rainfall is moderate throughout the year, except in coastal British Columbia and in the Alaskan **Panhandle,** where Juneau is located; rainfall here, as in the U.S. Pacific North-west, can be plentiful, especially in the late summer and during the fall.

As for tourist seasons, summer, as you would expect, is the most crowded. Temperatures are warm, sunshine is more common, and daylight lasts for long stretches each day. The number of tourists, especially in Canada, increases sharply around the last week of June and tapers off around Labor Day. For this reason, the best time to visit may be May, June, or September, because the weather can still be quite pleasant, yet the attractions are uncrowded.

Getting Around

To drive through Canada and Alaska can be an enjoyable experience, because intercity traffic is rarely a bother. Stray very far northward from the major highway systems, though, and it's a different story: Roads can leave something to be desired. (A few fine routes do stretch northward here and there.) To get to the north country, air taxis, helicopters, and seaplanes are more commonly used, though service isn't always timely (often because of weather). Of course, regular jet routes interconnect all the major cities of Alaska and southern Canada.

Climate at a Glance
ANCHORAGE, ALASKA

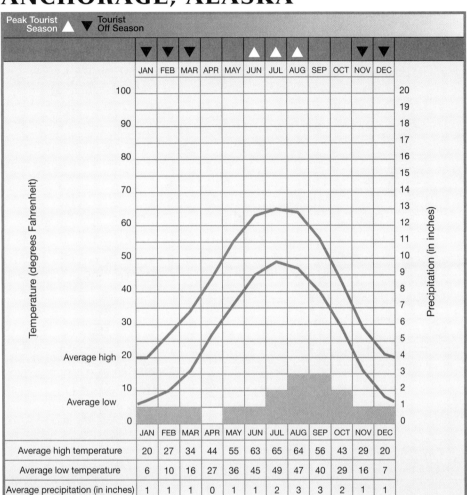

	JAN	FEB	MAR	APR	MAY	JUN	JUL	AUG	SEP	OCT	NOV	DEC
Average high temperature	20	27	34	44	55	63	65	64	56	43	29	20
Average low temperature	6	10	16	27	36	45	49	47	40	29	16	7
Average precipitation (in inches)	1	1	1	0	1	1	2	3	3	2	1	1

Figure 6–1

Two forms of transportation are especially useful in this region: trains and cruise ships. Canada's rail system, **VIA Rail Canada**, is a model of efficiency, and the seasonal Trans-Canada route is very popular. (In a way, the Vancouver to Toronto and Montreal portion of the trip is an attraction in itself.) **Rocky Mountaineer Railtours** operates between Vancouver and Jasper–Calgary. It follows an even more scenic route than VIA Rail's and does so during the daylight hours (not necessarily true with VIA Rail). Train service within Alaska, especially between Anchorage and Fairbanks, is also quite convenient. Alaska offers the "AlaskaPass," with unlimited travel on certain ferries, buses, and trains for one fee.

Cruises along the St. Lawrence River and beyond (between Montreal and New York City) are gaining in popularity. Multiday Alaska cruises, usually from Vancouver or Seattle, Washington, are especially popular: either roundtrip into Alaska's **Inside Passage**, or one-way into the **Gulf Coast** region to the Anchorage area. (A cruise can also be done in reverse, starting in Anchorage and ending in Vancouver or Seattle.) Seeing glaciers, snow-capped peaks, dense forests, and animal life along the way is an overwhelming experience. Larger ships offer many entertainment options for passengers. On the other hand, smaller vessels are able to get into narrower (and often more scenic) inlets and call on less visited ports. Cruise passengers can take plane or helicopter trips as excursions.

The short ferry ride to Toronto Island affords relaxing beauty and unparalleled views of Toronto.

Climate at a Glance
VANCOUVER, BRITISH COLUMBIA

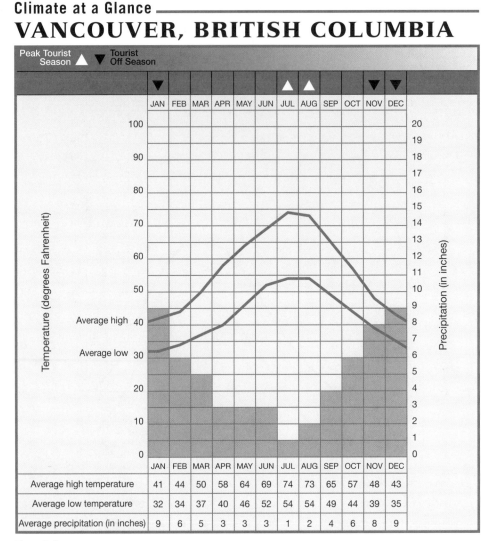

Figure 6–2

Local transportation, especially in Canada, tends to be exemplary. Subways, buses, streetcars, and taxis serve most Canadian cities, with inexpensive fares and clean, modern comfort. Another interesting transportation service is a helicopter tour of the Canadian Rockies: Passengers are set down on glaciers, alpine meadows, and mountain summits. Motorcoach tours of both Canada and Alaska are also extremely popular.

Important Places

As we mentioned in the chapter's introduction, tourists tend to visit only certain parts of Alaska and Canada. The highlights are as follows:

Alaska

Alaska appeals to a particular type of person: someone who loves natural beauty, can afford what could turn out to be a rather expensive trip, and doesn't mind a possibly slow-paced but certainly dramatic adventure. Among the highlights of any trip to Alaska are:

■ **An Inside Passage cruise,** with striking views and stops at **Sitka** (featuring remnants of Russian influence), picturesque Juneau (at the base of towering mountains),

Climate at a Glance
MONTREAL, QUEBEC

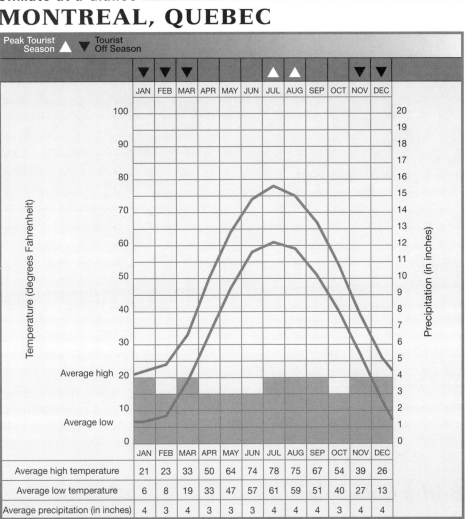

	JAN	FEB	MAR	APR	MAY	JUN	JUL	AUG	SEP	OCT	NOV	DEC
Average high temperature	21	23	33	50	64	74	78	75	67	54	39	26
Average low temperature	6	8	19	33	47	57	61	59	51	40	27	13
Average precipitation (in inches)	4	3	4	3	3	3	4	4	4	3	4	4

Figure 6–3

Glacier Bay (where passengers may see icebergs tumbling into the water from glaciers), Skagway (a key town in Alaska's gold-rush era), and Ketchikan (a rustic center of Native American culture).

■ Mendenhall Glacier, a dramatic sight visited as a half-day trip from Juneau.

■ Anchorage, Alaska's largest city and close to major glaciers (Portage Glacier is the best known), parks, and a zoo featuring Alaskan wildlife.

■ The Anchorage-Fairbanks Alaska Railroad, a 356-mile trip which crosses several awe-inspiring national parks, most notably Denali [den-AH-lee], a home to grizzlies and the location of Mt. McKinley (or Denali), North America's tallest peak. This journey is often part of a cruise tour.

■ Fairbanks, a gold-rush frontier town that features stern-wheeler trips, old gold camps, and Pioneer Park (formerly Alaskaland). Fairbanks is also a popular site in the winter for viewing that famous atmospheric phenomenon, the Northern Lights.

■ Nome, a northern gold-rush center; and Point Barrow, the northernmost spot in the United States. Both places—known for their summer "Midnight Sun"—are visited via plane as day trips from Fairbanks or Anchorage.

Japanese tourists like to visit Fairbanks in the winter. The reason: so they can see the colorful Northern Lights.

Ketchikan is a popular port on Alaska cruises
Image copyright Anthony Ricci, 2008. Used under license from Shutterstock.com

Yukon Territory

This territory to the north of British Columbia is often accessed via a motorcoach–train journey from Skagway, Alaska, as part of a cruise shore excursion. Yukon's frontier gold-rush spirit is best experienced at its two principal cities, **Whitehorse** (Yukon's capital) and **Dawson City**.

British Columbia

This western province is a prime destination for west coast residents of the United States and Canada. Its mist-shrouded mountains and graceful bays make it one of North America's most pleasant places to visit. Highlights include:

- **Vancouver**. Like many Canadian cities, Vancouver is an urban wonder, with neat homes, tree-lined streets, and flowering gardens. Late spring and summer would be the best times to visit. Among its attractions: the restored **Gastown** area, the **Granville Island** district, **Chinatown**, and the beautiful grounds of **Stanley Park**. Nearby (20 minutes from downtown) is **Grouse Mountain**, a popular ski spot. Vancouver has many wonderful dining and shopping opportunities.

> **Near Grouse Mountain is the Capilano Suspension Bridge, a swinging 400-foot-long bridge that spans a deep chasm. It looks as if it's right out of an Indiana Jones movie.**

- **Victoria**. On Vancouver Island, British Columbia's capital is a city of legendary beauty. Its most astonishing attraction: the **Butchart Gardens**, a 200-acre private park carved out of an old limestone quarry. To reach Vancouver Island, visitors can take a ferry from Tsawwassen (about 30 miles from Vancouver), from Port Angeles, Washington, or from Seattle. Even faster are large catamaran ships that sail between Victoria and Vancouver.

The Canadian Rockies

Every bit as scenic as the Alps, the Canadian Rockies are a magnet for both winter and summer visitors. Most attractions are found along the western boundary of the province of Alberta. Travelers will probably start from either Calgary or Edmonton. Each summer, Calgary hosts a renowned rodeo, the **Calgary Stampede**; a long stay in Calgary probably isn't warranted at other times of the year. Edmonton is quite famous for its shopping mall

> **Alberta's ski season begins as early as November and can extend into May.**

(one of the largest in the world), several good museums, an excellent zoo with polar wild-life, and the dozens of major events it stages each year. To the west of these two gateway cities are the following attractions (which are connected by the scenic **Icefields Parkway**):

- **Banff National Park** and **Lake Louise**, considered by some to be among the most pic-turesque places on earth, and a prime ski destination.
- **Jasper**, just northwest of Banff, Lake Louise, and Calgary (and due west of Edmonton), a gateway to several overwhelming glaciers, ice fields, and national parks. Jasper is also the departure point for helicopter trips into the Canadian Rockies, both in Alberta and into nearby British Columbia.

Ontario

Ontario is often confused with **Ottawa**. Ontario is a large eastern province, and Ottawa is Canada's capital (which happens to be on Ontario's easternmost border). To further compli-cate things, Ontario is also the name of a large airport east of Los Angeles. On occasion, travelers have been sent to this airport, instead of to Ottawa.

Toronto's Bata Shoe Museum has perhaps the world's biggest display of historical footwear.

The CN Tower offers an unparalleled view of Toronto, Lake Ontario and, on a clear day, the distant, rising mists of Niagara Falls
Image copyright Olga Skalkina, 2008. Used under license from Shutterstock.com

Ontario is fast becoming a major tourist destination. Among its many features are:

- **Toronto**, a culture-filled metropolis that designer Buckminster Fuller once called "the only modern city that works." Its restaurants and theater life are rich and diversified. The **Casa Loma** castle and lofty **CN Tower** are essential attractions to visit. **Rogers Centre** (formerly SkyDome) is home to baseball's Toronto Blue Jays. It has the world's first fully retractable roof (it can open or close in under 20 minutes) and a hotel that overlooks the playing field. The **Royal Ontario Museum** (or ROM) is Canada's largest museum. Its structure has recently been remodeled into a bold combination of traditional and modern architectural elements.

- **Niagara Falls** is one of North America's best known attractions. The only really full views of the two major Niagara cascades are from the Canadian—not the United States—side. The parkland that lines both sides of the Niagara River is also beautifully maintained, though the areas just inland from it are touristy. Niagara Falls is now also the site of two huge and popular casinos. Many small attractions, such as the **Journey Behind the Falls**, the **Whirlpool Aero Car**, and the *Maid of the Mist* boat ride, should be recommended. For the more adventurous, a high-powered jet boat challenges the river downstream from the Falls. Niagara can also be a day trip from Toronto or Buffalo, New York.

- **The Thousand Islands**, dotting the area where the St. Lawrence River flows out of Lake Ontario, are well worth visiting via cruises from **Gananoque** [gan-ah-NAH-kway], **Rockport**, and **Kingston** (where there's also a famous fort). (On the New York side, the access port is Alexandria Bay.)

- **Ottawa**, Canada's splendid capital, has much charm, several dramatic museums, and stately **Parliament** buildings (where there's a changing of the guard every morning in the summer). The 5.5-mile **Rideau Canal**, which bisects the city, becomes the world's longest skating rink during winter months. Ottawa is often bypassed by tourists, but it's definitely worth a one- or two-day stay. (It can also be a day trip from Montreal.)

The first person to go over Niagara Falls in a barrel was a woman, Annie Taylor.

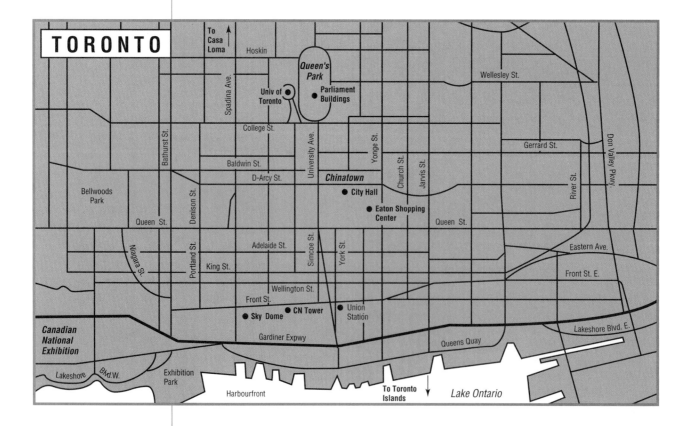

Quebec

Here's another easy mistake to make: Quebec is a province, **Quebec City** is its capital and quaintest place, and Montreal is its largest and most cosmopolitan city. Canada is a country of many heritages, but the English and the French predominate. And as you may know, Quebec is the bastion of French influence (though French–Canadian communities can be found in many other Canadian regions). Many residents of the U.S. Northeast know what other Americans do not: that a trip to Quebec is the next best thing to a trip to Europe. Here are its three most popular places:

- **Montreal** has remarkable churches (especially **Notre Dame**), a restored "Old Montreal" district, and hundreds of great eateries. A major casino is located in Montreal (as well as at several other Quebec locations). Several day trips from Montreal are possible, usually to Ottawa, the **Laurentian Mountains** (which have good winter skiing), and Quebec City.

- **Quebec City** can be a Montreal day trip, but most visitors prefer to lodge here. Quebec City is what sixteenth-century French towns must have been like; its ambience invariably charms visitors.

- **Gaspe**, with its rolling hills, Breton-like villages, and quaint little shops, is a frequent trip extension from Quebec City.

Montreal's Mt. Royal Park was designed by Frederick Law Olmsted. He also designed New York's Central Park, the U.S. Capitol Grounds, and the parks lining the U.S. side of Niagara Falls.

Roadside homemade-bread stands are a delight on the drive eastward from Quebec City.

The Atlantic Provinces

The easternmost provinces of Canada have long associated themselves with their seafaring traditions. They're all uncrowded and scenic, appealing to those who want to get away from it all. The Atlantic Provinces include the following:

- **New Brunswick** resembles Maine in many ways. Its most famous cities are the port city of **St. John**; **Fredericton**, the provincial capital; and **Moncton**, famous for several natural oddities that are nearby, including the "Reversing Falls," "Magnetic Hill" (where things seem to roll *up* inclines), and the awesome tides of the **Bay of Fundy** (which are more commonly viewed in Nova Scotia). A half-hour drive from Moncton is the **Hopewell Rocks Ocean Tidal Exploration Site**, where the Bay of Fundy's tides created the sandstone pillars called "flowerpots."

- **Nova Scotia**, the focal point of Canada's fishing industry and a province significant in both history and literature. Its best-known attractions: the **Cabot Trail**, a scenic drive along Nova Scotia's northernmost point; **Halifax**, the provincial capital; and **Peggy's Cove**, a picture-perfect fishing village not far from Halifax.

- **Prince Edward Island** (also called PEI) is Canada's smallest province. The island can be toured in a day, with stops at fishing villages, rolling beaches, and the **Anne of Green Gables Home**.

- **Newfoundland and Labrador**, a genuinely rustic area of Canada, with many picturesque spots, friendly villages, and ruins of settlements. (The island portion of the province is called Newfoundland; the mainland is called Labrador.) **L'Anse Aux Meadows** [lance oh MED-doze] **National Park** is home to the only validated Viking settlement in North America. Whales (and icebergs) can also be seen in **Iceberg Alley**, 250 miles southeast of Newfoundland.

The Bay of Fundy recorded the greatest tide change in history: 70 feet.

Possible Itineraries

A common way to visit many Canadian and Alaskan areas is simply day-tripping from key cities. Among the most popular multiday itineraries would be a week to 10 days in the Rockies, starting in Calgary and traveling northward, overnighting at Banff and Lake Louise, and then continuing through scenic roads up to Jasper (for possible side trips to

Juneau, Alaska, covers the largest area of any U.S. state capital, but has the smallest population.

The Hopewell "flowerpots" are one of several unusual attractions in New Brunswick
Image copyright V. J. Matthew, 2008. Used under license from Shutterstock.com

Edmonton, various ice fields, and perhaps a helicopter excursion into the Rockies). Another popular one- to two-week itinerary: Niagara Falls to Toronto, the Thousand Islands, up to Ottawa or Montreal, and finishing in Quebec City.

Lodging Options

Alaska has many hotels and motels, but they can be expensive (as are many things in Alaska). This is one more reason why cruises are an excellent option to recommend. Canada has a full range of lodging choices, from luxury hotels to campgrounds. Most U.S. chains have properties here. **Delta** and **Four Seasons** (both Canadian companies) offer at least one property in each major city. Tourists seem especially intrigued by the castle-like hotels (now owned by **Fairmont**) that the railroads built across Canada in the early 1900s. The most famous (and all of them are landmarks): the **Empress** (Victoria), the **Banff Springs Hotel**, the **Chateau Laurier** (Ottawa), and the **Chateau Frontenac** (Quebec City).

Niagara Falls bears special attention. The best lodging is on the Canadian side, preferably in one of several hotels that offer falls-view rooms. These view rooms can be expensive, but almost all Niagara Falls properties charge exorbitant summer prices. (There are real bargains off season, though.)

Allied Destinations

The interesting destinations that can be combined with a trip to Alaska or Canada don't usually occur to people. Your suggestions may lead to an expanded, more enjoyable, and more profitable itinerary.

Alaska lends itself to combinations with the Pacific Northwest, British Columbia, the Yukon, and the Canadian Rockies. Remember, too, that Alaska airports are occasionally stopovers for flights bound for Asia from the United States or Canada. Travelers often break up their trip with a brief stayover. In the east, Quebec and the Atlantic Provinces can be consolidated with a stay in New England or New York. Ontario is close to New York,

Pennsylvania, Ohio, and Michigan. Both Toronto and Montreal are occasionally stopover points on the way to Europe from west coast or Midwest points of origin. Again, a brief stay might be appropriate.

Factors That Motivate Visitors

Canada and Alaska have a specialized touristic appeal. Here are some of the reasons for going there:

- The area's natural beauty is stunning, especially in the Rockies, along the shore, and into the wilderness.
- Toronto, Montreal, Quebec City, and Vancouver are especially safe, clean, historic, beautiful, and lively.
- The area is "foreign" (especially Quebec) yet familiar, comparatively near and generally English-speaking.
- The people are friendly and welcome visitors.
- The winter sports, fishing, and camping opportunities are plentiful.
- Canada is, in many respects, a travel bargain.
- Wildlife, especially in Alaska, is relatively easy to observe.
- Transportation in the southern portions of the area is convenient.
- Cruise possibilities are numerous.

Alaska has about 100,000 glaciers.

French Canadians are generally patient with Americans who try out their high-school French.

Qualifying the Traveler
Alaska

For People Who Want	Appeal			Remarks
	High	Medium	Low	
Historical and Cultural Attractions		▲		Native American and Russian
Beaches and Water Sports			▲	Great fishing, though
Skiing Opportunities		▲		Mostly cross-country
Lots of Nightlife			▲	Anchorage and on cruises
Family Activities			▲	
Familiar Cultural Experience	▲			
Exotic Cultural Experience		▲		Native culture especially
Safety and Low Crime	▲			
Bargain Travel			▲	Alaska is expensive
Impressive Scenery	▲			Greatest strength
Peace and Quiet	▲			
Shopping Opportunities		▲		
Adventure	▲			
To Do Business			▲	Natural resources and tourism industries

Qualifying the Traveler
Eastern Canada

For People Who Want	Appeal			Remarks
	High	Medium	Low	
Historical and Cultural Attractions		▲		
Beaches and Water Sports			▲	Summer lakeside resorts
Skiing Opportunities		▲		North of Montreal
Lots of Nightlife		▲		Mostly Montreal and Toronto
Family Activities		▲		
Familiar Cultural Experience		▲		Enough like U.S.
Exotic Cultural Experience		▲		Especially Quebec Province
Safety and Low Crime		▲		
Bargain Travel		▲		
Impressive Scenery	▲			
Peace and Quiet		▲		Outside Toronto, Montreal, Quebec City
Shopping Opportunities		▲		Crafts in countryside
Adventure		▲		
To Do Business		▲		Especially Toronto and Montreal

Possible Misgivings

The appeal of Canada and Alaska does have its limitations. Among those concerns that you may have to address are:

- "What is there to see up there?" This will be the most common question you'll hear. Paint a clear picture of whatever attractions you think will appeal to the person: majestic scenery, sophisticated cities, uncrowded roads, natural wonders, great winter sports, and so on.

- "It's boring, isn't it?" Toronto, Montreal, and to a lesser extent, Anchorage, Vancouver, and Quebec City are energetic, lively, good-sized cities.

- "Isn't it expensive?" Alaska can be expensive, but stressing the all-inclusive nature of a tour or cruise may be the right approach. Lodging in Canada is relatively reasonable (though less a bargain than it used to be). For the budget minded, suggest spring or fall travel.

- "Aren't there political problems in Quebec?" The separatist movement, for now, remains dormant. Canada is a relatively safe and peaceful country, where locals are especially friendly to foreign visitors.

- "I'd love to see Niagara Falls, but isn't it a tourist zoo?" Summer is truly hectic. Things quiet down a bit the rest of the year, though Niagara Falls' popular casinos have ensured that off-season is much busier than it used to be. One option: lodging in Toronto, with Niagara as a day trip.

Captain Kidd's treasure is said to be buried on Oak Island in Nova Scotia's Mahone Bay (but no one has found it—or even a map—yet).

Sales Strategies

Several obvious recommendations can enhance profitability from a trip to Canada or Alaska. Among them are cruises, escorted tours, train trips, and ski packages. Some of the most popular ski destinations are **Whistler** (near Vancouver), **Mt. Tremblant** (north of Montreal), and the Banff area. People who wish to stay in Niagara Falls should be upsold to a falls-view room. Niagara Falls is also a long-standing honeymoon destination, though that reputation has become somewhat tarnished because of the place's touristy feel and the rising popularity of tropical honeymoon destinations. To those who do want to honeymoon in Niagara, a suite is an obvious upsell.

Few can resist the stunning natural grandeur of the Canadian Rockies and Alaska. You should also take into consideration how special events can attract tourists even in supposedly off seasons. Examples: Niagara Falls' **Festival of Lights** (November to January), Quebec City's **Winter Carnival** (late January to mid-February), and the Anchorage-to-Nome **Iditarod Sled Dog Race** (March).

For any destination in the area, mention the many potential allied destinations and stopovers that are possible. And for those bound for Alaska or the Rocky Mountains, suggest excursions via helicopter or air taxi; both can be booked in advance.

Watch a ship or boat go through a lock. Ottawa has several small locks; bigger ones can be found near Montreal, Niagara Falls, and several places in Ontario.

Travel Trivia

Oddly Named Canadian Specialties

- Caribou—a French–Canadian drink made of one part red wine to six parts grain alcohol
- Solomon Gundy—herring (Nova Scotia)
- Digby Chicks—smoked herring (Nova Scotia)
- Fiddleheads—the unopened fronds of the ostrich fern (Nova Scotia and New Brunswick)
- Dulse—dried seaweed
- Screech—a potent alcohol made in Newfoundland and Labrador
- Scrunchions—fried pork dish from Newfoundland and Labrador
- Ciapille—a French–Canadian pie containing fowl, game, or beef mixed with vegetables
- Beaver Tails—deep-fried pastries shaped like—you guessed it— beaver tails and served with condiments (sold in downtown Ottawa)
- Figgy Duff—steamed pudding with sauce

NAME _____   **DATE** _____

MAP ACTIVITY

A traveler wants to visit the places listed below. Which number represents each on the map?

Place/Attraction	In/Near Which City?	Number on Map
A. The Stampede	A. _____	A. _____
B. The capital of Alaska	B. _____	B. _____
C. The capital of Canada	C. _____	C. _____
D. The Chateau Frontenac	D. _____	D. _____
E. The capital of Nova Scotia	E. _____	E. _____
F. The northernmost point in the United States	F. _____	F. _____
G. The CN Tower	G. _____	G. _____
H. The *Maid of the Mist*	H. _____	H. _____
I. A major city south of the Laurentians	I. _____	I. _____
J. The Butchart Gardens	J. _____	J. _____

NAME _____   DATE _____

CASE STUDY

The Winter Wonderland Ski Club has approached you to set up air and lodging reservations for their ski trip to Banff. They're open to suggestions for things to do while they are there.

Circle the answer that best suits their needs.

1 Which would be an appropriate enhancement to their trip?

Car rentals   A train trip to Halifax

Full ski packages   An Alaska cruise

Why?

2 They could also travel up to Jasper. What might you recommend to them to do?

A shopping spree at a huge mall   A Yukon holiday

Helicopter rides   A stay in igloos

Why?

3 The nearest natural attraction to Banff is:

Niagara Falls   Edmonton

Lake Louise   Grouse Mountain

Why?

4 It turns out that Banff is fully booked at the only time the group can go. To what alternative place could you send them to ski?

Northern Nova Scotia   The escarpment near Niagara

The Laurentian area   Vancouver Island

Why?

NAME _____   **DATE** _____

CREATIVE ACTIVITY

Train travel has long been important to tourism in both Alaska and Canada. The president of the Railroad Buffs of America comes to you to help plan a 21-day Anchorage-to-Halifax rail journey using a private train with sleeper cars. This trip will be unique; no regular train service on this long route is sold to the public.

The club wishes to make only five stops between Anchorage and Halifax. What should the stops be and why? (Note: The train can go up to 60 mph. Also, Vancouver to Toronto takes three days on a train.)

1st stop   Reason:

2nd stop   Reason:

3rd stop   Reason:

4th stop   Reason:

5th stop   Reason:

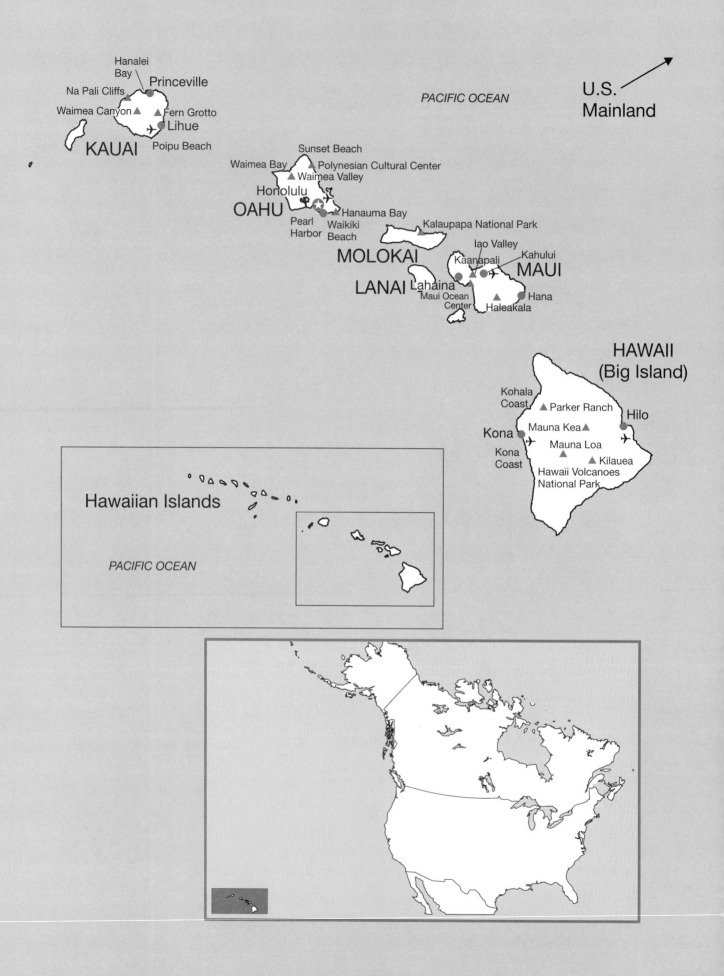

U.S.
Mainland

PACIFIC OCEAN

Hanalei
Bay
Princeville
Na Pali Cliffs
Waimea Canyon ▲
▲ Fern Grotto
Lihue
Poipu Beach
KAUAI

Sunset Beach
Waimea Bay ▲ Polynesian Cultural Center
▲ Waimea Valley
Honolulu
OAHU
Hanauma Bay
Pearl
Harbor
Waikiki
Beach
Kalaupapa National Park

MOLOKAI
Iao Valley
Kahului
Kaanapali
MAUI
LANAI
Lahaina
Hana
Maui Ocean
Center
Haleakala

HAWAII
(Big Island)

Kohala
Coast
▲ Parker Ranch
Hilo
Kona
Mauna Kea ▲
Kona
Coast
Mauna Loa
▲
▲ Kilauea
Hawaii Volcanoes
National Park

Hawaiian Islands

PACIFIC OCEAN

Chapter 7

Hawaii
Paradise Found

It must have been an astonishing trip: Around 700 A.D., hundreds of natives from the Marquesas Islands in the South Pacific set sail in great double-hulled canoes and crossed more than 2,000 miles of open ocean to arrive at what we now call the Hawaiian Islands. How did they know that the islands were there? Did they go back and forth many times, as legends insist? How did they interact with subsequent voyagers, who sailed in greater numbers from the Society Islands between the eleventh and fourteenth centuries?

No one really knows. But we do know that tens of thousands of tourists now cross that same Pacific each week to visit Hawaii—in jets, of course. What they'll find there: perhaps the most sweet, gentle, and majestic islands in the world.

Don't assume, as do many, that there are only one or two islands. In reality, 312 Hawaiian islands stretch in an arc of almost 1,500 miles in the middle of the Pacific. But only six, at the southernmost tip of the arc, attract visitors: **Kauai** [kah-WAH-ee], **Oahu** [oh-WAH-hoo], **Molokai** [mo-lo-KYE], **Lanai** [lah-NAH-ee], **Maui** [MAU-ee], and **Hawaii** (also called Hawaii's Big Island). Each has its own personality: Kauai is the wettest and most tropical; Oahu is the bustling center of tourism and commerce; Molokai and Lanai are sleepy little islands off the typical tourist path; Maui is an island of great resorts and breathtaking beauty; and Hawaii's Big Island boasts an active volcano and vast ranches.

How Travelers Get There

Dozens of North American and foreign carriers service the islands. Several airlines permit a traveler to stop off at no charge in Hawaii on the way to and from Asian or South Pacific destinations. (Passengers can't fly on foreign carriers from the U.S. mainland to Hawaii unless they're continuing across the Pacific.) Most flights from the mainland to **Honolulu**, Oahu (HNL), are nonstop or direct, with connections to the other islands. It takes about five hours to get from the West Coast to Honolulu; almost 11 hours from New York. Some carriers operate nonstop flights from the mainland to the other islands as well. Occasionally, passengers can sail from the mainland to Hawaii, especially when a cruise ship is repositioning itself, say, from Alaska to Asia.

Weather Patterns

Hawaii's climate barely varies all year (see Figure 7–1). The average high in August is 83 degrees and in January it's 77 degrees. Though it's generally humid, a strong east-to-west trade wind keeps the islands breezy and pleasant. It can get cool (in the mid-60s) at night in the winter, and it's liable to shower at any time—though rain is much more likely in the winter, which is, ironically, a peak tourist season. Summer, a time of minimal rain but greater heat, is also busy. Hawaii is least crowded in the spring and especially in the fall. Note: Hurricanes occasionally reach Hawaii in late summer or early fall.

Hawaii is the southernmost state in the United States, but Alaska extends farther west.

The statue of King Kamehameha was once lost at sea off the Falkland Islands, then retrieved and erected on Hawaii's Big Island.

Honolulu has the lowest air pollution of any major U.S. city.

Hawaii's climate is so varied that it offers 11 of the earth's 13 recognized climate zones. Only the Arctic and Saharan zones are missing.

Climate at a Glance _____
HONOLULU

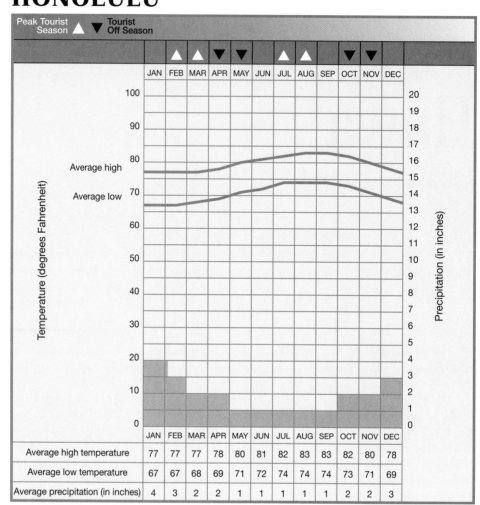

Peak Tourist Season ▲	▼ Tourist Off Season											
	▲	▲	▼	▼		▲	▲		▼	▼	
	JAN	FEB	MAR	APR	MAY	JUN	JUL	AUG	SEP	OCT	NOV	DEC

	JAN	FEB	MAR	APR	MAY	JUN	JUL	AUG	SEP	OCT	NOV	DEC
Average high temperature	77	77	77	78	80	81	82	83	83	82	80	78
Average low temperature	67	67	68	69	71	72	74	74	74	73	71	69
Average precipitation (in inches)	4	3	2	2	1	1	1	1	1	2	2	3

Figure 7–1

On Kauai, no building is taller than a palm tree.

The weather does vary from place to place. The western, leeward side of each island tends to be dry (it's where most of the lodging is), whereas the windward side and central mountainous areas have more frequent rain. Kauai's tourist areas, especially, are quite wet. And **Mauna Kea** mountain, on Hawaii's Big Island, is snow capped much of the winter and sometimes offers skiing (it's accessed by helicopter). So here's a unique opportunity for a real ski buff who loves the offbeat.

Getting Around

Seventy percent of all visitors to Hawaii rent a car for at least one day.

As well as service between Hawaii and the mainland, **Hawaiian Airlines** (HA) provides inter-island flights. Regional carriers also do inter-island flights. Swarms of small planes and helicopters fly tourists into the scenic but hard-to-access canyons of Hawaii's Big Island, Maui, and, especially, Kauai. Cruise ships act as "portable hotels" on cruises among the islands. Traveling by bus in Oahu is convenient, but for all other islands, visitors should book a car rental. Atlantis Submarines provide an unusual way to experience the waters off Oahu and Maui. All manner of rides on outrigger canoes, yachts, and rubber boats can be arranged upon arrival.

Important Places

Most tourists will already know of **Waikiki Beach**, which lies to the southeast of Honolulu's center. But spending all of one's time here is like visiting Las Vegas and thinking you've seen the United States. Each of the main Hawaiian Islands offers a unique environment and wonderful experience.

Oahu

This is the most visited island, the most populated one, the location of Honolulu (the state capital), and a central transportation hub. Most business is conducted in downtown Honolulu. Most tourists, though, stay in Waikiki, which offers many hotels, stores, and restaurants. Once considered a bit tacky, Waikiki has undergone a billion-dollar "facelift" and has a more refined feel to it than before. The island's sparsely populated **north shore** is well known for its surfing. And its windward northeastern beaches, though often cloudy or rainy, are spectacular and uncrowded; on a sunny day they make for a wonderful alternative to the tourist-packed sands of Waikiki. Among Oahu's other principal attractions are:

- **The Polynesian Cultural Center**, near the town of **Laie**, with its villages, crafts, and shows that try to convey Pacific Island life; the presentation is polished and exuberant.
- **Hanauma** [hah-NOW-mah] **Bay**, a paradise for even novice snorkelers.
- **Pearl Harbor**, with its boat ride to the U.S.S. *Arizona* Memorial and to the retired battleship U.S.S. *Missouri*.
- **The Bishop Museum** (with its displays on the geology and culture of Hawaii) and **Iolani Palace** (principal home of Hawaiian royalty), both within Honolulu city limits.
- **Waimea Bay** and **Sunset Beach**, two north shore areas, with occasionally massive waves and always expert surfers; nearby is the lush **Waimea Valley** and its picture-perfect falls.

Waikiki was originally rocky. Most of its sand was imported from Molokai and, of all places, Manhattan Beach, California.

Quiet Kailua and Lanikai beaches, on Oahu's windward coast, are considered by some to be the best beaches anywhere.

Rent a car on Oahu for at least one day and drive around the island, perhaps pausing at the beaches on the north shore or the windward side.

Waikiki hotels, with Diamond Head in the background
Photo by Marc Mancini

Maui

An island of condos and resorts, Maui—Hawaii's second–most visited island—features a broad stretch of wonderful beaches along its western coast. Most notable is the **Kaanapali** area, a planned development dotted with numerous resorts and hotels, anchored by **Lahaina** [lah-HIGH-nah]. The island's northeast coast is tropical and spectacular. The island's major airport is at **Kahului (OGG)**. Among Maui's attractions are:

- **Lahaina**, an old, picturesque whaling village. At its heart is a giant banyan tree that measures a quarter-mile in circumference.
- **The road to Hana**, a winding, overwhelmingly beautiful drive past waterfalls, pools, and vine-covered trees.
- **Iao** [ee-AH-o] **Valley State Park**, a picturesque spot where a major ancient battle took place.
- **Maui Ocean Center**, a marine park with an underwater viewing tunnel.
- **Haleakala**, where a drive to the top offers spectacular views, especially at dawn to see the sun rise. Located in the center of the island, Haleakala is the world's largest dormant volcano.

Hawaii's Big Island

Vast in size and with a wide variety of scenery, Hawaii's Big Island is a good recommendation for almost anyone (except those who seem chiefly attracted to Waikiki). The western **Kohala** and **Kona** coasts are rapidly developing resort areas. The island's largest city, **Hilo** (ITO), once a prime tourist destination, has somewhat lost its appeal and is now primarily a gateway to the volcanic area. For these reasons, Kona's airport (KOA) has become the choice (over Hilo's) for most tourists. Among the attractions are:

- **Hawaii Volcanoes National Park**, with its steaming craters, most notably that of active **Kilauea** [kih-lah-WAY-ah]. Tourists should call ahead to find out whether they can visit an active lava flow.
- **A drive from Hilo**, across the island's north shore, through the **Parker Ranch** area, and down through the moon-like lava field of **Waikoloa** [why-koh-LOH-ah].

There are no billboards in Hawaii. A 1926 law banned them.

At the Big Island's Kealakekua Bay is a 5,682-square-foot area that was deeded to Britain for a monument to Captain James Cook. So you can literally swim from Hawaii to England in Kealakekua Bay.

Because of Kilauea's lava flow, Hawaii is the only U.S. state that's still growing.

The town of Lahaina on Maui was once the principal port for whaling in the Pacific
Image copyright Christophe Testi, 2008. Used under license from Shutterstock.com

Many of the Big Island's beaches are rocky. For this reason, it offers fewer water-sport opportunities than do some of the other islands.

Kauai

Kauai is lush, moist, and dramatic—precisely what people picture a tropical island to be. Hotels are concentrated on the somewhat drier **Poipu Beach** area, in the area north and south of **Lihue** (LIH), and in the scenic **Princeville** area on the north shore. Among the attractions are:

- **The Fern Grotto**, with its beautiful fern-lined cliffs and cave. It can be accessed on a short boat cruise up the Wailua River. It's a popular site for weddings.
- **The Waimea Canyon**, a 14-mile-long, Grand Canyon–like spectacle that can be viewed from a road lookout, helicopter, or light plane.
- **The Na Pali Cliffs**, looming majestically over the island's nearly inaccessible northwest coast. Visitors can see them only if they hike, boat, or fly there.
- **Hanalei Bay**, a striking and serene area next to the resort city of Princeville.

Molokai and Lanai

With their small populations, few attractions, and limited lodging choices, these islands should be recommended only to those who want to get away from it all or who are veteran Hawaii tourists who've seen the other islands. Molokai is famous for its **Kalaupapa** [kah-laow-PAH-pah] **National Historical Park**, once the site of a famous leper colony and sometimes accessed by a mule trip down a series of cliffs. Lanai, through most of its history, was one big pineapple plantation; it's perhaps the only Hawaiian Island where visitors can most easily mix with the locals. Several relaxed but upscale hotels are located on Lanai.

Possible Itineraries

First-time visitors should spend a week on one island or split time between Oahu and another island. More experienced Hawaii travelers may bypass Oahu to see those islands they're unacquainted with. A seven-day, four-island itinerary via cruise ship is a popular option.

There's a theory that menehune—Hawaii's counterpart to the leprechaun—might have been real. They might have been Japanese fishermen blown off course and marooned in Hawaii before the arrival of Polynesians. The Polynesians, often well over 6 feet tall and weighing 300 pounds, would have considered these fishermen "little people."

The world's highest sea cliffs are on Molokai.

About 20 percent more women than men visit Hawaii.

Kauai is the most lush and tropical of the Hawaiian islands
Image copyright Caleb Foster, 2008. Used under license from Shutterstock.com

Lodging Options

Virtually every major hotel chain has numerous properties on the islands, though **Sheraton, Hyatt, Hilton, Marriott**, and the Hawaii-based **Outrigger, ResortQuest** (formerly **Aston**), and **Castle** predominate. Sheraton owns many restored historic properties. Hyatt fills its resorts with fine art. Hilton has most of the truly huge resorts. **OHANA** is Outrigger's moderate-level brand. ResortQuest and Castle have an unusually wide spectrum of properties, from budget to luxury.

Oahu has the most hotels, nearly all of which are concentrated along Waikiki Beach. Waikiki is a popular recommendation, especially for budget-minded travelers, because lodging is available at all price levels. Hotels and condos on the other islands tend to be somewhat more expensive, with few low-end properties. Maui's hotels are mostly clustered along its western coast, as are those of Hawaii's Big Island. Kauai's are along its wet southern and eastern sides, because the somewhat drier west coast is mostly cliffs. Molokai and Lanai have limited accommodations (though the Lanai properties are quite elegant).

Travelers may already know about certain Hawaiian properties, since several well-publicized hotels and resorts dot the islands. Oahu's list would be virtually endless, though the **Royal Hawaiian**, the **Moana Surfrider**, the **Halekulani**, and the **Kahala** are best known (and quite pricey). Three huge and extraordinary resort properties are located on the islands: the **Hyatt Regency** and the **Marriott** on Kauai, and the **Hilton** in the Waikoloa area of Hawaii's Big Island. Also on the Big Island is the unique **Kona Village**, upscale huts perched on stilts.

Mark Twain once sat under the banyan tree in the Moana Surfrider's courtyard.

Allied Destinations

Because the Hawaiian Islands are in the middle of the Pacific Ocean, no allied destinations are nearby. As we mentioned, however, travelers often go on from Hawaii to Southeast Asia, Australia, or New Zealand. There's also the possibility of continuing on to the South Pacific islands, including Tahiti and Fiji.

Cultural Patterns

Even though Hawaii is a U.S. state, its way of life is much more relaxed; jackets and ties, for instance, are rarely worn. Also, visitors shouldn't expect primitive, South Sea island conditions. Hawaii is a sophisticated, modern destination. Above all, don't refer to the U.S. mainland alone as the United States; Hawaii is also a part of the country. Hawaiians are very sensitive about this.

Hawaiians are becoming increasingly proud of their own history, and this is showing up in hotel decor, accuracy of entertainment, and the like. Visitors could read James Michener's *Hawaii*—or rent the movie based on it—to find out more about Hawaii's remarkable history and culture.

Factors That Motivate Visitors

Hawaii is a unique destination within the United States, and as such, there are unique reasons vacationers want to go there:

- They want to visit an exotic and romantic tropical paradise, but one that will still be relatively familiar.
- Hawaii affords a wide selection of accommodations (from budget to luxury), flights, independent tours, and natural attractions.
- Hawaiian fly-lodge-drive packages, especially those on Oahu, represent a value.
- Hawaii's climate is predictably warm and pleasant, even when it's cold and wintry on the mainland.
- Water sports and beach activities are readily available.

More than half of the marriages performed in Hawaii are for nonresidents.

- The opportunities to practice other sports, such as hiking, tennis, golf, and horseback riding, are almost limitless.
- Visitors have a choice of the intensely busy nightlife of Waikiki or the more relaxed possibilities of the other islands.

Possible Misgivings

Though Hawaii is, in many ways, a magical destination, there may be things about it that raise questions in a potential visitor's mind:

- "Hawaii is too touristy." Recommend Maui, Kauai, or Hawaii's Big Island.
- "There's not enough to do." This type of person should be steered to Waikiki, an adventure tour or package, a major outer island resort, a cruise, or (perhaps) an escorted tour, especially if he or she is older and has taken tours before.
- "I've heard it's expensive." Waikiki's budget hotels and low-cost independent tour packages may appeal to this traveler. Free tourist magazines are widely available and contain many discount coupons for food and entertainment.
- "There's nothing left of old Hawaii." Suggest a stay on Lanai, Molokai, or at the Kona Village. Point out that pride in Hawaiian history and culture has become strong and reflects itself in tours, lodging design, shopping, and so on.

Qualifying the Traveler
Hawaii's Big Island

For People Who Want	Appeal			Remarks
	High	Medium	Low	
Historical and Cultural Attractions		▲		Polynesian culture
Beaches and Water Sports		▲		Many beaches are rocky
Skiing Opportunities			▲	Downhill on Mauna Kea
Lots of Nightlife		▲		In hotels
Family Activities	▲			Especially resort hotels
Familiar Cultural Experience	▲			U.S. state
Exotic Cultural Experience		▲		Asian influences are strong
Safety and Low Crime		▲		Petty crime in certain areas
Bargain Travel		▲		Everything from budget to luxury
Impressive Scenery	▲			Mountains, rain forests, seascapes, volcanoes
Peace and Quiet	▲			One of the quieter islands
Shopping Opportunities			▲	Much better in Honolulu
Adventure		▲		More "extreme" sports opportunities these days
To Do Business			▲	Oahu, however, is a major business center linking Asia and North America

- "There's nothing cultural to see." Many small attractions underscore Hawaii's cultural heritage, but if someone's idea of a great vacation is visiting Europe's museums and cathedrals, Hawaii may indeed not be appropriate. One tour operator, Tauck, offers escorted tours of Hawaii.

- "I'm too old to hang out and sun on the beach or at a pool all day." A surprising fact: More than half of those who visit Hawaii say they never spend much time on the beach. This type of visitor may enjoy a packaged escorted tour that involves sightseeing and will keep him or her occupied. Oahu and Hawaii's Big Island are especially appropriate.

- "Locals aren't friendly and there's a lot of crime." There's some resentment and crime against tourists, but it's rarely encountered. A little prudence can lessen the chance of an unpleasant experience.

- "Bugs are everywhere." As with any tropical destination, this is true. In rainforest areas, the mosquitoes can be ferocious; visitors should take insect repellent. Roaches are indeed numerous; an occasional sighting even in luxury hotels or rental cars can be expected.

Sales Strategies

Hawaii can be a bargain destination, but often a low-cost hotel or subcompact car can undermine that dream vacation in "Paradise." Offer upgraded lodging; this is especially appropriate for Waikiki, where low-cost hotels may leave much to be desired. Ocean-view rooms are an upgrade that often appeals to guests. And for those going to Oahu for the first time, why not mention the possibility of a second or third island stay? Since they've gone that far, they likely will be receptive to having a longer and fuller Hawaiian experience. Here, knowledge of the distinct character of each island is imperative for a multi-island stay, because people may think that all the islands are the same.

Car rentals are extremely useful on all islands. Even Oahu warrants one for at least a day. Upselling someone to a convertible, jeep, or larger car may be an attractive strategy. And a multitude of cross-sell options (helicopter rides, dinner cruises, luaus, submarine rides, etc.) can often be booked and sold in advance.

Finally, remember that independent tours and inter-island cruises (most operated by Norwegian Cruise Line) often enable you to secure bargains for visitors while deriving commissions from an entire package of services. There are escorted tours of the islands; such tours often appeal to seniors who prefer not to drive around or to simply bake on the beach.

Travel Trivia

Surprising Facts about Hawaii

- Hawaiians didn't invent the ukulele. The Portuguese brought it to them in the 1880s.
- A new volcanic island is now forming underwater off the coast of the Big Island. It already has a name: Loihi.
- Though the first Pacific islands were "discovered" by Europeans in the early 1500s, the Hawaiian chain wasn't reached by them until 1778.
- Grass skirts aren't native to Hawaii. Micronesian immigrants brought them in the 1880s.
- The majority of Hawaii's land is owned by the U.S. government and by the descendants of five missionary families.
- The famous song "Aloha Oe" was written by Hawaii's last reigning monarch, Queen Liliuokalani.

NAME _____ **DATE** _____

MAP ACTIVITY

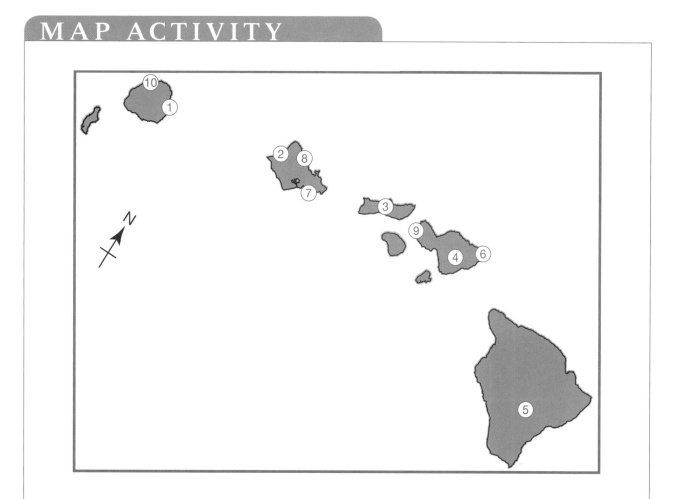

A traveler wants to visit the places listed below. Which number represents each on the map?

Place/Attraction	On Which Island?	Number on Map
A. Hana	A. _____	A. _____
B. The Fern Grotto	B. _____	B. _____
C. Waimea Bay	C. _____	C. _____
D. A mule trip	D. _____	D. _____
E. Princeville	E. _____	E. _____
F. The Halekulani Hotel	F. _____	F. _____
G. The Polynesian Cultural Center	G. _____	G. _____
H. Haleakala	H. _____	H. _____
I. Hawaii Volcanoes National Park	I. _____	I. _____
J. An old whaling village	J. _____	J. _____

NAME _____ **DATE** _____

CASE STUDY

Sharon and Marc, a couple in their early 30s from Buffalo, plan to honeymoon in Hawaii. They've been to Waikiki and didn't like it. They once visited Tahiti and loved its tropical splendor. Because this is a special trip, they're not afraid to spend money. They can take off only five workdays, but they want to get away from it all. They also want to stay in only one hotel during their trip.

Circle the answer that best suits their needs.

1 How many days would you recommend for their total trip, from departure to return home?

    Three   Seven

    Five   Ten

    Why?

2 If they went to only one island, which would you suggest?

    Maui   Corfu

    Kauai   Oahu

    Why?

3 If they wanted to see an active volcano, you could cross-sell a day trip air package to which island?

    Lanai   Oahu

    Hawaii   Kauai

    Why?

4 Which of the following would probably *not* be a good service to offer to book for Sharon and Marc?

    An escorted tour   A helicopter flight

    A hotel suite   First-class air reservations

    Why?

NAME _____   **DATE** _____

CREATIVE ACTIVITY

You're a reservationist for a large, California-based independent tour wholesaler to Hawaii. A caller has read an ad in the Sunday newspaper for a competitor's tour. The price is incredibly low: $599 per person, including air fare and six days in a hotel in Honolulu. The caller wants to know if you have something similar, as she's unfamiliar with the company in the ad, but knows yours well. She'll be traveling with her husband and 10-year-old son. This will be their 12th wedding anniversary.

You know you can't match the price and for a good reason: This is a bare-bones, cheapo trip that would almost surely displease the caller. The hotel might be in a poor location with no view, the available days might not be at a good time, and so on.

What five possibilities might you suggest to the caller to convince her that you could offer her a trip that would cost more, but would offer so many more pleasing features (and make more profit for your company via your upselling and cross-selling)?

For example: We could offer you a hotel that's right on the beach and a room with an ocean view. Wouldn't that be much nicer? And it would cost you only $29 more per night.

1

2

3

4

5

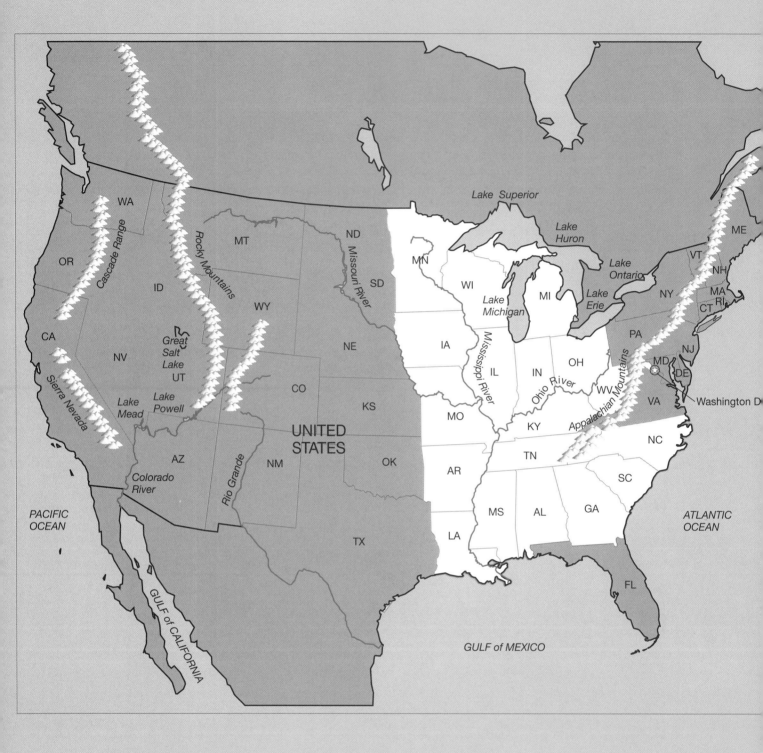

Chapter 8

North American Potpourri (East)

Pretend you're a British tourist. What would be the best place to visit in North America? A city? An entire state or province? A manmade attraction? A natural wonder? The point is this: North America is a continent of vastly diverse attractions. There's something for just about everyone.

In the preceding chapters, you've read about major tourist centers in the United States and Canada. However, dozens of other locations we haven't mentioned yet are fiercely appealing to tourists. Indeed, this chapter and the next address many of the most popular cities in the United States, including New Orleans, Chicago, Atlanta, Santa Fe, Seattle, and Las Vegas.

What follows isn't a compendium of every popular tourist attraction. Some, though wonderful, simply won't be places you'll be called on to book often. Others are visited mainly by business travelers, or by tourists who live nearby and who know the area well enough that they won't come to you for help.

There's a lot of information to digest about the United States. That's why we've divided American Potpourri into two chapters: East and West. Read each chapter slowly and carefully. Highlight as many important points as possible. Follow along on the regional maps.

The South

In many ways, it's unfair to gather all the Southern states not covered in previous chapters into one collection. They're all so different. But we can make at least a few generalizations about the South. Its many major cities have convenient air service, and an excellent network of highways criss-crosses the area. In fact, driving may be the best way to see this vast area.

The South's climate is generally temperate, especially along the coasts of the Atlantic Ocean and the Gulf of Mexico. Summers can be uncomfortably hot and humid; winters are chilly at worst, but pleasant. Spring can be a particularly beautiful time throughout the region—the magnolia blooms are legendary. Fall is very nice as well, but hurricanes and rain may occasionally interfere with a trip here.

The South has many forests, rivers, and hills, especially where the southern **Appalachian Mountains**

145

are prominent. Hiking, camping, and fishing are popular activities. The South is, in general, a rural land of quiet small towns; however, there are large, sophisticated cities, too. Elegance, pride, and a strong sense of history are what the South is all about.

Important Places

The commercial, transportation, and convention gateway to the South is **Atlanta**, Georgia (ATL). Many other cities have large airports, including **Charlotte**, North Carolina (CLT), and **New Orleans**, Louisiana (MSY).

Among the most popular areas in the South are the following, listed clockwise by state, starting with Georgia:

- **Atlanta, Georgia.** This affluent, cosmopolitan city has impressive cultural venues for symphony, ballet, and theater; the fascinatingly designed **High Museum of Art**; the many Olympic sports facilities; lovely magnolia tree-lined streets; and **Stone Mountain Park**, with its plantation, riverboat, small museums, and huge mountain carving of Confederate leaders. At the **Martin Luther King, Jr. National Historic Site**, visitors can attend services at the church where Dr. King preached.

- **Savannah, Georgia.** A beautifully restored and preserved city, Savannah has retained much of the charming heritage of the Old South. There are several museums and countless buildings in a 2-mile national landmark district that predates the Civil War.

- **Huntsville, Alabama. The U.S. Space and Rocket Center** located here is one of the largest space museums in the country. Alabama is noted for its grand old homes and wide spectrum of outdoor recreational activities.

- **Natchez, Mississippi.** This city boasts hundreds of pre–Civil War mansions that are best visited on one of the city's "pilgrimage" tours. (They occur only during certain seasons.)

- **Biloxi, Mississippi.** Gaming has made this port city a popular destination. In addition to its casinos and 26-mile-long beach, Biloxi has several small museums.

- **Vicksburg, Mississippi.** Vicksburg is famous for its military park commemorating the famous Civil War battle.

- **New Orleans, Louisiana.** A 2005 hurricane and subsequent flooding devastated this low-lying city. But much of it—especially the areas that tourists frequent—has returned to what made New Orleans one of the world's unique cities, with a strange, heady mixture of elegance, raucousness, great Dixieland jazz, and internationally renowned cuisine. The **French Quarter** is home to much of the city's entertainment, shopping, and dining. **Jackson Square** is the Quarter's focal point, and **Preservation Hall** features jazz performances. A world-class aquarium is located here, and day and multiday riverboat cruises are very popular. There are also tours of the surrounding bayou swamps and old, graceful plantations. The Tuesday before Ash Wednesday is when the spectacular, wild **Mardi Gras** festival is held. The astonishing floats used in the festival are then stored in a vast series of warehouses, called **Mardi Gras World**, an attraction open to the public.

- **Hot Springs National Park, Arkansas.** This famous resort has long been a favorite of vacationers. The **Ozark Mountains**, in northern Arkansas, have equally dramatic scenery and spas.

- **Nashville, Tennessee.** Nashville proudly calls itself "Music City USA," home of country music. Here's where tourists will find that great showcase for country and western music: the **Ryman Auditorium** (former home of the Grand Ole Opry), the immense **Gaylord Opryland Resort** and adjoining **Opry Mills** (a huge entertainment and shopping mall), and a first-rate **Country Music Hall of Fame and Museum**. President Andrew Jackson's home, the **Hermitage**, is nearby, and the **Parthenon** (an almost exact reproduction of the one in Athens) sits in a Nashville park.

The airport at Charlotte, North Carolina, was one of the first airports to have rocking chairs.

Underground Atlanta is a subterranean shopping, entertainment, and dining area on the original nineteenth-century site of the city.

Try a *beignet* at the Cafe Du Monde in New Orleans.

Alma, Arkansas, the "Spinach Capital of the World," prominently displays a statue of Popeye.

St. Louis Cathedral anchors one end of Jackson Square
Image copyright David Davis, 2008. Used under license from Shutterstock.com

- **Memphis, Tennessee.** Like Nashville, this city is best known for its contributions to America's musical heritage. **Beale Street** boasts an active nightlife and many "blues" cafes. **Graceland**, the legendary home of Elvis Presley, features two of Elvis's private jets, a collection of his cars, his outrageously decorated mansion, and his burial site.

- **Pigeon Forge, Tennessee.** This town is home to the **Dollywood Theme Park** and a spectacular yearly "Winterfest" of lights. Pigeon Forge and nearby **Gatlinburg** (another quaint town) are just north of the **Great Smoky Mountains**, one of the most visited national parks in the United States.

- **Mammoth Cave National Park, Kentucky.** With its 300 miles of massive underground caves, this attraction is the world's largest cave system. Kentucky's two key cities, **Lexington** (famous for its horse farms) and **Louisville** (home of the Kentucky Derby), are gracious and charming.

- **Harpers Ferry, West Virginia.** This historic city is where John Brown made his ill-fated attempt to arm a slave rebellion. To its west are some of the South's most beautiful outdoor recreation areas.

- **Cape Hatteras National Seashore, North Carolina.** Cape Hatteras features remarkable scenery and excellent beaches. The Wright Brothers made the first plane flight from nearby **Kitty Hawk**.

- **Asheville, North Carolina.** Location of the largest privately owned home in the United States, the 250-room **Biltmore House**, built over 100 years ago by George Vanderbilt.

- **Hilton Head Island, South Carolina.** With 12 miles of superb beaches, wind-swept scenery, and countless opportunities for water sports, Hilton Head is one of the most popular resorts in the country. Like **Myrtle Beach**, another resort in this state, it draws golfers, tennis players, and families looking to vacation.

- **Charleston, South Carolina.** Charleston is one of the most elegant and charming cities in the United States; the **Battery** is its historical district of beautiful antebellum houses. **Fort Sumter**, where the first shots of the Civil War were fired, is off the coast. Tourists often visit the spectacular plantations and gardens that are near Charleston.

Ducks parade twice a day in the lobby of the Peabody Hotel in Memphis.

Paducah, Kentucky, is famous for its quilts.

Greenbrier, a luxury resort in West Virginia, has a once-secret military base buried beneath it.

Sales Considerations

The Southern United States appeals strongly to travelers looking for music-themed experiences, water sports, historic sites, and a genteel way of life. The many offshore islands that stretch from Virginia through the Carolinas and down the coast of Georgia provide remarkable settings for a number of outstanding resorts.

The South offers convenient jumping-off points to other vacation spots. West Virginia is a gateway to Washington, D.C., Philadelphia, New York City, and beyond. Louisville is not far down river from Cincinnati; in fact, Kentucky borders not only Ohio but also Indiana and Illinois. Louisiana is an excellent extension of a trip to Texas. And any of the coastal states could lead to a Caribbean holiday. Atlanta is a major destination for business travelers, so popular hotels should be booked ahead of time. All hotels should be booked far in advance for those interested in visiting New Orleans during Mardi Gras. Several river- and sea-going cruise ships call New Orleans their home port.

Remember: The South's great charm, strong tradition of preserving history, splendid outdoor recreation areas, and vital urban centers can each attract a different kind of traveler.

The Midwest

The Midwest is what the region is best known as, but to some, this may seem like a misnomer. At the area's eastern end, Ohio could almost be considered a part of the East. Missouri was a part of the South during the Civil War. Even the area's westernmost boundary barely reaches the center of the country. Perhaps a tourist might be more comfortable calling the region the Prairie States, but even that doesn't fully apply to much of the territory. And so, the Midwest it is.

Without question, the centerpiece of the Midwest is **Chicago**, Illinois, the third-largest city in the United States. Not only is it the major gateway to the region but also its **O'Hare International Airport (ORD)** is one of the busiest in the United States. (Chicago's **Midway International Airport** [MDW] is an alternative.) However, there are many other large Midwestern urban centers set within rich farmland and beautiful forests. Parts of Minnesota, Wisconsin, and Michigan are a bit hilly, offering some winter skiing possibilities, but for the most part the Midwest is flat.

It's very easy to fly into the Midwest, with major terminals not only in Chicago but also in **Detroit**, Michigan (DTW); **Milwaukee**, Wisconsin (MKE); **Cleveland**, Ohio (CLE); **Cincinnati**, Ohio (CVG); **St. Louis**, Missouri (STL); and **Minneapolis–St. Paul**, Minnesota (MSP). The highway network is excellent for car or bus travel; however, since the region is so very large, distances might make that prohibitive. Chicago is also the major hub of train travel in the country.

The Midwest can be hot in the summer and somewhat humid; winters can get quite cold and snowy. Spring is rainy and usually chilly. Fall is beautiful, especially when the leaves change.

An important note: Though such states as Minnesota and Michigan have beautiful and popular recreation areas, they depend mainly on local Midwesterners for their tourism. Scenic as they are, they're not likely to be destinations you'll deal with as often as others. (Unless, of course, you live here!)

Important Places

Beginning with Illinois in the center and going clockwise from Missouri at seven o'clock, the most popular attractions in the Midwest include:

- **Chicago, Illinois**. This huge, cultured city is the Midwest's focal point. There's a strong theater community and a superb collection of museums. The most notable are the **Museum of Science and Industry**, one of the world's finest, with hands-on exhibits, an indoor farm, an underground coal mine, and a German submarine among its huge collection; the **Art Institute**, with its famous French Impressionist wing; the **Field Museum of Natural History**; and the **Shedd Aquarium**. The city also offers great shopping on the **Magnificent Mile** along North Michigan Avenue, excellent ethnic cuisine, and tours (by bus or boat) of its significant architectural landmarks.

- Lincoln Country, Illinois. This is the region where Abraham Lincoln lived. It includes **New Salem**, where Lincoln grew up and made his famous long walk to return a book, and **Springfield**, the state capital and Lincoln's home. Springfield is home to the high-tech **Abraham Lincoln Presidential Library and Museum**.

Michigan has more lighthouses (116) than any other U.S. state.

Try deep-dish pizza where it was invented: Chicago.

Metropolis, Illinois, has a Superman town square, a newspaper called *The Planet*, and a prominent bronze statue of the "Man of Steel."

Charleston is well known for its stately mansions
Image copyright Matty Symons, 2008. Used under license from Shutterstock.com

- **Hannibal, Missouri**. This charming town was Mark Twain's boyhood home.
- **St. Louis, Missouri**. The "gateway to the West" for nineteenth-century pioneers is commemorated by the famous **Gateway Arch**. The city's ornate cathedral has the largest collection of mosaics in the world.
- **Branson, Missouri**. This small town attracts millions of visitors a year with dozens of entertainment venues. It's nestled in one of the most scenic areas of the Ozark Mountains. Visitors usually fly into Springfield, Missouri, then drive to Branson. Branson is one of the United States' most popular motorcoach tour destinations.
- **The Amana Colonies, Iowa**. This is a communal society of seven small towns founded by a strict European religious sect. There are good cultural museums, and excellent local food and crafts are available.
- **Minneapolis–St. Paul, Minnesota**. The twin-city area is justly proud of its excellent symphonies, opera, and theater, especially the famed **Guthrie Theater**. Also here are a great zoo and several architecturally noteworthy museums. St. Paul celebrates a famous **Winter Carnival** each February.
- **Milwaukee, Wisconsin**. The most important city in the state has a new, architecturally daring **Milwaukee Art Museum**.
- **The Wisconsin Dells**. An hour north of the state capital of Madison and northwest of Milwaukee, this is an extremely popular recreation area where the Wisconsin River runs through scenic cliffs. Other impressive Wisconsin recreational areas include **Lake Geneva** and the **Door Peninsula**.
- **Mackinac Island, Michigan**. A charming and famous resort, the island has retained an Old-World feel. No automobiles are allowed here; people get around in horse-drawn carriages or on bicycles. The ornate **Grand Hotel** is wonderful; its 660-foot porch is legendary.
- **The Henry Ford Museum and Greenfield Village** in **Dearborn, Michigan**. Some of the country's most famous edifices have been brought here intact, including those of Thomas Edison, Noah Webster, the Wright Brothers, and Ford himself. This unique indoor-and-outdoor facility also includes a great collection of classic cars.

The Grand Hotel is Mackinac Island's signature building
Image copyright Vince Ruffa, 2008. Used under license from Shutterstock.com

- **The Pro Football Hall of Fame** in **Canton, Ohio**. This museum honors football's greats. Also in Ohio, just north of **Cincinnati**, is **Kings Island**, the nation's most visited seasonal amusement park. **Dayton**'s **U.S. Air Force Museum** is the largest of its kind in the world. And Cleveland, on a beautiful lakeside location, is home to the immensely popular and entertaining **Rock and Roll Hall of Fame and Museum**.

- **Indianapolis Motor Speedway, Indiana**. The famous Indy 500 (Memorial Day), Brickyard 400 (late July or early August), and U.S. Grand Prix (September) auto races are held here. A museum traces the history of racing.

Sales Considerations

The Midwest is a strategic spot from which to start a driving trip to Canada. Ferries that take cars across the Great Lakes can save travelers a tremendous amount of driving time. Because it's so spread out, different areas of the Midwest also lead into trips to the East, the South, and the Great Plains. Chicago is a major business and convention destination, and business travelers may want to extend their visits or even bring their families along. The Midwest can be a particularly good area for those who seek a mix of rural vacation and urban culture.

Martinsville, Indiana, is the world's largest producer of goldfish.

The Mall of America, with its 500 stores covering an area greater than 78 football fields, is in Bloomington, Minnesota. More people visit it each year than Walt Disney World.

Travel Trivia

Where the Brand-Name Museums and Tours Are

- Corning Museum of Glass, Corning, New York
- Ben & Jerry's, Waterbury, Vermont
- Crayola Factory, Easton, Pennsylvania
- World of Coca-Cola, Atlanta, Georgia
- Jack Daniel's Distillery, Lynchburg, Tennessee
- Louisville Slugger Museum and Factory, Louisville, Kentucky
- Anheuser-Busch Museum, St. Louis, Missouri
- Boeing Aircraft, Everett, Washington
- Hershey's Chocolate World, Hershey, Pennsylvania
- Celestial Seasonings, Boulder, Colorado

NAME _____   **DATE** _____

MAP ACTIVITY

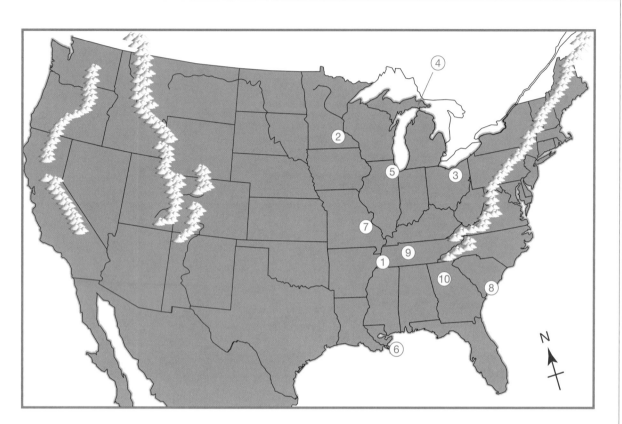

A traveler wants to visit the places listed below. Which number represents each on the map?

Place/Attraction	In/Near Which City/State?	Number on Map
A. The Rock and Roll Hall of Fame	A. _____	A. _____
B. The French Quarter	B. _____	B. _____
C. Graceland	C. _____	C. _____
D. The High Museum of Art	D. _____	D. _____
E. Mackinac Island	E. _____	E. _____
F. The Hermitage	F. _____	F. _____
G. Fort Sumter	G. _____	G. _____
H. The Museum of Science and Industry	H. _____	H. _____
I. The Guthrie Theater	I. _____	I. _____
J. The Ryman Auditorium	J. _____	J. _____

NAME _____ **DATE** _____

CASE STUDY

Marcia Wilkinson is attending a three-day business conference in New Orleans. It ends on a Friday and leads right into the Labor Day weekend. Her husband, Greg, has rearranged his schedule so that he can do some of his own business there and join her. These successful people, both in their late 20s, have never been to the South. The last time they did something like this was when Greg had to go to Boston, where they loved traveling around and visiting the historic sites.

Circle the answer that best suits their needs.

1 What attraction would you recommend they see?

Harper's Ferry   The Ryman Auditorium

Graceland   Jackson Square

Why?

2 To where would you suggest they make a day trip?

Savannah   Natchez

Charleston   Lexington

Why?

3 Which would *not* be an activity that could enhance their trip?

A trip through the bayous   A one-day riverboat cruise

A city tour   A trip through the Everglades

Why?

4 To which historic site should they make an overnight visit?

Hannibal   Fort Sumter

Vicksburg Battlefield   Kitty Hawk

Why?

NAME _____ **DATE** _____

CREATIVE ACTIVITY

Jurassic Park is a reality! Scientists have actually found a way to clone dinosaurs. But the investor who bankrolled the research wants to open the park not on an island off the coast of Costa Rica, but somewhere in the United States or Canada.

He has hired you to recommend where it should be located! You are given the following guidelines:

- It must be in a place remote enough that if the dinosaurs escape, they're unlikely to get very far or do any harm before being captured. Yet it must be close enough to lodging, transportation hubs, and so on, to guarantee a considerable number of visitors. No tourists will be housed at the park. They'll have to drive, bus, or sail in from somewhere else.

- Climate, terrain, accessibility to foreign tourists, and so on, should also be considered.

- You may consider any place in North America, even those covered in other chapters.

NAME _____   **DATE** _____

BONUS ACTIVITY

How's your knowledge of landmarks? Identify the city and/or country that each photo depicts. Write your answer on the line beneath each. Answers are at the bottom of this page.

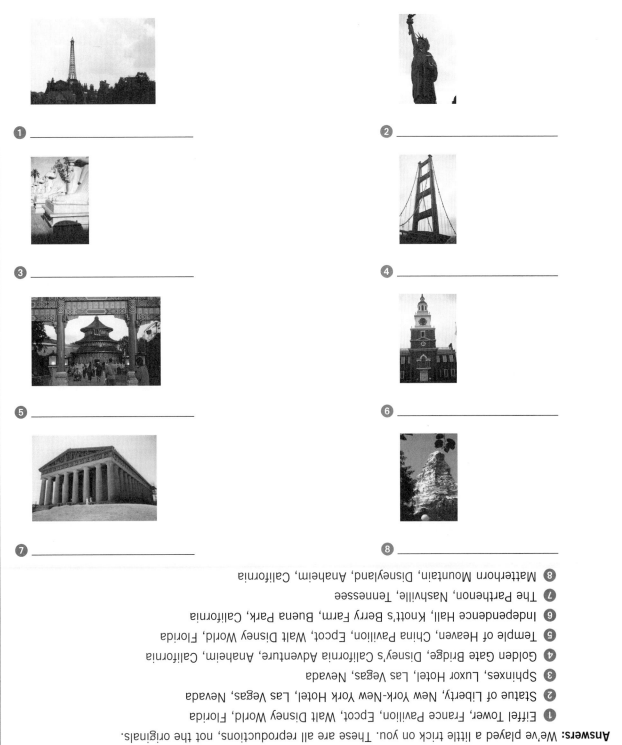

1 _____

2 _____

3 _____

4 _____

5 _____

6 _____

7 _____

8 _____

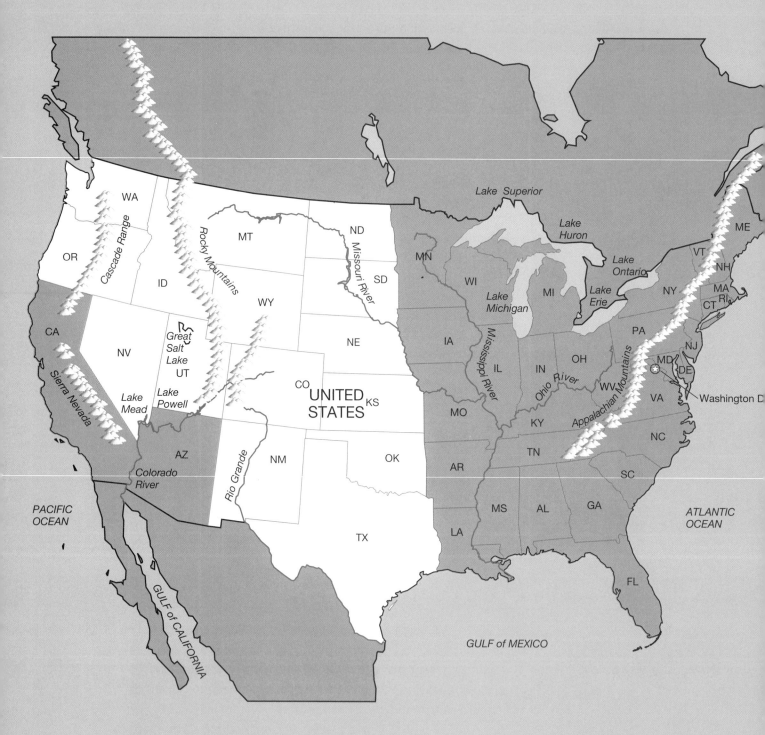

PACIFIC
OCEAN

WA

Cascade Range

OR

Rocky Mountains

MT

ND

MN

Lake Superior

Lake
Huron

Lake
Ontario

ME

VT

NH

ID

WY

SD

Missouri River

WI

Lake
Michigan

MI

Lake
Erie

NY

MA

CT

RI

CA

NV

Great
Salt
Lake

UT

NE

IA

IL

IN

OH

PA

NJ

MD

DE

Sierra Nevada

Lake
Mead

Lake
Powell

CO

UNITED
STATES

KS

MO

KY

WV

Appalachian Mountains

VA

Washington D

AZ

Colorado
River

Rio Grande

NM

OK

AR

TN

NC

SC

Ohio River

Mississippi River

GULF of CALIFORNIA

TX

MS

AL

GA

ATLANTIC
OCEAN

LA

FL

GULF of MEXICO

Chapter 9

North American Potpourri (West)

In the West, everything seems extreme: the vast plains, the towering mountains, the huge forests, the endless deserts. Even the cities can be overwhelming. Some of the country's most dramatic attractions, both natural and manmade, are here, too: Mt. Rushmore, the Stratosphere Tower, Yellowstone, and Carlsbad Caverns.

The West isn't just about major destinations. It has its subtleties, too; modest places with remarkable personalities: Santa Fe, Sun Valley, Taos, and Telluride. Indeed, the West is one of the most diversified and interesting places to visit in the world.

So let's look at those places we left out of previous chapters, those destination gems that warrant a special look.

The Great Plains

The Great Plains states are rocky in the north but flatten out toward the south. Winters are cold and snowy, and summers are hot. The farther south you go, the higher the temperatures get. The interstate highway network is good but limited; and because there are fairly long distances between urban centers, driving should perhaps be recommended only to those who want to enjoy the rural scenery. There are no gigantic cities in the region, though **Omaha**, Nebraska (OMA); **Wichita**, Kansas (ICT); and **Kansas City**, Missouri (MCI), are of respectable size and interest. They're the main gateways to the area.

Important Places

The Great Plains region offers some famous attractions. Some of the most recognizable, from north to south, are:

- **Theodore Roosevelt National Park, North Dakota.** The park's badlands offer a beautiful rocky landscape and feature some of the largest bison herds in America. North Dakota is home to many other impressive recreation areas, wildlife preserves, and state parks.

- **Mt. Rushmore National Memorial**, just outside **Rapid City, South Dakota**. One of the country's most

La Crosse, Kansas, has a barbed-wire museum.

Most of Mt. Rushmore was carved by using dynamite
Photo by Justus Ghormley

North Dakota has the lowest crime rate in the United States.

Mt. Rushmore's sculptor originally intended to carve the four presidents' full bodies, not just their heads.

Kansas is 0.9997 flat, making it flatter than a pancake.

familiar tourist sites, Mt. Rushmore is where huge busts of four former presidents have been carved out of the mountainside. Nearby are three other attractions: **Wind Cave National Park**, **Jewel Cave National Monument**, and the surreal landscape of **Badlands National Park**. To the north is **Deadwood**, a preserved Old Western town that sits in a canyon and that features gambling. And to the southwest, another huge carving is being created: the **Crazy Horse Memorial**.

■ **Fort Robinson State Park, Nebraska**. This remote park is one of the most interesting in the Great Plains. The site of an old cavalry post, it's strategic to several lovely recreation areas and to intriguing prehistoric fossil beds.

■ **Dodge City, Kansas**. The famous Western town, now restored, features the Boot Hill Museum, Boot Hill Cemetery, and historic areas like Front Street and the Long Branch Saloon. Another reconstructed cowboy town is **Wichita Cowtown**.

Sales Considerations

The Great Plains is wedged between the Midwest and the Rocky Mountain states, and offers a handy gateway to Canada. There's a pioneer history and spirit here, which may appeal to certain vacationers, especially Old West buffs. Anyone flying to the Great Plains should consider a car rental, since it's the best way to travel the great distances.

Texas and Oklahoma

These states are an anomaly. Together or separately, they could be considered part of the Great Plains, the Southwest, or even the South. Because these two states are so closely related, for tourism purposes it's best to look at them together.

Both states are quite hilly, though Texas has long stretches of desert in its southwestern region. The Gulf Coast on the southeast of Texas offers popular resort recreation areas. The climate in these two states is quite hot in the summer, with chilly winters; spring and

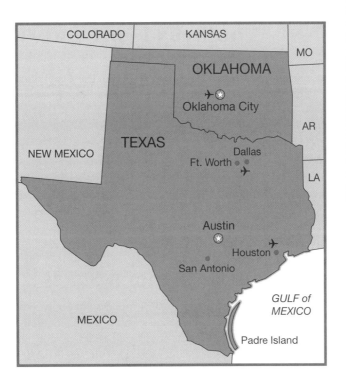

fall are generally pleasant. Temperatures in Oklahoma are usually cooler. The eastern portion of both states tends to be rainier than the west, which is arid.

Texas is easily reached via major gateways in **Dallas–Fort Worth** (DFW) and **Houston** (IAH), with other airports in smaller markets. **Oklahoma City** (OKC) is the main air route into Oklahoma. A few major interstates crisscross Texas, but because of the state's size, driving distances are long, and many areas don't have easy access. However, three important cities, **Houston**, **San Antonio**, and **Austin**, are reasonably close to one another.

Important Places

Both states are renowned for their strong cowboy traditions. Texas, the second-largest state in the country, offers many attractions, the most popular of which are in Dallas, Houston, and San Antonio. These attractions include:

- **Dallas, Texas**. A cosmopolitan and sophisticated commercial center, Dallas offers quite a few museums, the popular **Six Flags over Texas** theme park (in nearby Arlington), and a popular **Texas State Fair** from late September to mid-October. Its sister city, Ft. Worth, has some excellent Western art museums. Dallas is linked with the death of President Kennedy, and the **John F. Kennedy Memorial** commemorates that tragedy.

- **Houston, Texas**. The fourth-largest city in the United States, Houston is home to the **Johnson Space Center**, NASA's training facility for astronauts and tracking center for space flights (**Space Center Houston** houses the visitors center). Houston boasts the world's first indoor stadium, the **Astrodome**.

- **San Antonio, Texas**. This very popular city harbors the legendary centerpiece of Texas's struggle for independence: the **Alamo**. The **Riverwalk** is a unique attraction: A river several miles long, lined with dozens of restaurants and nightspots, twists and turns through the city's downtown.

- **Austin, Texas**. The state capital, Austin is famous for its music clubs and is the self-proclaimed bat capital of the world. (At sunset, 1.5 million bats set out for their evening hunting.)

A car rental is almost essential to get around the Dallas–Ft. Worth area.

Six flags have flown over Texas (thus the amusement park chain name). Whose flags? The United States, Mexico, Spain, France, Texas, and the Confederacy.

The capitol building of Texas is taller than the United States Capitol in Washington, D.C.

- **Padre Island, Texas**. Actually two separate islands, Padre is made up of a pristine national seashore area and clusters of rapidly developing resort areas. Padre Island is 115 miles long and stretches from Corpus Christi to Port Isabel.
- **Oklahoma City, Oklahoma**. The capital of Oklahoma boasts the **National Cowboy and Western Heritage Museum**, with an excellent collection of Old West mementos.

Sales Considerations

Texas is a logical gateway for those interested in a trip to Mexico. In addition, Houston is within a day's drive of New Orleans. Easily packaged with a trip to the Southwest, the region is particularly well suited for people who like Western history and the rugged outdoors. Dallas and Houston are both major urban centers, with sophisticated lodging (Dallas's **Mansion on Turtle Creek** is legendary). An interesting place to stay is at a ranch outside either of these cities.

The Rocky Mountain States

The name clearly defines the region's topography: rocky. From western Canada through the northern border of the United States, this massive mountain range twists down through the Rocky Mountain states. Areas of Montana and Wyoming also contain huge grasslands that spill over from the Great Plains. With its truly wide-open spaces, the area offers some of the most magnificent scenery and distant horizons in the country. The winters get quite cold and snowy, especially in the north, but summers are warm and pleasant. Surprisingly, eastern Wyoming and Montana, as well as southwestern Colorado, can get quite hot in the summer.

Denver, Colorado (DEN), serves as the main entrance into the area for air travelers. Driving, though it accesses dramatic scenery, can be difficult, especially in the winter when many mountain roads may be closed. Even under good conditions, interstate highway connections are few, and distances long.

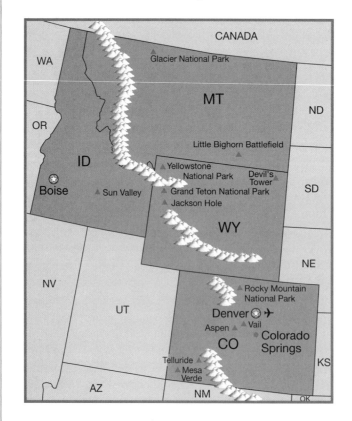

"Tex-Mex" cuisine is much spicier than Mexican food found elsewhere.

Important Places

The natural wonders of this area represent many of the top attractions, which include (going from south to north and then turning west to Idaho)

- **Mesa Verde National Park, Colorado**. In the thirteenth century, Native Americans built cliff dwellings in the canyon walls of Mesa Verde (Spanish for "green table"). The archaeological sites here are among the best in the country.

- **Denver, Colorado**. With spectacular mountains as a backdrop, Denver has an interesting combination of modernity and Old West past. There are fine museums and excellent nearby skiing. **Rocky Mountain National Park** is 70 miles northwest of Denver, and the **U.S. Air Force Academy** is 65 miles to the south in **Colorado Springs**.

- **The ski resorts of Colorado**. One of the prime skiing areas in the country, Colorado has dozens of popular slopes, including **Aspen, Vail,** and **Telluride**.

- **Yellowstone and Grand Teton National Parks**, in **northwestern Wyoming**. Together, these two parks provide some of the most breathtaking scenery to be found anywhere in the world. Yellowstone, whose most famous attraction is Old Faithful Geyser, was the world's first national park. Within the park are some fine lodges, which must be booked well in advance.

- **Jackson Hole, Wyoming**. Just south of the Grand Tetons, Jackson Hole is one of the country's top ski resorts. Here, too, is the Snake River, which offers many fishing and rafting opportunities.

- **Devils Tower National Monument, Wyoming**. The country's first national monument, it was featured in the classic movie *Close Encounters of the Third Kind*.

- **Little Bighorn Battlefield National Monument, Montana** (formerly known as Custer Battlefield). The famous battle took place here.

- **Glacier National Park, Montana**. With some of the most extraordinary scenery in the United States, the park has dozens of glaciers, hundreds of lakes, a huge diversity of floral life, and herds of virtually every large animal to be found in the country. Together with Alberta's Waterton Lakes National Park, it forms the Waterton-Glacier International Peace Park.

- **Sun Valley, Idaho**. In a region known for winter sports, Sun Valley was one of America's first great ski resorts.

Sales Considerations

Because many of the Rocky Mountain states could easily be considered parts of either the Great Plains or the Southwest, they clearly are excellent places to visit in conjunction with those areas. The great mountain ranges here will particularly appeal to those who ski or appreciate dramatic scenery.

The Pacific Northwest

Oregon and Washington, two of the best-loved states in the United States, are notable for their lush farmland, rugged coastline, lofty mountains, high waterfalls, and charming towns. The region's coastal strip is especially rainy, particularly from late summer through early spring. The climate is temperate near the coast, but colder in the eastern mountains. **Seattle**, Washington (SEA), and **Portland**, Oregon (PDX), are the major cities here; they're also the major air gateways. Driving along the coast is actually the preferred mode of travel in the region, but venturing to the picturesque outer areas of the states can be more challenging, since the highway network is limited.

Colorado means "red color" in Spanish.

Between 1978 and 1992, 12 people were injured by bears in Yellowstone, and 56 by buffalo.

Montana is Latin for "mountainous."

Yellowstone National Park has about 500 geysers.

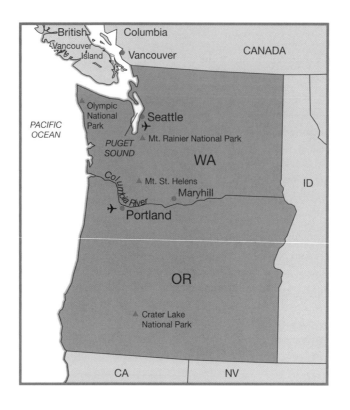

Important Places

This region covers only two states, but the overall beauty of the area is impressive. Its highlights include:

- **Seattle, Washington**. This cosmopolitan, beautiful city rests on Puget Sound. The **Space Needle** tower is the city's most recognizable landmark. Next to it is the **Experience Music Project**, an interactive music museum housed in an astonishingly shaped structure designed by architect Frank Gehry. Also part of the facility is the **Science Fiction Museum and Hall of Fame**, with the world's greatest collection of sci-fi movie props. Other attractions include the **Museum of Flight** (a fabulous collection of aircraft), **Pike Place Market**, **Pioneer Square** (a restored historic district), and, to the northwest, **Olympic National Park**. It's just a few hours' drive or ferry ride to either Vancouver Island or the city of Vancouver in Canada.

- **Mt. St. Helens, Washington**. The volcano that erupted in 1980 is now a starkly troubling national monument. Another volcano, **Mt. Rainier**, is a glacier-coated national park.

- **The Oregon Coast**. This area offers a breathtaking drive along the Pacific Ocean. Travelers can take a leisurely trip past grassy dunes, rugged cliffs, national forests, and picturesque towns.

- **Portland, Oregon**. The state's largest city has a restored old town and many impressive rose gardens. Nearby is the road along the **Columbia River Gorge**, with its towering cliffs and ribbon-like waterfalls. Many believe that this is one of the most beautiful drives in the United States. Along the Gorge, on the Washington State side, is **Maryhill**, a chateau-like museum that boasts a surprisingly rich collection of paintings and Rodin sculptures.

Sales Considerations

The Pacific Northwest combines naturally with a trip to western Canada. The region is also an excellent jumping-off point for cruises to Alaska. In addition, Oregon borders California

Oregon's Crater Lake is the deepest lake in the United States.

The most common town name in the United States is *Fairview*.

The Experience Music Project's strange, organic architecture contrasts with the
more traditional geometry of the Seattle Space Needle
Image copyright Glenn R. McGloughlin, 2008. Used under license from Shutterstock.com

to the south, and the Rocky Mountain states and their superb skiing opportunities lie
directly to the east. (There's some skiing in Oregon and Washington, too.) River-rafting
tours are very popular in the Pacific Northwest. Small cruise ships ply the area's waters.

The Southwest

The Southwest is noted for its deserts and arid climate. However, its range of conditions is
wider than this. Utah is extremely mountainous, as is the western portion of New Mexico.
Summers get blisteringly hot in the desert area, whereas the mountains are cold and snowy
in the winter. The major air terminals in these states are **Las Vegas**, Nevada (LAS); **Salt
Lake City**, Utah (SLC); and **Albuquerque** [AL-beh-ker-kee], New Mexico (ABQ). It's common to drive from Albuquerque to **Santa Fe**, New Mexico, but most other sites are far
apart and require long driving times.

Important Places

The most popular places for tourists in the Southwest tend to be in California and Arizona. However, the remaining states in the region offer some superb attractions. Among them are Las Vegas (profiled in its own section) and the following places:

- **Reno, Nevada.** This little brother to Las Vegas also offers gambling and shows, though on a smaller scale. Reno is near the resort area of **Lake Tahoe** (which also has a few casinos). Other Nevada gaming centers are **Laughlin** (on the Colorado River near Arizona), which caters to an older, budget-seeking clientele, and **Primm** (at the California–Nevada border), which attracts budget-minded families.

- **Virginia City, Nevada.** Museums, mine tours, and mansions are attractions in this old mining town, where visitors stroll a wooden boardwalk street full of shops and saloons.

- **Utah's National Parkland.** Some of the country's most spectacular national parks are in this state: **Zion, Bryce Canyon, Arches, Canyonlands**, and **Capitol Reef**. In southern Utah (and northern Arizona) is a popular recreational area, **Lake Powell**.

- **Salt Lake City, Utah.** The capital of Utah, Salt Lake City is the heart of the Mormon religion. The most important buildings are on and around **Temple Square**. Tours of the famous **Mormon Tabernacle** are available. The **Family History Library** is probably the greatest collection of genealogical resources in the world. It's open to visitors of all faiths. Salt Lake City was home to the 2002 Winter Olympics. Superb ski resorts— including **Snowbird, Park City, Deer Valley**, and **Alta**—are close by.

- **Santa Fe, New Mexico.** This absolutely charming capital city (the oldest capital in the United States) is famous as an arts and crafts center. Native American crafts are available everywhere; the dining facilities of the city—birthplace of "Southwestern cuisine"—are first rate. From July to August, the city hosts the internationally acclaimed **Santa Fe Chamber Music Festival**. To get to Santa Fe, travelers must fly into Albuquerque, then drive or bus to Santa Fe. (Air service into Santa Fe's modest airport is limited.)

- **Taos, New Mexico.** This artists' colony is also one of the most popular ski resorts in the country. In addition, **Taos Pueblo** is a classic Pueblo village.

- **Carlsbad Caverns National Park, New Mexico.** Its underground rooms (one of them could accommodate 11 football fields) and 21 miles of rocky passages carved out of the rock are renowned.

Many hotel rooms in Santa Fe come equipped with distinctive, funnel-shaped fireplaces.

Sales Considerations

The Southwest region is easily combined with a trip to Mexico or the Rocky Mountain states. The Southwest is of particular interest to those fascinated by Native American culture. Skiers will be drawn here as well. Keep in mind that Nevada's gambling cities are extremely popular for weekend trips (hotel rates are much lower on weekdays), and many special packages are available.

Visitors sometimes sprawl out at the point where Utah, Colorado, Arizona, and New Mexico meet, so they can say they were in four states at once.

Las Vegas, Nevada

A unique, desert-situated spectacle of neon, themed hotels, nonstop activity, and endless entertainment, Las Vegas has become one of the world's most visited cities. For that reason, we've given it its own mini-chapter:

Weather Patterns. Las Vegas is extremely hot in the summer, with daytime temperatures typically around 100 degrees. Because it's so dry, however, the heat—at least in short doses and with air conditioning in all buildings—is tolerable. Spring and late fall are much more pleasant. Daytime temperatures in the winter are in the 60s, but nights can be surprisingly cold and rain is a remote possibility.

Tourism Patterns. Summer is somewhat of a shoulder season; late November through January usually sees the fewest visitors (and the best values). The rest of the year is very popular. Year-round, weekends are busier (and more expensive) than weekdays. Las Vegas is one of the country's top convention destinations.

Getting There and Getting Around. People who live within a 400-mile radius (e.g., southern Californians) often drive or motorcoach to Las Vegas. Many low-priced flights and air–hotel packages are also available. Once in Las Vegas, visitors without a car can rent one (parking—even valet parking—is usually free), take taxis, or ride the local monorails and buses. Tours to nearby attractions are available.

Why People Go. Gambling, entertainment, and quick weddings used to be the big draws. They're still very much factors in this town, "a place where you go to do the opposite of what you do at home," as writer David Lansing put it. However, lodging bargains (what you get for your money is often remarkable) and theme park-like hotels have made Las Vegas an attractive place for families, too. Major shopping venues are everywhere.

About 150 couples get married in Las Vegas each day.

The bell tower of St. Mark's at the Venetian Hotel is a landmark of the Las Vegas Strip
Photo by Marc Mancini

Most of the large hotels stage lavish production shows and/or host world-famous performers. Many have extensive spa facilities. Dining choices are plentiful: World-class restaurants (with prices somewhat lower than they would be elsewhere), inexpensive coffee shops, fast-food outlets, and some absolutely astonishing buffets are just a few of the options.

Important Places. Las Vegas is a city where the hotel-casinos themselves are the attractions. (More about that next.) The 100-story **Stratosphere Tower** is a more conventional attraction, but it too has lodging, gaming, shopping, amusements, and dining at its base (and some small but scary thrill rides at its top). Nearby are two interesting day-trip destinations: the **Valley of Fire** (dramatic scenery) and **Hoover Dam**, as well as hiking, rock-climbing, and other sports possibilities.

Lodging. Las Vegas has over 130,000 hotel rooms. Its lodging can be divided into three geographic regions: the Strip, downtown, and peripheral areas.

The 3.5-mile-long Strip (Las Vegas Boulevard South) features over 20 gigantic hotel-casinos, most of which are dramatically themed. Among them are **Mandalay Bay** (and its "beach" with artificial waves), the **Luxor** (a huge glass pyramid), **New York–New York** (with a scaled-down New York skyline), **Paris Las Vegas** (with its own Eiffel Tower), **Bellagio** (boasting a huge fountain show in its "lake"), **Caesars Palace** (like an ancient, decadent Roman city), the **Venetian** (yes, canals and gondolas), the **Mirage** (with erupting volcano), **TI-Treasure Island** (a show with sirens and pirates takes place in front every 90 minutes), and **Circus Circus** (a family property with rides and circus acts).

The downtown area has lower-cost lodging and more modest casinos. Four blocks of its **Fremont Street** (seen in countless TV shows and movies) is covered with a canopy made up of 12.5 million light bulbs that perform hourly sound-and-light shows each evening. Other hotels and casinos are scattered about the greater Las Vegas area. Some are relatively near the Strip and downtown. Many of these are budget properties and are more modestly scaled. Among the exceptions are the **Rio** (Mardi Gras themed), the **Hard Rock Hotel** (trendy, with well-known performers), and the **Palms** (trendy, too).

Sales Strategies. Air–hotel packages are a natural here. Enhanced lodging (e.g., a suite) is often very affordable, as are car rentals. (Parking—even valet parking—in Las Vegas is almost always free.)

Travel Trivia

10 Inexplicable Airport Codes—Explained

1. CVG (Cincinnati): CVG is taken from Covington, Kentucky, the airport's location
2. MCI (Kansas City): Stands for Mid Continent International
3. MCO (Orlando): Stands for McCoy Airfield, the name of the military base once located there
4. MSY (New Orleans): Once the location of Moisant Stock Yard
5. OGG (Maui): Named after veteran Hawaiian Airlines pilot, Bertram Hogg
6. ORD (Chicago O'Hare): The airport's former name was Orchard Field
7. EWR (Newark): Derived from the E, W, and R in Newark
8. DCA (Reagan National, Washington, D.C.): Stands for District of Columbia Airport
9. & 10. IAD and IAH (Dulles; Washington, D.C.; and Bush Intercontinental, Houston): The IA stands for international airport, D for Dulles, and H for Houston

Source: Marc Mancini

NAME _____   **DATE** _____

MAP ACTIVITY

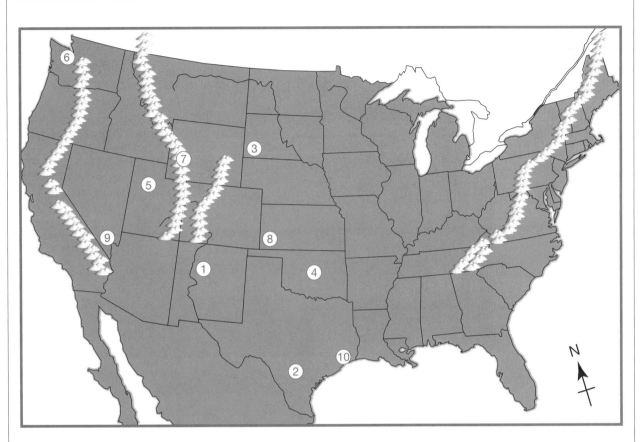

A traveler wants to visit the places listed below. Which number represents each on the map?

Place/Attraction	In/Near Which City/State?	Number on Map
A. Mt. Rushmore	A. _____	A. _____
B. The Space Needle	B. _____	B. _____
C. Taos Pueblo	C. _____	C. _____
D. The Johnson Space Center	D. _____	D. _____
E. Pike Place Market	E. _____	E. _____
F. Jackson Hole	F. _____	F. _____
G. Boot Hill	G. _____	G. _____
H. The Mormon Tabernacle	H. _____	H. _____
I. The Alamo	I. _____	I. _____
J. A glass pyramid, a volcano, and canals	J. _____	J. _____

NAME _____   **DATE** _____

CASE STUDY

Tiffany and Grant Mitchell are in their early 40s and live in Nashville. Grant's parents, who live in London, are coming to see them in February. Though the parents have traveled extensively, they've never been to the United States. They've told Grant that "they'd like to see something different," so Grant has decided to take them to Las Vegas for three days and perhaps extend that stay to at least one other destination.

Circle the answer that best suits their needs.

1   At which of the following lodging areas should they stay?

     The Strip   The Laughlin area

     Downtown   An off-Strip location

     Why?

2   They should expect weather similar to

     London in February   Frankfurt in November

     Athens in March   Nairobi in April

     Why?

3   What other city might appeal to them and be a real contrast to Las Vegas?

     Reno   Omaha

     Santa Fe   Seattle

     Why?

4   The parents have decided to come in June instead. Which national park might be the most interesting for them and wouldn't overly complicate their trip to Las Vegas?

     Yellowstone   Zion

     Mt. Rainier   Theodore Roosevelt

     Why?

NAME _____ DATE _____

CREATIVE ACTIVITY

You're a documentary filmmaker. You're currently scripting a one-hour special for PBS called "America's 'Personality' Cities." You intend to choose 10 cities that have unusual character and distinctiveness. Your first five choices are San Francisco, New York City, Miami, Los Angeles, and Orlando. What would the other five be? Give reasons for your choices.

City

1

2

3

4

5

Reason

1

2

3

4

5

NAME _____ **DATE** _____

PUTTING IT ALL TOGETHER

The Matching Game

Below is a list of places and attractions, some that we have covered and some that we haven't. There are all manner of connections among them. You have exactly 10 minutes to come up with as many connections as possible. (Items may be used more than once.) Write your answers below. Note: There are at least 20 possible connections. For example, the CN Tower and the Space Needle—both are tall towers.

Mt. Rushmore	Padre Island	West Point
Greenfield	Clearwater	High
Hudson	Washington, D.C.	Hilton Head
Yellowstone	CN Tower	Columbia
Aspen	Juneau	Santa Fe
San Diego	Hermitage	Sturbridge
Dulles	Williamsburg	Mt. Vernon
Space Needle	Shenandoah	Branson
San Simeon	Barnes Foundation	Stowe
Huntsville	Vizcaya	Logan
Orlando	Annapolis	Port Everglades
Valley Forge	Mackinac	Mammoth
Carlsbad	Cape Kennedy	Ottawa
Monticello	Vancouver	Stone Mountain

UNITED STATES

ATLANTIC OCEAN

Baja Penninsula

GULF of MEXICO

MEXICO

Sierra Madre Ranges

GULF of CALIFORNIA

BELIZE

HONDURAS

CARIBBEAN SEA

GUATEMALA

NICARAGUA

EL SALVADOR

Lake Nicaragua

COSTA RICA

PANAMA

GUYANA

SURINAME

Lake Maracaibo

Orinoco River

FRENCH GUIANA

VENEZUELA

PACIFIC OCEAN

Canal

COLOMBIA

Galapagos Islands

ECUADOR

Amazon River

Andes

BRAZIL

PERU

Lake Titicaca

Easter Island

BOLIVIA

Rio Parana

PARAGUAY

Atacama Desert

Mountains

Rio Uruguay

CHILE

URUGUAY

Rio de la Plata

ARGENTINA

Strait of Magellan

Falkland Islands

PART III

LATIN AMERICA AND THE CARIBBEAN

Rhythms of Culture

Read this sentence carefully: Mexico is South America's most popular destination, Costa Rica is that continent's hottest new place to visit, and Bermuda is perhaps the Caribbean's most gracious destination.

Find any mistakes? There are three: Mexico is not in South America; it's in North America. Costa Rica isn't in South America either; it's a Central American country. And Bermuda, though generally lumped together with the Caribbean islands, is actually in the Atlantic—at about the same latitude as Charleston, South Carolina.

For many of us, Latin America and the Caribbean are enticing destinations. But they're complicated. We're talking about dozens and dozens of countries, each with its own history, ambience, culture, and "personality." To be able to successfully sell these places, you'll have to bring their assets into better focus. The chapters that follow will help you do that. And once you do, you'll realize how much there is: from ancient cultures to magnificent beach resorts; from jungles, islands, and mountains to cosmopolitan cities. The nations we cover in Part III can be as enticing as the pulse of the tango or the beat of a steel drum band.

The world's largest rain forest (the Amazon), driest desert (the Atacama), and longest mountain range (the Andes) are all found in South America.

Where the Countries Are

Mexico is the nation just south of the U.S. border. Continuing south (and connecting Mexico to the continent of South America) is the cluster of countries making up Central America. From north to south, they're **Belize, Guatemala, Honduras, El Salvador, Nicaragua, Costa Rica**, and **Panama**. Then comes South America. Except for **Bolivia** and **Paraguay**, both of which are landlocked in the center of the continent, South America's countries are located almost in a circle along the coast: **Brazil** is by far the largest country in South America (indeed, slightly larger than the contiguous United States), occupying nearly half the continent as it protrudes to the east; continuing clockwise, we have **Uruguay, Argentina, Chile, Peru, Ecuador, Colombia, Venezuela**, and the **Guianas** (**Guyana, Suriname**, and **French Guiana**).

The geography gets more challenging when we examine the Caribbean islands. In Chapter 11, we'll fully sort out the Caribbean picture for you. For now, you should remember that the Bahamas and Bermuda are not officially part of the Caribbean islands. They're actually north of the Caribbean Sea, in the Atlantic. (They are, however, all generally viewed as part of the same sales market by the travel industry.)

A Satellite View

From above, Latin America's landscape seems amazingly diverse. Two of the world's great natural wonders are obvious: the Amazon River and the Andes mountain range. Their impact on the region, as you'll see, is profound. Many lakes also dot the land, wide grasslands sprout up, rivers crisscross the countryside, even a bleak desert area edges the continent's west coast. And of course, there are thousands of islands, some floating isolated in the Caribbean Sea, others seemingly broken off from the South and Central American mainland.

Bodies of Water

If you were in the space shuttle, you'd first notice the vast bodies of water flanking Central and South America: the **Pacific Ocean** to the west and the **Atlantic Ocean** to the east. The **Gulf of Mexico** is bordered by Mexico to its west and the United States to its north. Southeast of the Gulf is the **Caribbean Sea**, which opens onto the Atlantic.

Another gulf, though much smaller than the Gulf of Mexico, also stands out from your vantage point: Splitting the Baja Peninsula from the rest of Mexico is the Gulf of California (also called the Sea of Cortes).

Your eye will likely next be drawn to one of the world's major rivers, the Amazon. This mighty river runs from west to east almost across the entire breadth of northern South America, finally emptying into the Atlantic. Many tributaries flow into the Amazon, creating the massive Amazon Basin, which affects much of the continent's (and, for that matter, the world's) weather. It's here in the north that you can see South America's lush, tropical jungles. A few other major rivers are noteworthy. In the south, the Rio Parana and Rio Uruguay connect to the major estuary, Rio de la Plata, which in turn flows into the Atlantic. In the north, Venezuela's Orinoco River also empties into the Atlantic, just east of the Caribbean.

A few good-sized lakes interrupt the landscape. In Central America is Lake Nicaragua. As you gaze down to northern parts of South America, there's Lake Maracaibo. And finally, at the western bend of the continent is Lake Titicaca, a popular resort area between Peru and Bolivia. Farther south, just east of the Andes, is the Lake District of Argentina; this is a major resort region.

There are no rivers on any of the 700 islands in the Bahamas.

The Portuguese name for Iguazu Falls is Cataratas do Iguacu
Photo by Marc Mancini

The southwestern portion of the continent breaks up into a mass of islands (separated at its tip by the Strait of Magellan). Far west (2,300 miles, actually) is Easter Island, a fascinating destination. Two other island groupings catch your eye: the Galapagos Islands (a popular expedition site), off the northwest coast; and the Falkland Islands, off the coast to the southeast, which sometimes serve as a stop for cruises bound for Antarctica.

One final feature is highly significant. Splitting the isthmus connecting Mexico and South America is the manmade Panama Canal.

Mountains

From your satellite view, there's only one major mountain range of any note. But what a range: the **Andes** begin in the northwest corner of South America and follow the western coast down to the very southern tip. These mountains greatly influence life in the western part of the continent. A few popular ski resorts can even be found in their southern reaches. One other range is apparent: Two branches of the **Sierra Madres** parallel Mexico's east and west coasts, finally joining south of Mexico City.

Climate

As a rule, the weather in much of Latin America and the Caribbean is hot and humid, with frequent summer afternoon cloudbursts (though winters in the south can get chilly). The Amazon Basin is extremely hot, humid, and rainy year-round. Mexico is also hot, but the central plateau area tends to be more temperate and dry. Mountain temperatures, of course, are colder. And on the west coast of South America, from the northern border of Chile southward for about 600 miles, is the **Atacama**, perhaps the driest desert in the world.

Ocean temperatures on South America's east coast are quite warm, though waters off the west coast can be chilly, because the prevailing currents carry water up from the Antarctic. Even the Galapagos Islands, which lie virtually on the equator, are surrounded by surprisingly cool ocean waters.

Set elsewhere, the 5,500-mile-long Andes would stretch from London to San Francisco.

One of the engineering marvels of all time: the Panama Canal
Image copyright Jim Lipschutz, 2008. Used under license from Shutterstock.com

One other point must be made concerning the area's weather. Much of the region lies south of the equator, which bisects the northern part of South America. As a result, most of the continent has seasons that are opposite to those of the Northern Hemisphere: Summer is December through March, and winter (which tends to be the rainiest season) is June through September.

Tourism Patterns

Of all the countries we're examining in Part III, Mexico attracts more visitors than any other. As a group, the Caribbean islands are the second most popular.

In South America, Brazil is by far the most visited destination. Second is Peru, with several world-class attractions; Argentina isn't far behind. In recent years, many other Central and South American countries have seen increases in the number of visitors.

Latin American Distances

Because many people think of the region only in terms of its highly popular cities, such as **Rio de Janeiro, Buenos Aires**, and **Acapulco**, Latin America may seem far smaller than it is. In truth, it spills over two continents and covers an area several times greater than that of the United States.

All the major cities have very good air connections, which helps shrink the distances. In addition, many smaller cities within each country can be reached by air, as almost every country has its own national airline. Cruises are one efficient way to see Mexican and Caribbean beach resorts; ships also stop at many ports in Central and South America. A number of Mexican and Caribbean cruise patterns exist; we'll review them in Chapters 10 and 11.

As for South America, three cruise itineraries seem to predominate. The first starts in Florida or a Caribbean island, such as Barbados or Puerto Rico, sails past French Guiana, then up the Amazon River. The second begins from the same area, but bypasses the Amazon and continues down the coast, calling at several Brazilian ports along the way and, perhaps, ending in Argentina or Uruguay. The third is the most ambitious, entirely circling the continent.

There are other ways of getting around, but not all are efficient or comfortable; even when they are, the great distances to be covered may make them prohibitive. Tour travel is recommended.

Rail service, for example, is inconsistent, though there are a few fine and popular routes. Buses are for the more adventurous. In a few instances (usually between islands or through the river-crowded jungles), small boats and ships are the most useful way of getting around. They're slow, of course, but the scenery can be very beautiful.

Driving is always an alternative, too; plenty of rental cars are available. However, again, except for a few short distances over rather well-maintained roads (including the Pan-American Highway), this is a less likely recommendation. Major cities are very crowded, and in rural areas roads often aren't in good shape; moreover, heavy rains commonly wash out the roads in some places.

Remember, too, that the climate plays an important role in travel. Tropical rains, hurricanes, or snow in the Andes can dramatically affect travel plans.

Some Miscellaneous Considerations

Latin America has a very distinct culture. Some important factors to keep in mind are:

■ Spanish is the national language in most of these countries. (It's called Latin America because Spanish was derived from ancient Latin.) A few exceptions exist: Brazilians speak Portuguese; Belize's and Guyana's national language is English; Dutch is the official language of Suriname; and French Guianese speak French. The Caribbean is an even greater potpourri of languages, and all have been somewhat altered by African and Indian influences. However, English is widely spoken in the major cities and by most travel personnel.

Each autumn, millions of Monarch Butterflies fly thousands of miles from all across North America to several small areas north and west of Mexico City, where they mate.

In a 1493 decree, the Pope decided which parts of South America should belong to Spain and which to Portugal.

The huge Christ the Redeemer statue, which overlooks Rio, was
recently voted one of the "new seven wonders of the world"
Image copyright Franck Camhi, 2008. Used under license from Shutterstock.com

- Some areas in Latin America are off-limits to photography. Visitors must be discreet when taking pictures (especially of government buildings) and when talking about politics.

- Economic inflation—often occurring suddenly—is a major problem in certain Latin American nations. One way to offset this is by booking packages early, thus locking in prices.

- Political turmoil can flare up in many of these countries, turning an attractive destination into a dubious one. Keep up on the news and consult travel advisories.

- The concept of personal space and time in South America is different from that in the United States. Travelers are often surprised when a South American stands very close to them during a conversation. Though visitors should strive to be on time for an appointment, they shouldn't get offended if someone they are supposed to meet is late; time is very elastic here.

- In some South American countries, such as Chile and Bolivia, it's an insult not to hold eye contact with the person to whom you're talking.

- Crime is, unfortunately, a problem in some Latin American and Caribbean countries. Simple precautions and common sense will avert most predicaments.

- Many people mistakenly believe that all of the Caribbean and Latin America is a bargain. Not true. Venezuela and several Caribbean islands (e.g., St. Martin) are somewhat pricey. On the other hand, Brazil, Peru, Argentina, Colombia, and the Dominican Republic offer many value-priced opportunities.

NAME _____ DATE _____

CREATIVE ACTIVITY #1

You work for a tour wholesaler that specializes in independent tours to Latin America. Anticipate five possible objections—either real or imaginary—that a customer might have to going to Latin America, then come up with information that might overcome each objection.

Customer Objection

Example: I don't know Spanish. I'll have trouble being understood.

1

2

3

4

5

Overcome Objection with . . .

English is widely spoken in major cities and by most travel personnel.

1

2

3

4

5

NAME _____   DATE _____

CREATIVE ACTIVITY #2

Consult your city's Yellow Pages (online or in-print). Identify every restaurant that appears to feature cuisine from one of the countries we're covering in Part III. (Consult the map that opens Part III.) Then list them below, selecting only one from each nation. Unless you must, do not list fast-food providers.

Country	Name of Restaurant	Location
Example: Peruvian	The Incan Trail	52 N. Main

Travel Trivia

The World's Top 10 Cruise Destinations

1. Caribbean
2. Mediterranean
3. Europe
4. Alaska
5. Mexico West
6. Bahamas
7. Hawaii
8. Transatlantic
9. Trans canal
10. South America

SOURCE: Cruise Lines International Association

Chapter 10

Mexico
Tropical Fiesta

Sure, every tourist has heard stories of how you can eat, drink, and dance all night at Mexico's beach cities, then take a siesta all day under the hot tropical sun. But there's much more to the country than that. Mexico, for example, is rich with historical attractions and archaeological sites. There are some drawbacks, though. The biggest problem: Poverty is widespread. Indeed, this may be the greatest misgiving people have about a trip to Mexico.

First, some geography. Mexico is quite large—about a quarter the size of the United States—and it's not all palm-lined beaches. Mexico is a land of diverse landscapes: craggy canyons and cliffs, vast and arid deserts, dense tropical rain forests, and broad, high plateaus. Mexico is sandwiched between the United States to the north and Guatemala and Belize to the south. To the west are the warm waters of the Gulf of California (also called the Sea of Cortes) and the Pacific Ocean, and to the east are the even warmer waters of the Gulf of Mexico and the Caribbean Sea.

So much water is diverted from the Colorado River, that by the time it reaches its mouth at the Sea of Cortes, there's no water in it.

FYI
FOR YOUR INFORMATION

MEXICO

CAPITAL: Mexico City

AREA (SQUARE MILES): 761,600

TIME ZONES: GMT: −6 to −8

DRIVE ON: Right

POPULATION: 110,000,000

RELIGION: Roman Catholic

LANGUAGE: Spanish

CURRENCY: 1 peso = 100 centavos

ELECTRICITY: 110 volts, 60 cycles AC

CAPSULE HISTORY: Mayas, Toltecs, and Aztecs rule, pre-1519; Cortes conquers, 1519–1521; Mexicans overthrow Spaniards, 1821; war with U.S., 1846–1848; French invade and rule, 1861–1867; Juarez is president, 1855 and 1867; Civil War, 1920; major oil deposits discovered, 1975; political unrest, 1996; PAN party voted in, after 70 years of PRI party ruling Mexico, 2000.

For reference sources, tourist bureaus, and suggested lengths of stay, see the Appendices.

It's useful to divide the country into five major tourist areas. The Baja [BAH-hah] Peninsula stretches southward from California for nearly 700 miles. On the northern part of Baja, just south of the California border, is **Tijuana** [tee-WAH-nah], a city that's usually seen as a day trip from San Diego, California. Toward the southernmost tip are several resort cities: **La Paz**, **Cabo San Lucas**, and **San Jose del Cabo** (as a group, they're often called Los Cabos). To Baja's east and south is a second major tourist destination, the Mexican Riviera: a string of resort cities that lines Mexico's long western coast.

The Yucatan Peninsula, which curves out from Mexico's east coast, is a third key destination and is often considered part of the Caribbean. **Cancun** [kan-KOON] is its chief resort. The Yucatan is also the location of many of Mexico's most dramatic ruins. West of the peninsula are Veracruz, Tampico, and other port cities that are less visited, except perhaps as a cruise stopover. But not all of Mexico's attractions are along the beach. The **Copper Canyon**, in Mexico's north-central area, is a fourth major destination. And the fifth is Mexico's colonial region, which includes **Guadalajara**, **Cuernavaca**, **Taxco** [TAHS-ko], and **Mexico City**, the nation's capital.

How Travelers Get There

Mexicana (MX), the country's national carrier, flies out of several U.S. gateways, as does **Aeromexico** (AM), Mexico's other large airline. Quite a few U.S. carriers fly into Mexico; some people feel that service will be more reliable on these airlines than on Mexico's own. Unlike many countries, there's no real hub to the Mexican air system. There are enough connections that travelers can just fly into the cities they wish to visit. Among the principal airports are Mexico City (MEX), **Acapulco** (ACA), **Puerto Vallarta** (PVR), **Ixtapa/Zihuatanejo** (ZIH), and Cancun (CUN).

To take a train, bus, or car into Mexico is usually inadvisable. Its trains and buses leave something to be desired, and driving can be perilous. (Visitors who get into an accident or break a traffic law in Mexico might be detained indefinitely in jail.) Cruises, usually out of Los Angeles or San Diego, are an extremely popular way to see **Ensenada**, Cabo San Lucas, and the Mexican Riviera. Mexico's Gulf-Caribbean ports—especially Cozumel and Playa del Carmen (Cancun's port)—are stops for cruises, usually on Western Caribbean itineraries.

Weather Patterns

Most people imagine all of Mexico to be hot and humid. Not so. Mexico City, for example, sits on a high plateau. The city can certainly be warm (though rainy) in the summer, but it's quite cool in the winter, with an average daytime high around 60 degrees in December. And at almost any time of the year, Mexico City is cool at night. The beach cities are indeed hot and humid in the summer and early fall, with frequent afternoon downpours and an occasional hurricane. (As you can guess, this is the season for travel bargains.) But winter, Mexico's high tourist season, is pleasantly warm and dry (see Figures 10–1 and 10–2). The only exceptions are the smaller resorts along the Baja Peninsula and on the Gulf of California, where winter air and water temperatures can be a bit chilly.

Getting Around

In general, it's best to fly from place to place in Mexico. But there are a few exceptions: The Copper Canyon train ride is a first-rate trip. And several tour companies operate comfortable enough motorcoach trips between the major beach resort of Acapulco and Mexico City, with stops at interesting towns in between.

Getting around each city is relatively easy. There's a major subway in Mexico City, though taxis, as in all cities in this country, can be an inexpensive option. Beware: As with most things in Mexico, the fare should be negotiated in advance, especially if the taxi has no meter.

Climate at a Glance
MAZATLAN

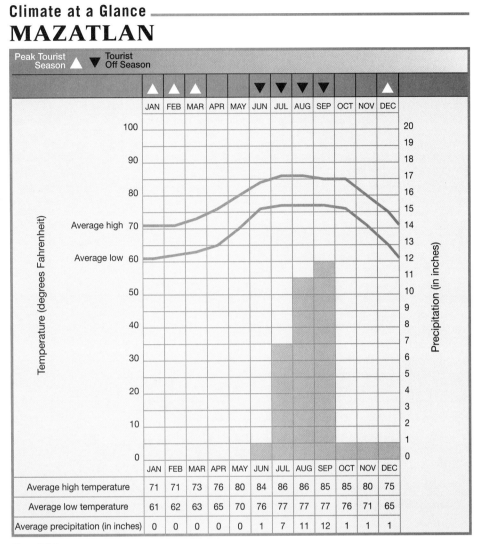

| Peak Tourist Season ▲ | ▼ Tourist Off Season |

	JAN	FEB	MAR	APR	MAY	JUN	JUL	AUG	SEP	OCT	NOV	DEC
Average high temperature	71	71	73	76	80	84	86	86	85	85	80	75
Average low temperature	61	62	63	65	70	76	77	77	77	76	71	65
Average precipitation (in inches)	0	0	0	0	0	1	7	11	12	1	1	1

Figure 10–1

Important Places

Carefully probe travelers' likes and dislikes. This will guide you in tailoring a Mexican vacation to their preferences. Those destinations you're most likely to deal with follow.

The Baja Peninsula

Visitors who intend to travel from San Diego to Tijuana must prepare to encounter a run-down environment as soon as they cross the border. (They should park their cars on the U.S. side and walk or taxi into town.) Why do people visit Tijuana? To bargain at the thousand little shops, to engage in the nightlife, and to say they've been to Mexico—if only for a few hours. In recent times, well-publicized crimes have dampened tourism there. Ensenada, a beach and college "party town" down the coast, is a frequent weekend getaway from southern California, either by car or by three- or four-day cruises out of Los Angeles or San Diego.

The area between Ensenada and the tip of Baja can be an arduous drive. It's better to fly either to Loreto, a quiet resort, or to the Los Cabos area, where tourists can visit and swim in several beautiful coves. The big attractions here are the superb deep-sea fishing

Climate at a Glance
MEXICO CITY

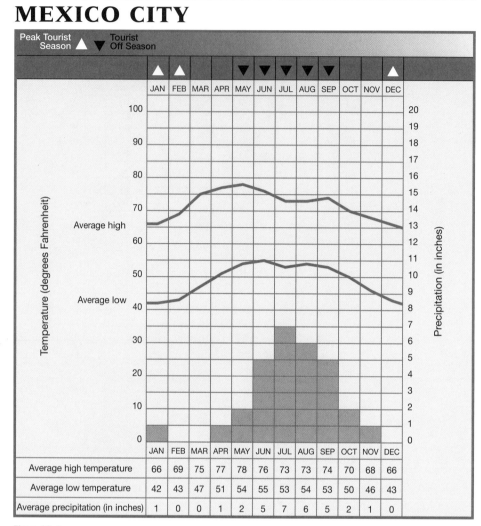

	JAN	FEB	MAR	APR	MAY	JUN	JUL	AUG	SEP	OCT	NOV	DEC
Average high temperature	66	69	75	77	78	76	73	73	74	70	68	66
Average low temperature	42	43	47	51	54	55	53	54	53	50	46	43
Average precipitation (in inches)	1	0	0	1	2	5	7	6	5	2	1	0

Figure 10–2

and the many dramatic resorts that dot the 22-mile "corridor" between San Jose del Cabo and Cabo San Lucas.

The Mexican Riviera

Mexico has an astonishing 6,000 miles of warm, tropical coastline. Most of its famous resorts are along the Pacific coast. From north to south, they are:

- **Mazatlan**. This mid-priced resort has a large harbor that easily accommodates big cruise ships. It's most famous as a fishing paradise, but also offers quite a few nonwater activities, including jungle tours, shopping, an aquarium, rodeos, and well-known Mardi Gras festivities. A ferry crosses daily from Mazatlan to La Paz, on the Baja Peninsula.
- **Puerto Vallarta**. Puerto Vallarta is more active than Mazatlan, with many fine hotels, a market, and superb beaches. Tours into the mountainous interior jungle are popular here, too.

A 12-foot, 988-pound marlin was once caught off Mazatlan.

One of Acapulco's famous cliff divers takes a death-defying plunge
Image copyright Alysta, 2008. Used under license from Shutterstock.com

- **Manzanillo**. The beach is small and the lodging choices limited. So why do people go to Manzanillo? Because **Las Hadas**, one of the world's most elaborate and romantic resort hotels, is located here. Deep-sea fishing is also excellent at Manzanillo.

- **Ixtapa** [is-TAH-pah]. A quieter and more exclusive beach resort than either Mazatlan or Puerto Vallarta, Ixtapa is a destination of great beauty. It offers several very good hotels, some shopping, and a few beaches. Nearby is the picturesque fishing village of **Zihuatanejo** [zee-WAT-ah-nay-ho], which also has lodging.

- **Acapulco**. This is the grand old resort of Mexico; it's been popular for many decades. A wall of large hotels lines Acapulco's many beaches; numerous nightspots, countless restaurants, and several moonlight cruises are available. And of course, there are the famous cliff divers. The city has been spruced up, though beggars and pickpockets still patrol the streets and beaches. If Mexico is a fiesta, Acapulco is its brash featured act.

- **Huatulco** [wah-TOOL-ko]. A government-planned beach resort, Huatulco faces a string of nine secluded bays and 10 miles of beach. Snorkeling is a prime activity.

Las Hadas hotel was made famous by the 1979 movie *10*.

The Yucatan Peninsula

Few destinations combine beaches and history so tantalizingly as the Yucatan Peninsula. Its chief city is Merida, but most travelers never see this bustling inland urban center. They usually arrive directly at Cancun. Among the peninsula's attractions are:

- **Cancun**, a vast government-planned seaside resort, boasting glorious beaches, dozens of first-rate hotels, many lively restaurants and nightspots, a wildlife reserve, and clean prosperity. Cancun is strategically located: By air, it's only a few hours from Dallas and Miami, less than four hours from New York, and about five hours from Los Angeles. The beach area south of Cancun has developed rapidly as well. Centered on the cruise port of Playa del Carmen, it often goes by the name **Costa Maya**.

- **Cozumel Island**, not far off the coast from Costa Maya and Cancun, also offers quite a few resort hotels, though the ambience is a bit more low key. Cozumel has a few small Mayan ruins and is a haven for divers and snorkelers. It's reached by air, ferry, or cruise ship.

- **The archaeological ruins** that dot the Yucatan, often seen on day trips via bus from Cancun. As dramatic as any in the world, they include **Chichen Itza** (with its well-known ball court and ancient observatory), **Uxmal** [oos-MAHL] (with an astonishingly steep pyramid), and **Tulum** (one of the only major ruins in Mexico to overlook the Caribbean Sea). The other ruins that are becoming increasingly popular to visit are Kabah, Sayil, Labna, Coba, and Dzibil Chaltun.

The Copper Canyon

Almost as dramatic as Arizona's Grand Canyon or Hawaii's Waimea, the Copper Canyon stretches through north-central Mexico. A train ride (which should be booked only through well-known tour operators) starts in **Chihuahua**, in the north, and finishes in **Los Mochis**, on the Gulf of California. The multiday Copper Canyon tours take passengers through dramatic scenery and make stops in various villages and towns along the way. Chihuahua is less than an hour's flight south of El Paso, Texas; Los Mochis is across the Gulf of California

On Isla Mujeres (off Cancun), there's a cave where divers can actually pet sharks; the water's natural mineral content makes the fish groggy and therefore unthreatening.

Climbing a pyramid is challenging, but the toughest part is coming *down*.

Trains are the most popular way for tourists to see the Copper Canyon
Photo by William and Marie Rourke

from La Paz and a relatively short flight from Mazatlan. In other words, you can easily combine the Copper Canyon trip with stays at Baja and Mexican Riviera resorts.

The Colonial Region

Mexico was long a Spanish colony and briefly a French one; remnants of this colonial past mark many of Mexico's inland cities, most of which lie on the country's somewhat cooler central plateau. Among its most popular cities:

- **Guadalajara**, a city of lovely flowering parks, graceful European architecture, and one of Latin America's largest zoos.
- **Cuernavaca**, a charming town inhabited by many retired Americans. It has several interesting buildings, including Cortes's Palace. It's an easy day trip from Mexico City.
- **Taxco**, the "Silver City," often visited on a motorcoach trip between Mexico City and Acapulco.
- **Oaxaca** [wah-HAH-kah], the most southerly of the Mexican colonial cities, best known as a center for arts and crafts. It has an impressive church (**Santo Domingo**), a fascinating museum, and several nearby ruins (especially **Monte Alban**).

Mexico City

Only a few sights of Mexico City's colonial past remain; earthquakes, traffic congestion, exploding population, and smog have seen to that. Yet Mexico City has a European-like, cosmopolitan air that's unique in the country. And it does have many famous, first-rate attractions, including:

- **The National Museum of Anthropology**, one of the world's great museums, with its dazzling collection of Olmec, Mayan, and Aztec artifacts.
- **The Zocalo**, a huge town square bordered by the city's dramatic cathedral and governor's palace.
- **The Floating Gardens of Xochimilco** [so-she-MEEL-ko], a charming attraction that visitors boat through. Popular with locals, it's all that's left of the system of canals that crisscrossed Mexico City in ancient times.

Several day trips from Mexico City are popular. The most interesting one takes you to the Toltec Pyramids of **Teotihuacan** [tay-oh-tee-wah-KAHN]—a major archaeological

Each year, on the evening of December 23, Oaxaca celebrates "The Night of the Radishes."

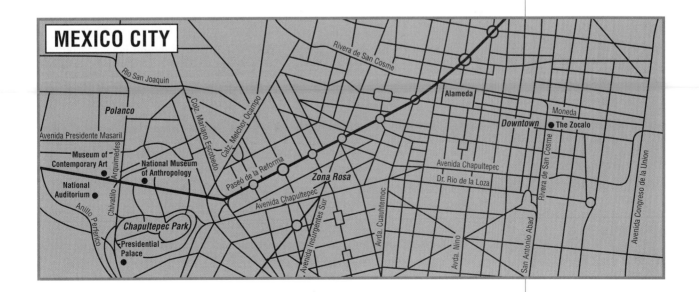

site about an hour away. America's first planned city, it housed 200,000 people in 500 A.D., and covered an area larger than imperial Rome.

The Border Towns

Many tourists envision Mexico through her border towns: Tijuana, Mexicali, Nogales (south of Tucson, Arizona), Ciudad Juarez (across from El Paso, Texas), and Nuevo Laredo (next to Laredo, Texas). Though these dusty, bustling places have their interesting points, they're hardly representative of the rest of Mexico.

Possible Itineraries

Booking a trip to any Mexican destination almost always requires the use of a wholesaler; the package is usually a bargain, and Mexican hotels are more likely to honor a reservation made through a large tour company. The itinerary, therefore, will probably be shaped by a prearranged tour package. Mexico City, the Copper Canyon, or the inland colonial cities are almost always combined with a single beach resort in a four- to nine-day itinerary. You can also package together two beach resorts, though it would be good to set up a contrast, say, Acapulco with Ixtapa or Cabo San Lucas. People who prefer to stay at one place can book at a resort for anywhere from a weekend to a week. One-week packages to beach resorts are very popular; many are all-inclusive.

Lodging Options

Oaxaca's Camino Real hotel is a converted convent.

Lodging in Mexico ranges from superdeluxe properties to budget hotels. To ensure clean, satisfying lodging, favor first-class and deluxe hotels whenever possible. Mexico's mid-priced chains include **Calinda, Fiesta Inn**, and **Real**. Upscale chains include **El Presidente, Krystal, Camino Real, Fiesta Americana**, and **Melia**, along with many prominent U.S. and Canadian hotel groups. Such hotels as **Las Hadas** (Manzanillo) and **Las Brisas** or **Princess** hotels (Acapulco) are world famous. Remember: Modified American Plans (MAPs), where breakfast and one other meal are included in the room rate each day, are typical in Mexican hotels during high season.

Three other lodging options are open to travelers. Club Med has all-inclusive properties in many Mexican beach cities. Cruise ships offer lodging that moves from one resort port to another. And condos, timeshares, and private homes are a useful option for some.

Allied Destinations

Mexico's east coast resorts combine readily with vacations in the Caribbean, Texas, Louisiana, and Florida. Central and west coast destinations often precede or follow stays in California, Arizona, New Mexico, and Texas. Mexico can also be a stop-off point for journeys into Central and South America.

Cultural Patterns

Though it borders the United States, Mexico presents unique cultural experiences:

- The custom of *manana* (putting off a task until tomorrow) persists. Don't confuse this with laziness. Time is perceived differently here; the pace is slower, more relaxed.

- A popular time to do business is during a long lunch. Business is commonly brought up after an extended period of socializing.

- If a traveler visits the home of a local, it's customary to bring a small gift.

- Mexicans give starting times for parties that are rarely observed. If a party is to start at 7 P.M., few will arrive before 8:30 P.M. This is especially true at beach resort cities.

This pyramid at Chichen Itza is one of the best-preserved structures from the ancient Mayan world
Image copyright Hannamariah, 2008. Used under license from Shutterstock.com

- Almost anything is negotiable in Mexico, especially souvenir purchases. Don't be intimidated; what may seem like impatience, anger, or obstinacy in the seller is simply part of the "game." Counter with a price that's 50 percent of the original quote and work from there.

Factors That Motivate Visitors

A wide spectrum of reasons motivates a traveler to visit Mexico:

- The beaches are, in most places, glorious.
- All manner of water-sport options are available.
- Mexico is a shopping and lodging bargain, especially off-season.
- Archaeological treasures are everywhere. (In fact, one estimate claims that the jungle still covers 90 percent of all ancient Mayan and Aztec sites.)
- Air and cruise transportation into and around Mexico is convenient, plentiful, and relatively inexpensive.
- Superdeluxe resorts in Mexico are a bargain compared to similar properties in other parts of the world, especially in the summer off-season.
- The foreign, exotic culture of Mexico is less than a six-hour flight away from most U.S. locations.
- The winter weather is warm, dry, and inviting.

Possible Misgivings

Mexico elicits both positive and negative reactions in potential visitors. Among the objections you may hear are:

- "I'll get sick." For possible intestinal problems—"Montezuma's Revenge" is genuine—travelers should consult their doctor about medication to take along. (Several over-the-counter remedies are highly effective.) And of course, they should avoid drinking

The Aztec emperor Montezuma reputedly drank 50 cups of chocolate a day.

Qualifying the Traveler
Cancun

For People Who Want	Appeal			Remarks
	High	Medium	Low	
Historical and Cultural Attractions	▲			Ruins are nearby
Beaches and Water Sports	▲			Warm, clear water
Skiing Opportunities			▲	None
Lots of Nightlife	▲			In hotels
Family Activities		▲		
Familiar Cultural Experience		▲		
Exotic Cultural Experience	▲			
Safety and Low Crime	▲			One of the safest Mexican destinations
Bargain Travel		▲		Expensive for Mexico
Impressive Scenery		▲		Primarily seascapes
Peace and Quiet		▲		Active, but not overwhelmingly so
Shopping Opportunities		▲		Crafts markets
Adventure		▲		
To Do Business			▲	Low in Cancun (but high elsewhere in Mexico)

the water. Even brushing teeth with tap water or having ice cubes in a drink may cause problems. Coffee, tea, canned soft drinks, and bottled wine or beer are generally safe. Instruct travelers never to eat uncooked meats, fish, or vegetables and to eat only fruit that they peeled themselves.

■ "I don't speak Spanish." Many people in major cities and at tourist facilities speak English.

■ "Poverty is a problem in Mexico." Poverty and its symptoms—crime, corruption, street begging, and unsanitary conditions—do plague many Mexican cities. Suggest Cancun, which is largely free of such problems. Self-contained mega-resorts such as the Acapulco Princess or Club Meds also can insulate tourists from most of the poverty.

■ "The food disagrees with me." Mexican food has great diversity. Familiar American-style food is available in many places. Nonspicy food is usually available in many locations, especially in the Yucatan.

■ "The only time I can afford a Mexican vacation is when it's hot and rainy." Late spring or early autumn is a good compromise: Rain isn't as frequent, the weather may not yet be very hot, and low- or shoulder-season rates may still be in effect.

Sales Strategies

Cruises, all-inclusive resorts, Copper Canyon packages, and high-season hotel MAPs maximize the potential profit from a Mexican vacation. Independent and escorted tours also offer efficient ways to profit from as many components as possible. Diving, fishing, or day-trip excursions can be booked in advance. Because most people are somewhat leery of budget or even moderate-class hotels in Mexico, the possibility to sell them superior or luxury accommodations is strong.

Travel Trivia

Places with Unlikely Names

- Yucatan, Mexico—the response that natives gave to Spanish explorers who landed here; it means, "I don't understand you."

- Singapore—means "city of the lion," even though there have never been any lions here.

- Cape of Good Hope—near the southern tip of Africa, with intensely rough seas.

- Greenland—one of the coldest, snowiest places on earth.

- Iceland—much less icy (and greener) than Greenland.

- Nome, Alaska—miscopied from a map that indicated "Name?" at this spot.

- The Pacific—called this by Magellan, who crossed at a time of no storms; of course, it has many dramatic ones.

- The West Indies—Columbus called the Caribbean islands this name because he thought he had reached the islands off the coast of India.

NAME _____ **DATE** _____

MAP ACTIVITY

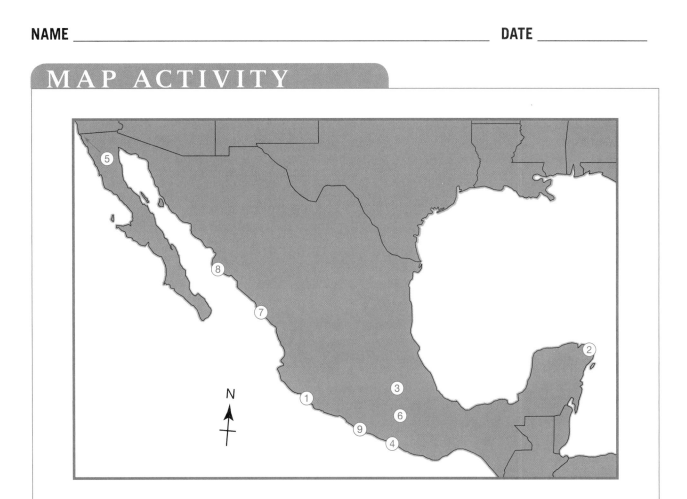

A traveler wants to visit the places listed below. Which number represents each on the map?

Place/Attraction	In Which City	Number on Map
A. A major Yucatan resort	A. _____	A. _____
B. City closest to San Diego	B. _____	B. _____
C. Resort near Zihuatanejo	C. _____	C. _____
D. The "Silver City"	D. _____	D. _____
E. A ferry crosses from La Paz to . . .	E. _____	E. _____
F. The Copper Canyon train ride begins in Chihuahua and ends in . . .	F. _____	F. _____
G. The Zocalo	G. _____	G. _____
H. Las Hadas Hotel	H. _____	H. _____
I. Cliff divers	I. _____	I. _____
J. Taxco is on the road between Mexico City and . . .	J. _____	J. _____

NAME _____   DATE _____

CASE STUDY

Ray and Connie Hernandez are a young couple in their late 20s. Ray is a successful electrician and Connie is a paramedic. Connie has just read a book, *Heritage of the Maya*, which has prompted her to consider spending an eight-day vacation at a Mexican destination. Ray wants mostly to relax: to enjoy some sun, perhaps do some snorkeling, eat well, and enjoy at least a little night entertainment.

Circle the answer that best suits their needs.

1 Which of the following hotels would be the poorest choice for them?

Las Hadas   The Calinda in Cuernavaca

The Acapulco Princess   The Fiesta Americana in Cancun

Why?

2 Which of the following would be the best destination for them to explore the Mayan heritage?

Cancun   Acapulco

Manzanillo   Los Cabos

Why?

3 Which would probably *not* be something they should consider?

A Club Med vacation   A day trip to Chichen Itza

A cruise   A stay in Mexico City

Why?

4 Rain would definitely dampen things for the Hernandez couple. What month would be the best recommendation?

September   April

February   June

Why?

NAME _____ **DATE** _____

CREATIVE ACTIVITY

Mexico has decided to release a series of 10 commemorative stamps that portray tourist-related places, landmarks, and activities for which the country is famous. If you were hired as a consultant, what 10 things would you recommend be put on the stamps? Use the Internet to find photos of your suggestions, with URLs. Be prepared to say why.

1

2

3

4

5

6

7

8

9

10

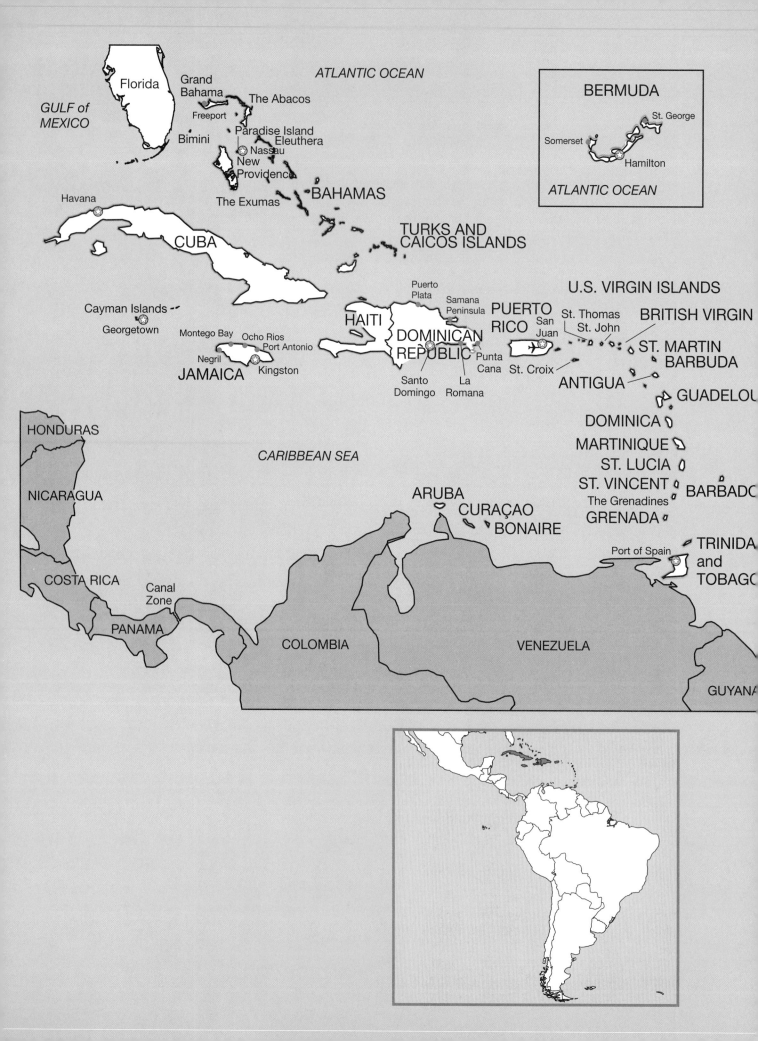

Chapter 11

The Caribbean
A Sea of Nations

Let's face it, Caribbean geography is complicated.
Hundreds of islands arc across this vast tropical region. Remembering which is where isn't easy. Furthermore, each island may have its own government, culture, value level, range of services and accommodations, topography, and language. To match a Caribbean destination to a traveler's needs takes great skill and knowledge. In this chapter we sort out and organize information about the Caribbean so that you'll feel far more confident about your understanding of the area and your ability to sell it.

A good way to start is to divide the Caribbean into six destination groupings. The first two, **Bermuda** and **the Bahamas**, aren't even part of the Caribbean, though many think of them as such. Bermuda is way off in the Atlantic, at about the same latitude as Charleston, South Carolina, and the Bahamas is a string of 700 islands that stretches southeastward from Florida into the Atlantic (and not into the central Caribbean Sea, which is farther south). Geographers label the third cluster the Greater Antilles ("greater" because most of the islands are large). Just south and southeast of Florida, they are, from left to right on the map, **Cuba**; the **Cayman Islands**; **Jamaica**; **Haiti** and the **Dominican Republic** (which together make up one island, Hispaniola); and **Puerto Rico**.

The fourth set of islands forms a crescent on the Caribbean's eastern side, starting near Puerto Rico and curving gently southward toward the shores of Venezuela. Because of their comparatively small size, they're called the Lesser Antilles. Trying to memorize them all would be quite a chore, so we concentrate on the most popular ones. They are, from north to south: **the Virgin Islands**, **St. Martin**, **Antigua**, **Guadeloupe**, **Martinique**, **Barbados**, and **Trinidad and Tobago** [tuh-BAY-go].

The fifth cluster of destinations is just northwest of Caracas, Venezuela: **Aruba**, **Bonaire**, and **Curacao**, often called the ABC Islands because of their first letters. The Caribbean destinations forming the sixth group aren't islands at all; they're the mainland cities that encircle the Caribbean, especially those of Mexico, Colombia, Venezuela, Belize, Honduras, and Costa Rica. These latter destinations we treat under their respective countries' chapters.

Two historical notes: The Caribbean islands were once called the West Indies, since early explorers thought that they had arrived in India. And the origin of the word Antilles is shrouded in mystery, though it's certainly French and probably means "land near the continent."

How Travelers Get There

Visitors reach the Caribbean islands through major U.S. and Caribbean airlines, several small commuter airlines companies (most out of Florida), chartered boats, and cruise ships. Cruise vessels have become the principal means of visiting the islands. They usually stop at

Almost half of all people who take a cruise each year do so in the Caribbean.

Set aside some local money for the airport departure taxes that are common at Caribbean airports.

several major ports and perhaps a few obscure, out-of-the-way ones. Four cruise patterns predominate: Short three- or four-day cruises into the Bahamas, almost always out of Florida; seven-day Eastern Caribbean or Western Caribbean sailings, again usually out of Florida; and seven-day Southern Caribbean cruises, mostly out of Puerto Rico. Longer itineraries also exist, and Caribbean cruises are often the final (or initial) leg of a trans-Canal cruise. Bermuda sailings are in a separate category: Usually seven days long, they generally depart from and return to New York City or Boston.

Most flights to the Caribbean are from Miami, though other mainland cities may serve as a point of departure (especially to San Juan, Puerto Rico). Travelers flying to the Caribbean should limit their trip to only a few islands (perhaps all serviced by the same airline). Otherwise, the airfares may turn out to be very high; inter-island flights can be quite expensive, especially when using more than one carrier or small local planes. A cruise is the best bet for tourists who want to visit multiple islands.

Weather Patterns

At one point the Caribbean is almost 5 miles deep.

The Caribbean is a year-round destination. Winters are pleasant and dry, though Bermuda gets chilly and the southernmost islands (such as Trinidad and the ABC Islands) can still remain uncomfortably warm (see Figure 11–1 for an example). High tourist season extends

Climate at a Glance
KINGSTON, JAMAICA

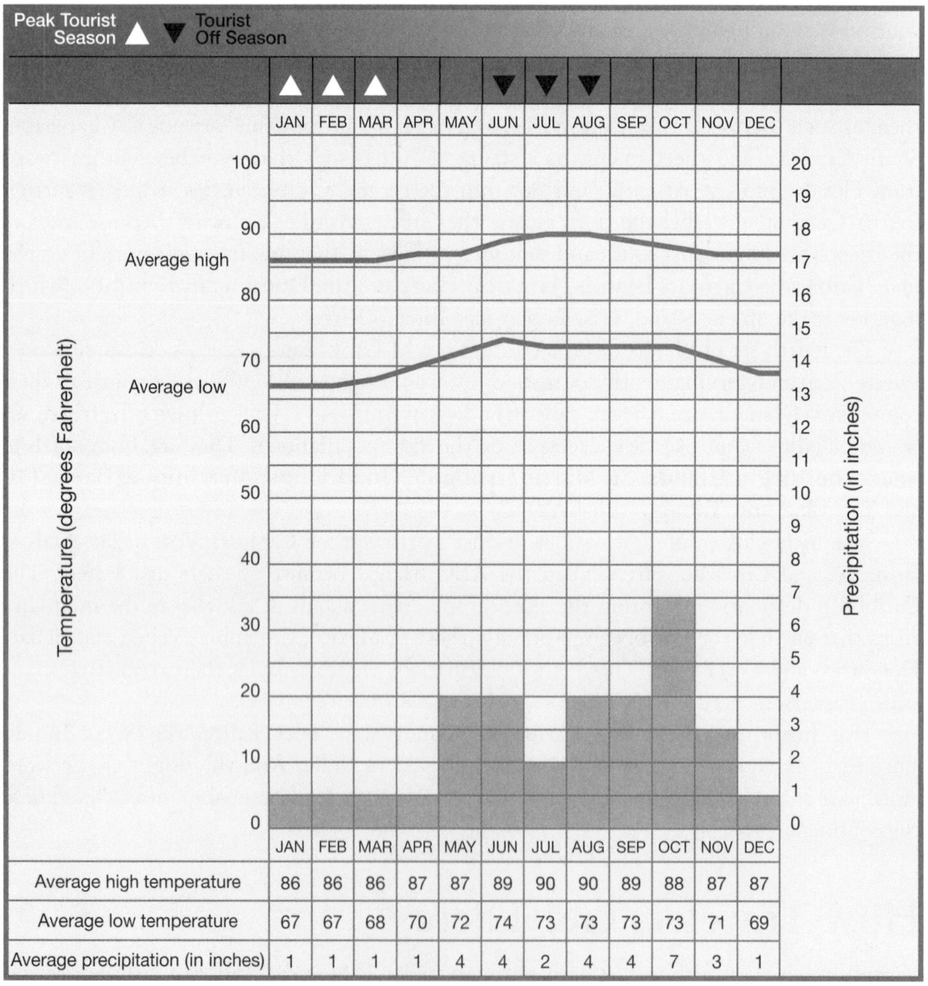

	JAN	FEB	MAR	APR	MAY	JUN	JUL	AUG	SEP	OCT	NOV	DEC
Average high temperature	86	86	86	87	87	89	90	90	89	88	87	87
Average low temperature	67	67	68	70	72	74	73	73	73	73	71	69
Average precipitation (in inches)	1	1	1	1	4	4	2	4	4	7	3	1

Figure 11–1

from just before Christmas to around April, except for Bermuda, which attracts more people in the summer. Summers can be quite hot and humid almost everywhere in the Caribbean (and even in more northerly Bermuda), with fierce hurricanes tearing through the area mainly from July through September. For this reason, summer and fall are considered off-seasons, with hotel rates dropping as much as 60 percent. (Again, it's just the opposite for Bermuda.)

Trade winds are important to the Caribbean's climate. They generally blow, as in all tropical regions, from east to west, bringing some relief even on the hottest days. The winds along the southernmost islands (e.g., the ABCs) are especially strong. Those islands with mountains (just about all of them except Bermuda, the Bahamas, the Caymans, and the ABC Islands, which are of coral, not volcanic origin—and are therefore flat) tend to be drier on their western and, in some cases, northern shores.

Getting Around

The means of transportation on each island are quite informal: mopeds, jeeps, buses, and car rentals. Off several islands, glass-bottom boats and even mini-submarines take tourists to view the underwater life. When reserving a car rental, remember to check whether the island is one of the many where traffic flows on the left, not the right; some people who normally drive on a trip won't if the driving is on the left. (If the island has a British heritage, it probably has left-side driving.) Remember, too, that tourists aren't allowed to rent cars in Bermuda; it's a way to control traffic.

Charter yachts are a popular way to get around the islands. The yacht-chartering capital of the Caribbean is the U.S. Virgin Islands, though some visitors charter vessels out of other islands or Florida. Generally, there are two options: a crewed charter, on which the yachting company provides all staff to operate the boat; and a bareboat charter, on which the renters actually do the sailing.

A few things to remember: First, Caribbean destinations aren't exactly into time and efficiency management. Their relaxed way of doing things can lead to lost reservations, especially for car rentals. The renter should have the confirmation number (and maybe even a printout of the confirmation, if possible). Second, taxis are very expensive on certain islands; visitors should determine the approximate price before getting in. Third, mopeds are a great way of getting around, but beware: People who aren't used to them frequently get into accidents.

Important Places

Here's a thumbnail sketch of each major Caribbean and Caribbean-related island destination. There's also a section on some of the minor destinations.

Bermuda

Even though Bermuda isn't part of the Caribbean, it does share much with its southerly neighbors: fine beaches and resort hotels, gorgeous weather and the like. What makes Bermuda special, though, is how it differs from Caribbean destinations: its mixture of temperate and tropical climates (including all manner of vegetation), the surprising combination of formal and informal elements, the neat little houses with white coral roofs, and the pink-sand beaches and azure waters that look straight out of a campy 1950s painting.

Remember three things about Bermuda: The hotels are expensive (though less so in the winter); both the air and water are chilly in the winter, when the only bargains can be had; and most visitors get around in taxis or on mopeds because rental cars aren't allowed.

The capital of this English-speaking country is **Hamilton**. **St. George** and **Somerset** are historical, often-visited towns. The island is dotted with several modest attractions, including a limestone cave, lighthouses, and several churches. A politically stable and safe island, Bermuda is ideal for those who want a little formality and culture to go along with their beach vacation. It's also a popular honeymoon, incentive, and convention destination.

St. Croix is very popular with bicyclists.

The coral roofs of Bermuda's houses help capture rainwater for home use.

Bermuda's 362-foot tall Gibb's Hill Lighthouse is made entirely of cast iron.

The Bahamas

Only 50 miles off Florida's southeast coast, the Bahamas are perfect for those who don't want to travel far from the mainland for their tropical vacation or who are first-time visitors to the area. Though the Bahamian chain is composed of hundreds of islands, only 22 are inhabited and even fewer attract tourists. The most popular Bahamian destinations are:

- **Nassau**, on the island of **New Providence**. This port city offers many opportunities to visit historical places, gamble, and shop (especially in and around its **Straw Market**). **Cable Beach**, 10 minutes from Nassau, is a major beach development with several large resort hotels.

- **Paradise Island**, a complex of resort and gambling facilities, reached by ferry, taxi, or on foot from Nassau. Paradise Island is sometimes called the Bahamian Riviera. The **Atlantis** megaresort is an attraction in its own right.

- **Freeport**, on the quiet island of Grand Bahama, another shopping treat. Freeport has no beaches, so to get some sun, tourists have to travel about 5 miles to **Lucaya Beach** and its world-class golf course.

- **Bimini** [BIM-uh-nee], made famous by author Ernest Hemingway and a legendary place for fishing.

- **The Out Islands**, also called the **Family Islands**, lining the eastern Atlantic edge of the Bahamas. These relaxed and scenic islands are havens for yachting, sports-fishing, and diving enthusiasts. The principal ones are **Eleuthera**, the **Abacos**, and the **Exumas**. A few of the smaller islands have been converted into "private" islands, where cruise ships anchor for the day.

The Cayman Islands

Another legendary place (especially for divers and snorkelers) is the Cayman Islands. It's a great destination, with some quaint (but expensive) restaurants and shops, dozens of water-sport opportunities, but virtually no scenery. (The Caymans are, in fact, large, flat coral reefs.) **Grand Cayman Island** and the capital, **Georgetown**, offer the most conventional diversions, including a **Maritime and Treasure Museum** that displays artifacts taken from the 325 shipwrecks that surround the island. Other Grand Cayman attractions: a **Turtle Farm** and **Stingray City**, where divers can swim with the ominous-looking yet

Paradise Island's original name was Hog Island.

At Nassau's Ardastra Gardens, you can see the world's only performing flamingos.

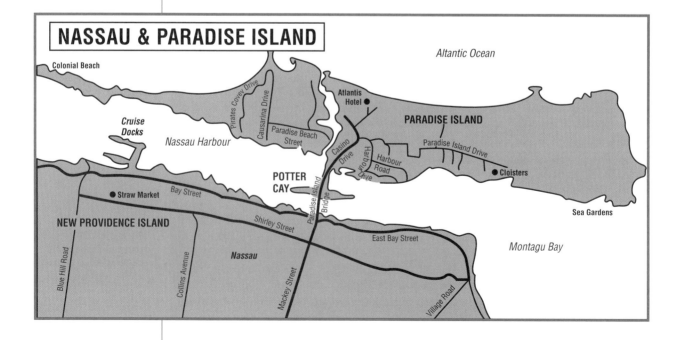

gentle creatures. North of Georgetown is **Seven Mile Beach**, where most resort hotels are located. **Cayman Brac** and especially **Little Cayman** are small, tranquil islands that draw snorkelers, divers, and fishing enthusiasts in droves.

Jamaica

Jamaica, a large island of wide terrain variations that's due south of Cuba, certainly has a high recognition factor, which can be both good and bad. Its reggae music, jungle water-falls, many golf courses, and sweeping beaches have made it a major Caribbean destination. But it also has many social problems. Here's information that will help clarify the picture:

- **Negril** has become Jamaica's favorite beach. Once a hangout for counterculture types, it has become much more respectable and upscale.

- **Montego Bay** is a major cruise port and air gateway. Shopping and nightlife are good, the **Rose Hall** tour is fascinating, but the beaches are so-so. Lodging here should serve as a base for excursions to the rest of the island, including to the **Blue Mountains** and to **Kingston**, the capital city. (Most travelers who fly into Kingston are visiting friends and relatives or are there on business.)

- **Ocho Rios** is another cruise port, with pleasant beaches, several outstanding hotels, and a dramatic mountain backdrop. Nearby is **Dunn's River Falls**, Jamaica's most famous attraction. Here, a river cascades down a series of stone steps that visitors can climb, usu-ally as part of a hand-holding "chain" of people.

- **Port Antonio**, a great beach area, has several minor attractions. Visitors can get to Port Antonio from Kingston by car (a two-hour drive), hotel shuttle bus, or air.

Two hotel hints: Jamaican lodging taxes are very high. Many major all-inclusive resorts are here, including **SuperClubs** and several **Sandals** (for couples only) resorts.

The Dominican Republic

Occupying the eastern two-thirds of the large island of Hispaniola is the Dominican Re-public (also known as D.R.), a nation with a rich diversity of natural environments. The big draws here are the many golf courses, bargain prices, great beaches, casinos, and historical sites. **Santo Domingo** (the nation's capital, with a restored colonial district), **La Romana** (its **Casa de Campo** resort was designed by Oscar de la Renta), the **Samana Peninsula**, and **Puerto Plata** (home to **Fort San Felipe**) are ports on some western Caribbean cruise itineraries. **Punta Cana** is a beach destination with several large resorts. Visitors who fly there will have plenty of accommodations to choose from: The Dominican Republic has the greatest number of hotel rooms in the Caribbean.

Puerto Rico

Puerto Rico is relatively inexpensive, accommodations are first-rate, many Americans trace their roots to its soil, and, because it's American, there's no need to deal with immigration and customs. This island is noted for its dining, nightlife, casinos, historical sites, good beaches, and Spanish heritage.

Two lodging options exist: to stay in bustling and historic San Juan, or at the resort beach complexes of **Palmas del Mar**, **Dorado**, or **Cerromar**. The most popular sightsee-ing attraction is **El Yunque** [YOON-kay], a 28,000-acre rainforest. (It's a bit less impres-sive in the dry summer.) Nearby is **Luquillo Beach**, probably Puerto Rico's loveliest. **Old San Juan**'s historic ambience is worth experiencing, too, as is its adjoining **El Morro** fort.

The Virgin Islands

One thing to know right away: There are *two* sets of Virgin Islands. The **British Virgin Islands**, sleepy little destinations, appeal primarily to yachters and divers, or to

Jamaica was the birthplace of reggae (and of singer Bob Marley).

Amber jewelry is a specialty in the Dominican Republic.

The world's largest radio telescope (seen in movies such as *Contact* and *Goldeneye*) can be visited at Arecibo, Puerto Rico.

The Sir Francis Drake Channel, within the British Virgin Islands, offers fantastic sailing.

Nelson's Dockyard in Antigua served as the hub of British naval activity in the Caribbean
Image copyright Thomas Crosley, 2008. Used under license from Shutterstock.com

beach-loving vacationers who are seeking to really get away from it all. Two of its better-known islands are **Tortola** (a haven for yachters) and **Virgin Gorda**, which feature one of the Caribbean's most remarkable attractions, a pile of seaside boulders called **The Baths**.

The **U.S. Virgin Islands** are just west of their British counterparts. Sailing, fishing, and diving are also major attractions here, but these islands are livelier than the British islands. The U.S. Virgin Islands are relatively clean and prosperous. They can be accessed by boat from the British Virgin Islands or San Juan. Like Puerto Rico, Americans do not need passports to visit the U.S. Virgin Islands.

Three principal islands make up the U.S. Virgin Islands. Each has its own character and can be used as a lodging base:

- **St. Thomas** is where most visitors to the U.S. Virgin Islands stay. It's the busiest and most developed of the three, with the city of **Charlotte Amalie** [ah-MALL-yah] providing most of the tourist attractions and extensive duty-free shopping. St. Thomas is a convenient port for many cruise ships.

- **St. Croix** [CROY] is quieter than St. Thomas, though it harbors several minor but appealing points of interest. It's also a cruise port.

- **St. John** is the least developed of all. Its campgrounds (in a U.S. national park) are highly popular. St. John has the most dramatic scenery, with dense rain forests, sharp reefs, and extinct volcanoes. Ferries run between St. Thomas and St. John.

St. Martin/Sint Maarten

St. Martin is perhaps the most unusual and satisfying of the Caribbean islands. Both France and the Netherlands govern it. The northern portion is French and the southern portion (where it's spelled *Sint Maarten*) is Dutch, but the island's informality leads to relaxed co-government over the entire island. The south is more commercialized, while the north is more relaxed, upscale, and scenic. There's a little sightseeing to do in St. Martin's two principal towns, **Philipsburg** (Dutch) and **Marigot** (French). But mostly it's the food, shopping, nightlife, and sun that occupy visitors.

Charlotte Amalie was the name of a Danish queen.

The town of Grand Case features some of the finest restaurants in the Caribbean.

Vacationers can also get away by plane or boat to one of the several attractive (but quiet) nearby islands:

- **St. Kitts** is a lush, flowery place with rustic plantations and a relaxed lifestyle. Two miles away is the island of **Nevis**, which has the same atmosphere and feel of St. Kitts.
- **St. Barts** has fine beaches, gourmet restaurants, rolling hills, and pricey lodging.
- **St. Eustatius**, also called Statia, has several historical points of interest and some good snorkeling areas.
- **Saba** boasts a picturesque blend of seascapes and cottage-dotted hills.
- **Anguilla** [an-GWILL-ah] is a favorite of many upscale Caribbean visitors for its fabulous beaches, excellent restaurants, and quiet lifestyle.

Antigua

Usually pronounced "an-TEE-gah," not "an-TEE-gwah," this major cruise destination claims that it has a beach for every day of the year: 365. Antigua is well developed for its size, with many good hotels and casinos, and one unique historic attraction: **Nelson's Dockyard** at **English Harbour**. In the eighteenth century, Antigua was homeport to the British Caribbean naval fleet; Admiral Lord Nelson commanded it from English Harbour, which has been energetically restored by the Antiguans. Another attraction is sparsely settled **Barbuda**, a coral island 30 miles north of Antigua that boasts pink sand beaches reminiscent of those on Bermuda. Those who like sailing, diving, and get-away-from-it-all beaches may like a stay on Antigua. Many tourists visit it as part of a cruise itinerary.

Guadeloupe and Martinique

Both of these islands have much in common: French culture, volcanoes, dramatic deep green scenery, and so-so beaches. For those who want French ambience to go along with their water activities, both islands will be intriguing.

The largest cities, Pointe-a-Pitre (Guadeloupe) and Fort-de-France (Martinique), are not where most visitors stay. They're hectic and a bit rundown. Major resort hotels aren't far away, though, and the all-inclusives are an excellent option, especially because lodging and food can be quite expensive in the French West Indies. An island in this area for those who want a quieter tone: lush **Dominica** [doh-mih-NEE-kah], with waterfalls, mountains, and a boiling lake.

The only remaining Carib Indians live on the island of Dominica.

St. Lucia

Picturesque **St. Lucia** [LOO-shah] has excellent beaches and a well-known sight: the twin mountain peaks of the **Pitons**. Tourists can also visit an active volcano, mineral baths, plantations, a rain forest, and forts. The island is popular with honeymooners, hikers, bikers, bird-watchers, golfers, and water-sport enthusiasts. **Castries** is the capital and main cruise port.

Barbados

Most of the Caribbean islands have been tourist destinations for only a few decades. Not so Barbados. This most easterly of the Antilles has been attracting tourists for centuries. So it's not surprising that Barbados offers many small but fascinating historical attractions (including several plantations), as well as the usual great beaches, water-sport opportunities, golf courses, and an underground wonder, **Harrison's Cave**.

Most people stay on the island's warm west Platinum Coast shore; the east can be windy and rainy. Who will most like Barbados? Those who want the calm, prosperous ambience of a very British, surprisingly formal island. Indeed, Barbados is quite reminiscent of Bermuda, but on a smaller scale.

Barbados is the Portuguese word for "bearded ones." (The island's fig trees have a beard-like appearance.)

Two of the most famous natural formations in the Caribbean: St. Lucia's Piton mountains
Image copyright James Beach, 2008. Used under license from Shutterstock.com

Trinidad and Tobago

Mention these islands and you're sure to elicit visions of steel drum bands, calypso music, and limbo competitions. Among the Caribbean islands, Trinidad is one of the liveliest and most prosperous, with a broad selection of international cuisine, entertainment, and shopping. Nearby Tobago, on the other hand, is a quiet, fantasy-like desert island, accessed by ferry or flight.

The principal city, **Port of Spain**, is filled with architectural surprises. The rest of Trinidad is best explored by car rental. Most of Trinidad's hotels are up in the hills, rather than on the island's only adequate beaches. Most of the upscale lodging is on Tobago.

The ABC Islands

Just north of Venezuela are Aruba, Bonaire, and Curacao [koor-ah-SOW], the ABC Islands. Two things about these tidy little islands are surprising: They're very dry and desertlike, rather than lush; and they combine Dutch and Hispanic influences in a most unusual cultural blend. Aruba is best known for its fine beaches and casino-resort hotels, Bonaire for its superb dining and diving, and Curacao for its fine dining, extensive shopping, and **Hato Caves**. Curacao's beaches are only so-so.

Lodging choices are very good in Aruba and Curacao, but limited in Bonaire. There are casinos on all three; the ABCs are quite popular among gamblers. They're also a great choice for those concerned about a hurricane ruining their trip. Hurricanes rarely cross these islands. Many flights connect the mainland to Aruba; fewer are available to Curacao and Bonaire. Inter-island flights and ferries are also available.

Miscellaneous Islands

Here's a list of some of the less visited islands in the Caribbean:

■ **Haiti**, on the western side of Hispaniola, is poorer and politically more unstable than its neighbor, the Dominican Republic. Its blend of French and African cultures, though,

Trinidad and Venezuela to the south are involved in oil exporting. This is where steel drums originated.

The Portuguese gave Curacao its name because sailors were *cured of* scurvy there.

is intriguing. Haiti has become the folk-art capital of the Caribbean. Attending voodoo ceremonies is becoming a common tourist activity.

- **Grenada** [grah-NAY-dah] (not to be confused with Granada, a city in Spain) is a sleepy little island with excellent beaches and a wide variety of water-sport activities. It's just north of Trinidad and Tobago, in the southern portion of the Lesser Antilles. Its nickname: The Spice Island.

- **St. Vincent and the Grenadines** are a collection of more than 100 islands, 100 miles west of Barbados. These casually formal destinations have great beaches, snorkeling, yachting, and a broad variety of volcanic landscapes.

- **The Turks and Caicos Islands** are, geographically, a southeasterly extension of the Bahamas (but under a different government). They have some of the same features of the Bahamas, but without the crowds. They're ideal for those who seek an isolated getaway or superb diving and yachting opportunities. The island of **Providenciales** (nicknamed Provo) is the most developed.

Possible Itineraries

Because many people visit the Caribbean as part of a cruise, their itineraries will be predetermined. Other travelers might like to combine a stay on one island with a side excursion to another island. Remember, though, that air or sea connections between islands aren't always convenient. Concentrate on islands that are easily combinable yet contrasting: St. Martin with, say, Anguilla; Barbados with St. Vincent; or Antigua with Barbuda. Keep in mind that Caribbean cruises don't only visit islands, but also mainland ports, especially in Central America. They also may visit ports that border the Gulf of Mexico, rather than the Caribbean. Also remember that the Caribbean isn't just about sightseeing. It's very much about *doing* things, too, like diving, playing golf, riding in a mini-submarine, hiking, kayaking, sailing, and biking.

In the Turks and Caicos Islands, there are giant frogs called "mountain chickens."

Most experts believe Columbus first landed in the New World at San Salvador Island in the Bahamas.

Among the attractions at the Atlantis Paradise Island are a water park and a marine habitat
Photo by Marc Mancini

Lodging Options

A few things to remember: First, good rooms are hard to get during high season; for last-minute types, a cruise is often the best option (if space is still available). Second, booking the highest affordable classification possible is usually best; budget lodging in most of the Caribbean is dicey. Third, more all-inclusive properties are located in the Caribbean than anywhere else in the world. The quality is relatively dependable, the activities endless, the beaches good, and the price (especially on some of the islands where food is costly) a bargain. Virtually every Caribbean island has at least one all-inclusive resort.

Most international hotel chains also have presences here. The two best-known lodging groups are Sandals and SuperClubs. (SuperClubs has three main "brands": Breezes, Grand Lido, and Hedonism.) The Atlantis megaresort, on Paradise Island, Bahamas, is the largest hotel in the Caribbean area.

Pusser's is a world-famous bar at Virgin Gorda.

Allied Destinations

The Caribbean islands are a natural extension of a visit to Miami, New Orleans, Houston, Mexico, or South America. Disney Cruise Lines offers cruises combined with a stay at a Walt Disney World property—ideal for families wishing to cruise the region. And of course, the islands are natural allied destinations for one another, as long as the air or sea connections are convenient.

Cultural Patterns

The relaxed pace of the islands is renowned. This will present an especially unusual environment for business travelers.

The branches of divi-divi trees (on the ABC Islands) grow horizontally because of the strong winds.

- Though informality marks most of the Caribbean, some of the islands have a reputation for showing a genteel, conservative side as well. For example, visitors shouldn't wear clothes that are too casual wherever they go; a few restaurants and nightspots may even require a jacket and tie for men and dresses or skirts for women.
- Those interested in experiencing the local lifestyle closely, perhaps even staying with a family, might consider either the **People-to-People** program in the Bahamas or the **Meet the People** program in Jamaica.
- A number of colorful festivals occur throughout the year in the Caribbean. The three most famous: the Bahamian **Junkanoo** (a Mardi Gras–like celebration on December 26 and January 1, but often beyond that), Trinidad's **Carnival** (just before Ash Wednesday), and Jamaica's **Reggae Sunsplash** (a music festival in August).

Factors That Motivate Visitors

Why do people visit the Caribbean? Here are some reasons:

For hikers, Guadeloupe offers the most extensive and well-maintained trails in the Caribbean.

- A tropical island stay beguiles almost anyone.
- The region features a wide variety of cultural experiences.
- No area in the world has more cruise options.
- The diving, fishing, and yachting possibilities are virtually endless.
- Many all-inclusive resorts dot the islands, as do several superdeluxe hotels.
- The weather is almost always warm.
- Several of the islands offer a great deal of nightlife and gambling opportunities.
- Shopping and lodging bargains are possible, especially in the off-season.

Qualifying the Traveler
The Caribbean

For People Who Want	Antigua	ABC Islands	Bahamas	Barbados	Bermuda	British Virgin Islands	Cayman Islands	Dominican Republic	Guadeloupe	Haiti	Jamaica	Martinique	Puerto Rico	St. Lucia	St. Martin	Trinidad	U.S. Virgin Islands
Cultural Attractions	▲	▲	▲	▲	◉	▲		◉	▲	◉	◉	▲	◉		▲	◉	
Lots of Nightlife		▲	◉		◉			▲			◉	◉	◉			◉	▲
Familiar Cultural Experience			▲				▲						▲				◉
Safety and Low Crime	▲	▲	▲	◉	◉	▲	▲								▲		▲
Impressive Scenery	▲			▲	◉	▲		▲	◉		◉	▲	▲	◉	▲		▲
Peace and Quiet	▲	▲	▲	▲		◉	▲		▲					▲	▲		▲
Shopping Opportunities		◉	◉	▲	◉		▲	▲	▲	▲	◉	▲		◉	▲		◉
Gambling	▲	◉	◉					▲	▲	▲		▲	▲		▲		
Sailing	◉		◉			◉						▲		▲	▲		◉
Diving	◉	▲	◉	◉	▲	◉	◉		▲	▲	▲	▲	◉	◉		▲	◉
Fishing	▲	▲	◉	▲	▲	▲	◉	◉	◉	▲	◉	▲	◉	▲	▲	▲	◉
Friendly Locals	◉	◉	▲	◉	▲	▲								▲	▲	◉	▲
Cleanliness	▲	▲	▲	◉	◉	▲	◉								◉		▲
Golfing		◉	▲	◉			◉				◉		◉				▲
Hiking		▲						▲	◉		◉	◉	▲	◉		▲	▲
To Do Business		▲	◉	▲			◉				▲		◉			◉	▲

▲ = Better than average   ◉ = Excellent

SOURCE: Miseyko Consultants

Possible Misgivings

As popular as the Caribbean is, some people will have concerns:

- "The islands are unsafe." Political unrest and petty crime plague some of the islands, but in most destinations, serious problems arise only once in a while. Those worried about this should visit islands such as Bermuda or the Bahamas, which have been stable for decades.

- "What about hurricanes?" For those with this concern, the winter months or cruises are popular; ships can usually reroute their itinerary in response to a hurricane's predicted path.

Montego Bay was once called the Bay of Lard.

Bermuda has more golf courses per square mile than any other nation.

■ "Lying on a beach bores me." Cruises or all-inclusive resort lodging take care of that. Islands such as the Bahamas, Bermuda, Jamaica, Puerto Rico, and Trinidad are more lively than most.

■ "Do they speak English?" About a third of the islands in this area are English-speaking. French, Spanish, and Dutch are spoken on other islands, but people involved in tourism usually speak English.

■ "Aren't the islands rather dirty?" Poverty and squalor do plague a few of the islands, especially those with a Spanish or French heritage. The situation is better in many of the U.S.- or British-influenced destinations, such as Bermuda, Barbados, the Caymans, or the Virgin Islands.

■ "Aren't many islanders resentful of tourists?" On some of the poorer islands, the constant flood of affluent visitors provokes a quiet—though apparent—resentment. On some of the smaller islands, such as Antigua, friendliness is the norm.

Sales Strategies

Few destinations offer as many sales opportunities as the Caribbean. Cruises and all-inclusive resort packages yield commissions on virtually everything the traveler will do. Yacht charters, a popular option for many, can be booked in advance. Submarine excursions, helicopter flights, and dive packages can also be prearranged. Because of poverty, crime, and unrest, visitors usually offer little resistance to deluxe lodging. Car rentals are popular on some of the larger islands. (Taxis are the mode of choice on the smaller islands.)

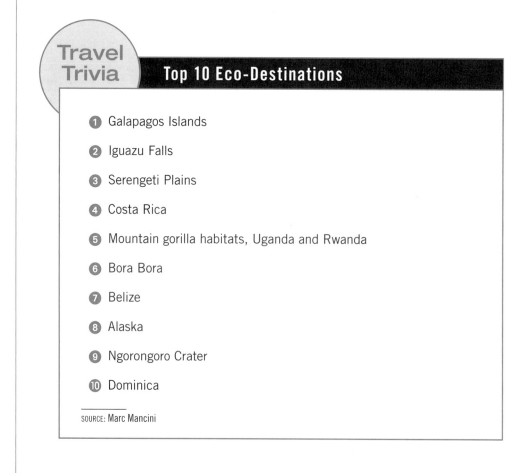

Travel Trivia

Top 10 Eco-Destinations

1. Galapagos Islands
2. Iguazu Falls
3. Serengeti Plains
4. Costa Rica
5. Mountain gorilla habitats, Uganda and Rwanda
6. Bora Bora
7. Belize
8. Alaska
9. Ngorongoro Crater
10. Dominica

SOURCE: Marc Mancini

NAME _____   DATE _____

MAP ACTIVITY

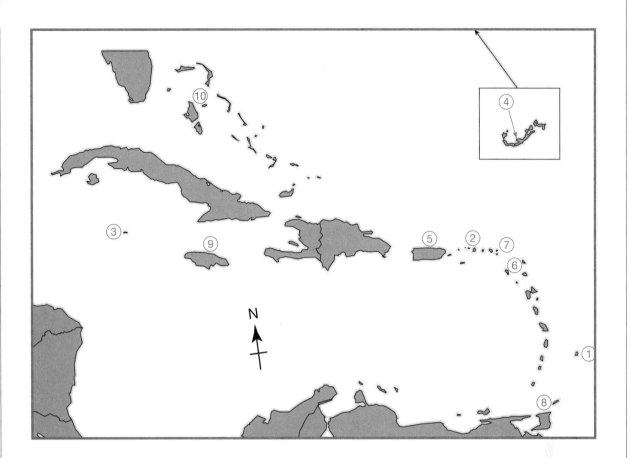

A traveler wants to visit the places listed below. Which number represents each on the map?

Place/Attraction	On Which Island/Group?	Number on Map
A. Negril	A. _____	A. _____
B. Nassau	B. _____	B. _____
C. Georgetown	C. _____	C. _____
D. Hamilton	D. _____	D. _____
E. Dutch and French culture	E. _____	E. _____
F. The easternmost part of the Lesser Antilles	F. _____	F. _____
G. St. Thomas	G. _____	G. _____
H. Nelson's Dockyard	H. _____	H. _____
I. El Yunque	I. _____	I. _____
J. Sister island to Tobago	J. _____	J. _____

NAME _____   **DATE** _____

CASE STUDY

Vickie and Larry Minkoff, who live in Bozeman, Montana, want to go to the Caribbean to celebrate their 10th wedding anniversary. They want to get completely away from it all, though Vickie wouldn't mind at least two nights on a second island with plenty of nightlife. They have a week off from work. They're both experienced divers.

Circle the answer that best suits their needs.

1 Which island should be their principal, get-away-from-it-all destination?

Nassau   Trinidad

Little Cayman   Jamaica

Why?

2 What relatively nearby island could serve as the lively second destination?

Cuba   Tobago

Jamaica   Anguilla

Why?

3 Which of the following would probably be most appealing to them?

A cruise   A four-day car rental

A week at Club Med   Upgraded accommodations

Why?

4 Which would be the most likely month for bad weather?

March   September

May   November

Why?

NAME _____   **DATE** _____

CREATIVE ACTIVITY

Slogans are a key to promoting destinations. For example:

Korea: More Than Seoul!

Mexico: Something Old, Something New

New Orleans: Come Join the Parade

Invent a clever and evocative slogan that could help sell each of the following destinations:

Destination   **Slogan**

1 Bermuda   **1**

2 The Bahamas   **2**

3 St. Martin   **3**

4 Aruba   **4**

5 The Caymans   **5**

6 Puerto Rico   **6**

7 Grenada   **7**

8 Trinidad   **8**

9 Martinique   **9**

10 Jamaica   **10**

Chapter 12

Brazil
Where Everything Sizzles

What do people imagine when they think about Brazil? The blistering temperatures along the Amazon River? The frenetic Carnival atmosphere of **Rio de Janeiro**? Such sizzling images come easily to mind, but they're only part of the picture.

Brazil is a huge country. Larger than the contiguous United States, it covers almost half of the South American continent. Visitors to Brazil will encounter dazzling diversity: lush rainforests (so dense in places that sunlight can't even reach the ground); some of the world's greatest beaches (on 4,603 miles of coastline, more than 1.5 times the distance from New York to Los Angeles); and warm, cosmopolitan cities.

Brazil is shaped a little like a triangle, with the base at the top. The northern region's largely jungle landscape is dominated by the **Amazon**, arguably the longest river in the world. **Belem** is at the Amazon's mouth; **Manaus** is located in the interior, just upriver on the Amazon's major tributary, **Rio Negro** [NAY-gro]. Northeastern Brazil conveys a strong African influence, centred primarily in the city of **Salvador**, located in Bahia province. The southeast is the cultural, commercial, and industrial heart of the country: There you can

The Amazon was named after female warriors who reputedly lived in a region east of ancient Greece. Supposedly, female warriors also lived in the Amazon Basin. Both stories are probably myths.

Brasilia is laid out in the shape of an airplane.

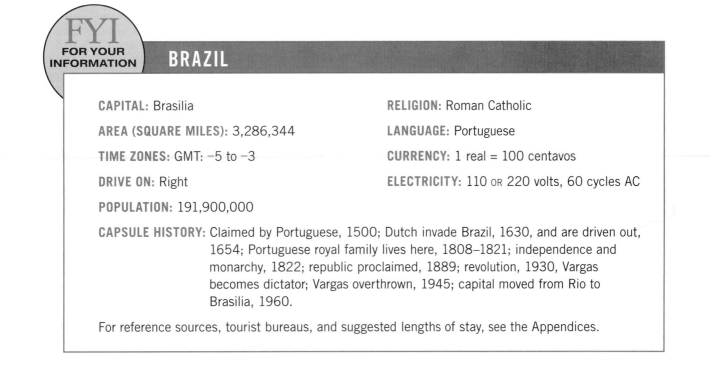

FYI
FOR YOUR INFORMATION

BRAZIL

CAPITAL: Brasilia

AREA (SQUARE MILES): 3,286,344

TIME ZONES: GMT: −5 to −3

DRIVE ON: Right

POPULATION: 191,900,000

RELIGION: Roman Catholic

LANGUAGE: Portuguese

CURRENCY: 1 real = 100 centavos

ELECTRICITY: 110 OR 220 volts, 60 cycles AC

CAPSULE HISTORY: Claimed by Portuguese, 1500; Dutch invade Brazil, 1630, and are driven out, 1654; Portuguese royal family lives here, 1808–1821; independence and monarchy, 1822; republic proclaimed, 1889; revolution, 1930, Vargas becomes dictator; Vargas overthrown, 1945; capital moved from Rio to Brasilia, 1960.

For reference sources, tourist bureaus, and suggested lengths of stay, see the Appendices.

Brasilia's capitol buildings
Photo by Justus Ghormley

find the joyous spirit of Rio de Janeiro and the international business of **Sao Paulo**, one of the largest cities in the world. Brazil's southern tip is where most of its agriculture and coffee-growing is found. And finally, the central and western regions are largely lush wilderness, with the capital, **Brasilia**, at the center. Though a modern, unusual city, Brasilia attracts few tourists.

The national language is Portuguese. Portuguese is indeed different from Spanish, but those who do speak Spanish should be able to get along fairly well (especially when reading signs, menus, and the like). English is widely spoken in the major cities.

How Travelers Get There

Brazil's national airline is **Varig** (RG), but several other foreign and domestic carriers also serve the country. **Galeao International Airport** (GIG) in Rio is the main gateway into the country, with flying time from New York 8 hours, from Los Angeles 12 hours, and from Miami 7 hours. Rio's domestic airport is **Dumont Airport** (SDU). There are also two major airports in Sao Paulo: **Guarulhos International Airport** (GRU) and **Viracopos International Airport** (VCP). Flying time is 8 hours from Miami (where connections to Brazil are often made). In addition, Brazil has extensive air service throughout the country, with airports at most major destinations (including Manaus, by the Amazon). Another way to reach Brazil is via a long cruise from Miami, San Juan, or even New York City. It's usually part of a larger cruise of South America.

Weather Patterns

Brazil experiences three climate patterns. The Amazon Basin, which includes Belem and Manaus, has a year-round temperature range of 80 to 90 degrees, with high humidity and rain most of the year. (The period from June through November is less rainy.) The plateau area (where **Iguazu Falls** is located) can be hotter, but there's less rain and humidity, and nights can be cool. There's almost no rainfall here from May through September. The coastal region (e.g., Rio) is a little cooler (mid-70s to 80s), with sea breezes to offset the humidity. Rain comes here from October through May, though showers can occur anytime (see Figure 12–1). Reminder: In most of Brazil, the seasons are opposite those in North America.

Climate at a Glance
RIO DE JANEIRO

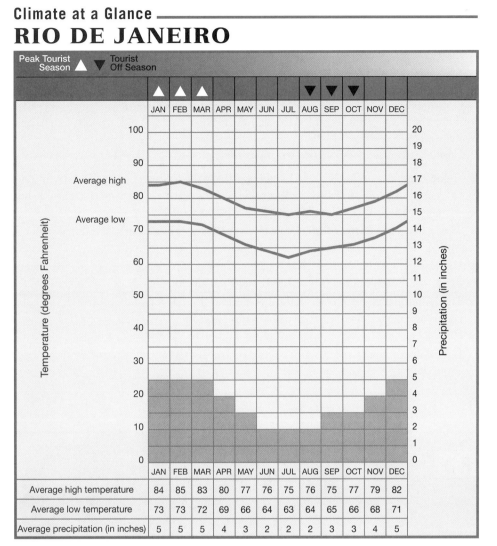

	JAN	FEB	MAR	APR	MAY	JUN	JUL	AUG	SEP	OCT	NOV	DEC
Average high temperature	84	85	83	80	77	76	75	76	75	77	79	82
Average low temperature	73	73	72	69	66	64	63	64	65	66	68	71
Average precipitation (in inches)	5	5	5	4	3	2	2	2	3	3	4	5

Figure 12–1

Getting Around

There's extensive air service within Brazil. Intercity buses are less expensive, but probably not up to the standards visitors expect. Driving is no picnic either: Cities are very crowded, streets can be confusing, breakneck speed is the rule among drivers, and, outside the cities, heavy rains can wash out roads. Trains are very limited.

In a country with extensive waterways and a long Atlantic coastline, ships and boats often represent an alternative means of travel. The most famous water journey is up the Amazon, all the way to Manaus. Many cruise lines include this adventurous trip as part of their South American itineraries.

Brazil's major cities feature inexpensive buses, but they can get very crowded. Taxis are a good way to get around. Private cars are considered safer and more reliable, but are more expensive than taxis. Tour packages to Brazil often include multiple forms of transportation.

Important Places

Most visitors center their Brazilian trip in one of three areas: around Rio de Janeiro, along the Amazon, and in the Salvador region.

Since 1900, at least 19 indigenous groups in Brazil have become extinct.

Rio de Janeiro

Rio is one of the world's great cities. If it were only for the stunning location—oddly shaped mountains, a picturesque lagoon, and lush vegetation intertwine through the city, with superb beaches and the glistening Atlantic Ocean at its doorstep—Rio would be famous. But Rio offers more. It's a cosmopolitan city with rich culture, warm people, wonderful cuisine, and a frenetic nightlife, all wrapped in a casual yet elegant charm. Rio, though, isn't perfect: The city is very crowded; it has slums, plenty of petty crime, and, like all of Brazil, an unpredictable economy.

Among the most popular Rio attractions are:

- **Sugar Loaf**, the strangely shaped mountain that's the city's landmark. The summit offers beautiful views and is reached by cable car. It's best to go on a weekday; weekends are crowded and the waiting line for the cable car is long.

- **Tijuca National Park**, which claims to be the "world's largest urban, forested national park."

- **World-renowned beaches**, most notably **Copacabana** (the biggest) and two more trendy beaches: **Ipanema** [ee-pah-NEE-mah] and **Leblon**.

- **The Botanical Gardens**, which features a rich collection of plants and trees brought by Portuguese navigators from their many world voyages.

- **Corcovado Mountain**, serving as the base for the city's other famous landmark, the 120-foot-high, open-armed statue of **Christ the Redeemer**. The views from here are astounding.

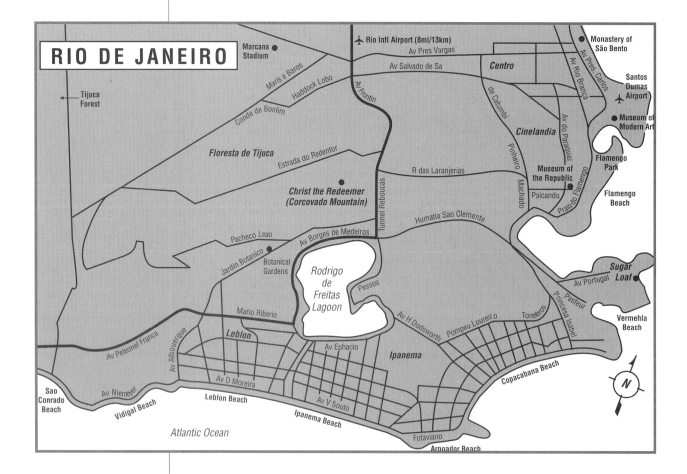

Recife is interlaced with waterways
Image copyright Travel Bug, 2008. Used under license from Shutterstock.com

- **Carnival**, a spectacular four-day festival starting the Saturday before Ash Wednesday and ending Tuesday evening. Visitors in the area at this time should not miss it. The city virtually shuts down, no one seems to go to bed, and anything goes.

Several **day trips** from Rio de Janeiro would add to a visit to this area:

- **Sao Paulo**, the business and industrial center of Brazil, which is about 170 miles southwest of Rio. It has world-class international restaurants and shopping, some of South America's best museums, and a good nightlife. (Unfortunately, it also has considerable traffic and pollution problems.) The **Sacred Art Museum** has the largest collection of religious art outside the Vatican, while the **MASP** museum boasts a huge collection of Impressionist paintings. The zoo's great menagerie of animals from the Brazilian jungle is impressive. Visitors shouldn't carry valuables or go walking at night (taxis or private cars should be taken instead), because street robberies, sadly, happen far too often.

- **Guaruja** [gwah-ruh-ZHAH], a sophisticated beach town, actually a day trip from Sao Paulo.

- **Petropolis**, once the summer retreat for the emperor of Portugal, with its **Imperial Palace**. The 45-mile drive from Rio to Petropolis is very scenic.

- **Costa Verde**, the beautiful coastal area between Rio and **Santos** (a coastal village just south of Sao Paulo). The beaches here are much quieter than those in Rio.

- **Iguazu Falls** (spelled Iguacu in Portuguese), a breathtaking attraction on Brazil's border which merits at least a two-night stay. To get there from Rio requires a short flight. Nearly 300 falls cover 2.6 miles and span an area much higher and wider than Niagara Falls. For movie buffs, this is where the film *The Mission* was shot. January through March is peak season, but it's also the hottest, steamiest time of year. August through October may be best for visiting Iguazu.

The Amazon

A trip up the Amazon promises one of the world's legendary tourist adventures. The river is about 4,000 miles long and up to 8 miles wide. The dense jungles and lush rainforests are home to wildlife seen nowhere else on earth, with fishing villages and small islands dotting the river's length. There are also a few major cities along the way:

- **Manaus**, deep in Brazil's hot interior, is a crowded city. Surprisingly, many Victorian buildings remain from the city's early rubber boom days. Today, the city is a free port with popular duty-free shopping; it's also a launch point for Amazon River boat trips to jungle lodges and for hunting expeditions. Manaus is also an inland stop for cruise ships.

    The sites of Manaus include the **Teatro do Amazonas**, an ornate opera house built in 1892, where many of history's great opera singers and actors have performed; **Mercado Municipal**, a marketplace of fascinating design; interesting museums and zoos; and **Salvador Lake**, just outside town, a nature preserve with a remarkable array of wildlife. The **Wedding of the Waters**, 12 miles from town, is where the Amazon, the Rio Solimoes, and the Rio Negro meet. Each has water of a different color, and the colliding swirls of separate hues provide a unique attraction. Half-day boat excursions can be taken from Manaus to visit this area.

- **Belem**, at the mouth of the Amazon, is home to a huge open-air market, **Ver-O-Peso**, which features all manner of items for sale. Lush parks and interesting old buildings decorate the city. A boat excursion to the ranches on the vast nearby island of **Ilha de Marajo** is popular.

- **Santarem** is a quiet city about halfway between Manaus and Belem. Although not offering anywhere near the attractions of those two cities, it's less crowded, less developed, and quite charming. A bit of trivia: Santarem was originally settled by people from South Carolina and Tennessee.

Salvador

Salvador, the capital of the **Bahia** district, is a baroque city with a strong African heritage. This coastal city, with perhaps the finest climate in the country, has excellent beaches, old neighbourhoods with winding streets, fine museums, and 365 churches. The city is built on two levels into a cliff, connected by the **Lacerda Elevator**. The views are gorgeous, the locals are extremely friendly, and the unique African-European cuisine is great. And like Rio, the city holds a festive Carnival for the week before Ash Wednesday. Its most interesting sites include:

- **Many churches**, the finest of which are the **Basilica Cathedral**, a wonderful 400-year-old structure; the ornate **St. Francis Church**, with a remarkable gold-leaf interior; and the **Church of Our Lord of the Good Ending**, whose congregation often wear the traditional clothes of their culture.

- **The Mercado Modelo**, with good buys on silver, rosewood, and fabric souvenirs.

- **Superb beaches**, the best of which are **Itapoa** and **Piata**.

There are a few interesting **day trips** from Salvador:

- **Excursions** to the numerous islands off the coast. **Itaparica** is probably the best known; it's quiet, lovely, and virtually undeveloped.

- **Recife**, reachable from Salvador in a day, but probably requiring an overnight stay. This city has been compared to Venice because of its canals and bridges though, unlike Venice, there's also normal vehicle traffic. There are many classical churches, an old fort, an eighteenth-century prison that's been turned into a shopping center, and great beaches. The lovely artist colony of **Olinda** is nearby. Farther north is **Fortaleza**, a beach area that has grown in popularity.

The Amazon Basin contains 20 percent of the world's fresh water.

Salvador once belonged to the Dutch.

Perhaps one of the most unexpected buildings to be found in the Amazon region: Teatro do Amazonas
in Manaus
Image copyright Rafael Martin-Gaitero, 2008. Used under license from Shutterstock.com

Possible Itineraries

For first-time visitors, Rio de Janeiro is a must-see. A very common itinerary is to spend
three or four days in Rio, fly to Iguazu for a two- to three-day stay, and continue on to Buenos Aires, Argentina. Travelers visiting Brazil for a second time might enjoy visiting the
exotic Bahia region around Salvador for three or four days or could spend up to six days
taking a cruise up the Amazon.

Lodging Options

Hotels in Brazil run the gamut from deluxe to budget, but the lower down the ladder you
go, the greater the chance for disappointment. (Of course, during Carnival, everything is
expensive.) The major luxury chains include **Othon** and hotels represented by **Leading
Hotels of the World**. **Luxor** is a popular first-class chain. A few North American companies are also present in Brazil.

In Rio de Janeiro, the largest hotel grouping is along Copacabana Beach, with other
clusters on Ipanema Beach, Leblon Beach, and upscale Gavea Beach. Lodging is expensive by South American standards, but less so than many other top resort areas around
the world. The turn-of-the-century, deluxe **Copacabana Palace Hotel** is internationally
renowned.

Most Sao Paulo hotels are in the western part of the city. Visitors to Manaus should
stay in the better-class hotels. Those staying in Salvador can save some money by lodging
in hotels off the beach, because most of the finest beaches in the area, notably Itapoa and
Piata, are out of town. At Iguazu Falls, several hotels are very close to the Falls, with some
offering a direct view of the cascades. Other hotels are located in nearby towns.

An interesting alternative for lodging in Rio: furnished apartments, called *apartotels*,
which have complete hotel services. There are also ranches and jungle lodges in many areas
of the country.

Rio's inhabitants are
called *Cariocas.*

Rio is a noisy city. A
beachfront or interior
room will shield you
from the constant din.

Allied Destinations

Taking up half of South America, Brazil is the ideal connection to the other countries on that continent. To the north, it borders French Guiana, Suriname, Guyana, Venezuela, and Colombia. Peru and Bolivia are to its west. And to the south are Paraguay, Argentina, and Uruguay. In fact, the only South American countries it doesn't border are Chile and Ecuador. Brazil is also close to Central America and the Caribbean. A cruise, especially, would be an excellent way to extend a trip between those areas.

Cultural Patterns

Brazil is an adventurous, lively country. Understanding the customs here will go a long way toward making a trip, business or otherwise, even more rewarding:

- Brazilians are physically and emotionally open. Shaking hands, embracing, and so on, are the rule.
- The OK sign in North America—made with the thumb and forefinger—is an obscenity in Brazil (and many other countries).
- Brazilians have a lax attitude toward time. Visitors should nonetheless be punctual for business appointments, even if they turn out to be the only ones there on time.

Soccer is a Brazilian passion. Attend a soccer match in one of Sao Paulo's or Rio's huge stadiums.

Qualifying the Traveler
Brazil

For People Who Want	Appeal			Remarks
	High	Medium	Low	
Historical and Cultural Attractions		▲		Especially Rio and Amazon; Carnival
Beaches and Water Sports	▲			Legendary beaches
Skiing Opportunities			▲	None
Lots of Nightlife		▲		Especially Rio
Family Activities			▲	
Familiar Cultural Experience			▲	
Exotic Cultural Experience	▲			
Safety and Low Crime			▲	Petty theft common
Bargain Travel		▲		Air/hotel packages excellent
Impressive Scenery	▲			Seascapes and jungle
Peace and Quiet		▲		Cities noisy, but outlying areas not
Shopping Opportunities		▲		Semiprecious stones, rosewood, leather
Adventure	▲			Amazon and Iguazu Falls
To Do Business		▲		In large cities

- To be invited to a Brazilian's home is an honor. Guests shouldn't plan to drop by for a brief visit; rather, they should be prepared to stay for many hours. It's also customary to arrive a little late. In addition, some small gift should be brought along. (An important note here, especially concerning flowers: Purple, in Brazil, is the color of death.) Brazilians are very conscious of keeping their hands on the table when dining.

Factors That Motivate Visitors

Among the reasons that motivate people to visit Brazil are:

- Rio de Janeiro promises excitement, fun, fine dining, and much nightlife.
- There are great beaches throughout the country.
- Considering what its great cities offer, Brazil is a relative bargain.
- The locals are extremely warm, open, and friendly.
- The Amazon is adventurous and unique.
- There's great cuisine and good shopping (especially for precious stones).
- The history and culture of Brazil are fascinating.
- Rio's Carnival is world renowned. Salvador's is almost as impressive.

Possible Misgivings

The culture of Brazil offers up a very foreign experience. The concerns that usually arise are:

- "There's malaria, cholera, and other diseases in the Amazon." Most of the worst areas are well away from the typical tourist areas. Travelers should check with a doctor before coming here.
- "They only speak Portuguese." Portuguese is somewhat similar to Spanish. More important, English is widely spoken in the major cities and by travel professionals.
- "I'm afraid to drink the water." Bottled soft drinks (including some very exotic Amazon fruit flavors) can be purchased everywhere. And Brazilian beer is excellent.
- "I won't like Brazilian food." Brazil is a mix of cultures. There is wonderful international cuisine. A special treat: *Churruscaria* restaurants that serve up barbecued meats carved at the diner's table.
- "There's a lot of street crime." Unfortunately, it's true. Commonsense precautions should be taken, such as leaving valuables in the hotel, dressing casually, keeping wallets protected, and not walking outside at night, except in clearly safe places.

Sales Strategies

The unique qualities of Brazil lend themselves to special ways to upsell and cross-sell a trip here. Because of the economic uncertainty and sometimes high inflation, an escorted tour package or cruise may lock in prices early, as well as help ease a vacationer's fears about traveling alone in such an exotic country. At the very least, booking city tours can be helpful, as driving in Brazilian cities is not recommended. (For that matter, driving *anywhere* in Brazil is not recommended.) Because intercity bus and train service is limited, flights between cities are preferable. Accommodations in lower-rated hotels can be risky; upgraded lodging should be the choice. For those visiting the Amazon, a boat trip is a must; a special excursion to the Wedding of the Waters would be a worthwhile addition. For those going to Iguazu Falls, a local helicopter tour or jet boat ride is exciting.

The Feirarte, a great open-air market, is held on Sundays in the Ipanema area of Rio.

Never leave your valuables unattended on the beach.

Travel Trivia

Places Famous for Pre-Lenten Carnivals

- Rio de Janeiro, Brazil
- New Orleans, USA
- Venice, Italy
- Nassau, Bahamas
- Salvador, Brazil
- Oruro, Bolivia

- Caracas, Venezuela
- Beuel, Germany
- Trinidad
- Nice, France
- Martinique
- Corrientes, Argentina

NAME _____   **DATE** _____

MAP ACTIVITY

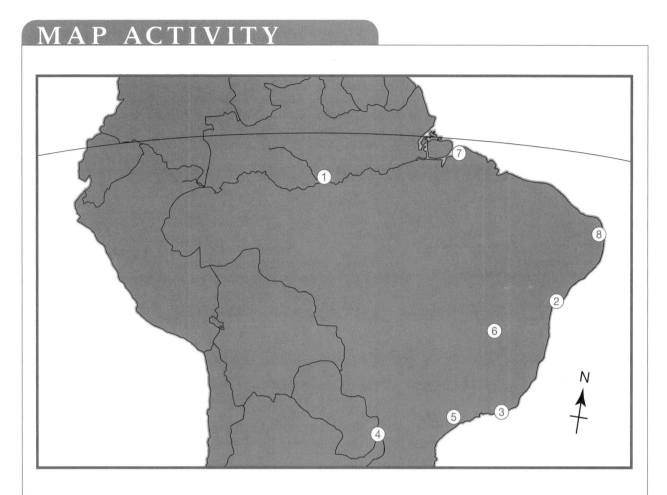

A traveler wants to visit the places listed below. Which number represents each on the map?

Place/Attraction	In/Near Which City?	Number on Map
A. Teatro do Amazonas	A. _____	A. _____
B. Sugar Loaf	B. _____	B. _____
C. Itapoa Beach	C. _____	C. _____
D. Leblon Beach	D. _____	D. _____
E. Falls bigger than Niagara	E. _____	E. _____
F. Capital of the Bahia District	F. _____	F. _____
G. The Wedding of the Waters	G. _____	G. _____
H. Sacred Art Museum	H. _____	H. _____
I. Brazil's capital	I. _____	I. _____
J. Ipanema	J. _____	J. _____

NAME _____ **DATE** _____

CASE STUDY

Nancy and Mark Aston are in their early 40s, with a daughter in college. They haven't had a vacation in three years—since they went to Paris and enjoyed the fashionable city very much. After their daughter returns to school in the fall, they'll be spending 11 days in South America, split between Brazil and Peru. They're a professional couple and don't like hassles on their trips. They plan to base their Brazilian stay in Rio.

Circle the answer that best suits their needs.

1 Which special tip would *not* be appropriate?

Be sure to see Carnival   Keep your valuables in the hotel

Don't drive in cities   Take along an umbrella

Why?

2 What good news could you tell the Astons?

The beach at Itapoa, where you're lodging them, is beautiful.

They're going during Brazil's bargain season.

Because Nancy speaks Spanish, Brazil's national language, they should have no trouble.

Like them, Brazilians dress conservatively.

Why?

3 The Astons decide that they want to see the Amazon. Which city would you suggest they fly to?

Salvador   Sao Paulo

Manaus   Brasilia

Why?

4 Which of the following services would *not* be good for the Astons?

A city tour   A helicopter ride

A boat cruise   A budget hotel

Why?

NAME _____ **DATE** _____

CREATIVE ACTIVITY

At Epcot in Orlando, many nations maintain pavilions that reflect their heritage and culture. For example, Morocco has reproduced a bazaar; Mexico, a Mayan pyramid (with a ride inside); France, a cafe-lined street. If you were a pavilion designer for the Walt Disney Company (which owns Epcot), what concept would you propose if Brazil decided to set up a pavilion? Describe or even draw it below.

BELIZE
Belmopan
GUATEMALA
HONDURAS
Guatemala City
Tegucigalpa
EL SALVADOR
NICARAGUA
Managua
Lake Nicaragua
Canal
Zone
COSTA RICA
San Jose
Panama
PANAMA
CARIBBEAN SEA

Caracas
Lake Maracaibo
Orinoco River
Georgetown
Paramaribo
FRENCH GUIANA
Cayenne
Bogota
VENEZUELA
GUYANA
SURINAME
COLOMBIA
Quito
ECUADOR
Andes
Amazon River

Galapagos
Islands

PERU
Lima
Lake Titicaca
BOLIVIA
La Paz
BRAZIL

PACIFIC OCEAN

Mountains

PARAGUAY
Asuncion

Easter Island

Rio Uruguay

CHILE
URUGUAY
Montevideo
Santiago
Buenos Aires
Rio de la Plata
ATLANTIC OCEAN

ARGENTINA

Falkland Islands

STRAIT of
MAGELLAN

South Georgia

Chapter 13

Latin American Potpourri

Too often when travelers from the United States think of heading south, they will consider only certain well-known destinations: Rio, the Mexican beach resorts, or the principal islands of the Caribbean. Yet Central and South America boast many first-rate but little-known attractions, many off the beaten tourist track.

There's a waterfall nearly three times the height of the Empire State Building, and another almost as wide as the Grand Canyon. There's the world's second-biggest coral reef, huge mysterious drawings on a vast plain, an island covered with giant stone heads, and an abandoned city at 8,000 feet in the Andes.

Do you know the names of these places? If not, you soon will. And you'll be able to use your knowledge to enhance the trip for anyone bound for Latin America.

Central America

The Central American isthmus, which connects Mexico to the South American continent, will probably be low on the priority list of most travelers. Though the land itself can be quite lovely and the weather tropical, the historical and cultural attractions are relatively undeveloped. More important: Some of the area's countries have been torn by enough intermittent wars and unrest to keep tourists away.

Air connections to and throughout Central America are the best bet for those who wish to visit the area. Car rentals are available and occasionally offer a good way to see the countryside; however, driving can be difficult in some places and dangerous in others. Bus service is widespread, but not recommended. Cruises may stop here as well, especially in **Costa Rica** and **Panama**. Indeed, cruises that pass from the Pacific to the Atlantic through the Panama Canal are quite popular.

Spanish is the national language in all Central American countries except **Belize** [beh-LEEZ], where English is the official language. English, however, is commonly spoken by travel personnel throughout the region.

The Pacific Ocean is at the Panama Canal's *eastern* end.

Important Places

Here are the countries, from north to south, you should know about:

Guatemala. Guatemala has had political instability. Its rich Mayan culture reached its high point at **Tikal** [tee-KAHL], an astonishing group of ruins that's right out of an Indiana Jones movie. Most of Guatemala's other ruins remain covered with earth and vines. **Guatemala City** (GUA), the capital, has several museums that explain Mayan civilization.

Belize. Belize is a tiny, politically stable country on the Caribbean coast with many Mayan ruins, meandering rivers, a lush jungle landscape, and some of the best diving spots in the world. It has become a popular stop for Western Caribbean cruises. Belize has the world's second-largest coral reef. At the reef's northern end is **Ambergris Cay**, with fine beaches, good fishing, and great diving. In the reef's middle are the **Turneffe Islands**, which feature what some consider the world's best dive site, the **Blue Hole**.

Honduras. Honduras has a poor economy and has been affected, in the past, by fighting in neighboring countries, some of which occasionally spills over its borders. However tourism (especially from cruise ships) has helped its economy. Its capital, **Tegucigalpa** (TGU), is quite pretty. The town of **Copan** is renowned for its Mayan ruins. The **Bay Islands** off Honduras (especially **Roatan Island**) offer good dive sites, including one where visitors can dive with dolphins.

El Salvador. El Salvador had been strife ridden for many years, but is now courting tourism. This scenic, mountainous country has much to offer. There are fine beaches, Mayan ruins are everywhere, and the capital of **San Salvador** (SAL) is beautiful.

Nicaragua. Nicaragua has also suffered on occasion from war and crime. The **Mosquito Coast** (the setting for the novel of the same name) lies on this country's Caribbean shore. Mayan ruins, abandoned gold mines, beach activities, and an old pirate settlement are among its attractions.

Costa Rica. Costa Rica is the success story of Central America: It's stable, prosperous, and has decent tourist facilities. In the country's central highlands is the capital city of **San Jose** (SJO), which contains some interesting museums and churches, a lovely national theater, and plenty of shopping. The climate here is pleasant. There are also interesting tours through the countryside and jungle: Costa Rica has a wealth of national parks and rain-forest reserves, which makes it appealing for ecotourists. The most famous of these is **Monteverde Cloud Forest Reserve**. Cruise ships call on the ports of **Limon** and **Puerto Caldera**, usually on Panama Canal itineraries. Offshore sports-fishing in Costa Rica is especially attractive.

Panama. Panama wavers between substantial tourism and no tourism at all; politics greatly affect tourism here. A common destination is **Panama City** (PTY), the capital, near the **Panama Canal**. This city—with a history strongly influenced by the Spanish, Indians, and pirates—is a popular cruise stop. Panama City boasts interesting Spanish colonial structures, old churches, and colorful plazas. **Balboa** is the American district: There's not much history to be found here, but it's safe and comfortable. Off Panama's Pacific coast is pretty **Taboga** Island; off its Caribbean side are the **San Blas** islands, a haven for Indian culture.

Sales Considerations

The area lends itself to cruises, particularly through Panama; along Costa Rica, Honduras, or Belize; or to some of the nearby islands. Book only the finest hotels in Central America. Tourists seriously interested in the local culture or ecotourism, those on cruises to South America or the Caribbean, or those who have relatives or ancestors from here will likely be the travelers visiting Central America. Vacationers who love fishing, secluded beaches, and diving are rapidly "discovering" Central America; its safer destinations are an appealing recommendation for those who've seen the more traditional ocean-oriented spots. A few fine

Belize was formerly known as British Honduras.

Lake Nicaragua is the only freshwater lake in the world that contains sharks.

Costa Rica means "rich coast," based on the hope that there was much gold there. (There wasn't.)

resorts have opened or are under development in Central America. There are many packages to Roatan Island, Costa Rica, Panama City, and the San Blas islands. Two-stay, city–beach tours in Costa Rica are also popular.

Colombia

The legendary El Dorado, stocked with golden riches, was reputedly in this region. It has never been found. But with three Andes ranges, broad beaches, extensive coffee plantations, and an Amazon jungle, Colombia has a wealth of another kind. Unfortunately, the country's long history with crime may discourage vacationers from sampling its attractions.

For those who *are* interested, **Avianca** (AV) is the national airline, flying into the capital of **Bogota** (BOG), on an Andean plateau. Major airports are also in the Caribbean port city of **Barranquilla** (BAQ) and the resort port of **Cartagena** (CTG), once a walled fortress. Good air connections crisscross the country, along with so-so rail service, crowded buses, and poor driving conditions. The national language is Spanish.

Bogota's residents live in a cool, spring-like, almost unchanging climate. The El Dorado tradition lives on here in the huge collection of the city's famous **Gold Museum.** A half-day trip from the city is **Zipaquira**, with its "Salt Cathedral" carved out of rock 450 feet below ground. Astonishingly large, it can hold almost 10,000 people. **San Agustin Park** is a 150-square-mile archaeological reserve dotted with stone monoliths. **Leticia**, accessible only by air or boat, is a gateway to Amazon adventure cruises. **San Andres Island**, about 300 miles of Colombia, was the base of English pirate Captain Henry Morgan.

Venezuela

Caracas, Venezuela's capital, lies in a northern Andean valley. Venezuela's other major geographic feature is the Orinoco River, which flows through the grassy plains (the *llanos*), into the Atlantic. **Simon Bolivar Airport** (CCS) in Caracas is the gateway into the country, though cruise ships also call on the nearby port of **La Guaira. Merida** (MRD) is the Venezuelan air gateway to the Andes, where visitors can ride the world's highest cable car. There's good air and bus service, but no train service to speak of. Though renting a car is easy, driving is difficult. *Por puestos* (taxis that pick up and drop off passengers along their routes, like a shuttle bus) are a popular way of getting around. Spanish is the national language.

The climate in Venezuela is very steady; in Caracas, for example, daytime temperatures average in the upper 70s year-round. Jungle areas are hotter and Andes destinations cooler.

Venezuela named its unit of currency, the bolivar, after Simon Bolivar.

Venezuela has a dry season from December to early May, with moderate and occasional rainfall the rest of the year.

Important Places

Venezuela has a number of interesting destinations:

■ **Caracas**, for the most part, is a handsome, modern city with many notable churches. It retains a strong Spanish influence and has an active, international nightlife. The birthplace and grave of Venezuela's national hero, Simon Bolivar (who helped free South America from Spain), is here. **Mt. Avila** offers great views of the city. **Colonia Tovar**, an interesting, German-like village, is nearby.

■ **Angel Falls**, at 3,212 feet, is the world's loftiest waterfall. (It's nearly 18 times higher than Niagara Falls.) Located in the southeast jungle, and reached by plane, the area also has thousands of varieties of orchids.

■ **Beach resorts** are found along the Caribbean coast. Two of the most popular are **Macuto**, not far from Caracas, and the very popular **Margarita Island** (in the Caribbean just east of the ABC Islands).

Sales Considerations

Venezuela is particularly convenient as an extension to a trip into the Caribbean. It's sometimes a stop on Southern Caribbean and trans-Canal cruise itineraries. Tourist services tend to be first-rate. An air tour to Angel Falls is an intriguing option; the drama of this attraction appeals to those who seek off-the-beaten-path experiences.

The Guianas

These three very small countries—**Guyana** [guy-AH-nah], **Suriname** [SUR-eh-nahm], and **French Guiana** [ghee-AH-nah]—huddle together on the Atlantic coast. The Guianas are largely jungle, with many rivers (especially in Guyana) and savannahs. Guyana's air gateway is the capital of **Georgetown** (GEO); Suriname's national airline, **Surinam Airways** (PY), lands in **Paramaribo** (PBM), the capital. Other airlines service the region as well.

Angel Falls, which plummets from "Devil Mountain," was discovered by and named after an American, Jimmy Angel.

The Dutch traded Manhattan for Suriname (originally Dutch Guiana).

The gateway into French Guiana is its capital, **Cayenne** (CAY). These three countries' ports are occasionally stops on Southern Caribbean or South American cruise itineraries. Train, bus, and boat are the easiest ways to get around; there are also some air connections. Rental cars are available, but driving conditions aren't good.

Each of these countries has its own national language: English in Guyana, Dutch in Suriname, and French (of course) in French Guiana. The climate is tropical, with conditions steadily humid and hot (though nights from December through February can get chilly). July through November might be the best time to visit here. May and June also have pleasant temperatures, but this is the rainiest season.

Important Places

Here are the most popular attractions in these exotic destinations:

- **Guyana** offers excellent trout and ocean fishing opportunities, and some interesting sites—notably in Georgetown. There's also **Kaieteur Falls**, which cascades down from a height of 740 feet.

- **Suriname** has a strong mix of cultures and religions, including Hindu, Muslim, and Catholic. In Paramaribo, a fairly sophisticated city, there are many interesting churches, marketplaces, and colonial buildings. Jungle excursions into Suriname's nature parks and reserves appeal to ecotourists. Suriname has occasional civil unrest.

- **French Guiana** is the least-developed country of the three. Its most noted attraction: a tour of the notorious penal colony, **Devil's Island**, which is offshore from **Kourou**. This is where French soldier Alfred Dreyfus was unjustly imprisoned at the turn of the twentieth century. Devil's Island is a frequent stop for cruise ships heading to or from South America. On the mainland, jungle and river excursions are possibilities. But since poverty, heat, and crime are ever-present problems, such trips are suitable only for the hardiest of adventure travelers.

Sales Considerations

Because these are such challenging destinations, people who are not very adventurous travelers should visit the Guianas via a cruise or well-established tour operator.

French Guiana is the launch site for France's aerospace program.

The world's tallest wooden structure is Georgetown Cathedral.

In the book Papillon, Henri Charriere wrote of his adventures as a convict on Devil's Island.

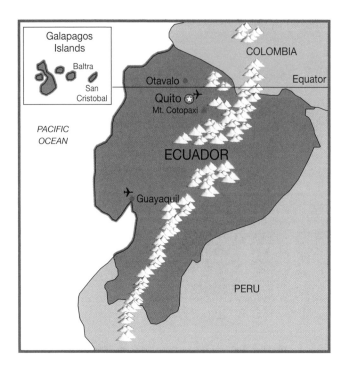

Ecuador

Located in the northwest corner of South America, Ecuador borders the Pacific Ocean. The Andes mountain range shapes much of the country's geography. The climate stays fairly steady all year, though different areas vary greatly. The highlands—which include the capital, **Quito** (often called the City of Eternal Spring)—tend to have cool temperatures. The west coast—where **Guayaquil** is located—is much warmer, with highs in the 90s. Ecuador has a rainy season from January to April; the rest of the year it's very dry.

Major North and South American carriers provide service to **Mariscal Sucre International Airport** (UIO) in Quito and **Simon Bolivar Airport** (GYE) in Guayaquil. Cruise ships dock at Guayaquil. There's good air service within the country. Visitors to the **Galapagos Islands** can fly to either **Baltra** or **San Cristobal** or take a boat there. Train service is limited in Ecuador, but there's a complicated series of connections between Quito and Guayaquil; the winding route through mountain passes is spectacular. Buses are very crowded, and though car rentals are widely available, road conditions aren't good. Taxis are a good way to navigate cities. Spanish is the national language.

Important Places

Though Guayaquil is Ecuador's largest city, its attractions are limited to some interesting Spanish buildings and a few cultural museums. Ecuador has two major destinations: Quito and the Galapagos Islands.

Surrounded by immense mountains, Quito has a natural setting that few country capitals can match. A strong Spanish architectural influence marks the city. Quito boasts some fine museums specializing in pre-Columbian art and a great many churches. The city's historical district, "Old Quito," is quite interesting. A beautiful day drive will take visitors to **Mt. Cotopaxi**, a national park. A half-day trip is 15 miles north to visit a large monument that marks the equator—it's sort of a required ritual for tourists visiting Quito to stand in the Northern and Southern Hemispheres at the same time. Some interesting ruins are along the way. Farther to the north and south lie a string of colorful towns, each with a popular marketplace (**Otavalo** is the best known).

Panama hats actually originated in Ecuador.

Ecuador supplies one-quarter of the world's bananas.

The Galapagos Islands possess some of the world's most remarkable wildlife. Its famous giant tortoises are believed to be the world's oldest living animals. The tortoises, iguanas, sea lions, penguins, and all sorts of birds (including the oddly named but famous blue-footed booby) have a "mater-of-fact" attitude toward humans. It's one of the rare places in the world where animals in the wild are neither fearful of nor aggressive toward humans. The Ecuadorian government sets a limit on the number of visitors to the Galapagos, so tours and trips should be booked well in advance.

Sales Considerations

Ecuador is a bit less developed than some of the more popular nations in South America. However, it's also less crowded and is relatively stable. For ecotourists, the Galapagos are a must-see, usually on a multiday small-ship cruise among these islands. (Visitors fly to one of two airports at the Galapagos from either Quito or Guayaquil.)

Peru

Few Latin American countries can boast as many well-known, first-rate attractions as Peru. Most tourists land first in **Lima** [LEE-mah] (LIM) or, via cruise ship, in the port city of **Callao** [cah-YAH-oh]. They encounter a nation of dramatic contrasts: the warm, dry Pacific coast; the mighty Andes just inland (which can get quite cold during the June-to-September, south-of-the-equator winter); and the hilly, rainy jungles of the eastern lowlands, where the Amazon finds its source.

Important Places

Lima, a huge, sprawling city that was the hub of Spain's New World government, retains much of its colonial architecture, especially at the **Plaza de Armas**. The city brims with fine museums and several ornate churches. Nearby are **Pachacamac**, an Incan ruin; **Miraflores**, a charming seaside town; and the **Nazca Lines**, huge mysterious designs drawn on the ground that have intrigued archaeologists and tourists for decades. Visible only from

The Galapagos Islands was where Charles Darwin did much of his research for his theories on evolution.

On Ecuador's Trans-Andean railroad, passengers are sometimes allowed to ride on the train's rooftop.

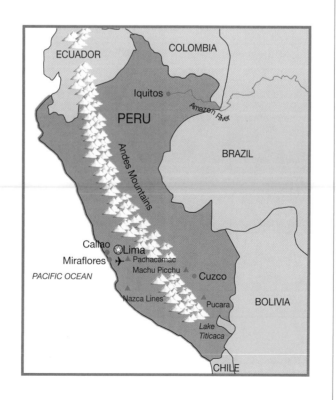

the air, the drawings of animals, people, and geometric shapes are best seen via local char-ter plane expeditions that you can book in advance.

Cuzco, the former capital of the Incan Empire, is another of Peru's well-known desti-nations. About 400 miles southeast of Lima at a more than 10,000-foot altitude, it features ancient buildings, colonial mansions, markets, a Renaissance-style cathedral, and a world-class hotel, the **Monasterio**. (It's probably the only hotel in the world where the main con-ference room is a converted chapel, complete with silver-and-gold-plated altar.) Not far is **Pucara**, an ancient Incan fortress.

But Pucara pales in comparison to Peru's most remarkable attraction, **Machu Picchu**. Hidden and forgotten until it was rediscovered in 1911 by former U.S. Senator Hiram Bingham, Machu Picchu boasts Incan temples, terraces, and residences. What sets it apart from other ruins is its setting: Machu Picchu sits atop a steep, lofty hill and is surrounded by dramatic mountains and, in the distance, even bigger snowcapped peaks. It seems like something an art director created for a movie—but it's very real. Most tourists visit it via a special morning train from Cuzco, returning in the late afternoon. Hardier types hike an Inca Trail to get there.

Iquitos [ee-KEE-tos], a city on the Amazon in northeast Peru, is the jump-off point for "Green Hell" boat tours up the Amazon River into the jungle.

Sales Considerations

What draws visitors to Peru? The country's felicitous climate, accessible location, startling scenery, budget prices, and high-recognition attractions make it one of Latin America's easi-est "sells." It's frequently an add-on destination to such bordering countries as Ecuador, Colombia, Brazil, Bolivia, and Chile. Many escorted tour packages are available to this "soft" adventure country.

There *are* problems related to a trip to Peru. As with many Latin American destina-tions, poverty leads to some petty crime, occasional terrorism, and health concerns—even in Lima and Cuzco. These problems, as well as inflation and limited hotel space, make booking packaged tours an advisable sales strategy. Because budget hotels leave much to be desired, upselling to luxury-class accommodations is an attractive option. Travelers to the region should talk with their physicians about medicines that prevent or minimize altitude sickness, since both Cuzco and Machu Picchu are at extremely high altitudes.

Some hotels in Cuzco offer oxygen-enhanced rooms.

Soroche is what Peruvian locals call altitude sickness. It's the number-one problem for visitors to Peru and is much worse than you might think.

Machu Picchu is known as the Lost City of the Incas
Photo by Justus Ghormley

Bolivia

Located in the center of the continent, Bolivia is one of the two landlocked countries in South America. (The other is Paraguay.) It's dominated by the Andes and is at extremely high altitudes; in fact, the thin air might be difficult for most visitors until they adjust. **La Paz**, the world's highest capital city, is in the far west-central portion of the country, not far from **Lake Titicaca**.

Visitors can reach Bolivia by air, usually connecting through another South American city and landing at **El Alto Airport** (LPB) in La Paz. The railway network is chaotic and trains are slow. There are air connections between major cities, as well. Because of the high altitudes, the climate in Bolivia is cooler than in the rest of South America; June through August, especially, is extremely chilly. The regions deepest in the mountains get quite cold. Spanish is the national language.

Important Places

The two main sites for tourists in Bolivia are around La Paz and Lake Titicaca. Here are some of the most popular attractions:

- **La Paz** is a modern, fairly sophisticated city. The main boulevard and hotel area, **El Prado**, provides fascinating markets of all kinds, including a legal "black market." The city also has many fine cultural museums. The drive to **Chacaltaya** mountain is breathtakingly stunning, but its steep and winding curves should be recommended only to the fearless.

- **Tiwanaku** (Tiahuanaco), with its famed ancient stone ruins and the unusual rock formations of the **Valley of the Sun**, is 40 miles from La Paz.

- **Lake Titicaca** is shared by Bolivia and Peru, though it's most commonly accessed from Bolivia. It's the highest navigable lake in the world. **Copacabana** is a popular, lively resort on its southwestern shore.

Sales Considerations

Bolivia is a beautiful country, but quite challenging. It should be recommended especially to more adventurous travelers. It's very well suited as an extension of a trip to Peru, because Lake Titicaca covers parts of both countries. Bolivia has begun to take advantage of its

Because of the lack of oxygen at its 12,000-foot altitude, La Paz is nearly fireproof.

Bolivia's Aymara Indians were the first to cultivate the potato.

appeal to ecotourists. Many specialized tour companies are developing and selling adventure tours that appeal to hikers, campers, and lovers of nature. Because so much of Bolivia is at high altitudes, visitors may need some time to adjust.

Paraguay

Paraguay, just east of the Andes, is the second of South America's two landlocked countries. The capital city, **Asuncion** (ASU), is the gateway into Paraguay; buses are the most common means of getting around. The climate is hot from September to April, with rain possible at any time of the year. It's also fairly humid. From May through August, the temperature finally cools down to the 70s during the day. The national language here, too, is Spanish.

Important Places

Paraguay offers some pleasing attractions for those who visit:

- **Asuncion** is a charming city. There's an odd, small-town feel here, with trees and gardens everywhere. The city's slow pace is especially evident during a three-hour siesta at midday. There are some churches, parks, and museums. A particularly charming train ride leads to the botanical garden and zoo. For cruise lovers, the Paraguay River connects Asuncion to Buenos Aires, Argentina.
- **The Golden Triangle** is the eastern farmland area of Paraguay. Visitors will find small, old villages throughout the Golden Triangle.
- **Iguazu Falls** is at Paraguay's eastern border. Very few tourists, however, access the Falls from Paraguay, choosing instead Brazil or Argentina, which are more strategically located to the Falls.

Sales Considerations

Because it's often missed on the larger "sampler" tours of South America's highlights, Paraguay is a good recommendation for travelers returning to this southerly continent for a second visit. A jungle safari trip is often part of a more general escorted tour package. Paraguay is well known for its shopping opportunities. Because of holiday festivities, it's not advisable to go during December and January. May through September (winter) probably offers the most pleasant weather and the fewest crowds.

Dueling is legal in Paraguay if both parties have registered as blood donors.

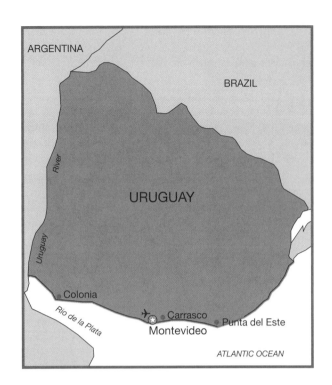

Uruguay

Tucked between Brazil and Argentina, Uruguay is one of the most European countries of South America. Its capital, **Montevideo** [mon-tay-vee-DAY-o] (MVD), on the southern coast, is where most visitors arrive, either by air or by cruise. Ninety miles east is **Punta del Este**, the most famous beach resort on Uruguay's 200-mile-long "Riviera of South America."

Uruguay has a very comfortable, temperate climate. Its lengthy summer lasts from November until March. July is the coldest month, with daytime temperatures in the 50s. Rental cars are widely available and visitors might enjoy driving around the countryside. (Montevideo's traffic, though, can be insane.) Spanish is the national language.

Important Places

Though small, Uruguay has some particularly interesting sites:

- **Montevideo** is a friendly and spacious city. Many of its most interesting buildings surround the **Plaza Independencia**. There are also very good parks, markets, and museums. The nearby resort town of **Carrasco** has excellent beaches and grand old mansions. And a half-hour away is **Tablada**, often called the "Town of the *Gauchos*."

- **Colonia** is about 70 miles west of Montevideo, a one-hour trip, via catamaran, from Buenos Aires, Argentina. The historic town—well off the beaten path of tourists—preserves the cobblestoned and walled ambience of Spanish and Portuguese colonial times.

- The "Riviera" runs east from Montevideo. Punta del Este is its most popular resort. Trendy and lively, it offers gambling and has many nightclubs. Excellent fishing is nearby.

Sales Considerations

Uruguay is a good choice for people interested in exotic nature and for those who want to visit a South American country largely free of crime and political turmoil. It's also a wonderful add-on to a visit to Brazil and/or Argentina. Punta del Este is popular with sun-seekers who love "discovering" a new resort destination. Air day trips from Montevideo to Buenos Aires or to Iguazu Falls are potential cross-sell opportunities.

Montevideo is well known for its cuisine.

A hovercraft carries passengers between Buenos Aires and Montevideo.

Many find the country's blend of cultures rather intriguing. (Uruguay, like Argentina, has many people of Italian and German descent.) This—and the availability of fine meats from Uruguay's ranches—makes for an especially diversified cuisine.

Argentina

Argentina, South America's second-largest country, is about one-third the size of the United States. The country shares its western border with Chile; the Andes serve as a border between the two. Its major city and capital is **Buenos Aires**. The popular beach resort **Mar del Plata** is south of Buenos Aires. The **Lake District** is in the western part of the country, near the Andes.

There's a very strong European influence in Argentina, where a local is almost as likely to have an Italian name as a Hispanic one. Though Spanish is the national language, English is widely spoken in the major cities. Buenos Aires is the gateway into Argentina for cruises and for flights, at **Ezeiza Ministro Pistarini Airport** (EZE). Flying time from New York is 9 hours; from Los Angeles it's 14 hours. **Aerolineas Argentinas** (AR) is Argentina's large national carrier, though many other airlines serve the country. Within Argentina,

Over one-third of all Argentineans are of Italian descent.

Climate at a Glance
BUENOS AIRES, ARGENTINA

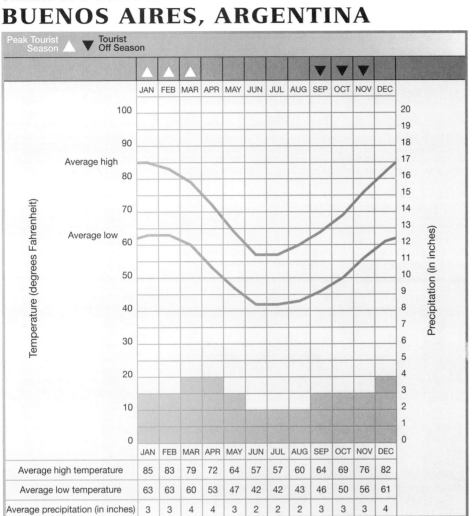

	JAN	FEB	MAR	APR	MAY	JUN	JUL	AUG	SEP	OCT	NOV	DEC
Average high temperature	85	83	79	72	64	57	57	60	64	69	76	82
Average low temperature	63	63	60	53	47	42	42	43	46	50	56	61
Average precipitation (in inches)	3	3	4	4	3	2	2	2	3	3	3	4

Figure 13–1

there's very good air, bus, and railroad service. Car rentals are widely available, but distances can be long and challenging in some areas, and city traffic is hectic. The weather in Buenos Aires is wonderful: The summer months of December through February hit the mid-80s and descend to the mid-60s at night. Winter (June through August) is cooler but still pleasant (see Figure 13–1).

Important Places

No visitor to Argentina should miss a stay in Buenos Aires, one of the world's great cities. Considered by some to be a South American Paris (some of the buildings even have gray mansard roofs), sprawling Buenos Aires is very cosmopolitan and has wonderful cuisine, top fashion, good museums, many parks, wide boulevards, and a lively nightlife. The city is also fairly safe for tourists. Notable attractions are:

- **Plaza de Mayo**, the political heart of the city, with colonial buildings and the city's cathedral. Its **Casa Rosada** (Pink House) is a landmark government building.
- **Avenida 9 de Julio**, reputedly the widest boulevard in the world.
- **Colon Theatre**, a huge, world-class opera house that has hosted the likes of Toscanini, Nijinski, and Baryshnikov. Tours are offered regularly.

On Calle Florida is a replica of Big Ben's tower, given to Buenos Aires by the city of London.

Gaucho ranches feature barbecued meals and horseback riding on the *pampas* (broad, grassy plains).

- **Diverse neighborhoods**, such as **San Telmo**, the old colonial section with cobblestone streets, tango nightclubs, and markets. Another interesting neighborhood to visit is **La Boca**, the Italian district, noted for its intensely colored buildings, fine art galleries, al-fresco dining opportunities, and lively restaurants.

- **Calle Florida**, a popular pedestrian-only street of shops and stores (including many leather manufacturers who will provide custom-made coats).

Some of Argentina's other destinations include:

- **Mar del Plata**, about 250 miles south of Buenos Aires, with 5 miles of great beaches. There are hundreds of hotels, excellent shopping, and a huge casino.

- **Iguazu Falls**, probably the widest series of waterfalls in the world. The falls are shared by Argentina, Brazil, and Paraguay, but are more often visited from Brazil.

- **The Lake District**, often compared to Switzerland. The town of **Bariloche**, just south of **Lake Nahuel Huapi** [nah-WEL wah-PEE], is a popular year-round resort; summer

Two of the hundreds of strange stone carvings that cover Easter Island
Image copyright Andrzej Gibasiewicz, 2008. Used under license from Shutterstock.com

offers great fishing, whereas the winter season (from June through October) provides excellent skiing. Other major ski resorts are **Las Lenas** and **Chapelco**.

- **Patagonia**, a vast stretch of land in southern Argentina, is famous for its animals, birds, and rolling, largely unspoiled countryside. To its south is the **Strait of Magellan**, **Tierra del Fuego** (shared with Chile), and the port of **Ushuaia**—important destinations on cruises around the tip of South America or to Antarctica.

Sales Considerations

Argentina will appeal to those who want a European flavor to their Latin American experience. It's safer than many other South American destinations, an important consideration for some. For those planning to travel around the country, an air package is ideal. Argentineans love sports of all kinds; sports packages are, therefore, an attractive cross-sell for Argentina-bound travelers. Tourists almost always visit one of the tango clubs in Buenos Aires, and it's usually worth the experience.

Chile

This pencil-thin country—at one point, it's only 56 miles wide—snakes down the west coast of South America to the tip of the continent. Chile is separated from Argentina by the Andes. Most of the interesting sites are in the central plains of the country. The area is flanked by bone-dry desert to the north, whereas the south (split by the Strait of Magellan and reaching almost to Antarctica) breaks up into little islands and fjord-like inlets. Chile's capital, **Santiago**, is located almost directly in the center of the country. Northwest of it is the major port of **Valparaiso** and the popular beach resort, **Vina del Mar**. A bit farther north is **Portillo**, a major ski resort. Another of Chile's most famous sites is actually more than 2,000 miles west of the mainland: **Easter Island**, with its mysterious, giant statues.

Lan Airlines (LA) is the major Chilean airline and flies into the gateway of Santiago (SCL). Valparaiso is the port of entry for cruises. Air service and trains connect the major cities. Chile has an excellent bus system. Car rentals are widely available, though some of the conditions off the Pan-American Highway can be quite difficult. Spanish is the national language.

The weather in Santiago from November through March (summer) is pleasant and dry, but it can get hot. Winter gets chilly, dropping to as low as the 30s at night. Vina del Mar's climate tends to be milder throughout the year. On Easter Island, the weather is temperate, ranging between 60 and 80 degrees.

Important Places

Santiago, surrounded by the Andes, offers beautiful scenery, lovely colonial architecture, and many modern structures. The city has good museums and an excellent planetarium. The most interesting sites include:

- **Plaza de Armas**, where many of the finest colonial buildings are found, including the huge cathedral and the **National Historical Museum**.
- **San Francisco Church and Colonial Art Museum**, a fascinating complex.

In addition to Santiago, Chile provides tourists with other wonderful places to visit, including:

- **Vina del Mar**, an expensive, fashionable beach resort.
- **Portillo**, one of the world's finest ski resorts, open at full operation from June through September and on a more limited basis the rest of the year.
- **Easter Island**, far off in the Pacific, with a volcanic, tree-stripped landscape. The most famous attractions here are huge statues, erected most probably for religious purposes. The island can be reached via air (a five-hour flight from the mainland of Chile) or cruise.

Southern Argentina's indigenous people wrapped their feet in furs. So Spanish explorers called them *patagones,* or "big feet." Hence Patagonia.

The tango originated in Argentina at the end of the nineteenth century.

Chile is 2,650 miles long and has no rivers of any size.

The leader of Chile's war of independence was named Bernardo O'Higgins.

Easter Island may have been the world's first manmade ecological disaster. The natives completely deforested the island.

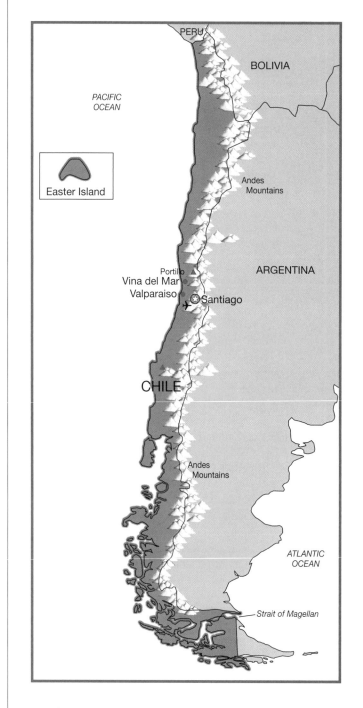

Sales Considerations

For many years, Chile was under military rule. However, it's once again a democracy, and tourism is on the rise. The country provides opportunities for skiers as well as beach lovers. Expeditions to Easter Island are popular with culture seekers.

Travel Trivia

Salty Attractions

- Salt Cathedral, Zipaquira, Colombia
- The Dead Sea, Israel/Jordan
- Bonneville Salt Flats, Utah
- Salt Cay, Turks & Caicos
- Kansas Underground Salt Museum, Kansas
- Etosha Salt Pan, Namibia
- Great Salt Lake, Utah
- Hallstatt Salt Mine, Austria
- Pekelmeer Salt Flats, Bonaire
- Wieliczka Salt Mine, Poland

NAME _____   **DATE** _____

MAP ACTIVITY

A traveler wants to visit the places listed below. Which number represents each on the map?

Place/Attraction	In Which Country?	Number on Map
A. Montevideo	A. _____	A. _____
B. Quito	B. _____	B. _____
C. Tikal	C. _____	C. _____
D. Cartagena	D. _____	D. _____
E. Machu Picchu	E. _____	E. _____
F. World's highest capital	F. _____	F. _____
G. Angel Falls	G. _____	G. _____
H. Buenos Aires	H. _____	H. _____
I. Santiago	I. _____	I. _____
J. The Golden Triangle	J. _____	J. _____

NAME _____ DATE _____

CASE STUDY

German and Leah Ruiz are a couple in their late 30s. Though they were both born in the United States, German's grandparents are from Venezuela and he has relatives there whom he's never met. The couple plan to take a 10-day trip; six days will be spent in Venezuela and the remaining time they'll spend in Buenos Aires. They don't have to worry about an itinerary in Venezuela; the relatives will take care of that. Buenos Aires is another matter and that's where they'll need some help.

Circle the answer that best suits their needs.

1. They want to visit an old Italian district known for its colorful houses. Where should they go?

    La Boca   Plaza de Mayo

    San Telmo   Portillo

    Why?

2. They'd like to squeeze in a natural wonder on their way from Venezuela to Buenos Aires. Which would be impossible for them to visit?

    Angel Falls   Iguazu Falls

    The Amazon   The Sea of Tranquility

    Why?

3. Which of the following services would be most appropriate for you to book for them in Buenos Aires?

    A cruise on Lake Titicaca   A city tour

    An Amazon cruise   A ski package

    Why?

4. They decide that they want to drive down the coast for a couple of days and spend some time at a beach resort. Which should it be?

    Mar del Plata   Punta del Este

    Vina del Mar   Villa D'Este

    Why?

NAME _____ DATE _____

CREATIVE ACTIVITY

A new *Star Wars* movie is in the works. Here's the plot: Luke Skywalker, now an old man, must find a successor to carry on the Jedi tradition. At the same time he is pursued by the evil clone of Darth Vader. First, Skywalker goes to a planet of mountains and ice. Then he travels to a hot, jungle planet. He leaves its lowlands, crosses a parched desert, and climbs to a mysterious ruined city in the cliffs, where a Yoda-like creature gives him many clues. But his pursuers catch up to him here. They chase him behind vast waterfalls and corner him in a fjord.

What? Did you think we'd give away the ending?! Anyway, you're the producer for this movie. You must find the necessary locations to shoot the scenes described. Why not shoot the entire film in Latin America? It will save money, and it has all the scenery needed.

In which Latin American place would you put up cast and crew for each location, assuming that you could take them by train or bus to and from the location each day? (Don't worry about the routing from base to location.) Assume flights are available to all places—no need to look up schedules.

Setting	Place
1 Mountains and ice	**1**
2 Jungle	**2**
3 Desert	**3**
4 City in the cliffs	**4**
5 Waterfalls	**5**
6 Fjord	**6**

What might be your flight itinerary for this shoot, assuming it starts and ends in Los Angeles?

NAME _____   **DATE** _____

PUTTING IT ALL TOGETHER

The Matching Game

Below is a list of cities, attractions, and so on; some we have covered, some we haven't. There are all manner of connections among them. With your group, you have exactly 10 minutes to come up with as many connections as possible. (Items may be used more than once.) Place your answers below. Note: There are at least 20 possible connections; for example, Sugar Loaf and Corcovado—both are mountains.

Dunn's River	Bogota	Bariloche
Galapagos	Vina del Mar	Iguazu
Machu Picchu	Las Hadas	Sierra Madres
Las Brisas	Asuncion	Sugar Loaf
Angel	Corcovado	French Guiana
Copacabana	Andes	Easter
Plaza de Mayo	Chichen Itza	Cayman
Copan	Mar del Plata	Haiti
Portillo	Bonaire	Zocalo

PART IV

EUROPE

Continental Flair

If an American decides to voyage overseas, it will in all probability be to visit Europe (often called "the Continent"). Indeed, Europe is a magnet for tourists from all countries. Most of the top-10 destinations for world travelers are in Europe. Celebrated historical monuments, sun-baked beaches, sparkling ski resorts, landmark hotels, gourmet restaurants, intriguing cultures and people—Europe has all of these. Many jets crisscross the Atlantic, so it's easy to get there. And once travelers arrive in Europe, they find an efficient network of railroads, highways, buses, motorcoach tours, and subways to get around. This broad array of services offers you, the travel professional, countless opportunities to enhance a person's European vacation.

According to the European Travel Commission, the number-one objection to visiting Europe is the cost.

Where the Countries Are

Over 40 countries comprise Europe; many of them have their own language and way of life. Don't be intimidated, though. Their locations can be mastered easily, especially when you sort them into logical geographical groupings.

Look at the map. Across the north are the **Scandinavian countries**: **Iceland**, **Norway**, **Sweden**, **Denmark**, and **Finland**. (Greenland, a seldom-visited destination to the west of Iceland, is usually considered part of North America.) On the Baltic Sea, just beneath the Scandinavian Peninsula, are the **Baltic nations** of **Estonia**, **Latvia**, and **Lithuania**. In the northwest are the **British Isles**, which consist of **Great Britain** and **Ireland** (which isn't really British at all).

In western Europe are **France** and the **Benelux countries** (*Be*lgium, the *Ne*therlands, and *Lux*embourg), as well as the **Iberian Peninsula**, which features **Portugal** and **Spain**. Spain is also sometimes included as part of the **Mediterranean countries**, which curve along the northern shore of this legendary sea. Among them are **Italy**, **Greece**, and **Turkey** (which spills over from Asia).

The Eastern European countries are **Poland**, the **Czech Republic**, **Slovakia** (also known as the Slovak Republic), **Hungary**, **Romania**, **Bulgaria**, and **Albania**. The former nation of Yugoslavia is also among these, but it has broken down into a series of smaller countries: **Slovenia**, **Croatia**, **Bosnia and Herzegovina**, **Macedonia**, and what remains of the original Yugoslavia (usually called **Serbia**). In the easternmost portion of Europe is **Russia** and its co-nations in the **Commonwealth of Independent States** (most of the former Soviet Union), which stretches well into Asia. And in the middle of Europe are the nations of Alpine Europe: **Germany**, **Switzerland**, and **Austria**.

About 60 cities and towns around the world promote themselves as "Little Switzerlands."

That's about all you need remember now. We'll mention Europe's smaller countries and principalities in the chapters that follow. Meanwhile, practice filling in a blank map of Europe to master where each country is situated. Do it over and again: You'll master their locations more quickly than you would expect.

A Satellite View

If you were looking down from space, it would be impossible to tell one European country from another. Borders, after all, aren't painted across the face of the earth. But things like mountains, oceans, lakes, and rivers have long defined Europe's national boundaries. And these geographic features affect travel plans in major ways.

Bodies of Water

The first thing you'd see from a satellite would be the broad blue expanse of the **Atlantic Ocean**, which lies along Europe's western shore. In the north, the **Baltic Sea** separates Scandinavia from Russia and the Baltic States; and the **North Sea** cuts off Great Britain from the Benelux countries, Germany, and Scandinavia. The **Irish Sea** lies between Ireland and Great Britain. From space, the narrow blue line that separates Great Britain from France, the **English Channel**, wouldn't seem very significant, but it has been a critical body of water for centuries and is crossed by numerous ferries, hovercraft, and the Channel Tunnel (or "Chunnel").

And of course, you'll easily make out the **Mediterranean Sea**, that long, azure feature that splits Europe from Africa. In several places, it stretches long fingers into Europe, including those of the **Adriatic** and **Ionian Seas** (between Italy, Greece, Croatia, and Albania) and the **Aegean Sea** (between Greece and Turkey). The Mediterranean is peppered with islands, many of which are beach or cruise destinations. Finally, the blue oval to the east is the **Black Sea**, a major resort for Eastern European and Russian tourists, as well as an increasingly popular destination for cruise ships.

If you have keen eyes, you could also spot a few major rivers crisscrossing Europe. The **Danube**, celebrated in literature and music, snakes its way eastward out of Germany through Eastern Europe and empties into the Black Sea. Down through Europe's middle is the **Rhine**, a river that finds its source in Switzerland and flows northward through Germany and the Netherlands, and eventually into the North Sea. Both rivers offer major cruise opportunities.

You may even be able to spot the lakes of northern Italy and of Switzerland, the fjords of western Norway, and the *lochs* (lakes) of northern Scotland. Many manmade waterways course through the continent, too: Barge rides on canals are an increasingly popular option for vacationers.

Mountains

It's critical to know where the mountains of Europe are; they have a significant impact on weather, travel times, and vacation activities. The most obvious are the **Alps**, the thick, lofty mountains that ripple across Switzerland, Austria, southern Germany, eastern France, and northern Italy. The **Pyrenees**, massive ridges that separate Spain from France, are important, too. Medium-sized mountains and hills are in many other areas; only Denmark, Poland, Hungary, and the Benelux countries are relatively flat.

Climate

Europe's weather varies immensely according to latitude, altitude, and season. The Alpine mountain areas tend to be cold in winter and cool in summer. Skiers favor the winter, of course, but a surprisingly large number of vacationers visit in the summer. (Late spring or early fall, though, can be glorious and uncrowded.) Northern France, the Benelux countries,

At the English Channel's narrowest point, only 21 miles separate Dover, England, from Cape Griz-Nez, France.

There are about 40,000 ski runs in the Alps.

Conwy Castle in Wales is a classic example of a medieval castle
Image copyright Chris Green, 2008. Used under license from Shutterstock.com

Eastern Europe, much of Germany, and the Alpine lowlands are similar to America's Pacific Northwest: cool to cold in winter, with much dampness and cloudiness; cool to warm in the spring or fall. The Mediterranean rim is an all-year destination, though summers can get hot; winters are mild, but cold weather is not unheard of here. Mediterranean water temperatures are chilly, and rain is more common in the winter months.

Precipitation also varies greatly. As you'd expect from what you learned in Part I, Europe's west coasts are wet; this is especially true of Norway's fjord area, the west coasts of Scotland and Ireland, northwestern Portugal, and the eastern shore of the Adriatic. There are also some very dry areas, especially southeastern and central Spain and the area northeast of the Black Sea. Rainfall in the rest of Europe tends to be like that of the northeastern United States: humid and showery in the summer; rainy, snowy, or cloudy in the winter, with brief, welcome spells of crisp sunshine.

Tourism Patterns

The United Kingdom is the most popular destination among North Americans, with France, Italy, and Spain not far behind. But these days, just about every country in Europe attracts both leisure and business travelers.

One important pattern: Europeans tend to take very long summer vacations, usually from mid-July to late August. And they generally head south to Spain, the French Riviera,

Many cities in New York State are named after ancient Mediterranean cities. Some examples: Utica, Ithaca, Syracuse, Troy, Carthage, and Rome.

Italy, and Greece. As a result, northern European cities seem somewhat empty at this time. Hotel room availability in central and northern Europe is, therefore, surprisingly good in late summer.

European Distances

Because Europe brims with so many countries, it seems enormous. Yet Europe is about the same size as the United States. A good comparison would be to think of each European nation as a geographic equivalent of a U.S. state.

Remember, too, that certain cities in totally separate countries can, in reality, be very close to each other. For example, Brussels, the capital of Belgium, is less than a half-day drive or a 1.5-hour train ride from Paris; Paris is a mere one-hour flight from London; and Munich, Germany, is quite close to Salzburg, Austria.

Once Europe's compactness sinks in, however, it's easy to mistakenly think that traveling times within Europe are always short. Not so. Some nations—like Germany, Belgium, and the Netherlands—do have complex and modern highway systems; that's why car rentals are very popular there. On the other hand, Spain, Portugal, Greece, Ireland, Scotland, most of Scandinavia, and Eastern Europe have a more limited network of highways. As a result, to drive from, say, the Italian Riviera to Rome would take at least two days—even though the distance is about the same as from Boston to Washington, D.C., which (because of the highway system) is only about an eight-hour drive.

Trains can be a direct and swift alternative, but not always. Europe's high-speed trains are a wonder: They whoosh from Paris to Geneva in 3.5 hours and at speeds approaching 200 mph. On the other hand, Lisbon to Madrid (a distance equal to that of Paris to Geneva) takes about 11 hours by train. Old tracks, curving routes, and awkward train connections can make some rail trips long and slow. For most tourists, this wouldn't be acceptable. (However, a slow, leisurely trip might be exactly what some want.) Several luxurious train excursions exist in Europe, including the most legendary of all: the Venice Simplon-Orient-Express. A principal route is London to Venice, but there are many alternative itineraries.

Cruises are very popular. Major cruise areas are the Eastern Mediterranean (including Greece, Turkey, and sometimes Israel and Egypt); the Western Mediterranean (Italy, France, and Spain); a route from Barcelona, Spain, along Portugal and France, and on to Great Britain; a British Isles itinerary; and several routings that call on ports in France, the Netherlands, Germany, Scandinavia, the Baltics, and Russia. Most European cruises are 7 to 14 days in length. In addition to cruise ships, Europe's waterways also feature small barges, large riverboats, and very large ferries, which sometimes offer overnight accommodations.

And what of aircraft? Of course, they provide rapid European connections, though sometimes high-speed trains are just as fast. Air travel, however, doesn't provide those features that make train travel and motoring attractive: the scenery along the way, travel unaffected by snow or fog (especially true for trains), and the option to stop and see some magnificent castle or fairytale town. One offbeat option: short or multiday balloon trips, most often staged in France and Italy, but also available in Switzerland, Austria, and Turkey.

Some Miscellaneous Considerations

Certain bits of knowledge can help fine-tune your understanding of Europe. Here are a few considerations:

- Many European hotels are old and lack elevators, have small rooms, and feature only single-sized beds. Always check standard industry references before making reservations and make sure the lodging matches what the traveler wants.

- Eurail Passes are handy (though not quite the bargain they used to be) and an important item to cross-sell. These passes often cover airport transfers and ferries, too. Consult the Internet for rates, countries covered, services offered, and the like. First class is probably

Europe is the smallest continent after Australia.

The most famous high-speed trains are Eurostar (Transchunnel), ICE (Germany), TGV (France), X2000 (Sweden), AVE (Spain), and Pendolino (Italy).

According to a study by psychology professor Adrian White, the happiest people on earth live in Denmark, followed by Switzerland and Austria. The United States ranked 23rd.

Eurail Global Passes (and many single-country and regional passes) can be purchased only in North America.

The Eurostar train carries passengers at speeds well beyond 100 mph
Image copyright Thor Jorgen Udvang, 2008. Used under license from Shutterstock.com

better for American visitors, because in many countries second-class cars can be crowded, uncomfortable, or both. (The second-class Youth Pass is available for travelers under 26 years of age and may be a reasonable alternative.) Keep in mind that some privately run trains do not accept Eurail passes.

■ A single-country or regional train pass is a better value for a person traveling extensively in only one area. Some countries even offer rail-drive-lodging packages.

■ Seeing Europe by car appeals to those who are used to driving when they vacation. It offers much more routing, scheduling, and sightseeing flexibility than do trains. The same applies to camper rentals, which have become an increasingly popular way of motoring through Europe. One warning, though: European driving—with its very high-speed highways, twisting secondary roads, narrow city streets, limited parking, many tolls, and high gasoline prices—can challenge the best driver. Also, travelers who rent a car in central or northern Europe may be told when they pick up the car that they cannot drive it in southern Europe, or that their insurance will not cover them in the south. It's important to know in advance if such conditions will apply.

Cars in most European nations tend to be small. The reason: so they can navigate the very narrow streets in city centers; and gasoline is much more expensive than in the United States.

- Most European countries have their own airlines, which offer regular service to major U.S. gateways and are partners in the frequent-flyer programs of American carriers—a major consideration for some travelers.

- In the past, flights between countries in Europe were expensive. This has changed, however, as low-fare airlines have appeared throughout Europe.

- European carriers often offer fly-drive packages at substantially discounted rates.

- Most major European cities are quite expensive, with Paris, Milan, Venice, London, and the Scandinavian capitals among the most costly in the world. Portugal, Ireland, Greece, Turkey, and some places in Eastern Europe are still relative bargains.

- In the following chapters, under "Lodging Options," you'll be reading about hotel chains that have major presences in Europe, such as Novotel, Le Meridien, Golden Tulip, and Movenpick. U.S. and Canadian companies include Sheraton, Marriott, Holiday Inn, Best Western, Hyatt, Fairmont, Four Seasons, and Hilton. Be aware that there are many European hotels that are part of no official chain, but are represented by reservation organizations. For example, some of Europe's (and the world's) most exclusive hotels are booked via Leading Hotels of the World and Preferred Hotels. Even some hotels that *are* part of major chains can also be affiliated with these two organizations for the prestige it brings. A service that represents a broader range of hotel values in Europe is Utell International.

- Europe is striving to become a more unified political and economic unit. It has become easier for tourists to cross borders; intra-Europe flight costs are dropping, and more multicountry high-speed train lines have been built. Much of Europe has a single currency (the euro), standardized electrical outlets, uniform value-added taxes (VAT: taxes on goods and services), and passport-free travel. But longstanding traditions have made these tourism-facilitating breakthroughs a bit slow to achieve.

Travel Trivia

You Know It's Spring In . . . When . . .

- The Netherlands and Ottawa: The tulips bloom.

- Rome: Outdoor Easter Mass is celebrated at St. Peter's.

- Alaska: You hear the sound of ice breaking up on the rivers.

- Washington, D.C., and Tokyo: The cherry blossoms bloom.

- Sydney: People start planning their Christmas shopping.

- New York City: The Easter Parade takes place on Fifth Avenue.

- Guatemala: The Passion Play is performed in the city of Antigua.

- Daytona Beach, Palm Springs, Fort Lauderdale, Clearwater, and South Padre Island: Students pour in for spring break.

- London: Someone first sights a cuckoo bird.

NAME _____   DATE _____

CREATIVE ACTIVITY

The kinds of people who prefer to visit Europe via rental car are different from those who wish to do so by train, plane, or ship. What do you think are the advantages and disadvantages of each way of getting around?

	Advantages	**Disadvantages**
Car Rental:	❶ Stop where/when you want	❶ Dealing with traffic
	❷	❷
	❸	❸
Rail Travel:	❶	❶
	❷	❷
City-to-City Air Travel:	❶	❶
	❷	❷
Cruise Travel:	❶	❶
	❷	❷

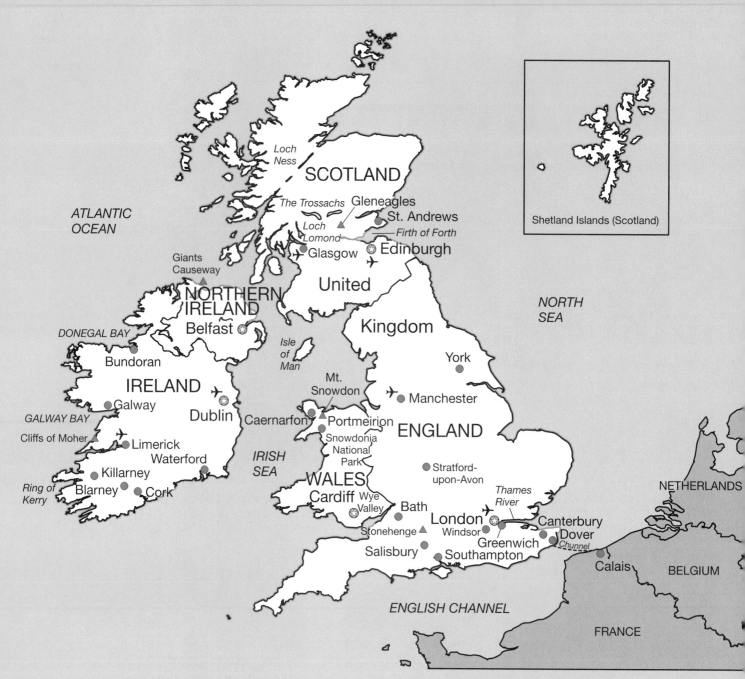

ATLANTIC OCEAN

SCOTLAND

Loch Ness

The Trossachs
Gleneagles
St. Andrews
Loch Lomond
Firth of Forth
Glasgow
Edinburgh

United

Giants Causeway

NORTHERN IRELAND

Belfast

Kingdom

DONEGAL BAY

Bundoran

IRELAND

Galway

GALWAY BAY

Cliffs of Moher

Dublin

Limerick
Waterford

Killarney

Blarney   Cork

Ring of Kerry

Isle of Man

York

Mt. Snowdon
Caernarfon
Portmeirion
Snowdonia National Park

Manchester

ENGLAND

IRISH SEA

WALES

Cardiff

Wye Valley

Stratford-upon-Avon

Thames River

Bath

Stonehenge

London
Windsor
Greenwich
Salisbury
Southampton

Canterbury
Dover
Chunnel

NORTH SEA

NETHERLANDS

Calais

BELGIUM

ENGLISH CHANNEL

FRANCE

Shetland Islands (Scotland)

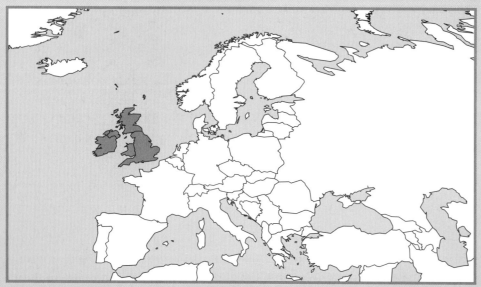

Chapter 14

Great Britain and Ireland

Foreign, Yet Familiar

Great Britain and Ireland may be a perfect first visit for someone who hasn't yet been to Europe. Far across the Atlantic, they're distant and different enough to be intriguing, yet their language and familiar culture offer a sense of security and comfort.

How do England, Great Britain, and the United Kingdom differ? The *United Kingdom* is made up of four quasi-independent countries. Three of them constitute the island of *Great Britain*: **England**, the largest (about the size of New York State), is to the southeast (the term *England* is sometimes used—incorrectly—for all of Great Britain); **Wales** is southwest; and **Scotland** is to the north. The fourth is **Northern Ireland**, across the Irish Sea on the northeast corner of the island of Ireland. (In this chapter we'll use the term *Great Britain*, because we're focusing on England, Scotland, and Wales.) The nation of **Ireland** is distinct from Northern Ireland. It's a separate country from the United Kingdom and feels very strongly about its independence.

Nearly the size of Oregon, Great Britain has two centers of tourism. **London**, a world unto itself, is a base for day trips in England, and **Edinburgh** [ED-in-bur-ro] is the heart of Scottish touring. Ireland has no real hub; visitors travel from town to town.

Names in Great Britain aren't always pronounced the way they look. For example, the Scottish town of Kirkcudbright is pronounced "kuh-KOO-bree."

How Travelers Get There

There's extensive service to London on domestic and foreign carriers. Most travelers arrive at **Heathrow Airport** (LHR), but **Gatwick** (LGW) and **Stansted** (STN)—which are farther out—also offer many flights. All three offer rail service into the city. Visitors heading directly to Scotland may fly into **Glasgow** (GLA), Edinburgh Airport (EDI), or even to **Manchester** (MAN), which lies halfway between London and Scotland. Travel time to London from New York is 6.5 hours, from Chicago it's 7.5 hours, from Los Angeles it's 10.5 hours. The national airline, **British Airways** (BA), flies throughout the world; **Virgin Atlantic** (VS) services North America and Europe; and **British Midland** (BD) flies domestically and to the Continent.

A hovercraft crosses the English Channel from Dover to France, and many ferries operate from other towns along both coasts. The **Channel Tunnel** (or "**Chunnel**") connects **Folkestone** (west of Dover) to Calais, France, and permits passengers to travel between Paris and London via the high-speed **Eurostar** train in under 2.5 hours.

Even though **Dublin** (DUB) is Ireland's capital and has a major airport, the country's principal air gateway is **Shannon** (SNN), outside **Limerick**. The national airline, **Aer Lingus** (EI), is the major carrier from Boston and New York into Shannon, but service

257

FYI
FOR YOUR INFORMATION

GREAT BRITAIN AND IRELAND

CAPITALS: Great Britain: London
Ireland: Dublin
AREAS (SQUARE MILES): Great Britain: 94,500
Ireland: 27,000

TIME ZONE: GMT: +0
DRIVE ON: Left
POPULATIONS: Great Britain: 60,900,000
Ireland: 4,200,000

RELIGION: Great Britain: Protestant
Ireland: Roman Catholic
LANGUAGE: English
CURRENCIES: Great Britain: 1 pound = 100 pence
Ireland: 1 euro = 100 cents
ELECTRICITY: 220 volts, 50 cycles AC

CAPSULE HISTORY: Great Britain: Rome invades, first century B.C.; Angles and Saxons invade, fifth century; England united, eleventh century; Normans invade, 1066; Magna Carta signed, 1215; Church of England breaks from Pope, sixteenth century; formation of Parliament, eighteenth century; World War I, 1914–1918; World War II, 1939–1945; first woman prime minister, 1979; greater autonomy given to Scotland and Wales, 1997.

Ireland: St. Patrick introduces Christianity, 432; Norsemen defeated, 1014; becomes separate republic, 1921.

For reference sources, tourist bureaus, and suggested lengths of stay, see the Appendices.

is also provided by many other air carriers. Flights are just over six hours; some continue on to Dublin, which takes approximately 35 minutes more.

Cruises to Great Britain and Ireland from Spain, France, Germany, and other countries are numerous. England's three major embarkation ports are **Southampton, Tilbury**, and **Tower Bridge** (in London itself). Cunard Line offers regularly scheduled cruise sailings from New York City to Southampton. Ships on repositioning or round-the-world cruises also often stop at ports in the British Isles.

Weather Patterns

Visitors can tour the interior of London's famous Tower Bridge.

Because of the warming influence of the Gulf Stream, Great Britain's generally moderate climate is similar to Oregon's, even though it's almost at the latitude of southern Alaska. The famous London fog is a memory of the past; it was actually smog, which has been brought under control. English summers hover around 70 degrees. Conditions change often between sunshine and rain. Winters are sharp (in the 40s) and wet, with occasional snow (see Figure 14–1). Most tourists visit between mid-April and mid-October; the peak tourist season extends from June to September. Scotland is cooler and rainier than England in winter, but summers are about the same. The best time to see Great Britain may be spring or fall, when the weather is still pretty good and crowds are somewhat thinner. The period just after New Year's is particularly slow; it's one of the only times to get bargains in London.

Ireland's weather is similar to Great Britain's, but runs slightly cooler, cloudier, and wetter. As a result, the tourist season is a bit shorter: May to September. Summers are in the 60s, with frequent rain showers and fog (but long periods of daylight). Winters have more misty, rainy, or overcast days. It's hard to avoid precipitation here, but that's why the land is such a deep green. Ireland isn't called the Emerald Isle for nothing.

Climate at a Glance
LONDON, ENGLAND

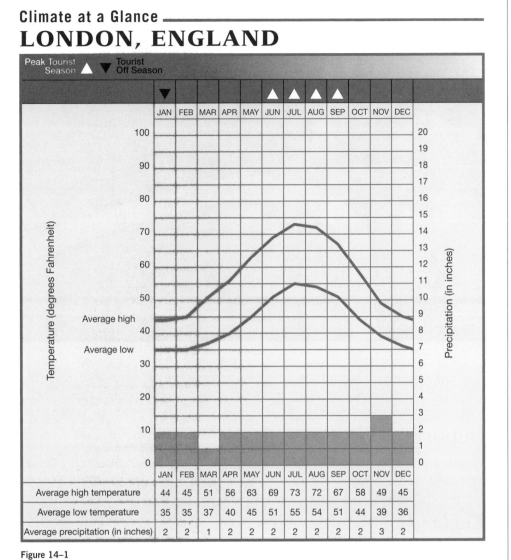

	JAN	FEB	MAR	APR	MAY	JUN	JUL	AUG	SEP	OCT	NOV	DEC
Average high temperature	44	45	51	56	63	69	73	72	67	58	49	45
Average low temperature	35	35	37	40	45	51	55	54	51	44	39	36
Average precipitation (in inches)	2	2	1	2	2	2	2	2	2	2	3	2

Figure 14–1

Getting Around

Many airlines and flights connect the area's major cities. The excellent rail system links towns throughout Great Britain, as do many buses. (Some high-speed trains cover distances in half the time a car would.) Visitors can also reach Ireland by ferry, and once there, travel by train and bus.

London, despite its size, is easy for tourists to navigate. The subway system (called the Underground or the Tube) goes almost everywhere. Visitors can use two of the great transportation icons: the lumpy taxis and the red double-decker buses. London is also a very walkable city.

What about driving? Car rentals are widely available, but mastering the art of tooling down the "wrong" side of the road is, without question, one of life's challenges. Actually, though, driving down a quiet country lane can be a joy—except for the odd, circular intersections called roundabouts—but in major cities there are saner ways for a tourist to get around.

City and multiday tours are popular. Boats along the **Thames** [TEMZ] **River** in London are common, leisurely barge cruises through the countryside are delightful, and several cruise lines operate itineraries that call on English, Scottish, Welsh, and Irish ports.

BritRail passes for unlimited train travel in Britain can be bought only in North America. The Eurail Pass does not cover Britain (but does cover Ireland).

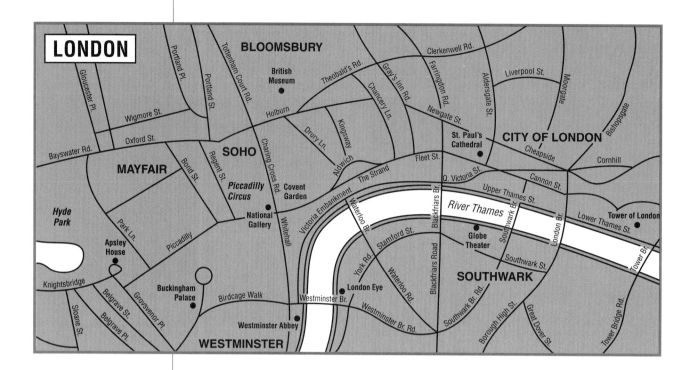

Important Places

Great Britain and Ireland abound with charming cities, villages, and attractions. There are some unique treasures here, even a few that are tied closely to the history of North America.

England

London—one of the largest and most lively cities in the world—offers a remarkable range of culture, history, and arts. First-time visitors will probably spend most of their time within the city. However, because London is also the central hub for seeing England, day trips offer veteran tourists even more opportunities. Return visitors to London will always find new plays to see (theater tickets are reasonably priced), as well as unexplored museums, shops, and streets. Among the most important attractions:

- **The Tower of London**, home of the Crown Jewels, infamous prisons, and armories. There are lots of tourists here and lots of historic pageantry, too. The Tower is, after all, one of Britain's top tourist attractions.

- **St. Paul's Cathedral**, the largest church in London, designed by Christopher Wren. In its Whispering Gallery, a word whispered to the wall can be heard clearly on the other side, over 100 feet away.

- **The British Museum**, a vast, legendary collection of such items as the Rosetta Stone and the Elgin (Parthenon) Marbles.

- **Buckingham Palace**'s Changing of the Guard, perhaps what tourists think of most when they think of London. Parts of the palace are occasionally open to tourists.

- **Westminster Abbey**, housing within its magnificent Gothic architecture the burial places of many of Great Britain's royalty, historical figures, and literary giants. Nearby are the **Houses of Parliament** and **Big Ben** (which isn't the famous tower or clock, but the bell).

The huge abstract form of London's Swiss Re building (nicknamed the Gher-
kin) contrasts with a traditional English church
Image copyright David Burrows, 2008. Used under license from Shutterstock.com

- ■ **The London Eye**, a tall, modern observation wheel on the south bank of the
  Thames. The 30-minute ride gives passengers great views of London and the surrounding countryside.
- ■ **Several well-known shopping districts and stores**, including Harrods and Selfridges
  (two famous department stores), Oxford Street, Regent Street, and Covent Garden.

When shopping, ask
the salesperson about
refunds on the VAT
(a tax on all goods
and services). Many
stores participate in a
service that mails you
a check or credits your
credit card account for
the VAT on purchases
over a certain amount.

London offers a wealth of **day-trip** options:

- **Stonehenge**, the strange, mystical circle of huge stones, a close drive to **Salisbury** (with its beautiful cathedral).
- **Stratford-upon-Avon** [AY-ven], a charming town that's Shakespeare's birthplace and home of the Royal Shakespeare Company.
- **Hampton Court Palace**, the expansive estate of Henry VIII, with its famous garden maze.
- **Windsor Castle**, home to Britain's monarchs for nearly 1,000 years. It's the oldest inhabited castle in the world.
- **Greenwich** [GRIH-nij], just down-river from London, site of the **National Maritime Museum**, the **Old Royal Observatory**, and the famed clipper ship *Cutty Sark*.
- **Bath**, an elegant city of Georgian architecture and Roman baths.
- **Canterbury**, an ancient, picturesque city with a magnificent cathedral that's the centerpiece of the Church of England and the destination of the pilgrims in Chaucer's famous work *The Canterbury Tales*. Minutes away are the **White Cliffs of Dover**.
- **York**, a walled medieval city that boasts the **National Railway Museum** (the world's largest), **York Minster** (a huge Gothic cathedral with impressive stained glass), the **Castle Museum** (with a recreated Victorian street), and the **Jorvik Viking Centre** (a reconstruction of the ninth-century Viking settlement that became York).

Scotland

Edinburgh, the capital of Scotland, has a regal, medieval ambience. It's a port city located on the Firth of Forth and is a good jumping-off point for the area. Among its best attractions:

- **Edinburgh Castle** looks the way a person imagines a castle should look, looming high above the city and built out of the rock it sits on.
- **The Palace of Holyroodhouse** is the residence of Queen Elizabeth II when she is in the city; it retains an infamous association with Mary, Queen of Scots.
- **The Royal Mile** connects Edinburgh Castle and Holyroodhouse. It's the oldest and most historic area of the city.

Some of the best **day trips** are:

- **The Trossachs** [TRAH-sacks], the area of Scotland's most beautiful moors and *lochs* (lakes), are a long drive and deserve more than one day.
- **Glasgow** is an industrial town, but with excellent theater, fine arts, and the superb **Burrell Collection** museum. It's near famous **Loch Lomond** and is surrounded by very pretty countryside.
- **The Glasgow–Edinburgh area** is considered a virtual shrine for golfers. There are many championship courses, including the legendary **Old Course** at **St. Andrews**, and **Gleneagles**.
- **Loch Ness** is well known for its often-sighted but never-found monster.

Wales

Though perhaps not as familiar as other parts of Britain, Wales nonetheless contains interesting sights. It's a land of mountains and castles, with a strong Celtic influence. Many residents of North Wales speak Welsh as their first language. Among the attractions in Wales:

- **Snowdonia National Park**. Steam trains climb to the summit of **Mt. Snowdon** for spectacular views of North Wales.
- **Caernarfon** [kyre-NAR-von]. The town is still partially encircled by its walls and is dominated by the huge castle where Charles was invested as Prince of Wales.

In York, streets are called "gates," gates are called "bars," and bars are called "pubs."

The British Open golf tournament, held in mid-July, is usually played in Scotland at St. Andrews or Gleneagles.

The village with the longest place name in the world is in northern Wales: Llanfairpwllgwyngyllgogerychwyrndrobwllllantysiliogogogoch, known locally as Llanfair P.G.

Tintern Abbey inspired poets such as Wordsworth
Photo by Karen Fukushima

- **Portmeirion** [port-MARE-ee-on]. This extraordinary Italian-style village overlooking the sea was the setting for the 1960s cult TV series "The Prisoner." It's now a hotel and is also famous for Portmeirion china.
- **The Wye Valley.** In this valley on the English border are many semi-ruined castles and churches, including well-known **Tintern Abbey. Hay-on-Wye** is a book-lover's dream; most of the town consists of second-hand bookstores. World-famous authors give readings at its annual literary festivals.
- **Cardiff.** The capital of Wales, Cardiff boasts a whimsically restored castle and the **Welsh Folk Museum** at **St. Fagans**. Buildings from all over Wales were reassembled here, providing a living history of the nation.

Remember, too, that **Northern Ireland**, despite its political problems, still manages to attract many travelers. Visitors to Scotland or to Ireland often sidetrack for a few days to see Northern Ireland's scenic countryside or to play on its many golf courses. **Giants Causeway**, a natural formation of volcanic columns in the sea off Northern Ireland's north coast, is fascinating.

Ireland

Ireland's attractions are scattered about the country, not concentrated in one or two places. Among the towns and attractions to visit:

- **Dublin**, the capital of Ireland, has a stormy and vibrant past. It offers a rich collection of medieval history, modern arts, and pubs. Among its attractions are **St. Patrick's**

According to local legend, Giants Causeway was built by a giant.

Members of the Irish rock band U2 own Dublin's Clarence Hotel.

Cathedral, containing many monuments and plaques; **Christ Church**'s vaulted crypt; **Dublin Castle**, part of which dates back to the Celts; **Trinity College**, with a collection of old book treasures (including the Book of Kells); and the **National Museum**, holding one of the world's great gold collections (with some Bronze Age pieces).

- **Bundoran**, a popular resort, is located on **Donegal Bay**. Nearby is picturesque **Glenveigh National Park**.
- **Galway**, a beautiful and charming town on **Galway Bay**, is best visited by taking a relaxed walking tour. Just southwest of Galway are the dramatic **Cliffs of Moher**.
- **Limerick** is the first stop in Ireland after arriving at Shannon Airport. Historic, ancient architecture is everywhere, including **St. Mary's Church**.
- **Killarney** is renowned for its magnificent scenery of lakes, forests, and mountains. Nearby are **Bourne Vincent Memorial Park**, a national park; **Gap of Dunloe**, a stunning gorge; and the **Ring of Kerry**, a scenic drive past cliffs, mountains, lakes, and villages.
- **Cork** has extensive arts and cultural activities, including choral and drama festivals, ballet, and opera.
- **Blarney** is the town—only 6 miles from Cork—that's famous for its **Blarney Stone**, which is said to give the gift of eloquence to anyone who kisses it.
- **Waterford** is best known for its world-famous **Waterford crystal factory**.

Possible Itineraries

First-time visitors should spend about a week in London, including time for day trips through the area. The more experienced will still probably want to spend some time there before (or after) exploring the English countryside, Scotland, and Wales. Ireland could stand on its own for a full week. To visit the entire area of Great Britain and Ireland requires a stay of at least two weeks.

Lodging Options

Some of the most famous (and expensive) hotels in the world are in London's West End: **Claridge's**, the **Dorchester**, the **Ritz**, and the **Savoy**. Many interesting lodging alternatives exist, including bed-and-breakfasts, flats (apartments), manors and castles, and even working farms.

If conventional hotels remain the lodging of choice, there are other wonderful places to choose from, such as the very-English **Brown's** in London and the **Caledonian** in Edinburgh (though these, again, are costly). Among the most popular chains in Great Britain are **Millennium & Copthorne, Swallow, Moat House, Thistle**, and **Premier Inn**. North American chains also have a very large presence.

Ireland offers its own wide range of accommodations, and prices are lower than in Great Britain. There are still, of course, many first-class hotels, like Dublin's **Shelbourne**. **Jurys** is a large Irish chain. However, like Great Britain, Ireland offers wonderful alternative housing. Notable among these are the spectacular **Ashford Castle** near Galway and **Dromoland Castle** near Limerick, both of which offer stunning grounds. Other castles and manors, as well as bed-and-breakfasts, farmhouses, and cottages, can be found.

Allied Destinations

Great Britain and Ireland are an ideal starting point for a visit to the rest of Europe. France, especially, is an easy connection. And just across the North Sea are Denmark and the rest of Scandinavia, the Netherlands, and Belgium. Travelers can get to these places via air, ferry, cruise, and (through the Chunnel) train.

The world's first traffic lights were installed in London in 1868.

An exact reproduction of Shakespeare's Globe Theatre has been built in London near its original site.

The Giants Causeway in Northern Ireland is one of the strangest natural formations in the world
Image copyright Joe Gough, 2008. Used under license from Shutterstock.com

Cultural Patterns

Yes, visitors find Great Britain and Ireland to be comfortable and familiar destinations. Nonetheless, these nations have distinct cultural patterns as well. Here are a few tips:

- Business appointments must be booked well in advance.

- Honorary titles are *always* used, even among friends.

- Words for food are often different from those used in North America. *Pudding* can refer to dessert in general. *Biscuits* are cookies. *Beer* is generally bitter, dark, and tepid. (What North Americans call beer is known as *lager.*) *Crisps* are potato chips; while *chips* are French fries.

- Don't talk shop over drinks and dinner unless a local does it first.

- The British are generally reserved and subdued. Politeness is still the standard here.

- The peoples of Great Britain and Ireland are proud of their respective histories. Any visitor would do well to show an interest in these countries' pasts as well as current events.

- Promptness is important, especially for business appointments.

- When visiting the home of a local, it's not necessary to bring a gift; however, it's considered a thoughtful gesture. Any gift should be presented to the lady of the house.

- Scotland, Wales, and Northern Ireland are *not* England; they are all distinct regions of the United Kingdom. People here are very sensitive to these distinctions.

- Clearly, it's impossible and inappropriate to stereotype how people in each of these countries will act in every instance. There are, however, generalizations: Scotland tends to be more open, independent, and fun loving than England. Be careful about discussing religion and politics in Northern Ireland, where it's an extremely sensitive subject. And Ireland is generally a friendly, exuberant land.

Whisky is distilled in Scotland; *whiskey* (with an *e*) is distilled in Ireland.

Factors That Motivate Visitors

The major reasons for Americans to choose these destinations are cultural ties and ease of language; however, there might be other reasons, too. Understanding them all is essential in setting up a memorable trip:

- There are more air connections from North America to London than to any other international city.
- Convenient public transportation and cruise options make the countries easy to get around.
- Picturesque villages are just about everywhere.
- A diverse span of accommodations and price levels is available.
- London is a major center for cultural attractions and the theater.
- Ireland is relatively inexpensive and can be the choice of budget-minded vacationers.

Qualifying the Traveler
London

For People Who Want	Appeal			Remarks
	High	Medium	Low	
Historical and Cultural Attractions	▲			London's chief asset
Beaches and Water Sports			▲	So-so beaches to south
Skiing Opportunities			▲	None
Lots of Nightlife	▲			Especially theater
Family Activities		▲		Mostly sightseeing
Familiar Cultural Experience		▲		Foreign, but English-speaking
Exotic Cultural Experience		▲		
Safety and Low Crime		▲		Some clients fear terrorism
Bargain Travel			▲	London is one of the most expensive cities in the world; many museums are free, though
Impressive Scenery		▲		Especially the countryside
Peace and Quiet			▲	Some parts quiet
Shopping Opportunities	▲			Antiques, china, woolens, legendary department stores
Adventure			▲	Outside of the city
To Do Business	▲			Many U.S. businesses are British-owned and vice versa

- The region is well known for its lush scenery.
- Many visitors have retained a close family association to Ireland and Great Britain and want to trace their roots here.
- The locals are known to be courteous and hospitable.
- And, yes, of course, English is spoken and the culture is familiar.

Possible Misgivings

For any destination, including Great Britain and Ireland, people will always have concerns you'll have to address:

- "Driving on the left intimidates me." The public transportation infrastructure of trains, buses, subways, and taxis is excellent.
- "Isn't the food really bland?" The best meals, especially in London, tend to be foreign; try Indian, Italian, Asian, or African restaurants. Even traditional English food has improved. The new cuisine emphasizes the fresh foods readily available throughout the country.
- "It's extremely expensive there." Bed-and-breakfasts are a reasonable alternative, as are tourist-class hotels. Suggest Scotland, Wales, Ireland, or the English countryside, where costs are much lower than in London.
- "I've been to London and seen everything." The many other areas of Great Britain and Ireland offer a wealth of options.
- "The political unrest in Ireland frightens me." The country of Ireland is calm. The serious problems in Northern Ireland seem to have abated for now and rarely affected tourists.
- "Ireland's so rainy." This is precisely why it's so green and beautiful, but for sun seekers, there are better choices.

Sales Strategies

The unique qualities of Great Britain and Ireland provide many selling opportunities. Motorcoach tours free visitors from the anxiety of driving on the left side of the road. Cruises call on most of the essential places, as well as a few less visited ports. Lodging in castles might be that rare treat that makes a trip especially memorable. Barge cruises afford tourists a slow but special view of the country. Theater packages in London solve the problem of getting tickets to hit shows. An overnight ferry ride to Scandinavia turns yet one more connection into an adventure.

And remember: For those who are hesitant about visiting Europe because it's a "foreign" place, Great Britain and Ireland are ideal choices. The familiarity of language and customs make this a comfortable recommendation, whether as a stand-alone destination or as a first stop on the way to other European countries.

An especially interesting London pub is the Mayflower, which has on display an old copy of the passenger list of its namesake ship.

In 1300, the Pope declared that pilgrims should keep to the left on roads. The reason: so they could reach their swords easily if they passed a bandit. In the 1700s, the French began keeping to the right to let carriages go by. Napoleon spread the custom throughout Europe and it was copied by the newly formed United States. But the British never changed, nor did many of their colonies. Today, only 30 percent of the world travels on the left.

The Edinburgh International Festival, a huge arts festival, is held in late August.

Travel Trivia

Great Britain's Hidden Gems

1. Newstead Abbey, Nottinghamshire: The ancestral home of poet Lord Byron.

2. Sir John Soane's Museum, London: Eclectic collection (including the sarcophagus of pharaoh Seti I) of this historic architect.

3. The Wallace Collection, London: An impressive collection of art and armor in the former home of the Marquess of Hertford.

4. The National Railway Museum, York: One of the finest collections of railroad artifacts in the world.

5. Bede's World, Jarrow: Attraction at the site of the monastery where the Venerable Bede, England's first historian, lived.

6. St. Bartholomew-the-Great, London: Atmospheric 900-year-old church seen frequently in movies.

7. Avebury, Wiltshire: A stone circle that's larger than Stonehenge (though with smaller stones). It's so large that most of a village sits inside it.

8. Iona, Inner Hebrides, Scotland: The island where many ancient kings of Scotland are buried (including Macbeth).

9. Merton College, Oxford: One of Oxford's oldest colleges, where J.R.R. Tolkien, who authored *The Lord of the Rings*, was a professor.

10. Castell Coch, South Wales: Thirteenth-century castle rebuilt in the nineteenth century with fanciful interiors.

SOURCE: Marc Mancini

NAME _____   DATE _____

MAP ACTIVITY

A traveler wants to visit the places listed below. Which number represents each on the map?

Place/Attraction	In/Near Which City?	Number on Map
A. Stonehenge	A. _____	A. _____
B. Palace of Holyroodhouse	B. _____	B. _____
C. Italian-style village famous for china	C. _____	C. _____
D. The Blarney Stone	D. _____	D. _____
E. The Burrell Collection	E. _____	E. _____
F. St. Paul's Cathedral	F. _____	F. _____
G. A crystal factory	G. _____	G. _____
H. The Crown Jewels	H. _____	H. _____
I. Trinity College	I. _____	I. _____
J. The Royal Mile	J. _____	J. _____

NAME _____   DATE _____

CASE STUDY

Don and Karen Robinson are a couple in their late 30s, living in Orlando. They were in London 13 years ago, when they were first married; now, however, they have a 12-year-old son and are planning to return to the area. They would like to see some new sights, but don't want their son to miss out on anything. They have great curiosity and love theater, but Karen is not very adventurous in traveling. They can take off five workdays. They're staying in a hotel in London's Mayfair district. (To do this case study fully, you'll need to do a little research, either on the Internet or in print resources.)

Circle the answer that best suits their needs.

1 How many days total would be best for their trip?

Three   Five

Eight   Ten

Why?

2 On what area would you suggest they concentrate?

London and environs   London and Scotland

London and Ireland   Wales and Northern Ireland

Why?

3 Which of the following would you *not* recommend?

A trip to Stonehenge   A BritRail pass

A barge cruise   A city tour

Why?

4 Which of the following statements would be correct?

You'll probably have a nice view of the Tower of London from your hotel room.

Hyde Park will be just a short stroll from your hotel.

Your hotel is right on the River Thames.

The Royal Mile, where you're staying, is lined with wonderful shopping.

Why?

NAME _____ DATE _____

CREATIVE ACTIVITY

You're studying to be a London city Blue Guide. Blue Guides are considered to be among the world's most knowledgeable tour guides. Using the Internet and/or reference books (refer to the appendixes for suggestions), answer the following questions regarding sights in London for which you'll need to be informed.

1 How big is the "City of London"?

2 What is the Rosetta Stone?

3 What is Piccadilly Circus?

4 Where is London Bridge?

5 Whose statue is in Trafalgar Square?

6 Which art museum is housed in a converted power station?

7 Where does the Changing of the Horse Guards take place?

8 Who lives at 10 Downing Street?

9 Where was Anne Boleyn beheaded?

10 What is the Serpentine?

11 Where is Chaucer buried?

12 What is Hamleys?

13 Near which park is Madame Tussaud's?

14 When during the year does the Wimbledon tennis tournament take place?

15 Where is the *Magna Carta* kept?

Your research sources:

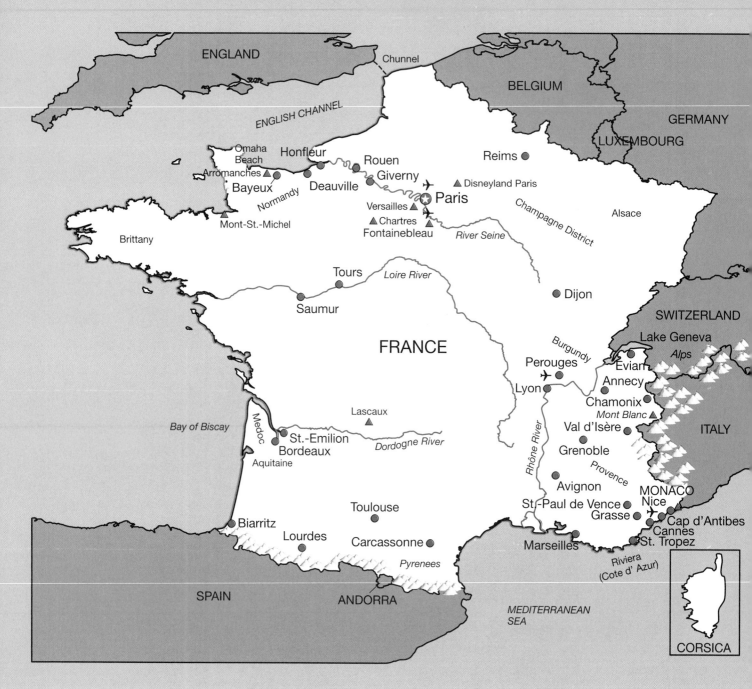

ENGLAND

Chunnel

BELGIUM

ENGLISH CHANNEL

GERMANY

LUXEMBOURG

Omaha
Beach
Honfleur
Rouen
Reims
Arromanches
Deauville
Giverny
Disneyland Paris
Bayeux
Normandy
★ Paris
Versailles
Alsace
Champagne District
Mont-St.-Michel
Chartres
Fontainebleau
River Seine
Brittany

Tours
Loire River
Dijon
Saumur
Burgundy
FRANCE
Perouges
SWITZERLAND
Lake Geneva
Alps
Evian
Lyon
Annecy
Lascaux
Chamonix
Bay of Biscay
Medoc
Mont Blanc
ITALY
St.-Emilion
Bordeaux
Dordogne River
Val d'Isère
Aquitaine
Grenoble
Provence
Avignon
MONACO
Toulouse
St.-Paul de Vence
Nice
Biarritz
Grasse
Cap d'Antibes
Lourdes
Carcassonne
Cannes
St. Tropez
Marseilles
Pyrenees
Riviera
(Cote d' Azur)
SPAIN
ANDORRA
MEDITERRANEAN
SEA
CORSICA

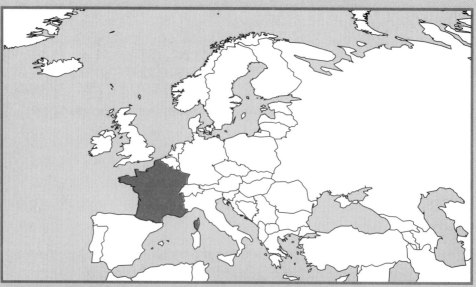

Chapter 15

France
The Movable Feast

Ernest Hemingway, in a bit of memorable phrasing, called **Paris** "a movable feast." The same can be said for all of France. Whether it's because of food, culture, language, or history, visitors bring back with them strong, fond memories of their feast-like visit to this rich country. Paris clearly is the focal point of most trips to France. However, to acquire a full appreciation of this country, you have to go beyond Paris. Indeed, its eight richly diverse regions could each merit a separate vacation.

France is the largest country completely within Europe; it's about the size of Indiana, Illinois, Iowa, and Missouri combined. Cosmopolitan, unique Paris sits in the north-center of the country. Heading west (and counterclockwise) are the beaches of **Normandy**, with their seaside towns, war memorials, and medieval architecture. Below Normandy and Paris are the magnificent *chateaux* (castles) of the **Loire** [LWAHR] **River Valley**. South of the Loire region is the **Aquitaine** district, with its legendary wines, Roman ruins, and prehistoric sites.

The French wine industry dates back to around 600 B.C.

FYI
FOR YOUR INFORMATION

FRANCE

CAPITAL: Paris

AREA (SQUARE MILES): 212,841

TIME ZONE: GMT: +1

DRIVE ON: Right

POPULATION: 60,900,000

RELIGION: Roman Catholic

LANGUAGE: French

CURRENCY: 1 euro = 100 cents

ELECTRICITY: 220 volts, 50 cycles AC

CAPSULE HISTORY: J. Caesar conquers Gaul, 57–52 B.C.; becomes distinct country, 843; Louis XIV reigns, 1643–1715; revolution, 1789; Napoleon becomes emperor, 1804; Louis XVIII begins reign, 1815; second revolution, 1848; second empire, 1852; Germany invades, 1940; France liberated, 1944; DeGaulle begins rule, 1946; DeGaulle loses election after violent demonstrations and strikes, 1969.

For reference sources, tourist bureaus, and suggested lengths of stay, see the Appendices.

Along France's border with Spain are the **Pyrenees**, a place of scenery, shrines, and skiing. In southeastern France is the **Provence** region.

Stretching along France's Mediterranean coast are the chic beaches of the **French Riviera**, also known as the **Côte d'Azur**. To the north are the fashionable ski resorts of the French Alps. Then, stretching northward toward Paris is France's **Eastern Wine Country**, including the **Burgundy** and **Champagne** districts. To the southeast, off the coast, lies the French island of **Corsica**.

English is commonly spoken by those in the tourist trade; however, though many citizens of this country have a strong command of English, they are *passionately* partial to speaking their own language.

How Travelers Get There

Many carriers, both domestic and foreign, serve Paris, including the national airline, **Air France** (AF). Flights from the United States land at **Charles de Gaulle** (CDG). **Orly** (ORY) is Paris's other major airport. In addition, flights from New York via Paris to the Riviera land in **Nice** at the **Côte d'Azur Airport** (NCE). **Lyon** [lee-OHN] (LYS) is a gateway to the Eastern Wine Country and the Alps.

Flying time to Paris from New York is 7 hours; from Miami and Chicago, it's 8.5 hours; and from Los Angeles, it's 11 hours. Flights to the Riviera take 90 minutes longer. Travelers can get from London to Paris via a brief air flight (a little over an hour) or on the **Eurostar** train through the Channel Tunnel (under three hours). The high-speed **Thalys** train connects Paris with Brussels (Belgium) and Amsterdam (the Netherlands). Hovercraft and ferries connect southern England to various French ports. Cruise ships regularly call at ports on the Riviera, along the Atlantic Coast, and in northern France.

Weather Patterns

By and large, the climate of France is temperate. Paris has weather similar to London, though slightly warmer, ranging from the mid-70s in summer to near 40 degrees in winter. Temperatures do vary, however, in certain regions of the country. The Riviera's climate is somewhat similar to that of Los Angeles: summers in the 80s and winters in the 50s. In the Alps, winters are cold with snow—but then, that's exactly what skiers want (see Figures 15–1 and 15–2).

Who hasn't heard of April in Paris? It's famous. And rainy, which most people are surprised to learn. September is a better month to visit; the weather is usually nice and crowds are smaller. The main tourist season is June to September, peaking in July. Parisians go on vacation in August; the city empties and the Riviera gets packed.

Getting Around

France has some of the finest transportation systems in the world. The **TGV** is a premier rail system with 200-mph trains. For those who prefer to do their own driving, France has many good highways. Car rentals are readily available.

What the TGV is to France, the Metro is to Paris. One of the world's great subways, the Metro is simple to use: Each station has a map, and pushing a destination button lights up the best route. Paris buses are cheap but slow; the huge tour buses, though, give first-rate city tours. Taxis are a bit expensive and drivers can be selective about where they'll go. What about driving a car in Paris? Aggressive drivers, nonexistent lanes, and expensive parking make it a challenging experience. Beyond Paris, though, a car rental can be an attractive choice.

France offers adventurous travel alternatives. Bicycle tours through the wine regions and balloon trips over farmland and chateaux are quite memorable. Barges—with cabins onboard for passengers—cruise down the Loire and through the Wine Country. River Seine tours are a wonderful way to see Paris.

Except for a few private sandy beaches that visitors have to pay to use, the Riviera's beaches are quite pebbly.

Storms born in North Africa sometimes suck up Sahara sand. The storms then drift northward to France. The result: rainfall that coats southern France with sandy dirt.

The TGV covers the 250 miles between Lyon and Paris in two hours.

Motor homes are an increasingly popular way to visit the French countryside.

Climate at a Glance
NICE

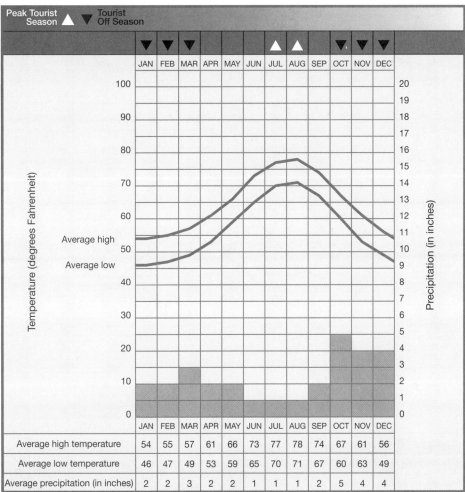

Figure 15–1

Important Places

Think of France and you think of Paris. But the country offers many other regions, too, all of which should be considered when planning a trip.

Paris

The French are fiercely proud of their culture and nowhere more so than in Paris. From history to arts, from architecture to haute cuisine and fashion, Paris has earned its reputation. The capital and largest city in France, the "City of Lights" is also the nation's business center and perhaps the most romantic city in the world. The list of Paris attractions is lengthy. Among those that are must-sees:

- **The Eiffel Tower**, maybe the most famous icon of any city in the world. Built for the 1889 World's Fair, it rises high above the Seine and offers panoramic views.
- **Notre Dame**, the Gothic cathedral on the Ile de la Cite, guarded by its stone gargoyles (best viewed by climbing up the staircase in one of the towers). The nearby **Sainte-Chapelle** church has stained-glass windows that are renowned.

Lunch, not dinner, is the Parisian's main meal.

On a hot day, the Eiffel Tower is 6 inches taller than it is on a cold day.

Climate at a Glance
PARIS

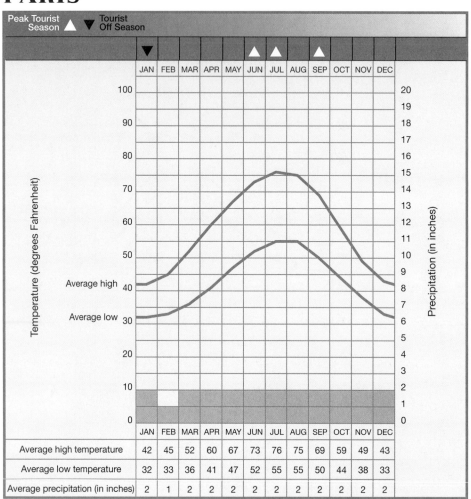

	JAN	FEB	MAR	APR	MAY	JUN	JUL	AUG	SEP	OCT	NOV	DEC
Average high temperature	42	45	52	60	67	73	76	75	69	59	49	43
Average low temperature	32	33	36	41	47	52	55	55	50	44	38	33
Average precipitation (in inches)	2	1	2	2	2	2	2	2	2	2	2	2

Figure 15–2

■ **The Arc de Triomphe**, commemorating Napoleon's victories. The top offers a grand vista over Paris, especially down the **Champs-Elysees** boulevard to the **Place de la Concorde**.

■ **The Paris Opera (Palais Garnier)**, the ornate setting for *The Phantom of the Opera*.

■ **Montmartre**, with its twisting streets, once the bohemian part of Paris. This district and its famous **Sacre Coeur** (a white marble basilica) are depicted in many famous Impressionist paintings.

■ **The Louvre**, perhaps the greatest museum in the world. It houses such masterpieces as the *Mona Lisa*, *Winged Victory*, and the *Venus de Milo*. A half-dozen other great museums exist in Paris, including the **Centre Georges Pompidou**, with its modern art and bold exterior; and the **Musee d'Orsay**, a converted railway station with Impressionist works (including *Whistler's Mother*).

The following **day trips** from Paris are very popular:

■ **Versailles** [vehr-SIGH], a sprawling, opulent palace with spectacular grounds.

■ **Chartres** [SHART], one of the world's great medieval cathedrals, with its stained-glass windows.

The foundations of the original Louvre Palace can be viewed in the museum's Sully Wing.

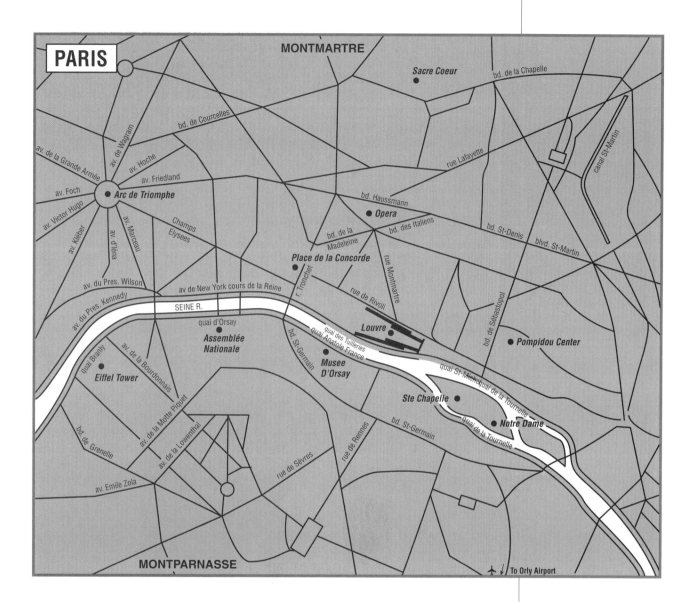

- **Fontainebleau**, the home of Napoleon, Marie Antoinette, and many others, with its beautiful gardens.
- **Giverny** [zhee-ver-NEE], with its gardens made famous by the painter Monet. (His home is here, too.)
- **Disneyland Paris** and the adjoining **Walt Disney Studios**, east of Paris on the main route to Brussels, Belgium. It's oddly disorienting for an American to see a European version of Disneyland.

Normandy

This area along the English Channel will forever be a monument to the World War II D-Day landing. Normandy is a place of green farmland and medieval architecture. Among the attractions:

- **Omaha Beach**, the site of the Allied Invasion, is made up of what were originally three separate beaches. It is often seen along with **Arromanches** and its invasion museum.
- **Rouen** [roo-AHN], the "City of 100 Steeples," is famed for medieval architecture. Indeed, many of its fifteenth-century homes are still occupied.

Paris's Musee Rodin has virtually all of the Great Master's works, including *The Thinker*.

Across the English Channel is the British abbey, St. Michael's Mount, which was modeled after Mont-St-Michel.

Some Loire Valley chateaux close between noon and 2 P.M., as do many other French attractions.

- **Deauville** [doh-VEEL], a restored seaside resort, is to northern France what St. Tropez is to the southern Riviera. It has a mile-long boardwalk.
- **Honfleur** is a highly picturesque fishing port, often depicted in paintings.
- **Bayeux** [bye-YOO] boasts a Gothic cathedral. The remarkable **Bayeux Tapestry**, housed in an adjacent museum, depicts the Battle of Hastings.
- **Mont-St-Michel** is a stunning fortified abbey from the eleventh century—perched, like a spired silhouette, on a rock cut off from the mainland at high tide. Mont-St-Michel also borders the peninsula of **Brittany**, with its many castles and strange, prehistoric monuments.

The Loire Valley

Spread throughout the Loire River area are more than 100 majestic chateaux. The gateway of the area is the charming town of **Tours**. Some chateaux offer *son et lumiere* (sound-and-light) shows at night. The sites you might recommend include:

The odd proportions of Montmartre's Sacre Coeur intrigued many of France's greatest painters
Image copyright Angelina Dimitrova, 2008. Used under license from Shutterstock.com

Mont-St-Michel seems impossibly perched on a rocky outcropping, surrounded at high tide by the sea
Image copyright Jakez, 2008. Used under license from Shutterstock.com

- **The chateaux.** Among the most famous are **Amboise, Blois, Villandry,** and **Azay-le-Rideau.** If there's time for only one or two chateaux, the awesome **Chenonceau** and **Chambord** are *the* ones to see.
- **Saumur,** famous for its **National Riding School,** many wine cellars, and, of all things, a mushroom museum.

The Aquitaine Region

The Aquitaine (also called Perigord) is one of France's most diversified tourist centers. It's famous for its vineyards, Roman ruins, prehistoric cave paintings, and *bastides* (quaint towns built on hillsides). Recommend the following:

- **Bordeaux** [bor-DOH], a sophisticated port city of parks, salons, bistros, casinos, and beaches.
- **The St-Emilion area,** in the heart of Bordeaux's Wine Country. The medieval town of St-Emilion itself is one of the most charming in all of France.
- **The Medoc,** another of the major wine regions, known for some of France's top vintages. More formal than St-Emilion, many of the estates have extremely grand chateaux.

The following **day trips** from the Aquitaine region are very popular:

- **The Dordogne** [dor-DOI-ing] **River Valley,** with its prehistoric cave paintings. The most famous, at **Lascaux,** are now closed to the public, but an exact reproduction can be visited nearby.
- **Biarritz,** a lovely beach town near the Spanish border on the Bay of Biscay. It's one of Europe's few surfing venues.

The Pyrenees

In the lofty mountains that separate France from Spain are several ski resorts. The shrine of **Lourdes** draws Catholic pilgrims seeking cures and is one of the most visited sites in

According to city measurements, the Peripherique expressway is the noisiest thing in Paris. The Pere-Lachaise Cemetery, where many notables are buried, is the city's quietest place.

France. As in the Aquitaine, a number of *bastides* dot the hillsides. The city of **Toulouse**, called the "Rose City," boasts Europe's largest Romanesque church. And **Carcassonne** is a huge, hulking medieval fortress of a town—the largest in all of Europe. Within its walls is the impressive **Castle of the Counts.**

The French Riviera

The Mediterranean-hugging Riviera offers an unusual blend of features. Its stunning beaches, wonderful weather, superb dining, and many art galleries have long enticed the jet-setting elite. It's also the most popular spot for the French themselves during their July and August holidays. Among the towns and attractions of the Côte d'Azur are:

- Nice [NEECE], the largest city on the Riviera, is crowded but still charming. Fine museums are around Nice, including the **National Museum Marc Chagall, Matisse Museum**, and **Museum of Modern and Contemporary Art.**

- Cannes [KAHN] is famous for its international movie festival, beaches, and boardwalk. With casinos and nightclubs, it's trendy and perhaps a bit noisier than other Riviera towns.

- St-Tropez [SAN troh-PAY] is very chic, but beginning to get crowded and just a bit aged.

- Cap d'Antibes [CAHP dahn-TEEB] is for those looking for an especially luxurious seaside vacation. The nearby town of Antibes has a **Picasso Museum.**

One of France's greatest art collections is in a restaurant, La Colombe d'Or, just outside the wall of St-Paul de Vence. The reason: Artists like Matisse, Picasso, and Modigliani would pay for their meals or a room here with one of their works of art.

- St-Paul de Vence and **Grasse** lie in the hills above the Riviera. St-Paul—a walled medieval village atop a hill—has many galleries, boutiques, fine restaurants, and hotels. It's a gem of a town. The nearby **Maeght Foundation** is a world-class museum. Grasse is famous for its perfume factory.

You should advise visitors to take the following **day trips** from the French Riviera:

- Marseilles [mahr-SAY] is over 2,500 years old. It's quite attractive, though a bit scruffy on the edges. Many museums dot this spirited city.

- Monaco, an independent principality close to the Italian border, is best known for its **Casino** and for the **Monaco Grand Prix** auto race, held in late May. The road between Nice and Monaco goes through an area called the **Corniches**, a series of three winding roads—each at a different level. Along the way is a picture-perfect medieval town, **Eze** [AIZ], that rises above a steep cliff.

- The inland **Provence** [pro-VAHNS] **Region** features many spas and Roman structures (including the astonishing 2,000-year-old **Pont du Gard** aqueduct). In **Avignon** [ah-vee-NYOWN] is the **Palace of the Popes** (where popes lived in the fourteenth century) and a bridge made famous by a children's song.

The French Alps

Skiers love the Alps for their winter facilities, and those who enjoy scenery are likely to visit at any time of the year. Among the towns most visited are:

- Chamonix [shah-mo-NEE] (near **Mont Blanc**, one of Europe's highest mountains), a large, trendy resort town with spectacular views. There's also a casino.

- Val d'Isere [VAHL dee-ZARE], a charming village with fewer tourists. It's an ideal place for serious skiers.

- Grenoble, most notable of the country's world-class ski resorts, the site of the 1968 Winter Olympics. Accessible from Geneva, Switzerland, it's one of the most picturesque towns in the Alps.

- Several charming cities, including **Annecy** (the Flower City) and lakeside **Evian** (of the famous spa and bottled water).

Monte Carlo's casino was designed by Charles Garnier, the architect of the equally extravagant Paris Opera
Image copyright Paul Vorwerk, 2008. Used under license from Shutterstock.com

The Eastern Wine Country

France's legendary Wine Country extends all the way from near Reims in the Champagne District, southeasterly through the **Alsace** region, and down through Burgundy into the Rhone River Valley. Among its major attractions, from south to north:

- **Lyon**, France's second-largest city and a center of business and gastronomy. Nearby is **Perouges**, one of Europe's best-preserved medieval villages.
- **Dijon**, another place of fine cuisine and the heart of Burgundy. Between Dijon and **Beaune** (a medieval town) are numerous wineries.
- The **Alsace** area, with its melding of German and French ambience. Here is the fabled "**Route du Vin**," a 75-mile drive through vineyards and mountains.
- **The Champagne District**, another region of vineyards and wine cellars. It's anchored by the city of Reims. Several wineries in the area offer tours of their vast underground tunnel systems, where wines and champagne are left to age.
- **Reims**, at the northern tip of the Wine Country. Its Gothic cathedral is where most French kings were crowned.

Possible Itineraries

First-time visitors should spend a week in Paris—with day trips to Versailles, Chartres, and perhaps the Loire Valley. Seasoned tourists could put aside two weeks to visit a broader area. Starting in Paris, they could travel to the Loire, then continue down through the Aquitaine region, perhaps ending up in the Riviera.

Each area of France can easily sustain a five- to seven-day stay. In the winter, France offers the skiing splendor of the Alps and in the summer, the pleasant beaches of the Riviera.

In Paris, it's against the law to honk your car horn except in an emergency; blink the headlights instead.

Lodging Options

The French pride themselves on having the best: haute cuisine, haute couture, great novelists, and trend-setting artists. France's hotels are no different: Some of the world's best are here. In Paris, many hotels are on the Right Bank, especially the areas just off the Champs-Elysées and near the Opera. Among them are the world-class **Ritz**, **George V**, **Bristol**, **Crillon**, and **Plaza Athenee**. On the Riviera, the **Negresco** in Nice is an official national monument.

The French government officially rates lodging, with four-star luxe as the highest rating, down to one-star. Alternatives to hotels are abundant. In Paris, for instance, visitors can rent apartments. In the countryside, farmhouses, castles, manors, and monasteries have been converted to upscale lodging facilities and have banded together into a network called **Relais et Chateaux**.

Many North American hotel chains serve France. Among the other major chains are the upscale **Sofitel**, **Le Meridien**, and **Concorde**. At the other end of the budget are the economy chains of **Hotel Campanile**, **Libertel**, **Mercure**, and **Ibis**.

Allied Destinations

France borders Spain, Andorra, Italy, Switzerland, Germany, Belgium, and Luxembourg. The Netherlands is just around the corner, and Great Britain is right across the English Channel. Although closely related to France, Monaco has its own separate government. (It's officially a principality.) A France itinerary can be expanded to include any of these countries.

Cultural Patterns

The French are proud of their country's cultural heritage. This isn't limited to artistic endeavors but to all French customs. A business traveler, especially, wouldn't want to commit a *faux pas* (literally, a false step).

- The French prefer somewhat formal greetings. They regularly use such titles as *Monsieur, Madame,* and *Mademoiselle*. Once a French person knows someone, he or she may give the traditional kiss *by* the cheek. (The cheek isn't kissed, but the air next to it.)

- The French are proud of their language. Although many speak English, they far prefer French. Visitors should ask, *"Parlez-vous anglais?" not* "Do you speak English?"

- Visitors should be careful about using the OK sign. The thumb and index finger together means zero here, almost the opposite of what may be intended.

- Gift giving should be done carefully. A business gift should not be embossed with a corporate logo; a hand-written note should accompany it; and flowers must be in an uneven number (not 13, though). Gifts that are intellectual or artistic in nature make a great impression on the French.

- The French admire promptness. On the other hand, the idea of standing in line is somewhat foreign to them.

Factors That Motivate Visitors

Many would-be visitors know of France by its reputation. However, it's important to think about the reasons why the country truly intrigues them. Among these reasons:

- It's romantic.

- The cultural and artistic attractions are seemingly endless.

- The cuisine and wines are legendary.

- There are many airline flights into Paris.

Several hotels in the Loire region have rooms cut into rock cliffs. In effect, guests there stay in caves.

The French rarely eat full breakfasts. Their *petit dejeuner* usually consists of rolls, perhaps orange juice, and coffee.

Leonardo da Vinci spent his last years in Amboise.

Qualifying the Traveler
Paris

For People Who Want	Appeal			Remarks
	High	Medium	Low	
Historical and Cultural Attractions	▲			Superb museums
Beaches and Water Sports			▲	Must go to the Riviera
Skiing Opportunities			▲	Must go to the Alps
Lots of Nightlife	▲			Nightclubs expensive
Family Activities		▲		Mostly sightseeing and Disneyland Paris
Familiar Cultural Experience			▲	
Exotic Cultural Experience		▲		
Safety and Low Crime		▲		Petty crime
Bargain Travel			▲	In the countryside
Impressive Scenery		▲		Mostly in countryside
Peace and Quiet			▲	Sidestreets quiet
Shopping Opportunities	▲			Especially luxury items
Adventure			▲	Outside of the city
To Do Business		▲		

- Easy public transportation makes it simple to get around.
- Winter skiing, especially in the Alps, is readily available.
- The beaches are trendy.
- Picturesque villages dot the countryside.
- The casino in Monaco offers gambling in sophisticated surroundings.
- Some want to see the cutting edge of fashion and arts.
- There's great shopping.

Possible Misgivings

No matter how graceful France might appear, visitors still have concerns. Here are the most common ones:

- "The French are rude." Parisians—like many big-city residents—can seem abrupt, but they're usually polite if treated with respect. Locals in the countryside tend to be friendlier.
- "All there is in France is Paris." There's also the Wine Country, Loire Valley chateaux, Normandy memorials and architecture, the Riviera, and the Alps.
- "They don't speak English and are intolerant of French that isn't flawless." Most people in any way connected to tourism speak English and prefer doing so to dealing with a foreigner's French.

Be aware of pickpockets—which include young children—in Paris.

- "Traffic and parking in Paris is a problem." Public transportation is excellent, and there are many wonderful city motorcoach tours.

- "France is expensive." It's true that Paris and the Riviera (in spring and summer) are among the most expensive places in the world. However, bargains can be found (especially off-season). Other areas of France are generally more reasonable.

Sales Strategies

Tours are offered of the sewers of Paris.

The diversity of France generates many ways to upsell and cross-sell. Balloon trips offer a spectacular way to see the country. Staying in a chateau would be memorable for just about anyone. Renting a car to drive through the countryside or booking train travel lets visitors see more than just the well-known highlights. Barge cruises, too, are a unique way of getting around. City tours of Paris make that sprawling city more manageable. A few extra days added on to a Paris trip will allow a tourist to visit the chateaux country or other regions. Cruises let you easily combine a trip to, say, the Riviera with visits to Italy and Spain.

Travel Trivia

Where the Famous Paintings Are

- *The Mona Lisa* (da Vinci)—The Louvre, Paris

- *The Starry Night* (Van Gogh)—Museum of Modern Art, New York City

- *The Last Judgement* (Michelangelo)—The Sistine Chapel, Vatican City

- *Syndics of the Drapers' Guild* (Rembrandt)—Rijksmuseum, Amsterdam

- *Three Musicians* (Picasso)—Museum of Modern Art, New York City

- *The Artist's Mother* (Whistler)—Musee d'Orsay, Paris

- *The Blue Boy* (Gainsborough)—The Huntington Library, Pasadena, California

- *Campbell's Soup Cans* (Warhol)—The Andy Warhol Museum, Pittsburgh, Pennsylvania

- *Luncheon on the Grass* (Manet)—Musee d'Orsay, Paris

- *The Last Supper* (da Vinci)—Santa Maria Delle Grazie Church, Milan, Italy

NAME _____   **DATE** _____

MAP ACTIVITY

A traveler wants to visit the places listed below. Which number represents each on the map?

Place/Attraction	In/Near Which City?	Number on Map
A. The Seine River	A. _____	A. _____
B. Sainte-Chapelle	B. _____	B. _____
C. An abbey on top of a rock	C. _____	C. _____
D. The Negresco Hotel	D. _____	D. _____
E. The heart of Burgundy	E. _____	E. _____
F. The Louvre	F. _____	F. _____
G. The site of a film festival	G. _____	G. _____
H. Mont Blanc	H. _____	H. _____
I. The Arc de Triomphe	I. _____	I. _____
J. The Castle of the Counts	J. _____	J. _____

NAME _____ DATE _____

CASE STUDY

Nicole and Matthew, both in their mid-20s, have just gotten married. Only Nicole has traveled outside the United States, and that was five years ago (through Great Britain). They each have a week off from work, but could possibly stretch the goodwill of their employers, considering the circumstances.

Circle the answer that best suits their needs.

1 What area would you suggest they concentrate on?

Paris   Normandy

The Riviera   Paris and the Loire Valley

Why?

2 Which of the following tips should you *not* pass along to Nicole and Matthew?

Go in April when the weather is best.   French trains can be very fast.

Order prix fixe lunches.   *Bastides* can be seen in Aquitaine.

Why?

3 Which of the following should you probably recommend?

Taking a barge to Toulouse   Staying at the Negresco

A first-day city tour   Visiting the Hermitage

Why?

4 Which is *not* a day trip from Paris?

Versailles   Fontainebleau

Chamonix   Chartres

Why?

NAME _____   **DATE** _____

CREATIVE ACTIVITY

You're the travel planner for Ice Cadettes, a skating show that has entertained audiences around the world for decades.

Experience has taught you that in order to turn a profit, only cities with a greater-metropolitan population of 300,000 or more are worth a visit. There's even a "divide-by-two" formula: Cities with 400,000 warrant two nights performance; 600,000, three nights; and so on. The maximum the show stays in any city is seven nights.

The company has decided to stage Ice Cadettes in France. They want to spend no more than 40 days there. You also need one day off between each city engagement for traveling (by air, train, or road—as the distance warrants).

Below, write in the names of the cities in which Ice Cadettes will perform for this French road tour. Apply the day-population formula; look up the population of French cities in whatever reference sources you have access to. Also, try to make an itinerary that's geographically efficient. Don't have the group constantly flying back and forth across France. We've started you off, to show you what we want:

1. Fly into Strasbourg	15.	29.
2. Strasbourg	16.	30.
3. Strasbourg	17.	31.
4. Travel to	18.	32.
5.	19.	33.
6.	20.	34.
7.	21.	35.
8.	22.	36.
9.	23.	37.
10.	24.	38.
11.	25.	39.
12.	26.	40.
13.	27.	
14.	28.	

Chapter 16

Italy
Pisa and Pizza

How often have you heard a child confuse the words *Pisa* and *pizza*? Well, that child grows up and one day becomes a tourist. Even as adults, people think of Italy in terms of ancient ruins and pasta. The country, however, is much more; indeed, it's one of the richest experiences in Europe. Just pizza? Hardly. It's a banquet.

Italy is about the size of Arizona and is easily recognized by its famous boot shape. The country is so full of attractions that there's really no center point to tourism. In fact, it could be said that there are *four* Italys: First, there's northern Italy, with its mix of mountains, lakes, and the **Italian Riviera**; then comes the Italy of great cities, including the art, history, fashion, and commerce of **Venice** (Venezia), **Florence** (Firenze), and **Milan** (Milano); next are **Rome** (Roma) and its environs, the country's political and cultural center and once the hub of the world's most powerful empire; finally, there's southern Italy, with the area that surrounds **Naples** (Napoli), as well as the islands of mountainous **Sicily** and resort-lined **Sardinia**.

Visitors to St. Peter's must not wear shorts.

How Travelers Get There

The major international gateways into Italy are **Rome-Fiumicino "Leonardo da Vinci" Airport** (FCO) and Milan's **Malpensa Airport** (MXP). Venice (VCE), Pisa (PSA), Florence (FLR), and Naples (NAP) all mostly handle shorter flights.

Alitalia (AZ) is Italy's major airline; the country is also served by several North American carriers. Flying time to Rome from New York is 8 hours; from Chicago, 9.5 hours; and from Los Angeles, 12 hours. Cruises also stop at dozens of Italian mainland and island ports. Indeed, Rome's **Civitavecchia** [chee-vee-tah-VECK-ee-ah] and Venice are two of the Mediterranean's busiest ports. Visitors can also drive into the country from the north, often via trans-Alpine tunnels.

Weather Patterns

Who hasn't heard of "sunny Italy"? It's a well-earned reputation, but Italy's climate is a little more complicated than that.

Italy has three climate patterns. The northern Alpine area has cold winters and mild, sometimes rainy summers. The region between Milan and Venice has hot, sunny summers,

> Many attractions and most businesses, except restaurants, close between 1:00 P.M. and 3:30 P.M., but stay open as late as 8:00 P.M.

Climate at a Glance
ROME

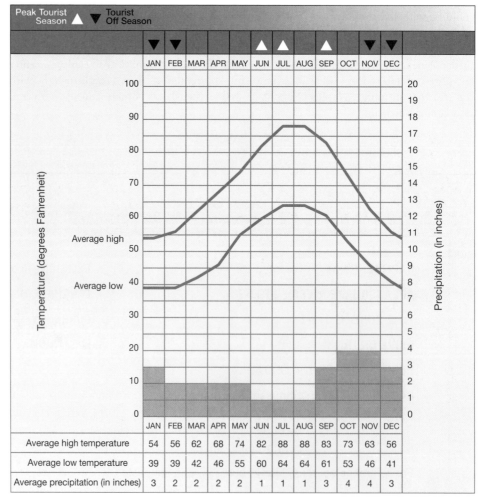

	JAN	FEB	MAR	APR	MAY	JUN	JUL	AUG	SEP	OCT	NOV	DEC
Average high temperature	54	56	62	68	74	82	88	88	83	73	63	56
Average low temperature	39	39	42	46	55	60	64	64	61	53	46	41
Average precipitation (in inches)	3	2	2	2	2	1	1	1	3	4	4	3

Figure 16–1

What remains of the most important public place in the entire ancient Rome Empire, the Forum
Image copyright Motordigitaal, 2008. Used under license from Shutterstock.com

but winters are chilly and misty. The rest of Italy is like California, with dependably hot, dry summers. Winters are mild, with changeable, unpredictable weather (see Figure 16–1). Occasionally in the summer and fall, a hot, humid sirocco wind blows from the south, while in the winter, a hot, dry *foehn* wind from the north sometimes increases temperatures and lowers humidity in the Alps. Waters around Italy are pleasantly warm from May to October, but chilly the rest of the year.

June, July, and September are the busiest tourist months. There's a small drop-off in major cities in August, when Italian tourists head for other countries or for the Riviera.

Getting Around

Italy's train system is inexpensive and fast, though efficiency is not its strong suit. The **Pendolino**, or **ETR**, is Italy's swiftest train. Travelers can also fly the short distances between major cities. Car rentals are readily available; however, Italian cities, especially Rome and Milan, are treacherous for "amateurs." Multiday escorted tours or short city tours are good alternatives. Taxis are fairly priced, but they can be expensive for long distances, and cab drivers have been known to play loose with the meters.

In Rome, the subway and bus system are extensive, with many lines traveling beyond the city. Buses and trolleys are also good in Florence, but just so-so in Milan (which also has a subway).

A unique transportation system, of course, is found in Venice. No cars are allowed in the city. (Travelers driving to Venice must park in one of several huge garages on the city's perimeter.) Boats are the way to get around. The most famous, romantic, and expensive are gondolas. (If you want a singing gondolier, you'll have to pay extra.) Water taxis are fast but also expensive. *Vaporetti* are slow "water buses" and *motoscafi* are express ones.

Important Places

Italy is a treasure trove of diverse places to experience. Among its most popular cities and attractions are:

Eurail passes and Italy rail passes for unlimited train travel can be bought only in North America.

By law, Venice's gondolas must be painted black. The one exception: those owned by city officials.

Rome

The Eternal City was originally built on seven hills along the **Tiber River**; its center today is on the river's left bank. Rome is the political, cultural, and religious heart of Italy. Among its attractions are:

- **The Colosseum**, one of the most recognizable structures in the world. It's an ancient stadium where gladiators fought and Christians were martyred.

- **The Forum**, once the center of the Roman Empire and now a broad area of ruins that only hints at the glorious buildings that once were here.

- **The Spanish Steps**, a place where locals and tourists have gathered for centuries.

- **The Trevi Fountain**, of *Three Coins in the Fountain* fame. Throw a coin over your left shoulder and you'll return to Rome, says the legend.

- **The Pantheon**, renowned as a remarkably preserved domed Roman building from the second century A.D. Its dome was the world's largest until Florence's Duomo was built in the fifteenth century.

The Forum is best viewed from Capitoline Hill.

A 2,000-year-old underground aqueduct feeds many of Rome's most famous fountains.

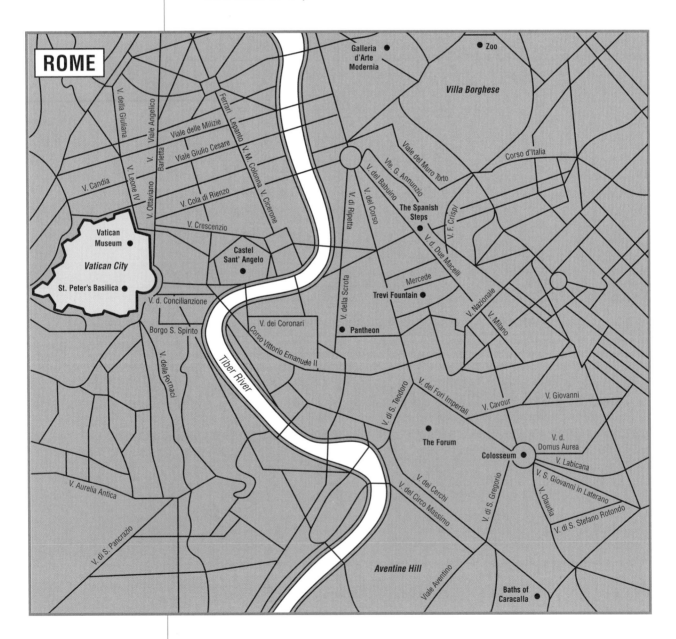

- **Vatican City**, actually one of the smallest nations in the world. The seat of Roman Catholicism and home to the pope, it's the site of **St. Peter's Basilica** (the largest church in the world) and the overwhelming **Vatican Museums**. Michelangelo's *Creation* is painted on the **Sistine Chapel** ceiling, his *Last Judgement* on its wall.

Outside Rome are wonderful attractions. Some popular **day trips**:

- **The Villa d'Este** in **Tivoli** is famed for its majestic, terraced water gardens and fountains. Nearby is **Hadrian's Villa**, a remarkable archaeological find.
- **Ostia Antica** contains the vast excavated ruins of an ancient port.
- **The Catacombs**—where early Christians secretly buried their dead—are located just outside town (there's a smaller version near the Via Veneto), as is the Roman Empire's principal road, the **Appian Way**.

Venice

Venice could never happen again. One of the truly unique cities of the world, it was built on 118 islands connected by 150 canals and more than 400 bridges. Located on the Adriatic, the city is expensive, with polluted waters and crowds of tourists (over 20 million each year, for a city whose population is about 63,000). Yet a walk through its back alleys opens up a quiet, romantic, fragile world of another time. Among its attractions:

- **St. Mark's Square** is the city's busy gathering place. It's enclosed at one end by the fanciful **St. Mark's Basilica** and has numerous outdoor cafes, each with "dueling" orchestras.
- **The Doge's Palace**, near the basilica, reflects a Moorish architecture. It houses one of the world's great collections of maps and globes. The famous **Bridge of Sighs** is nearby.
- **The Rialto Bridge** is one of Venice's most photographed bridges. It crosses the **Grand Canal**, the city's main waterway.
- **The Lido**, a trendy, luxury beach resort, is on its own island across from the Grand Canal.

Here are some of the most popular **day** or **half-day trips**:

- **Murano** is a touristy island where glass has been made for some 700 years. (The sales push to buy can be very aggressive.)
- **Burano** is the quaint island-capital of lace making.
- **Padua** [PAD-yoo-wah] is a town with charming medieval buildings.
- **Verona** has noteworthy architecture and a renowned outdoor opera festival. "Juliet's balcony" is here, as well. Verona can also be visited en route to Milan or the **Lake District**.

Florence

A city of art and architecture with a strong intellectual community, Florence is where the Renaissance began and flourished in the fifteenth century under the Medici family. It's located on the **Arno River** in the beautiful **Tuscany hills**. This international city remains, in many ways, a town of artisans and elegance. Among the many sites to see are:

- **The Duomo**, one of the most architecturally important cathedrals in the world. Started in 1296, it took 173 years to finish. One of the reasons for the delay: At first, no one knew how to engineer and build its huge dome.
- **The Accademia Gallery**, with its very fine collection of Florentine art, best known for Michelangelo's *David*.

Best time to see the Sistine Chapel: at opening (bypass the museum, go straight to the Chapel, then work your way back) or in February.

The view from the tower at St. Mark's is best at sunset.

The famous architect Frank Lloyd Wright applied for permission to build a home on Venice's Grand Canal. He was refused.

Duomo is an Italian term for any large cathedral.

A gondola passes beneath Venice's Rialto Bridge
Image copyright Paul Reid, 2008. Used under license from Shutterstock.com

■ **The Basilica of Santa Croce**, where Michelangelo is buried.

■ **The Vecchio Palace**, an opulent "town hall" built by the Medicis.

■ **The Ponte Vecchio**, the renowned bridge over the Arno, lined with gold and jewelry shops.

■ **The Pitti Palace**, a lavish home of the Medicis, which is so large it houses several museums.

■ **The Uffizi Gallery**, a Renaissance palace housing one of the premier collections of art in Italy.

The following **day trips** from Florence are very popular:

■ **Pisa** is world renowned, of course, for its leaning tower.

■ **Fiesole** [FYAY-zo-lay] is a beautiful old Etruscan village. Concerts still take place in the amphitheater, built in 80 B.C.

■ **Siena** is a pretty Renaissance village in the hills of the Tuscany wine country.

Because of the noise from mopeds, it's best *not* to have a room facing a busy street in Florence.

San Gimignano, outside Siena, is famous among architects for its many medieval towers.

The Italian Riviera

An extension of the French Riviera, the Italian Riviera offers stunning scenery along a mountainous coast. It's very crowded in the summer.

Portofino, an exclusive and high-priced resort town, is perhaps the most beautiful on Italy's Riviera. **Santa Margherita Ligure** and **San Remo** are popular beach resorts, as well. **Genoa** is a major Italian port and the birthplace of Christopher Columbus. It has many fine museums and Gothic architecture.

The Portofino Bay Hotel in Orlando, Florida, was built to look like Portofino, Italy.

Milan

Milan is the financial, business, fashion, and publishing center of Italy. The city has a sophisticated cultural life and is the gateway to the Alps and the Lake District. Among the major attractions are:

- **The Church of St. Mary of Grace**, the location of da Vinci's restored *The Last Supper*.

- **The Duomo**, an intricate marble structure and one of the world's largest cathedrals. The square that fronts it is famous for its pigeons.

- **La Scala**, perhaps the world's most famous opera house. Its season runs from December to July.

- **The Galleria Vittorio Emanuele II**, an ornate, glass-domed shopping mall built in 1861.

Milan is closer to London than it is to the tip of Italy's boot.

To see its intricate carvings, go up to the roof of Milan's Duomo.

The Lake District

This Alpine region near Switzerland is one of magnificent scenery and charming villages. The many lakes and surrounding Alps are part of the same geologic development, which glaciers carved out millions of years ago. Among its key towns are:

- **Como**, on **Lake Como** (one of two main lakes in the district). Its notable structures include a 700-year-old palace and a Renaissance Gothic cathedral.

- **Stresa**, the largest town on the area's other major lake, **Lake Maggiore**, with beautiful villas.

- **Bergamo**, a two-level city. Its main plaza is surrounded by stunning medieval buildings.

Not far from the lakes are the ski resorts of the Italian Alps. Among the favorites are beautiful **Cortina d'Ampezzo** and **Courmayeur**, the area's largest ski resort, with a very busy nightlife.

Aosta is off the tourist-beaten path, but has a picture-perfect location in the Italian Alps.

Naples

Naples is crowded and a bit run down, but it does boast some interesting churches and museums. Though it may not be Italy's most popular place to visit, the region nearby offers fascinating attractions, including:

- **Mt. Vesuvius** and **Pompeii**, whose histories intertwined in 79 A.D., when the volcano (now dormant, but potentially still active) erupted and buried the town. The ruins have since been excavated. A second nearby town, **Herculaneum**, was also buried. Like Pompeii, it has been uncovered and can be visited.

- **The Isle of Capri**, a trendy resort. Though there aren't many beaches, it's an area of charming villages and great vistas. Here, too, is the **Blue Grotto**, a watery cave of eerie azure light.

- **Sorrento**, which has long been one of the most beautiful, romantic, and famous resort areas in Italy. Unfortunately, it's becoming rather crowded, worn, and expensive.

Ancient Romans placed chickpeas and bacon in sealed jars and exported them to the rest of the Empire. That's where our pork and beans comes from.

■ **Amalfi Drive**, along the peninsula of the **Amalfi Coast**, offering breathtaking views past cliffs, coves, and villages.

Sicily

Located just off the toe of Italy's boot, this beautiful island is mountainous and dry. It's excellent for water sports and has very good beaches. In the winter there's also some good skiing in the mountains. Among its attractions are **Mt. Etna**, a still-active volcano; **Taormina**, a charming and popular beach resort town; and **Palermo**, Sicily's seaport capital, with ancient buildings and Norman palaces.

Sardinia

About 100 miles off Italy's west coast, this sparsely populated island is known for its beaches and water sports, especially fishing. The beautiful countryside and picturesque villages hold remnants of many ages. Easily the most popular beach area on Sardinia is **Costa Smeralda** (the Emerald Coast), long one of the trendiest luxury resorts in all of Europe.

Address an Italian by his or her first name only when invited to do so.

The Duomo is a distinctive feature of the Florence skyline
Photo by H. Fukushima

Possible Itineraries

First-time travelers to Italy visit Rome and other great cities, perhaps Venice and Florence. A week is the bare minimum. Seasoned travelers will probably want to explore the other areas of the country, as well as spend perhaps a bit more in-depth time in the major cities. A week concentrated in any one area, such as the Lake District or the region south of Rome, is just about right. Two weeks in Italy, however, provides ample opportunity to visit several major regions and cities.

Lodging Options

There's a wide range of hotel chains to choose from in Italy. At the upper end are such organizations **Atahotels**, **Starhotels**, and **Jolly Hotels** (many of whose hotels are more moderately priced than others). Many North American chains are also represented in Italy.

Hotels in Rome are concentrated around the rail station, the Spanish Steps, and the Via Veneto (famed for its many sidewalk cafes). In Venice, the best (and costliest) lodging is along the Grand Canal and near St. Mark's Square. Among the most famous: the **Cipriani**, **Danieli**, and **Gritti Palace**. Hotels in Florence are mostly to the north, along or near the Arno River. On Sicily and Sardinia, most of the accommodations are on the northern parts of the islands.

Although lower-rated hotels may present unwelcome surprises, Italy does offer wonderful alternative lodging, notably the chance to stay in old villas.

Request rooms in the oldest section of the Danieli.

Allied Destinations

Although most of the country is surrounded by water, Italy is bordered on the north by France, Switzerland, Austria, and Slovenia. The lovely and historic French island of Corsica is just off the west coast, and the island-nation of Malta is to the south of Sicily. Moreover, located as it is at the southern tip of Europe, Italy is also a perfect jumping-off point to Africa across the Mediterranean Sea. Nearby are Morocco, Tunisia, and Egypt. Note that many Eastern Mediterranean cruises start out in Venice, while Western Mediterranean cruises often begin at Civitavecchia.

Cultural Patterns

Italy has a rich, exuberant culture, but with traditions that can be quite different from those to which most Americans are accustomed. Business travelers should pay close attention to the customs.

- The daily pace is slower in southern Italy than in the north.
- Dinner can be a long, social event, but lunch is generally the day's biggest meal. Visitors shouldn't rush their meal and they should try their best to eat everything placed before them.
- When doing business, travelers should wear their finest clothes. In Italy, great clothing is a badge of success.
- It's appropriate for a guest to bring a small gift to an Italian home.
- The North American gesture for one (the index finger raised) means two in Italy, since the thumb is counted as one.

Extra tips are expected for most service-related jobs. Waiters should be tipped a little in addition to the service charge on the bill.

Factors That Motivate Visitors

For as diverse a country as Italy, it's important to understand precisely what motivates people to go there. Among their reasons might be:

- Some of the world's best-known ancient sites are here.
- The food is familiar and wonderful.

Trattorias **are less expensive for dining than** *ristorantes* **and offer very good food.**

- The country serves as a center for Christian religious pilgrimages.
- The culture is rich with opera, art, architecture, and history.
- There's the opportunity for water sports in summer and skiing in winter.
- There's great shopping.
- Many North Americans have their cultural roots in Italy.
- Some of the world's finest resorts are here.
- Italy is a major departure point for cruises.

Possible Misgivings

For all Italy's attributes, certain concerns regularly arise:
- "Everything's so expensive." Italy is indeed expensive; prebooked tours and cruises can blunt the cost a bit.
- "It's so disorganized." Book an escorted tour; the tour manager will deal with whatever problems may arise.
- "There's a lot of crime." Most are petty offences. But crime does happen, and normal precautions must be taken.

Qualifying the Traveler
Italy

For People Who Want	High	Medium	Low	Remarks
Historical and Cultural Attractions	▲			Cities are virtual museums
Beaches and Water Sports		▲		Especially Riviera and Sardinia
Skiing Opportunities	▲			Northern Alps
Lots of Nightlife		▲		Especially Rome
Family Activities		▲		Mostly sightseeing
Familiar Cultural Experience			▲	
Exotic Cultural Experience	▲			
Safety and Low Crime			▲	Petty crime frequent
Bargain Travel			▲	Venice especially costly
Impressive Scenery	▲			Especially countryside and the North
Peace and Quiet		▲		In countryside
Shopping Opportunities	▲			Designer items, glass, gold, jewelry, high fashion
Adventure		▲		
To Do Business		▲		

- "It's so hot." Spring or fall offers nice weather. Italy's northern regions are cooler.

- "Driving in cities is dangerous." Fine public transportation helps visitors get past this concern.

Sales Strategies

Italy offers unique selling avenues. With city driving so treacherous, city tours and train transportation become especially attractive. For that matter, with so many different attractions in Italy, escorted tours or day trips can be excellent ways to see the country. So, too, are cruises, which often call on Italy's less visited areas (e.g., Sicily and Sardinia) before continuing on to other countries.

Lodging in villas ranges from inexpensive to costly, but all offer a way to help make Italy memorable. Hotels along Venice's Grand Canal or with views in Florence may be expensive, but they're worth it. Their drama can cap off any guest's trip.

Buy detailed guidebooks for each city. Many of Italy's attractions have poor signage and no guided tours.

Travel Trivia

Where Famous People Are Buried

- Michelangelo: Basilica di Santa Croce, Florence

- Napoleon: Les Invalides, Paris

- Jim Morrison: Pere Lachaise Cemetery, Paris

- Karl Marx: Highgate Cemetery, London

- Marilyn Monroe: Westwood Village Memorial Park, Los Angeles

- Leornardo da Vinci: Chapel of Saint-Hubert, Chateau Amboise, France

- St. Peter: St Peter's Basilica, Vatican City

- William Shakespeare: Holy Trinity Church, Stratford-Upon-Avon, England

- Abraham Lincoln: Oak Ridge Cemetery, Springfield, Illinois

- Elvis Presley: Graceland, Memphis, Tennessee

- Henry VIII: Windsor Castle, Windsor, England

- Christopher Columbus: Seville Cathedral, Seville, Spain or Faro A Colon, Dominican Republic; also possibly Havana, Cuba

SOURCE: Marc Mancini

NAME _____   **DATE** _____

MAP ACTIVITY

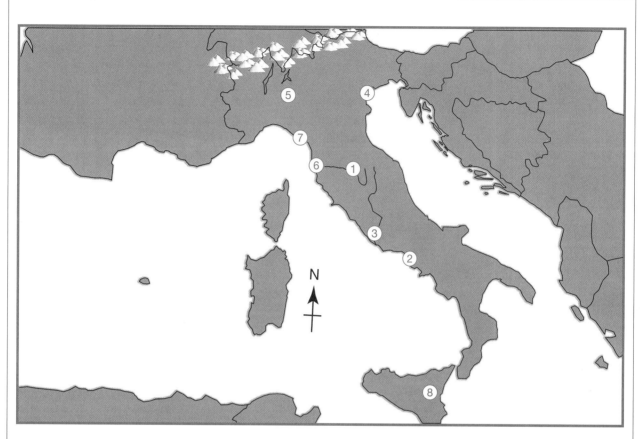

A traveler wants to visit the places listed below. Which number represents each on the map?

Place/Attraction	**In/Near Which City?**	**Number on Map**
A. St. Mark's Basilica	A. _____	A. _____
B. The statue of David	B. _____	B. _____
C. The Trevi Fountain	C. _____	C. _____
D. Pompeii	D. _____	D. _____
E. La Scala Opera House	E. _____	E. _____
F. Gondolas	F. _____	F. _____
G. *The Last Supper*	G. _____	G. _____
H. A leaning tower	H. _____	H. _____
I. The Doge's Palace	I. _____	I. _____
J. The Spanish Steps	J. _____	J. _____

NAME _____   **DATE** _____

CASE STUDY

Thomas and Jeannette Blair love food; they're taking a two-week culinary trip to Europe with Nancy and Sam Armato, who are also gourmets. Both couples are in their early 60s and have been to the Continent many times. What attracts them, in addition to the food, is the history of the cultures. They plan to go to Italy, France, and Spain.

Circle the answer that best suits their needs.

1 How many total days in Italy would you recommend for their trip?

Two   Three

Five   Ten

Why?

2 Which of the following Italian destinations could you suggest?

Costa Smeralda   Bimini

Corsica   Santorini

Why?

3 Which of the following tips would the couples find most useful in Italy?

Vatican City is right next door to the Colosseum.

Leave a tip, even when there's already one on the bill.

Car rentals in Rome are inexpensive.

Milan's Last Supper is its finest restaurant.

Why?

4 Which of the following services should you *not* offer?

A hotel suite   A city tour

A luau   A Eurail Pass

Why?

NAME _____   **DATE** _____

CREATIVE ACTIVITY

Thanks to television, nearly a billion people see the Rose Parade each year. That's why so many countries sponsor Rose Bowl floats. This year, Italy will create a float. What do you think it should look like? Describe it very specifically or, if you're artistic, draw it below.

BAY of BISCAY

FRANCE

Guernica

Bilbao
San Sebastian
Basque Region

Pamplona

ANDORRA

Pyrenees Mountains

Ampurias
Figueres

Costa
Brava

SPAIN

Montserrat ▲
Catalonia

Barcelona

Segovia

Avila

PORTUGAL

San Lorenzo ▲
de El Escorial

✹ Madrid

Toledo

Majorca

Menorca

Valencia

Ibiza

Balearic Islands

Sintra

Lisbon ★

Alicante

Costa
Blanca

Formentera

Córdoba

Seville

Portimão

Albufeira

Sagres
Lagos   Faro

Algarve

Andalusian Region

Granada

Nerja

Málaga

Marbella

Torremolinos

Costa del Sol

MEDITERRANEAN SEA

Strait of Gibraltar

GIBRALTAR

ALGERIA

ATLANTIC OCEAN

MOROCCO

Azores
(Portugal)

Madeira
(Portugal)

Canary Islands
(Spain)

Chapter 17

Spain and Portugal
Everything under the Sun

Have you ever been faced with so many choices you didn't know where to begin? That's the problem with Spain. There are so many different cultures, climates, and topographies that it's almost impossible to determine where to start.

The one constant: all the sunshine. Though the climate changes in Spain from area to area, it's almost always a case of good, better, best. And though that fact may not be well known in the United States, Spain is one of the top vacation destinations for European tourists.

Actually, there may be a logical place to start in Spain: right in the center of the map, at **Madrid**, the country's capital. If you view Spain as a clock, one o'clock would be **San Sebastian** (center of the Basque region). Moving around the country clockwise, there's the beach resort of **Costa Brava**, followed by charming **Barcelona**. Off the coast in the Mediterranean Sea, at three o'clock, are the **Balearic** [bah-lee-AIR-ik] **Islands** of **Majorca** [mah-YOR-kah] and **Ibiza**.

There are two more exquisite beach regions: the **Costa Blanca**, along Spain's southeastern coast, and the **Costa del Sol**, along the southern coast. Then comes the mountainous area that most people imagine when they think of Spain—the **Andalusian** region, the home of bullfighting and flamenco. Centered in **Seville**, this area also includes **Granada**.

Spain is about the size of Arizona and Utah combined. It's also only one part of what's known as the **Iberian Peninsula**; Portugal occupies the remainder. Bordering Spain on the west, Portugal is the size of Indiana. It, too, has its own beach resort area: the **Algarve** [all-GARVE-ah] on the southern coast. The capital of Portugal, **Lisbon**, rests up against the Atlantic Ocean. Several Spanish- and Portuguese-controlled islands lie far offshore in the Atlantic. The Portuguese **Azores**, about 800 miles west of Lisbon, are gentle islands with a few spas and beach resorts. The **Madeira Islands**, also Portuguese, are farther south— 400 miles west of Morocco. And Spain's **Canary Islands** are southwest of the Madeiras.

In major tourist areas, English is spoken by many. Elsewhere, however, it's far less common; the national languages of Spanish (in Spain) and Portuguese (in Portugal) predominate.

How Travelers Get There

The major gateway into Spain is Madrid's **Barajas Airport** (MAD), served by several North American carriers and **Iberia** (IB), the Spanish national airline. Flights originate from New York and Boston (6.5 hours each), Chicago and Miami (8 hours each), and

> Spain is one of the few countries whose capital is at its center.

> Spain was once considered the wealthiest and most powerful country in the world.

FYI
FOR YOUR INFORMATION

SPAIN AND PORTUGAL

CAPITALS: Spain: Madrid
               Portugal: Lisbon

AREA (SQUARE MILES): Spain: 197,897
                          Portugal: 35,387

TIME ZONES: Spain: GMT +1
                 Portugal: GMT +0

DRIVE ON: Right

POPULATION: Spain: 40,500,000
                 Portugal: 10,700,000

RELIGION: Roman Catholic

LANGUAGES: Spain: Spanish
                Portugal: Portuguese

CURRENCY: 1 euro = 100 cents

ELECTRICITY: 220 volts, 50 cycles AC

CAPSULE HISTORY: Spain: Part of Roman Empire, 201 B.C.; barbarians invade, 412; Muslims invade, 711; last Muslims defeated, 1492; defeat of Spanish Armada by British, 1588; republic declared, 1931; civil war, 1936–1939; Franco rules, 1939–1975; parliamentary system takes effect, 1982.

Portugal: Independence from Spain, twelfth century; Age of Discovery, early fifteenth through early seventeenth century; world power, 1433–1581; republic, 1910.

For reference sources, tourist bureaus, and suggested lengths of stay, see the Appendices.

Los Angeles (11 hours). In addition, several carriers fly into Malaga's **Picasso Airport** (AGP) on the Costa del Sol, and into Barcelona's **El Prat Airport** (BCN).

Flights to **Portela Airport** (LIS) in Lisbon can be booked on the Portuguese national airline, **TAP Air Portugal** (TP), and on a few North American and international carriers.

Tourists can also access the Iberian Peninsula from France via railroad and highways. Many ships end (or begin) their Western Mediterranean cruises in Barcelona. Several lines sail regularly from Great Britain, down Europe's Atlantic Coast, to ports in Portugal and Spain.

Weather Patterns

A hot, dry wind, called the *leveche*, sometimes blows from Africa across southern Spain and Portugal.

Most of Spain is very warm and dry in the summer, but during the rest of the year, three separate patterns occur. In the north and northeast, winters are a bit rainy, with plenty of snow in the mountains. Central Spain (where Madrid is located) has chilly winters, with frequent showers. (After all, the rain in Spain stays mainly on the plain.) (See Figure 17–1.) The coastal areas and Balearic Islands have a climate similar to southern California, with mild, occasionally rainy winters and hot, dry weather the rest of the year (when tourism is heaviest).

Portugal's climate has less temperature variation year-round, with more winter rain than in Spain (especially as one goes farther north). Water temperatures along the Algarve are warmer than on Portugal's Atlantic coast (see Figure 17–2).

Climate at a Glance
MADRID, SPAIN

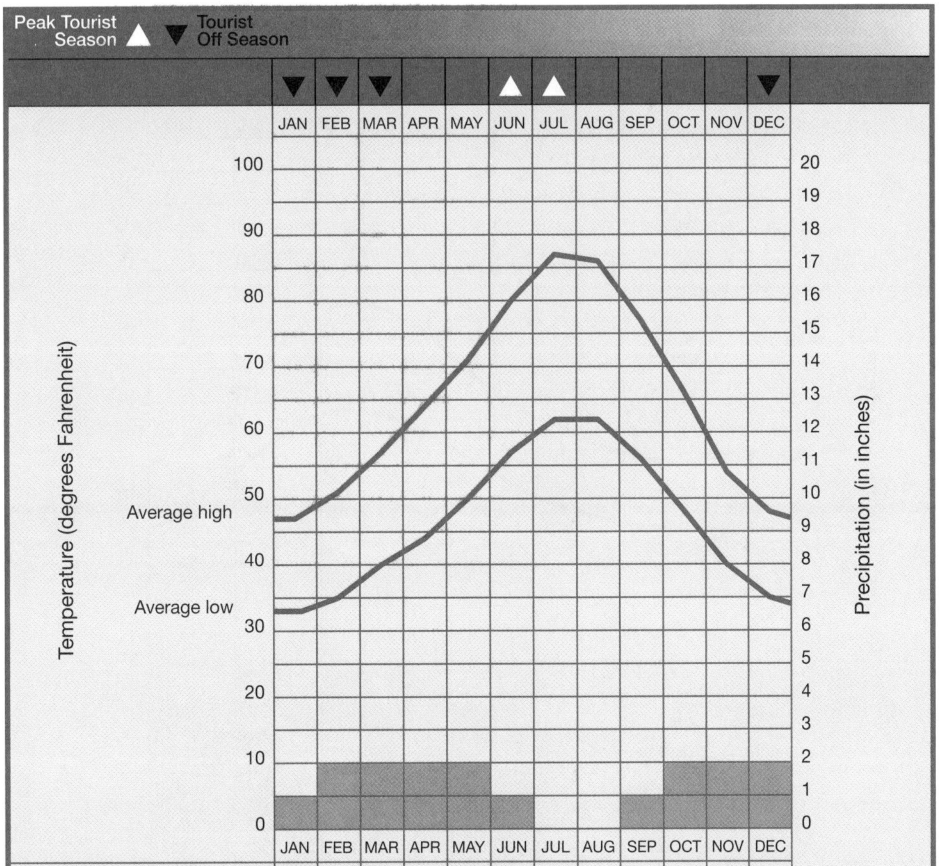

Peak Tourist Season ▲ ▼ Tourist Off Season											

	JAN	FEB	MAR	APR	MAY	JUN	JUL	AUG	SEP	OCT	NOV	DEC
	▼	▼	▼			▲	▲				▼	
Average high temperature	47	51	57	64	71	80	87	86	77	66	54	48
Average low temperature	33	35	40	44	50	57	62	62	56	48	40	35
Average precipitation (in inches)	1	2	2	2	2	1	0	0	1	2	2	2

Figure 17–1

Getting Around

Spain is the second-largest country in Europe (only France is larger). Therefore, visitors may do better to fly from one area to the next, especially since the highway and rail systems aren't quite as extensive or efficient as in some other European countries. The Spanish national railway uses good equipment mostly on its high-speed long-distance **AVE** routes. Shorter runs can be slow and uncomfortable.

Trains in Portugal, however, are generally modern and comfortable (though the many daily runs on the pretty ride from Lisbon to the Algarve can get crowded). There's also a connection between Lisbon and Madrid. Buses are quite comfortable in Portugal. For those who want to drive themselves, car rentals in both countries are widely available—though a self-driving trip may not be prudent: Portugal and Spain have high accident and car break-in rates.

Cruises are a good way to see many of Spain's and Portugal's coastal and offshore sites, usually in combination with other European countries. In addition to Barcelona and Lisbon, ships call on the Balearic Islands, **Valencia**, the Costa del Sol, the Madeiras, and the Canaries (the latter two often in combination with Morocco).

Spain's unlimited rail passes are available only in North America.

Climate at a Glance
LISBON, PORTUGAL

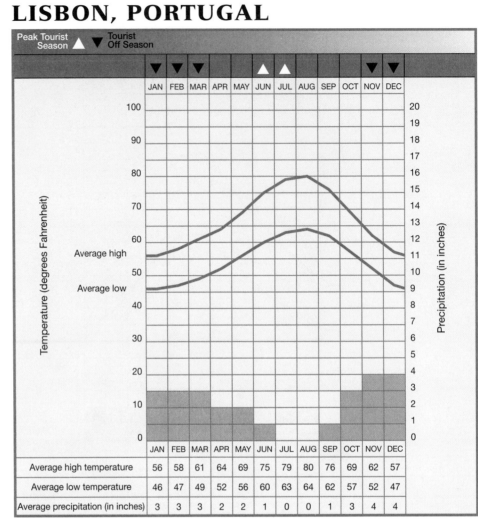

Peak Tourist Season ▲	▼ Tourist Off Season										
▼	▼	▼			▲	▲				▼	▼
JAN	FEB	MAR	APR	MAY	JUN	JUL	AUG	SEP	OCT	NOV	DEC

	JAN	FEB	MAR	APR	MAY	JUN	JUL	AUG	SEP	OCT	NOV	DEC
Average high temperature	56	58	61	64	69	75	79	80	76	69	62	57
Average low temperature	46	47	49	52	56	60	63	64	62	57	52	47
Average precipitation (in inches)	3	3	3	2	2	1	0	0	1	3	4	4

Figure 17–2

Madrid has a good, inexpensive bus system and a fine Metro subway. Barcelona's buses and Metro are well run. Lisbon's subway, the Metropolitano, is good. Taxis in Lisbon are reasonably priced.

Important Places

Each region of Spain is virtually a world of its own. And Portugal, closely related, has its own unique charm and beauty. These countries offer a wealth of interesting cities and attractions.

Madrid

The largest city in Spain, Madrid is the center of Castilian culture. Free enterprise, new personal freedoms, and burgeoning arts and industry have revitalized this beautiful and strong city. Among the major attractions:

- **The Prado**, one of the world's premier and most influential museums. Its collection of Spanish art, especially, is superb.
- **The Plaza Mayor**, an imposing square in the city's Old Madrid section.
- **The Royal Palace**, once home to King Charles III and today an art museum with one of the finest medieval arms exhibits in the world.

Madrid's Botin Restaurant claims to be the world's oldest restaurant. It opened in 1725.

The following **day trips** from Madrid are popular:

- **San Lorenzo de El Escorial**, an awesome monastery and palace. This sprawling six-teenth-century edifice, burial place of Spanish royalty, is 30 miles northwest of Madrid.
- **Avila**, a fully walled medieval city with an impressive cathedral and monastery.
- **Toledo**, a multicultured city with a famous cathedral. The beautiful town was home to the painter El Greco. Its **Alcazar** fortress was where the legendary leader El Cid was reputedly stationed.
- **Segovia**, a 2,000-year-old town famous for its imposing castle and Roman aqueduct.

San Sebastian

Built on three hills, San Sebastian lies at the heart of the picturesque Basque region, near the French border. The area is known for excellent cuisine. San Sebastian has fine beaches and an elegant casino, and is a popular summer resort. It's an excellent base for exploring the Basque country. Among possible **day trips** are:

- **Pamplona**, a charming, hilly village best known for the famous "running of the bulls" in July.
- **Bilbao**, a port city on the Bay of Biscay, with a Gothic cathedral and many museums. Most noteworthy: the architecturally daring **Guggenheim Museum Bilbao**.
- **Guernica**, made famous by the Picasso painting (in the Museo Nacional Reina Sofía, in Madrid) memorializing the town's devastation in the Spanish Civil War.

The only language related to Basque is a language spoken in Pakistan.

Barcelona

The second-largest city in Spain, Barcelona was once a major seaport. The harbor has been renewed and the city today is also a thriving business center and the heart of the distinctive Catalan culture. Barcelona is a city of diverse art museums, unusual architecture, fine music, and excellent food. Among the attractions that dominate this intriguing city are:

- **The Picasso** and **Miro Museums**, with collections that span the careers of each of these great artists.
- **La Rambla**, one of the great walking streets of Europe, with many little restaurants and shops.
- **Barri Gotic**, the old Gothic quarter, with fourteenth-century buildings and churches.
- **Montjuic Park**, with dramatic structures and gardens from the 1929 World's Fair and the 1992 Summer Olympics.
- **Sagrada Familia (Holy Family) Church**, a wonderfully bizarre edifice by architect Antonio Gaudi (who fashioned several other odd, striking buildings in Barcelona).

Most signs in Barcelona are in two languages: Catalan and Spanish.

The following **day trips** from Barcelona are popular:

- **Montserrat** is the mountainous site of a monastery where pilgrims have come for 800 years. Housed here is a famous statue, the Black Madonna.
- **Andorra** is a charming, tiny country in the nearby Pyrenees, with great shopping buys.

Gaudi never created a blueprint for the Sagrada Familia Church. He worked from a few rough sketches and simply instructed workers on what to build as they went along.

Costa Brava

This popular stretch of beach resorts north of Barcelona also features two attractions:

- **Ampurias**, with excavation sites of rare Phoenician ruins. There's also an impressive archaeological museum.
- **Figueres**, which houses the **Dali Theatre-Museum**, ingeniously converted from an old castle.

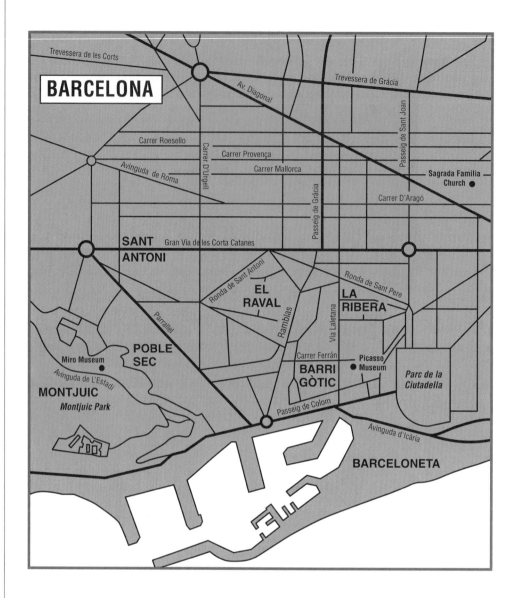

Balearic Islands

This group of Spanish islands is best known for the trendy and touristy resort island of Majorca. However, another island, Ibiza, has become popular with club goers. **Menorca** and **Formentera** are also part of the Balearic group; their tourism is a little less developed. Lodging is plentiful.

Costa Blanca

The second of the mainland beach resorts, Costa Blanca is to the south of Barcelona. At its center is the popular beach town of **Alicante**. The Costa Blanca is one of Spain's driest regions; it enjoys more than 3,000 hours of sunshine a year.

Costa del Sol

Located on the south coast, the Costa del Sol is one of the preeminent beach resorts in Europe. Highly developed with condominiums and high-rises, the area is known for having a very busy nightlife. Among its attractions:

Bilbao's Guggenheim museum was designed by American architect Frank Gehry and resembles several of his other signature buildings
Image copyright Luis M. Seco, 2008. Used under license from Shutterstock.com

- **Malaga**, the picturesque transportation center of the area, is Picasso's birthplace and home to the Malaga vineyards.
- **Torremolinos** is the most popular (and crowded) beach town in the region.
- **Marbella**, the trendiest and most luxurious of the resorts, has been able to keep much of its Old-World architecture.
- **Nerja** became famous in 1959 when children discovered its underground caves.

Not far from the Costa del Sol are Granada and Seville. Tourists can visit them as day trips, but these cities are more commonly seen as part of a trip to Andalusia.

Andalusia

This mountainous region is the land of flamenco dancing, bullfighting, and lavish Moorish palaces. Among its cities and attractions:

- **Granada** boasts one of Spain's great structures, the **Alhambra**, a spectacular fortress and palace, built by the Moors and graced by some of the most famous gardens in the world.
- **Cordoba** is home to **La Mezquita**, a magnificent Moorish mosque so huge that a cathedral was later built inside it.
- **Seville** has a fifteenth-century cathedral that is the world's largest medieval Gothic structure. The **Reales Alcazar** is a fortress remodeled to look like the Alhambra.

Lisbon

The capital of Portugal has an ancient history—possibly going back to the time of Ulysses, who legend says founded the city. However, Lisbon is also in many ways relatively new.

A highlight of Seville's cathedral is Christopher Columbus's tomb. Yet the Dominican Republic claims he is buried on their island.

In Lisbon, the Feast of St. Anthony revelry on the night of June 12 and all day June 13 is as festive as New Year's Eve.

Antonio Gaudi, who designed this unusually shaped apartment complex, is better known for Sagrada Familia Church
Image copyright Graca Victoria, 2008. Used under license from Shutterstock.com

An earthquake devastated much of the town in 1755 and since then it's been rebuilt. Lisbon is an easygoing place, gentle and less expensive than Madrid. Among the attractions you might recommend are:

- **The Alfama** and the **Bairro Alto**, famous for their cobbled streets and ancient medieval buildings. The **Baixa**, below them, is Lisbon's main shopping district.
- **Belem**, a riverside district that features the landmark **Tower of Belem**, the **Monument to the Discoveries**, and the white marble **Jeronimos Monastery**, a striking building whose sea-inspired architecture is unique to Portugal.
- **St. George's Castle**, a huge structure atop the city, with 10 towers, beautiful gardens, and great views.
- **Estoril**, a major seaside resort about 15 minutes from Lisbon.

A great **day trip** from Lisbon is picturesque **Sintra**, in the middle of the **Serra de Sintra mountains**. The **National Palace** and the sprawling **Pena Palace**, with its extravagant 500-acre gardens, are located here.

The Algarve

The beaches of this south-coast resort area are quainter and quieter than those of Spain, though tourism to the region is escalating fast. Surrounded by high cliffs, the area is one of the most popular in Portugal. Its air gateway is the town of **Faro** (FAO). Among its towns are:

- **Lagos**, a walled seaside village with a rich history. It has wonderful beaches that are getting a little touristy.
- **Sagres**, a historical navigation center. Vasco da Gama, Magellan, and Diaz all studied here.
- **Portimao**, with fine beaches. It has an active fishing trade and is fairly crowded.
- **Albufeira**, perhaps the busiest of the resorts. It's faster paced and has more of a nightlife.

Though Portugal is small, its seafaring tradition enabled it to have a worldwide empire. Its former colonies include Macau (near Hong Kong), Brazil, Goa (in India), Formosa (now Taiwan), Angola, and Mozambique.

The Tower of Belem is one of Portugal's most recognizable structures
Image copyright Matt Trommer, 2008. Used under license from Shutterstock.com

Possible Itineraries

First-time visitors to this part of Europe might enjoy a week that starts in Madrid before heading down to Seville and Granada or, instead, over to Barcelona. A few days could be added for one of the adjacent beach resorts. Return travelers could easily spend two weeks exploring: adding Portugal to a trip to Madrid, Seville, and the Costa del Sol; or including the Basque country with a trip to Madrid, Barcelona, and the Costa Brava. Furthermore, any beach resort or Balearic Island would make a wonderful four- to five-day visit, or as a one-day cruise stop.

Lodging Options

Spain offers a wide range of accommodations; however, the lower-rated hotels may be a bit iffy. Many of the deluxe hotels are costly but very special.

Madrid's most famous lodging is the **Hotel Ritz**, an extraordinary Edwardian-style property. In Seville, there's the classically elegant **Alfonso XIII**. In Barcelona is another elegant **Ritz** (now the **Hotel Palace**), as well as the old-world luxury of **Avenida Palace**.

The following chains offer the most lodging options in Spain: **Melia** (upscale), **Sol**, **NH**, and **Tryp**. Several North American and international hotel chains are also represented. Alternative accommodations include the *paradores* (converted castles and monasteries that are fairly priced).

Most of the world's major hotel chains have a few properties in Portugal. The country has a surprising number of opulent five-star hotels. An excellent alternative type of lodging here are the *pousadas*—inexpensive government-sponsored inns, many of which are castles.

There are more people of Portuguese descent in New England than there are in Lisbon.

Allied Destinations

At the very southern tip of Spain is British-controlled Gibraltar (and its famous rock) and across the Strait of Gibraltar is Morocco. Sandwiched between northern Spain and southern France is the tiny country of Andorra, a wonderful place to do some duty-free shopping.

Cultural Patterns

Though Western nations, Spain and Portugal present unique cultural challenges. Business travelers especially should be sensitive to a few unique customs:

- An invitation to a Spanish home is often made out of courtesy and shouldn't be accepted until one's host insists.

- Visitors should bring a small gift to a Spaniard's home. They may receive a gift in return, which should be opened on the spot.

- Many businesses close from 1:30 P.M. to 4:30 P.M. in Spain for siesta; in Portugal, they close from noon to 3 P.M.

- Dinner is served very late in Spain, where restaurants often do not open until 9 P.M. and don't fill until 11 P.M.

- One's appearance is given meaningful attention in Spain and shouldn't be taken lightly; visitors should dress carefully and well for business occasions.

- After a meal, diners must place their utensils together on their plate. To do otherwise would suggest that they weren't satisfied.

- Punctuality is not high among Spanish and Portuguese virtues. Yet the Portuguese do expect people to arrive on time for meetings (even if they start late).

Qualifying the Traveler
Spain

For People Who Want	Appeal			Remarks
	High	Medium	Low	
Historical and Cultural Attractions	▲			World-class museums
Beaches and Water Sports	▲			Both southern and eastern shores and islands
Skiing Opportunities		▲		Northern mountains
Lots of Nightlife		▲		Especially Madrid and Barcelona
Family Activities			▲	
Familiar Cultural Experience			▲	
Exotic Cultural Experience	▲			
Safety and Low Crime		▲		Much petty crime
Bargain Travel		▲		
Impressive Scenery countryside	▲			Seascapes and
Peace and Quiet		▲		In countryside
Shopping Opportunities		▲		Leather, lace, pottery
Adventure		▲		
To Do Business		▲		

Factors That Motivate Visitors

Among the reasons a vacationer might be eager to visit Spain and Portugal are:

- The weather is sunny and beautiful.
- The countryside can be inexpensive, with great bargains for shopping and lodging. Portugal is an even greater bargain than Spain.
- The locals are extremely friendly.
- Portugal has some great golf courses.
- Both countries are easily accessible from North America.
- Water sports, beach activities, and cruise opportunities are readily available.
- The food is wonderful (though different from the Hispanic foods Americans are familiar with).
- There's rich cultural and artistic diversity to be found.

Possible Misgivings

Of course, as with any country, would-be visitors have concerns about Spain and Portugal. Among these concerns are:

- "It's much too hot in summer." Northern Spain is cooler than the rest of the Iberian Peninsula. The heat elsewhere tends to be dry.
- "It's crowded in the summer." The beach resorts are indeed crowded in the peak seasons. Vacationers can visit at a different time, find a less famous beach, or choose another area of the country.
- "The Basque separatist groups commit terrorist acts." The few incidents that occur make the news. The chance of a tourist being affected is slim.
- "It's expensive." Madrid and Barcelona—once bargains—have become pricey. However, many secondary Spanish cities and most of Portugal are less expensive.
- "There's a great deal of petty crime there." Unfortunately, there's crime in most big cities of the world. Normal precautions will reduce risk.

Sales Strategies

Lower-rated hotels can be unpleasant, so more highly regarded lodgings can make the difference between a successful and an unsuccessful trip. Deluxe hotels in Spain are expensive but luxurious and special. *Paradores* can make a visit memorable. Because of the size of Spain especially, tours can be appropriate. On the Costa Brava or Majorca, chauffeured cars are a much safer way of getting around the dangerous, winding roads. Motorboats or cruises along the coast and to the islands are also an enjoyable way of seeing the country.

Tapas are hors d'oeuvres-like treats that Spaniards often combine to form a meal. They developed out of a nineteenth-century custom of topping glasses of sherry with toast to keep the flies out.

Over 3,000 feasts and festivals take place each year in Spain.

Travel Trivia

Museums with the Greatest Collections of Picasso Paintings

- Metropolitan Museum of Art, New York
- Centre Georges Pompidou, Paris
- The Hermitage, St. Petersburg, Russia
- The Kunstmuseum, Basel, Switzerland
- Musee Picasso, Paris

- Museu Picasso, Barcelona
- Museum of Modern Art, New York
- National Gallery, Prague, Czech Republic
- National Gallery of Art, Washington, D.C.
- Philadelphia Museum of Art, Philadelphia

NAME _____ **DATE** _____

MAP ACTIVITY

A traveler wants to visit the places listed below. Which number represents each on the map?

Place/Attraction	In/Near Which City?	Number on Map
A. The Alhambra	A. _____	A. _____
B. Transportation hub of the Costa del Sol	B. _____	B. _____
C. The Prado	C. _____	C. _____
D. The major city closest to Andorra	D. _____	D. _____
E. The Baixa	E. _____	E. _____
F. Picasso Museum	F. _____	F. _____
G. The Alfama	G. _____	G. _____
H. The town where the bulls run	H. _____	H. _____
I. The world's largest medieval Gothic church	I. _____	I. _____
J. The busiest of the Algarve's resorts	J. _____	J. _____

NAME _____   DATE _____

CASE STUDY

Mary-Jo and Bud Reid, in their early 30s, are planning a three-week trip to Europe, concentrating on Spain. It's their first visit there and their first big vacation in five years, so they're willing to spend money.

Circle the answer that best suits their needs.

1 How many days would you recommend for Spain?

    Three   Six

    Seven   Fourteen

    Why?

2 Which of the following countries would you be *least* likely to combine with a trip to Spain and Portugal?

    Morocco   Gibraltar

    Andorra   Grenada

    Why?

3 If they especially wanted to see a bullfight and flamenco dancing, where would you suggest Mary-Jo and Bud go?

    Granada   San Sebastian

    Ibiza   The Spanish Riding School

    Why?

4 Of the following tips you could propose to Mary-Jo and Bud, which would be most useful?

    Visit the Prado in Ibiza   Shop at midday

    Go in July   Plan to eat late dinners

    Why?

NAME _____   **DATE** _____

CREATIVE ACTIVITY

Your Atlanta-based public relations company has been hired to create the tourist promotional campaign for the Iberian Tourist Office, which represents Spain, Portugal, and all of their islands.

You've decided to "target" your market to figure out which kinds of American travelers are most likely to find Spain and Portugal appealing. You create the grid below to guide you.

Fill out the grid, circling a number according to the given rating system. Give your reasoning in the right column. (An example is provided.)

Kind of Traveler	Appeal (5 highest, 1 lowest)					Comments
Sun-and-fun types	⑤	4	3	2	1	Mediterranean beaches and Balearic Islands
Value seekers	5	4	3	2	1	
Quick-getawayers from the United States	5	4	3	2	1	
Families with children	5	4	3	2	1	
Single travelers	5	4	3	2	1	
Cruisers	5	4	3	2	1	
Affluent travelers	5	4	3	2	1	
Ethnic tourists	5	4	3	2	1	
Ecotourists	5	4	3	2	1	
Business travelers	5	4	3	2	1	
People seeking seclusion	5	4	3	2	1	
People who take tours	5	4	3	2	1	
Art lovers	5	4	3	2	1	

DENMARK

BALTIC SEA

NORTH SEA

POLAND

✈ Hamburg

Elbe River

Berlin ⊛
Potsdam ● ✈

NETHERLANDS

Rhine

✈ Dusseldorf

Cologne

Leipzig ●

Dresden

Bonn

GERMANY

BELGIUM

Koblenz

CZECH REPUBLIC

Rudesheim
Rhineland

✈ Frankfurt

LUX.

Mainz

Wurzburg

Worms

Mannheim

Nurnberg

Heidelberg

Rothenburg

SLOVAK

Heilbronn

Neckar River

Dinkelsbuhl

Black Forest

✈ Stuttgart

Nordlingen

FRANCE

Rhine

Baden-Baden

Bavaria

Passau ●

Danube River

▲ Dachau
● Munich

Freiburg

Lake Constance

✈ Oberammergau

Fussen

AUSTRIA

HUNGA

SWITZERLAND

Alps

Garmisch-Partenkirchen

Chapter 18

Germany
Romantic Roads

Germany is a culture-rich land of fairytale sights. Whether driving the **Romantic Road** or cruising the **Rhine River**, visitors can discover charming hamlets, delicate or imposing castles, and, in at least one city, people who—on occasion—still dress in medieval clothing.

Germany was divided into two separate governments after World War II, but was reunified in 1990. German, of course, is the national language, though many Germans do have a good command of basic English.

When people think of Germany, the area they probably envision is **Bavaria**, in the south. With **Munich** [MYOO-nik] (Munchen) as its center, this is the land of Alpine terrain, oom-pah bands, beer halls, and mountain skiing. Meandering north from Bavaria is the Romantic Road, so named because of its enchanting medieval villages. Running down the west side of Germany is the legendary **Rhineland**, with its stunning scenery along the Rhine River. This leads into the **Black Forest**, found in Germany's southwest corner.

Binoculars are essential for a Rhine cruise.

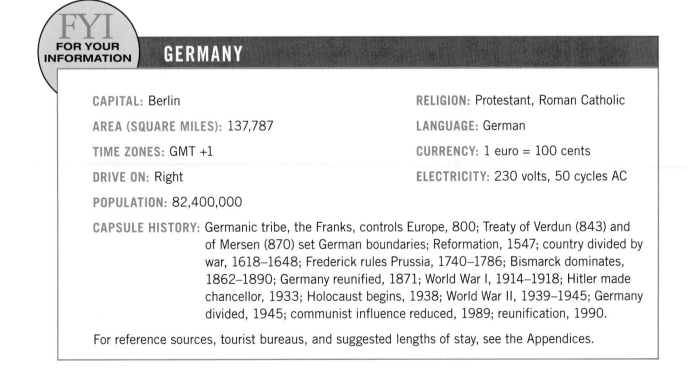

FYI
FOR YOUR INFORMATION

GERMANY

CAPITAL: Berlin

AREA (SQUARE MILES): 137,787

TIME ZONES: GMT +1

DRIVE ON: Right

POPULATION: 82,400,000

RELIGION: Protestant, Roman Catholic

LANGUAGE: German

CURRENCY: 1 euro = 100 cents

ELECTRICITY: 230 volts, 50 cycles AC

CAPSULE HISTORY: Germanic tribe, the Franks, controls Europe, 800; Treaty of Verdun (843) and of Mersen (870) set German boundaries; Reformation, 1547; country divided by war, 1618–1648; Frederick rules Prussia, 1740–1786; Bismarck dominates, 1862–1890; Germany reunified, 1871; World War I, 1914–1918; Hitler made chancellor, 1933; Holocaust begins, 1938; World War II, 1939–1945; Germany divided, 1945; communist influence reduced, 1989; reunification, 1990.

For reference sources, tourist bureaus, and suggested lengths of stay, see the Appendices.

Cutting east to west across the country's center are the rolling hills and magical palaces of the **Castle Road**. Nearby, in the middle of Germany, is **Frankfurt**. The flat, northern part of the country is less visited by foreign tourists; travelers do go to **Hamburg**, but it's mainly for business. And **Berlin**, once divided, has regained its status as Germany's preeminent city.

How Travelers Get There

The major gateway into Germany is **Frankfurt Airport** (FRA). **Munich Airport** (MUC) and **Dusseldorf Airport** (DUS) are also used heavily. Secondary airports are in Berlin (BER), Hamburg (HAM), and **Stuttgart** (STR).

Germany's airlines are **Lufthansa** (LH) and **L.T.U. International Airways** (LT). The country is also well serviced by North American carriers. Flying time from New York is 7.5 hours; from Chicago, 8.5 hours; and from Los Angeles, 11.5 hours.

Hamburg is an important port of arrival and departure for cruises to the British Isles, Scandinavia and the Baltics, and other European destinations. **Passau** is a launch point for Danube cruises into Eastern Europe.

Lake Constance, at the border of Germany, Austria, and Switzerland, is also called Bodensee.

Climate at a Glance
FRANKFURT

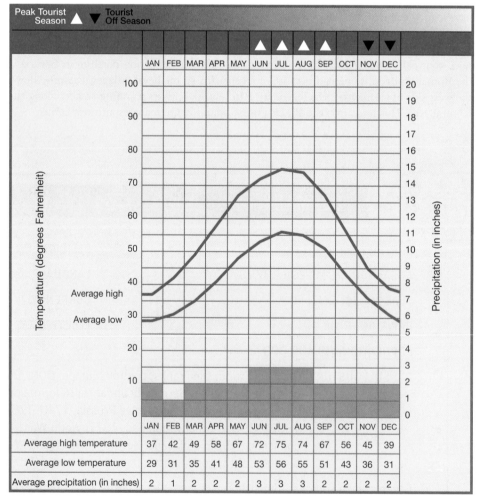

	JAN	FEB	MAR	APR	MAY	JUN	JUL	AUG	SEP	OCT	NOV	DEC
Average high temperature	37	42	49	58	67	72	75	74	67	56	45	39
Average low temperature	29	31	35	41	48	53	56	55	51	43	36	31
Average precipitation (in inches)	2	1	2	2	2	3	3	3	2	2	2	2

Figure 18–1

Weather Patterns

Summer days are very pleasant, with temperatures in the 70s, but nights can drop to the 50s (see Figure 18–1); temperatures in Bavaria can run even cooler. Winters are cold and often overcast or foggy, with rain and (especially in Bavaria) snow. Indeed, when the sun comes out, it seems as if every German heads outdoors. Fall and spring are chilly, but in general quite lovely and less crowded. Summers are the peak tourist season, whereas winters see a drop-off in tourism. One exception: The Alpine area gets very busy in the winter with skiers.

Getting Around

Germany's rail system is one of the world's finest—so good that it often beats traveling between cities by air, though most major cities have excellent airport connections. Travelers can even get off their plane and get on a train, because rail terminals are located at several airports. The **autobahn** is a wonderful way to travel through Germany. On some of its stretches, speed limits are nonexistent or only "suggested." Car rentals are widely available. Tourists who plan to buy a German car can order it before leaving home, pick it up at the factory in Germany, and then drive the vehicle around the country.

Rhine River cruises have been popular for well over a century. Cruises down the Elbe (from Hamburg to Dresden and into the Czech Republic) provide a creative way to sightsee in eastern Germany.

In Munich, the U-Bahn is a very good subway system that connects with the S-Bahn local trains. There's also a well-run bus system. Taxis tend to be a little expensive. Berlin is usually reached by air, car, or train.

Important Places

Though most people think of Germany in terms of Bavaria, the country's many regions are diverse in their attractions.

> On the autobahn, stay in the slower right-hand lanes—unless you're prepared to hurtle along at breakneck speeds.

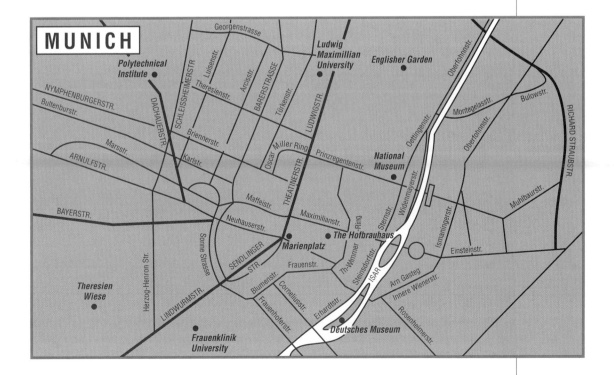

Bavaria

Surrounded by the **Alps**, Bavaria is a robust area, with picturesque castles and medieval villages. The heart of Bavaria is the region's capital, Munich.

Like the rest of Bavaria, Munich is a lusty place, with beer halls, cabarets, and a lively nightlife, especially during the renowned **Oktoberfest** celebration. It's also a sophisticated city with world-class opera and symphonies, high fashion, excellent museums, and important centers of learning. This 800-year-old riverfront city appeals to almost everyone. Among its best attractions are:

- **The Marienplatz**, the heart of Munich, a town square with its famous glockenspiel clock.
- **The Deutsches** [DOY-ches] **Museum**, the world's largest science and technology museum.
- **The Hofbrauhaus**, a renowned huge, lively beer hall.
- **Nymphenburg Palace**, a seventeenth-century castle with vast gardens and a museum. Located just outside town, it also houses a china factory.

Here are some interesting **day trips**:

- **Fussen** [FEW-sen] is famous for the spectacular castles built by King Ludwig II. Just about every country has a castle that claims to have inspired the one in Disneyland, but **Neuschwanstein** [NOYSH-vahn-shtine], the most remarkable of Fussen's castles, is *the* one.
- **Oberammergau** has put on its legendary passion play since the 1600s. The drama is presented the first year of every new decade.
- **Dachau** is a stirring and disquieting memorial to the victims of Nazi concentration camps.
- **Garmisch-Partenkirchen** was the site of the 1936 Winter Olympics. It's a modern yet charming town—beautiful in summer and a premier Alpine ski resort in the winter.

The Romantic Road

Beginning in Fussen, in the heart of Bavaria, and winding north more than 200 miles to **Wurzburg**, the Romantic Road is a string of medieval cities and Roman ruins. Suggest a visit by car or motorcoach tour. Among the attractions you might recommend are:

- **Nordlingen** and **Dinkelsbuhl**, with city centers that evoke the Middle Ages.
- **Rothenburg** [ROTE-en-burg], perhaps the finest preserved medieval village in all of Europe.

The Castle Road

Stretching east from **Mannheim** to **Nuremberg** (Nurnberg) and on to Prague in the Czech Republic, the Castle Road is a path of castles and fortresses dating to medieval times. It's also a fine wine district. The route can be driven or taken as part of a cruise along the **Neckar River**. More commonly, this area is visited as part of a shorter version, from Mannheim to **Heilbronn**. Among its key towns are:

- **Heidelberg**, home to one of the world's great universities. Its medieval castles and churches are the setting of the operetta *The Student Prince*.
- **Rothenburg**, the well-preserved medieval town.
- **Nurnberg** (or **Nuremberg**), remembered as the site of the World War II war-crimes trials. It's also famous for its gingerbread, toy making, medieval structures, and massive **Christmas Market** in December.

Street names change often in Munich, and these names are very long. Always carry a street map with you.

In the seventeenth century, the villagers of Oberammergau vowed to stage the play every decade to give thanks for being spared during the Black Plague.

In Rothenburg's oldest structures, tourists regularly bump their heads on overhead beams and door overhangs. The reason: People were much shorter when Rothenburg was built.

This structure near Fussen is one of the world's most famous castles: Neuschwanstein
Image copyright Yan Ke, 2008. Used under license from Shutterstock.com

Although not precisely on the Castle Road, **Worms**, a historical town associated with Attila the Hun and Martin Luther, has the oldest synagogue in Germany and is the center for Liebfraumilch wine.

The Rhineland

The 825-mile Rhine River is one of Europe's oldest trade routes. The Rhineland proper is generally considered to stretch from **Mainz** to **Koblenz**, though some feel it goes all the way up to **Cologne** (Koln). Winding its way past charming villages, castles high on cliffs, and vineyards, this river passes through the region from which many German legends spring. Though the Rhineland can be seen by train or car, perhaps the most popular way of visiting this scenic area is on a cruise. Most cruises are run by **KD Rhine** and range from half to full day. Other companies operate four- to eight-day trips (the multiday cruises cover more of the river and use ships with overnight accommodations). Among the Rhineland's most interesting towns are:

- **Cologne**, with its renowned thirteenth-century Gothic cathedral and beautiful stained-glass windows.
- **Rudesheim**, a very charming but touristy wine center.
- **Bonn**, the capital of the former West Germany and the birthplace of Beethoven.
- **Dusseldorf**, a fashionable city with an active nightlife and good shopping.

Near the Rhineland is Frankfurt, the main air gateway to Germany. Although not a major tourist destination, the house of famed author Johann Wolfgang von Goethe is here, as are a few nice museums, a good opera company, and Gothic buildings.

The Black Forest

This beautiful region is rich with mountains, meadows, deep valleys, cool lakes, and dense forests. Beginning south of Frankfurt and continuing down to the thoroughly charming

On the banks of the Rhine River is the Lorelei Rock. According to legend, a siren (sea nymph) would sing to lure sailors to the rock, where they'd shipwreck and drown.

This graceful bridge marks the entrance to the quaint town of Heidelberg
Image copyright siegfried boes, 2008. Used under license from Shutterstock.com

town of **Freiburg**, the area is particularly noted for spas, cuckoo clocks, and ski resorts. Among the towns associated with the Black Forest are:

- **Stuttgart**, with its art and automobile museums, ballet and opera companies, and the nearby **Mercedes-Benz car factory**.
- **Baden-Baden**, one of the world's oldest and most famous spas, with an elegant casino.

Berlin

This city sits in Germany's northeast corner, in the middle of what was East Germany. It's a dynamic center of culture, with a world-class orchestra, noted theaters, and some of the finest museums in Europe. Among its attractions:

- **The Wall** (or what little is left of it), the infamous 30-mile structure that once prevented East Berliners from going to the West.
- **The Reichstag**, the original, ornate German parliament building, now capped with a modern glass dome.
- **Charlottenburg Palace**, a grand, opulent structure built in the late seventeenth century.
- **East Berlin** (which used to be a separate area), with many worthwhile attractions. Sights include **Unter den Linden**, the soul of the city and its main boulevard, lined with linden trees and many historic buildings; the **Brandenburg Gate**, which once linked East and West Berlin; and an entire island of museums. Among the most visited of these museums is the **Pergamon Museum**, a huge indoor space that harbors three astonishing structures that, piece by piece, were relocated here: the **Pergamon Altar** (a temple dedicated to Zeus in the second century B.C.), the **Processional Way and Gateway of Ishtar** (from ancient Babylon), and the **Market Gate of Miletus**.
- **Sans Souci Palace**, a monument to the fanciful and elaborate excesses of the Rococo architectural style. Located in nearby **Potsdam**, Sans Souci sits in a charming park.

Eastern Germany

This formerly communist region has opened itself wide to tourism. In addition to Berlin, Eastern Germany features two other intriguing places:

- **Dresden** is a jewel of a city. Firebombed into near-oblivion during World War II, Dresden rose from the ashes and is largely rebuilt. Its palaces, art galleries, and opera are first rate.

- **Leipzig**'s musical heritage is legendary. This graceful city is most often associated with composer Johann Sebastian Bach.

Possible Itineraries

Because it borders so many countries, Germany is often included as part of a larger trip. First-time visitors should either spend at least five days exploring the Romantic Road and Bavaria, or take a few days on or along the Rhine. These destinations can, of course, be combined for a longer stay.

Return travelers may like to explore areas they haven't seen yet, such as the Black Forest or the Castle Road. A trip to Berlin would also be fascinating. You should keep in mind that Germany is very rich in attractions and can easily be visited in-depth for two weeks on its own.

Lodging Options

Germany can be a fairly expensive country to visit, and lodging is a large part of that cost. Germany's luxury chain is **Kempinski Hotels**. For those looking for something less costly, **Queens**, **Dorint**, and **ArabellaSheraton Hotels** are available. **Steigenberger** hotels range from first class to deluxe. Quite a few North American chains are present as well. In Munich, hotels are clustered south and east of the rail station. In Berlin, many hotels are near the **Europa Centre**.

Germany offers assorted lodging alternatives. Many castles have been converted into hotels; they're beautiful, but can be expensive. **Gast im Schloss** is an association of somewhat reasonable castles that you might want to look into. In addition, spas (especially in the Black Forest) are popular. For those on a budget, *pensions* offer pleasant and inexpensive lodging.

Allied Destinations

Germany is centrally located in Europe, which is one reason it's often combined on a vacation with other countries, both by land and by sea. It borders Denmark, Poland, the Czech Republic, Austria, Switzerland, France, Luxembourg, Belgium, and the Netherlands. Switzerland and Austria, because of their similar cultures and proximity to Bavaria, are the most frequent add-ons to a trip to Germany.

Cultural Patterns

Located in the heart of the continent, Germany represents a rich mixture of Western European traditions and Eastern European ways of thinking. With the major changes this area has undergone in recent years, it's particularly important that business travelers, especially, are sensitive to its cultural diversity:

- Germans tend to be somewhat reserved. First names should be used only when one has been given permission or knows the person well; if uncertain, a visitor should follow the lead of the person to whom he or she is talking.

- Punctuality and thoughtfulness (e.g., acknowledging a birthday) are very important to Germans.

A small German–English dictionary is especially useful when ordering from a menu; remember to bring one along.

The Kiel Canal, which connects the Baltic and North seas, carries more traffic than any other canal in the world.

Fasching, usually held in February or March, is the Munich version of wild Mardi Gras revelry.

The Pergamon Altar came from the ancient city of Pergamon, in what is now Turkey
Photo by Marc Mancini

- It's considered rude to talk with one's hands in one's pockets.
- Prepare for an unusual custom: To show their appreciation at the end of a meeting, Germans will often bang their fists on the table.

Factors That Motivate Visitors

Among the reasons for wanting to visit Germany might be:

- Bavaria's scenery is spectacular.
- Germany is very accessible, clean, and organized.
- The country is filled with cultural riches and architectural landmarks.
- The people are friendly.
- The food is wonderful and hearty.
- Hamburg is a major cruise port and the Rhine is an important cruise waterway.
- There are lively festivals.
- Winter sports facilities are extensive, especially for skiing.

Possible Misgivings

As spectacular as Germany is, some may feel reservations toward this destination. Among their concerns:

- "It's expensive." Yes, but there are bargains, and certain areas, like the Romantic and Castle Roads, can be a bit less costly. All-inclusive tours help minimize unexpected costs.
- "The Nazis caused World War II and the Holocaust. Neo-Nazi sentiments still exist." This is a very sensitive topic. Some people, indeed, will *never* want to go to Germany. For those who might, but have some reservations, a visit to the Dachau Memorial might be appropriate. A new generation now leads the country and only a small (but vocal) few still harbor Nazi-like sentiments.

Munich's Oktoberfest begins in late September and runs through the first week of October.

Qualifying the Traveler
Germany

For People Who Want	Appeal			Remarks
	High	Medium	Low	
Historical and Cultural Attractions	▲			
Beaches and Water Sports		▲		Scenic lakes
Skiing Opportunities	▲			Bavarian Alps
Lots of Nightlife		▲		Mostly Munich
Family Activities		▲		Primarily sightseeing
Familiar Cultural Experience			▲	
Exotic Cultural Experience		▲		
Safety and Low Crime	▲			
Bargain Travel			▲	
Impressive Scenery	▲			Especially in south
Peace and Quiet		▲		Only in countryside
Shopping Opportunities		▲		Steins, cameras, cuckoo clocks, porcelain
Adventure		▲		
To Do Business		▲		A major trade partner with the United States

- "Germans are a cold people." In fact, the locals are quite friendly toward visitors.
- "They don't speak English." Germans are very well educated, and many people do indeed learn English as a second language.
- "It's so far from the United States." Germany is almost as close as Paris and is closer than Rome; a trip can easily be combined with one of those cities.
- "The weather's bad and there are no sun resorts." The weather is nice in the summer. A Bavarian resort or spa may be just fine; otherwise, Germany may be the wrong place for sun-and-fun types.

Sales Strategies

Germany's strengths lend themselves to a great many sales enhancements. For instance, staying in a castle high above a forest, though expensive, would be magical. A cruise down the Elbe, Rhine, or Neckar may be the best way to see those regions. Spas have long been popular in Germany, and they're now catching on with Americans. Because there's so much history spread out across the country, an escorted tour or river cruise might be perfect for some. City tours (especially of Berlin) are a good option.

A rail pass, too, provides efficient travel among Germany's far-flung attractions. Car rentals, because of the autobahn system, appeal to many. And "European Delivery" Mercedes and BMWs appeal to the upscale.

German Rail Passes and Eurail Global Passes can be bought only in North America.

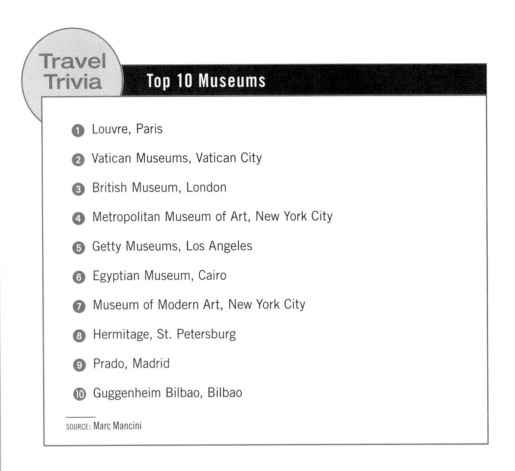

Travel Trivia

Top 10 Museums

1. Louvre, Paris
2. Vatican Museums, Vatican City
3. British Museum, London
4. Metropolitan Museum of Art, New York City
5. Getty Museums, Los Angeles
6. Egyptian Museum, Cairo
7. Museum of Modern Art, New York City
8. Hermitage, St. Petersburg
9. Prado, Madrid
10. Guggenheim Bilbao, Bilbao

SOURCE: Marc Mancini

NAME _____   **DATE** _____

MAP ACTIVITY

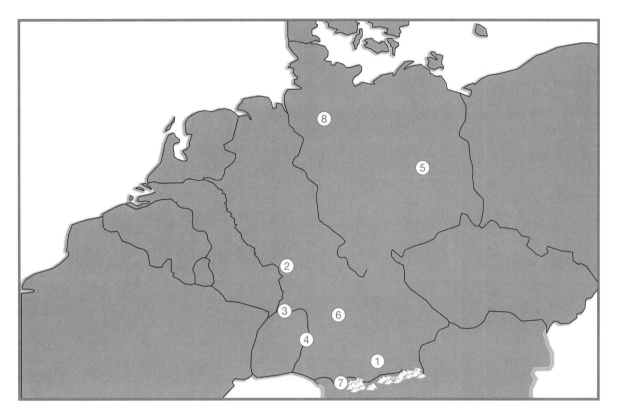

A traveler wants to visit the places listed below. Which number represents each on the map?

Place/Attraction	In/Near Which City?	Number on Map
A. Charlottenburg Palace	A. _____	A. _____
B. Europe's best-preserved medieval town	B. _____	B. _____
C. Neuschwanstein	C. _____	C. _____
D. The Marienplatz	D. _____	D. _____
E. An automobile museum	E. _____	E. _____
F. The university town where *The Student Prince* is set	F. _____	F. _____
G. The Hofbrauhaus	G. _____	G. _____
H. Goethe's house	H. _____	H. _____
I. The remains of the Wall	I. _____	I. _____
J. The Deutsches Museum	J. _____	J. _____

NAME _____ **DATE** _____

CASE STUDY

Clark and Ellen Griswold and their two teenage boys are planning a 21-day excursion to Germany, France, and Italy. The parents have been to France and Italy, but it's their boys' first trip to Europe. With four people traveling for three weeks, they don't plan to be extravagant, but they do want to be comfortable.

Circle the answer that best suits their needs.

1 How many total days in Germany would you recommend for their trip?

    Three   Six

    Fifteen   Twenty

    Why?

2 If they want to concentrate on only one area, which would you suggest?

    The Castle Road   Bavaria

    Eastern Germany   Vienna

    Why?

3 Which region should they visit if they want to take a cruise, as well as see some castles?

    The Lowenbrau River   The Elbe River

    The Loire   Rhineland

    Why?

4 If they wanted to see medieval towns, to which of the following should they *not* go?

    Rothenburg   Nordlingen

    Garmisch-Partenkirchen   Dinkelsbuhl

    Why?

NAME _____ DATE _____

CREATIVE ACTIVITY

Which German city should you recommend to a traveler who likes each of the following? (Be prepared to justify each choice.)

For Travelers Who Like . . .   **Recommended City**

1 Medieval history   **1**

2 Recent history   **2**

3 Drinking wine   **3**

4 Visiting castles   **4**

5 Skiing   **5**

6 Cuckoo clocks   **6**

7 Christian religious pageantry   **7**

8 Literature   **8**

9 Spas   **9**

10 Festivals   **10**

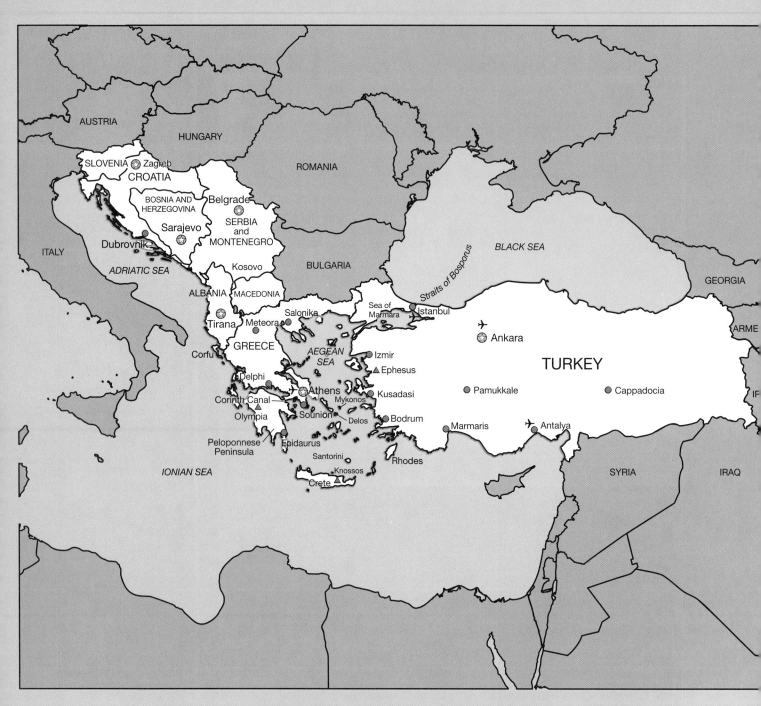

AUSTRIA

HUNGARY

SLOVENIA
CROATIA ⊛ Zagreb

ROMANIA

BOSNIA AND
HERZEGOVINA
Belgrade ☆

ITALY

Sarajevo ☆
Dubrovnik

SERBIA
and
MONTENEGRO

ADRIATIC SEA

Kosovo

BULGARIA

BLACK SEA

Straits of Bosporus

GEORGIA

ALBANIA MACEDONIA

Sea of
Marmara

Istanbul

ARME

Tirana

Salonika

Meteora

✈

GREECE

AEGEAN
SEA

Ankara ⊛

Corfu

Izmir

TURKEY

Delphi

▲ Ephesus

Pamukkale

Cappadocia

Corinth Canal
Olympia

Athens ⊛

Mykonos

Kusadasi

Sounion

Delos

Bodrum

Peloponnese
Peninsula

Epidaurus

▲

Santorini

Marmaris

✈ Antalya

Rhodes

IONIAN SEA

Knossos

SYRIA

IRAQ

Crete ▲

Chapter 19

Greece and Turkey
An Odyssey of Culture

Homer's classic tale *The Odyssey* is perhaps the most famous adventure story ever told: It traces the travels of Odysseus through some of Western civilization's most famous places. Present-day travelers can take the same trip—with fewer obstacles. The land of *The Odyssey*—the Eastern Mediterranean from Greece and its islands to Turkey—remains as classic today as it was in the time of Homer.

Greece, which altogether is about the size of New York State, spreads over a broad area. The country is made up not only of its mainland but also of more than 2,000 islands. Turkey is larger: It's nearly as big as Texas and Louisiana combined. A small part of Turkey occupies a little portion of Europe, but most of the country is in Asia. The two sections are separated by the **Straits of Bosporus** (which connect the Black Sea with the Sea of Marmara and, eventually, the Aegean).

Most American tourists are interested in three areas: **Athens** and the region around it, the **Greek islands**, and western Turkey. Northern Greece, with cities such as **Salonika** (also called Thessalonika) and **Meteora** (with its hilltop monasteries), is interesting, but somewhat off the beaten path. **Istanbul**, Turkey, is a fascinating, unique city often visited on cruises. Other Turkish destinations are the ports of **Izmir** and **Kusadasi**, and the inland ruins. In both countries, English is spoken by those in the tourist trade.

Greece and European Turkey are often cited as part of a larger group called the **Balkans**. The Balkans include Bulgaria (discussed in Chapter 20), **Albania, Slovenia, Croatia, Bosnia and Herzegovina, Serbia,** and **Macedonia**.

Turkey is 3 percent in Europe and 97 percent in Asia.

How Travelers Get There

Olympic Airlines (OA) is Greece's main airline and flies into the country's main gateway in Athens (ATH). A few North American airlines fly here, as well. Secondary airports operate on the islands of **Corfu** (CFU), **Mykonos** (JMK), and **Rhodes** (RHO). **Turkish Airlines** (TK) flies into Istanbul (IST), **Ankara** (ANK), and **Antalya** (AYT).

Most American tourists to Greece, however, visit the Greek islands and Turkey via cruises, most of which operate from May to October. During the other months the seas can be very rough; cruise opportunities, therefore, are limited beyond the high summer season. Most cruises arrive at Athens's **Piraeus** (the Mediterranean's number-one cruise port) or Istanbul.

FYI
FOR YOUR INFORMATION

GREECE AND TURKEY

CAPITALS: Greece: Athens
Turkey: Ankara

AREA (SQUARE MILES): Greece: 50,944
Turkey: 301,382

TIME ZONE: GMT +2

DRIVE ON: Right

POPULATIONS: Greece: 10,700,000
Turkey: 71,900,000

RELIGION: Greece: Greek Orthodox
Turkey: Islam

LANGUAGES: Greece: Greek
Turkey: Turkish

CURRENCY: Greece: 1 euro = 100 cents
Turkey: 1 Turkish lira = 100 kurus

ELECTRICITY: 220 volts, 50 cycles AC

CAPSULE HISTORY: Greece: Ancient Greece reaches peak, fifth century B.C.; Roman colony from second century B.C.; Greece becomes Turkish (Byzantine Empire) province, 1460; wins independence, 1827; becomes kingdom, 1832; becomes republic, 1924; monarchy restored 1935; Italy and Germany invade, 1941; liberated, 1944; military rule, 1967–1974; new republic, 1975.
Turkey: Captured by Alexander the Great, fourth century B.C.; Romans establish Ephesus, first century B.C.; Constantine founds Constantinople, 330; Muslims begin converting country to Islam, eleventh century; Ottoman Empire established, fifteenth century; becomes republic, 1923; economic and political problems, late 1970s; military rule, 1980–1983; returns to civilian rule, 1983.

For reference sources, tourist bureaus, and suggested lengths of stay, see the Appendices.

Weather Patterns

Sudden strong winds often occur in the seas southeast of Greece. (They're what blew Odysseus off course.)

Greece is renowned for its wonderful temperate weather (see Figure 19–1). Summers are hot and dry, in the upper 80s, whereas winters can drop into the mid-50s, with occasional rain and gusty winds. Coastal areas and the islands are cooled slightly by their proximity to the water. Northern Greece runs about 10 degrees cooler than the south. Summer is the peak tourist season. Spring and fall are good times to visit; the climate is still lovely and the country is less crowded. Tourism drops off in the winter, when bargains are available (and the waters get chilly).

Turkey has almost the same weather patterns as Greece. Istanbul, like Salonika, has cool winters and warm summers, with some winter rain and occasional summer showers. Izmir is like Athens—with hot, dry summers and cool, more humid winters; spring and fall are pleasant shoulder seasons.

Getting Around

Most ancient Greek buildings and statues were originally painted in bright colors.

Olympic Airlines connects most major cities in Greece. However, cruises are the most common form of transportation among the islands, and many well-known cruise lines operate there. Inter-island ferries are also a way to get from island to island; most leave the mainland from Piraeus.

On the Greek mainland, the rail system is extensive, but not the best way for tourists to get around; English isn't commonly spoken, which can make trips difficult. There are,

Climate at a Glance
ATHENS, GREECE

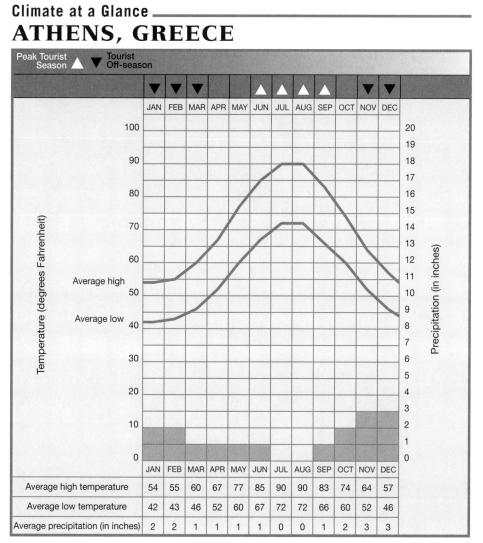

	JAN	FEB	MAR	APR	MAY	JUN	JUL	AUG	SEP	OCT	NOV	DEC
Average high temperature	54	55	60	67	77	85	90	90	83	74	64	57
Average low temperature	42	43	46	52	60	67	72	72	66	60	52	46
Average precipitation (in inches)	2	2	1	1	1	1	0	0	1	2	3	3

Figure 19–1

however, excellent trains from major European cities to Athens. Buses are not recommended for anyone but seasoned travelers. That goes for travel within Athens and Istanbul, as well, where a ride can be a crowded adventure. Taxis are inexpensive and a good way to get around. Car rentals are widely available; they're best for excursions beyond Athens. One small warning: Greece has among the highest traffic accident rates in Europe. For that and many other reasons, escorted motorcoach tours are a popular way to experience mainland Greece.

Most tourists get around Turkey via cruise ship or on escorted motorcoach tours to the interior. Turkish Airlines services the major cities. Buses and trains connect many cities in Turkey. And, as in Greece, car rentals (outside the major cities) and taxis (within them) are viable alternatives.

Important Places

Most of the best-known sights of Greece are located in the southern part of the country. On the mainland, there are the attractions of Athens and its environs and, for the seafaring, the magnificent Greek islands. For those venturing farther, Turkey offers many intriguing spots to visit.

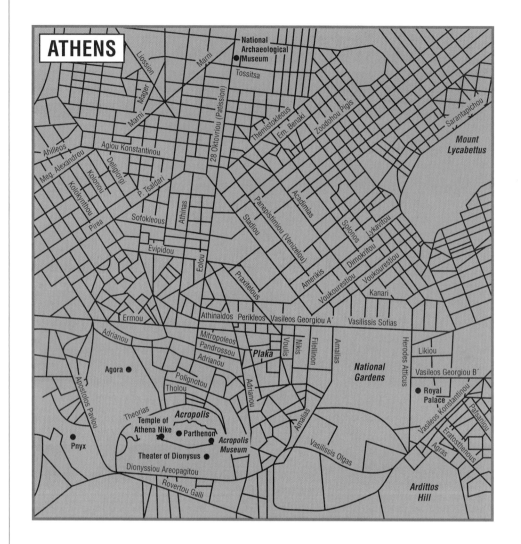

Athens

Athens is the heart and soul of Western civilization. Philosophy, architecture, drama, and democratic government took root in Athens 2,500 years ago. The people of Athens are warm and friendly. The pace of the city can be either relaxed or frenetic, according to the situation. Things can become almost like a nonstop party, especially when both locals and tourists dance late into the night to *bouzouki* music in the taverns. Among the attractions of Athens:

■ The **Acropolis** is one of the world's most magnificent and inspiring places. Towering over the city, this rocky hill is covered with monuments and temples. At the top is its main temple, the legendary **Parthenon**, many of whose treasures can be found in the **Acropolis Museum**. (The Parthenon has probably influenced more buildings in the Western world than any other.)

■ The **Agora** was the commercial center of ancient Athens. With fascinating ruins, the area is still active today. Even more active is the city's business and entertainment district, the **Plaka**.

■ The **National Archaeological Museum** is a world-class museum with a rich collection of Greek art and culture.

Athens is a hub for many memorable **day trips**. Among them are:

■ The **Peloponnese Peninsula**, in 1400 B.C. the home of the Mycenean civilization, with the citadel of Agamemnon and an unusual structure called the **Beehive Tomb**.

The Parthenon was built for the goddess Athena, patron of Athens
Photo by Justus Ghormley

On the way from Athens to the Peloponnese is the **Corinth Canal**, begun by the ancient Romans and completed by Greece in the late nineteenth century.

- **Delphi**, amid magnificent scenery, where the shrine of Delphi once housed a renowned oracle of the ancient world. There are also other temples and an amphitheater.

- **Olympia**, where the well-preserved ruins of the first Olympic Games (held in 776 B.C.) are found.

- **Epidaurus**, famous in ancient times as a spa and a center for drama. Its 15,000-seat amphitheater, still in use today, is renowned for its stunning acoustics.

- **Cape Sounion**, with its **Temple of Poseidon** overlooking the rushing seas.

- **The Saronic Islands**, between Athens and the Peloponnese Peninsula, covered with fascinating ruins of fortresses and Doric temples, as well as beautiful forests.

The Greek Islands

Of the more than 2,000 islands, about 230 are inhabited. Most of the islands are off the mainland's east coast in the Aegean Sea, although a scattered group lies to the west in the Ionian Sea. Most tend to be quite arid and none are really tropical looking. They're most often visited on cruises or by ferry.

- **Crete**—the largest Greek island—is a mountainous place with beautiful gorges, wonderful beaches, and caves to explore. The famous **King Minos's Palace**, dating back 3,500 years, has been reconstructed in **Knossos**. There's also a good archaeological museum.

- **Mykonos** is a fashionable island with excellent beaches, abundant nightlife, and many churches. Bright, colorful, with whitewashed houses, it looks the way people most likely envision Greece to be.

- **Delos** is usually reached through Mykonos. Once a sacred island, Delos is small, but covered with ruins and grand temples honoring Apollo (believed by the ancients to have been born here).

- **Santorini** (sometimes known as **Thira**) is one of the most dramatically beautiful places on earth. The island is formed by the blown-out cone of a huge volcano, with blue water

The ancient Greeks believed that the center of the world—and of the universe—was at Delphi.

Delos may have more ruins per square inch than any other place in the world.

within, several excavation sites, and bleached white buildings lining the slopes of what remains of the volcano's rim. Historians believe that, in ancient times, the island's volcanic eruption killed most of its inhabitants and perhaps created a tsunami that destroyed other nearby places. This catastrophe, they suspect, may be the source of the "lost continent of Atlantis" tale.

- **Corfu**, off the mainland's west coast, is another trendy resort. Because it's more lush than Greece's other, drier islands, many call it the most beautiful spot in the country. It has great beaches, a lively nightlife, and a semiformal casino. There are churches, a palace, and a very good museum.

- **Rhodes** lies off the coast of Turkey. At **Lindos** is a remarkable amalgam of Greek, Byzantine, European, and Turkish ruins, with a commanding view of the countryside and sea. There are excellent beaches, a busy nightlife, and the **Palace of the Grand Masters**, a fully restored fourteenth-century Crusader fortress. One of the Seven Wonders of the Ancient World, the Colossus of Rhodes (a giant statue that inspired the Statue of Liberty), stood here before being felled by an earthquake. None of it remains.

Turkey

Turkey is a remarkable blend of European and Middle Eastern influences. It has some wonderful sites for travelers to explore. Among the destinations are:

- **Istanbul**, the capital of the old Byzantine Empire, and once called Constantinople. Sultans' palaces, minarets, and two important mosques (the **Blue Mosque** and the much older **Hagia Sophia**) grace the city's skyline. Istanbul is an active city with bazaars and a busy nightlife. **Topkapi Palace** is renowned for its spectacular jewels, Muslim relics, and countless (but mostly empty) chambers.

- **The Turquoise Coast**, with its white sands and pine forests, facing both the Aegean and Mediterranean seas. It can be accessed by air (via Izmir or Antalya), charter yacht, or cruise ship (the principal ports are Izmir and **Kusadasi**). Among the Turquoise Coast's most visited seaside cities—often near ancient ruins—are **Bodrum**, **Marmaris**, and Antalya.

The Palace of the Grand Masters was inspired by Avignon's Palace of the Popes.

Until St. Peter's in Vatican City was built, the Hagia Sophia (then a Christian church) was for centuries the world's largest religious structure.

Above Ephesus is a site where legend says Mary, the mother of Jesus, spent her last years.

Santorini: the "lost continent of Atlantis"?
Photo by Marc Mancini

The most important ruins, however, are at **Ephesus** (mentioned in the Bible), about 30 miles south of Izmir and about the same distance north of Kusadasi. There's no better place to experience what ancient Roman cities must have been like. Several other important (but less preserved) ruins are nearby.

- **Inland Turkey**, including **Pamukkale**, with its hot springs and the white calcium terraces that look like "cotton castles"; **Cappadocia**, a place of hundreds of cave churches and dwellings; and Ankara, the nation's capital.

The Balkans

During the 1990s, there was great strife in this part of the world. Yugoslavia—rich in attractions and once a major tourist destination—broke up into a series of countries with conflict among various ethnic and religious groups. However, the region's conflicts have largely abated. The Balkans have once again become a viable destination.

- **Slovenia** has Alpine scenery, fine beaches, distinguished architecture, and bargain prices. The country's proximity to Italy makes it an intriguing add-on destination.
- **Croatia** borders the Adriatic Sea and is a destination for many cruise ships on the way to or departing from Venice. **Dubrovnik**, a medieval port on the Dalmatian Coast, has been restored and has regained tourist appeal. The capital city of **Zagreb** boasts many museums, art galleries, and outdoor cafes.
- **Bosnia and Herzegovina** was deeply affected by war. Its capital, **Sarajevo**—once a historic gem of a town and a major ski center—was severely damaged but has been restored.
- **Serbia**, what remains of the original Yugoslavia, was also much involved in the fighting. Its capital, **Belgrade**, lies on the Danube and is famous for museums, cafes, and cabarets. **Macedonia** is considered by most to be an independent nation, by others as part of Yugoslavia. In 2008, **Kosovo** declared its independence from Yugoslavia. Some countries have recognized it as independent, others have not.
- **Albania**, long a "mystery" country (it intentionally cut itself off politically from both East and West), now courts tourism. Its assets include Adriatic beach towns, Greco-Roman ruins, and the capital city of **Tirana**.

Possible Itineraries

Because of the length of time needed to get to Greece from the United States, travelers should ideally plan an extended visit.

However, if time is a constraint, first-time tourists can center a week-long trip in Athens and its environs. But to go to Greece and not experience its islands would be unfortunate. Seven days should be a minimum and twelve would be ideal. Travelers could see Istanbul and Kusadasi on an Eastern Mediterranean cruise, but to see Turkey in depth, visitors should take a week, starting in Istanbul, heading south to Pamukkale, then west to Ephesus, returning back to Istanbul. Return visitors would probably want to see new islands, explore old ones in greater depth, or take the occasion to see more of Turkey, including Ankara, Cappadocia, and Antalya.

Lodging Options

Greece's more upscale hotel chains include **Astir**, **Divanis**, and **Chandris**. Many North American companies have properties in Greece as well. Several hotels face the Acropolis, providing a memorable view.

Some tourists prefer an alternative type of accommodation. There are beautiful villas throughout Greece, but they aren't bargains and many have maintenance problems. Other lodging choices include bed-and-breakfasts and spas.

Angora (as in cats and sweaters) is derived from the word Ankara.

Dubrovnik is famous for its red tile roofs.

Fifty-nine percent of Greece's hotels are located on islands.

Istanbul's Hagia Sophia was first a church, then a mosque, and is now a museum
Photo by Marc Mancini

In Turkey, such international chains as **Hilton** and **Mercure** predominate. Istanbul's better hotels cluster around Taksim Square (including the Hilton, with its fine view) and along the Bosporus. The famous **Ciragan Palace Hotel** was once a sultan's palace.

Allied Destinations

Because Greece, Turkey, and the Balkans are so far from the United States, visitors often choose to add other nearby countries to their trip. Italy is a good add-on, as it's right across the Ionian Sea. Because the Middle East is just on the other side of the Mediterranean Sea, a trip to Israel or Egypt is a common add-on as well. Remember that you can break up a trip to Greece or Turkey from the United States (especially the West Coast) by connecting through and pausing for a few days at a European gateway city—sometimes at no extra airfare.

Cultural Patterns

Many vacationers are apprehensive about Greece and Turkey. And business travelers may have concerns about what will be expected of them in their daily contacts:

- Greeks and Turks are extremely hospitable to visitors. Handshaking is very important upon meeting someone.

- Many businesses close at midday for a few hours.

- A small nod of the head upward means *no*, not *yes*.

- If invited to visit a Greek home, bring a small gift as a token of appreciation. Also, if the host insists that you try a particular food, do so.

- Be careful about overpraising any item when visiting a Greek home. The host may feel obligated to present it as a gift.

- When on business, it's important to deal with the person who has the most authority. This isn't snobbery; it's the way Turkish society is structured.

- There is sporadic political discord between Turkey and Greece. It's a subject that should be sidestepped, as should the tensions among the other Balkan countries.

Istanbul's vast Covered Bazaar may be the world's oldest indoor shopping center.

Factors That Motivate Visitors

To assume that tourists want to visit the area only because of its cultural history would be shortsighted. Among their many reasons might be:

- The culture and history of the region form the basis for Western civilization.
- It's one of the world's finest destinations for sunshine.
- Greece, Turkey, and the Balkans are comparatively inexpensive places to visit.
- Many water sports and cruise options are available.
- The people are extremely friendly.
- There are many shopping bargains.

Possible Misgivings

The rewards of visiting these countries are considerable. However, they may not be for everyone. Among the concerns to address are:

- "I don't like long flights." Greece or Turkey can be part of a flight package that includes other countries, breaking up the length of travel.
- "The area is dirty and there's poverty." Some of the Greek islands are quite upscale, as are certain areas in major cities.

Qualifying the Traveler
The Greek Islands

For People Who Want	Appeal			Remarks
	High	Medium	Low	
Historical and Cultural Attractions		▲		Some ruins, but mainland is better
Beaches and Water Sports	▲			Many opportunities
Skiing Opportunities			▲	None
Lots of Nightlife		▲		On larger islands
Family Activities			▲	
Familiar Cultural Experience			▲	
Exotic Cultural Experience	▲			
Safety and Low Crime		▲		
Bargain Travel		▲		
Impressive Scenery	▲			But not tropical or lush
Peace and Quiet		▲		On smaller islands
Shopping Opportunities		▲		Pottery, jewelry, leather
Adventure		▲		
To Do Business			▲	

It can get hot when touring; bring bottled water along.

■ "It's so hot." The climate is temperate and dry most of the year. Humid heat is rare. Spring and fall are beautiful.

■ "There's nothing to do there except see ruins." The nightlife can be quite impressive for those looking for excitement.

Sales Strategies

First-time visitors to Greece should consider taking either a cruise among the country's islands or a multiday stay on one island. For a special way of getting from island to island, they may even go by yacht: A private one is expensive, but others will take up to 30 people and are more reasonable. Cruises calling on Istanbul and Kusadasi are also popular. City tours in Athens are a good choice because public transportation isn't great. For seeing remote areas, car rentals and trains are always available (though, again, trains are not the best mode of transportation in Greece). Escorted tours are a very good option, too. Budget hotels throughout the region can leave something to be desired. Better accommodations are preferable. Most of the Balkans are appropriate mainly for those who want something off the beaten path, usually in connection with cruises that visit Greece and, sometimes, Israel and Egypt.

Minnesota's Mall of America has more than 500 shops and the West Edmonton Mall—North America's largest—has about 800. Istanbul's Covered Bazaar has more than 4,000 shops.

Travel Trivia

Top 10 Remarkable Ruins

1. Machu Picchu, Peru
2. Tikal, Guatemala
3. Ephesus, Turkey
4. Petra, Jordan
5. Luxor, Egypt
6. Forum/Colosseum, Rome
7. Teotihuacan, Mexico
8. Borobudur, Indonesia
9. The Parthenon, Greece
10. Angkor Wat, Cambodia

SOURCE: Marc Mancini

NAME _____   **DATE** _____

MAP ACTIVITY

A traveler wants to visit the places listed below. Which number represents each on the map?

Place/Attraction	In/Near Which City or Island?	Number on Map
A. King Minos's Palace	A. _____	A. _____
B. The Parthenon	B. _____	B. _____
C. Site of a famous oracle	C. _____	C. _____
D. The Blue Mosque	D. _____	D. _____
E. A small island near Mykonos	E. _____	E. _____
F. The Temple of Poseidon	F. _____	F. _____
G. Where the first Olympic Games were held	G. _____	G. _____
H. A resort island off Greece's west coast	H. _____	H. _____
I. Topkapi Palace	I. _____	I. _____
J. A city on a volcano rim	J. _____	J. _____

NAME _____   DATE _____

CASE STUDY

Every year, Jason St. Amand, a high school history teacher, takes a vacation. This year, the 32-year-old resident of Los Angeles wants to go to Greece. Because he has his summers free, his schedule is very flexible. Although he doesn't have a great deal of money to spend, he has enough to make such a long trip worthwhile. Jason is single.

Circle the answer that best suits his needs.

❶ Which place would you *not* recommend he visit?

Athens   Crete

Mykonos   Salonika

Why?

❷ If he decided to lengthen his trip, which city would be the *least* likely for an additional stop?

Martinique   Istanbul

Rome   Cairo

Why?

❸ Jason's hotel is near the Acropolis. Which of the following would be the farthest away?

The Plaka   The Parthenon

The National Archaeological Museum   The Temple of Poseidon

Why?

❹ Which would be the best month for him, all things considered?

September   June

November   August

Why?

NAME _____ **DATE** _____

CREATIVE ACTIVITY

A contest! A travel magazine prints the grid below. It contains at least 18 words that refer to Greek or Turkish places. The words can read left-to-right, top-to-bottom, or diagonally. They can even be backwards—right-to-left, or bottom-to-top. Circle every word you can find and list it the bottom.

Z	O	R	B	A	C	R	H	O	D	E	S
M	Y	K	O	N	O	S	E	L	B	A	O
A	S	C	D	S	R	L	H	A	I	R	N
R	A	S	R	K	F	U	Y	X	P	I	E
M	N	U	U	A	U	M	P	M	I	M	R
A	T	S	M	E	M	S	E	A	P	Z	A
R	O	E	L	U	B	N	A	T	S	I	K
I	R	H	I	H	P	L	E	D	N	T	A
S	I	P	M	I	K	I	T	A	A	A	L
S	N	E	H	T	A	D	E	L	O	S	P
P	I	T	A	N	K	A	R	A	S	T	I
S	O	U	N	I	O	N	C	O	M	O	P

Chapter 20

European Potpourri

Collectors of countries—that's what tourists bound for Europe often are. Their motto: The more countries we see during our trips, the better. Sometimes, that's easy: A visit to Germany is readily combined with one to **Austria** and **Switzerland**; a trip to France can be easily side-tracked to **Belgium**; the **Netherlands** lends itself logically to a side trip to **Denmark** and on to the **Scandinavian countries** or to the **Baltics**. (Of course, travelers can also choose to spend an entire vacation in just one country for a more in-depth experience.)

It's very probable that a tourist will consider adding at least one of the above-mentioned destinations to the itinerary. So you need to know them especially well. Here goes.

Belgium

One of the three Benelux nations, Belgium could be a robust addition to a European itinerary. Its capital, **Brussels**, is only 1.5 hours northeast of Paris by train or five by car. It's easy to get around this nation, not only because it's relatively small and flat, but also because an efficient system of highways, trains, bus routes, canals, and small rural roads criss-crosses it. Those who prefer driving will find Belgium a good choice.

Brussels Airlines (SN) is Belgium's major air carrier, but many other airlines fly into Brussels (BRU). (In fact, Brussels is a prime European gateway.) **Eurostar** trains run between Brussels and London via the Chunnel in less than two hours. The climate is mild, with cool days in winter (snow is infrequent) and mildly warm summers. The area has a tendency toward fog, drizzle, and rain. French and Flemish are spoken here, but English is also commonly understood in key tourist cities.

Important Places

Brussels is a convenient base for visiting all of Belgium. The city bills itself as a "living museum" and it's certainly that: Medieval structures are everywhere. But modern buildings have shoved their way into this fast-paced city. Brussels is, therefore, not the uniformly quaint city that

There are more than 2,000 chocolate shops in Belgium.

349

people may imagine. To discover that quaintness, tourists must visit some of Belgium's outlying towns. The following attractions are the most important in Brussels:

- **The Grand Place** [PLAHS], reputed to be Europe's most beautiful town square and the model for Munich's Marienplatz.
- **The Manneken-Pis**, the fountain with a statue of a small boy "relieving himself." The statue is often dressed in different outfits (it has a wardrobe of over 700).
- **Several museums**, especially the **Museum of Ancient Art** and the **Museum of Modern Art**.
- **Erasmus House**, a classic sixteenth-century home and garden.
- **City tours** of Brussels, a particularly appropriate choice, since the city features dozens of small, fascinating attractions scattered about which tourists might miss on their own.

To really see Belgium, **day trips** out of Brussels are essential. Here are some highlights:

- **Bruges** [BROOJ], one of Europe's best-preserved medieval cities, often called the Venice of the North because of its many canals.
- **Ghent**, a picturesque city of flowers, gardens, and bridges.
- **Antwerp**, well known as an outlet for diamonds, but also graced by many museums, galleries, and churches.
- **The Ardennes** [ar-DEN] **Forest**, with its handsome vistas and Battle of the Bulge memorials.

Sales Considerations

Belgium is a logical extension of a vacation in France or the Netherlands. It's especially appropriate for people who like escorted tours. The country is also a shopper's paradise: Belgian chocolates, linen, ceramics, and precious stones are well known. Because Brussels is a major destination for European government officials and business executives, its hotels tend to fill up—especially on weekdays. Book lodging, therefore, well in advance. Tours, both escorted and independent, are a great way to access hard-to-get hotel space.

The Netherlands

Another Benelux country, the Netherlands (also called **Holland**, though technically, Holland is only the western part of the country) conjures a ready image of tulips, windmills, dikes, and canals. The Netherlands is indeed a congenial destination, though its climate is often damp and its days gloomy.

Getting to **Amsterdam** (AMS), the center point of Dutch culture, is easy. The country's carriers **KLM** (KL) and **Martinair** (MP) have frequent and convenient service, as do many other airlines. In fact, Amsterdam is one of Europe's major gateways. Most Dutch attractions are within a day's trip from Amsterdam—accessed by convenient rail and bus service, as well as by a well-developed highway system. The locals speak Dutch, though knowledge of English is widespread.

Important Places

Amsterdam is the must-see city of the Netherlands. Its most important attractions are:

- **The Rijksmuseum**, with its magnificent collection of Dutch Masters.
- **Anne Frank House**, where the famed young diarist hid from the Nazis for two years.
- **Van Gogh Museum**, with the world's finest collection of works by the noted Dutch artist.
- **Rembrandt House**, where the artist lived and worked for two decades.

Venturing into the countryside provides a good sense of the country. Key places include:

- **Delft**, the world-famous pottery and tile center.
- **Haarlem**, a well-preserved old city. Nearby is the vast **Keukenhof Garden**, where seven million flower bulbs are planted annually. It's open for two months in the spring.
- **Zaanse Schans**, with its collection of working windmills.
- **The Hague**, a splendid city (and home of the **World Court**) that boasts the **Madurodam**, a city fashioned in miniature.

Sales Considerations

Virtually every type of vacationer will find the Netherlands appealing, except perhaps those exclusively drawn to beach resorts or adventure travel. One possible objection: The country has a well-founded reputation for permissiveness. Drugs, prostitution, and pornography are tolerated and in many places are legal. It's unlikely, though, that visitors will find trouble unless they go looking for it. Two other points: The Netherlands has an unusually extensive system of camping facilities, and diamonds are a shopping specialty.

Switzerland

Central and small, Switzerland boasts no real tourist hub city (like, say, England's London). Gingerbread hamlets, silvery lakes, and dazzling vistas dot this entire mountainous Alpine country. You might be able to get a handle on Switzerland by dividing it up into its three linguistic areas: the German-speaking north, central, and east; the French-influenced west; and the Italian-inspired south.

The Swiss are known for their efficiency; transportation to, within, and from Switzerland operates with clock-like precision. **Swiss (LX)** is the national carrier; both **Geneva (GVA)** and **Zurich (ZRH)** are major air gateways. Not even Alpine peaks interfere with the country's superb rail and highway system; giant tunnels bore through wherever appropriate. Except for its high mountain areas, Switzerland has a pleasant climate. Summers can even

The Dutch buy more books and bicycles per capita than any other people in the world.

The number one weekend getaway for the Dutch is the beautiful city of Maastricht, a culinary and shopping magnet.

In Switzerland, Swiss cheese is called Emmentaler cheese.

The many canals of Bruges have caused it to be compared to Venice, Italy
Image copyright Tom Davison, 2008. Used under license from Shutterstock.com

be quite hot (especially in the south), but without the humidity that makes other destinations uncomfortable. The *foehn* wind also sometimes brings unseasonably warm and dry weather to Switzerland's mountain valleys and it may occur in any season.

Important Places

Though small in size, Switzerland has distinct regions. It's important to understand their differences:

- **Northern and eastern Switzerland** is anchored by Zurich, Switzerland's largest city and its financial center. Not far away is one of Europe's most visited natural attractions, tumultuous **Rhine Falls**. Also in northern Switzerland—on the Rhine, near both the

In a little town 30 miles south of Zurich is a huge surprise: the ornate church monastery at Einsiedeln.

French and German borders—is **Basel**, with its many first-rate museums, an excellent zoo, and spectacular winter carnival. **St. Gallen** is a picturesque Alpine city that is often a stopover between Zurich and Innsbruck, Austria.

■ **Central Switzerland**, just southwest of Zurich, is often called the **Interlaken District**. The city of **Interlaken** itself would perfectly satisfy the expectations of what tourists think of a Swiss town: cute chalets, imposing clocks, and views of the **Jungfrau Mountains**. The country's charming capital, **Bern**, with its arcaded streets, fountains, and mascot bears, is to the west. Nearby is **Lucerne**, a medieval lakeside city whose landmarks include the **Lion Monument** and **Chapel Bridge**.

■ **Western Switzerland** feels far more French. Most of the attractions border **Lake Geneva**, including **Lausanne** [low-ZAN], **Chillon** [shee-ON] (a famous, dank castle), **Montreux** (the site of many music festivals), and Geneva itself (whose most recognizable feature is the **Jet d'Eau**, a fountain in the lake that shoots water over 400 feet in the air).

■ **Zermatt** highlights the part of Switzerland that borders Italy to the south. Located at the foot of the well-known **Matterhorn** mountain, this town is quaint and car-free. Farther to the east but still along the border is the **Lake District**, which more fully captures the Italian influence on Switzerland. Chief lake cities are **Lugano** and **Locarno**.

Sales Considerations

With its ski areas, palm-lined southern lakes, beautiful villages, and cities filled with culture, Switzerland is a genuinely easy country to sell. Sports enthusiasts especially relish the thought of a trip to Switzerland, which offers many opportunities for boating, hiking and, of course, skiing. The prime Swiss ski resorts are:

■ **Zermatt**, a massive winter-sport development.

■ **St. Moritz**, a pricey resort in Switzerland's southeast, and beautiful **Arosa**, which is nearby.

■ **Gstaad**, a resort beautifully set in a valley in southwestern Switzerland.

Usually there's enough snow on the Matterhorn to ski in summer.

In 1471, in Basel, Switzerland, a chicken was arrested, tried, found guilty, and burned at the stake. Its crime: It laid an egg so brightly colored, it was judged to be possessed by the devil.

Lucerne's Lion Monument honors the members of the Swiss Guard who were killed in the French Revolution
Photo by Karen Fukushima

For those who prefer trains, the **Glacier Express**—which slices through some of Europe's most spectacular countryside between Zermatt and St. Moritz—is a must. And for lovers of service and luxury, Switzerland's fine hotels are a strong selling point.

Austria

Though small (it's about the size of the state of Maine), Austria ranks as a first-rate tourist destination. About 70 percent of its surface is mountainous, making it a prime ski destination. Its strategic position—bordering Germany, Switzerland, and Italy—makes it easily combinable with these major destinations. Its cultural legacy is rich, especially in music. Try to think of Austria without imagining the music of Mozart, Strauss, and Haydn. You probably can't.

Austrian Airlines (OS) and other carriers connect into Austria's two principal cities, **Vienna** (VIE) and **Salzburg** (SZG). Rail transportation into and within the country is good. The climate is better than most people expect. Late spring, summer, and early fall are temperate, with occasional hot and dry *foehn* winds in south-facing valleys. Winters are very cold and snowy in the high Alpine regions, but other areas are surprisingly mild. Austria is a German-speaking country, though many locals know some English.

Important Places

Austria boasts many intriguing destinations, but three top the list: Vienna, Salzburg, and the Alpine ski resorts.

Vienna, Austria's capital, is a jewel-box of a city. Located in Austria's northeast corner on the legendary Danube River, it's filled with elegant palaces, graceful fountains, quaint cafes, huge museums, and world-class hotels. (The magnificent **Hotel Sacher** is famous for its tortes.) Yet imposing as it is, Vienna is a comfortable, civil city. Among its must-sees are:

- **The Hofburg Palace**, whose Vienna Boys' Choir is world famous.
- **St. Stephen's Cathedral**, whose soaring Gothic spire is a Vienna landmark.
- **The Spanish Riding School**, with its renowned white Lipizzaner stallions. (They perform there only in the spring and fall.)
- **The Schonbrunn**, a palace often called the Versailles of Austria.

During World War II, the Lipizzaner stallions were rescued by the U.S. Army under the command of General George Patton.

- **The National Library**, whose main hall is a baroque architectural wonder.
- A day trip to **Melk**, where a huge Baroque monastery perches on a high ridge overlooking the Danube.

Salzburg, near the German border (and not all that far from Munich), is a remarkable destination. Though Mozart moved from Salzburg at the age of 25, his spirit still breathes through this picture-perfect city. Its attractions include:

- **Mozart's Birthplace**, the apartment where he composed his earliest works.
- **Hellbrunn Palace**, a wonderfully eccentric place with "surprise" fountains that spritz visitors when they least expect it.
- **Mirabell Palace**, with its vast marble decorations and gardens.
- **Day excursions**, most especially to **Werfen**, with 25 miles of dramatic ice-lined caves; to **Hallstatt**, where visitors dress as miners and ride a tunnel train; and into the countryside on an ever-popular *Sound of Music* tour.

The Austrian Alps, with their superb skiing, are also celebrated summer destinations. Key resorts are at **Innsbruck, Kitzbuhel, Lech, St. Anton Am Arlberg**, and **Zurs**. This mountainous region is often called the **Tyrol**.

Sales Considerations

Austria is ideally combined with trips to its neighboring countries; its powerful appeal makes it an ideal way to expand an itinerary. Vienna is a key stop on many tours and Danube cruises. Skiers often extend their trips with visits to Vienna and Salzburg; both cities offer lively cultural attractions, even in the dead of winter.

Austria appeals strongly to those who seek safety, comfort, and well-organized facilities. Lovers of music, art, food, and winter sports will be especially drawn to Austria. Some, however, remember its close relationship to Nazi Germany in World War II and for this reason find Austria an unappealing destination.

Vienna's many coffeehouses are the legacy of a seventeenth-century occupation by the Turks.

The Alps are especially dramatic in the Tyrolean region
Image copyright Carsten Medom Madsen, 2008. Used under license from Shutterstock.com

Scandinavia

Held together by a common cultural heritage, the five countries of Scandinavia spread broadly across northern Europe. **Norway, Sweden,** and **Finland** compose the Scandinavian Peninsula, a fan of land that stretches from the North Sea on the west to Russia on the east. **Denmark** (a peninsula and series of islands that stretch northward from Germany) and **Iceland** (way out in the North Atlantic) round out this nation grouping. Most tourists who visit Scandinavia are from Germany; Scandinavia, however, is becoming a more popular destination for North Americans, due, in part, to its reputation as a very safe, clean, and organized place to visit.

Scandinavia is cold most of the year. In summer the weather is generally pleasant: Real heat is a rarity and daylight lasts from very early to very late. Precipitation isn't excessive, except on Norway's west coast, which is rainy and snowy. Iceland, despite its name, isn't impossibly cold. (On the other hand, Greenland, despite its optimistic name, has extremely cold weather.)

Several national carriers service Scandinavia, including **Icelandair** (FI), **SAS** (SK), and **Finnair** (AY); many other carriers go there, too. Internal transportation is excellent, with a wonderful system of trains, ferries, steamships, cruise ships, buses, and subways. The one weak link: Except for certain areas, Scandinavia's roads tend to be rural and marked with hard-to-decipher signs.

Important Places

Here are Scandinavia's nations and what each has to offer:

Denmark. Denmark, Scandinavia's most popular tourist destination, is a friendly little country; it's impossible to visualize it without thinking of Hans Christian Andersen's fairytales. It was also once an immensely prosperous nation; all that wealth brought fine

castles, rich artistic achievements, enlightened government, and the ability to create the ultimate open-faced sandwich. **Copenhagen**, the capital, is the focal point of travel; city tours and day-trip excursions are popular enhancements. Most tourists visit the **Little Mermaid** statue and **Tivoli Gardens**, which served as a major early influence on Walt Disney's amusement park plans.

Norway. Norway is an outdoorsy nation with few real urban centers. Oslo, its cozy capital, features a **Viking Ship Museum**, the **Kon-Tiki Museum**, and **Vigeland**, a park of unusual sculptures. You should offer to cross-sell Norway's prime attraction: a cruise through the fjord area. Fjords are steeply cliffed inlets from the sea; they're majestic and humbling. Most local fjord cruises depart from the city of **Bergen**, which can be accessed via a scenic train ride from Oslo. The most famous fjord for visitors: **Hardangerfjord**, about 47 miles from Bergen. Hurtigruten cruise line's ships run year-round. Other cruise lines occasionally offer fjord cruises, as well. It's rainy along Norway's western fjord coast. Winter-sports enthusiasts also enjoy Norway. The Olympic center at **Lillehammer** is especially popular.

Sweden. Sweden is a friendly, modern country, and **Stockholm**, its capital, is cosmopolitan and charming. Three highlights are the **Royal Palace**, the **Old Town district**, and the **Wasa Ship** (a seventeenth-century galleon that was hauled up from the bottom of Stockholm harbor). A day trip to **Uppsala**, a historic university town only about an hour north of Stockholm, is an interesting option.

Finland. Finland and its capital, **Helsinki**, are often thought of as merely a stopover to Russia and the Baltics. That's unfortunate, for Finland has a lot to offer. The **Lakeland Region** to Helsinki's north is truly picturesque. More adventurous travelers are drawn to **Lapland**, Finland's northern wilderness. (Lapland also extends across Norway and Sweden.) Helsinki itself has many interesting attractions; again, a city tour is an excellent option.

Iceland. Volcanoes, geysers, earthquakes, boiling cauldrons—that's not what most visitors will expect, but that's exactly what they'll find in Iceland. Indeed, all this geothermal drama constitutes Iceland's prime tourist attraction. **Reykjavik**, the capital, has many appealing though modest architectural points of interest.

Sales Considerations

Lack of knowledge about Scandinavia is the major factor that prevents many people from considering it for a European vacation. Another objection may be the costliness of visiting Scandinavia; the budget-minded *can* visit these countries, but their choices will be limited. However, even moderate lodging is usually clean and comfortable. And hotel rates are surprisingly reasonable in summer, when business travel in Scandinavia drops and many residents head south for their holidays.

Would-be visitors may also worry about the language barrier, especially if they've seen or heard any of the Scandinavian languages, which are often quite incomprehensible to Americans. But most Scandinavians know at least some English and love to practice it. Emphasize the clean, safe, friendly, and orderly nature of these countries. Suggest a fjord sailing, or the more extensive cruises that call on Scandinavia (usually out of Copenhagen, Stockholm, or ports in England or Germany). And remember that many Scandinavian airlines route their flights to the rest of Europe and to the Middle East through their capital cities; a brief stopover can often be easily arranged.

Eastern Europe

To list this many Eastern European nations under one heading is probably unfair; each does have a distinct character. These former communist countries were long closed to outsiders. But most of the nations involved are now doing an excellent job of serving tourists.

Several national airlines serve Eastern Europe, as do some North American and Western European carriers. Eastern European countries, though, are quite a long distance from the United States and often involve connecting flights.

In Helsinki is the Temppeliaukion, a large church carved entirely into a huge rock.

The most northerly capital in the world is Iceland's Reykjavik.

Danish, Norwegian, and Swedish are similar. But Finnish is from a different language family and Icelandic is so much like Old Norse, people there can read stories that were written almost 1,000 years ago.

Winston Churchill popularized the phrase "Iron Curtain."

Once visitors get there, they'll find it a bit difficult to get around on their own, because few locals speak English and major highways are rare. Escorted tours are, therefore, the best way to sightsee. A Danube cruise that starts in Germany or in Vienna and continues through much of Eastern Europe is an inspired way to visit the area's great cities.

We can divide Eastern Europe into two groups. The northern group includes **Poland**, the **Czech Republic**, **Slovakia** (also called the Slovak Republic), **Hungary**, and **Romania**. These nations are hilly, with cool-to-cold winters and mild summers (though areas of Romania can get hot). The southern tier of countries has a climate and topography more akin to Greece. They are the Balkan countries (which were covered in Chapter 19) and **Bulgaria**.

Important Places

The most likely destinations are:

Poland. A rapidly changing country, Poland has taken on greater tourist importance of late. The following cities are the most visited in Poland:

- **Warsaw**, the capital, with more than 30 museums, many coffeehouses, casinos, and a restored old-town section.
- **Cracow**, a beautiful medieval town, 200 miles south of Warsaw. **Wawel Royal Castle** was where Polish royalty lived for centuries. Near Cracow is **Auschwitz**, the former Nazi concentration camp that is now a museum.
- **Poznan**, with its fifteenth-century town hall and old market square.

The Czech Republic. This western portion of the former nation of Czechoslovakia is a magnet for tourists visiting Eastern Europe. Its scenery, spas, villages, ski areas, and hundreds of castles give it a wide appeal. Key cities and towns include:

- **Prague** [PRAHG], the capital, a city of elegant architecture, parks, and shopping. It has become one of the most popular cities to visit in Europe. Its two most famous attractions: **Prague Castle** and the statue-lined **Charles Bridge**.
- **Cesky Krumlov** and **Tabor**, both ancient, atmospheric medieval towns.
- **Brno** [BUR-nah], with its mixture of ancient and modern attractions.

The Wieliczka Salt Mine, near Cracow, is filled with religious and historical carvings.

Czechoslovakia broke apart and became the Czech Republic and Slovakia in 1993.

Prague's Charles Bridge was built with egg-based cement.

To the Czech Republic's east is Slovakia. Slovakia has appealing villages, castles, mountains, and a splendid capital, **Bratislava**, that's often a stop on Danube cruises.

Hungary. A country rich in historical and cultural attractions, Hungary has become one of Eastern Europe's most popular tourist destinations. It's a romantic country with legendary food, lovely musical performances, many hot-spring spas, and hundreds of historical structures. Among Hungary's chief destinations are:

- **Budapest**, a graceful city and the seat of Hungary's government. Its **Parliament building** is one of Europe's most elegant. Budapest's attractions include **Buda Castle Palace** (which contains several museums), **Budapest Central Synagogue** (one of the world's largest), and **Fisherman's Bastion** (which provides a great view of the river and the city). The Danube bisects Budapest, creating two sections: Buda, all hilly and historical, and Pest, a center of business and commerce. Almost all the rest of Hungary can be a day trip from Budapest.

- **The Danube Bend**, a short trip north of Budapest, with its picturesque scenery. Nearby is **Esztergom**, where Hungarian kings resided and river cruise vessels now regularly visit. A huge church is Esztergom's chief attraction.

- **Lake Balaton**, a resort-lined lake offering all manner of water sports.

- **Pecs** [PAYCH], a southern city blessed with an unusual blend of Turkish and European architecture.

Romania. Romania, a mountainous nation that borders the Black Sea, has made a good effort to attract tourists. Most visitors are interested in the following:

- **Bucharest** [BOO-kah-rest], the capital, a city of huge palaces.

- **Brasov**, a medieval town at the foot of the Carpathian Mountains in Transylvania. A day trip away is **Bran Castle**—associated with a Count Dracula, who, though not a vampire, contributed to the legend through his merciless rule and violent cruelty.

- **The Black Sea Coast**, with its nearly 200 miles of coastline and flourishing resorts. Its key city is **Constanta**, a well-known cruise port.

Bulgaria. One of the smaller Eastern European countries, pleasant Bulgaria has the most ancient history of any Eastern European nation. Its best known attractions include:

- **Sofia**, the capital, with its Moorish and Byzantine influences. Near Sofia are many spas and monasteries, most especially the **Rila Monastery**, with more than 1,000 frescoes painted on its exterior walls.

- **The Black Sea Coast**, with some 200 miles of sandy beaches and so many resort hotels that it's often called the "Second Riviera."

Sales Considerations

Eastern Europe appeals to those who have already seen the major attractions of the rest of Europe, who are seeking bargain travel (though several of its cities are expensive), or who may be drawn to this area for ancestral reasons. An escorted tour or a Danube River cruise are efficient options. Skiers and spa enthusiasts who seek more offbeat destinations may find Eastern Europe appealing. People who normally resist tours will gladly book one to any of these countries. Hotel rooms must be booked well in advance; Eastern Europe has somewhat of a lodging shortage.

The Commonwealth of Independent States and the Baltics

Like Yugoslavia, the Soviet Union politically "came apart" in the post–Cold War era. Most of the "new" nations that resulted banded together to form the **Commonwealth of Independent States**, or **CIS** (though that title is not used much today).

Many buildings in Budapest still have bullet holes from the 1956 uprising against communism.

Romanian is the only Latin-based language spoken in Eastern Europe.

A number of airlines serve these nations, most notably Russia's **Aeroflot** (SU) and **Transaero** (UN). Cruise ships call on Russia's St. Petersburg and the ports of the Baltic nations.

Russia is the biggest and most important country of the group. The **Baltic nations**, huddled in the northwest, consist of **Estonia, Latvia**, and **Lithuania**. To their south are **Belarus, Ukraine**, and **Moldova**. Another group—wedged on an isthmus between the Black and Caspian seas—is composed of **Georgia, Armenia**, and **Azerbaijan**. A final group of countries with tongue-twisting names flows eastward from the Caspian Sea: **Turkmenistan, Uzbekistan, Kazakhstan, Kyrgyzstan**, and **Tajikistan**. These latter five, all Muslim influenced, belong more properly to Asia than to Europe.

Important Places

Let's take a look at the most likely destinations:

Russia. This huge nation—the world's largest—stretches across 7,000 miles and 11 time zones. The disintegration of the Soviet Union put a brief damper on Russian tourism, but the many attractions that grace this area have now become quite popular. Its two most important cities to visit are:

- **Moscow**, the capital, with **Tretyakov Gallery, Red Square**, and its most important attraction, the **Kremlin**, which contains government buildings and ornate churches. Two very different places—the Bolshoi Ballet and the Moscow Circus—are prime attractions. The **Cathedral of Christ the Savior**, which was destroyed in 1931, has been rebuilt. And **St. Basil's Cathedral**, just outside the Kremlin, is a Moscow landmark.

- **St. Petersburg**, an elegant, Western European–like city and cruise port that boasts one of the world's great museums (the **Hermitage**) and Russia's own version of the Tower of London (the **Peter and Paul Fortress**). Several huge "summer palaces" outside St. Petersburg are well worth the visit.

Other CIS Nations. Which CIS countries are most likely to interest tourists? Here are a few:

- **Ukraine**, a country of great agricultural wealth, featuring two interesting cities: **Kiev** boasts many fine monasteries and churches, most notably **St. Sophia's**. And **Yalta**, on the Black Sea, is a resort town of surprising sophistication.

- **Georgia**, which has suffered political infighting. Its cities of **Batumi, Sukhumi**, and **Tbilisi** used to be part of a popular itinerary through the southern part of the old Soviet Union. They are becoming viable destinations again.

- **Azerbaijan**'s capital of **Baku**, a Caspian seaside city that was also a popular tour destination before strife began in the region.

- **Uzbekistan**'s cities of **Bukhara, Samarkand**, and **Tashkent**. All three were important economic and religious centers located on the legendary "Silk Road" that connected Europe with China. As a result, fine architecture and good museums are everywhere.

The Baltics. The first three nations to break from the Soviet Union—Estonia, Latvia, and Lithuania—have energetically begun to court tourism. **Riga** (Latvia) and **Tallinn** (Estonia) have become major cruise ports. To accommodate land-bound travelers, these three nations have developed a "Via Baltica" road system that begins in Warsaw, Poland, and works its way northward near **Vilnius** (Lithuania), then on to Riga and Tallinn.

The world's biggest bell is at the Kremlin.

St. Petersburg was called Petrograd from 1914 to 1924, changed to Leningrad in 1924, and was renamed St. Petersburg in 1991.

Kiev's St. Sophia's was named after the one in Istanbul.

Sales Considerations

The Baltics and Russia continue to be attractive destinations for those who want something a little different in their European vacations. Tours and cruises appeal to many visitors. Be alert for political instability in all these countries. Many American "necessities" are in short supply and crime is a problem in the former Soviet Union (one more reason for an escorted tour).

Little Countries

Ever wonder how a weeklong European tour could visit nine countries? The answer is simple: Europe is peppered with little countries, some of which are principalities under the protection of a larger country. Little countries make excellent day trips or places to pass through on a voyage from one major destination to another. Most offer duty-free shopping opportunities. Here's a thumbnail sketch of each:

- **Andorra**—ruggedly perched in the Pyrenees on the border between France and Spain—offers wonderful scenery, good-sized ski resorts, quaint villages, and great duty-free shopping. It's most often visited as a day trip from Barcelona, Spain.

- **Cyprus**, in the far eastern portion of the Mediterranean, lost some tourism because of internal strife between its two ethnic groups, the Greeks and the Turks. (The island is divided between the two.) But peace talks have eased the decades-long tension between the two sides. Cyprus is an air connection point between Europe and the Middle East, and a stop for several cruise lines. Among its attractions are the walled capital of **Nicosia**, the mosaic-decorated ruins at **Paphos**, the **Tomb of the Kings**, and many beaches and water-sports activities.

- **Gibraltar** has a high recognition factor among travelers—it's the symbol of Prudential Insurance. This British-ruled promontory is 3 miles long and less than a mile wide. Its caves, beaches, ruins, and monkeys (yes, monkeys) are its principal attractions. The "Rock of Gibraltar" can be reached by ferry from southern Spain or Tangier, Morocco. It's included in many escorted tours of Spain and Portugal.

- **Liechtenstein** [LICK-ten-shtine], a 62-square-mile patch of land on the Swiss–Austrian border, has much of the same appeal of its two neighboring countries: a prince's castle, hamlets, vistas, mountain paths, and chalets.

- **Luxembourg** sits squarely at the intersection of France, Germany, and Belgium. Dense forests, flowering meadows, and quaint towns cover its 999-square-mile terrain. It's easy to reach Luxembourg from Brussels, Belgium; Reims, France; or Frankfurt, Germany. It's also an important air gateway to all of Europe.

- **Malta** is a cluster of islands about 60 miles south of Sicily. Its climate is ideal, its beach resorts many, and its historical attractions plentiful. Most visitors reach Malta from Italy by air or boat.

- **Monaco**, on the extreme eastern edge of the French Riviera and near Italy, has long attracted the upscale crowd and is a popular stop for tourists traveling along the Italian and French coasts. It's well known as the gaming center of Europe. **Monte Carlo** is its capital. The closest major city is Nice, France.

- **San Marino** is a rocky, mountaintop country completely surrounded by Italy. (It's near the northeast Italian coast.) This, the world's oldest republic (founded in 301 A.D.), is a frequent stop for travelers on their way from Venice to Florence. It's very close to the seacoast town of Rimini. Prepare visitors for the crowds they'll probably encounter there: San Marino is a major shopping area.

Moscow's subways are surprisingly ornate, with marble and chandeliers.

The Sovereign Order of Malta, which occupies a building in Rome and has 80 people, claims to be the world's smallest country.

Because of an incomplete peace treaty, Liechtenstein is still at war with Prussia, a nation that no longer exists.

The world's oldest freestanding stone structures are on Malta.

Travel Trivia

Signs Encountered by Travelers

- Fur coats made for ladies from their own skin. (Sweden)
- When passenger of foot heave in sight, toot the horn. Trumpet him melodiously at first, but if he still obstacles your passage, then tootle him with vigor. (Japan)
- Our wine leaves you nothing to hope for. (Switzerland)
- We take your bags and send them in all directions. (Denmark)
- Swimming is forbidden in absence of the Savior. (France)
- Please do not feed the animals. If you have any suitable food, give it to the guard on duty. (Hungary)
- Ladies may have a fit upstairs. (Hong Kong)
- Please leave your values at the front desk. (France)
- Because is big rush, we will execute customers in strict rotation. (Greece)
- This hotel is renowned for its peace and solitude. In fact, crowds from all over the world flock here to enjoy its solitude. (Italy)
- The provision of a large French widow in every room adds to visitors' comfort. (Spain)

NAME _____   **DATE** _____

MAP ACTIVITY

A traveler wants to visit the places listed below. Which number represents each on the map?

Place/Attraction	In Which Country?	Number on Map
A. The Spanish Riding School	A. _____	A. _____
B. The town of Bruges	B. _____	B. _____
C. Cracow	C. _____	C. _____
D. The Anne Frank House	D. _____	D. _____
E. Zermatt	E. _____	E. _____
F. Budapest	F. _____	F. _____
G. A famous boy's choir	G. _____	G. _____
H. The port of Tallinn	H. _____	H. _____
I. The Kremlin	I. _____	I. _____
J. Tivoli Gardens	J. _____	J. _____

NAME _____ DATE _____

CASE STUDY

Mr. and Mrs. Navratilova—a wealthy retired couple in their 70s—have seen much of the world. They've just returned from an Alaska cruise, which they enjoyed very much. They want to return to Europe, though Mr. Navratilova complains he hates seeing things twice. They have already visited France, Great Britain, Scandinavia, the Alpine countries, Italy, and Greece.

Circle the answer that best suits their needs.

1 What area would you recommend to them?

Norway   Eastern Europe

The Greek islands   The little countries

Why?

2 What primary means of transportation would you recommend?

A Danube cruise   A rail journey

A rental car   Flying from city to city

Why?

3 What destination would probably be appropriate to combine with your recommendation?

Czech Republic   Italy

Austria   Sweden

Why?

4 Which places would Mr. Navratilova probably *not* want to visit?

The Rila Monastery and the Parliament in Budapest

Chillon Castle and the Spanish Riding School

Lake Balaton and the Hermitage

Red Square and Prague

Why?

NAME _____ **DATE** _____

CREATIVE ACTIVITY

You've been a tour conductor for years, taking groups of Americans across Europe. You're very proud of your knowledge of European history and culture; many tour passengers on your motorcoach have commented on how you make the past come alive.

It's your day off. You live in Brussels and decide to sort through the cluttered attic of your recently deceased aunt, Marie-Louise Wells. Marie-Louise was the granddaughter of the famous British author and thinker H. G. Wells.

But what's this in a dark dusty corner? A weird contraption with a brass plate that says . . . this is a time machine! Could it be that what Wells wrote about is real? Attached is a note from your aunt. It tells you that, indeed, this time machine works. You can visit any person or place in the past. Though the machine's *time* range is unlimited, its distance is not. The farthest away, geographically, you can go from Brussels is 2,000 miles. You must also return to Brussels after each single "time trip."

You decide on your first excursion to visit six famous people and places from the past. Your first trip will be to visit Mozart in Salzburg. What will the other five be? (You may need to use an atlas to calculate distances.)

Person	Place	Reason
1 Mozart	Salzburg	To see a young musical genius at work
2		
3		
4		
5		
6		

NAME _____ DATE _____

PUTTING IT ALL TOGETHER

The Matching Game

Below is a list of cities, attractions, and so on, some of which we have covered, some of which we haven't. There are all manner of connections among them. With a group of fellow students, you have exactly 10 minutes to come up with as many connections as possible. (Items may be used more than once.) Write your answers below. Note: There are at least 20 possible connections. For example, Andorra and Gibraltar— both are "little countries."

Hofburg Palace	Rothenburg	British Museum
Red Square	Turkey	Prado
Lillehammer	Yalta	Venice
Delft	Salzburg	Wasa
Malta	Madurodam	Ardennes
Istanbul	Santorini	Carcassonne
Courmayeur	Kitzbuhel	Bruges
Chillon	Grand Place	Hermitage
Andorra	Legoland	Albufeira
St. Peter's	Sherwood	Russia
Kiev	Parthenon	St. Moritz
Schonbrunn	Blarney	Waterford
Liechtenstein	Marienplatz	Gibraltar

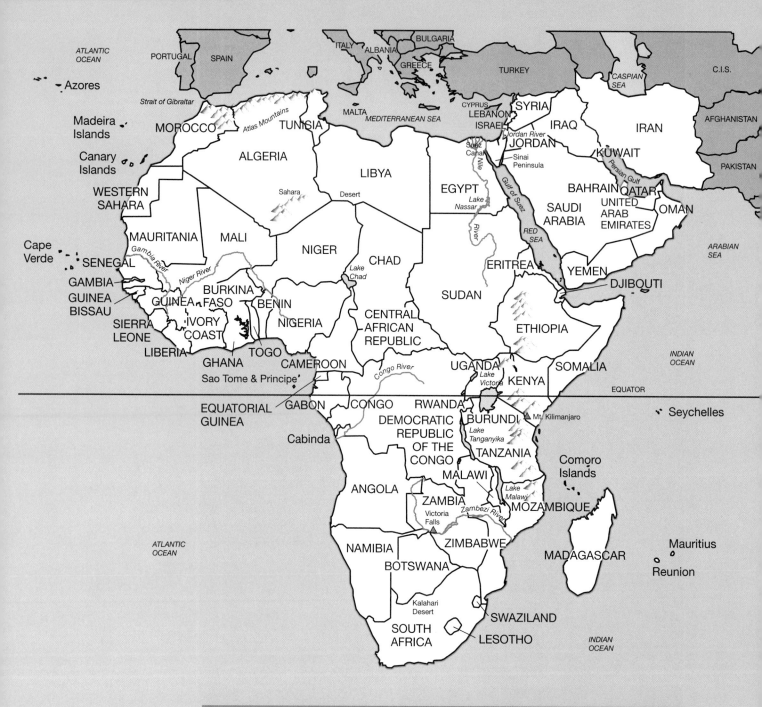
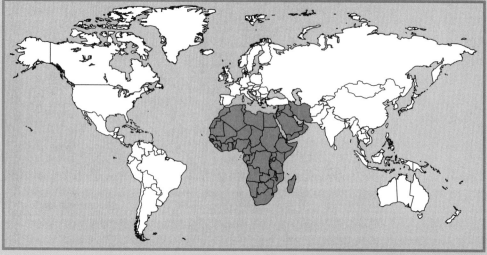

PART V

AFRICA AND THE MIDDLE EAST

Savannahs and Sand

Just about everyone has wished to visit Africa and the Middle East. To see the homelands of the Bible and the Koran; to travel back in time to the palaces and pyramids of ancient pharaohs; to trek across the ever-shifting dunes of the Sahara; to witness the spectacle of vast, migrating herds; even to pay a quiet visit to a family of mountain gorillas: These are the experiences a visitor can have in Africa and the Middle East.

But few travelers ever get to this region. It's so far, so distant, so different. But those who do go to these exotic, foreign lands bring home powerful, eternal memories of these genuinely exotic places.

Where the Countries Are

Africa is the world's second-largest continent, yet most people have only the dimmest ideas about what it contains or even where it is. Africa is directly south of Europe, across the Mediterranean Sea. Indeed, some of the countries in northern Africa can be visited as day trips from Spain, Italy, or Greece. And what of the Middle East? It's to the northeast of Africa and officially is part of Asia.

Africa and the Middle East theoretically offer many countries as options for travel. Some, however, are developing nations with meager tourist facilities. Others, because of political turmoil, aren't attractive possibilities. Some are simply too small and don't offer enough places of interest. As a result, we'll concentrate on only those countries with at least some tourism.

Remember, too, that things change quickly in Africa and the Middle East: Today's tourist hot spot can be abandoned at the first sign of political upheaval; sleepy little countries can suddenly begin courting tourism with a vengeance.

The many African nations can be grouped into seven regions. The first, **Northern Africa**, is a place of deserts, oases, and Islamic culture. The countries we'll cover are, roughly from west to east, **Morocco, Mali, Tunisia, Libya, Egypt** (which is sometimes grouped with the Middle East), **Eritrea**, and **Ethiopia**. The second region is just northeast of Egypt: the **Middle East**. Here you'll find the Biblical lands of **Israel** (and the self-governing **Palestinian territories**) and **Jordan**. Other destinations, for both leisure and business travelers, are **Saudi Arabia, Lebanon, Bahrain**, and the **United Arab Emirates**—among others.

The Sahara is the hottest, largest, and most desolate desert on earth.

The part of Africa that sticks out on its east coast and includes Somalia and Ethiopia is called the "African Horn."

369

Devout Muslims are expected, at least once in their lives, to visit the holy city of **Mecca** in Saudi Arabia.

A third touristic region is the massive, curved peninsula of **West Africa**. Highly influenced by French culture, these countries include **Senegal**, the **Gambia**, **Sierra Leone**, **Liberia**, the **Ivory Coast**, **Ghana**, **Togo**, **Benin**, and **Nigeria**. The fourth area, located just to the east of these nations, is often thought of as the **Central Safari Belt**. Its most visited countries: **Cameroon**, the **Democratic Republic of the Congo** (formerly Zaire), **Tanzania**, **Kenya**, **Rwanda**, and **Uganda**. A fifth magnet for tourism is the more southerly **Central Victoria Falls Region**, flanked by **Zambia** and **Zimbabwe**.

A sixth prime destination is **Southern Africa**. **South Africa** dominates tourism here, but **Namibia**, **Botswana**, and the small nations of **Lesotho** and **Swaziland** have become popular, too. The seventh and final category isn't an area at all. It comprises the many islands that lie off the shores of Africa. The best known are east of Africa in the Indian Ocean and include the **Seychelles**, **Madagascar**, and **Mauritius**. The others are northwest of Africa and can be stop-off points on flights between Europe and North America: the **Azores**, the **Canary Islands**, the **Madeira Islands**, and the **Cape Verde Islands**.

A Satellite View

From space, Africa is a distinctive-looking continent. What would be its most prominent feature? Probably the **Sahara Desert**, which covers most of the continent's northern third. In addition, the **Kalahari Desert** takes up much of southern Africa. And most of the Middle East is desert as well, notably the **Sinai** region. Although too many old Tarzan movies lead people to think that the remainder of Africa is dense jungle, much of the rest of the continent is actually grassy savannah and veldt, with rivers and a few large lakes here and there. Furthermore, most of Africa consists of flat coastal and plateau regions, though some major mountains rise up in the northwest and along the continent's eastern side. And the equator cuts an imaginary line almost directly across its center.

The features of Africa and the Middle East that we've just reviewed are a major part of what makes these lands so interesting. Those same features dramatically shape the conditions travelers face when they venture here.

Bodies of Water

Two oceans lie on either side of Africa: the **Atlantic Ocean** on the west and the **Indian Ocean** on the east. Along the northern boundary is the **Mediterranean Sea**, and dividing the continent in the northeast from the Middle East (which is connected to Europe and Asia) is the **Red Sea**.

Two large bodies of water, the **Black Sea** and the **Caspian Sea**, form partial boundaries between the Middle East and Europe. The **Persian Gulf** juts into the center of the Middle East and flows directly into the **Arabian Sea**, which in turn divides the region from western Asia. In the area separating the Middle East from Africa, you'll also notice the **Suez Canal**, which connects the Mediterranean with the **Gulf of Suez**.

Though much of Africa is desert, there's quite a network of rivers. Indeed, some of the most famous rivers in the world flow here. Emptying into the Mediterranean is the mighty **Nile River**, which dominates northeastern Africa. The **Jordan River** courses through the western part of the Middle East (and runs into the **Dead Sea**, a popular resort area). Several major rivers flow off the west coast of Africa into the Atlantic, including the **Congo** and **Gambia** rivers. A major rainforest surrounds the Congo River basin. The **Niger River** runs through northwestern Africa. Emptying at the east coast is the **Zambezi River**, which begins in central Africa and flows southward, then eastward, tumbling at midpoint over mighty **Victoria Falls**, a major tourist destination. Victoria Falls is often visited in conjunction with stays in Zambia or Botswana.

Africa and the Middle East have few lakes, but **Lake Victoria** is quite large and stands out in eastern Africa. Below it are a couple of long, thin lakes: **Lake Tanganyika** and **Lake Malawi**. In the north, just south of the Sahara, is **Lake Chad**. One warning: Water in Africa is generally for viewing, not swimming. As picturesque and even pure as the water may seem, bacteria and who knows what other creatures may lurk there. They may be harmless to locals (who often are resistant) but not to tourists. Ocean water is usually safe, but pollution and sharks can, in some places, be a danger.

Mountains

If you were to visit Africa and the Middle East, it would become clear that they're not as mountainous as, say, Europe or Asia. Though much of Africa is very hilly or has plateaus, only two major ranges interrupt its surface: the **Atlas Mountains** in the northwest corner and the many mountains (most volcanoes) of the eastern regions. Indeed, lofty **Mt. Kilimanjaro**, the highest mountain in Africa, rises more than 19,000 feet above sea level. One other prominent feature stands out: the **Great Rift Valley**, which begins in the Middle East and continues down to east-central Africa.

Climate

To fully summarize the climate of Africa and the Middle East is a challenge. Why? Because just about every conceivable climate exists.

First, because the equator bisects Africa, the region has two seasonal patterns. North of the equator, the seasons are those that Americans are used to: Winter is December through March, and summer is June through September. South of the equator, though, winter starts in June, summer in December.

What about temperatures? Winters in the desert areas of northern Africa and the Middle East, as well as in southern Africa, are warm to cool, with chilly temperatures especially at night. Summers in the north can be broiling, though southern Africa's summers are relatively pleasant. As you get closer to the equator, however, temperatures tend to be warmer year-round, with only minor temperature fluctuations between summer and winter.

The Great Rift Valley is a treasure trove of early human artifacts.

Depending on the criteria, Djibouti may be the hottest inhabited place in the world, and Aswan, Egypt, the driest.

Zebras: Are they white-striped on black, or black-striped on white?
Photo by Sharon Blair

But altitude is a component, too. The plateau and mountainous areas of southern and eastern Africa tend to be cooler in general than land closer to sea level. (There are even snow-capped African mountains on or near the equator.) The Atlas Mountain region can also be quite cold in the winter, hence the ski resorts there. And what of rain? Northern Africa tends to be dry year-round, as is Namibia, on the southwestern coast. On the other hand, the coastal areas of western and central Africa are very rainy (here are the rain forests and jungles). The rest of Africa has moderate rainfall patterns. One final point: Rainy seasons vary widely from place to place in Africa. Certain countries near the equator, like Kenya, even have two distinct rainy seasons.

Tourism Patterns

The Middle East—though comparatively small—attracts more visitors than vast Africa. Among North Americans (and when the political climate is calm) Israel is the most popular destination, with South Africa a fast-rising second.

Political turmoil, acts of terrorism, and other negative events in the Middle East or Africa usually impact tourism intensely—not only in the immediate area of that event, but thousands of miles away. For example, a crisis in, say, Kuwait, can cause a 50 percent drop in tourism in Cairo, which is over 800 miles away. Even Morocco would suffer a major downturn, though it's thousands of miles distant from the Middle Eastern turmoil.

African and Middle Eastern Distances

Africa and the Middle East are big. Africa alone is larger than South America and Europe combined. That, by itself, is enough to make point-to-point travel there a major undertaking. Adding to the challenge is that, overall, the transportation networks here aren't always reliable. This is still a developing region. Even the most progressive of the nations discussed in this section haven't reached the standards most American tourists are accustomed to. Finally, the delicate political climate in many of the countries may necessitate roundabout travel plans. (Some governments, for instance, don't allow visitors to enter directly into their country from another rival nation; visitors have to reroute through a third, neutral country. Be sure to check government advisories on this.)

In short, traveling through Africa and the Middle East is an adventure. Traveling times can be easily miscalculated: A short direct road may be washed out or in poor condition. A simple flight between countries can become a circus of connections. In Africa and the Middle East, anything can change on a moment's notice.

Most public transportation (specifically, buses and trains) should be viewed with healthy skepticism. The vehicles can be uncomfortably crowded; in many cases English won't be spoken. Taxis are a better bet, but the fares can be quite slippery. Rental cars are widely available. However, a car rental can present challenges, especially because road conditions are so uncertain; some areas might not even be safe to drive through or are poorly marked. Namibia and, especially, South Africa are among the few places where car rentals are a prudent option. A popular way for tourists to get around is by hiring a car and driver for the day, perhaps through their hotel's concierge, or to set things up via a reputable tour operator. And for visitors staying at a safari lodge, the hotel will provide a jeep, driver, and "tracker" to take them out on daily drives to see the wildlife.

Air travel to Africa and the Middle East has become easier. Though most itineraries must be built via European gateways, a few nonstop jets do fly from U.S. cities. For example, Tel Aviv is a 12-hour flight from New York City.

Perhaps the best option is an escorted tour and/or safari. Africa and the Middle East lend themselves ideally to such travel packages, and even independent spirits may greatly appreciate how much easier their trips are when someone else handles the logistics. And what about air travel? Service is fairly good between major cities; however, scheduling can be uncertain. Many secondary routes are flown by "bush pilots" who fly small aircraft.

Libya is the only nation whose flag is one solid color: green.

A shrine in Ethiopia claims to have the Ark of the Covenant.

Until a few thousand years ago, lions, elephants, and other large animals lived in North Africa. Because the Roman Empire captured them for its spectacles and because the area became drier, these animals disappeared from the area.

Motor coaches at the Great Pyramid in Giza, Egypt
Photo by Marc Mancini

Trains are a viable way of getting around in Egypt and South Africa. Indeed, South Africa's luxurious "Blue Train" is legendary, traveling between Cape Town and Pretoria. Cruises are even more reliable. Three cruise itineraries dominate: Morocco, Tunisia, and the Atlantic islands, often out of Spain; a routing that features Kenya and the Indian Ocean islands, often in combination with South Africa or, occasionally, India; and the highly popular Nile cruises.

One last thing to remember when setting up schedules: The weather can play an important part in transportation. Rainy seasons can wash out roads, hurricanes brush along Africa's eastern coast, and desert dust storms can make traveling difficult or dangerous.

Some Miscellaneous Considerations

People usually have a clear notion of only the most obvious destinations in this part of the world—the pyramids, for example, or Jerusalem. As for the rest—well that's another matter. Some situations you should be most aware of are:

- Health conditions here are often far below the standards to which many people are accustomed. Tourists should visit their physician before leaving on their trip to get appropriate inoculations and medicines.

- Surprising to most tourists: Some extremely luxurious lodging is available in Africa and the Middle East. Even some "tents" and "huts" are very upscale.

- By North American standards, Africa and most of the Middle East are a bargain. Costs in Israel and certain Middle Eastern countries are somewhat higher.

- Crime and theft are a definite problem in some countries, decidedly not in others. The normal precautions should be taken. Begging, often by little children, is aggressive and common.

- AIDS has reached epidemic proportions in Africa (but not in the Middle East). Unsafe sex here is a potentially deadly mistake.

- Many tourists hear of wonderful exchange rates on the local black markets and decide to take advantage of the prices. But many nations here severely punish the practice. Indeed, the person offering that terrific exchange rate may be an undercover police officer.

In 900 A.D., the world's most populous city was Baghdad.

The first beers were brewed in Ancient Egypt and Babylon.

- Similarly, drug use in many of these countries is a very serious crime.

- These destinations are informal. Yet tourists shouldn't dress too casually, especially when visiting temples and mosques. Shorts or sleeveless dresses are often a no-no.

- Bargaining at shops is usually lively and expected. But not always. Hotel personnel can clarify the situation.

- Africa and the Middle East can be very hot; insects are everywhere; malaria and polio are a problem, especially in West Africa. Sunscreen and insect repellent are essential.

- Outbreaks of lawlessness, warfare, or political fighting sporadically occur across much of Africa. Keep abreast of travel advisories.

- Taking photographs is one of life's great pleasures for many travelers. In many of these nations, however, certain sites (such as some government buildings or a special place of worship) may be off-limits. Visitors should ask about any restrictions when they reach their destination or consult a tour operator in advance. Also, you'd be surprised how close safari jeeps get to lions, hippos, elephants, baboons, and other wild animals. The opportunity for wonderful photos is great, but certain rules of behavior—usually explained by the guide—have to be followed. Otherwise, you may discover exactly why they're called *wild* animals. . . .

- When booking a safari, find out how many vehicles are used per trip. A safari should have at least two vehicles traveling near one another, in case one breaks down, or should have a two-way radio to call another for help.

- Travelers should reconfirm their next flight, if practical, immediately on arrival—and in person, *not* by phone. Travelers must arrive for flights very early so they'll be at the front when boarding occurs. (Seat reservations are sometimes ignored.)

- The hotel chains with the largest presence in Africa and the Middle East include Hilton, Sheraton, Inter-Continental, Le Meridien, and Holiday Inn.

- Most tourists go to Africa primarily to see wildlife. They usually conclude, however, that meeting the locals is a major benefit of their trip.

Africa has over 50 countries—more than any other continent.

Spanish is the official language of only one African nation: Equatorial Guinea.

Tourists in Africa often travel from place to place in small aircraft
Photo by Sharon Blair

Travel Trivia

What They Said

- "Everything in Africa bites, but the Safari bug is worst of all."—Brian Jackman

- "In the winter, Venice is like an abandoned theater. The play is finished, but the echoes remain."—Arbit Blatas

- "Russia is the only country in the world you can be homesick for while you're still in it."—John Updike

- "Prague is like a vertical Venice—steps everywhere."—Penelope Gilliatt

- "Whether you go to Heaven or Hell, you still have to transfer in Atlanta."—Anonymous

- "I'm leaving because the weather's too good. I hate London when it's not raining."—Groucho Marx

- "Rome was a poem pressed into service as a city."—Anatole Broyard

- "He who rides the sea of the Nile must have sails woven of patience."—William Golding

NAME _____ **DATE** _____

CREATIVE ACTIVITY

You won the lottery! You can now indulge in your lifelong fantasy: to visit all seven touristic regions of Africa during a month-long trip. You have to plan your packing. What 10 special items do you think you'll need to bring, other than essentials (e.g., don't list shirts, a toothbrush, and so on), for this African holiday?

Item

① Binoculars

②

③

④

⑤

⑥

⑦

⑧

⑨

⑩

Reason

① To see distant animals at wildlife reserves

②

③

④

⑤

⑥

⑦

⑧

⑨

⑩

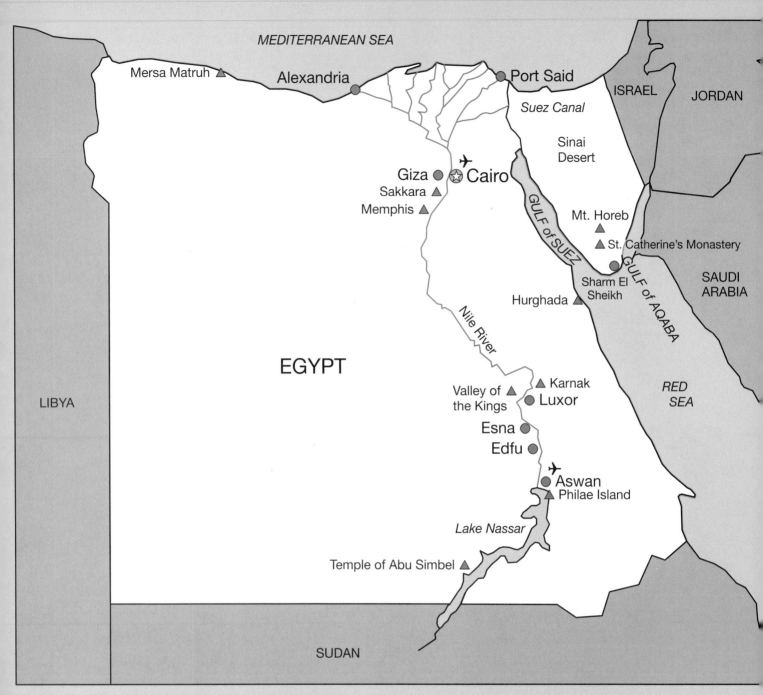

MEDITERRANEAN SEA

Mersa Matruh ▲   Alexandria ●   ● Port Said

ISRAEL   JORDAN

Suez Canal

Sinai
Desert

Giza ● ✈ ☆ Cairo
Sakkara ▲
Memphis ▲

GULF of SUEZ

Mt. Horeb
▲
▲ St. Catherine's Monastery

SAUDI
ARABIA

Sharm El
Sheikh ●

GULF of AQABA

Hurghada ▲

Nile River

EGYPT

RED
SEA

LIBYA

Valley of ▲ ▲ Karnak
the Kings ● Luxor

Esna ●

Edfu ●

✈
Aswan ●
▲ Philae Island

Lake Nassar

Temple of Abu Simbel ▲

SUDAN

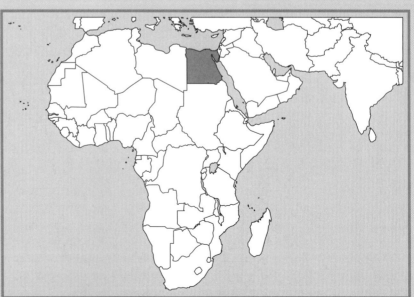

C h a p t e r   2 1

Egypt
Riddles in the Sand

It's perhaps the most famous riddle of all time: the riddle of the Sphinx. "What is it," the Sphinx asked passersby, "that walks on four legs in the morning, two legs during the daytime, and three legs at night?" If travelers couldn't answer the question, the Sphinx would slaughter them.

The Sphinx was a mythical creature and the only big Sphinx left in Egypt is a stone statue, anyway. Tourists are safe. But riddles do remain. How were Egypt's great monuments built? Why were they built? What was ancient Egypt really like? These are the riddles that continue to draw tourists today (and provide a seemingly endless topic for cable TV networks).

Egypt is located in the northeast corner of the African continent. It's a large country—about the size of California, Nevada, and Arizona combined. Yet most of the population lives in the narrow, fertile **Nile River Valley**. Depending on how you measure, the Nile may be the world's longest river. (The Amazon is the other possibility.) The Nile flows south to north through the eastern portion of the country and empties into the Mediterranean Sea. The country's capital, **Cairo**, is on the Nile in northern Egypt. Indeed, most of the destinations that tourists are interested in—**Luxor**, in the center of the country, and **Aswan**, in the south—are on the Nile. (Those who fly between cities will see an astonishing sight: a blue and green ribbon of a river cutting through the tan, dusty surface of Egypt.)

Western Egypt, which makes up the bulk of the country, is desert and largely uninhabited. The nation's eastern border is marked by the **Red Sea**, which (with the **Gulf of Suez** to the west and the **Gulf of Aqaba** [ACK-ah-bah] to the east) helps form the border of the **Sinai (Peninsula)** desert. The famous **Suez Canal** lies to the north, between the Gulf of Suez and the Mediterranean. Arabic is the national language, but English is widely spoken by tourist personnel.

The answer, incidentally, to the Sphinx's riddle is "man." For it's man who crawls on all fours during infancy, stands upright through the prime of life, and uses a cane in old age. The rest of Egypt's riddles are left for visitors to ponder on their own, during a fascinating journey to this faraway land.

How Travelers Get There

The national airline is **Egyptair** (MS), though other North American and foreign carriers also fly into the main gateway at **Cairo International Airport** (CAI). Flying times from the United States are long, usually with connections: 12 hours from New York, 15 hours from Chicago, and nearly 17 hours from Los Angeles.

Travelers may also reach Egypt following a stopover visit in Europe; it takes five hours to fly into the country from Paris, for example. It's also possible to arrive in Egypt via ship; Egypt is a stop on certain Eastern Mediterranean cruise itineraries, usually out of Piraeus

The "Lower" Nile is in the north of Egypt, and the "Upper" Nile in the south.

Tolls paid by cruise ships and freighters going through the Suez Canal are a major source of income for Egypt.

The original Library of Alexandria, established in 288 B.C., is said to have included all the knowledge of the ancient world.

379

FYI
FOR YOUR INFORMATION

EGYPT

CAPITAL: Cairo

AREA (SQUARE MILES): 386,101

TIME ZONE: GMT +2

DRIVE ON: Right

POPULATION: 81,700,000

RELIGION: Islam

LANGUAGE: Arabic

CURRENCY: 1 Egyptian pound = 100 piastres

ELECTRICITY: 220 volts, 50 cycles AC

CAPSULE HISTORY: Upper and Lower Kingdoms united, 4000 B.C.; "Golden Age," sixteenth to thirteenth century B.C.; Alexander conquers Egypt, 332 B.C.; Rome takes over, 30 B.C.; Islam introduced, 641; Turks take over, 1517; Napoleonic occupation, 1798–1801; Suez Canal, 1869; British occupy, 1882; independence, 1922; monarchy ends, 1953; various Israeli–Egyptian wars, 1956–1973; fundamentalist unrest and acts of terrorism, 1993–1998.

For reference sources, tourist bureaus, and suggested lengths of stay, see the Appendices.

(Athens) or Istanbul. The main port in Egypt is **Alexandria**, in the center of the nation's northern coast. A secondary port is **Port Said** [sah-EED], on the Suez Canal.

Weather Patterns

Most tourists to Egypt spend their time at destinations along the Nile, whose climate is far more comfortable than that of the Western and Sinai deserts. For example, the temperatures in Cairo during winter (the main tourist season) will reach only the 70s and cool down to as low as the upper 40s at night (see Figure 21–1). Late fall can be pleasant as well, reaching 80 degrees or more. Visitors should avoid the summer, however, unless they're willing to put up with intense heat and air pollution in order to take advantage of bargain rates; the average summer highs are in the mid-90s, and it's dry (and it gets even hotter in southern Egypt). In addition, March through May is usually uncomfortable—not only because of shifting temperatures but also because of shifting sand; lung-searing winds (called the *khamsin*) can occur during this time. Rain, though, is unlikely to dampen a visit; it rains, on average, only one day a month in Cairo and a little more than that along the northern coast, where Alexandria is located.

Getting Around

The most popular ways for tourists to visit Egypt's highlights is on a Nile cruise and/or an escorted tour. There are also good air connections between the major cities. Egypt has adequate train and bus service. Travelers who decide to go by rail should take first class only; second class can be very uncomfortable. Ditto for the crowded buses that cross the country. (Those bus routes used predominately by tourists are OK.) And remind visitors that donkeys, horses, and, yes, camels are commonly used for getting around in certain areas (especially around the pyramids).

Taxis are an inexpensive way to see Cairo. However, meters are often ignored; the cost of the ride should be firmly set at the beginning (and it often depends on the age, condition, and make of the vehicle!). Car rentals are widely available, but driving can be

Over a million people live in structures within one of Cairo's cemeteries. It's called the "City of the Dead."

When setting up a camel ride, negotiate the price first and wait until the end to pay and tip. The same applies for trips in feluccas (small sailboats) and taxis.

Climate at a Glance
CAIRO

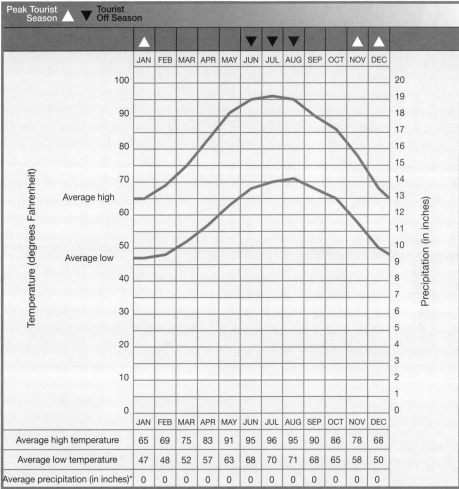

	JAN	FEB	MAR	APR	MAY	JUN	JUL	AUG	SEP	OCT	NOV	DEC
Average high temperature	65	69	75	83	91	95	96	95	90	86	78	68
Average low temperature	47	48	52	57	63	68	70	71	68	65	58	50
Average precipitation (in inches)*	0	0	0	0	0	0	0	0	0	0	0	0

*Occasional rain, but never totaling more than ½-inch in any given month.

Figure 21–1

a nightmare of crowded streets and lonely desert roads. Many visitors hire a driver for the day; car rental companies and hotels can facilitate this. The jam-packed city buses should be avoided. There's an adequate subway system and visitors can also travel through the city by boat along the Nile.

Important Places

Several remarkable destinations are typically on the tourist agenda.

Cairo

Located on the Nile, Cairo is a historic, bustling city (Africa's largest, by far). Visitors should be prepared for the squalor of certain sections of the area. Among Cairo's attractions are:

■ **The Egyptian Museum**, near the Ramses Hilton Hotel, with perhaps the world's greatest collection of ancient Egyptian artifacts, including the mummies of most of the great pharaohs and the dazzling treasures of King Tutankhamun. It's best to get there early and to go directly to King Tut's room on the second floor, then to the mummy room, and on to the rest of the collection.

At Cairo's Egyptian Museum, you can actually look upon the face of Ramses II (mummified, of course), who may have been the pharaoh referred to in the story of Moses.

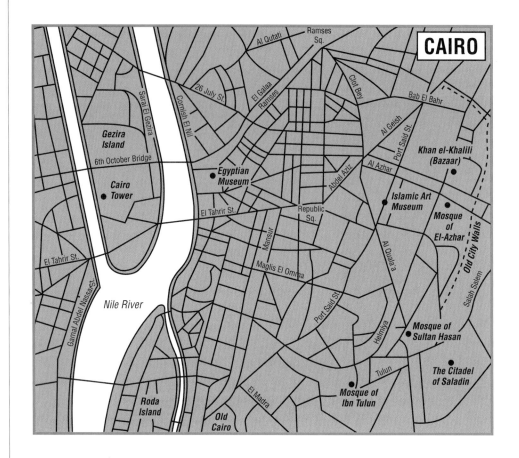

- **Great mosques**, the most notable of which are the ancient **Mosque of Ibn Tulun**, the renowned **Mosque of El Azhar** (near the old bazaar), and the colossal **Sultan Hassan Mosque**.

- **The Citadel of Saladin**, a walled, hilltop fort built in the twelfth century. Within it is the legendary **Alabaster Mosque**, the Citadel's central attraction.

- **The Museum of Islamic Art**, perhaps the finest exhibit of its kind in the world.

- **The Coptic Quarter**, with its old narrow streets, ancient Christian churches, and a museum. (The Coptic Church is an ancient Christian sect.)

- **The Three Great Pyramids and the Sphinx**—among the most renowned attractions anywhere—located in the town of **Giza**, just west of Cairo. The pyramids were one of the Seven Wonders of the Ancient World and they're the only "wonder" still in existence. The most famous is the pyramid of **Cheops**. The dramatic sound-and-light show (given in English on certain nights) is impressive. Early morning visits are good, too, since the heat is reduced and the crowds still thin.

A short day trip from Cairo is to **Sakkara** and its famous **Step Pyramid**, the world's oldest intact stone structure. Nearby is **Memphis**, which in ancient days was the capital of Egypt; brooding monuments and a huge statue of Ramses II are the attractions that remain from this city, now largely gone.

Luxor

Upriver (south) from Cairo, Luxor features some of the most remarkable ruins in all of Egypt. In ancient days this city was known as Thebes. It was in the **Valley of the Kings**—across the river from Luxor—that King Tut's tomb was discovered. Other ancient pharaohs were buried here, as well. Though their tombs are now mostly empty, the astonishing wall

Thebes was also the name of the ancient Greek city-state conquered by Alexander the Great.

The Great Pyramid and the Sphinx are two of the most famous attractions at Giza
Photo by Marc Mancini

decorations remain. The area boasts two of the world's finest temple complexes: the **Temple of Luxor** and the nearby **Temple of Karnak**.

Aswan

Farther upriver from Luxor, Aswan today is most recognized as home to one of the world's biggest structures: the **Aswan High Dam**. The temples on **Philae** [FIE-lee] **Island** provide the backdrop to a superb sound-and-light show. A number of temples can be reached from Aswan; the best known is the towering **Temple of Abu Simbel**, where the figure of Ramses II is cut into a bluff. (The entire temple was cut into pieces—its original site was flooded when the Aswan Dam was built—and reassembled at its present location.)

Nile Cruises

Cruises can be taken in either direction (or both), but it's most efficient to fly south and then cruise north with the current. For those with plenty of time, the week-long voyage from Aswan to Cairo is unforgettable. More common, however, is the shorter four-day trip between Aswan and Luxor. The ship will stop at such sites as **Esna** (with the **Temple of Khnum**) and **Edfu** (with the superbly preserved **Temple of Horus**). Passengers will also get a real feeling for everyday Egyptian life. Hotels operate most cruise ships; the cruise price will include a cabin and most meals.

> Even on the finest Nile cruise ships, stomach disorders are common.

Though these are the main destinations in Egypt, other areas draw tourists, including:

- **The Sinai Desert**, where many biblical sites are found, including **Mt. Horeb**, which some believe to be Mt. Sinai where Moses received the tablets of the Ten Commandments. **St. Catherine's Monastery**, at the presumed site of the Burning Bush, is nearby.

- **Alexandria**, Egypt's second-largest city and its main cruise port. Though attractions are rather limited, there are some fine museums, a stunning new library, several palaces, and some ancient ruins. Divers have begun to find intriguing artifacts in Alexandria's harbor, some of which are now on display.

> It's believed that Alexander the Great is buried somewhere under Alexandria. No one knows where.

Karnak is a triumph of detail
Image copyright Vova Pomortzeff, 2008. Used under license from Shutterstock.com

■ **Resorts,** most notably **Mersa Matruh** (on the Mediterranean, west of Alexandria), **Sharm El Sheikh** (at the southern tip of the Sinai Peninsula), and **Hurghada** [HOOR-gah-duh] (on the Red Sea), a fine snorkeling and diving site.

Possible Itineraries

Deciding on the length of stay in Egypt depends not only on the destinations to be visited but also on the mode of transportation. A good itinerary would be 10 days for first-time visitors. They would start in the area around Cairo and then fly to Aswan, where they'll take a ship downriver to Luxor, then return by air to Cairo. Experienced travelers may wish to take excursions to some of the lesser-known sites, visit the Sinai Desert, take a longer cruise, or even spend some time at one of Egypt's fine resorts.

Lodging Options

Budget accommodations in Egypt can provide guests with unwelcome surprises. Very good lodging, though, is reasonably priced. There's a wide selection of North American chains in Egypt, especially in Cairo. Perhaps the best hotel in Cairo is the **Marriott**, with a converted palace at its center. Most Cairo bars and nightclubs are in the hotels.

Most of Cairo's lodging is situated around the Egyptian Museum and along the Nile. Quite a few hotels line the road to the airport. For those planning to spend much time exploring the Great Pyramids and the Sphinx, you might recommend accommodations in Giza, where there are several hotels and resorts. (The most famous is the **Mena House Oberoi**.) For those taking a Nile cruise, the ship acts as the hotel; passengers stay onboard at night.

The mummy of Ramses I, the grand-father of Ramses II and a major pharaoh in his own right, had long been missing. In 1999 it was found, unidentified, in an obscure Niagara Falls museum. It has since been "repatriated."

Allied Destinations

It's not uncommon for a visit to Egypt to be combined with a trip to its neighbor, Israel, and to nearby Jordan. Egypt is also just across the Red Sea from Saudi Arabia. Because of the great distance to Egypt from the United States, visitors often prefer to break up the flight by stopping over in Europe for a few days before continuing. The country can also be visited as part of a Mediterranean cruise.

Cultural Patterns

Egypt's culture is different from what visitors are likely to be used to. This is most relevant to business travelers.

Many people expect small tips, called *baksheesh*, for favors that they've done; this includes letting their photographs be taken. Even museum guards may ask.

■ The use of titles (e.g., Doctor, Professor) is important when addressing people in Egypt. And dress is fairly formal and conservative.

Alexandria's new library honors its famous predecessor
Image copyright Holger Mette, 2008. Used under license from Shutterstock.com

- Parties, dinners, and other gatherings often don't start until 10 P.M. When staging a social gathering, have nonalcoholic beverages available for Muslim attendees.
- Building trust is important to Egyptians. As a result, visitors should be prepared to engage in extended conversation and coffee before starting a meeting. Even shopkeepers will offer customers a free coffee or cola.
- It's quite acceptable to ask an Egyptian's opinion about something. However, to ask about personal matters is rarely done, except among close friends.
- If visitors are invited to someone's home, it's polite to bring a gift, and good manners to leave some food on their plates. (It's a sign of abundance.)
- When exchanging an item (such as food or a gift) with another person, never use the left hand alone; it's considered ill mannered.
- Many businesses close on Friday, the Muslim day of rest. Workweeks begin on Saturday and run through Thursday. Some places close completely (or early) on Sunday.

Factors That Motivate Visitors

Certain predictable reasons prompt people to visit Egypt:

- It has a unique and rich cultural history.
- Costs within the country are relatively low, and shopping is a bargain.

Qualifying the Traveler
Egypt

For People Who Want	High	Medium	Low	Remarks
Historical and Cultural Attractions	▲			Legendary sights
Beaches and Water Sports		▲		Seacoast resorts; Red Sea diving
Skiing Opportunities			▲	None
Lots of Nightlife		▲		In Cairo, especially in hotels
Family Activities		▲		Primarily sightseeing
Familiar Cultural Experience			▲	
Exotic Cultural Experience	▲			
Safety and Low Crime			▲	Safer than most tourists think
Bargain Travel		▲		After airfare, can be inexpensive
Impressive Scenery		▲		The Nile and desert
Peace and Quiet			▲	Cairo very noisy; rest of country is quieter
Shopping Opportunities		▲		Pottery, handicrafts, false antiquities, cotton
Adventure	▲			
To Do Business			▲	Must understand the culture

- The locals are warm and friendly to foreign visitors.
- It appeals to those who like cruises. Nile cruises are attractive to people who usually reject water travel because of seasickness; the Nile is quite calm.
- The weather is warm and pleasant during the winter.

Possible Misgivings

A trip to Egypt is a unique experience. But it does generate concerns—some genuine, some unfounded:

- "Hasn't there been crime and terrorism directed against tourists?" Serious but sporadic incidents by terrorists have occurred and have dramatically impacted tourism, but overall, Egypt is an astonishingly crime-free country.
- "The hostilities in the Middle East worry me." Wars in the Middle East are not affecting Egypt.
- "I've been told that the water is very bad." Drink bottled liquids instead, and be careful with fresh fruits and vegetables.
- "There's widespread disease there." Check with a physician before making the trip and get any necessary shots.
- "It's blisteringly hot." Avoid Egypt during the summer; visit in the winter or late fall, when the weather is usually lovely.
- "The country is dirty and crowded." Book a first-class or deluxe hotel, or take an upscale package tour. Cairo's traffic, smog, and crowds are real, though; those with this concern should perhaps stay only briefly in Cairo and move on to other Egyptian areas.
- "Aren't there aggressive salespeople and beggars everywhere?" Much of this is a sort of game that locals play to make a meager living. Everyday Egyptians are among the most friendly, hospitable, and helpful people in the world.

Sales Strategies

What's the most obvious way to enhance a trip to Egypt? By booking a memory-of-a-life-time Nile cruise. An escorted tour is a good choice for those who feel a certain hesitancy about their visit. Because the flight to Egypt from the United States is so long, stopovers in Europe will break up the voyage. A trip to Egypt combines well with a visit to Israel or Kenya. Further, because many budget hotels can be unpleasant, better hotels are advisable. Cruises are a grand way to maximize profits from a traveler's trip.

Obelisks were first erected in Egypt. The world's tallest contemporary one is the Washington Monument, in Washington, D.C.

The most famous bazaar to see in Cairo is the Khan El Khalili.

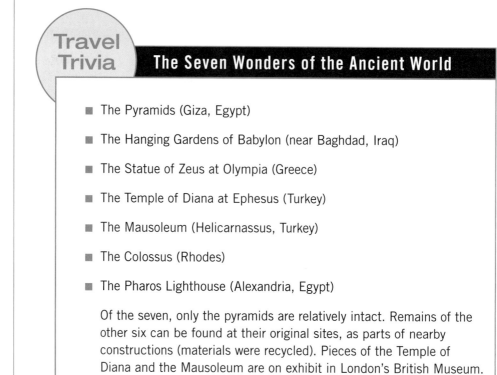

Travel Trivia

The Seven Wonders of the Ancient World

- The Pyramids (Giza, Egypt)

- The Hanging Gardens of Babylon (near Baghdad, Iraq)

- The Statue of Zeus at Olympia (Greece)

- The Temple of Diana at Ephesus (Turkey)

- The Mausoleum (Helicarnassus, Turkey)

- The Colossus (Rhodes)

- The Pharos Lighthouse (Alexandria, Egypt)

Of the seven, only the pyramids are relatively intact. Remains of the other six can be found at their original sites, as parts of nearby constructions (materials were recycled). Pieces of the Temple of Diana and the Mausoleum are on exhibit in London's British Museum.

NAME _____ **DATE** _____

MAP ACTIVITY

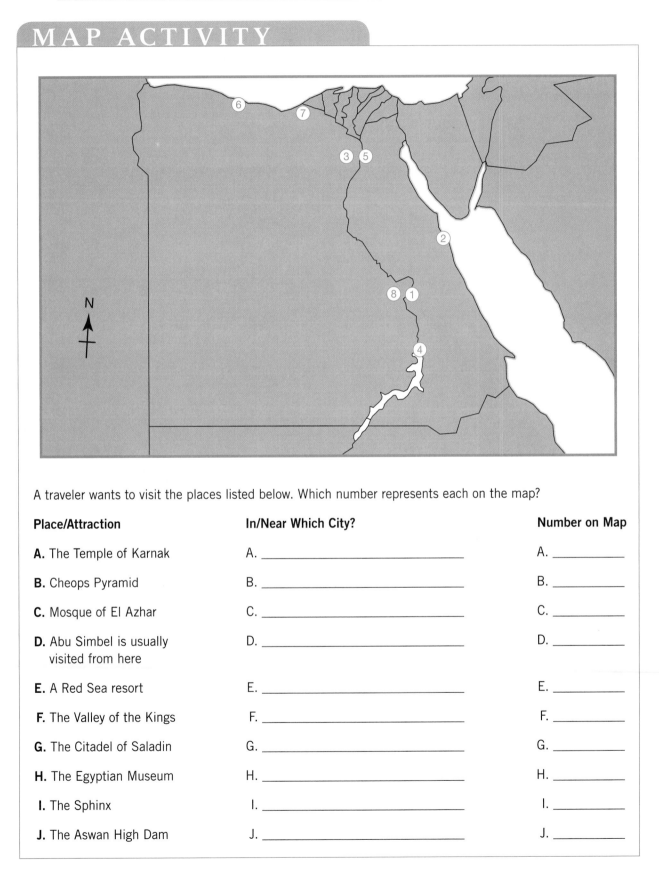

A traveler wants to visit the places listed below. Which number represents each on the map?

Place/Attraction	In/Near Which City?	Number on Map
A. The Temple of Karnak	A. _____	A. _____
B. Cheops Pyramid	B. _____	B. _____
C. Mosque of El Azhar	C. _____	C. _____
D. Abu Simbel is usually visited from here	D. _____	D. _____
E. A Red Sea resort	E. _____	E. _____
F. The Valley of the Kings	F. _____	F. _____
G. The Citadel of Saladin	G. _____	G. _____
H. The Egyptian Museum	H. _____	H. _____
I. The Sphinx	I. _____	I. _____
J. The Aswan High Dam	J. _____	J. _____

NAME _____ **DATE** _____

CASE STUDY

Elizabeth and John Apicella enjoy the region around the Mediterranean. They've been to Italy and Israel and have cruised the Greek Isles, but they've yet to visit Egypt. This year, at last, they plan to go for 11 days.

Circle the answer that best suits their needs.

1 The Apicellas enjoy cruises. Which of the following do you suggest they take as a trip?

Aswan to Luxor   Cairo to Aswan

The Dead Sea   The Eastern Mediterranean

Why?

2 While staying in Cairo, they want to see pyramids. To what town would you direct them?

Uxmal   Giza

Rhodes   Gaza

Why?

3 Which of the following tips would *not* be a good idea to pass along to the Apicellas?

Many businesses are closed on Fridays.   Pass gifts with the left hand only.

Remove shoes before entering mosques.   Carry a lot of spare change.

Why?

4 Which month would you suggest they go?

May   June

November   August

Why?

NAME _____ **DATE** _____

CREATIVE ACTIVITY

Using only the Internet, see if you can find the answers to the following. Give the answer and the URL of the site where you found it.

1 Name three companies that operate cruises on the Nile.

2 Is it possible to take trips into western Egypt's Sahara? How would you do it?

3 Who was the architect of the Sakkara Pyramid and what else was he known—and venerated—for?

4 You live in Los Angeles and want to fly to Cairo. Give three air itineraries you could take, including the airlines you would use and the cities in which you would connect.

5 Do you need a visa to visit Egypt?

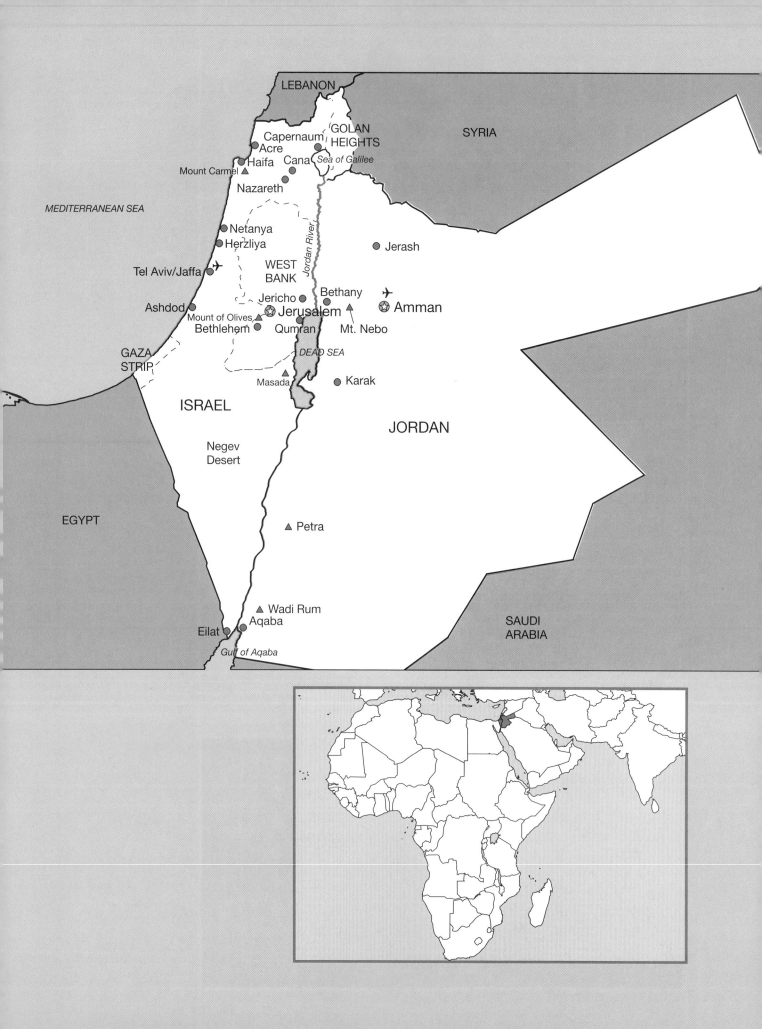

Chapter 22

Israel, Palestine, and Jordan

The Holy Lands

If Greece is the cultural heart of Western civilization, then the Holy Lands (Israel, Palestine, and Jordan), it can be argued, are its soul. Not only is this remarkable region the homeland of the Jewish religion, it holds a preeminent place among Christians—this is where Jesus lived. Moreover, **Jerusalem** is one of the holiest spots to those of the Islamic faith; for it's from here, Muslims believe, that Mohammed ascended to heaven. Perhaps what makes the region so emotionally unique is that it's where spiritual belief anchors itself to solid reality: The cities and sites where biblical events occurred and people lived are *right here*. They look almost exactly like you would imagine them.

This is a place of great contrasts and diversity, not only of religion and cultural history but also of topography; isolated and desertlike, it has been transformed into a flowering landscape. The fragile beauty and majesty of this region, praised in the Bible's poetic prose, continue to enchant visitors today.

Israel isn't as big as you might think; it's about the size of New Jersey. Bordered by the Mediterranean Sea on its west and surrounded by Egypt, Jordan, Syria, and Lebanon, the southern two-thirds of the country consists primarily of the **Negev Desert**. The capital, Jerusalem, is located in the north-central portion of Israel. Indeed, virtually all the major cities and tourist destinations are found in the north. **Bethlehem** is just southwest of Jerusalem, in Palestine. And a bit farther south is the historic site of **Masada**, near the major resort area of the **Dead Sea** (on the border with Jordan). **Tel Aviv**, Israel's second-largest city and a modern center of commerce and culture, is on the central coast; many government offices and foreign embassies are here.

To the north, on the coast, is **Haifa**, Israel's primary seaport. Southeast and east of Haifa are the biblical sites of **Nazareth** and the **Sea of Galilee (Lake Tiberias)**. The major city in the south of Israel is the port of **Eilat** (today a bustling resort destination) by the Gulf of Aqaba [ACK-ah-bah] and the Red Sea. The **Jordan River** marks much of Israel and Palestine's eastern boundary with Jordan.

The 1993 peace accords between Israel and the Palestinians gave self-governing status to parts of several regions taken over by Israel in previous wars. (See dotted areas on map.) The final form the governing will take, what areas it will extend to, and how it will impact tourism (as well as everyday life) still remains in dispute and sometimes cause military conflict within the three "occupied" territories: the **Gaza Strip, West Bank**, and **Golan Heights**.

Jordan is slightly smaller than Indiana. In addition to Israel and Palestine, it borders Syria, Iraq, and Saudi Arabia. Most of its cities (including the capital, **Amman**) and attractions are in the country's western regions, not far from its borders with Israel and Palestine.

All Jews throughout the world have the automatic right to be Israeli citizens.

There are 1,204 synagogues, 158 churches, and 73 mosques in Jerusalem.

ISRAEL, PALESTINE, AND JORDAN

CAPITALS: Israel: Jerusalem
Jordan: Amman

AREA (SQUARE MILES): Israel: 8,302
Palestine: 2,239
Jordan: 35,637

TIME ZONE: GMT: +2

DRIVE ON: Right

POPULATION: Israel and Palestine: 7,100,000
Jordan: 6,200,000

RELIGIONS: Judaism, Islam, Christianity

LANGUAGES: Hebrew, Arabic

CURRENCY: Israel: 1 shekel = 100 agorot
Jordan: 1 dinar = 1,000 fils

ELECTRICITY: 200 volts, 50 cycles AC

CAPSULE HISTORY: Hebrew kingdom, 1000 B.C.; Rome takes control and rules 400 years, 63 B.C.; numerous invasions until 634–640, when Muslims take control; Crusaders arrive, 1099; Turks control, 1516–1917; Britain governs region as "Palestine," 1923–1948; Jordan becomes independent, 1946; Jewish state founded, 1948; wars between Israel and Egypt, 1956–1973; war between Israel and Lebanon, 1982–1983; Israeli-Palestinian Interim Agreement, 1993; major hostilities between Israelis and Palestinians, 2001–present.

For reference sources, tourist bureaus, and suggested lengths of stay, see the Appendices.

In Israel, Hebrew is the national language, but Arabic is also an official language. Arabic is the national language of Jordan and Palestine, though Hebrew is spoken by many Palestinians. English is widely spoken in all three nations.

How Travelers Get There

The main air gateway into Israel and Palestine is Tel Aviv's **Ben Gurion International Airport** (TLV), which also serves Jerusalem. **El Al Israel Airlines** (LY), Israel's national airline, is considered one of the safest in the world; the security checks it employs are so extensive that a very early arrival for a flight is essential. Jordan's air gateway, **Queen Alia International Airport** (AMM) in Amman, is served by **Royal Jordanian** (RJ). Several North American carriers and many European ones service Israel and Jordan.

Flying times, often involving connections in Europe, are around 10.5 hours from New York, 15 hours from Chicago, 14.5 hours from Miami, and 18 hours from the West Coast. Many cruise ships on Eastern Mediterranean itineraries call on the ports of Haifa (gateway to Nazareth and the Galilee area) and **Ashdod** (gateway to Jerusalem). Many people visit Jordan by land from Israel and Palestine, or via the Red Sea port of **Aqaba**.

Weather Patterns

Sharav winds can bring very hot, dry weather in the late spring or early fall.

The region has two distinct climates. Western Jordan and Israel's Negev Desert, in the south, are hot—it's likely that only those heading for Eilat or Aqaba will want to spend time visiting here. In the north, the weather is pleasant year-round—though spring and fall are the best seasons to visit (see Figure 22–1). Summer can be hot and dry, with highs

Climate at a Glance
JERUSALEM

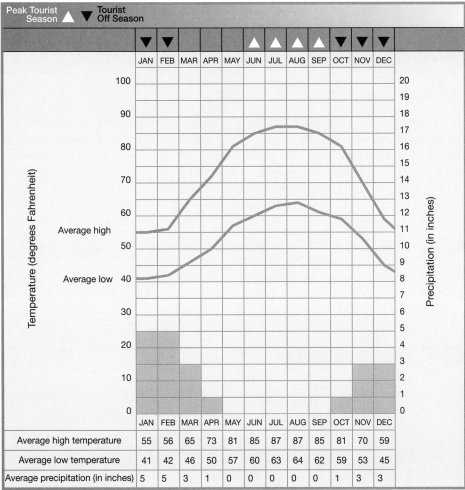

Peak Tourist Season ▲	▼ Tourist Off Season

	JAN	FEB	MAR	APR	MAY	JUN	JUL	AUG	SEP	OCT	NOV	DEC
Average high temperature	55	56	65	73	81	85	87	87	85	81	70	59
Average low temperature	41	42	46	50	57	60	63	64	62	59	53	45
Average precipitation (in inches)	5	5	3	1	0	0	0	0	0	1	3	3

Figure 22–1

averaging in the upper 80s (dropping almost 20 degrees at night). Summer rain is a rarity. Winter (which is somewhat a tourist off-season) gets cool and rainy. Average highs reach only the upper 50s (again, there's a big drop at night to as low as the 30s). Winter rainstorms are heavy but infrequent. Some areas, like Jerusalem and Bethlehem, can even get snow. So all those Christmas cards that show biblical landmarks dusted with snow are more accurate than you might have thought!

Getting Around

The bus system is quite good and fairly inexpensive in Israel and much of Palestine, both within cities and between them. Air service connects the major cities, but this is such a compact region that it's not usually necessary for visitors to fly. The train network is limited. Roads are well maintained and car rentals are extensively available. To get around within cities, taxis are another good means of transportation. An alternative mode of transport between cities in Israel is a *sherut* taxi, which is larger than the regular cabs and takes more passengers. Tours, both in cities and over the whole region, are popular for North Americans.

Visitors can rent cars in Jordan, but driving in Amman is difficult. Taxis are available in the major cities and can be hired for the day. Service cabs operate within cities and also connect major cities and towns; they tend to be less expensive than regular taxis. Buses (both government and private) and limousines operate within and between major cities and tourist sites.

Important Places

Following is a list of the destinations that are most popular in the Holy Lands.

Jerusalem

This is perhaps the world's holiest city, home to some of the most sacred sights of the Jewish, Christian, and Islamic faiths. Jerusalem is located in the Judean hills. Its attractions are sprinkled throughout the city; they can be categorized into two groups: those within the **Old City** and those outside. The Old City is a walled area, reached via several ancient gates (the most famous is the **Damascus Gate**); it's divided into Jewish, Christian, Muslim, and Armenian quarters, and is filled with historical and religious structures, ancient, narrow streets, and bustling markets. Among the many locations to visit in the Old City are:

- **The Wailing Wall** (or **Western Wall**), one of the most sacred sites in the world to Jews. It's all that remains of the legendary Second Temple, which was destroyed by the Romans in 70 A.D.

- **The Church of the Holy Sepulchre**, one of the most deeply sacred sites to Christians. The general location of Christ's crucifixion and burial.

The same family (the Nusseiba family) has been in charge of opening and closing the Church of the Holy Sepulchre since 636 A.D.

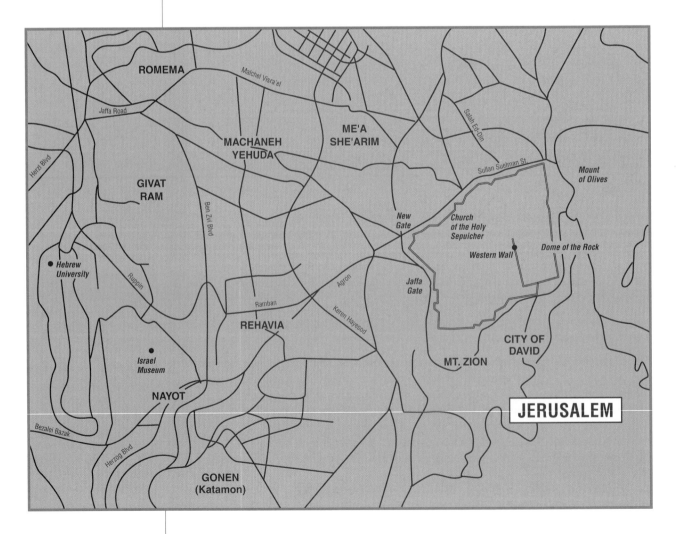

- **The Dome of the Rock**, sacred to Muslims, the third of Jerusalem's most holy places. It's from here that Mohammed is believed to have risen to heaven. This site is also holy to Jews, as the Dome was built on the Temple Mount.

- **Via Dolorosa**, the supposed path Jesus took on his way to the crucifixion.

Outside the Old City, the popular sites of Jerusalem include:

- **Mt. Moriah**, the location where Abraham prepared to sacrifice his son, Isaac, according to God's wishes.

- **The Dead Sea Scrolls**, held in the Shrine of the Book in the **Israel Museum**. These 2,000-year-old scrolls, found in a cave by a shepherd seeking his lost goat (in 1947), have shed light on early Jewish texts and practices. The museum also contains works by Picasso, van Gogh, and other world-famous artists. An instructive and inspirational museum is the **Holocaust History Museum**.

- **The Mount of Olives**, with the **Garden of Gethsemane** and what is believed to be the tomb of Mary, Jesus' mother.

- **The Garden Tomb**, considered by many to be Jesus' actual place of burial, not the Church of the Holy Sepulchre.

- **Mt. Zion**, the tomb of King David, as well as where the room of the Last Supper is thought to be. A newer addition is the **Chamber of the Holocaust**.

Men praying at Jerusalem's Western Wall (Wailing Wall)
Photo by Justus Ghormley

Among the **day trips** from Jerusalem are:

The door to the
Basilica of the Nativity
was made very small
so people couldn't ride
their horses into the
church.

- **Bethlehem**, by tradition, the birthplace of Jesus and also where King David was born. The **Basilica of the Nativity** at Manger Square supposedly sits on the place Jesus was born. Bethlehem is within the Palestinian West Bank.
- **Jericho** (also in the West Bank), considered the oldest city in the world, where Joshua fought the well-known battle. Northeast of Jerusalem on the Jordan River, it's now a favorite winter resort. Sites include **Herod's Winter Palace** and the **Mount of Temptation**. Nearby is **Qumran**, where the Dead Sea Scrolls were found.
- **Masada**, one of the world's most interesting archaeological sites. This promontory is where nearly 1,000 Jewish Zealots are purported to have barricaded themselves against the Romans in 73 A.D., ultimately choosing mass suicide to enslavement. **King Herod's Palace** is at Masada.

Tel Aviv

Tel Aviv was the first
capital of the modern
nation of Israel.

This cosmopolitan city is the major center of commerce and culture in Israel. Located on the Mediterranean coast, the area was nothing but sand dunes in 1900. Now there's a lively nightlife, many sidewalk cafes, and excellent shopping. Among its most interesting sites are:

- **Very good museums**, most notably the **Tel Aviv Museum** and the **Museum of the Diaspora** (for a compelling history of the Jewish people).
- **Independence Hall**, where David Ben Gurion declared Israeli independence in 1948.
- **Dizengoff Square**, with sophisticated shopping and cafes. Another interesting visit would be to the ancient adjacent town of **Jaffa**, which dates from before the time of King Solomon. This old port, with its cobblestone streets, is now an artists' colony.

Haifa

Haifa is Israel's major cruise port. It has some interesting temples, particularly the **Bahai Shrine**, the center of the Bahai faith. Biblical **Mt. Carmel** offers panoramic views; at the base of the mountain is **Elijah's Cave**.

Nazareth and the Sea of Galilee

These unique destinations in Northern Israel can easily be reached as a day trip from Haifa. **Nazareth** is the city where Jesus grew up, and is sacred to Christians. The **Basilica of the Annunciation** is, according to legend, on the spot where an angel told Mary that she was to be the mother of Christ. Other important sites are **Cana** (the site of one of Jesus' first miracles), **Capernaum** (with the ruins of a synagogue where Jesus may have taught), the legendary Sea of Galilee, and the Jordan River (where Jesus was baptized).

Visitors to **Tiberias** often try the town's famous St. Peter's Fish. Another popular destination in northern Israel is the **Crusader's Underground City** at **Acre**.

Resorts

There are many popular resorts in this region of the Middle East.

There are no fish in the
Dead Sea.

- **The Dead Sea**, shared by Israel, Palestine, and Jordan, is a popular resort area. It's often called the world's largest natural spa. This is the lowest point on earth, and its waters are far saltier than those of the Great Salt Lake.
- **Netanya and Herzliya**, located in Israel between Tel Aviv and Haifa on the Mediterranean coast, are among the trendiest and most deluxe resorts.

■ **Eilat (Israel) and Aqaba (Jordan)**, at the northern tip of the Red Sea, offer excellent diving, snorkeling, sandy beaches, and especially beautiful coral reefs. Surrounded by mountains, Aqaba is also popular with mountain climbers.

Jordan

Jordan is often visited in conjunction with a trip to Israel and Palestine. Among the highlights not yet mentioned are:

■ **Splendid archaeological sites**, including astonishing **Petra**, a superb attraction with buildings carved out of a stone mountainside over 2,000 years ago and accessed (via horse or on foot) through a long, dramatically narrow pass. Most impressive, too, are the ruins of an old Crusader fortress and castle at **Karak**. Greco-Roman ruins exist at **Jerash**, which presents a nightly sound-and-light show in the summer. The **King's Highway**, a 5,000-year-old route mentioned in the Old Testament, connects many of the sites.

■ **Amman**, Jordan's hilly capital, with a notable archaeological museum and an old **Roman amphitheater** still in use. Nearby are the ruins of the **Temple of Hercules** and many structures built by the Crusaders.

■ **Biblical sites**, such as **Bethany** (where John the Baptist lived) and **Mt. Nebo** (where Moses is purportedly buried).

■ **Wadi Rum**, with a "Valley of the Moon" landscape. The fort there is associated with Lawrence of Arabia.

Possible Itineraries

Seven days in the Holy Lands should be considered a minimum visit. After landing in Tel Aviv and spending a day or two there, visitors can head to Jerusalem for three or four days and explore the environs—including Bethlehem. They then can head up to Nazareth and the Sea of Galilee, over to Haifa, and down the coast back to Tel Aviv for a couple of days. Return visitors or those wishing to experience more of the area outside Jerusalem can head

Petra was used as the Holy Grail's resting place in the movie *Indiana Jones and the Last Crusade*.

Baptism site on the Jordan River
Photo by Marc Mancini

into the Negev (and down to Eilat and Aqaba), explore Amman and Petra, and/or add some resort stops at the Mediterranean or Dead Seas. It would be easy for a vacationer to fill up two weeks here.

Lodging Options

In Jerusalem, the largest clusters of hotels are near the Convention Center and Independence Park, west and north of the Old City. One of the most famous hotels in town is the **King David**, offering great charm and elegance. Tel Aviv hotels are packed along the coast, south of the Botanic Gardens. For alternative lodging, you might suggest an all-inclusive resort or a health spa. Many kibbutzes (collective farms) also offer accommodations for visitors. Jordan has recently built many new hotels in Amman, near Petra, and along the Dead Sea coast.

Allied Destinations

Because they border Egypt, Saudi Arabia, Syria, and Lebanon, the Holy Lands are an ideal gateway to the entire Middle East. European destinations are logical extensions of a trip to or from the region. Indeed, many Americans who visit here stop off somewhere in Europe or North Africa.

Cultural Patterns

It's important that visitors to the Holy Lands, especially those traveling on business, understand the customs.

- The Hebrew word *shalom* has at least three meanings: hello, goodbye, and peace.
- Israeli society is quite informal. Some examples: Ties are worn only for important occasions; titles are rarely used; schedules aren't strictly adhered to. A visitor should feel comfortable using an Israeli's first name soon after meeting the person.
- Despite Israel's informality, Israelis expect precision in conversation, expect appointments to be met, and take few things for granted.
- Visitors should bring a small gift when visiting a Jordanian's home.
- When an Israeli invites a guest to his or her home, it's an important gesture. It's not necessary to bring a gift, but a book as a gift is appropriate.
- Business dress is more formal in Jordan than in Israel. Men should wear a suit and tie for meetings. Though non-Muslim women aren't expected to cover their arms, legs, and hair as Muslim women do, they shouldn't wear very revealing clothing in public.
- The strife between Palestinians and Israelis is an explosive issue. Be very careful if you must discuss this topic.
- Jordanians are proud of their Arab heritage and are extremely hospitable to visitors.

Factors That Motivate Visitors

Among the reasons that people are inspired to visit the Holy Lands are:

- The region is very important to many different religious faiths. It boasts places many people have heard about from the time they were infants.
- The history, archaeology, and culture are fascinating.
- There are many resorts and thermal spas—more than most people realize.
- The climate at most times and in most places is very pleasant.
- There's great opportunity for outdoor activities and sports, including diving, desert trekking, and mountain climbing.

Many businesses in Israel close on the Sabbath (from sundown Friday to sundown Saturday).

Much of Israel's early biblical history isn't all that precise. The traditional religious sites may or may not be exactly accurate; after so many centuries, no one really knows.

Qualifying the Traveler
Israel

For People Who Want	Appeal			Remarks
	High	Medium	Low	
Historical and Cultural Attractions	▲			Sites appealing to Jews, Muslims, and Christians
Beaches and Water Sports		▲		Along Mediterranean and Red Seas
Skiing Opportunities			▲	Limited skiing in north
Lots of Nightlife			▲	Some in Tel Aviv and Jerusalem
Family Activities		▲		Primarily sightseeing
Familiar Cultural Experience			▲	
Exotic Cultural Experience	▲			
Safety and Low Crime			▲	Long history of strife; petty crime rare
Bargain Travel		▲		
Impressive Scenery		▲		
Peace and Quiet			▲	Jerusalem and Tel Aviv bustling
Shopping Opportunities		▲		Handicrafts, religious souvenirs
Adventure	▲			
To Do Business		▲		Strong trade ties with United States

Possible Misgivings

Though the Holy Lands provide some powerfully emotional reasons for people to visit, there are also some strong objections that can get in the way. A few of these objections and their counters are:

- "This is one of the most dangerous areas in the world." There's no denying the long history of conflict in the Holy Lands, primarily between Israel and the Palestinians. Relations between Palestinians and Israelis are sometimes good, and at other times quite tense. Keep up on news events in order to make appropriate judgments.

- "The Middle East is unsanitary." Health conditions in the Holy Lands are very good, and it's safe to drink the water.

- "The flight here is too long." It is far, but it's quite near Europe. Travelers can break up the lengthy flight between the United States and the region with stopovers on the continent.

- "I'm concerned about airport and airline bombings." Because of the threat of terrorism, security at Ben Gurion Airport is probably the best in the world, as is the antiterrorist safety record of El Al Israel Airlines. You could also suggest an Eastern Mediterranean cruise to someone with this worry.

Petra's wonders lie at the end of a long, narrow, rocky passageway
Image copyright OPIS, 2008. Used under license from Shutterstock.com

The legendary Ark of
the Covenant, said
to contain the Ten
Commandment tablets,
disappeared from the
Temple in Jerusalem.
A church in Ethiopia
claims to have it.
Some scholars believe
it to be hidden and
buried somewhere in
the Temple Mount.

Sales Strategies

Located on the Mediterranean, Israel lends itself to cruises. Even though it's fairly easy to drive in this region, many visitors feel safer on an escorted tour.

Because the Holy Lands are so close to Europe, you might suggest a stopover there. There are some interesting camel ranches, of all things, in the southeastern region of Israel, which some might enjoy staying at for a few days. Several organizations set up short archaeological digs, and some tourists might jump at the chance to participate. Others might enjoy a restful stay at an all-inclusive resort, a dive package at Eilat or Aqaba, or a stay on an Israeli kibbutz. Pilgrimages, often arranged by and for church congregations, are very popular.

Travel Trivia

The Official New 7 Wonders of the World

Recently, 100 million people voted online to determine the Seven Wonders of our world today, and the results were:

1. Great Wall of China
2. Colosseum, Rome, Italy
3. Taj Mahal, Agra, India
4. Petra, Jordan
5. Machu Picchu, Peru
6. Chichen Itza, Mexico
7. Christ the Redeemer statue, Rio de Janeiro, Brazil

SOURCE: www.new7wonders.com

The New7Wonders campaigns aim to encourage and foster global dialogue and mutual understanding, please vote in the current campaign at www.new7wonders.com.

NAME _____ **DATE** _____

MAP ACTIVITY

A traveler wants to visit the places listed below. Which number represents each on the map?

Place/Attraction	In/Near Which City?	Number on Map
A. The Dome of the Rock	A. _____	A. _____
B. Buildings carved in a mountainside	B. _____	B. _____
C. The Basilica of the Annunciation	C. _____	C. _____
D. The Wailing Wall	D. _____	D. _____
E. The Bahai Shrine	E. _____	E. _____
F. Associated with Lawrence of Arabia	F. _____	F. _____
G. The Museum of the Diaspora	G. _____	G. _____
H. Jaffa	H. _____	H. _____
I. The Church of the Holy Sepulchre	I. _____	I. _____
J. Mt. Zion	J. _____	J. _____

NAME _____   DATE _____

CASE STUDY

Deborah and Jerry Levin have wanted to visit Israel for years. This spring, they've saved up and are finally going for seven days. The couple, in their early 50s, has never traveled much, except mostly through the United States. They've been to Mexico and Canada a few times and went to Europe about five years ago. They've been reading all manner of history books and watching videos to get ready.

Circle the answer that best suits their needs.

1 Which of the following services would be most appropriate for the Levins?

    A Mediterranean cruise   A moderately priced hotel

    A two-day stopover in Europe   A stay at a seaside resort

Why?

2 Which of the following places would *not* be a good idea to recommend to the Levins for a day trip from Jerusalem?

    Bethlehem   Jericho

    Luxor   Masada

Why?

3 Which of the following tips would be the best one for you to recommend to the Levins?

    Go in August.   Drink bottled beverages.

    Do your shopping on Saturday.   Dress is very informal.

Why?

4 In addition to experiencing the history of Israel, the Levins would like to enjoy some of the modern-day culture. Where should you direct them?

    Tel Aviv   Eilat

    Haifa   Babylon

Why?

NAME _____   **DATE** _____

CREATIVE ACTIVITY

You're an American filmmaker who's been hired by the Holy Lands Tourist Board to shoot a 15-second commercial for broadcast on U.S. television. You must start by creating a "shot" list of images that will go along with the music and narration that the Board has already decided upon.

Complete the list of shots below. (A few are already filled in.) Your images may be of people, places, or things.

Soundtrack	Images
Slow, romantic, full orchestrated music, with slight Middle Eastern allusions	**1**
	2 Olive-treed garden
	3
	4
	5
Music changes to peppy, intense, active beat	**6**
	7 Cruise ship sailing into Haifa
	8
Narration: "The Holy Lands: So much to see, so much to do, so much to relive."	**9**
	10
	11 Smiling children
	12

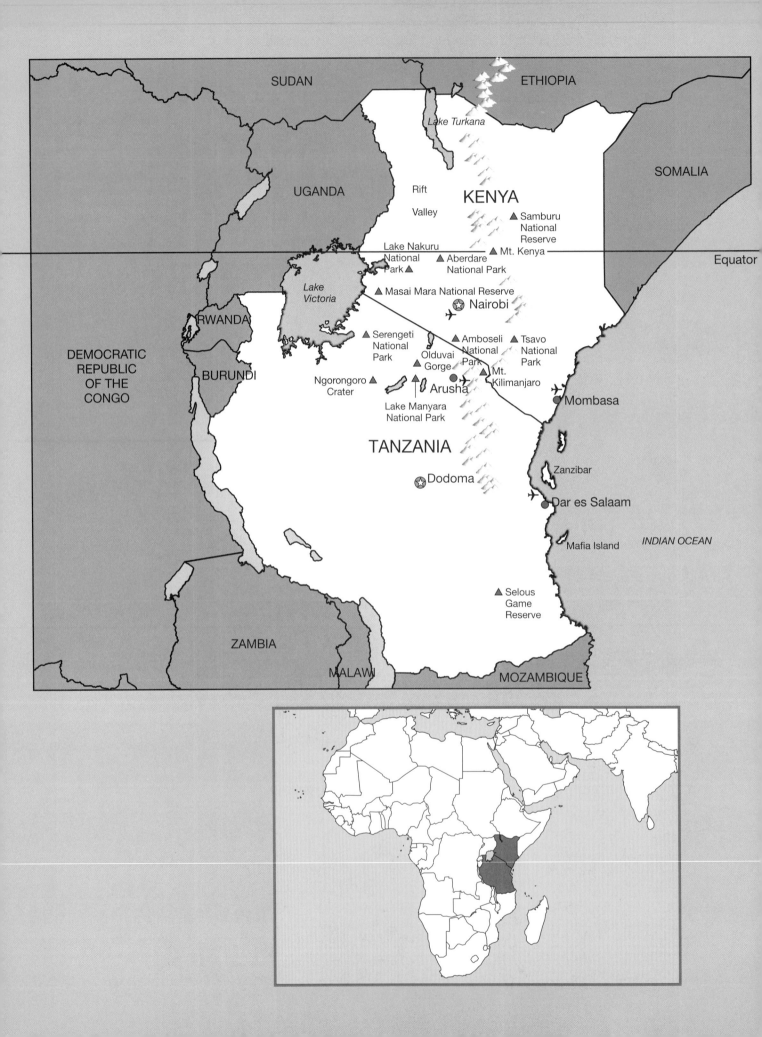

Chapter 23

Kenya and Tanzania
The Lion Sleeps Tonight

A herd of antelopes race and leap across the high grass of a seemingly unending savannah, as giraffes, zebras, and elephants rest at nearby watering holes. That one image defines both Kenya and Tanzania [tan-zah-NEE-ah], two of the most popular destinations for safaris in Africa. These countries not only protect and preserve their wildlife but also have made a mission of it. Their wildlife reserves and national parks attract considerable trade. That income has fuelled their drive to become among the greatest natural refuges for animals in the world. The lions do indeed sleep here—safely, majestically, and, unlike the title of the famous song, during the day as often as at night.

Kenya is located on the east coast of central Africa. Ethiopia lies to the north, Somalia and the Indian Ocean to the east. Uganda lies against Kenya's western border and Tanzania fronts the southern border.

About the size of Texas, Kenya is bisected by the equator. Also splitting the country, but from north to south, is the western region's **Rift Valley**, which continues south into Tanzania. **Nairobi**, the capital, is in south-central Kenya; most of the country's wildlife reserves can be reached in a few hours from here by road or by air. **Mombasa**, in the very southeast, along the coast, is Kenya's main seaport. Kenya also has nearly 400 miles of beaches along the warm waters of the Indian Ocean.

Tanzania is quite large: more than twice the size of California. To Tanzania's north are Kenya and Uganda, and to the south are Zambia, Malawi, and Mozambique; across Lake Tanganyika to the west is the Democratic Republic of the Congo. Also to Tanzania's west are the small countries of Rwanda and Burundi. Like Kenya, Tanzania is bordered on the east by the Indian Ocean, and has even more beaches. **Dodoma**, in the center of the country, is the new capital. **Dar es Salaam**, the former capital, is the major seaport and air gateway.

There's a wide mix of cultures and tribes in Kenya and Tanzania. Kenya's national language is Swahili, though English is widely spoken. Swahili and English are the official languages of Tanzania.

The name *Tanzania* is a composite of Tanganyika (the country's original name) and Zanzibar.

How Travelers Get There

The main gateway into Kenya is Nairobi, at **Jomo Kenyatta International Airport** (NBO). Flights also land in Mombasa (MBA). Flying time from New York is 13.5 hours. Many travelers will connect through Europe; because the flight to Kenya is so long, you might suggest a stopover. The national airline, **Kenya Airways** (KQ), and many international carriers fly here, most notably European ones. Mombasa is a common cruise departure

KENYA AND TANZANIA

CAPITALS: Kenya: Nairobi
            Tanzania: Dodoma

AREA (SQUARE MILES): Kenya: 225,000
                         Tanzania: 364,899

TIME ZONE: GMT +3

DRIVE ON: Left

POPULATION: Kenya: 38,000,000
              Tanzania: 40,200,000

RELIGIONS: Traditional, Christianity, Islam

LANGUAGES: Swahili, English

CURRENCY: Kenya: Kenyan shilling
            Tanzania: Tanzanian shilling

ELECTRICITY: 240 volts, 50 cycles AC

CAPSULE HISTORY: Kenya and Tanzania: First occupied by bushmen; herdsmen arrive from the north, Bantu tribesmen from the west, early A.D.; Arab traders settle on the coastal area, pre-Middle Ages; Portuguese explore, late 1400s.
Kenya: British occupy, late 1800s; British protectorate, 1895; British Crown colony, 1920–1963; Mau Mau revolt, 1952–1955; independence, 1963.
Tanzania: Portuguese and Arabs create Sultanate of Zanzibar, through mid-1800s; Tanganyika becomes German protectorate, 1886; becomes British protectorate, 1920; gains independence, 1961; merges with Zanzibar to become Tanzania, 1964.

For reference sources, tourist bureaus, and suggested lengths of stay, see the Appendices.

or return point for ships visiting the islands of Madagascar, Mauritius, and the Seychelles. Several European carriers land in Tanzania at **Kilimanjaro Airport (JRO)** or **Dar es Salaam International Airport (DAR)**. **Air Tanzania (TC)** services travelers within the country. Tanzania is also often accessed by land via Nairobi (and vice-versa).

Weather Patterns

The equator bisects Kenya; however, because of its generally high altitudes, the climate in much of the nation is cooler than you'd expect in an equatorial country (see Figure 23–1). The desertlike northerly regions of Kenya tend to be drier and hotter than the southern highlands; temperatures are fairly constant year-round.

Nairobi, in the south, ranges from an average high in the 70s to an average low in the 50s; the north runs about 10 degrees warmer. The only truly tropical climate is along the coast, where Mombasa is located. The main tourist season is November through February, but July through September is also popular.

Kenya's rain pattern is quite unusual. There are two rainy seasons: March through May (Kenyans call it "the long rains") and October through early December (called "the short rains"). Tanzania's daytime temperature is fairly steady year-round, with days in the low 80s, nights in the low 70s. Winter is the driest season; fall is the wettest. The mountain areas can get quite cold.

Getting Around

Because most people visit Kenya or Tanzania to see the wildlife, the most common way for them to travel is by minibus, four-wheel-drive vehicle, or small plane—usually as part of an organized safari tour (often booked through tour operators and/or hotels). Driving in

Safaris are no longer taken to kill animals, but to photograph them.

Climate at a Glance
NAIROBI, KENYA

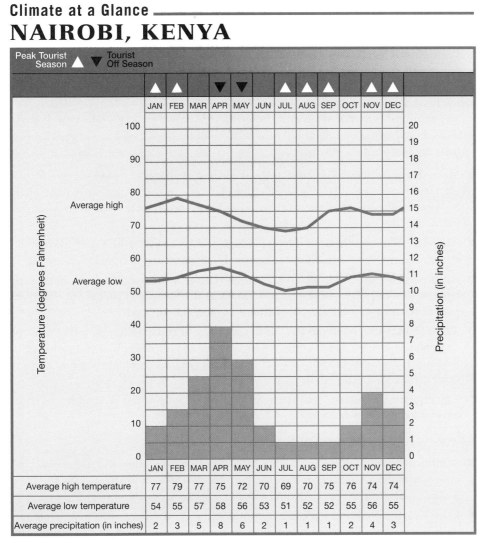

	JAN	FEB	MAR	APR	MAY	JUN	JUL	AUG	SEP	OCT	NOV	DEC
Average high temperature	77	79	77	75	72	70	69	70	75	76	74	74
Average low temperature	54	55	57	58	56	53	51	52	52	55	56	55
Average precipitation (in inches)	2	3	5	8	6	2	1	1	1	2	4	3

Figure 23–1

Kenya and Tanzania is on the left. The roads are often narrow, and unpredictable road conditions may make driving an unwise idea.

There's a fairly good rail system here, but very few tourists use it. Buses are crowded and uncomfortable. In Nairobi, the taxi system is good: Visitors have the choice of taking normal everyday cabs, or *matatus*, which pick up passengers and go to more than one destination. Finally, hot-air balloon trips over the sprawling grasslands have become increasingly popular, often as part of a safari.

People often ask what a safari is like. In brief, the group heads out into the bush to sleep in comfortable lodges and sets out early in the morning along bumpy, dusty roads to spot the animals when they're most active. The vehicles sometimes leave the road to get to where the animals are; the vehicle roof opens, which permits passengers to view the animals from safety, yet at close range.

Important Places

Most tourists visit Kenya in order to experience its remarkable wildlife. In fact, it helped pioneer travel safaris. Kenya has lost some of its tourism to Tanzania and other African countries (like South Africa, which we'll cover in Chapter 24). Nonetheless, it continues to have one of the most extensive tourism infrastructures on the continent.

Africa's tallest mountain and part of its largest lake are located in Tanzania.

Kenya

Nairobi, lying relatively near the equator, is a city of contrasts: at once sophisticated and primitive. The **Nairobi National Museum** has a top collection of African arts and crafts, as well as a superb explanation of Kenya's prehistory. **Nairobi National Park** provides a wide range of animals in their natural habitat and serves as a quick "sampler" of the safaris beyond.

The national parks and reserves are beautiful year-round, especially when vast herds of wildebeests and zebras are migrating. Almost 40 wildlife reserves exist in Kenya. The most popular of them are the following:

- **Masai Mara National Reserve**—perhaps the best of all—is the northern extension of the Greater Serengeti Plains, which borders Tanzania in the southwest. A particularly wide range of animals gathers here. Nearby is **Lake Victoria**, the world's second-largest freshwater lake.

- **Aberdare National Park**, in the central highlands, is noted for its waterfalls, rain forests, and banyan trees. **Mt. Kenya**, the second-highest mountain in Africa, is nearby.

- **Amboseli National Park** is on the Tanzanian border, southeast of Nairobi. In the early morning of a clear day, visitors can look across its flat borderland and see Mt. Kilimanjaro. Elephants are found in especially large numbers in Amboseli.

- **Tsavo [TSAH-voh] National Park** is in the southeast corner of Kenya, and also on the Tanzanian border. It's Kenya's largest national park and is divided into two parks: Tsavo East and Tsavo West. Tsavo is closer to Mombasa than it is to Nairobi and may be more easily accessed from that coastal city.

- **The equator** is a popular destination for tourists—if only to say, "I stood on the equator." It's located a few hours north of Nairobi.

Among the other destinations that Kenya offers:

- **Samburu National Reserve** looks a little different from other wildlife reserves; it's hilly and has thick foliage. It also has particularly exotic animals, such as the blue-necked Somali ostrich, Grevy's zebra, and all manner of crocodile.

- **Lake Nakuru National Park** is a beautiful refuge for a variety of animals, especially birds. It's located in southwestern Kenya, in the Rift Valley, northwest of Nairobi. It's most noted for its grand flock of pink flamingos.

- **Mombasa** is Kenya's main cruise port. Largely a Muslim city, it has a great many mosques. Excellent crafts shopping and some fine beaches and coral reefs are nearby.

Tanzania

The large town of Arusha usually serves as the departure and return point for the multiday safaris that visit Tanzania's many wildlife preserves.

The country's prime attractions lie mostly along the "Northern Crescent," which starts in Nairobi:

- **Serengeti National Park** is one of the world's most famous and finest wildlife preserves. Located in the north, this 5,700-square-mile park is best known for its herds—especially wildebeests and zebras—which migrate during May and June, and again in September. Serengeti National Park is also famous for its black-maned lions. Relatively nearby is the renowned **Olduvai [OLE-de-vay] Gorge**, where Dr. Louis Leakey discovered some of the earliest known fossils of humans.

- **Other wildlife reserves** can be visited here, as well. Among the best: the huge **Selous Game Reserve**, noted for its elephants, and **Lake Manyara National Park**, a small reserve with spectacular pink flamingos.

The snowcap and glaciers atop Mt. Kilimanjaro are receding. Global warming may be the cause.

Tanzania's Selous Game Reserve is bigger than Switzerland.

Zanzibar has some of Africa's finest beaches
Image copyright vera bogaerts, 2008. Used under license from Shutterstock.com

- **Ngorongoro** [eng-gore-on-GOH-roh] **Crater**, 10 miles across, shelters large numbers of lions, zebras, elephants, and rhinos; visitors can view them in the crater from four-wheel-drive vehicles. Most lodges are on the crater's rim, affording a great view and chilly nights (because of the altitude). The animals here are used to tourists, so it's easy to get very close viewings.

- **Zanzibar**, a large and pretty island that once was an independent country, has fine beaches and interesting Arabic architecture, notably in **Stone Town**. (Wonderful beaches are also found at Dar es Salaam and **Mafia Island**.)

- **Mt. Kilimanjaro**, the highest mountain in Africa, is a stunning sight. Adventurous visitors can hike to its snow-capped top in about six days, either on their own or, preferably, as part of a hiking group. September, October, January, and February are ideal for such hikes, because clouds often obscure the mountain at other times. (The best view, though, is from Kenya.)

Tribespeople (who had never seen snow) thought Mt. Kilimanjaro was topped with salt.

Possible Itineraries

Unlike most destinations, Kenya and Tanzania may be a different experience each time a visitor arrives—depending on which herds are migrating and which animals can be seen. Because each area of the region specializes in different species, tourists can easily spend at least a week here. Travelers visiting Kenya could start in Nairobi, visit Masai Mara and Aberdare, then head up to Mt. Kenya and Samburu. Those who want to spend more time could add Amboseli and Tsavo, or Mombasa and the coral beach towns. Visitors to Tanzania use Arusha as a gateway to Serengeti National Park, Ngorongoro Crater, and Mt. Kilimanjaro. Extensions to this itinerary could include Selous Game Reserve, or the beaches of Zanzibar (which also boast historical sites) and Mafia Island.

Lodging Options

Several major North American and European chains have hotels in the major cities of Kenya and Tanzania. What distinguishes lodging in both countries are the unique "lodges" that are near or in the wildlife reserves. Often built like large tribal huts—but more luxurious—these lodges offer wonderful meals, cultural entertainment, and the vehicles and guides that take visitors into the parks for wildlife-viewing safaris. Some are located near bodies of water or salt licks—it's sometimes possible to see animals right near the guestrooms. **Treetops**, a famous lodge located in Aberdare National Park, is built into trees.

Kenya's largest lodging chain is **Serena**. However, many hotels and lodges in Tanzania and Kenya are independently owned and operated and aren't part of chains.

Allied Destinations

If a trip to Kenya is to be extended, it most commonly would be to Tanzania, and vice versa. Most of the other countries in the region have political problems or limited tourist facilities, which make them improbable add-ons. (However, Ethiopia, Uganda, Malawi, and the Democratic Republic of the Congo are beginning to attract visitors.) Two other major

Princess Elizabeth was staying at the Treetops lodge when her father, King George VI, died. So she climbed up to her room as a princess and climbed down as queen.

Don't even consider sneaking home ivory or wildlife items (such as skins). It's illegal and it encourages poaching.

A lioness and her cub seem unbothered by a safari jeep just 20 feet away
Photo by Sharon Blair

destinations, Israel and Egypt, can be a stopover on the way from North America, as can various cities in Europe.

Cultural Patterns

Most tourists visiting Kenya and Tanzania do so on an organized safari. Still, it's important that they understand the special traditions of the region.

- In Kenya, pointing with an index finger is very insulting; use the whole hand. Don't use the left hand alone when passing or receiving an item. (This is true in Tanzania, as well.)
- Be prepared to give hearty handshakes on greeting a Kenyan. A "soft" handshake is considered effeminate. So, too, is the use of cologne by men, especially to those Kenyans who live outside urban centers.
- Some people feel that Tanzania now offers a better experience than does Kenya. Their belief: Tourism in Tanzania has been going on for less time than in Kenya. As a result, travel personnel are more eager to please and less jaded than those in Kenya.

Factors That Motivate Visitors

It's easy to figure out why people might want to visit Kenya and Tanzania. Among these reasons are:

- The wildlife is among the finest and most accessible in the world.
- Safaris are easily booked and provide safety in an adventurous environment.
- The culture is intriguing.
- Shopping choices are quite interesting.
- English is commonly spoken.
- Tanzania has sites of historical interest.
- There are lovely beaches.
- There's warm, pleasant weather year-round.
- Mombasa is a prime cruise embarkation and debarkation port.

Kenyans and Tanzanians greet people with the word *jambo!*

Mt. Kilimanjaro is actually made up of three volcanic cones
Image copyright enote, 2008. Used under license from Shutterstock.com

Qualifying the Traveler
Kenya and Tanzania

For People Who Want	High	Medium	Low	Remarks
Historical and Cultural Attractions		▲		Wildlife primary attraction but local cultures are fascinating
Beaches and Water Sports		▲		Near Mombasa; impressive coral reefs
Skiing Opportunities			▲	None
Lots of Nightlife			▲	Some in Nairobi
Family Activities		▲		Children love safaris
Familiar Cultural Experience			▲	
Exotic Cultural Experience	▲			
Safety and Low Crime			▲	Some turmoil in Kenya; check news for recent information
Bargain Travel			▲	Airfare and safaris can be expensive
Impressive Scenery	▲			A little of everything
Peace and Quiet		▲		Quietest on wildlife reserves; though animals can get noisy at night
Shopping Opportunities			▲	Local handicrafts
Adventure	▲			Safaris
To Do Business			▲	

Possible Misgivings

Kenya and Tanzania are beautiful yet challenging countries. Some typical objections are:

- "It's so far." Break up the trip with European or Middle Eastern stops.
- "There's a danger of disease." Kenya and Tanzania can be quite safe so long as the traveler checks with a doctor before leaving the United States and takes necessary precautions. And be sure to pack insect repellent and sunscreen.
- "African languages make it impossible to communicate." English is widely spoken in both countries.
- "The water and food can make you sick." Drink bottled liquids and make sure that food is properly prepared.
- "All there is to do is go on a safari." There are also some very nice coral beaches off the east coast. However, this may be the wrong destination for people who don't like safaris, though hiking, shopping, and cultural exploration are all valid reasons to visit these countries.
- "It's so expensive to get there." It can be expensive, but costs within the countries are reasonable. An all-inclusive package tour can help keep prices under control.

Most tourists travel between wildlife reserves via small, fixed-wing aircraft. The pilot will also serve as baggage handler and flight attendant.

■ "It's dangerous." Crime does occur, often with a great deal of publicity and usually in big cities, like Nairobi. Check on any advisories. An escorted safari with a reputable company minimizes danger.

Sales Strategies

The best way to enhance a trip to Kenya or Tanzania is to book a package safari through a tour operator. For travelers who would rather take a less-structured trip, a private guide is a good alternative. A higher-class hotel is advisable; budget accommodations can be chancy. Because getting to Kenya and Tanzania takes so long and there's so much to see, tourists should lengthen their stay a few days to take full advantage of the region and to explore the less-visited reserves or coastal towns. A cruise would be a fine way to extend a trip. A multiday stopover in Europe might be a good way to break up the long flight from the United States. Finally, travelers may wish to offset the long flight by flying in first or business class.

Travel Trivia

Cultural Surprises

- In Kenya, the verbal "tch, tch" sound is considered an insult.

- The North American "OK" sign is obscene in Russia.

- In Switzerland, asking for salt and pepper while dining is an insult to the cook.

- The North American hitchhiking sign is obscene in Yugoslavia.

- To drink ice water with a meal is a peculiarly North American custom.

- In France, a salad is served after the main course, not before.

- In Japan, one should accept a gift with two hands.

- In Muslim countries, to show the soles of one's shoes while seated is very rude behavior.

NAME _____ **DATE** _____

MAP ACTIVITY

A traveler wants to visit the places listed below. Which number represents each on the map?

Place/Attraction	In/Near Which City/Park?	Number on Map
A. The tallest mountain in Africa	A. _____	A. _____
B. Kenya's National Museum	B. _____	B. _____
C. Wildlife reserve in northern portion of Serengeti Plains	C. _____	C. _____
D. Mt. Kenya	D. _____	D. _____
E. The major cruise port of Kenya	E. _____	E. _____
F. National park near Olduvai Gorge	F. _____	F. _____
G. Crater with many animals in it	G. _____	G. _____
H. Kenya's air gateway	H. _____	H. _____
I. Gateway to Tanzania's animal preserves	I. _____	I. _____
J. A Muslim city with many mosques	J. _____	J. _____

NAME _____   DATE _____

CASE STUDY

Dr. Ernest Rollo and his wife, Anne, are a couple in their late 60s. They've always taken their annual vacation on their own. This year they want to go to Kenya, but are wary about traveling there alone, so they've decided to take a package tour. They can go only in February.

Circle the answer that best suits their needs.

1 They want to visit as many national parks as possible. Which of the following would they probably *not* go to?

    Amboseli   Aberdare

    Mombasa   Tsavo

Why?

2 Which of the following tips would *not* be appropriate to pass along to the Rollos?

    You'll need to bring sweaters.   Zebra skins are great bargains.

    Exchange money only in a bank.   Drive on the left.

Why?

3 Which of the following services would *not* be good for you to book?

    Business class airfare   Accommodations in a lodge

    An Amazon cruise   A hot air balloon trip

Why?

4 The Rollos decide to extend their trip beyond just Kenya for a few days. What other nearby country might you suggest they visit?

    Tanzania   South Africa

    Morocco   Ivory Coast

Why?

NAME _____   **DATE** _____

CREATIVE ACTIVITY

Do you think the following famous people would like visiting Kenya and Tanzania? Why or why not? What specifically would appeal to them?

❶ Donald Trump (multimillionaire):

❷ Madonna (singer-actress):

❸ Homer Simpson (cartoon character):

❹ Oprah Winfrey (talk-show host):

❺ Tom Cruise (actor):

❻ Your teacher:

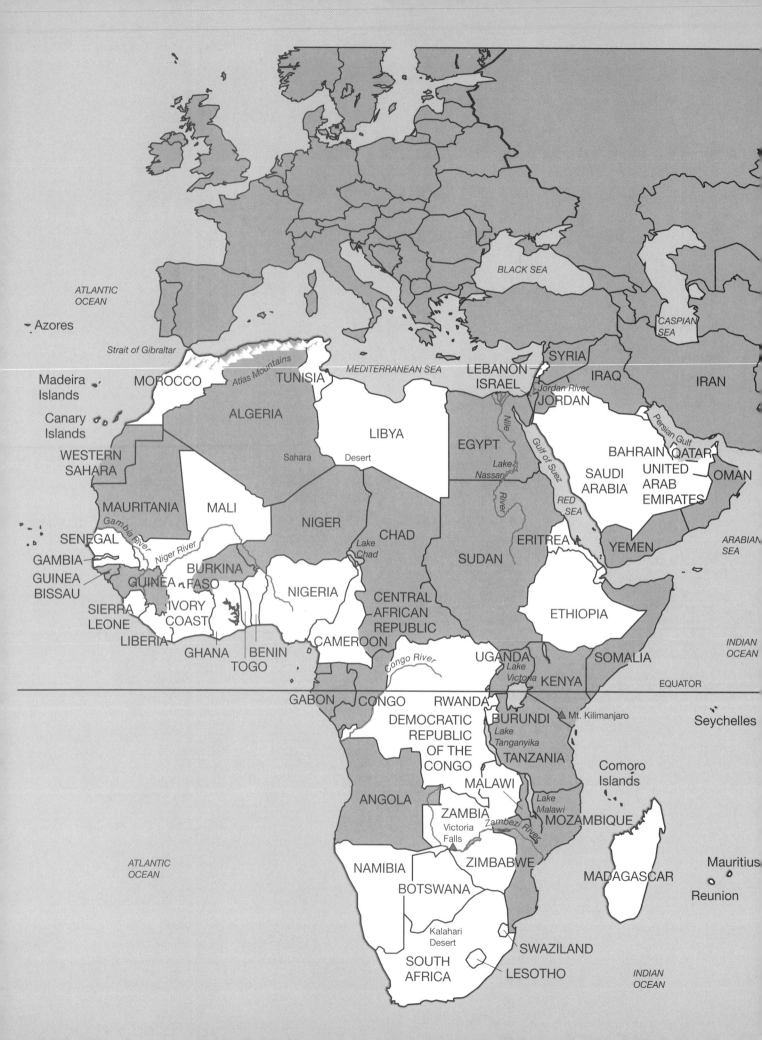

ATLANTIC
OCEAN

BLACK SEA

CASPIAN
SEA

Azores

Strait of Gibraltar

Atlas Mountains

MEDITERRANEAN SEA

LEBANON
ISRAEL

SYRIA

IRAQ

IRAN

Madeira
Islands

MOROCCO

TUNISIA

Jordan River

JORDAN

Canary
Islands

ALGERIA

LIBYA

EGYPT

Nile

BAHRAIN QATAR

WESTERN
SAHARA

Sahara   Desert

Lake
Nassar

Gulf of Suez

SAUDI
ARABIA

UNITED
ARAB
EMIRATES

OMAN

MAURITANIA

MALI

NIGER

CHAD

River

RED
SEA

Persian Gulf

ARABIAN
SEA

Gambia River

SENEGAL

Niger River

CENTRAL

Lake
Chad

SUDAN

ERITREA

YEMEN

GAMBIA

BURKINA
FASO

GUINEA
BISSAU

GUINEA

NIGERIA

AFRICAN
REPUBLIC

ETHIOPIA

INDIAN
OCEAN

SIERRA
LEONE

IVORY
COAST

LIBERIA

GHANA   BENIN
TOGO

CAMEROON

Congo River

UGANDA
Lake
Victoria

SOMALIA

KENYA

EQUATOR

GABON

CONGO

RWANDA

Mt. Kilimanjaro

Seychelles

DEMOCRATIC
REPUBLIC
OF THE
CONGO

BURUNDI

Lake
Tanganyika

TANZANIA

Comoro
Islands

MALAWI

ANGOLA

ZAMBIA

Lake
Malawi

Victoria
Falls

Zambezi River

MOZAMBIQUE

ATLANTIC
OCEAN

NAMIBIA

ZIMBABWE

Mauritius

BOTSWANA

MADAGASCAR

Reunion

Kalahari
Desert

SWAZILAND

SOUTH
AFRICA

LESOTHO

INDIAN
OCEAN

Chapter 24

African and Middle Eastern Potpourri

In describing the vast area that is Africa and the Middle East, writer John Gunther once said, "One travels like a golf ball, hopping from green to green." To Gunther, each "green" was a unique and exotic tourist destination: sacred sites, archaeological wonders, thundering waterfalls, great herds of exotic beasts. And such attractions aren't limited to the places we've already covered: Egypt, Kenya, Tanzania, Palestine, Jordan, and Israel. Africa and the Middle East constitute a huge region, brimming with attractions. So, to make Africa as easy as possible for you to know, we've divided this chapter into eight important regions of tourism.

Many of the emerging nations discussed in this section suffer from political and economic uncertainties. Each country's political situation can become dangerous, and quite quickly. You should continually check government travel warnings on current situations and keep up on the news. Remember, too, that disorganization and unpredictable levels of service often mark emerging countries such as these.

Morocco

American travelers are finding out what Europeans have long known: Morocco is one of Africa's most exotic yet accessible destinations. Often visited as a southern side trip from Spain or on a cruise, it's just a few miles across the Strait of Gibraltar. Most of its attraction cities lie along the cool and dry Mediterranean coast, while its inland area features broad, hot deserts and the **Atlas Mountains**. French and Arabic are the principal languages.

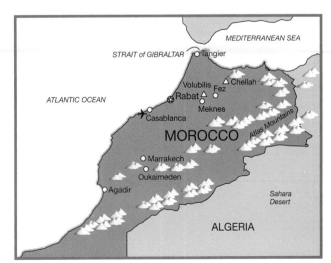

Important Places

- **Casablanca** (CAS) is Morocco's air gateway. All the ambience made famous by the film of the same name—the dimly lit nightclubs, narrow streets, frenetic **Casbah**—is really here. It also has several noteworthy churches and mosques (especially the **Hassan II Mosque**).

- **Rabat**, the capital, is a worthwhile day-trip destination from Casablanca. Its most famous landmark: the **Hassan Tower**, a lofty, 800-year-old minaret whose construction was halted upon the death of a sultan. Nearby is **Chellah**, the site of Roman ruins.
- **Tangier**, just across from Spain and Gibraltar, has long been a prime port of entry. As a result, cultures have mixed freely, resulting in Tangiers's renowned, diversified cuisine.
- **Fez** is Morocco's oldest city and a major center of the Islamic religion. Its *medina* (Arabic for marketplace) and old walled city section are usual tourist stops. Two major day trips from Fez: **Meknes**, often called the Versailles of Morocco; and **Volubilis**, the site of some of the best Roman ruins in North Africa.
- **Marrakech**, Morocco's most popular tourist destination, is usually reached by train from Casablanca. Its most fanciful attraction is **Djemaa el Fna Square**—with snake charmers, fortune tellers, food vendors, and nearby bazaar. Marrakech is also noted for its daily **Fantasia**—a feast of food, music, dance, and horse-mounted guards who, while firing their guns in the air, charge at people. Marrakech is also poised strategically between mountain and sea: **Oukaimeden**, an Atlas Mountain ski resort, is to the south; and **Agadir**, a beach resort, is to the southwest.

Sales Considerations

Morocco is relatively inexpensive, so it appeals to bargain hunters. It's sufficiently exotic for the adventurous, yet geographically and culturally close enough to Europe to make it appealing to more timid travelers. Street crime and health problems can be vexing; high-quality hotels, lodging in better areas, and escorted tours largely protect tourists from unpleasantness.

Northern Africa

This region—much of it covered by the **Sahara Desert**—exhibits a strong Arab influence. Bordered to the north by the Mediterranean Sea, a few of its destinations are close enough

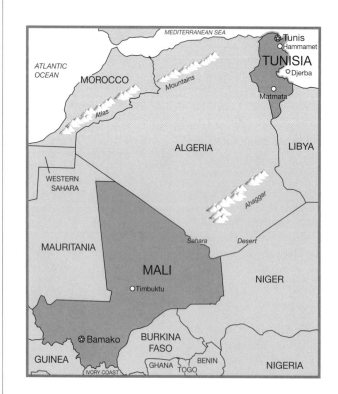

to Europe to be booked as day trips from there. And east of Northern Africa is the Middle East—technically a part of Asia.

Important Places

Northern Africa's destinations are among the most unusual on the continent. We've already discussed Egypt (in Chapter 21) and Morocco (in the previous section). We now cover the other countries.

Tunisia. On Africa's northern coast is Tunisia. Arabic and French are its national languages. With a long, winding coastline, much of the country is graced by a warm, breezy Mediterranean climate that's ideal for resorts; in fact, the first Club Med was built here. Winters can be rainy.

Tunis, the capital, lies in an area that in ancient days was part of the powerful city-state of Carthage. (You may remember from your history books how its general, Hannibal, nearly defeated the Roman Empire.) Today, Tunis boasts the **Bardo Museum** (with archaeological treasures), the **Medina** (the city's old quarter), and the **Great Mosque**. It's also an occasional port for Mediterranean cruises. About 10 miles away from Tunis are the ruins of Carthage itself. Most of the structures are Roman, not Carthaginian, as the Romans destroyed just about everything in 146 B.C. A visit to Tunisia often includes a visit to **Matmata**, an underground city where more than 6,000 people live. The island of **Djerba** has interesting ruins and beaches and is very popular among Europeans. In the north is **Hammamet**, a modern beach resort.

Libya. Long considered a hotbed for terrorism, Libya is becoming more friendly with the rest of the world. As a result, some adventurous tour operators have begun to offer trips there. Libya has some notable ancient Roman sites.

Mali. Mali's national languages are French and Bambara. Not much English is spoken here and tourist services are somewhat unreliable. It does have a city that almost everyone has heard of: Timbuktu, once one of the world's most inaccessible places. Timbuktu doesn't offer much to see—but then, that's sort of the point.

Ethiopia. Far to the east is Ethiopia, a country that features some interesting mosques, tombs, and palaces. **Addis Ababa** is the capital. The ancient town of **Aksum** (a major religious site) features ruins, the country's crown jewels, the **Palace of the Queen of Sheba**, and the **Church of St. Mary of Zion** (the *supposed* resting place of the Ark of the Covenant). Ethiopia is especially famous for its 11 remarkable churches carved out of solid rock. They're in the town of **Lalibela**. A visit to Ethiopia could coincide with a trip to Egypt or Kenya.

Eritrea. Eritrea has potential: Diving along its Red Sea coast is good and its capital, **Asmera**, has Italian-influenced architecture. The country has had on-again, off-again strife with its southern neighbor, Ethiopia.

The ancient Coliseum at El Jem, Tunisia, rivals the one in Rome.

Ninety-five percent of Libya is covered by sand.

Haile Selassie, Ethiopia's emperor from 1930 to 1974, once visited Jamaica and made such an impression that many Jamaicans still revere him deeply.

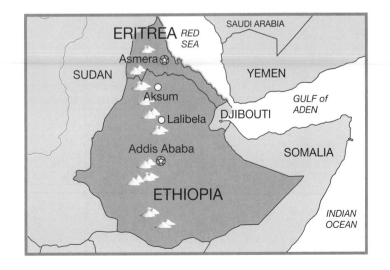

Sales Considerations

Northern Africa is strategically central to travel. The reason: It's just south of Europe (separated by only the Mediterranean), just west of the Middle East, and a gateway to the rest of Africa. Escorted tours, especially desert safaris, are popular here, because they wrap lodging and travel into one efficient package. This is a destination, though, that appeals mostly to bargain hunters, the adventurous, or those intrigued with desert culture. Its Mediterranean beaches offer some excellent opportunities for a resort stay, usually among European tourists.

The Middle East

The Middle East is one of the world's most newsworthy, volatile, and historically important regions. The political climate here fluctuates constantly. In normal times, tourists tend to visit Israel, Palestine, Jordan, and Egypt (all covered in previous chapters). Business travelers visit these countries, too, as well as those nations where oil is an important resource. The Middle East is bordered by Europe to the north, Africa on the west (in fact, Egypt—often considered part of the Middle East—is actually on the African continent), and Asia on the east. The Arabian Sea lies just to the south.

Important Places

Though few Westerners visit Syria, it has two remarkable ruins: a 2,000-year-old Roman city, Palmyra, and an 800-year-old Crusader castle, Crac des Chevaliers.

Religious sites and historical landmarks—that's what the Middle East is largely famous for. We've listed key nations in their order of importance to travelers.

Saudi Arabia. Taking up the bulk of the Arabian Peninsula is Saudi Arabia. In a region known for its religious significance, the Islamic beliefs and laws in Saudi Arabia—the birthplace of Mohammed—are among the strictest. Jordan and the Red Sea are to its west, Iraq and the Persian Gulf to the east, and Yemen and Oman to the south. There's limited direct air service here via North American carriers; more direct service is available via national carrier **Saudi Arabian Airlines** (SV) and by several European airlines. The main gateway is the capital, **Riyadh** (RUH), in the center of the country; travelers can also find international service on the western coast in **Jiddah** (JED), which is also the major port.

The climate in Saudi Arabia varies immensely from place to place, but daytime heat is a near constant. Temperatures in Riyadh climb from a spring and fall average in the 90s to the 100s in the summer; winters are cooler. Sandstorms can happen in any season. The national language is Arabic.

Some very significant religious destinations exist here, especially for Islamic pilgrims. Remember that Saudi Arabia conducts a great deal of business with Western countries.

- **Mecca**, Mohammed's birthplace, is the holiest city in the Islamic religion. This is a major pilgrimage destination—able-bodied Muslims must visit it at least once in their lives as part of a voyage called the *haj*—but it's closed to non-Muslim tourists. Two of the most sacred sites are the gigantic **Holy Ka'aba Shrine** and a huge mosque.

- **Medina**, where Mohammed is buried, is the second-holiest city to Muslims. Like Mecca, only Muslim pilgrims may enter the city.

- **Riyadh**, sitting in the middle of the desert, is a modern capital city. There are palaces, museums, and an old-city area.

- **Jiddah** is an interesting mixture of modern and old. There's lovely scenery, a good marketplace, several palaces, and an old-city quarter. Red Sea beaches are nearby. Snorkeling here is excellent.

The United Arab Emirates. Sitting on the eastern tip of the Arabian Peninsula is the small country of the United Arab Emirates (or UAE). Seven emirates (each led by an emir, an Islamic chief or commander) united to form this nation, which is extremely oil-rich. Like Kuwait to the north, it's mainly a business destination, but there are some historic buildings and small beach resorts for leisure travelers. **Gulf Air** (GF) has served the UAE for a long time. **Emirates Airline** (EK) has become a major airline, with an extensive network of long-distance air routes into and out of its hub city, **Dubai** (DXB).

- **Abu Dhabi**, one of the emirates and also the name of the capital of the UAE, has ancient ruins, an archaeological museum, and a popular open-air market. In addition, the city boasts a major Middle Eastern gateway at **Abu Dhabi International Airport** (AUH).

- **Dubai** (both a city and a UAE sheikhdom) has, in recent times, experienced astonishing growth. Its landmark building, the **Burj Al Arab Hotel**, rises just offshore like some gigantic ship's sail. Some consider it one of the most stunning achievements of modern architecture.

  What attracts people to Dubai other than business opportunities? Great shopping, safety, convenient air connections, and a few historical attractions, as well as to experience one of the most unusual places in the world. Some examples: Dubai has a 5.5-acre indoor ski slope with five ski runs on 3 feet of artificial snow. It has a manmade series of islands shaped like a palm tree, another like a giant world map. It will soon boast the world's tallest skyscraper. No idea seems too outrageous for Dubai.

Lebanon. Located north of Israel and west of Syria, Lebanon was once one of the most popular tourist destinations in the region, but decades of on-and-off strife have affected tourism. Potential attractions are **Beirut**, the capital city once known as the "Paris of the Middle East"; **Tyre**, with the remains of the ancient Phoenician civilization; **Baalbek**, with well-preserved Roman temple ruins; and **Byblos**, one of the oldest towns in the world.

Bahrain. Bahrain is a tiny, multi-island, oil-producing nation just off the east coast of Saudi Arabia in the Persian Gulf. Compared to many of its neighbors, the formerly British-dominated country is fairly sophisticated and has some active nightlife. **Bahrain Island**, where the capital city of **Manama** is located, has marketplaces, mosques, and minor archaeological sites. Bahrain's shores have some good beaches.

Sales Considerations

Leisure travelers may avoid this region because of its political volatility or the torrid climate. The Middle East will attract those who travel for religious or business reasons. It's also a prime location for those deeply interested in archaeology. Some good snorkeling, deep-sea fishing, and beach-resort opportunities exist here, though services aren't always up to Western standards. If political tensions ease, Iraq, Iran, and Syria—because their lands were so important in antiquity—could become viable tourist destinations.

Over four million Muslims visit Mecca each year.

There are bears in the mountains of Lebanon.

The ancient Babylonian civilization was centered on what is today Iraq.

The Burj Al Arab, a hotel that looks like a sailboat, was Dubai's first signature
building

West Africa

This region—largely of French culture—lies in the most recognizable area of Africa: along
the "crook" where the continent bends around the Gulf of Guinea. Reminder: Government instability, street violence, and other dangerous conditions can erupt in these places
quite suddenly.

Important Places

Though most of the nations in this coastal region are tiny, they offer many unique, seldom-
visited attractions.

Nigeria. The densely populated country of Nigeria is the most visited of western African countries, though most travelers come for business reasons (Nigeria is an oil producer)
or are tourists from places other than the United States. Its air gateway is **Lagos** (LOS), the
capital. Nigeria is often subject to political unrest.

Senegal. Steeped in Muslim culture, Senegal is the most westerly country in Africa.
Several European carriers offer limited service to **Dakar** (DKR), the capital. Summers here

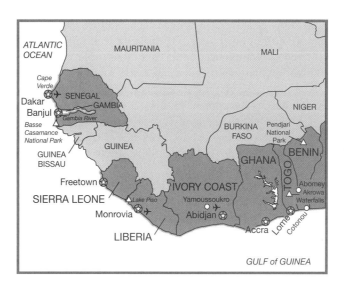

are quite hot and August is particularly rainy; Senegal's winters are very warm, with almost no rain. The official languages are French and several local dialects.

Among the places you should be aware of in Senegal:

- **Dakar**, a fairly sophisticated city on the central coast, was designed in a style reminiscent of Paris, with wide boulevards. Dakar is proud of its theater, ballet, museums, and fine beaches. Popular day-trip destinations include the historical harbor area of the **Island of Goree**, a place from which slaves were originally shipped out. Also, **Cape Verde** (not to be confused with the Cape Verde Islands, about 400 miles off the coast) features a rolling, volcanic landscape.

- **Cap Skirring** is a beach resort district not far from Senegal's best-known wildlife preserve, **Basse Casamance National Park**.

Ivory Coast. Also known as **Cote d'Ivoire** (its official name), Ivory Coast lies along the southern coast of Africa's western arm. The influence of French culture is even stronger here than in Senegal. There are limited flights from North America via a few European carriers. Its gateway is the capital of **Abidjan** (ABJ). Ivory Coast has a hot climate almost year-round; winters are largely rain free. French and various local dialects are the national languages. In recent times, Ivory Coast has suffered from severe political strife.

Ivory Coast does have one major attraction: **Our Lady of Peace**, a spectacular Roman Catholic cathedral that resembles St. Peter's in Rome and is one of the largest churches in the world. Located inland in **Yamoussoukro**, this granite, glass, and marble structure cost more than $200 million and was paid for by the country's then-president, Felix Houphouet-Boigny.

Liberia. Liberia began as a settlement of freed slaves from the United States. Its capital, **Monrovia** (founded in 1822), was named after U.S. President James Monroe. English is the official language; local dialects are also spoken. Monrovia boasts a fine museum and cultural arts center. **Lake Piso** is in a beautiful area on the northwest coast. Liberia occasionally suffers from serious political unrest.

Sierra Leone. On the west coast is the tiny nation of Sierra Leone. Settled by freed British slaves (English is one of its official languages), it is sometimes visited along with Liberia. Like its neighbor, it has suffered from sometimes severe political unrest. The capital, **Freetown**, is in a beautiful hilly area along the coast. A famous, centuries-old cotton tree stands near the **National Museum**, and several markets attract tourists. The country features wildlife preserves and several deluxe resorts.

The Gambia. The Gambia runs from the Atlantic Ocean through a thin slice of Senegal, along the **Gambia River**. English and tribal languages are spoken here. The country is best known as the starting point in Alex Haley's novel *Roots*; it remains a popular destination for African Americans. This former British colony has good beaches and fishing. **Banjul**, its quiet capital, is a base for trips through the country and along the river.

    Ghana. Well known for its colorful festivals, Ghana's capital is **Accra**. Scenic beaches (but with rough waters), oceanside castles and forts (which supported the slave trade), fishing, wildlife reserves, tribal ceremonies, and English-speaking locals account for Ghana's ever-increasing tourism.

    Togo. The tiny nation of Togo is wedged along the southern coast of the western arm. The country is known for its beaches and tribal culture. The capital, **Lome**, has much nightlife and an open-air market. The spectacular **Akrowa Waterfalls** is a bit of a challenge to get to from Lome.

    Benin. Formerly a French colony, Benin has begun to attract tourism. The country is generally visited out of **Cotonou**, where some modest lodging is available. Among the most popular day trips from Cotonou: **Ganvie**, a city of canals and houses on stilts; **Abomey**, with several ancient structures and offbeat shopping; and two wildlife parks.

> **Voodoo began in Benin, not Haiti.**

Sales Considerations

Though best known for wildlife safaris and the general friendliness of its people, West Africa presents some very good (and less-crowded) sites for adventurous tourists (though services are often below par). Beach resorts—some deluxe—dot the Gulf of Guinea. And ambitious travelers might like a trip up the Gambia River. Many of the nations here can be combined for an extended visit. Political unrest in some of these countries is often a problem; make sure to check current advisories.

The Central Safari Belt

The central portion of the African continent can be divided into two sections: the Safari Belt and the Victoria Falls region. The Safari Belt, especially, is what many people imagine when they think of Africa.

Important Places

> **Visitors to wildlife reserves hope to see Africa's "Big Five" animals: lions, leopards, rhinoceroses, elephants, and water buffaloes.**

Although Kenya and Tanzania are the most visited of the Safari Belt countries and are covered in their own chapter, they're not the only places with spectacular wildlife. The countries that follow are, in many ways, just as awe inspiring (though for the more adventurous). They're listed in order of importance to travelers.

Herds of elephants are a common sight on African safaris
Photo by Sharon Blair

Democratic Republic of the Congo. (Formerly Zaire, it must not to be confused with the Republic of the Congo, its neighbor to the west.) Almost directly in the center of the continent is the large Democratic Republic of the Congo. Once also known as the Belgian Congo, this is a nation of great tribal diversity (and rivalries). The country's transportation system is limited, often there's political unrest, and, unfortunately, crime is common. **Virunga National Park** is the country's finest and most scenic wildlife reserve. **Kahuzi-Biega National Park** is one of the few places in Africa where you can see gorillas in the wild.

Cameroon. Though considered part of central Africa, Cameroon lies on the hilly western coast, not far from the French-influenced West African nations. Less crowded than most other wildlife-reserve countries, Cameroon has a first-rate destination: **Waza National Park**, with its large herds of elephants.

Rwanda and Uganda. Most tourists to these two nations go to view mountain gorillas in the wild. The most popular parks for viewing these animals are **Parc National des Volcans** (Rwanda) and **Bwindi National Park** (Uganda). Both countries have suffered from political unrest. They're sometimes combined with trips to their neighbors: Kenya and Tanzania.

Sales Considerations

This region will appeal to the most hardy and adventurous travelers: animal lovers, mountain climbers, and water-sports aficionados. Escorted safaris are obviously popular. A trip here could be extended with a visit to the Victoria Falls region. Remember that political turmoil, banditry, disease, and unpredictable tourist services can be potential problems for those headed for the Safari Belt; as always, check for political advisories.

The Central Victoria Falls Region

South of the popular safari destinations of central Africa is another equally popular but vastly different area. The nations covered in this section are gloriously lush and harbor the awesome Victoria Falls.

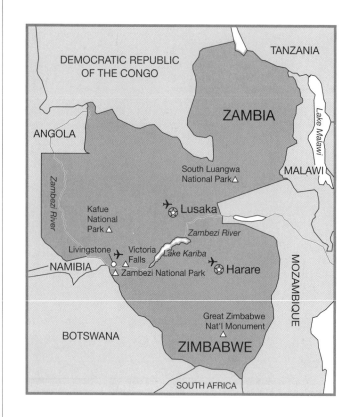

Important Places

Victoria Falls is one of the world's great natural wonders. However, this region offers many other beautiful attractions.

    Zambia. Located almost directly in the center of Africa's southern region is the land-locked country of Zambia (formerly Northern Rhodesia). **Zambian Airways** (Q3) is the major airline. European carriers bring travelers here via flights from Europe. The gateway is **Lusaka International Airport** (LUN) in the nation's capital. Zambia lies south of the equator, so its seasons are opposite those of North America. It's also mostly plateau country, so temperatures are less tropical than you'd think: in the 80s from September to December and in the 70s the rest of the year. Dry season extends from May to October. English and various tribal dialects are the national languages. Among the beautiful attractions in Zambia:

> *Victoria Falls is more than a mile wide.*

- **Victoria Falls,** on the **Zambezi River**, is an awesome sight. Period. It's many times the width of Niagara Falls. Visitors must not miss it if they're anywhere near the area. (They'll usually stay overnight at nearby lodging.) The Zambian town closest to the falls is **Livingstone**; the **Livingstone Museum** houses memorabilia of Dr. Livingstone, as well as 300-year-old African maps.

- **Kafue National Park** is a huge area with elephants and more than 400 species of birds.

- **South Luangwa National Park**, in the Luangwa Valley, is perhaps one of Africa's most richly stocked animal preserves. It's best visited during dry season.

> *The ruins of Great Zimbabwe are 1,200 years old.*

    Zimbabwe. Once known as Southern Rhodesia, Zimbabwe has had a troubling political situation for many years. Among the top attractions in Zimbabwe are **Victoria Falls** (seven-eighths of the Falls are on the Zimbabwe side), **Zambezi National Park** (along the shores of the Zambezi River), and **Great Zimbabwe National Monument** (featuring the most impressive African ruins south of the Sahara). Despite these remarkable attractions, tourism to Zimbabwe has plummeted because of deep political unrest and widespread violence.

Sales Considerations

Victoria Falls is what brings tourists to the region. When people visit the Falls, they often take a "Flight of Angels." This aerial view of the rushing waters is stunning. Though there are animal reserves in the region, its main attraction is the spectacular scenery. But the adventurous will surely have a great time here: Safaris, walking tours, river rafting on the Zambezi, and boat excursions are all popular.

Southern Africa

Though the nation of South Africa dominates the region's tourism, quite a few other countries are here as well. Nestled into the very bottom of Africa, the area is bordered by both the Atlantic and Indian oceans, ending in the south at the famous, scenic, and often visited **Cape of Good Hope**, a geographic attraction that marks where the two oceans meet.

The best time to take a safari here is in the winter, when more animals gather.

Important Places

With the elimination of its racial apartheid policy, South Africa—one of the most physically beautiful and Westernized nations of Africa—has regained its popularity as a tourist destination. In fact, South Africa has become a destination that rivals Kenya and Tanzania. The other countries within or near South Africa (**Lesotho, Swaziland,** and **Botswana**) are attracting many visitors, as well.

South Africa. South African Airways (SA)—the national airline—flies to South Africa, Africa's southernmost country, as do several European carriers (for East Coast cities) and Asian carriers (an alternative for West Coast cities). Air gateways are **Pretoria** (PRY), the administrative capital, located in the northeast; **Johannesburg** (JNB); and **Cape Town** (CPT), the legislative capital, on the southwest coast. In addition, cruises that visit southeast Africa and its islands start or end at Cape Town.

In South Africa, traffic signals are sometimes called "robots."

South Africa's subtropical, southern California–like climate is pleasant all year, though September to November (spring) is best. South Africa is south of the equator and its seasons are opposite those of North America. Most of the country is dry; indeed, the arid **Kalahari Desert** covers much of the northwest. The **Drakensberg Mountains** (lying southeast and east) and interior plateaus tend to have cooler temperatures and some rain, which falls from May to September. The official languages are Afrikaans and English. Among the remarkable attractions in South Africa:

Africa produces more gold and diamonds than any other continent.

- **Johannesburg** (often referred to as Jo'burg), south of Pretoria, is an active city and the nation's gold-mining center. There are tours and a museum at **Gold Reef City**, as well as other nearby mines. You can suggest a long day trip to **Kimberley**, the diamond-mining center, where tours of the mines are offered. A few miles from central Johannesburg is **Soweto**, a township where the anti-apartheid movement began and ultimately triumphed. (Apartheid was a countrywide policy of strict racial segregation.) A popular museum here explains the history of apartheid. The hero of the anti-apartheid movement, Nelson Mandela, was imprisoned at **Robben Island**, also now a popular tourist attraction. Johannesburg serves as a jump-off spot for trips to most of South Africa's major wildlife refuges. It does, however, have a problem with crime. It's best to stay at a hotel that's located in the safer, upscale parts of the city.

- **Sun City**, a two-hour drive northwest of Johannesburg, is sometimes known as the "Las Vegas of Africa." Its casinos, theme attractions, and resort hotels draw many visitors. Especially astonishing is the **Lost City Resort**, with fake ruins, a 62-acre forest, simulated ocean waves, and the immense, ornate **Palace of the Lost City** hotel.

The owner of the biggest hotel in Sun City also developed the giant Atlantis Paradise Island resort in the Bahamas.

- **Cape Town**, one of the world's most beautifully situated cites, lies near the edge of the Cape of Good Hope. It has good beaches, vibrant nightlife, a busy waterfront shopping area, and several excellent hotels. **Table Mountain**, reached by cable car, provides grand vistas. There's an especially beautiful "Garden Route" drive from Cape Town to **Port**

Elizabeth, which has great beaches and vistas. Several "wine routes" lie east of Cape Town—it's estimated that the region has over 3,000 wineries.

■ **Durban**, on the southeast coast, is a fashionable, multicultural resort that's very popular with vacationing South Africans. Its "Golden Mile" beach is lined with restaurants, gardens, and shops.

■ **Kruger National Park**, in the northeast, is a 7,722-square-mile wildlife reserve that matches those of Kenya and Tanzania for attracting foreign visitors. June through October are prime months for animal watching here.

■ **Zululand**, once a separate territory, provides seven wildlife reserves. Visitors learn about the Zulu culture at craft centers and the **Zululand Historical Museum**, and can even spend the night in a Zulu hut.

■ **The Kalahari Gemsbok National Park**, which is quite remote, has a varied collection of animals. The Kalahari Desert's boundaries cross over into Namibia and Botswana.

■ **Sabi Sand**—a collection of private reserves—is perhaps the finest place in South Africa for wildlife viewing. Its most famous reserve is **MalaMala**. Adjacent to Kruger National Park, Sabi Sand is also less crowded than many of the public preserves. Luxurious safari lodges are available and animals are viewed from open vehicles, with some of the most close-up viewing of animals in all of Africa.

Lesotho. Lesotho, sometimes called the "Switzerland of Africa," is surrounded by the nation of South Africa. Criss-crossing this tiny country are beautiful mountains and even ski facilities.

Swaziland. Like Lesotho, Swaziland is a small, independent, picturesque country. It harbors a surprising number of wildlife reserves.

Namibia. Lying along the Atlantic and bordering South Africa to the northwest is Namibia. It's becoming a popular safari destination: **Etosha National Park** is a beautiful park and wildlife preserve, as is **Fish River Canyon National Park**. The **Namib Desert** landscape and wildlife are magnificent. **Skeleton Coast**, nestled in the north between the ocean and desert, is the historical site of many sunken ships and moonlike landscapes.

Botswana. Sandwiched between Namibia and Zimbabwe, Botswana has some of the finest and most uncrowded wildlife preserves in Africa, as well as a wide spectrum of accommodations, from upscale lodges to tented camps. Two parks in the north are especially well known: **Chobe National Park** (with more than 100,000 elephants) and **Moremi Game Reserve**. The latter occupies a portion of the **Okavango Delta**, one of the greatest homes for wildlife in the world. Northern Botswana is relatively near Victoria Falls, too;

The Skeleton Coast got its name from the many ships that were wrecked and lost there.

The Okavango is one of the world's only inland deltas.

Yes, penguins—in Africa (near Cape Town)—and they make sounds like donkeys
Photo by Sharon Blair

a visit to Botswana's reserves is often combined with a trip to the Falls. Botswana has the oldest democracy and one of the most stable governments in Africa, and is especially concerned with preserving its wildlife.

Sales Considerations

Southern Africa will appeal to those who admire beautiful scenery, bargains, good weather, and safaris. There are also some world-class beach resorts and good skiing (though lodging tends to be simple, not luxurious). Gold- and diamond-mining tours are popular (but diamonds here are no less expensive than elsewhere). Reservations, especially at or near the wildlife reserves, need to be booked very far in advance. The **Blue Train** is legendary and offers a luxurious and unique way to see the region between Cape Town and Pretoria. The 1,000-mile trip takes about 27 hours, with passengers sleeping overnight in one of the train's private compartments. (Each compartment has a bathroom with shower or tub.) **Rovos Rail** operates vintage trains from Cape Town to Victoria Falls.

Afrikaans, a language spoken by many South Africans, was derived from Dutch.

The African Islands

In the Indian Ocean off the southeast coast of Africa are a number of islands that draw tourists; the largest of these by far is **Madagascar**, but others offer finer, more developed attractions. Indeed, **Mauritius** [moh-RIH-shus] is one of the world's more popular island destinations. There are also some islands off the northwest coast, most notably the **Canary Islands**.

Important Places

The islands that surround Africa are largely neglected by American tourists. Part of the reason is that they're simply not well known. These islands are wonderful destinations and are growing in popularity. We've ordered them in their importance to travelers.

   The Seychelles [say-SHELLS]. Nearly 1,000 miles east of Kenya and lying northeast of Madagascar, the Seychelles is actually made up of 115 tiny islands. There's limited service from North America by European carriers; **Air Seychelles** (HM), the national carrier,

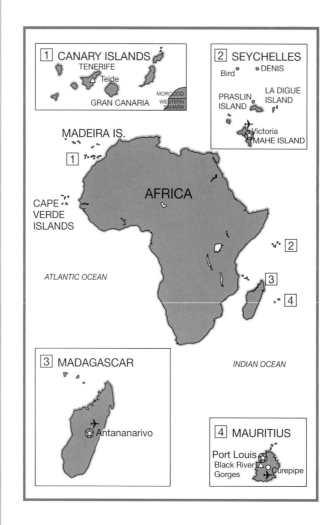

also flies from Europe, South Africa, and Singapore. The gateway is **Seychelles International Airport** (SEZ), near the capital of **Victoria** on Mahe [ma-HAY] Island. There's air service among the country's various islands.

The Seychelles' climate is generally warm and balmy, and its look is absolutely distinctive among tropical islands: unusually shaped granite boulders line many areas. Being south of the equator, its seasons are opposite those in North America. Creole English and French are the national languages in this British-influenced country. Among its finest sights:

- **Mahe Island**—the most populous—has great beaches, beautiful gardens, and a lovely, mountainous national park. Mahe offers especially superb snorkeling and diving. Suggest a car rental; the drive around the island is spectacular.

- **Praslin** [prah-LIN] **Island** has good facilities as well, to go with its wonderful scenery and beaches. Its **Vallee de Mai Nature Reserve** contains the remnant of a primeval palm forest. Twenty-one miles from Mahe, Praslin is reached by either boat or plane.

- **La Digue** [DIG] **Island**, a 15-minute boat ride from Praslin, has spectacular rock formations at **Union Beach**.

- **Animal sanctuaries** can be found throughout the Seychelles; among the most notable are **Bird Island** and **Denis Island**.

Mauritius. Mauritius lies 500 miles east of Madagascar. **Air Mauritius** (MK), the national carrier, flies here from Europe and Africa, and a few European airlines depart from their home countries, landing at **Sir Seewoosagur Ramgoolam Airport** (MRU) on the southeast coast. Spring and fall are lovely seasons here, with average temperatures in the 80s. June to August can get pretty chilly, whereas December through February is rainy. Once under British control, the dense population here is mixed, which is reflected by its

Mauritius was home to the weird dodo bird, which became extinct shortly after Europeans settled the island in the 1600s.

official languages: English, French, Creole, and Hindi. Mauritius is a major getaway destination for European vacationers. It features some lovely attractions, including:

- **Port Louis**, the capital, which is on the northwest coast. Several museums, gardens, and an aquarium are located in Port Louis. There are some examples of interesting architecture and an enjoyable marketplace.
- **Abundant beaches and coral reefs**. The resorts are low-key and relaxed, the diving and deep-sea fishing excellent.
- **Black River Gorges National Park**, with beautiful views and gorgeous scenery.
- **Curepipe** [cure-PEEP], a fairly cosmopolitan town that offers excellent shopping.

Madagascar. Madagascar, the fourth-largest island in the world, is almost the size of Texas. It lies east of Mozambique, about 240 miles from the coast of southern Africa. Formerly under French control, Madagascar has a wide variety of assets: rain forests, semideserts, mountains, and excellent beaches. It's very famous for its lemurs (primitive primates) and unique species of plant life. The national airline is **Air Madagascar** (MD). Attractions in the central capital and main gateway, **Antananarivo** (TNR), include a palace, a zoo, and botanical gardens. Remember that Madagascar's tourist facilities are much more limited than those on the nearby Seychelles.

The Canary Islands. In the Atlantic off the northwest coast of Africa are the Canary Islands. Provinces of Spain, they offer volcanic scenery, superb beach resorts, and a pleasant year-round climate, especially during the dry and warm summers. Its two most important islands are **Gran Canaria** and **Tenerife** (Spain's highest mountain, **Teide**, at 12,198 feet, is here).

Other islands off Africa's western and northwestern coasts are Portugal's **Cape Verde**, **Madeira**, and **Azores** islands. Of the three, only the Azores have any sort of major tourism. The Azores are most pleasant in the summer, with air temperatures in the 80s and water temperatures in the low 70s. However, winters tend to be gray, wet, and chilly.

Sales Considerations

Almost all the African islands have magnificent beaches and superb scenery. These islands are attractive to people looking for a warm, sunny destination with great water-sports opportunities and who are willing to traverse long distances to get there. Snorkeling and deep-sea fishing are ideal here. This is also a wonderful region for naturalists. Both the Atlantic and Indian Ocean island groups are often part of cruise itineraries; it's a great way to combine an island package with a mainland one.

Eighty percent of Madagascar's plants are found nowhere else.

Yes, canary birds are native to the Canary Islands.

Madeira wine is indeed named after the Madeira Islands.

Travel Trivia

What They Used to Be Called

Current Name	Old Name	Current Name	Old Name
Ethiopia	Abyssinia	Vanuatu	New Hebrides
Democratic Republic of the Congo	Zaire, Belgian Congo	Iran	Persia
		Zambia	Northern Rhodesia
Belize	British Honduras	Zimbabwe	Southern Rhodesia
Mali	French Sudan	St. Petersburg, Russia	Leningrad, U.S.S.R.
Sri Lanka	Ceylon	Thailand	Siam
Bangladesh	East Pakistan	Tanzania	Tanganyika and Zanzibar
Ghana	Gold Coast		
Suriname	Dutch Guiana		

NAME _____   **DATE** _____

MAP ACTIVITY

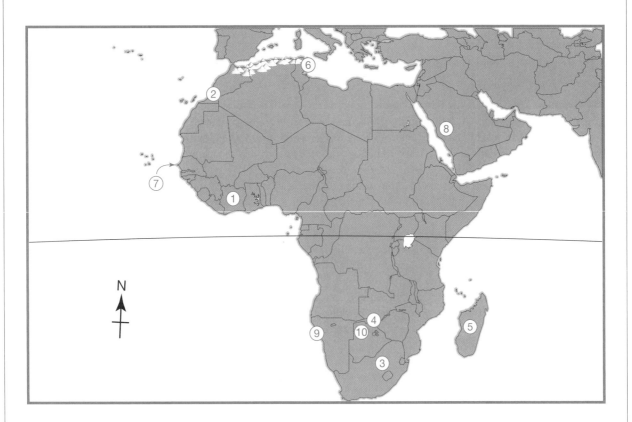

A traveler wants to visit the places listed below. Which number represents each on the map?

Place/Attraction	In Which Country?	Number on Map
A. Carthage	A. _____	A. _____
B. Victoria Falls and the Livingstone Museum	B. _____	B. _____
C. Djemaa el Fna Square	C. _____	C. _____
D. Our Lady of Peace Cathedral	D. _____	D. _____
E. Gold and diamond mines	E. _____	E. _____
F. Lemurs	F. _____	F. _____
G. The Island of Goree	G. _____	G. _____
H. Mecca	H. _____	H. _____
I. The Skeleton Coast	I. _____	I. _____
J. The Okavango Delta	J. _____	J. _____

NAME _____ **DATE** _____

CASE STUDY

Mike and Carolyn Robitaille usually take their vacations in Europe, but three years ago they tried something different: a safari in Kenya. The couple, in their early 50s, had a wonderful time. They loved the wildlife, and everything about the trip was so well organized that it was much easier than they thought it would be. They've decided to go back to Africa.

Circle the answer that best suits their needs.

1 Having gotten their feet wet, the Robitailles feel that it's time to get a little more adventurous. And as much as they enjoyed Kenya, they don't want to repeat the trip, preferring to see some different animals, if possible. Which country should they visit?

South Africa   Morocco

Niger   Ivory Coast

Why?

2 They decide not to limit their experiences in Africa merely to safaris; they want to enjoy a different part of the continent's dramatic attractions, as well. To what scenic area should they extend their trip?

Tarzan's tree house   Iguazu Falls

Victoria Falls   Lake Tanganyika

Why?

3 The Robitailles decide that, after all, they do prefer a more relaxed, less adventurous trip; it's been a hard year. They'd still like to see some wildlife, but also miss the charms of Europe and wouldn't mind stretching out on the beach for a few days. Where would you suggest?

Bahrain   Zambia

Ethiopia   Senegal

Why?

4 What services would be appropriate for the Robitailles?

An escorted tour   A budget hotel

A stopover in South America   First-class rail tickets to Mauritius

Why?

NAME _____   DATE _____

CREATIVE ACTIVITY

Ecotourism—tourism driven by a desire to see places in their natural state—has become a significant and profitable segment of the tour business. You're an itinerary planner for a tour company that has decided to sell a 15-day ecotour of Africa, starting and ending in Nairobi.

How would you construct the tour? Where would you go? Describe your tour below, remembering to set aside a day each time the group flies from one country to another. (Assume there are air connections between each place; no need to look them up.) And be sensitive to what ecotourists might want to see.

Day	City/Place or Country	Activity
1	Nairobi	Orientation meeting for group; reception dinner
2		
3		
4		
5		
6		
7		
8		
9		
10		
11		
12		
13		
14		
15	Nairobi	Free day; departure late in day

NAME _____   DATE _____

PUTTING IT ALL TOGETHER

The Matching Game

Below is a list of cities, attractions, and so on, some of which we have covered, some of which we haven't. There are all manner of connections among them. With a group of fellow students, you have exactly 10 minutes to come up with as many connections as possible. (Items may be used more than once.) Write your answers below. Note: There are at least 20 possible connections; for example, Dakar and Nairobi—both are capital cities.

Lost City	Haifa	Sinai
Sultan Hasan	Alexandria	Zambezi
Dome of the Rock	Eilat	Mt. Kilimanjaro
Kalahari	Jomo Kenyatta	Okavango
Masai Mara	Dakar	Nile
The Ark	Mombasa	Sacred Heart
Zanzibar	Great Mosque	Ngorongoro
Ben Gurion	Serengeti	Hurghada
Ka'aba	Canary	Tel Aviv
Nairobi	Madagascar	Our Lady of Peace

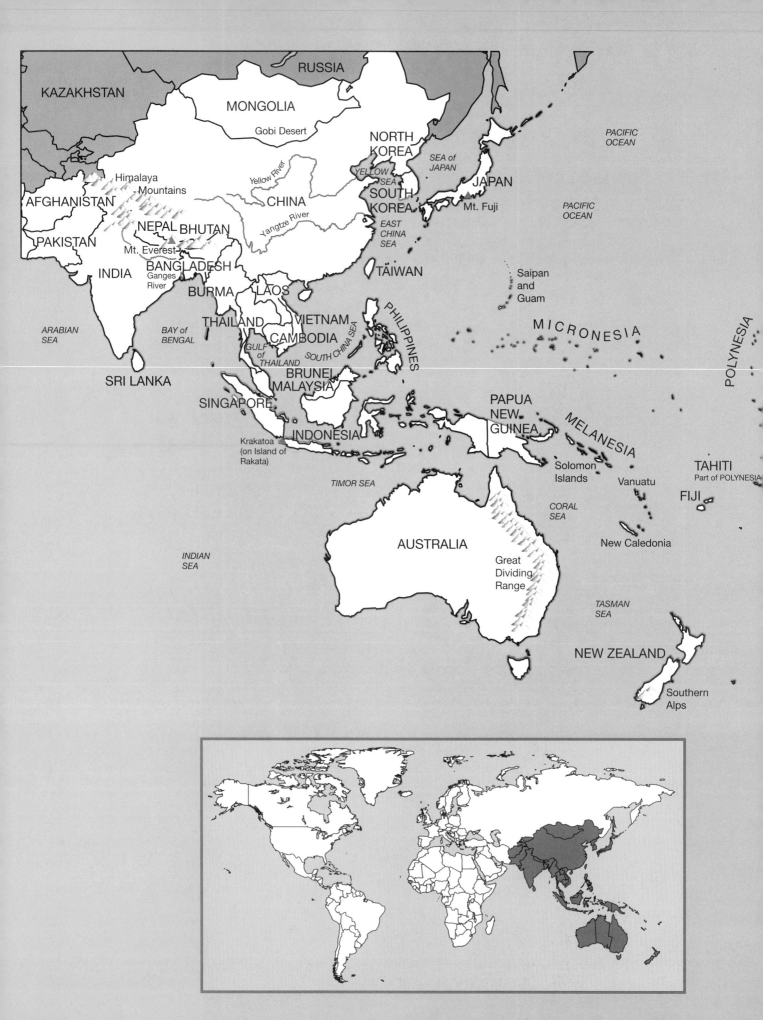

KAZAKHSTAN

RUSSIA

MONGOLIA

Gobi Desert

NORTH KOREA

SEA of JAPAN

PACIFIC OCEAN

Himalaya Mountains

Yellow River

CHINA

YELLOW SEA

JAPAN

AFGHANISTAN

SOUTH KOREA

Mt. Fuji

PACIFIC OCEAN

PAKISTAN

NEPAL BHUTAN

Yangtze River

EAST CHINA SEA

Mt. Everest

INDIA

BANGLADESH

Ganges River

BURMA

LAOS

TAIWAN

Saipan and Guam

ARABIAN SEA

BAY of BENGAL

THAILAND

VIETNAM

CAMBODIA

SOUTH CHINA SEA

PHILIPPINES

MICRONESIA

POLYNESIA

GULF of THAILAND

SRI LANKA

SINGAPORE

BRUNEI MALAYSIA

INDONESIA

PAPUA NEW GUINEA

MELANESIA

Krakatoa (on Island of Rakata)

Solomon Islands

Vanuatu

TAHITI
Part of POLYNESIA

TIMOR SEA

CORAL SEA

FIJI

INDIAN SEA

AUSTRALIA

Great Dividing Range

New Caledonia

TASMAN SEA

NEW ZEALAND

Southern Alps

PART VI

ASIA AND THE PACIFIC
Rim of Mystery

In the great courts of Europe, word had spread about the fabulous riches—both cultural and physical—that existed off in the far, mysterious East. But no one truly knew what was there until Marco Polo traveled to the Orient and returned with stories and treasures that dazzled the Europeans of his day.

Asia and the Pacific still offer treasured opportunities to those who visit the far rim of the Pacific. Yet 700 years after the great explorer made his journey, the Far East is still poorly understood by travelers, even though they may drive Japanese cars, buy Korean DVD players, and watch Australian movies.

With the growth in trade among Pacific Rim nations has come a major growth in travel. Fifty years ago, most North Americans would never have considered visiting Asia or the Pacific islands—not only because of closed cultures but also because of the sheer physical logistics. However, with the advent of long-distance jumbo jets, the Far East is not much more than a half-day away.

In days past, even crossing the International Date Line was a major event—a celebration. Today, a pilot merely informs the plane's passengers about it—assuming, of course, that they hear it through their mid-Pacific doze.

Where the Countries Are

Tourists and geographers don't always think alike. For instance, where exactly does Asia start and Africa and Europe end? Most geographers consider everything to the east of the Red Sea and the Ural Mountains to be Asia—and that includes the Middle East, Turkey, and the majority of Russia.

However, parts of the Middle East are often booked as part of a trip to Europe or Africa. Few tourists ever visit Russia in conjunction with a vacation to China; more likely, a Russian vacation is tied to a trip to Scandinavia. And Turkey is most commonly accessed as an extension of a Greek island cruise. As a result, we've covered some of Asia's 40 or so countries in previous sections, to relate them to realistic tourist itineraries.

What's the most obvious place on a map of Asia? **China**, which physically dominates most of the continent. It dwarfs **Mongolia**, which borders it to the north, and **North** and **South Korea**, which take up the peninsula on its northeastern corner. (Communist North Korea is rarely visited by Westerners and therefore won't be covered here.)

Off China's east coast is a string of island-nations; from north to south: **Japan**, **Taiwan**, and the **Philippines**. Continuing south, you encounter the multi-island nation of **Indonesia** and **Malaysia**, along with **Singapore**. On the Southeast Asian mainland are **Thailand**, **Vietnam** (with its swiftly emerging tourism), and the less visited **Cambodia**, **Laos**, and **Myanmar** (better known by its traditional name, **Burma**). Below China and to

The words *orient* and *oriental* come from the Latin word for the East, *oriens*, because Asia was to the east of the Roman Empire. This also explains the "Near East" (today's Turkey), "Middle East" (the now-Muslim nations beyond Turkey), and the "Far East" (China, Japan, etc.).

Some scholars now suspect that Marco Polo never actually reached China, but made up many of his descriptions.

the west of Southeast Asia is the large area known as the Indian subcontinent. From west to east, it includes **India, Nepal**, and **Bhutan** (as well as less-visited **Pakistan, Bangladesh**, and **Sri Lanka**). Also in Asia are five independent nations of the former Soviet Union. **Azerbaijan** and **Uzbekistan** are the most important of these.

The islands of the Pacific may seem to be a great distance from Asia, but some of them are much closer to the continents of Asia or **Australia** than to the Americas: **Papua New Guinea** and **Fiji** (both parts of Melanesia) are relatively close to Australia and Indonesia; the Micronesian islands of **Saipan** and **Guam** are to the east of the Philippines. For this reason, visits to Asia can easily be combined with stopovers at Pacific islands. Though the tens of thousands of Pacific islands are clearly much too numerous to mention, the major ones are (from west to east): **New Zealand, Fiji, Tahiti** (one of the Polynesian islands), and the state of Hawaii (which is closest—about five hours—to the North American mainland and which we covered in Chapter 7).

A Satellite View

Looking down on Asia and the Pacific, it would be easy to distinguish the larger islands among the area's oceans and seas. The Asian continent is another matter; it blends into Europe and the Middle East (and therefore Africa, as well).

Perhaps the most noticeable feature of the entire region is how flat much of it is. Most of western China is desert (notably the **Gobi Desert**), as is the western two-thirds of Australia. Much of Southeast Asia, too, is flat rainforest.

However, the exceptions to this flatness are dramatic and have an overwhelming impact on the region (e.g., the Himalaya Mountains). To properly plan trips to this region, it's essential to fully understand the lay of the land.

Bodies of Water

As you would imagine, the **Pacific Ocean** is critical to this vast region. Moreover, the continent of Asia, being as large and geographically situated as it is, is ringed by an assortment of seas.

Beginning at the western part of Asia is India, which is bordered on its west by the **Arabian Sea**, on its south by the **Indian Ocean**, and on its east by the **Bay of Bengal**. Farther east is the **Gulf of Thailand**, in the midst of Southeast Asia; the Gulf, in turn, flows into the **South China Sea**.

The **Sea of Japan** separates Russia and the Korean peninsula from Japan. The **Yellow Sea**—which forms a bay between northeast China and Korea—empties into the **East China Sea**, which in turn merges into the South China Sea. Bordering this whole region to the east is the vast Pacific Ocean.

The Pacific encompasses most of the South Sea islands. However, other major waters here bear note: The **Timor Sea** separates northern Australia from Indonesia; the **Coral Sea** lies northeast of the continent; and dividing southeast Australia from New Zealand is the **Tasman Sea**.

Asia, Australia, and the Pacific islands have only a few major rivers. The **Yellow** and **Yangtze** wind and twist their way through the center of China. They offer visitors a superb way of exploring the magnificent countryside. (There's also an important canal system in northeastern China that permits several popular excursions.) The **Ganges**, which flows through the northeast of India, is perhaps the most sacred river on earth, for Hindu pilgrims immerse themselves in its waters to spiritually cleanse themselves. Most of Australia's rivers are in its southeast corner. The **Murray** and the **Darling** are the two most important ones.

Mountains

The 2,000-mile **Himalaya Mountain range** is the loftiest range in the world. To put this in its proper perspective, Himalaya's **Mt. Everest** is the world's tallest mountain:

Mt. Fuji on a rare, perfectly clear day
Image copyright Olga Zaporozhskaya, 2008. Used under license from Shutterstock.com

It's 9,000 feet higher than the tallest mountain in North America, Mt. McKinley, and 7,000 feet higher than the tallest peak of the Andes. Of the world's 50 tallest mountains, virtually all are in the Himalaya. The challenging Himalaya are considered by adventurous travelers to be the finest trekking and mountain-climbing territory in the world. The Himalaya ripple through the top of Pakistan, northern India, Nepal, Bhutan, and the Tibet region of China, covering an area greater than all of Germany.

In addition, a spine of volcanic mountains runs down the length of much of Japan, the most famous of which is stately **Mt. Fuji**. There are also many mountains of volcanic origin in Indonesia (where the legendary **Krakatoa** erupted) and in Australia, with its **Great Dividing Range** down the east coast. The **Southern Alps** rise above New Zealand's South Island. Parts of western China are also somewhat mountainous—though few tourists visit there.

Climate

Because parts of Asia and the Pacific lie both north and south of the equator, two distinct patterns exist: North of the equator, seasons are the same as those in North America; south, they're the opposite. An important point to remember: Though many think of this entire region as hot and humid, Australia and New Zealand are exceptions. They both have temperate weather. In the winter, New Zealand's mountainous South Island gets plenty of snow. In addition, the Himalaya and other high regions can have very cold weather. One more exception: Western China and western Australia have largely desert climates.

The Indian subcontinent, most of China, the islands of Japan and Taiwan (all of which lie north of the equator), and northern Australia (to the equator's south) have a subtropical climate. Summers in these areas are very warm and humid; winters are drier and more pleasant. A fully tropical climate can be found in those countries that flank the equator—most of Indonesia and all the South Sea islands—as well as in Southeast Asia, the Philippines, and Micronesia (north of the equator).

A final note: The region is famed for its monsoons, typhoons, and cyclones. Monsoons are long-standing summer rainstorms, usually associated with the Indian subcontinent and Southeast Asia. Typhoons are what hurricanes are called when they occur in the China Sea and west Pacific area. Cyclones (the generic name for hurricanes and typhoons) often whip along Australia's northeast coastal areas.

The world's oldest rain forest is Malaysia's Taman Negara. It has remained unchanged for 130 million years.

The deepest place on earth is in the Mariana Trench. It's almost 7 miles below the surface of the Pacific Ocean.

Tourism Patterns

Two words summarize the pattern of Pacific Rim tourism: *explosive growth*. It has not been unusual to see a doubling of the numbers of tourists in a matter of a year or two. As a result, major hotels are being built everywhere. China (including Hong Kong) is by far the most popular destination in Asia. Japan, South Korea, and Australia are also popular with North American travelers. In addition to the leisure segment, business travel accounts for much movement across the Pacific between North America and the Far East.

What of the Pacific islands? The U.S. state of Hawaii is number one, but surprisingly, the Micronesian islands of Guam and Saipan are in second place (most of their tourists come from Japan). Fiji is the most successful destination in Melanesia, and Tahiti leads the Polynesian islands in tourism. Hawaii, Tahiti, and Fiji are all common stopover points on trans-Pacific travel itineraries, both on planes and on repositioning cruises.

Asian and Pacific Distances

For traveling through Asia, the mode of choice for most tourists is the escorted tour. Driving a rental car is not a good idea (except in Australia and New Zealand). Asia's rural roads are sometimes primitive and they can be washed out; city traffic may be impenetrable. Asian languages are usually indecipherable to Westerners. These can be real problems if you're a car renter, especially if you get lost and can't read the signs. Some trains are comfortable, even luxurious. Buses—except those used on tours—are usually a challenge.

Even though many in these countries do speak English fairly well, the language is still a critical—and very real—obstacle. Two ways around this: escorted tours and cruises have become a popular option for visiting key port cities in Asia, Australia, New Zealand, and the Pacific islands.

For those who are traveling on their own, distances in some Asian countries can be great—giant China and India being the obvious examples. However, in many Asian countries, the major destinations tend to be clustered in distinct, limited areas: In China, for instance, the sites typically visited are almost entirely in the east.

The Pacific islands, on the other hand, don't pose that much of a problem. The inhabitants of many of the popular islands speak English; for many (Fiji and Guam, among others), it's an official language. These islands are relatively small, so taxis, car rentals, and (perhaps) buses will do.

Certainly, roads on the smaller islands may be primitive, but again, distances are comparatively minor. The only modes of transportation of any great importance among the islands are planes that hop from one island to the next, ferries that weave their way among clusters of islands, and cruise ships that connect the islands.

Visitors must fly between sites in Australia that are far apart, unless they have a lot of time to spare. Australia is very big: It's about the size of the contiguous United States. Its attractions (except for a notable few) are along the east and west coasts, with much of the inland area desertlike and sparsely populated. The majority of New Zealand's most popular attractions, too, tend to be conveniently clustered. Train and bus travel in both countries (as well as in Japan) is excellent. Trains and buses are less predictable elsewhere, though luxury trains travel through India, and between Singapore and Bangkok.

Some Miscellaneous Considerations

Asia and the Pacific are often thought of as exotic. Usually travelers to this part of the world want some sense of security before they leave. Among the suggestions you can give are:

■ Health conditions in some of these countries are far below the standard that most tourists expect. Travelers should check health advisories and visit their physician before leaving on a trip to Asia and the Pacific.

Japan has the world's busiest rail system.

The Maldives, an island nation south of India, is the lowest-lying country on earth. Average elevation: 3 feet above sea level.

Some Muslims believe that when Adam was expelled from the Garden of Eden, he went to Sri Lanka.

The Shinkansen, Japan's Bullet Train
Photo by Brian Yokoyama

■ Shopping in Asia, in Australia, and among the islands is of great allure to many tourists. The best prices on brand names can usually be found in Hong Kong, South Korea, and Singapore, while crafts are a bargain in almost all of these places.

■ The engines of commerce are powerful in Asia. Nowhere in the world, these days, is business travel more important. The industrial nations of Asia, by the way, are often called "The Dragons."

■ Bargaining on prices is extremely common, indeed almost expected, in many of these countries—though not in Japan, Australia, and New Zealand. Check with hotel personnel about local customs.

■ Even though many locals understand English, visitors who are having a difficult time communicating should write out their questions. It's not uncommon for someone here to read English better than they speak it.

■ Tourists who plan to take photographs in China and in Southeast Asia should check ahead of time to make sure it's not prohibited in the area they're touring.

■ The water in Asian lakes, ponds, and rivers (including the mystical Ganges) is often filled with microbes that North Americans have no resistance to. Swimming in Asian waters is generally a bad idea.

■ Many of the regions here offer only the most basic conveniences; however, Australia, New Zealand, and Japan offer great luxury and comfort.

■ Uninformed tourists often think all Asian nations have the same general customs. Not so. Differences among Japanese, Chinese, Korean, Thai, and Philippine cultures are as pronounced as those among, say, French, British, Italian, and Greek cultures.

■ Treks have become a popular form of adventure travel; several areas in China, India, Nepal, and Bhutan offer trekking tours, but only hardy travelers who are prepared to walk for hours at high altitudes and sleep in a tent should consider a trekking tour.

■ Costs in this vast region vary widely. For example, Japan is expensive, while China, Thailand, and Southeast Asia tend to be bargains.

There's controversial evidence that in ancient times, Chinese vessels crossed the Pacific Ocean and landed in what is now Redondo Beach, California.

Climbers who reach the top of Mt. Everest spend an average of only a half-hour there.

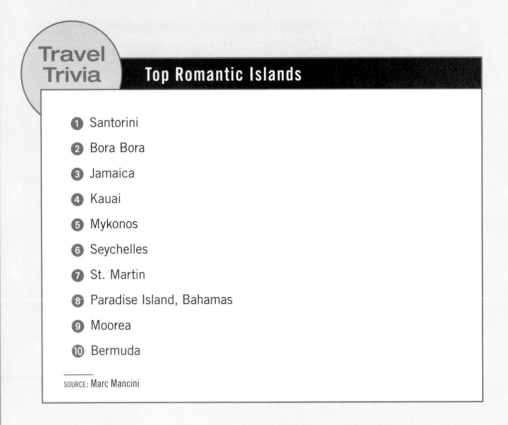

Travel Trivia

Top Romantic Islands

1 Santorini

2 Bora Bora

3 Jamaica

4 Kauai

5 Mykonos

6 Seychelles

7 St. Martin

8 Paradise Island, Bahamas

9 Moorea

10 Bermuda

SOURCE: Marc Mancini

NAME _____ **DATE** _____

CREATIVE ACTIVITY

Based on the information in this chapter and in other sources, which 10 different Asia/Pacific destinations would you suggest to someone looking for each of the following? Be prepared to justify your recommendations.

1 Hiking:

2 Dry, warm climate:

3 A river cruise:

4 A rarely visited tropical country:

5 Diving:

6 An exotic cultural experience:

7 A bargain vacation:

8 Luxurious accommodations:

9 A stopover between Honolulu and Sydney:

10 A country that can be seen on a one-day visit:

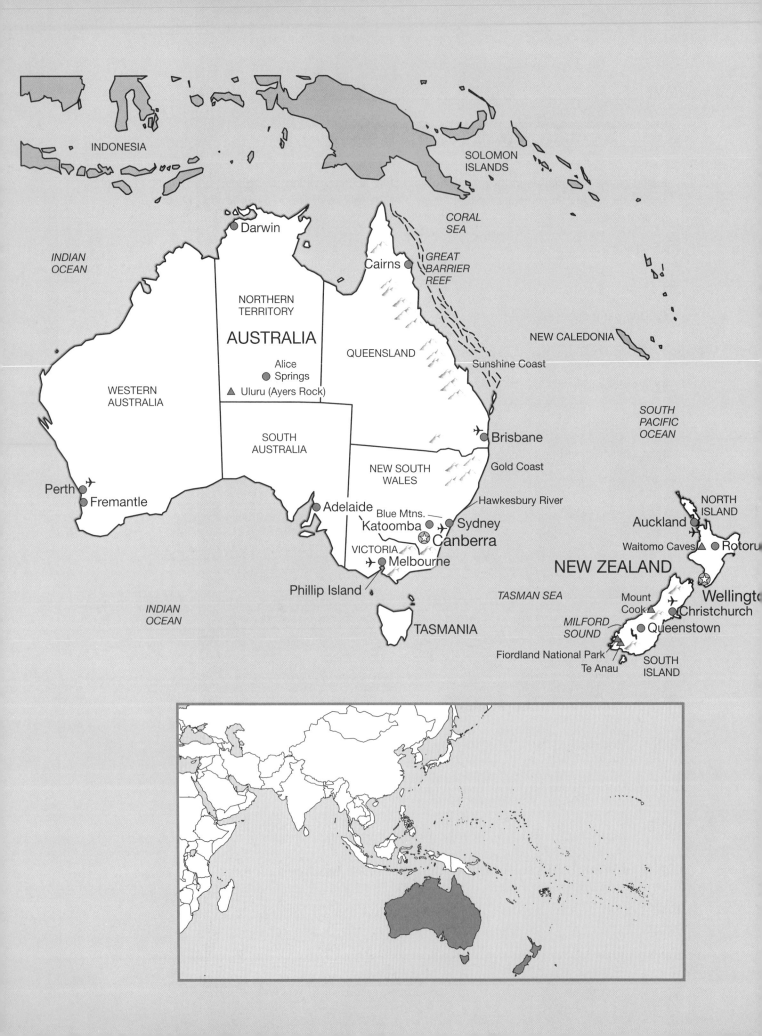

INDONESIA

SOLOMON
ISLANDS

CORAL
SEA

INDIAN
OCEAN

Darwin

GREAT
BARRIER
REEF

Cairns

NORTHERN
TERRITORY

AUSTRALIA

QUEENSLAND

NEW CALEDONIA

Alice
Springs

Sunshine Coast

WESTERN
AUSTRALIA

▲ Uluru (Ayers Rock)

SOUTH
PACIFIC
OCEAN

SOUTH
AUSTRALIA

Brisbane

NEW SOUTH
WALES

Gold Coast

Perth

Hawkesbury River

Fremantle

Adelaide

NORTH
ISLAND

Auckland

Blue Mtns.

Katoomba

Sydney

Waitomo Caves ▲ ● Rotoru

Canberra

NEW ZEALAND

VICTORIA

Melbourne

Wellingto

TASMAN SEA

Mount
Cook ▲

Phillip Island

Christchurch

INDIAN
OCEAN

MILFORD
SOUND

Queenstown

Fiordland National Park

TASMANIA

Te Anau

SOUTH
ISLAND

Chapter 25

Australia and New Zealand

Where Things Are Jumping

It was the late eighteenth century. European explorers were finally making serious excursions to the strange, distant lands of Australia and New Zealand. Other experiences had prepared them for much of what awaited them: fierce Maori [MAH-ree] warriors; the bleak, reddish, desert-like Outback; the Alpine peaks of New Zealand. Similar things they had seen before.

But nothing could prepare them for the animals they found in this "land down under": Kangaroos that can leap a span of 25 feet; the koala, a bear-like little creature that lives in (and on) eucalyptus trees; and the platypus, a mammal with webbed feet and a duck-like bill that lays eggs. Indeed, the platypus is so weird that European zoologists at first thought it to be a patched-together hoax sprung on them by prankish sailors.

Visitors of today still find the fauna and flora of these two countries astonishing. That and the friendly reputation of their people are a powerful magnet for tourism. Indeed, Australia and New Zealand still continue to draw more and more tourists, often as parts of a single lengthy trip.

When you sell this area, remember that it's much more vast than people may imagine. The continent of Australia is about the size of the contiguous United States. (But its population is only 21 million.) To its west is the Indian Ocean; to the east are the Coral and Tasman seas, which in turn open onto the Pacific Ocean.

The principal cities on Australia's charming but less visited western shore are **Perth** and nearby **Fremantle**. The nearer east coast is a more popular destination. Here are, from the northern state of **Queensland** to the southern state of **New South Wales**, the **Great Barrier Reef**, a 1,200-mile stretch of coral that's generally accessed from the city of **Cairns** (which Australians pronounce CANS); the **Sunshine Coast**, a beach resort area north of the key city of **Brisbane**; the **Gold Coast**, an even bigger, Miami-like beach area that starts about 50 miles south of Brisbane; **Sydney**, Australia's largest and liveliest city; and inland **Canberra**, Australia's capital. Along the southeastern coast are three popular destinations: **Melbourne, Adelaide**, and the island-state of **Tasmania**.

And what's in the middle? Several million square miles of bleak, desolate brush and desert, called the **Bush** and the **Outback**. Still, there are two Outback attractions that tourists visit: **Alice Springs**, a frontier town that's a showcase for the culture and art of Australia's original dwellers, the aborigines [ab-uh-RIDGE-uh-neez]; and **Uluru** (better known as **Ayers** [AIRZ] **Rock**), a massive red stone that's best seen in the crimson light of sunset. Even more remote (and less visited) is **Darwin**, a port on Australia's wet, tropical north coast. **Kakadu National Park**, 155 miles east of Darwin, is noted for its ancient cave paintings and wide spectrum of wildlife.

The genuinely bizarre creatures down under make a zoo or animal park visit an essential activity.

Tasmania was a British penal colony whose nickname was "Devil's Island."

449

AUSTRALIA AND NEW ZEALAND

CAPITALS: Australia: Canberra
New Zealand: Wellington

AREA (SQUARE MILES): Australia: 2,968,000
New Zealand: 103,736

TIME ZONES: Australia: GMT +8 to +10
New Zealand: GMT +12

DRIVE ON: Left

POPULATION: Australia: 20,600,000
New Zealand: 4,200,000

RELIGIONS: Protestant, Catholic

LANGUAGE: English

CURRENCY: Australia: 1 Australian dollar = 100 cents
New Zealand: 1 New Zealand dollar =
100 cents

ELECTRICITY: 240 volts, 50 cycles AC

CAPSULE HISTORY: Australia: Aborigine ancestors arrive, 30,000 B.C.; Dutch land here, 1606; British James Cook explores, leading to a British claim of possession, 1770; island remained a British penal colony until 1850s; gold discovered, 1851; Commonwealth declared, 1901; Australia Act severs many ties with Britain, 1986; Olympics held in Sydney, 2000.
New Zealand: Maoris, a Polynesian group, arrive and settle, 1300s; discovered by Dutch, 1642; Britain annexes from Maoris, 1840; Maori wars, 1845–1870; gold rush, 1861; declared "nuclear-free" zone, 1984.

For reference sources, tourist bureaus, and suggested lengths of stay, see the Appendices.

New Zealand, about 1,200 miles to Australia's southeast, used to be a more difficult sell, since it didn't elicit the strong mental pictures that Australia does. No more. *The Lord of the Rings* movies—mostly shot in New Zealand—helped the public visualize the country's intense beauty. Its **North Island** has rolling green hills and considerable geothermal activity. **Auckland**, New Zealand's largest city, is here; as is **Rotorua**, a center of Maori culture and powerful, steaming geysers. **Wellington**, at the southernmost tip of North Island, is New Zealand's hilly and increasingly cosmopolitan capital. The **South Island** (where much of *The Lord of the Rings* was filmed) is dramatically mountainous and colder, with many fjord-like inlets. Its chief cities are **Christchurch** and **Queenstown**.

How Travelers Get There

Virtually everyone from North America who visits the "land down under" arrives via jet. It's a long haul, though; from the West Coast it's more than 7,000 miles. And for travelers flying from any point farther east, it'll be even longer. Many flights stop in Hawaii, Fiji, or Tahiti to refuel. In fact, it's often possible to break up the long trip by stopping over for a pleasant day or two at one of several South Pacific island destinations.

Most Australia-bound travelers arrive through one of three gateway cities: Brisbane (BNE), Sydney (SYD), or Melbourne (MEL). Those heading to New Zealand usually land at Auckland (AKL) or Christchurch (CHC). And don't forget that travelers will be crossing the International Date Line (and therefore changing days) while airborne.

Several North American airlines fly to the region. A traveler can also be booked on the countries' principal carriers: Australia's **Qantas** (QF) and **Air New Zealand** (NZ). Cruise ships sailing from North America on repositioning cruises often cross the Pacific and terminate in New Zealand or Australia, where they'll begin to operate their "down under" summer itineraries.

Australia is the world's
smallest continent.

Weather Patterns

Remember that the seasons in these Southern Hemisphere destinations are the opposite of those in North America: The coldest weather is in June, July, and August, while summer heat arrives in January and February (see Figures 25–1 and 25–2). New Zealand's North Island has cool and occasionally rainy winters (June to August), but warm and sometimes humid summers (January and February). The South Island is somewhat colder all year, especially in the mountains.

Australia has a warmer and generally drier climate than that of New Zealand. Cities such as Melbourne and Sydney have wonderful warm summers and mild, chilly-water winters—with relatively modest amounts of rain year-round. (Melbourne is a bit drier than Sydney.) Brisbane and Perth are even warmer, with more rain. Cairns and especially Darwin have a tropical climate (somewhat like Florida's or Mexico's coastal regions) with hot and rainy summers (January to March) and warm, dry winters. The climate of Australia's vast interior is Sahara-like.

High tourist season is December, January, and February, when the locals take their summer holidays and snowbirds hope to get away from the cold. Bargain rates are most likely in June, July, and August, except in mountain resorts and Queensland, which (because of their weather) become winter getaways for Australians and New Zealanders.

A surprising 40 percent of Australia lies within the tropics.

Climate at a Glance
SYDNEY, AUSTRALIA

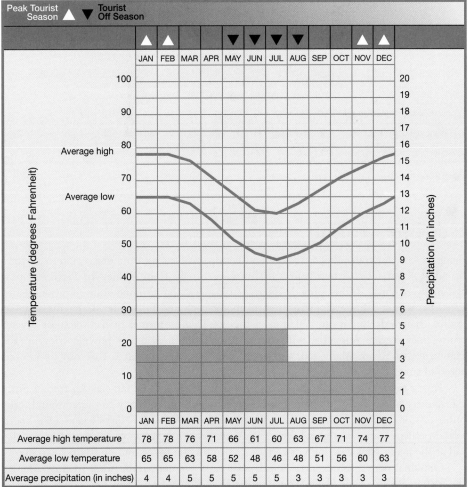

	JAN	FEB	MAR	APR	MAY	JUN	JUL	AUG	SEP	OCT	NOV	DEC
Average high temperature	78	78	76	71	66	61	60	63	67	71	74	77
Average low temperature	65	65	63	58	52	48	46	48	51	56	60	63
Average precipitation (in inches)	4	4	5	5	5	5	5	3	3	3	3	3

Figure 25–1

Climate at a Glance
WELLINGTON, NEW ZEALAND

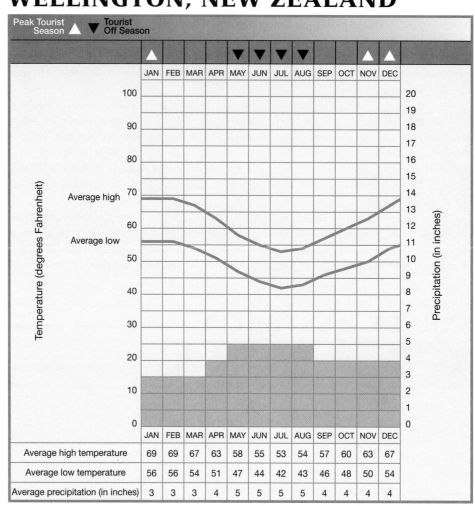

	JAN	FEB	MAR	APR	MAY	JUN	JUL	AUG	SEP	OCT	NOV	DEC
Average high temperature	69	69	67	63	58	55	53	54	57	60	63	67
Average low temperature	56	56	54	51	47	44	42	43	46	48	50	54
Average precipitation (in inches)	3	3	3	4	5	5	5	5	4	4	4	4

Figure 25–2

Getting Around

Being so vast, Australia almost always requires air travel to get from one region to another. (It takes about four to five hours, for instance, to fly from Sydney to Perth.) Qantas and many regional airlines provide internal transportation. Ground transportation is also excellent, with a well-developed system of motorcoach and rail routes. Car rentals are an option, though driving is on the left (as is the case in most former British colonies). Several cruise lines service Australia, with stops at major port cities, or provide trips up the **Hawkesbury River**. Many tour operators offer excellent packages that can be booked ahead of time.

New Zealand's internal transportation options are much the same as Australia's. Since the country is relatively compact, however, visitors are more likely to drive around, take buses, or ride the train from one city to the next, especially on the North Island. (The South Island perhaps warrants flights between its more far-flung points of interest.) Cruises also call at the major New Zealand ports, often continuing on to (or coming from) Australia.

One final note: Each country boasts some rather famous train rides. In Australia, it's the **Indian Pacific** route (from Sydney to Perth) and the **Ghan** (from Adelaide to Darwin). Each affords a comfortable way of experiencing Australia's Outback. New Zealand operates its **Overlander**, which connects Wellington and Auckland.

In Western Australia, 12 different aboriginal languages are spoken.

The Sydney Opera House now competes for attention with new, towering structures
Image copyright Sandra Caldwell, 2008. Used under license from Shutterstock.com

Important Places

Unlike some countries, Australia and New Zealand have clear-cut centers of tourism. Here are the most important:

Sydney

With nearly a fifth of Australia's population, Sydney is one of the world's most energetic, stylish, and progressive cities. Though enormous in area, most of Sydney's tourist sites are in a concentrated section near its fine harbor. Among the city's attractions are:

- **The Sydney Opera House**, an astonishing building with a design so unorthodox and original that it took years before anyone could figure out how to build it properly.
- **The Rocks**, the old, restored section of Sydney.
- **Kings Cross**, a nightclub, pub, and restaurant area that's Sydney's liveliest and rowdiest.
- **Harbor cruises** that afford a superb view of Sydney's lively waterfront area, hill-clinging skyline, and the landmark **Harbour Bridge**.
- **The Queen Victoria Building**, now converted into an attractive shopping center.
- **Several nearby beaches**, including Bondi [BON-dye] and Port Jackson.

    Short trips out of Sydney take visitors to **Botany Bay** (where Captain Cook's *Endeavour* anchored) and to several wild-animal parks (with up-close views of koalas and kangaroos). Similar parks exist throughout Australia. Three longer **day trips** can be recommended:

- **The Blue Mountains**, a scenic area that centers around the town of **Katoomba**, with its waterfall, railway (which travels steeply down into a valley), and skyway (a cable car that traverses between two cliffs).
- **Canberra**, Australia's sedate and isolated capital, which boasts some rather interesting modern architecture and a fountain jet not unlike Lake Geneva's.
- **Hawkesbury River cruises**, available out of ports north of Sydney. Ships take passengers along the river's rugged gorges and into a national park. One- or two-day cruises are available.

Because of its shape, the Sydney Harbour Bridge is called the "Coat Hanger." For a hefty fee, visitors can walk to the top of its high, arched superstructure.

The Blue Mountains got their name because of the blue haze given off by eucalyptus trees.

Melbourne

Australia's second-largest city—a melting pot of diverse ethnic groups—is as cosmopolitan as any of the nation's urban centers. It's well known for its gardens (Melbourne is sometimes called the Garden City), elegant stores, ever-present streetcars, sporting opportunities, and nearby ski resorts. Most hotels, restaurants, theaters, stores, and government buildings are within the city's "**Golden Mile**" district.

Just south off the coast from Melbourne is **Phillip Island**, one of Australia's most famous attractions. It's home to the "fairy" penguins—which, each day at dusk, march dutifully from the beach to their burrows. The area is well lit to ensure that tourists will see these creatures' waddling parade. (At certain times, though, the number of penguins dwindles, making for some disappointment.) Farther offshore is the island-state of Tasmania, with its slow pace, mild climate, and deep-green countryside.

Queensland

Queensland is to Australia what California and Florida are to the United States: a region of palmy splendor, striking seascapes, and booming growth. Queensland is vast: It's much larger than any U.S. state. The state's principal concentrations of tourism are, from north to south:

■ **The Great Barrier Reef.** This 1,250-mile strip is made up of hundreds of offshore coral islands. Resort hotels anchor many of the larger islands, and the diving, snorkeling, and marlin fishing here provide astonishing experiences. Cairns, at the Reef's northern end, is its principal gateway.

- **The Sunshine Coast**. This nearly 40-mile stretch of beaches, lakes, and mountains has a reputation for being less commercialized than its southerly competition. For vacationers who want relaxation or plenty of sporting opportunities, the Sunshine Coast is ideal.

- **Brisbane**. Queensland's capital is a lush tropical paradise, with superb landscaping and several animal sanctuaries just outside the city. It's about a 90-minute drive south of the Sunshine Coast.

- **The Gold Coast**. About an hour south of Brisbane, this beach resort area is Australia's most developed and crowded. It's somewhat reminiscent of Miami Beach, with many large hotels and resorts, as well as several family theme parks. (One well-known section is **Surfers Paradise**.) This is for the vacationer who wants seaside hustle and bustle, not a get-away-from-it-all vacation.

The Outback

The vast, arid, near-empty center of Australia has an otherworldly quality that many visitors find absolutely intriguing. The art and culture of the aborigines, too, layer the region with even more mystery. Though vastly separate, two Outback attractions (usually reached by plane) merit attention:

- **Alice Springs**, a frontier town with many art galleries, is surrounded by an almost surrealist landscape of red hills and hard, flat desert. Many natural wonders are nearby.

- **Uluru** (Ayers Rock), a massive stone outcropping that's best seen at sunset, when its reddish hue is most striking. It's more than 1,000 feet high and 6 miles around, and is a sacred site for aborigines. Nearby is the tourist oasis of **Yulara**, with its unorthodox, tent-like structures.

Perth

This, Australia's largest west coast city, is a sunny amalgam of parks, hills, and friendliness. Fremantle, a nearby town, is famous for its yachting, restored buildings, art galleries, and springtime flowers. Few American tourists visit the Perth area, however, since it's a nearly 10-hour roundtrip from Australia's east coast. Still, Perth appeals to just about everyone who decides to see all of Australia.

Perth is closer to Singapore and Jakarta than it is to Sydney.

New Zealand's North Island

New Zealand–bound tourists usually wish to see two cities: Auckland (New Zealand's largest city) and Wellington (its capital). Both cities, though lovely, are relatively small and quiet—the kinds of places with many little points of interest (best seen via a city tour).

Auckland's most notable sight is a waterfront theme attraction: **Kelly Tarlton's Antarctic Encounter and Underwater World**. Among the major attractions between Auckland and Wellington are:

- **The Waitomo** [why-TOE-mo] **Glowworm Caves**, where thousands of glow-worms turn the ceiling of a deep grotto into a night-sky-like fantasy.

- **Rotorua**, a small city whose numerous features make it a must-see. First, Rotorua is an important center of Maori native culture; its **Maori Arts and Crafts Institute** shows contemporary artists continuing the traditions of the country's first inhabitants. Second, Rotorua is the site of tremendous geothermal activity. Its thermal area boasts geysers, steam vents, and bubbling mud pots.

- **The Agrodome**, not far from Rotorua, an offbeat attraction where New Zealand's important sheep-raising industry is explained. It may sound boring, but it's not—visitors love it when 19 different breeds of "trained" sheep trot out to their appointed platforms on stage.

New Zealand experiences about 400 earthquakes yearly. Almost all of them are so mild that they're not felt.

Uluru: one of the world's most famous natural attractions
Image copyright mdd, 2008. Used under license from Shutterstock.com

New Zealand's South Island

Colder, larger, and more mountainous than its northern neighbor, the South Island claims several world-class attractions. Christchurch (with its graceful peaks) and Queenstown (a scenic mountain resort town that boasts a very active nightlife) are both essential stops on a South Island itinerary. So, too, are the following:

■ **Mt. Cook**, with its awe-inspiring glaciers, most frequently visited via ski planes.

■ **Milford Sound**, a dramatic, carved sea inlet that's part of New Zealand's picturesque **Fiordland National Park**.

Other possibilities: a visit to the **Te Anau** [TAY AH-now] glow-worm caves or whitewater rafting on any of several South Island rivers.

Possible Itineraries

Because Australia and New Zealand are so distant from the United States, vacationers, once they set out for this region, almost always wish to see as much as possible. Typical is a minimum 10- to 12-day itinerary that includes New Zealand's North or South Island and Australia's east coast, especially the areas around Sydney and Melbourne. Those with the time for a more extended vacation or on a second, in-depth trip will certainly want to see both of New Zealand's major islands and either Australia's west coast (with a stop at Alice Springs and Uluru) or the Queensland region. Finally, those seeking a tropical stay or wishing to drive often limit their stay to Australia's east coast, with perhaps a day or two in Sydney and the rest of the time along the Great Barrier Reef and the beach areas north or south of Brisbane.

Lodging Options

North American chains have a strong presence here, as do such local companies as Australia's **Rydges** and **Flag**. Both Australia and New Zealand have some deluxe properties (especially in Sydney and the Great Barrier Reef), but most of the accommodations in these countries tend to cluster at a mid-range, first-class level. Motels are popular; it's traditional here for motel rooms to have full kitchenettes, so this type of accommodation may appeal

Milford Sound is one of New Zealand's most picturesque destinations
Image copyright Martin Maun, 2008. Used under license from Shutterstock.com

to families and the budget-minded. Home and farm stays can also be easily arranged—they're a wonderful option, since Australians and New Zealanders are among the world's friendliest people. Lists of farm and home-style accommodations are available from each country's tourist bureau.

Allied Destinations

Arranging a visit to any of the many Pacific islands that lie between North America and Australia or New Zealand is a wise and popular sales strategy. It breaks up the long trip. But other options exist. Singapore, Malaysia, Indonesia, and several other less-visited countries lie just to the north of Australia. Even Japan, China, the Philippines, and the nations of Southeast Asia are potential add-on destinations, since visitors are already flying across the Pacific and may feel that they might as well visit other transoceanic places if they have the time. Perhaps the most exotic option of them all: Antarctica. Several companies operate summer cruises from New Zealand to this bottom-of-the-world continent of ice.

Cultural Patterns

Most Americans feel comparatively at home here. Yet Australia and New Zealand have their own customs:

- These are two friendly, very open nations, and visitors should feel comfortable about using first names in greetings.
- Though these countries are easygoing in their ways, customs are more formal than a visitor might expect. Punctuality, for example, is important in both countries. And New Zealanders tend to be more formal than Australians; for instance, they're likely to be restrained with strangers at first meeting.
- A gesture similar to the "thumbs up" sign is considered an obscenity here.
- Tipping in restaurants isn't common. As a visitor, you may wish to tip, but it's rarely expected.

Woolens are a relative bargain, but so are opals, which are mostly gathered and polished in Australia.

Australians call people with red hair "bluies."

Vegemite is a
yeast spread that
Australians slather on
their bread. (Frankly, it
tastes awful.)

- The food here was once considered bland. No longer. Foreign specialties have melded with post-British cuisine to create some wonderful culinary treats. Two major specialties: oysters and lamb-based dishes.

- Nightlife in New Zealand often features Maori-Polynesian entertainment. Australian nightlife ranges from informal pubs to several nightspots that pay homage to Australia's colorful frontier history, as well as to aboriginal music. It's all very touristy, but then again, the locals somehow give it an unjaded, gee-whiz treatment. (Visitors will probably tire of sheep-shearing demonstrations, though, which are done in so many tourist places that they'll half-expect the flight attendants to do it on the plane home.)

Factors That Motivate Visitors

Awareness of what Australia and New Zealand offer is growing daily. Among the features you should emphasize are the following:

- Increasingly, New Zealand and Australia are being viewed as adventure destinations, both for soft adventure activities and "extreme" ones, such as bungee jumping and white-water rafting.

- Though distant and offbeat, Australia and New Zealand are culturally very accessible.

- The plants and animals are unlike those anywhere else in the world.

- The people are extremely friendly to tourists, have a wonderfully informal attitude, and speak English.

- Food and lodging are bargains, especially for those staying in motor inns.

- The Queensland beaches are superb and especially uncrowded north of Brisbane, and the diving along the Great Barrier Reef is legendary.

- New Zealand and Australia rarely feel hectic or crowded, except perhaps in Sydney and along the Gold Coast.

- The Aborigine and Maori cultures are intriguing. (However, they're mainly experienced only in certain areas, such as Alice Springs and Rotorua, respectively.)

- These countries bask in their most pleasant summer weather when many Americans are shivering from winter's cold and are ready to get away for a warm-weather vacation.

- There's skiing in southeast Australia and in southern New Zealand, where many slopes are accessed only via helicopter.

- Both countries are extremely stable politically and have a relatively low crime rate.

Certain types of
kangaroos—especially
in the wild—can
be very dangerous.
They can easily kill a
person with one swift
kick or punch.

Possible Misgivings

Australia and New Zealand aren't for everyone. Here are some of the objections that may come up:

- "It's too far." These countries are indeed a long flight from anywhere in the United States. You could break up the trip, however, by adding a stop in each direction (generally with little or no additional airfare) at a Pacific island resort. Travelers from the East Coast could pause a day or two in Los Angeles, or San Francisco.

- "It's too expensive." Airfares can be hefty, but bargain rates appear in the off-season. Once there, tourists can drive around, staying at motels or farmhouses.

- "We can't be away from work that long." If visitors limit themselves to one area of Australia or New Zealand, a roundtrip can be done in about nine days.

- "There's not all that much to see and do." You must explain the many wonders of this part of the world to offset such preconceptions.

Qualifying the Traveler
Australia and New Zealand

For People Who Want	Appeal			Remarks
	High	Medium	Low	
Historical and Cultural Attractions		▲		Some cities; Maori and aboriginal culture
Beaches and Water Sports	▲			In Queensland
Skiing Opportunities		▲		In southern mountains
Lots of Nightlife			▲	Sydney and Queenstown
Family Activities		▲		Children will find animals interesting; motor hotels plentiful
Familiar Cultural Experience		▲		
Exotic Cultural Experience		▲		Aboriginal and Maori cultures
Safety and Low Crime	▲			
Bargain Travel		▲		Flight expensive, but other costs reasonable
Impressive Scenery		▲		Bush and Outback impressively bleak; mountains and seascapes
Peace and Quiet	▲			In countryside
Shopping Opportunities		▲		Opals, woolens, leather
Adventure		▲		Especially in the Outback, areas near Darwin and South Island
To Do Business		▲		A common language facilitates business

■ "We'd like to bring our children, but they'll have nothing to do." Again, most people don't know about Australia's beaches, New Zealand's family outdoor adventures, and so on. Furthermore, many children love animals, and both countries have plenty of weird ones. The one legitimate objection for families: the cost of airfare.

Sales Strategies

Expand a trip by suggesting that as long as they'll be going to Australia, why not add New Zealand, Fiji, Tahiti, or Hawaii? It will require just a short lengthening of their trip. Suggest a larger rental car, especially if the person expects to drive across Australia's vast stretches. Ski, cruise, and dive packages can all be sold in advance, as can city tours (especially appropriate in Sydney, Melbourne, and Auckland).

Tasmanian devils do indeed come from Tasmania, but they hardly look like or behave like the cartoon character.

Travel Trivia

Most Bizarre Questions Travel Agents Have Heard

- "When you travel to Australia do you have to fly backward or upside-down?"

- "Can I take a Greyhound bus to Europe?"

- "Do I need a visa for China? I prefer using MasterCard."

- "What time does the sun pass over the pool at the Flamingo Hilton in Las Vegas?"

- "Will there be any icebergs en route in the Caribbean?"

- "Could you book a room with an ocean view for me in Palm Springs?"

- "Can I take a seven-day Mediterranean cruise out of San Juan, Puerto Rico?"

- When an elderly lady was told she had to fly through Phoenix, she exclaimed, "Venus? I don't want to go to Venus!"

NAME _____   **DATE** _____

MAP ACTIVITY

A traveler wants to visit the places listed below. Which number represents each on the map?

Place/Attraction	In/Near Which City?	Number on Map
A. Australia's gateway to Queensland's beach resorts	A. _____	A. _____
B. A remarkable opera house	B. _____	B. _____
C. Fremantle's sister city	C. _____	C. _____
D. Geysers and steam vents	D. _____	D. _____
E. A famous rock	E. _____	E. _____
F. "Fairy" penguins can be seen south of this city	F. _____	F. _____
G. The Great Barrier Reef's air access city	G. _____	G. _____
H. The South Island's principal city	H. _____	H. _____
I. The Blue Mountains' principal city	I. _____	I. _____
J. Australia's capital	J. _____	J. _____

NAME _____   DATE _____

CASE STUDY

Geri Harding wants her two children to see the country where they were born, Australia. (The children were very young when the family moved from Sydney to San Diego.) This will be a costly trip, so Geri would like to find some bargains. Geri can take as long as two weeks from her job as a high-school teacher. She wishes to go to Sydney and then travel around a bit by car.

Circle the answer that best suits their needs.

1 When would you suggest that they go?

July   Christmas

November   April

Why?

2 Which of the following should you tell Geri about?

The attractions in Sydney   The motor vehicles she can book

The weather at the time she's going   The great driving distances between cities

Why?

3 Which add-on foreign destination might be the most appealing to them?

Fiji   Singapore

Perth   Tokyo

Why?

4 What might be the most appealing enhancement opportunity?

Business-class flights   Sheep-shearing lessons

A dive package   A larger-size car rental

Why?

NAME _____   **DATE** _____

CREATIVE ACTIVITY

You're reading a magazine and see that Qantas is running a "Down Under Mystery Tour" contest. You're supposed to read the "Mystery Tour" description, guess each city or region the tour will visit, fill out the contest blank, then wait to see if yours will be chosen from among the correct entries to receive an all-expenses-paid trip. Here's the description:

> On the first few days you'll let off a little steam, have the wool pulled over your eyes, and see "stars" at noon. Two days later you'll pretend you're in Norway. Then it's across the water to someplace that everybody says is filled with cans. Next stop: a big reddish thing in the middle of nowhere. The next place is even stranger: It's for the birds, tuxedoed ones at that. We finish off with a drink on the Rocks.

Places the Tour Will Visit:

1

2

3

4

5

6

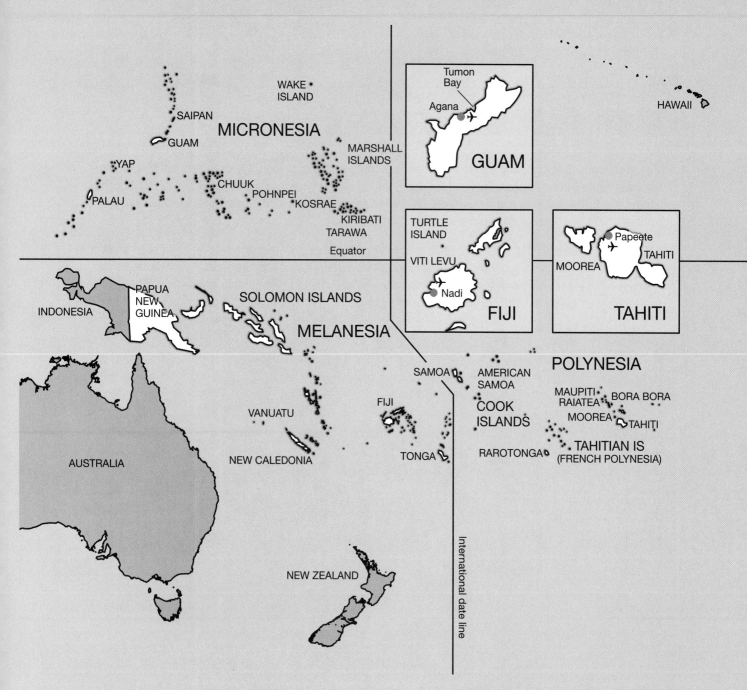

WAKE ISLAND

SAIPAN

GUAM

MICRONESIA

YAP

PALAU

CHUUK

POHNPEI

KOSRAE

MARSHALL ISLANDS

KIRIBATI

TARAWA

Equator

HAWAII

Tumon Bay

Agana

GUAM

TURTLE ISLAND

VITI LEVU

Nadi

FIJI

Papeete

TAHITI

MOOREA

TAHITI

INDONESIA

PAPUA NEW GUINEA

SOLOMON ISLANDS

MELANESIA

POLYNESIA

SAMOA

AMERICAN SAMOA

COOK ISLANDS

MAUPITI

RAIATEA

BORA BORA

MOOREA

TAHITI

VANUATU

FIJI

AUSTRALIA

NEW CALEDONIA

TONGA

RAROTONGA

TAHITIAN IS (FRENCH POLYNESIA)

International date line

NEW ZEALAND

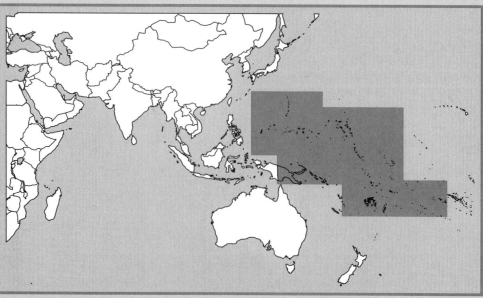

Chapter 26

The Pacific
Fantasy Islands

How many islands dot the Pacific? Thousands. In fact, tens of thousands. Either coral or volcanic in origin, spreading across vast stretches of ocean waters, these islands have been the subject of fantasy to the Western mind since 1521, when the explorer Magellan first passed through them. No, you'll not have to learn all of their names and locations. Probably the world's foremost geography experts would have trouble doing that. Only about a dozen or so have become significant tourist destinations. Some of these islands or island groupings are independent countries. Others are under various levels of administration by France, Great Britain, the United States, and others.

The islands of the Pacific can be loosely divided into three regions. (The whole area is sometimes called **Oceania**.) North and northeast of Australia are the islands of **Micronesia**. Tourism in Micronesia is limited, except for **Guam** and **Saipan**, which appeal strongly to Japanese tourists. **Chuuk**, **Kiribati** [kir-ih-BASS or kir-uh-BAH-tee], **Yap**, and **Palau** (also spelled Belau) have an almost legendary appeal for divers.

Melanesia—so named for the natives' dark skin (*mela* means *dark*)—draws quite a few North American tourists, though the islands of this group appeal most strongly to Australians and New Zealanders. **Fiji** [FEE-jee] is by far the most popular, but **Papua** [PAP-yuh-wah] **New Guinea** and **New Caledonia** also have their devotees.

Polynesia is perhaps the best known of the South Sea island groups. Legendary for its romantic scenery, soft climate, and graceful native lifestyle, it extends, technically, all the way north to Hawaii (covered in Chapter 7), to Easter Island on the east, and to New Zealand on the west. We concentrate mostly on those dots of land to the immediate east of Melanesia—**Tahiti** and its nearby islands are the big draw here, but **Tonga**, **American Samoa**, **Samoa** (formerly Western Samoa), and the **Cook Islands** all have their admirers.

Two significant geographic lines cross the region. One is the International Date Line, which we spoke of in Part I of this book. It zigs and zags among the islands so that it crosses no major destination. (Otherwise, you could find yourself in another day just by crossing the street!) It zags just to the east of Tonga. As a result, Tonga is technically the place where each new day starts. (That's why some Tongan stamps proclaim, "Tonga—Where time begins.") The other significant line is the equator. In this chapter, we discuss mostly those destinations south of it (they're called the South Seas), but remember that quite a few Pacific islands spill out north of the equator, including Hawaii and almost the entire area that is Micronesia.

> More languages are spoken in Papua New Guinea (700) than in any other country.

How Travelers Get There

Several major North American airlines fly to these destinations from the West Coast and Hawaii, as do such foreign carriers as Qantas, Air New Zealand, Air France, and a number of Asian carriers. After travelers fly on a major airline to a principal gateway—**Papeete**

Even into the 1900s, seashells were used as currency on many Pacific islands.

[pah-pee-AY-tee], Tahiti (PPT); **Nadi** [NON-dee], Fiji (NAN), or Guam (GUM)—they'll need to hop aboard one of the dozens of local airlines to get to the less visited islands. Some of these connections will be cited later; remember, though, that air service in the region is in a constant state of flux.

Several tour operators specialize in air–hotel packages to the South Pacific; they can often save travelers hundreds of dollars—and booking and itinerary-planning time, as well. Cruise ships visit the area (sometimes on repositioning cruises) and all manners of ferries, yachts, and cargo ships unite the islands.

Weather Patterns

Because virtually every one of the Pacific islands lies within the tropics, the climate is relatively predictable: for Polynesia and Melanesia, May through October (winter season) is warm, fairly dry, and high tourist season, whereas November through April (summer season) is hotter, wetter, and sees a thinning of tourism. (Remember that Polynesia and Melanesia are mostly in the Southern Hemisphere, so their seasons are the reverse of North America's.) On the other hand, Micronesia—being largely north of the equator—has the best weather in its winter season, from November through March, when temperatures are milder. The Micronesian summer season (July to October) is rainy; hurricanes are a threat in the summer and fall.

Topography and location, though, can produce variations within these patterns. For example, visitors to Papeete (Tahiti) in August can expect it to rain only about one day a week, but someone visiting **Pago Pago** [PONG-o PONG-o] (American Samoa) during that same month may experience rain just about every other day. To predict the leeward (and, therefore, drier) side of a mountainous island is not always as easy to do as in other parts of the world, because this region stretches across several opposite wind patterns. In general, though, the rule we learned in Part I applies to these tropical islands: Western shores will tend to be drier and eastern shores will be rainier. For an example of a South Seas climate, see Figure 26-1.

Getting Around

In South Pacific hospitals, a significant number of injuries treated are coconut tree–related.

Frequent flights and cruises connect the islands. On-island transportation is quite informal. Buses are usually a good option, because locals are often friendly and talkative. Mopeds and bicycles are a popular choice. Taxis are plentiful on the major islands, and visitors can often rent a car or taxi with driver for a day's sightseeing at a reasonable cost. How about car rentals? Well, they're available on the major islands; because of poor road conditions, a four-wheel-drive vehicle might be more practical. One thing to make clear: Don't expect the quality of service or efficiency of transportation to be anywhere near that of the United States. Other options: helicopter rides, glass-bottom boats, and even horseback riding.

Important Places

To bring some sense of order to this vast destination, we'll examine the principal islands according to their traditional cultural and geographic divisions: Polynesia, Melanesia, and Micronesia.

Polynesia

On the more remote French islands, locals often speak only French. But unlike many of France's residents, islanders will happily tolerate a tourist's high-school French.

Polynesia—the word itself conjures up the scent of plumeria blossoms, the sounds of friendly voices, and the feel of warm, azure waters lapping at your feet. Visitors favor five Polynesian island groups:

The Tahitian Islands. The Tahitian Islands, also known as the Society Islands (an older term), comprise the western part of French Polynesia. Tahiti itself (with its capital, Papeete) is the principal gateway to the region's 130 or so islands. Papeete is a bustling little city, with an open-air market, several fine resorts, and a small museum displaying the works of

Climate at a Glance
PAPEETE, TAHITI

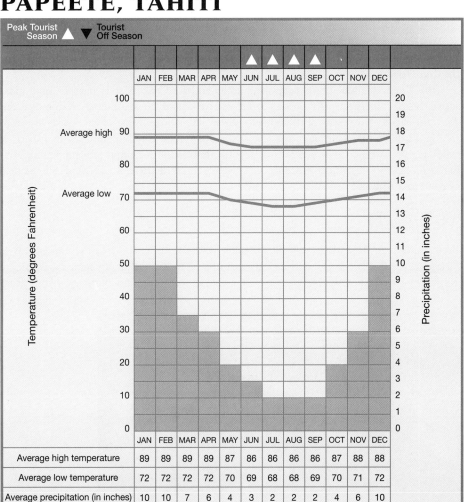

| Peak Tourist Season ▲   ▼ Tourist Off Season | | | | | | | | | | | | | |

	JAN	FEB	MAR	APR	MAY	JUN	JUL	AUG	SEP	OCT	NOV	DEC
Average high temperature	89	89	89	89	87	86	86	86	86	87	88	88
Average low temperature	72	72	72	72	70	69	68	68	69	70	71	72
Average precipitation (in inches)	10	10	7	6	4	3	2	2	2	4	6	10

Figure 26–1

French artist Paul Gauguin, who lived here. An interesting law—no building can be higher than a coconut tree—keeps Papeete and the rest of Tahiti free of view-spoiling high-rises.

There are many scenic areas on Tahiti itself, but even more dramatic scenery and the most extensive tourist lodging is on the nearby island of **Moorea** and on **Bora Bora** (which is 143 miles northwest of Tahiti). **Raiatea** and **Maupiti** have fewer lodging options, but are excellent get-away-from-it-all islands. One warning: French Polynesia is one of the most expensive island destinations in the South Pacific. Recommend French Polynesia to those who like water sports, all-inclusive resorts (which can blunt some of the high costs), and awesome scenery.

Tonga. Tonga has spectacular scenery—including several active volcanoes—and provides visitors with just about every water-sport opportunity available. Boaters love Tonga for its comparative absence of reefs. Tonga, which is still a monarchy, is made up of several islands; **Tongatapu**, where the capital is located, provides most of the modest lodging choices and, by Polynesian standards, is somewhat crowded. Travelers to Tonga will probably have to route through American Samoa, Samoa, Fiji, or Auckland.

American Samoa. Another mountainous (and picturesque) chain of islands, American Samoa has facilities even more limited than Tonga, but what is there feels more American than Polynesian. In other words, it's appropriate for those who want to retain at least some of the feel and comfort of home. Deep-sea fishing is good here, as are hiking opportunities.

Samoa was named
after a sacred chicken.

Virtually all accommodations are in the town of Pago Pago. Travelers can fly to Pago Pago's airport from Fiji, Samoa, the Cook Islands, or Hawaii.

Samoa. Samoa and its chief town, Apia, feel much more Polynesian than does American Samoa. Indeed, Samoa has the world's largest population of full-blooded Polynesians. Services, though, are limited; a growing influx of tourists may change that soon. For now, Samoa is still a bargain. Visitors can get here from Tahiti, Fiji, Tonga, American Samoa, or the Cook Islands.

The Cook Islands. Once sleepy and secluded, the Cook Islands have become more active, thanks to investment money from Australia and New Zealand. Rarotonga and Aitutaki islands have most of the hotels—several are deluxe. Most of the guests are from the "lands down under," though the Cook Islands are increasingly popular with American travelers. This would be an interesting, offbeat destination for those into snorkeling, diving, deep-sea fishing, or just beaching it. Travelers could be booked via Tahiti, Fiji, Samoa, or American Samoa.

Melanesia

Better known to Australians and New Zealanders (who are fairly close by), the islands of Melanesia are fast becoming destinations that appeal to Americans. In some cases, they're destinations unto themselves, but more often they're stop-off points on the way to or from

The South Pacific is a dream destination for divers
Image copyright Khoroshunova Olga, 2008. Used under license from Shutterstock.com

Australia and New Zealand. Two bits of trivia: 80 percent of the Pacific's islander popula-tion lives in Melanesia, and nearly 1,200 distinct languages are spoken throughout Melanesia—fortunately, English is one of them and it's spoken on many of the islands.

The Fiji Islands. The Fiji Islands have become among the most important of South Sea destinations. The large island of **Viti Levu** has many fine tropical hotels—especially on the west coast around Nadi (where the airport is located) and along the southern coast, which has come to be known as the **Coral Coast.** Hotels dot other shores of Viti Levu, as well as those of other islands in the Fijian chain, including **Turtle Island,** a well-publicized, very expensive private resort. The rest of Fiji, though, is a comparative South Sea bargain and is quite popular with divers, shoppers, and culture-seekers. (The islands' population is a not-always-harmonious blend of native Fijians, Polynesians, Indians, Chinese, and Europeans.)

Papua New Guinea. Papua New Guinea occupies the eastern half of the large island of New Guinea, which lies north of Australia (the western half is part of Indonesia). This trop-ical destination is especially interesting for its native culture: Until fairly recently, some of its natives were Stone Age headhunters. A few areas of the country are quite modern, with many conveniences, but most are thoroughly primitive. Papua New Guinea is an expensive destination, political and social turmoil is frequent, and crime can be a problem. But divers love its offshore areas and nature buffs appreciate its huge variety of orchids and birds. Air connections are generally made through several Australian east coast cities, though flights also arrive from Singapore and New Zealand.

New Caledonia. New Caledonia is famous for two things: Its superb diving (one of the world's largest barrier reefs lies offshore) and its capital city, **Noumea** [noo-MAY-uh]. Often called the Paris of the Pacific, Noumea has a few elegant boutiques, some gourmet restaurants, and, not far outside town, a casino. Don't fall into thinking that this is another French Riviera; New Caledonia seems elegant only in comparison to neighboring island destinations. Indeed, much of the island has a charming seediness about it. Yet, like other French islands, New Caledonia can be a rather expensive destination. A short flight north-east of New Caledonia are the islands of **Vanuatu,** with their impressive scenery, good div-ing, and surprising array of quality lodging.

Micronesia

Thousands of islands, but all of them isolated and small—that's the best way to describe Micronesia. The islands of Micronesia weren't exactly household words until World War II, when news reports from Guam, Yap, Truk (now Chuuk), and Saipan became commonplace. In the period following the war, nuclear testing took place here; one site, the island of Bi-kini (part of the seldom-visited Marshall Islands), became permanently associated with a scanty form of bathing suit. Micronesia continues to be of military interest, but American tourists are gradually finding out what Japanese tourists discovered decades ago: These is-lands are truly appealing destinations.

Guam. Part of a collection of islands geographically known as the Marianas, Guam is Micronesia's principal destination. The U.S. military's growing presence here helps ensure air connections to Hawaii—and many Western amenities. Water sports and dramatic scen-ery are Guam's principal attractions. Most tourist facilities are around the capital, **Agana,** and on **Tumon Bay,** which is highly frequented by Japanese and Taiwanese tourists. Guam is also a gateway to most of the other Micronesian islands. Travelers who are into water sports, history (especially that of World War II), golf, and other comforts typical of the United Stats will find Guam appealing.

Saipan. Also part of the Marianas, Saipan is Micronesia's other well-developed tour-ist center. It, too, owes its success to its reputation as a Japanese honeymoon destination. More so than Guam, Saipan is mostly geared to Japanese travelers, not Americans. A strong point for most: It feels less military. Divers, windsurfers, golfers, and scenery lovers will find Saipan quite pleasing.

Chuuk. Politically part of the Federated States of Micronesia (which also includes Pohnpei [PONE-pay], Yap, and Kosrae [KOSS-rye] and geographically part of the Caroline

Fijians are famous for their intricate tattoos and fire walking.

New Caledonia means "New Scotland."

Before World War II, Guam had no snakes. Now it has more snakes per square mile than anywhere else in the world.

Islands, Chuuk (formerly Truk) is a legendary destination for divers. Here, the United States bombed and crippled the World War II fleet of Japan; 60 wrecks lie on the bottom of Chuuk's 40-mile-wide lagoon harbor. Another diver's paradise in the Carolines (though accommodations are limited) is Palau, with its superb reef diving opportunities and picture-perfect tropical island scenery.

Kiribati. These flat atoll islands—stretching across almost 2,000 miles of the Pacific—include the Gilbert and Phoenix island groups. Still relatively uncommercialized, Kiribati appeals to divers and others who want to get away from it all. Basic lodging is available on several islands, especially **Tarawa**, where the capital is located.

Possible Itineraries

There are two ways to consider the islands of the Pacific: as "pause points" on the way to other places, or as a vacation's main destination. Polynesia and Melanesia can break up a trip to and from Australia and New Zealand. For example, travelers could fly to Fiji, where they might stay two or three days before they continue on to, say, New Zealand. They could then pause for a few days in Tahiti or Hawaii on the way back. Similarly, Guam or Chuuk could be a several-day pause between the mainland or Hawaii and such countries as Japan, China, the Philippines, Singapore, or any of the other Southeast Asian countries. Unfortunately, the flight connections may be a little difficult to arrange if the travelers need to use multiple airlines.

What of those travelers who want to visit only an island or combination of islands? It's best to keep them within one general island grouping. For example, a nine-day itinerary could include two flight days, four days on Moorea, and three days on Bora Bora. Another longer possibility would be to fly to Fiji for a three-day stay, then connect to two- or three-day stays in the islands to the east: Tonga, American Samoa, Samoa, or Rarotonga. Or hub out to the west, to such Melanesian destinations as New Caledonia and Papua New Guinea. Divers might enjoy a 9- to 14-day itinerary to the Micronesian islands of Guam, Chuuk, and Palau, with a more lively stay in Hawaii along the way. Cruises provide efficient itineraries between or among these island groupings.

Lodging Options

The Pacific islands' range of accommodations is staggeringly wide. On Bora Bora, for example, you can stay in a deluxe hut that sits on piers over a lagoon, sometimes on its own *motu*; at an all-inclusive resort, like **Club Med**; or in simple, inexpensive bungalows. Among the Fiji islands is super-exclusive Turtle Island Resort, once featured on *Lifestyles of the Rich and Famous*. Or you can book into a New Guinean guesthouse run by the descendants of headhunters. For those seeking more conventional accommodations, many North American and international chains have properties throughout the Pacific.

A few warnings: Even the most deluxe properties can be a bit disorganized and messy; reservations can be lost (bring a copy of the confirmation and pray); the locals on French islands sometimes don't speak English; bugs are everywhere in the tropics, including in the finest hotels; and some of the less-visited islands don't have anything but the most basic of lodging—one more reason to depend on independent tour packages that select hotels carefully and place more clout behind a guest's reservation.

Allied Destinations

Polynesia and Melanesia are easily combined with trips to Australia and New Zealand. Micronesia can be a stopover to the Philippines, Singapore, Malaysia, and all of mainland Asia. You can also combine several islands into one vacation package, including some South Sea destinations that few tourists visit and that we've not mentioned here. For information on such islands (including Nauru, Niue, the Solomons, Tuvalu, Wallis, and Futuna), consult a more detailed resource.

In the tropics, twice as many people are killed by falling coconuts than by sharks.

Little islands in Tahiti are called *motus*.

If you see geckoes (little lizards) in your room, encourage the creatures to stay. They chase insects while avoiding humans.

Mosquitoes are ferocious and roaches are ubiquitous throughout the islands; bring repellent and get your inoculations against mosquito-borne diseases.

Tahiti and other South Pacific islands feature over-water bungalows
Image copyright Marie Lumiere, 2008. Used under license from Shutterstock.com

Cultural Patterns

Each of these many islands has its own unique customs of which vacationers and business travelers alike should be aware. Among them are:

- In Fiji, time is informal and it may be acceptable to arrive quite late. Visitors to someone's home should remove their shoes before entering. The drink *kava* is often offered to guests; though it may taste harsh to Americans, it would be considered rude to refuse it. (This also applies in Samoa.) When talking with a Fijian resident, crossed arms is a sign of respect.

- Though it's not necessary to tip in French Polynesia, small gifts are often given.

- In Samoa, an elaborate greeting is considered very respectful. It's rude for a person standing to sway while talking to a Samoan; indeed, almost all conversation is held while sitting.

- Completely give up the notion of punctuality or efficiency while in the islands; nothing here seems to work as it should. (Consider that at some small island airports, the air traffic controller is also the ticket-taker and the skycap!)

- To Tahitians, shaking hands is very important. Visitors to the home of a local should taste at least a little bit of everything offered and be prepared to eat with their fingers. And they should not praise any item in the home too highly; it may be presented as a gift.

> Ask about tipping early on. On many islands, it's not the practice.

Factors That Motivate Visitors

Among the motives that people may have for traveling among the islands of the Pacific are:

- They seek the legendary beauty and romance of the islands.
- They want to break up a long trans-Pacific trip.
- The climate is spectacular.
- Water-sport, beach, adventure tour, and cruise opportunities are widely available.
- The cultural differences are fascinating.

> Bungee jumping originated on Vanuatu.

- It's a good way to visit many off-the-beaten-path, get-away-from-it-all destinations without too many inconveniences.
- The food is fresh and generally wonderful.
- Bargains can be had for those willing to put up with the barest of accommodations or with freighter transport.
- The scenery on the volcanic islands is dramatic.

Possible Misgivings

Perhaps you're in love with the South Pacific as a destination. Don't assume everyone else is. There are many potential objections to a South Sea vacation:

- "It's too expensive." This is a genuine concern; because most supplies are shipped to the islands, all costs are high, especially on French-governed islands. Suggest an off-season trip, when airfares are lower. Recommend one of the major islands, where a wide variety of services is available and air connections are easy. Suggest Fiji or Samoa, which are somewhat less expensive.
- "It's too far." The trip can indeed be long, with many potential connections if a lesser island is involved. A stopover in Hawaii can break up the initial long flight.
- "It seems too primitive for me." Suggest Fiji or Tahiti, where many conveniences are available.

When shopping, don't try to bargain for items. Among most islanders it's considered inappropriate.

Qualifying the Traveler
Fiji

For People Who Want	Appeal			Remarks
	High	Medium	Low	
Historical and Cultural Attractions		▲		Melanesian culture
Beaches and Water Sports	▲			
Skiing Opportunities			▲	None
Lots of Nightlife		▲		In hotels
Family Activities		▲		Families will enjoy it, but airfare prohibitive
Familiar Cultural Experience			▲	
Exotic Cultural Experience	▲			
Safety and Low Crime		▲		Some unrest
Bargain Travel		▲		Many bargains; flights costly
Impressive Scenery	▲			Seascapes, volcanic mountains, jungle
Peace and Quiet	▲			Much quieter than Hawaii
Shopping Opportunities		▲		Carvings, jewelry
Adventure	▲			Especially less-visited islands
To Do Business			▲	

- "I've heard of political unrest." On some islands, friction does sometimes occur between natives and the governing country or among different local factions. (This is especially true in Fiji.) Yet it seems that tourists are usually left alone here, even in revolutions. Still, check government advisories and give prudent, informed advice.

- "There aren't enough cultural attractions." The people and their way of life *are* the culture here, especially in the non-U.S. territories. If this is the type of person who loves Europe but not island stays, though, you may have to counter with a destination other than the South Seas.

- "We didn't like Hawaii and we won't like this." Find out why they didn't like Hawaii. Was it the overt commercialism? If so, perhaps the South Seas are exactly what they're looking for.

Sales Strategies

Independent tour packages and cruises are a great way to ensure maximum value and commission. All-inclusive resorts—common on some of these islands, not on others—often represent a good value. Dive packages, dive tours, and adventure jeep tours into an island's lush interior can often be booked in advance. Helicopter and even submarine rides are available on several islands. With someone who is worried about the quality of accommodations, upsell to the best hotel possible and suggest an ocean-view room. For those who dread long flights, suggest business or first class.

At some of the over-water hotel properties, room service is delivered by canoe.

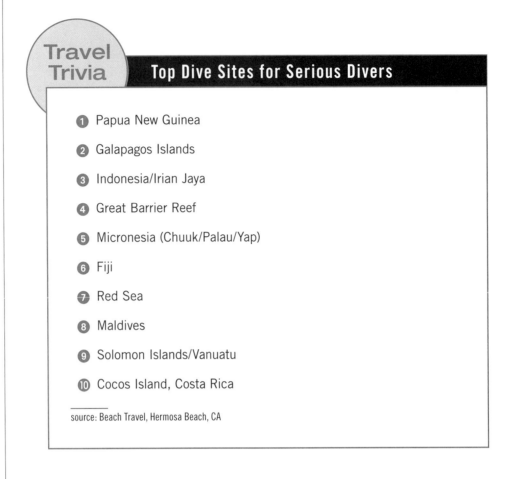

Travel Trivia

Top Dive Sites for Serious Divers

1. Papua New Guinea
2. Galapagos Islands
3. Indonesia/Irian Jaya
4. Great Barrier Reef
5. Micronesia (Chuuk/Palau/Yap)
6. Fiji
7. Red Sea
8. Maldives
9. Solomon Islands/Vanuatu
10. Cocos Island, Costa Rica

source: Beach Travel, Hermosa Beach, CA

NAME _____   **DATE** _____

MAP ACTIVITY

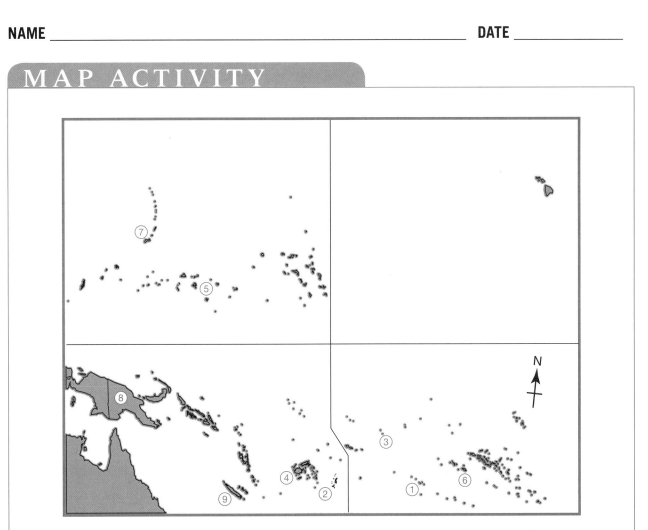

A traveler wants to visit the places listed below. Which number represents each on the map?

Place/Attraction	On Which Island or Island Group?	Number on Map
A. A monarch-ruled island	A. _____	A. _____
B. Nadi	B. _____	B. _____
C. A Gauguin museum	C. _____	C. _____
D. Descendants of headhunters	D. _____	D. _____
E. Noumea, the Pacific Paris	E. _____	E. _____
F. Micronesia's gateway isle	F. _____	F. _____
G. Papeete	G. _____	G. _____
H. A legendary dive site from World War II	H. _____	H. _____
I. Pago Pago	I. _____	I. _____
J. Rarotonga	J. _____	J. _____

NAME _____   **DATE** _____

CASE STUDY

Larry Olson, who loves diving, comes to you with vague plans to visit some Pacific islands. His wife, Adrienne, is also somewhat of a diver, but still feels the need for a culturally interesting place. Because she tells you that in college she was a French major with an art history minor, you think of several possibilities. They tell you they can be away for as long as nine days. Mr. Olson, by the way, owns a large building materials firm and drove up to your office in a Mercedes.

Circle the answer that best suits their needs.

1 Where would you suggest as a primary destination?

Chuuk   Palau

Fiji   New Caledonia

Why?

2 Which of the following would be a second destination that's nearby and would especially appeal to Larry?

Tokyo   Tahiti

The Philippines   Cairns

Why?

3 Adrienne states that perhaps a hard-core diving trip could be postponed to another vacation and that this time it might be nice to stay at a Club Med and have a variety of activities. Larry agrees. What might you recommend?

Bora Bora   The Thousand Islands

Papua New Guinea   Samoa

Why?

4 The Olsons like very comfortable lodging and you'd be glad to upsell them to a fine hotel. Of the following, which would be the *least* likely to have a selection of deluxe hotels?

Tahiti   The Cook Islands

Fiji   Palau

Why?

NAME _____ **DATE** _____

CREATIVE ACTIVITY

In the Creative Activity for Chapter 23, you judged whether a group of celebrities would like to visit Kenya and Tanzania. This activity is the reverse of that. Below are eight Pacific island destinations. Try to think of a famous person who might enjoy each destination (you must have a different celebrity for each one). Be prepared to explain how you arrived at your solution.

Destination	Celebrity	Why?
1 Moorea	**1**	**1**
2 Vanuatu	**2**	**2**
3 Tonga	**3**	**3**
4 Pago Pago	**4**	**4**
5 Papua New Guinea	**5**	**5**
6 Fiji	**6**	**6**
7 New Caledonia	**7**	**7**
8 Chuuk	**8**	**8**

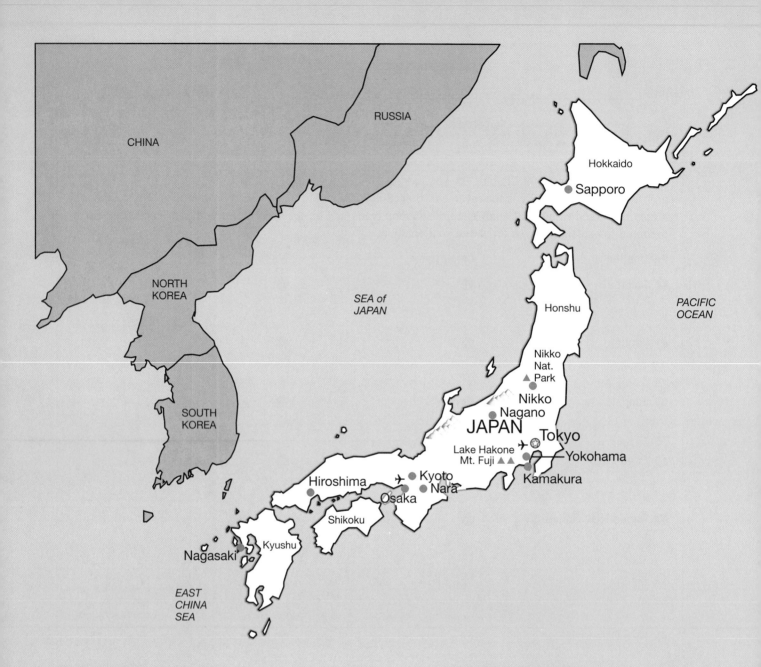

CHINA

RUSSIA

NORTH
KOREA

SEA of
JAPAN

Hokkaido

Sapporo

Honshu

PACIFIC
OCEAN

SOUTH
KOREA

Nikko
Nat.
Park

Nikko

Nagano

JAPAN

Tokyo

Lake Hakone
Mt. Fuji

Yokohama

Hiroshima

Kyoto

Kamakura

Osaka

Nara

Shikoku

Kyushu

Nagasaki

EAST
CHINA
SEA

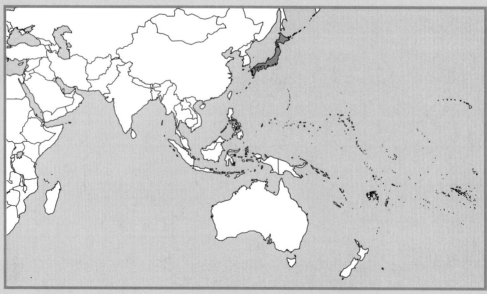

Chapter 27

Japan
Pearl of the Orient

Mitsubishi, Toyota, Sony—these are names that the whole world knows. Yet until the twentieth century, Japan—like some pearl hidden in an oyster—existed in almost complete isolation, a mystery to the world: small, unimpressive, largely unknown. Japan still is only a series of small islands in the shadow of that teeming behemoth, China. Yet a mere few decades after having faced defeat in World War II, Japan today powerfully influences world economics, business, and politics. It's a country of calm beauty and aggressive drive.

About the size of Montana, Japan is bordered by the Sea of Japan to its west and the Pacific Ocean to the east. A spine of volcanic mountains runs along the western length of the country; indeed, most Japanese live along the country's eastern flank. One surprising fact: Japan is made up of not one or a few, but more than 4,000 islands. Only four, however—**Hokkaido** [ho-KYE-doh], **Honshu, Shikoku** [she-KOH-koo], and **Kyushu** [KYOO-shoo]—are populated to any great degree. And of those, it's Honshu, the largest, that dominates the country.

On Honshu, **Tokyo**—the world's largest metropolitan area—lies near the center, on the east coast. **Kyoto**, an ancient city of great charm, rests in the south-central region of the island, and the port of **Osaka** (a major business destination) is just to its southwest.

Japanese products aren't necessarily cheaper in Japan, but you'll probably find many items not yet available in North America.

FYI
FOR YOUR INFORMATION
JAPAN

CAPITAL: Tokyo

AREA (SQUARE MILES): 145,766

TIME ZONE: GMT +19

DRIVE ON: Left

POPULATION: 127,300,000

RELIGIONS: Buddhism, Shintoism

LANGUAGE: Japanese

CURRENCY: yen

ELECTRICITY: 100 volts, 60 cycles AC

CAPSULE HISTORY: Contact with China, fifth century; first Shogun, 1185; Portuguese visit, 1542; trade between Japan and the West opens, 1854; parliamentary system, 1889; Pearl Harbor attack, 1941; Japan surrenders, after two atom bombings, 1945; full sovereignty, 1952.

For reference sources, tourist bureaus, and suggested lengths of stay, see the Appendices.

Although the national language of Japan is Japanese, many people (especially travel personnel) speak relatively good English and are eager to communicate.

How Travelers Get There

Tokyo is Japan's gateway. **Narita** (also known as New Tokyo) **International Airport (NRT)** is where most international flights land. It's 43 miles to the northeast and the fares into Tokyo in regular taxis are incredibly expensive. Limousine buses, cars (booked in advance), and an express train are the best alternatives and can cost much less than a taxi would. Osaka's **Kansai International Airport (KIX)** is another popular option for Japan-bound travelers.

Nonstop service is available to Japan from the United States. Several North American carriers fly here, as do many international airlines, especially those based in Asia. **Japan Air Lines** (JL) is the national carrier; **All Nippon Airways**, also called **ANA** (NH), provides service as well. Flying time from Los Angeles is just over 11 hours; from New York, it's over 13 hours. (It's common for travelers from the East Coast to stop over on the West Coast or in Hawaii.) Japan is also a cruise destination. A few cruises start in **Yokohama**, just south of Tokyo, while others stop off at various Japanese ports (especially **Nagasaki**) as part of a longer Asian itinerary.

Weather Patterns

Japan's climate is temperate, though conditions are less than ideal; gray and drizzly days are all too common (see Figure 27–1). Summers are warm and humid, whereas winters are chilly. (Winter in Hokkaido and the northern portion of Honshu, however, is very cold.) Rain is common from March through October; only winter is relatively dry, with about five rainy (and occasionally snowy) days per month. Spring is a legendary time to visit Japan; the cherry blossoms are in bloom, the temperatures are pleasant, and the rainy season hasn't quite reached its full strength. September to November can also be pleasant. Temperatures average in the range of 60s to 70s during the day, and precipitation, especially in late fall, is less likely. (Typhoons bring heavy rains in early fall.)

A warning: Avoid traveling in Japan during major Japanese holiday periods because accommodations and transportation get very crowded. The days before and after New Year's are one such vacation time; mid-August (the Obon Festival) is another. Finally, Golden Week, April 29 through the first week of May, is the third big holiday period. Tourism thins out a bit during winter, but rates—especially hotel costs—don't drop very much. There's no real budget season in Japan.

Getting Around

Japan Air Lines and ANA provide domestic flights between major cities. However, since most of the country's main tourist destinations are comparatively close to one another, air service may not be the most convenient mode of transportation. That honor falls to the famed bullet trains (*Shinkansen*), which hurtle down tracks at speeds up to 130 mph. Every visitor to Japan should travel on at least a part of the bullet train route between Tokyo and Osaka: The *Hikari* train offers near-express service, whereas the *Kodama* provides more stops (especially helpful for tourists who wish to see the sights en route). The **Japan Rail Pass** is a useful option for those who intend to spend a good length of time in Japan; it allows unlimited rail travel and can be purchased only in North America. There also are regular service trains throughout the country, some of which are highly luxurious. (Note: Some trains are private and aren't covered by the Japan Rail Pass.)

Though car rentals are widely available, they're not the best idea. Because driving is on the left and most road signs are in Japanese, conditions can be extremely confusing. A better (though costly) alternative: a private car with driver or guide.

Tokyo and Osaka offer superb subways. The systems are frenetic, but not nearly as confusing as some might fear. (They're fairly well marked for Westerners.) Kyoto has a limited subway.

Kansai Airport is on a huge manmade island. Unfortunately, it's slowly sinking.

During rush hours, Tokyo's subways have professional "pushers" who shove commuters into the packed cars.

Climate at a Glance
TOKYO

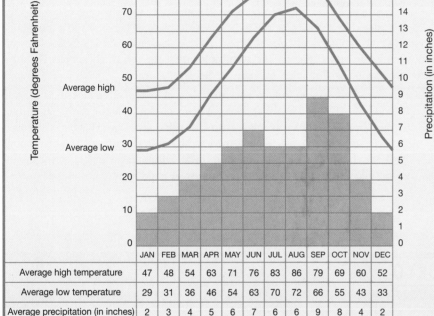

	JAN	FEB	MAR	APR	MAY	JUN	JUL	AUG	SEP	OCT	NOV	DEC
Average high temperature	47	48	54	63	71	76	83	86	79	69	60	52
Average low temperature	29	31	36	46	54	63	70	72	66	55	43	33
Average precipitation (in inches)	2	3	4	5	6	7	6	6	9	8	4	2

Figure 27–1

Bus service in Japan is good and moderately priced. Avoid public transportation during rush hours. The kind of crowding that goes on may come as quite a shock.

Important Places

Japan has many unusual places to enjoy. Keep in mind that the country is also an especially important destination for business travelers.

Tokyo

Tokyo, Japan's capital, is a paradox: futuristic yet deeply traditional; intensely crowded yet thoroughly efficient. It's Japan's center of commerce, education, publishing, and entertainment, as well. Major sites in Tokyo are:

- **The Ginza district**, one of the most recognizable areas of the city to Westerners. Its glittering neon shines on high-fashion shops, restaurants, theaters, and very expensive nightlife.

- **The Imperial Palace**, home of the emperor, in the center of the city. Though the palace itself is closed to tourists (except on special occasions), the sprawling grounds are open; they feature a moat, park, and museum.

For buying electronic gadgets, visit Tokyo's Akihabara district, which packs 1,000 shops into five square blocks.

- **Tokyo Tower**, over 1,000 feet high, offering the best view of the city (as long as it's clear, which it seldom is).
- **Temples and shrines**, the most popular of which are the **Meiji Shrine** (with its sacred Shinto gardens) and the large, impressive **Asakusa Kannon Temple** (Tokyo's oldest temple).
- **The Ueno** [oo-EH-no] **district**, where several museums and a zoo are located. One problem for Westerners: Most of the signs are in Japanese only.
- **Tokyo Disneyland**, just outside the city. It's similar to its overseas cousins, but there are a few differences—some cultural, some practical. (For instance, "Main Street, U.S.A." is covered with a canopy to keep out the rain.) Adjacent is **Tokyo DisneySea**, a maritime-themed amusement park.

Most visitors to Tokyo wish to travel out of the city and take some **day trips**. Among the attractions you can recommend are:

- **Nikko**, considered by many to be the most beautiful place in Japan. It's in a mountainous region two hours north of Tokyo by train. Its huge national park is spectacular, with glorious mountain views. The region is well known for the intricately carved **Toshogu Shrine** (the "see no evil" monkey carvings are here).
- **The Kamakura-Hakone region**, an hour southwest of Tokyo, often visited on the way to Kyoto and Osaka. Kamakura, an ancient government seat, is home to the **Daibutsu**, the Great Buddha (a 43-foot statue more than 750 years old). Lake Hakone (also called Lake Ashi) provides a spectacular setting to view **Mt. Fuji**, the famous volcanic mountain. (That is, of course, if it's not shrouded in mist.) Climbing excursions to the mountain's summit take place mostly in July and August. A good level of fitness is required.

> When Japanese children lose a tooth, they throw it onto the roof of their house.

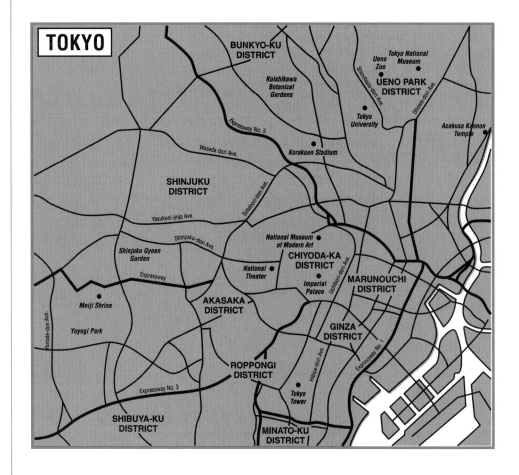

Kyoto

Surrounded by hills, this ancient, historical city—for 1,000 years it was Japan's capital—is noted for its architecture, folk arts, and graceful beauty. Kyoto claims to have 2,000 temples and shrines, not to mention many exquisite gardens. In addition to its shrines, Kyoto's popular sites include:

- **The Imperial Palace**, the ancient royal residence, which can only be visited by guided tour.
- **Nijo Castle**, a subtle seventeenth-century structure built for a shogun.

The following **day-trip** destinations are usually reached from Kyoto:

- **Nara**, the capital of Japan 1,200 years ago and the origin of much of the country's art, religion, and government. It's only about a half-hour from Osaka and Kyoto. Its most famous attraction is the **Todaiji Temple**, considered the largest wooden structure in the world: It houses a 49-foot bronze Buddha. **Kasuga Shrine** has a lofty pagoda and a path lined with thousands of lanterns. Legendary is Nara's 1,240-acre **Deer Park**, where the deer are so tame that they will nibble food right out of visitors' hands.
- **Hiroshima**, the first city ever to be devastated by a nuclear weapon. A very long day trip from Kyoto in southern Honshu, Hiroshima's **Peace Memorial Park** and other memorials are very moving.

Nara's deer are so aggressive that they'll poke into visitors' pockets and bags for food.

Osaka

Though often bypassed by tourists in favor of nearby Kyoto, Osaka—one of the main commercial and industrial centers of Japan—has much to offer. The city is one of the most frenetic in the world, with business people constantly hurrying from place to place and an astonishing array of stores and shopping malls. Among Osaka's main attractions are:

- **Osaka Castle**, a sixteenth-century structure that affords an excellent view of the city. A good museum is nearby.
- **Performances** of Kabuki drama, Noh theatre, and Bunraku puppet shows (all of which, frankly, can seem alien and perhaps boring to many Americans).

Osaka's corporate and cultural center is the Nakanoshima district.

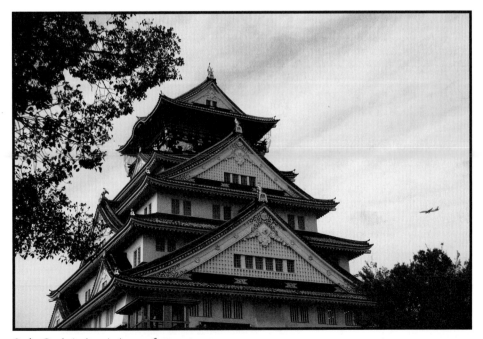

Osaka Castle is that city's most famous structure
Image copyright Chris McCooey, 2008. Used under license from Shutterstock.com

Possible Itineraries

Japan is often visited as a business destination, but tourism is still quite important. The country is fairly compact, with most major attractions centered on Honshu island. First-time visitors could spend about a week here: a couple of days in Tokyo, a day trip to the Kamakura–Hakone area, and three or four days in Kyoto, Osaka, and Nara. Return travelers may want to add visits to Nikko or Hiroshima. Some fine resorts are on the northern island of Hokkaido, including an excellent ski facility in **Sapporo**, where the 1972 Winter Olympics were held. (The 1998 Games took place in **Nagano**, on Honshu.)

Lodging Options

Hotel accommodations in Japan are among the best run—and most wallet thinning—in the world. To save money, you might look into voucher programs sponsored by tour operators: Participating hotels are usually in the first-class and tourist-class categories and offer substantial savings. Another possibility is a business-class hotel; these offer quite small and very basic accommodations that are popular among Japanese businessmen, though they wouldn't be suitable for families. One other alternative: *ryokans*, or Japanese-style inns, which offer soaking baths and thin futon mattresses. (They also have Western-style rooms and tend to assume that foreign visitors prefer such accommodations.)

Tokyo's hotels are scattered throughout the city. But the best ones are clustered in two places: the area around the Imperial Palace, and a section just west of the Shinjuku district. Plenty of lodging is available in the Narita Airport/Convention Center area.

Many North American and other international chains serve Japan. Among the best Japanese chains are **Okura, Akasaka, New Otani**, and **Rihga**.

Allied Destinations

Japan is just across the Sea of Japan from the nations of South Korea and China. Both are potential add-on destinations. Russia is also adjacent; most major Russian tourist destinations, however, are nearer Europe. The Philippines and the islands of Micronesia are sometimes add-on destinations for Japan-bound travelers. Southeast Asian countries such as Thailand, Malaysia, and Singapore aren't anywhere as close to Japan as many people imagine; however, considering the distance that most Americans travel to reach Japan, it might be reasonable to recommend any of these nations to expand a trip. And don't forget: Hawaii may be a convenient way to break up a flight to or from Japan.

Cultural Patterns

Customs are of great importance in Japan. It's necessary that business travelers, and people on holiday, understand them.

- The Japanese are very formal in their introductions. Though handshaking is acceptable, bowing is still the custom; moreover, visitors should bow as low as they are being bowed to in return. Titles are commonly used when addressing one another, and first names are used only among the closest of friends and family.

- One's position holds great meaning in Japan and business cards are widely exchanged; make sure to bring some along, even if on vacation—you never know when a business contact will be made. (Bilingual cards are preferable and can usually be ordered through the hotels.)

- All dealings and relationships should be handled with restraint and reserve. And be sure to treat the elderly with the utmost respect.

The Nara deer seem timid—until they start looking in your pockets for food
Image copyright Sam DCruz, 2008. Used under license from Shutterstock.com

- The Japanese are astonishingly helpful to foreign visitors. If you get lost, try to find someone who knows a smattering of English. That person will then probably escort you to wherever you're bound.

- This helpfulness extends to stores. Don't be surprised by all the attention you'll get from sales personnel.

- Bring a small gift when arriving at a business meeting or visiting a Japanese home; these gifts should be wrapped in pastel-colored paper with no bows, and items that come in pairs (e.g., pen-and-pencil sets) are often considered good luck. (By the way, overcomplimenting an object in a Japanese home is a bad idea: It may be presented as a gift.)

- Though there's active nightlife in Japan, it doesn't go on until the wee hours. Because the subways don't run all night, restaurants and nightclubs close relatively early.

- If offered a gift, refuse once, modestly and calmly. Then accept it using both hands.

Shoes should be removed before entering temples, homes, and rooms that have straw *tatami* mats.

- Punctuality is important, especially for business meetings.
- The Japanese don't like to say "no" if it can be avoided. Instead, they often answer "maybe" or "it is very difficult." This is an important distinction to understand, particularly for travelers here on business, for they may misinterpret this to mean agreement with their position.
- Although individualism is prized in North America, the welfare of the group predominates in Japan.
- It's considered rude to point with one finger; use the whole hand.
- Business is almost never discussed until the participants have socialized considerably—sometimes for days.

Factors That Motivate Visitors

It's important to understand why someone might want to visit Japan. This is a wonderful country, but it's not for everyone. Some reasons for wanting to visit Japan are:

- It's a very important business destination.
- Japan has a unique, exotic, and ancient culture.
- Some visitors can trace their ancestry here.
- There's beautiful art and architecture.
- It's very Westernized and comfortable.
- Its level of service, efficiency, and creature comforts is astonishingly high.
- The countryside has great natural beauty.
- It's an absolute heaven for golfers, though they may find courses to be somewhat smaller and more expensive than those at home.
- Japan is an extremely safe place to visit.
- The Japanese are incredibly helpful to visitors, who shouldn't be surprised if a local goes very much out of the way to help them.
- A full schedule of nonstop flights makes traveling from the United States convenient.

Possible Misgivings

Here are a few of the qualms that some people might have about Japan, and their counters:

- "Japan is extremely expensive, especially its restaurants." Prices certainly can be high. This country is not for the budget conscious. However, there are many ways to keep costs down: You can book hotels through a voucher program or as part of a tour; travelers can get a Japan Rail Pass and take subways instead of cabs. As for food, beef is particularly expensive. Try eating at regular neighborhood restaurants, sushi bars, and noodle shops rather than in fancy places. And, of course, tours—both escorted and independent—lock in prices and eliminate most financial surprises.
- "The Japanese language is terribly confusing." Many Japanese speak English, especially in business. English is often easier for many Japanese to read than to speak: If problems in communication do occur, you should write down what you wish to say.
- "I've heard that the Japanese don't get along with people who weren't born there." Travelers should know that the Japanese are exceedingly polite and gracious. Moreover, the country's relationship with North America is very good.
- "Japanese culture is different; I'll feel lost there." Of all the Asian nations, Japan may be the most Westernized. Read a book on Japanese customs; it's a simple effort and tremendously helpful.

The lyrics of the Japanese national anthem are over 1,000 years old.

Some of the rare shopping bargains: fine paper goods, toys, clocks, sugar novelties, children's clothing, and electric razors.

Qualifying the Traveler
Japan

For People Who Want	Appeal			Remarks
	High	Medium	Low	
Historical and Cultural Attractions	▲			Mostly related to Japan's fascinating history
Beaches and Water Sports			▲	Some, but not frequented by foreigners
Skiing Opportunities			▲	Some, but less frequented by foreigners
Lots of Nightlife		▲		Tokyo and Osaka
Family Activities			▲	Cost discouraging
Familiar Cultural Experience			▲	
Exotic Cultural Experience	▲			
Safety and Low Crime	▲			One of world's lowest crime rates
Bargain Travel			▲	One of world's most expensive destinations
Impressive Scenery		▲		Outside cities
Peace and Quiet			▲	Only in the countryside
Shopping Opportunities		▲		Wide selection, but costly
Adventure		▲		
To Do Business	▲			Must understand cultural differences

Figure 27–2

■ "I know I won't like eating there; I've never liked sushi." Japanese cuisine is much more than just raw fish. For example, *yakitori* is skewered and grilled meats and vegetables, and *tempura* is deep-fried. There are many other styles as well, not to mention Western restaurants and fast food. One interesting custom: Restaurants display in the window the dishes they serve so that you can know what you'll eat. (The display food is, of all things, plastic, but incredibly realistic.) Menus are also posted outside.

Sales Strategies

Because of its distance from the United States, Japan provides you with a wonderful option to break up the long flight by booking a stopover in Hawaii or, for East Coast travelers, on the West Coast. And because the country is so far away, some travelers might extend their trip—either within Japan or by visiting other nearby destinations. Because of Japan's unusual cultural, linguistic, and monetary conditions, vacationers are quite willing to consider all-inclusive escorted or independent tours. Though most tourists don't think of Japan as a resort or spa country, there are some fine ones here. A Japan Rail Pass is a good idea for those who intend to travel around the country over several weeks. Cruises are becoming a popular way to visit Japan's port cities.

In Japan there's one vending machine per 20 people. Some machines dispense beer and whiskey.

Plastic food in a restaurant window tempts diners
Photo by Marc Mancini

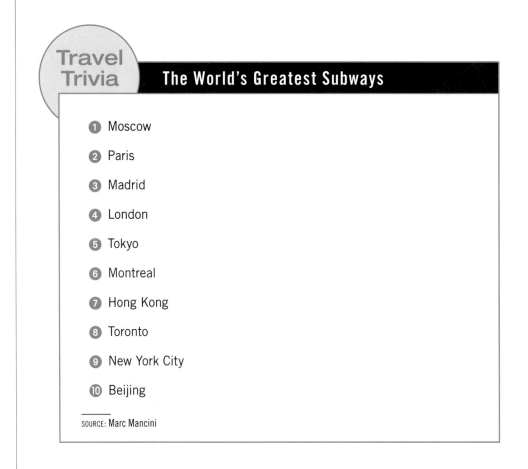

Travel Trivia

The World's Greatest Subways

1 Moscow

2 Paris

3 Madrid

4 London

5 Tokyo

6 Montreal

7 Hong Kong

8 Toronto

9 New York City

10 Beijing

SOURCE: Marc Mancini

NAME _____ **DATE** _____

MAP ACTIVITY

A traveler wants to visit the places listed below. Which number represents each on the map?

Place/Attraction	In/Near Which City?	Number on Map
A. Toshogu Shrine and "see no evil" carvings	A. _____	A. _____
B. Ueno Zoo	B. _____	B. _____
C. Todaiji Temple and tame deer	C. _____	C. _____
D. The Daibutsu (the Great Buddha)	D. _____	D. _____
E. Japan's capital for 1,000 years	E. _____	E. _____
F. Nijo Castle	F. _____	F. _____
G. The Ginza	G. _____	G. _____
H. Peace Memorial Park	H. _____	H. _____
I. DisneySea	I. _____	I. _____
J. Meiji Shrine	J. _____	J. _____

NAME _____ **DATE** _____

CASE STUDY

Jack Fujimoto has a small business in Seattle that's just starting out and he's trying to land a major Japanese account. Though it's a stretch for his company, he's decided to fly to Tokyo for three days. As long as he has to go over anyway, the 40-year-old executive and his wife, Grace, have decided to extend this trip into a personal vacation; they may not have another chance for a while. She will fly over with Jack, and they'll spend some extra days traveling around the country.

Circle the answer that best suits their needs.

1 What service would *not* be appropriate for the Fujimotos?

     A Japan Rail Pass   An independent tour

     A business-class hotel   A stopover en route

     Why?

2 Which of the following tips would benefit them?

     Buy a Japan Rail pass   Take a cab from Narita
     when you get there.   Airport into Tokyo.

     Be prepared to dine   Always tip at least
     relatively early.   10 percent.

     Why?

3 How many days would you recommend for their pleasure trip after business is completed, if they go only to Japan?

     Five   Twelve

     Nine   Four score

     Why?

4 The Fujimotos decide that because they'll already be going as far as Japan, they might as well extend their trip three days to visit another country. They have to return to Tokyo for their flight home, so they don't want to travel too far. Which of the following destinations would *not* be appropriate for them to visit?

     Thailand   South Korea

     Hong Kong   Taiwan

     Why?

NAME _____   **DATE** _____

CREATIVE ACTIVITY

Because you're in the travel industry, your friends often ask you for free advice. But this time the request is unusual: Your neighbors' daughter will be on her school's team in a state geography competition. She's been told that one of the destinations that will be focused on is Japan, but that any other global destination may also come up. Can you help coach her?

You discover that she knows plenty about the world's cities and attractions, but not much about Japan. You give her a book on Japan to study. You also set up a little training exercise for her. You create a list of Japanese attractions and challenge her to go online and come up with an equivalent somewhere else in the world. She must explain her choice. (You hope this will help her "connect" what she already knows about the rest of the world with what she's now learning about Japan.) You should also predict a possible answer for each, just in case she can't think of one.

Japanese Place/Attraction	Equivalent Elsewhere	Why
e.g., The Imperial Palace	Buckingham Palace, London	Both homes to monarchs, rarely open to public
1 Tokyo Tower		
2 Mt. Fuji		
3 The Ginza		
4 Hiroshima		
5 Osaka Castle		
6 Sapporo		
7 Tokyo Disneyland		
8 Yokohama		
9 Narita		
10 The *Shinkansen*		

Chapter 28

Singapore and Thailand
Crossroads of Asia

The great trader ships of yesteryear must certainly have been a sight, with their sails billowing in the wind. Bound for China and India from the South Pacific, they had but one direct route: through the **Strait of Malacca** at the tip of the **Malay Peninsula**. Lying at the peninsula's southern end was the major port of Singapore, and just to the north was Siam. Today, Singapore remains one of the world's busiest ports, and Siam, now known as Thailand [TIE-land], has stayed—through wars, massive migration, and an unending onslaught of trade—a strong, independent nation. At the cornerstone of a continent, both glory in their rich mix of cultures. And for both their past and present, they represent two of the world's most intriguing destinations.

Originally a British colony, Singapore is a unique island—it's both a city and a self-contained country. Thailand is approximately the size of Arizona and Utah combined. Its capital, **Bangkok**, lies slightly north of the Gulf of Thailand, just before the country thins out and winds its way down the peninsula. It's here that you'll find two of the country's popular resorts: **Pattaya Beach** on the south coast and **Phuket** [poo-KET] **Island** just off the west. **Chiang Mai**, the second-largest city, is in the hilly north.

Thailand's national language is Thai, though English is widely spoken, especially by travel personnel. In Singapore, because of the particularly diverse origins of its populace, there are actually several official languages: Malay, English (which is predominant in the business and travel industries), Mandarin Chinese, and Tamil.

How Travelers Get There

Two major gateways serve this region: Singapore and Bangkok. Singapore is accessed by its national carrier, **Singapore Airlines** (SQ), which flies into **Changi International Airport** (SIN) (praised by many as the world's finest airport), as do other North American and international airlines. Flights from Los Angeles take about 18.5 hours. Singapore is also one of the world's busiest seaports and is a common embarking and stopping point for cruises. In addition, Singapore is linked by causeway to the adjoining nation of Malaysia and can be reached from Malaysia by train. The national airline of Thailand is **Thai Airways** (TG); it and other North American and international carriers land at **Bangkok International Airport** (BKK). Many domestic flights land at the city's old international airport **Don Muang** (DMK). Flying time from Los Angeles is 18 hours. Cruises call near Bangkok and at Phuket.

Thailand is the only southeast Asian nation never to be colonized.

493

FYI
FOR YOUR INFORMATION

SINGAPORE AND THAILAND

CAPITALS: Singapore: Singapore
Thailand: Bangkok

AREA (SQUARE MILES): Singapore: 226.4
Thailand: 198,250

TIME ZONES: Singapore: GMT +8
Thailand: GMT +7

DRIVE ON: Left

POPULATION: Singapore: 4,600,000
Thailand: 65,500,000

RELIGION: Buddhism, Christianity, Islam,
Taoism, Hinduism

LANGUAGES: Singapore: Malay, Chinese,Tamil,
English
Thailand: Thai

CURRENCY: Singapore: 1 dollar = 100 cents
Thailand: 1 baht = 100 satangs

ELECTRICITY: 220 volts, 50 cycles AC

CAPSULE HISTORY: Singapore: Founded as separate entity by Sir Stamford Raffles, 1819; separate British Crown colony, 1946; independence, 1959; part of Malaysian federation, 1963; separate republic, 1965.
Thailand: Separate identity beginning sixth century; British dominate, 1824; absolute monarchy ends, 1932; Japan occupies, 1941–1945; many refugees migrate into Thailand, 1978.

For reference sources, tourist bureaus, and suggested lengths of stay, see the Appendices.

Weather Patterns

The climate of these two destinations are quite similar (see Figures 28–1 and 28–2). Both are generally hot and muggy year-round, with little variation in temperature. Singapore, particularly, is stunningly consistent, because it's so near the equator: It averages a high in the upper 80s, down to the mid-70s, 12 months a year. Though there's plenty of rain in every season, November to January are Singapore's wettest months. March and September are especially uncomfortable—cooling breezes are minimal or nonexistent.

Unlike Singapore, Thailand has relatively little precipitation from November through April; May through October are the rainiest months. The hottest months of the year are March through August, with highs in the 90s and lows in the 70s. November through February is the coolest time, with temperatures somewhat lower—though it's still pretty warm (but nights can get chilly). Typhoons and monsoons can affect travel in the late summer and fall.

Tourism is fairly consistent year-round in Singapore, though the period from June through August draws more tourists than any other. The same situation prevails in Bangkok, though January and February are off-season—a surprising fact because Bangkok weather is at its best in the winter. (It's because Thais leave Bangkok for the southern beach cities at this time of year; as a result, tourism peaks at beach resorts such as Phuket in the winter, in complete reversal of the patterns for the rest of the country.)

Getting Around

It's relatively easy to get around Singapore: Many taxis patrol the streets, and they're reasonably priced. (The main business district has a restricted area during early hours for vehicles with a minimum number of passengers; those who are there mainly for business

Climate at a Glance
BANGKOK, THAILAND

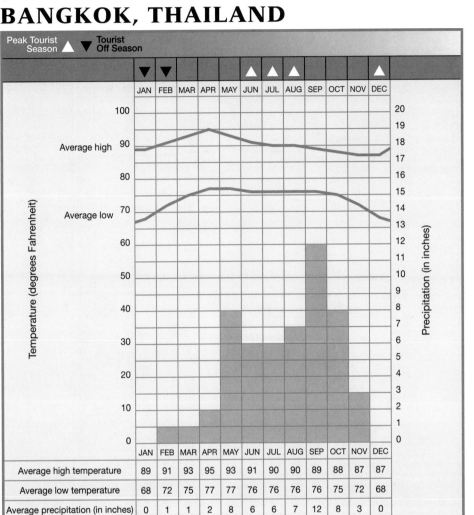

| Peak Tourist Season ▲   ▼ Tourist Off Season | | | | | | | | | | | | | |

	JAN	FEB	MAR	APR	MAY	JUN	JUL	AUG	SEP	OCT	NOV	DEC
Average high temperature	89	91	93	95	93	91	90	90	89	88	87	87
Average low temperature	68	72	75	77	77	76	76	76	76	75	72	68
Average precipitation (in inches)	0	1	1	2	8	6	6	7	12	8	3	0

Figure 28–1

should be sure to check the restrictions.) The bus system can be confusing. Three-wheeled "trishaws" can be an unusual way to travel; settle on a price first.

Thailand has a good bus system and fairly good trains. The roads are basically sound, but avoid them during the rainy season. In Bangkok, the hotel-run taxis are more expensive than private ones, but they're a little better. Because there are many canals through the city, river taxis can be a fun and inexpensive way to travel. The streets are crowded, so renting a car is a bad idea. Thailand's major cities are connected by air. And, of course, the two countries—and the nations around and in-between—are interconnected by flights and cruises. A luxury train, the **Eastern & Oriental Express**, makes the 1,200-mile run between Singapore and Bangkok; some departures continue on to Chiang Mai; others run between Bangkok and Vientiane, Laos.

Important Places

Singapore and Thailand offer visitors a rich mix of cultures, superb scenery, and many ancient monuments. Tourism concentrates on the following areas.

Bangkok's canals are called *klongs*.

Climate at a Glance
SINGAPORE

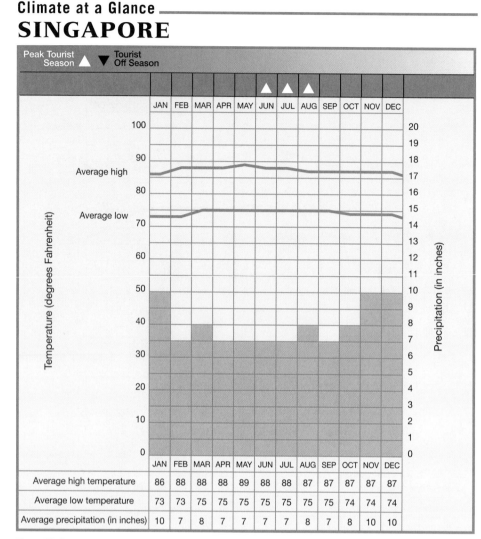

	JAN	FEB	MAR	APR	MAY	JUN	JUL	AUG	SEP	OCT	NOV	DEC
Average high temperature	86	88	88	88	89	88	88	87	87	87	87	87
Average low temperature	73	73	75	75	75	75	75	75	75	74	74	74
Average precipitation (in inches)	10	7	8	7	7	7	7	8	7	8	10	10

Figure 28–2

Singapore

Singapore is a very contemporary city—and one of Asia's most prosperous. (It's also the second-most densely populated country in the world, after Monaco.) It's one of the world's busiest ports and a major business destination. The 4.6 million residents are largely of Chinese descent; yet there remains a strong British influence left over from colonial days. Singapore boasts famous shopping, fine dining, active nightlife, and a well-scrubbed look. Among the most popular attractions:

- **Haw Par Villa** (formerly Tiger Balm Gardens), an offbeat attraction with grottoes, statues, amusement rides, and a superb view of the sea.

- **Chinatown, Little India**, and **Arab Street**, charming, fun, and interesting neighborhoods that offer excellent shopping and great food.

- **The National Museum of Singapore**, Singapore's oldest museum.

- **The Singapore Zoological Gardens**, considered one of the world's finest zoos. Next door is the **Night Safari**, where visitors can see nocturnal animals.

- **Jurong Bird Park**, a colorful and extremely large home to more than 9,000 birds from around the world.

There are stiff penalties in Singapore for jaywalking and littering, and smoking is prohibited in many public places.

The bold Esplanade building in Singapore houses a variety of performance venues
Image copyright Antonio M. Magdaraog, 2008. Used under license from Shutterstock.com

Among the several **day trips** from Singapore that you might want to suggest are:

- **Kusu**, a popular island resort. Turtles are a major attraction here. (According to legend, the island itself was a turtle at one time.)

- **Sentosa**, another active island resort located nearby, with many recreational activities and several major resort hotels. Also here is **Underwater World**, a $20 million oceanarium.

- **Malaysia**, which begins just across the Strait of Malacca. **Johor Bahru** is the Malaysian town closest to Singapore; a bazaar and sultan's palace are its prime attractions. (We examine Malaysia—a major destination in its own right—more fully in Chapter 30.)

Bangkok

Bangkok is a chaotic, noisy, densely populated city, yet its spirit, friendliness, and heritage make it a top-class travel destination. The **National Museum** has an excellent and extensive collection of Oriental artifacts. However, what visitors notice first are the temples. Hundreds of them embellish the city skyline. Among the most popular sites are:

- **The temples**, of course (called *wat* in Thai). The most striking ones are the soaring **Wat Arun** (Temple of the Dawn), which offers a great city view; **Wat Traimit** (Temple of the Golden Buddha), with its 5.5-ton, solid gold carving; and **Wat Pho** (Temple of the Reclining Buddha), with a 150-foot-long statue.

- **Cruises** on the city's meandering **Chao Phraya River** and canal waterways.

- **Jim Thompson's house**, the residence of an American silk merchant, which contains remarkable, beautiful Asian artwork.

- **The Grand Palace**, the royal residence, once a walled fortress. Also a part of the complex is perhaps Bangkok's most famous site, **Wat Phra Kaew** (Temple of the Emerald Buddha).

- **The Patpong**, the city's notoriously wild nightclub, bar, and shopping district.

While visiting Malaysia in 1967, Jim Thompson disappeared under mysterious circumstances.

Not far from Bangkok lie several fascinating destinations for **half-day trips**. Those you should be most aware of are:

- **The Damnoen Saduak**, an aromatic floating fruit and vegetable market, about two hours southwest of Bangkok.
- **The Rose Garden**, one hour west of the city, with its beautiful flowers, authentic dance performances, and array of outdoor activities. This is a comprehensive cultural experience that most visitors enjoy.

  Among the **day trips** from Bangkok are:

- **The Bridge on the River Kwai**, which many will recognize from the famed classic movie. It really does exist; it's in **Kanchanaburi**, west of Bangkok. Allied prisoners of war were forced to build the bridge during World War II in order for the Japanese to move their supplies into Burma.
- **Nakhon Pathom**, with the biggest Buddhist monument in the country. Nakhon Pathom can be combined with the trip to the River Kwai bridge.
- **Ayutthaya** [ah-yoo-TYE-uh], Thailand's capital until 1767. North of Bangkok and usually accessed by bus or a river cruise boat, it offers interesting archaeological sites, ruins, and museums.

River Kwai Bridge Week, held in late November–early December, features a sound-and-light show, exhibitions, and vintage train rides.

■ **Tropical resorts**, most notably the world-class Pattaya Beach—a somewhat polluted and unsavory, yet lively and (in most places) luxurious city that's a two-hour drive south of Bangkok; and Phuket—a lush tropical island with particularly lovely scenery and towns. Phuket is about a one-hour flight south of Bangkok. It seems to be going the same way as Pattaya: Overdevelopment and pollution are becoming a problem. Less crowded is **Ko Samui**, on the east side of the peninsula. Several of Thailand's beach resorts were hard hit by a 2004 tsunami, but reconstruction has helped them regain their vitality.

■ Beyond Phuket are a number of dramatic, rocky, uninhabited islands that tourists can visit via a "long-tailed" boat. **Phang Nga [PONG GAH] Bay**, with its gorges, caverns, grottos, and lofty limestone pillars, is one of Asia's greatest scenic wonders.

Chiang Mai

Located in the northwest corner of Thailand about an hour's flight from Bangkok, this compact walled town offers temples and museum art that are quite different from those of southern Thailand. It's home to the famous **Night Bazaar**, whose stalls are open from 7 P.M. to midnight. Chiang Mai is also an excellent base for trips through the nearby hills, national parks, teakwood forests, and tribal villages. Many modes of transportation are common: elephants, river rafts, and on-foot trekking. You should be sure, though, to book with a reputable guide or tour company; otherwise, this beautiful but primitive area can be unpleasant at best and dangerous at worst. The cities of **Chiang Rai** and **Mae Hong Son**, though less known, are perhaps better starting places for treks into the wilderness.

Possible Itineraries

For those travelers interested in visiting Singapore and Thailand as their sole destination (rather than as part of a larger tour of Southeast Asia), you should suggest a minimum of 10 days. Starting with two or three days in Singapore, they could then head up to Bangkok for a couple of days. A short jump to the north and to Chiang Mai would help round out the trip, as would a visit to one of Thailand's resorts, notably Phuket and the small offshore islands. Such a vacation could easily be extended, depending on how much the travelers would like to more fully explore the sites and ruins around Bangkok. Return visitors might wish to spend more time on the beaches.

Lodging Options

Singapore boasts the legendary **Raffles Hotel**, a place of English colonial gentility. After-noon tea here is a ritual, both for guests and visitors. The **Goodwood Park Hotel** is a Singapore national landmark. In addition to these two legendary hotels, Singapore boasts a number of other world-class luxury hotels. Many hotels here are clustered in the **Orchard Road** and downtown areas. Most North American chains are present in Singapore.

A first-class chain headquartered in Thailand is **Dusit Hotels**. The **Siam Lodge Group** is moderately priced. Most hotels in Bangkok are located on and especially to the east of the Chao Phraya River. Bangkok, like Singapore, features several hotels world-famous for their level of luxury and service. Phuket also has some super-deluxe lodging. One interesting practice at many Thai hotels: Christmas Eve and New Year's Eve lodging requires a supplementary charge for a mandatory dinner celebration at the hotel.

Allied Destinations

The most obvious allied destination for Singapore and Thailand is Malaysia, which is sand-wiched between the two countries. Burma (Myanmar) also borders them, as do Laos and Cambodia, though political turmoil may make it less likely that you'll book these countries.

The Singapore Sling cocktail was invented at the Raffles Hotel.

A *wat* in Bangkok, Thailand
Photo by Justus Ghormley

Nearby are Vietnam, the Philippines, Indonesia, and the island of Borneo. Parts of China and India are also a fairly short jet trip away. Thailand and Singapore are commonly reached as part of cruises of Southeast Asia.

Cultural Patterns

The customs of Thailand and Singapore will likely seem unfamiliar to most Westerners. Business travelers, especially, will want to understand the traditions of those with whom they will be dealing.

■ When visiting Thailand, always return a *wai* greeting (where one's hands are held together at the chest like a prayer and then a slight bow is given).

■ Certain gestures in Thailand and Singapore carry meanings different from those in North America. For instance, never point a finger or foot toward another person.

■ Remember to remove shoes before entering a temple. Female visitors should dress modestly and cover their heads when visiting religious attractions.

■ Don't pause on the doorsill of a house; this is where Thais believe a spirit lives. Guests shouldn't feel obligated to bring a gift when visiting. Moreover, they shouldn't overcompliment one of their host's possessions: It may later be presented to them.

Chiang Mai's *wats* reflect the city's important past
Image copyright Artur Bogacki, 2008. Used under license from Shutterstock.com

- Never pat a Thai child (or for that matter, an adult) on the head.
- Both countries expect punctuality for meetings.

Factors That Motivate Visitors

Among the reasons to visit these countries are:

- The culture is intriguing.
- The food is superb.
- They are easily visited as part of a cruise.
- The countryside is beautiful.
- The weather is consistently warm all year.
- There are several first-rate beach resorts and super-deluxe hotels.
- The people are friendly toward tourists.
- Singapore, especially, is one of the cleanest and most modern cities in Asia and a comfortable one for people apprehensive about the Far East.

> Food in Singapore, and especially in Thailand, can be very spicy.

Possible Misgivings

Here are a few of the objections some may have about the area:

- "It's polluted and crowded." Bangkok and Pattaya are indeed choked with traffic and pollution. Suggest only a short stay in Bangkok and more time in the countryside. Singapore is spotless.
- "I hear there are guerrillas and in-fighting in Thailand." Most of the dangerous areas are away from tourist areas and have diminished. If the itinerary emphasizes Bangkok and the major cities, visitors will likely be safe, though parts of Bangkok and Pattaya Beach are a bit rowdy and seedy.
- "Southeast Asians dislike Westerners." In fact, the locals are extremely friendly.

Qualifying the Traveler
Thailand

For People Who Want	Appeal			Remarks
	High	Medium	Low	
Historical and Cultural Attractions	▲			Especially Buddhist temples
Beaches and Water Sports		▲		Excellent, but less known outside Asia
Skiing Opportunities			▲	None
Lots of Nightlife	▲			Lively and even notorious
Family Activities			▲	
Familiar Cultural Experience			▲	Western amenities but exotic locale
Exotic Cultural Experience	▲			
Safety and Low Crime		▲		
Bargain Travel		▲		Especially outside Bangkok
Impressive Scenery		▲		Wide variety
Peace and Quiet		▲		Outside Bangkok
Shopping Opportunities	▲			Silks, precious stones, gold, antiques, wood items
Adventure		▲		Especially in the Chiang Mai region
To Do Business		▲		Singapore more so than Thailand

Figure 28–3

- "I don't like to rough it." Singapore is quite modern and Bangkok has most Western conveniences. However, excursions out of Chiang Mai shouldn't be recommended to such a person.
- "I'm afraid of drinking the water." The water in Singapore is very safe; in Thailand, drink only bottled beverages.
- "The Thai language is strange and I can't read their signs." English is widely spoken in Thailand and Singapore, especially by travel personnel. Many signs in Thailand have English printed along with the Thai words.

Sales Strategies

The region is a particularly good one for packaged tours—either city tours of Singapore or hosted tours of Thailand—and they are the best way to fully comprehend each place's cultural complexities. And because Malaysia is situated directly between these two countries,

Singapore has the highest rate of personal savings and home ownership in the world.

you could easily cross-sell a trip to Kuala Lumpur and Malacca. In addition, Vietnam, the Philippines, and Indonesia are nearby, as are some other interesting destinations; you might suggest that travelers extend their visit, as long as they're in the area. Because low-end hotels can be risky, higher-rated accommodations are far preferable. Cruises are a way to combine these two destinations into an efficient, high-commission package.

Travel Trivia

Places with Dramatic Views

- The Masada Plateau, Israel
- Machu Picchu, Peru
- The Pali Lookout, Oahu
- St. Mark's Campanile, Venice
- The Empire State Building, New York City
- Mont Royal, Montreal
- The 10th floor of the Samaritaine Dept. Store, Paris
- Telegraph Hill, San Francisco
- Swissotel Stamford Hotel (70th floor), Singapore
- Mulholland Drive, Los Angeles

- Victoria Peak, Hong Kong
- Pincio Hill, Rome
- The Eiffel Tower, Paris
- The Roof of St. Peter's, Vatican City
- The Skylon Tower, Niagara Falls
- Borobudur Tower, Indonesia
- Corcovado Mountain, Brazil
- Table Mountain, Cape Town
- Great Wall of China, Badaling

NAME _____   DATE _____

MAP ACTIVITY

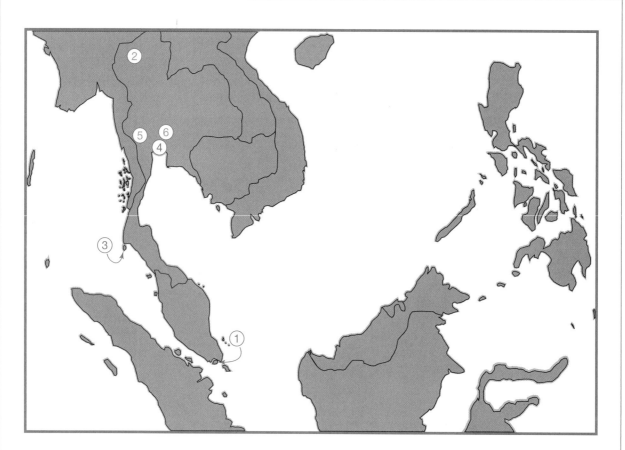

A traveler wants to visit the places listed below. Which number represents each on the map?

Place/Attraction	In/Near Which City?	Number on Map
A. Wat Arun	A. _____	A. _____
B. Night Bazaar	B. _____	B. _____
C. Haw Par Villa	C. _____	C. _____
D. The Bridge on the River Kwai	D. _____	D. _____
E. Jim Thompson's house	E. _____	E. _____
F. One of Asia's cleanest cities	F. _____	F. _____
G. The former Thai capital	G. _____	G. _____
H. Raffles Hotel	H. _____	H. _____
I. A Thai island resort	I. _____	I. _____
J. The Grand Palace	J. _____	J. _____

NAME _____ **DATE** _____

CASE STUDY

Karen Wise, age 29, will fly to Singapore in January on business. She hasn't had a real vacation in almost two years and has decided to stay in the area for eight days. She has money to spend and is interested in fairly active sightseeing. She's used to comfort, though, and doesn't particularly care to rough it.

Circle the answer that best suits her needs.

1 She wants to stay at a fine hotel while in Singapore, preferably one she's heard about that's English colonial style. Which of the following would be best?

Raffles Hotel   The Dusit

The Orchard Road   Underwater World

Why?

2 What cultural suggestion would *not* be appropriate for you to give to her?

Never point a finger at a Thai.   Try to return a *wai* greeting.

Don't ever jaywalk.   Meetings rarely start on time.

Why?

3 Karen decides that because she's been working so hard, she'd like to kick back and relax for a few days in Phuket. Which of the following should you tell her?

It will be high season.   Rent a car and do a day trip to Bangkok.

Thai food is very mild.   Visit Jim Thompson's house.

Why?

4 This business trip is a special one; Karen doesn't expect to get back to the area for quite a while. She'd like to see as much as possible. What destination could you suggest she add to her trip (from Singapore up to Thailand), without too much inconvenient flying?

Burma   Malaysia

Indonesia   Micronesia

Why?

NAME _____ **DATE** _____

CREATIVE ACTIVITY

You've taken tests on travel geography. Now is your chance to make a test. Pretend that you're a teacher and create a 10-question, multiple-choice quiz on Singapore and Thailand. Be sure your questions cover important information, use travel-related language, and are creative. Indicate the answers on a separate answer key. (Your instructor may ask you to swap tests with another student.)

For example: Which of the following would *not* be an easy add-on destination to Singapore?

       (a) Thailand   (b) Benin   (c) Malaysia   (d) Indonesia

①

②

③

④

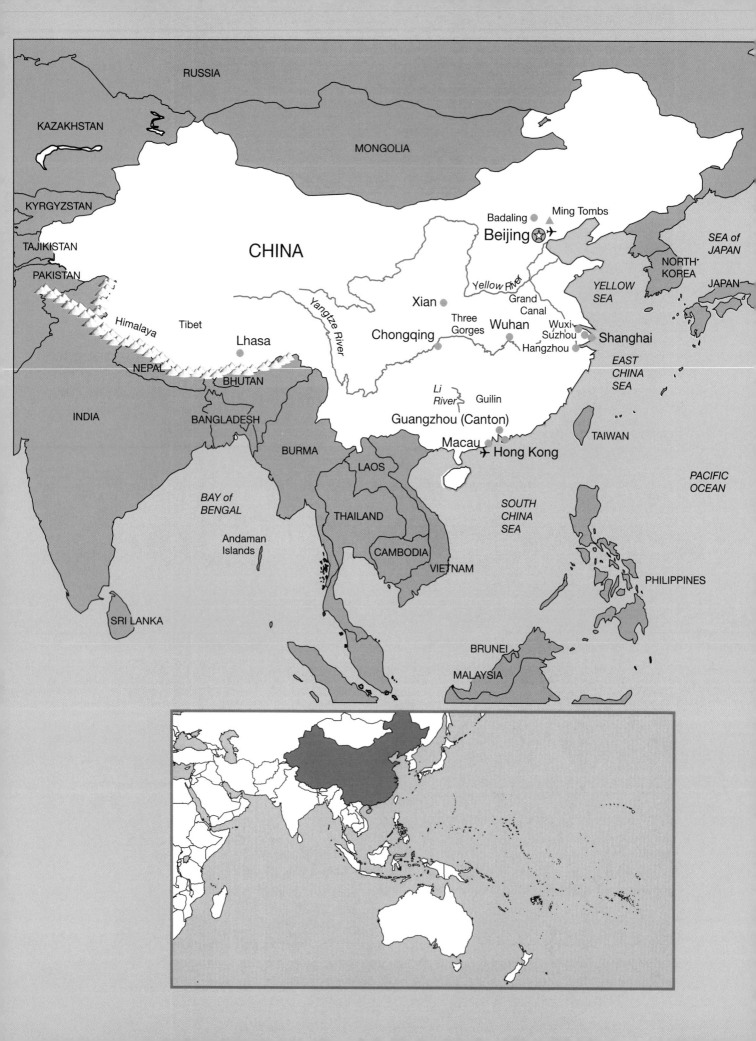

Chapter 29

China
Of Red and Gold

Two colors—red and gold—hold positions of great symbolic importance to the Chinese. In ancient times, red signified good luck, and gold was a color exclusive to the emperors. Today, these hues have taken on other meanings. Red is often used to refer to China's communist regime, begun under Mao Zedong. And gold is the perfect color to symbolize the money currently pouring into the vast, yet largely untapped, market that is China. And now that Hong Kong has become part of China, it is money, not an emperor, that rules.

China—or, more officially, the People's Republic of China—is a noteworthy land, not merely for its history, culture, size, and population but also the fact that so important a nation is so poorly known to outsiders.

China is the world's third-largest country, slightly bigger than the United States (including Alaska and Hawaii); its population is over 1.3 billion (more than four times the U.S. population). One-fifth of all the people in the world live here, providing a huge marketplace for investors, both Chinese and foreign.

Virtually the entire Chinese population lives in the arable eastern half of the country; the west is mountainous, sparsely populated, and extremely dry. Bordered on the east by Russia, North Korea, the Yellow Sea, the East China Sea, the Pacific Ocean, and the South China Sea, it's easiest to envision the major cities of China as if on the rim of a left-facing crescent. At the one o'clock position of the crescent, in northeast China not far from the coast, is **Beijing** (formerly Peking), the capital. Heading clockwise, **Shanghai**, the largest city and main port, is located at three o'clock. In the southeast is **Guangzhou** [GWANG-JOE], the city closest to **Hong Kong** and with the most contact with the West. **Macau** [muh-COW] (sometimes spelled Macao) is a close neighbor to Hong Kong.

Guilin, thought by many to be the most beautiful area of China, is near the crescent's bottom. Out at the crescent's far tip, at about seven o'clock, is mountainous **Tibet** in the Himalaya. Considered to be the basis of the Shangri-La legend, Tibet is a popular tourist destination. It's on the south-central border and is more often visited as part of a trip to Nepal and India. And in the center of this Chinese crescent are the astonishing archaeological treasures of **Xian** [she-AHN], the ancient capital of China.

Many regional dialects are spoken in China, but the main languages are Mandarin and Cantonese. Not many people here understand English, though some of the major tourist personnel may be helpful. This is one of the reasons escorted tours are almost always the mode of choice on a visit to China. English is spoken by almost everyone in Hong Kong.

How Travelers Get There

The two main Chinese gateways are **Hong Kong International Airport** (HKG) and Beijing's **Capital International Airport** (PEK). There is some nonstop service to Beijing from

China has only one time zone, though it spans six.

China's recorded history goes back 4,000 years.

CHINA

CAPITAL: Beijing

AREA (SQUARE MILES): 3,691,501

TIME ZONE: GMT +8

DRIVE ON: Right

POPULATION: 1.3 billion

RELIGIONS: Buddhism, Confucianism, Taoism

LANGUAGES: Mandarin Chinese, Cantonese, and English (in Hong Kong), Cantonese and Portuguese (in Macau)

CURRENCY: 1 yuan = 100 fen
Hong Kong: 1 Hong Kong dollar = 100 cents

ELECTRICITY: 220 volts, 50 cycles AC

CAPSULE HISTORY: Feudal states unite, 246–210 B.C.; arts flourish, 618–907; Mings rule, 1368–1644; Manchus invade and rule, 1644; Hong Kong ceded to Britain, 1841; Korea, Taiwan, and other areas ceded to Japan, 1895; Boxer rebellion, 1900; republic declared, 1912; communists take power, 1949; Tibet annexed by China, 1951; Red Guard revolts, 1966–1967; Mao dies, 1976; student revolt quelled, 1989; Hong Kong merges into China, 1997; Macau merges into China, 1999.

For reference sources, tourist bureaus, and suggested lengths of stay, see the Appendices.

---

the United States by both domestic and international carriers, as well as by China's two national air carriers, **Air China (CA)** and **China Eastern Airlines (MU)**. Both domestic and international carriers, including Hong Kong–based **Cathay Pacific Airways (CX)**, also serve Hong Kong. North American travelers will face long flights, often with connections. Flying time to Hong Kong or Beijing is about 13 hours from the West Coast and about 19 hours from New York; it takes 11 hours from Honolulu, a frequent stopover for cross-Pacific trips. A flight from Hong Kong to Beijing takes 2.5 hours; from Tokyo, it's 3.5 hours.

Shanghai and Hong Kong are also very popular ports for either extended cruises or general boat arrivals from Japan. China can be reached via train from Russia (which borders the country to the north). And travelers may access China from India, Nepal, or Vietnam.

Weather Patterns

The climate in much of China is similar to that of the United States, though the temperatures tend to be more extreme: hotter highs and colder lows. Generally, the north is colder and the south (except for Tibet, which can be extremely cold) is warmer, rainier, and more humid. Late fall to early spring can bring dust storms in the north, while monsoon rains sweep across the south coastal regions in late summer and early fall. Western China is very dry.

Beijing has a wide swing of temperatures, not only from season to season but also from morning to night. From March to May and again from September to November, the highs average in the 80s; nights, however, can drop to as low as 20 degrees. Summer in Beijing can be very hot—as high as 100 degrees during the day—whereas winter ranges from the

Among the best buys in Hong Kong are silks, porcelain, jade, watches, and some electronics.

mid-50s to zero or below. A somewhat hot rainy season takes place from June through August, making spring and fall the best times to visit Beijing.

The climate in Hong Kong and Guangzhou is much steadier (see Figure 29–1). Late fall, winter, and early spring are particularly nice, with temperatures in the 50s to upper 70s. Summer can be brutal: From May to September there's plenty of rain, occasional typhoons, high humidity, and daytime temperatures in the upper 80s to 90s.

As for tourism patterns, China generally sees a drop-off from early December to early April. Spring and fall are high season, with summer a slightly off-peak time.

Getting Around

China is so huge, air transportation is often the best way to get around. Air China, China Eastern, and Hong Kong-based **Dragonair** (KA) are the primary domestic air carriers. As for train travel, you should book a top-class "soft" berth. It's a bit expensive, but it's clean, comfortable, and worth the extra cost. Tourists can't rent a car (except in Hong Kong). You can book a driver with a car in advance, however; in fact, you can get a car, driver, and guide for a surprisingly reasonable price. Boat cruises are a popular way to travel along the **Yangtze**, **Li** [LEE], and **Yellow** rivers, as well as portions of the ancient **Grand Canal**.

The legendary ruler Kublai Khan had much of the Grand Canal constructed.

Climate at a Glance
HONG KONG

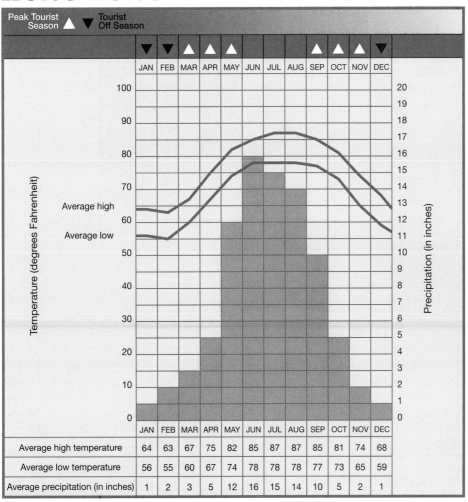

	JAN	FEB	MAR	APR	MAY	JUN	JUL	AUG	SEP	OCT	NOV	DEC
Average high temperature	64	63	67	75	82	85	87	87	85	81	74	68
Average low temperature	56	55	60	67	74	78	78	78	77	73	65	59
Average precipitation (in inches)	1	2	3	5	12	16	15	14	10	5	2	1

Figure 29–1

Some consider Beijing's Temple of Heaven one of the world's most perfect structures
Image copyright Lim Yong Hian, 2008. Used under license from Shutterstock.com

Within most cities, taxi service is good, but get a cab from a hotel; long waits anywhere else are common. (This is why it's often a good idea, on reaching the destination, to ask the driver to stay and keep the meter running, even if it might cost quite a bit.) Buses are very crowded.

Hong Kong is a different matter. The subway system is excellent and easy to use, with English signs and diagrams. Taxis are plentiful. Ferries are the easiest way to get around the harbor—the historic **Star Ferries** are renowned. Buses and double-decker trams are crowded, but visitors should take the cog railway up to **Victoria Peak** for the best view of the city. And car rentals are an option, though Hong Kong is so compact and crowded that renting a car isn't always a good idea.

Important Places

China offers superb, exciting, and dramatic destinations. Here are the most important ones:

Beijing

Beijing, the capital of China, is the country's economic and cultural center. Like many of China's major cities, it's extremely crowded. There's some good and diverse shopping in the city. Many temples are scattered throughout Beijing, and the zoo here is noted for its pandas. But it's the grand and graceful structures of Beijing that clearly stand out. Among them are:

- **The Imperial Palace** (once known as the Forbidden City), the home of 24 Chinese emperors. Commoners were not allowed inside (hence the "forbidden" city). One of the world's greatest attractions, this walled complex covers 250 acres and encloses 980 structures—each more dramatic than the last.

- **The Temple of Heaven**, a complex of structures whose pagoda-like **Hall of Prayer for Good Harvests** houses what may be China's most exquisite room.

- **Tiananmen Square**, the largest city square in the world and the centerpiece of Beijing. Here Mao raised the flag of the People's Revolution. A giant portrait of him still looms over this 122-acre plaza. The **Great Hall of the People**, site of the National People's Congress, sits on the western side of the square. Opposite it are several museums.

Beijing offers several **half-day trips**, including:

- **The Great Wall**, a structure that's perhaps even more spectacular than people imagine. This architectural wonder is, from end to end, more than 2,800 miles long. That's greater than the distance from Boston to Los Angeles. However, because the everwinding wall is full of twists and turns, some claim that it's actually about 10,000 miles long. The most popular site to visit this 2,300-year-old structure is at **Badaling**, 50 miles from Beijing. To walk along the wall's top is unforgettable—but also exhausting, for in Badaling it snakes up and down some rather steep hills.

- **The Ming Tombs**, 30 miles northwest of Beijing, usually combined with a visit to Badaling. Thirteen emperors are buried in its cavernous but now largely empty halls.

- **The Summer Palace**, on the outskirts of Beijing. The central palace and its extensive grounds are elegantly situated on a lake. One of the oddest sights here is a "stone boat" built with navy monies by an empress.

Shanghai

Shanghai is the largest city in China and its major port and commercial center. Because it was one of China's first international ports, Shanghai is one of the nation's most cosmopolitan cities. Its skyline is now dominated by many dramatically modern high-rises, visible symbols of China's new, booming economy. There are attractive gardens, open markets, museums, the **Bund** (a European-like, water-skirting boulevard), a zoo with pandas, and the famous Shanghai Acrobats. Among the other sites are:

- **Pudong New Area**, across the river from the Bund, affording great views of Shanghai.

- **The Temple of the Jade Buddha**, a particularly beautiful structure, with a six-foot-tall white jade Buddha brought from Burma.

- **Longhua Park**, a charming area that houses the ancient **Longhua Temple and Pagoda**.

- **The Shanghai Museum**, which contains one of the world's best collections of Chinese furniture, brass, and jade. The **Shanghai Art Museum** contains more contemporary works.

There are several interesting destinations near Shanghai. In fact, since many of these lie along the 1,400-year-old, 1,200-mile-long Grand Canal, the best way to enjoy them might be via cruise. Among the most popular **day trips** are:

KFC's slogan, "Finger lickin' good" originally was translated into Chinese as "Eat your fingers off."

Legend says that construction workers who died on the job were buried in the wall.

Bund sounds German, but it's actually a word from India that means "an embankment used to control the flow of water."

- **Suzhou** [SOO-JOE], a city known for its many gardens (the **Humble Administrator's Garden** is anything but humble), as well as numerous canals. Suzhou has also been renowned for silk since the Sung Dynasty.
- **Wuxi** [WOO-SHE], a graceful city of gardens, canals, and pagodas.
- **Hangzhou** [HAWNG-JOE], an exceptionally pretty city. Though its temples, canals, and lakes alone would make Hangzhou scenic, the city's abundance of gardens are what really make it stand out.

The Yangtze River

In its upper stretches, the Yangtze is 16,000 feet above sea level.

This legendary river (called Changjiang in Chinese) is a popular cruise destination; there's superb scenery along several parts of its 3,900-mile length. Though the river can be reached by a short flight from Shanghai to **Wuhan**, it's best to start farther west, at the historical city of **Chongqing** (also known as Chungking) and travel downriver to the east, ending at Wuhan. The 120-mile stretch known as the **Three Gorges** is dramatic and spectacular, as the river wends its way through the mountains. Unfortunately, a new dam has been built and the rising water will soon make the Three Gorges less impressive and may reduce tourism to this region.

Guangzhou

Because it's only 80 miles from Hong Kong, Guangzhou (better known to North Americans as Canton) has had much contact with Westerners. Guangzhou is a very active trading and commercial center. This is a frequent destination for business travelers; in fact, its Trade Fair attracts huge crowds from all over the world. (Check with Chinese travel authorities about the dates: Many business travelers will want to go at that time; everyone else will want to avoid it.) Guangzhou boasts great shopping, some fine temples, and a museum of history.

Guilin

Guilin offers exceptional, strange beauty—many consider it to have the most spectacular scenery in China. Li River cruises, which depart from Guilin and generally last seven hours, float past dreamlike rock formations that look like something out of a surrealist painting. Or as one Chinese poet put it, "The fantastic peaks grow like a jasper forest, the blue waters ripple like silken gauze." One of Guilin's major attractions is **Reed Flute Cave**.

Xian

Xian is the ancient capital of China. Until recently, that was its sole claim: enough to attract interest, but not enough to make it a major destination. All that has changed. And it all begins with a legend.

A mysterious businessman from Seattle built a 1/20th sized version of the Forbidden City in Katy, a town 30 miles west of Houston, Texas. Also on display are reproductions of Xian's terra-cotta warrior statues.

An old epic poem extolled the riches of Qin Shi Huang Di, China's first emperor. It detailed the fabulous wealth he had buried with him, guarded by more than 7,000 soldiers. For centuries this was viewed as a mere artistic and political myth. But no more. In 1974 a farmer struck something in the soil by accident. It proved to be a life-size terra-cotta statue of a soldier. Hundreds upon hundreds of other statues of soldiers in full battle dress, horses, and wagons were excavated. Archaeologists suspect even more wonders are to be discovered in a huge mound near the warriors (the Chinese are taking their time to be extremely careful); the artifacts that have already been found are now exhibited in a giant, roofed excavation. Other sites of interest in Xian include:

- **The Greater Wild Goose Pagoda**, a famous structure from the seventh century.
- **The Tomb of Emperor Qin Shi Huang Di**, with its stunning underground vaults and tombs.
- **Banpo Museum**, at the site of a 6,000-year-old prehistoric village.

Tibet

Once an independent country, Tibet is a very mountainous, underdeveloped area of China in the Himalaya. The air is thin here: The average altitude is 16,000 feet. **Lhasa**, the capital city, is Tibet's major attraction. Nestled in a valley, Lhasa was once home to the Dalai Lama, who resided in the huge, 13-story **Potala Palace**, which stands on a lofty cliff. The seventh-century **Jokhang Temple** is the holiest Buddhist temple in Tibet and attracts masses of pilgrims.

The lhasa apso dog, which comes from Tibet, was named after the city of Lhasa.

Hong Kong

Hong Kong, which had been a British colony, was returned to China in 1997. This port city is a place of legendary shopping, where you can buy electronics, custom-tailored suits, gems—you name it—and entrepreneurial Hong Kong will sell it to you, cut-rate. Hong Kong has two principal districts: **Hong Kong Island** (which probably offers the best shopping) and **Kowloon Peninsula**. The predominant languages are Cantonese and English. Among Hong Kong's attractions are:

- **Aberdeen**, a floating village on Hong Kong Island. People live here on junks, sampans, and fishing boats. There are also floating markets and restaurants.

- **Victoria Peak**, for the best view of the city. It can be reached via the "peak tram" cog railway. Another way to see the Hong Kong skyline is via a junk ride.

- **Stanley**, an upscale district, with a popular open-air market.

- **The Star Ferries**, boats that carry passengers across the dramatic harbor. Other means of transportation exist here for this purpose, but the Star Ferries are too famous to be missed.

One Hong Kong experience that's a *must*: a meal aboard one of the huge floating restaurants (though they're certainly not the best restaurants in Hong Kong).

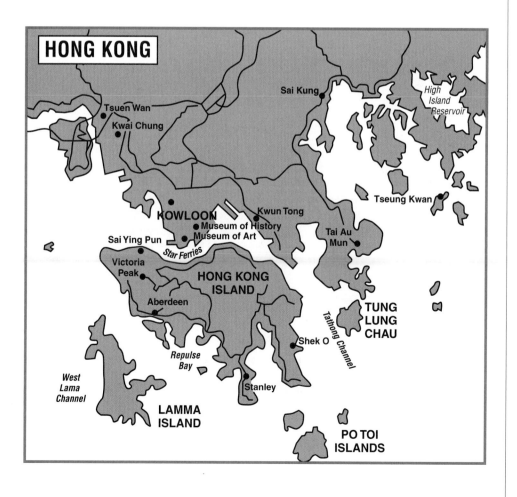

Three **day trips** from Hong Kong stand out:

- **Macau**, a former Portuguese colony that returned to Chinese rule in 1999. Macau used to present a quieter alternative to the hustle and bustle of Hong Kong. No longer: Macau, which can be easily reached from Hong Kong by ferry, has become a major gaming venue. The languages of Macau are Cantonese and Portuguese, but English is spoken by many.
- **The New Territories**, an outlying, surprisingly rural part of Hong Kong. One of the area's best-known attractions: the **Ten Thousand Buddhas Monastery** in **Shatin**.
- **Lantau Island**, home to **Po Lin Monastery** and the **Giant Buddha**, which is over 110 feet high and weighs 275 tons. Also on Lantau Island is Disney's newest theme park, **Hong Kong Disneyland**.

Possible Itineraries

China is a long way from the United States. Most tourists prefer to see as much as possible on a visit, presuming that they might not be back for a while, and typically trips take anywhere from 9 to 15 days. The country can be seen starting with three days in Beijing. Heading south, travelers could stop in the Grand Canal area of Suzhou for two days and then on to Shanghai for two more. They could spend two days in Xian. Then on to a few days in Guilin, cruising along the Li River, before ending their stay at Guangzhou and Hong Kong for three days. (Hong Kong is an ideal final stop, because purchases can be made at the end of the trip and not carried around throughout the journey.)

Return visitors, or those who'd like to take more time for their trip, may want to add a visit to Tibet, a cruise along the Yangtze River, and a stop in Macau. Trips to China are also often combined with a host of allied Asian destinations.

North America's largest Chinatown is in San Francisco; the second largest is in Vancouver.

The Star Ferries connect various parts of the Hong Kong region
Image copyright Thor Jorgen Udvang, 2008. Used under license from Shutterstock.com

Lodging Options

Be aware that accommodations in most of China range from adequate (in smaller cities) to deluxe (especially in Beijing and Shanghai). Even more impressive: Hong Kong has dozens of outstanding hotels—many experts claim that there are more world-class facilities and better service in Hong Kong than anywhere else in the world.

At one time, quality lodging was difficult to find in Beijing. That has changed dramatically. There are now very good hotels in numerous areas of the city. In Hong Kong, booking a room with a harbor view is worth it—the waterfront at night is an unforgettable sight. In Shanghai, hotels cluster near People's Square and the Pudong New Area. Hotels in other Chinese cities are often scattered about. It's best to try to book a hotel close to each city's center.

Shanghai's Grand Hyatt is on the 53rd through 87th floor of the Jin Mao Tower, making it the "highest" hotel in the world.

Allied Destinations

China is surrounded by many countries. In fact, it's so large that its allied destinations must be broken down into three separate regions. To the north are Russia and Mongolia (though most of Russia's main attractions are nearer Europe). In the northeast, you'll find South Korea (on the mainland) and Japan (across the Sea of Japan). And finally, there's the Indian subcontinent and Southeast Asia, with such nations as India, Nepal, Bhutan, Burma (Myanmar), Vietnam, Thailand, Singapore, and Malaysia. In addition, across the South China Sea are the Philippines and Taiwan (which for years claimed to harbor the legitimate government of China). Those traveling between Taiwan and the People's Republic of China should check any government advisories on travel and customs restrictions.

More countries (15) border China than any other nation in the world.

Cultural Patterns

Hong Kong has always been a key business center. Now, all of China is taking on that status. It has become increasingly important, therefore, to understand the cultural uniqueness of this land.

- The use of full titles when addressing people is important. In addition, remember that in a Chinese name, the family name is listed first. Bowing is common, though a handshake is also acceptable.

- Promptness is much prized in China; it's even praiseworthy to be early.

- The Chinese don't call their country Red China or Communist China, but the People's Republic (of China).

- Discussing business during a meal is considered improper by the Chinese. In addition, be prepared to make a little speech after a more formal occasion as an acknowledgment to the host.

- Use both hands when passing a gift or food. If one person in a business group is to receive a gift, all others within the group must also receive one.

- It's more likely to be invited to a home in Hong Kong than in the rest of the country, where government approval is often required. In any event, bring a small gift. At least taste every dish served.

- Generosity is important to the Chinese. And treat the elderly with respect.

- Social position is critical in China, and embarrassing situations are avoided, allowing people to save face and retain self-respect. Avoid awkward situations.

- White is the Chinese color of mourning and should be avoided in such things as gift-wrapping.

- The concept of lining up is foreign to the Chinese.

- Chinese point with an open hand, not with the index finger.

Chop suey and fortune cookies were actually invented in the United States.

The huge Potala Palace perches on a steep hill
Image copyright enote, 2008. Used under license from Shutterstock.com

Factors That Motivate Visitors

Among the factors that motivate people to visit China are:

- There are remarkable archaeological treasures and sites.
- Chinese architecture and art are beautiful and impressive.
- China is viewed as a "soft adventure" destination by many North Americans.
- Hong Kong, Shanghai, Beijing, and Guangzhou are major business centers.
- The regional cuisines of China are superb and familiar.
- Many Americans can trace their ancestry here.
- Cruise ships increasingly call on Chinese ports.
- Hong Kong has legendary, world-class lodging.
- There's great shopping, especially in Shanghai and Hong Kong.

Possible Misgivings

Because this region is so far away, some people might hesitate to visit. Some of their possible concerns include:

- "China has a repressive government." Events occasionally bring China's politics into the forefront of the news. Though this might concern some people, so far it has had virtually no effect on tourism.
- "The country isn't set up for tourism and the facilities are primitive." This was once true but no longer. China has been welcoming foreign visitors for many years now. The tourism infrastructure in major cities and at outlying attractions is now thoroughly modern. Taking a fully inclusive escorted tour—by far the most popular option—will go a long way toward making such a trip more convenient.
- "The Chinese don't like Westerners." The Chinese people are very friendly and (though for generations unaccustomed to outsiders) warmly welcome visitors.

It's hard not to buy a custom-made suit before leaving Hong Kong. Measurements will be taken one day and the completed suit delivered to the hotel the next. Hong Kong's most famous tailor shop is Baron Kay's.

Political regulations can change often. Always check the latest advisories before you leave.

Qualifying the Traveler
Beijing

For People Who Want	Appeal			Remarks
	High	Medium	Low	
Historical and Cultural Attractions	▲			Especially Great Wall and Imperial Palace
Beaches and Water Sports			▲	Few facilities
Skiing Opportunities			▲	None
Lots of Nightlife		▲		
Family Activities		▲		Mostly sightseeing
Familiar Cultural Experience		▲		
Exotic Cultural Experience	▲			
Safety and Low Crime		▲		Sporadic unrest; petty theft
Bargain Travel		▲		Packages are all-inclusive
Impressive Scenery		▲		In countryside
Peace and Quiet			▲	Bustling city; quieter in countryside
Shopping Opportunities		▲		Shanghai and Hong Kong much better
Adventure		▲		
To Do Business	▲			China is a huge market

Figure 29–2

- "I don't think I can take Chinese food every single day." Each region in China offers its own unique cuisine. It's possible to have five or six dishes at each meal, three times a day, for weeks, and never eat the same thing twice.
- "The language is undecipherable." Speaking English in Hong Kong is no problem at all. For those concerned about the rest of the region, you might suggest an escorted tour. Many Chinese guides are fluent in English.

Sales Strategies

Because of travel restrictions and language problems, China is ideal for all-inclusive escorted group tours (including those that specialize in trekking expeditions). Travelers seeking an upscale experience can book a custom-designed personal tour with driver and guide for a reasonable price. A river cruise adds a lot to an itinerary. You can enhance a visit to the Great Wall and Ming Tombs by booking a helicopter flight over the area. And because China is so distant from the United States, you might suggest that visitors extend their trip, either within China or to allied countries in Asia, often via a cruise. Similarly, you could consider booking a stopover (e.g., in Hawaii for travelers going west or in Europe for those flying east) to break up the long flight. Luxury lodging is especially attractive to travelers to this region.

Travel Trivia

More Signs, Brochures, and Memos Encountered by Travelers

- Teeth extracted by the latest Methodists. (Hong Kong)

- Visitors must complain at the office between 9 and 11 daily. (Greece)

- Please bathe inside the tub. (Japan)

- To move the cabin push button for washing floor. (Yugoslavia)

- Ladies are requested not to have children in the bar. (Norway)

- Ticket price for 0–2 year ache babys are 10% of normal price. (Turkey)

- The flattening of underwear with pleasure is the job of the chambermaid. (Yugoslavia)

- Not to perambulate the corridors in the hours of repose in the boots of ascension. (Austria)

- Bodrum Airlines is not able to caryout flight schadule if an unusual thinks take place like bed weather, float, fire, eath queke, war done of elefricity, natural disaster, etc. (Turkey)

- A sports jacket may be worn to dinner, but no trousers. (France)

- The lift is being fixed for the next day. During that time we regret that you will be unbearable. (Romania)

NAME _____   **DATE** _____

MAP ACTIVITY

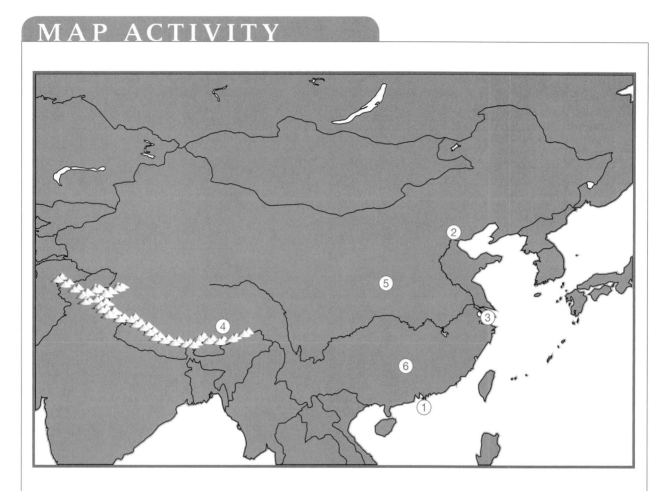

A traveler wants to visit the places listed below. Which number represents each on the map?

Place/Attraction	In/Near Which City?	Number on Map
A. The Temple of Heaven	A. _____	A. _____
B. A palace of the Dalai Lama	B. _____	B. _____
C. Star Ferry trips	C. _____	C. _____
D. Terra-cotta statues in the ground	D. _____	D. _____
E. The Imperial Palace	E. _____	E. _____
F. Dramatic and strange rock formations	F. _____	F. _____
G. The capital of Tibet	G. _____	G. _____
H. A famous floating village	H. _____	H. _____
I. Tiananmen Square	I. _____	I. _____
J. The Temple of the Jade Buddha	J. _____	J. _____

NAME _____ **DATE** _____

CASE STUDY

Terry and Sue Lee want to go on a trip to China. In their late 50s, they've done a bit of independent traveling in the United States and Europe. They could take up to three weeks, but have settled on 17 days, as they know the trip will be taxing.

Circle the answer that best suits their needs.

1 What Chinese attraction might you suggest to the Lees?

Chiang Mai   Sherwood Forest

Deer Park   Reed Flute Cave

Why?

2 The Lees, of course, prefer to go when the weather is at its best, but the tour they were hoping to get on is all booked up. As their second choice, they'd rather have the climate a bit colder than have to deal with the rain. In which month would you *not* recommend they go?

March   July

May   November

Why?

3 The Lees tell you that they want their last stop to be Hong Kong. What would logically be their destination just before getting to Hong Kong?

Guangzhou   Tibet

Macau   Singapore

Why?

4 Which would probably *not* be a useful recommendation to make to the Lees?

It's worth it to book a room with a view of Hong Kong's Victoria Harbour.

Rent a car and drive around the Beijing countryside.

While you're visiting Beijing, by all means visit the Imperial Palace and the Great Wall.

Use both hands when passing a gift or food.

Why?

NAME _____ **DATE** _____

CREATIVE ACTIVITY

Ancient historians compiled lists of the "Seven Wonders of the World" that every traveler should see. Among them were the Great Pyramids, the Colossus of Rhodes, and the Hanging Gardens of Babylon. (Only the Pyramids still exist.) The current government of China has decided that it, too, should boast of its own seven wonders in all of its promotional materials. What would you think these seven should be? Use the Internet to find photos of these "wonders," with URLs. Be prepared to justify your suggestions.

1

2

3

4

5

6

7

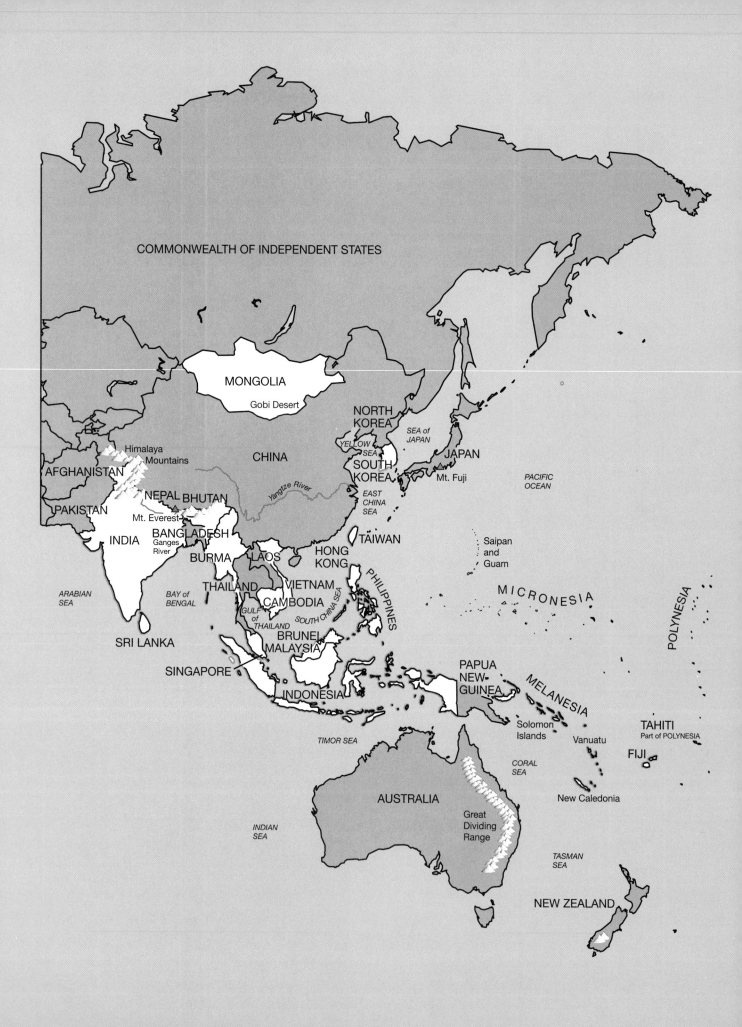

COMMONWEALTH OF INDEPENDENT STATES

MONGOLIA

Gobi Desert

NORTH KOREA

SEA of JAPAN

YELLOW SEA

CHINA

SOUTH KOREA

JAPAN

Mt. Fuji

PACIFIC OCEAN

Himalaya Mountains

AFGHANISTAN

NEPAL BHUTAN

Yangtze River

EAST CHINA SEA

PAKISTAN

Mt. Everest

INDIA

BANGLADESH

Ganges River

BURMA

LAOS

HONG KONG

TAIWAN

Saipan and Guam

MICRONESIA

POLYNESIA

THAILAND

VIETNAM

PHILIPPINES

ARABIAN SEA

BAY of BENGAL

GULF of THAILAND

CAMBODIA

SOUTH CHINA SEA

SRI LANKA

BRUNEI MALAYSIA

SINGAPORE

INDONESIA

PAPUA NEW GUINEA

MELANESIA

TAHITI

Part of POLYNESIA

FIJI

Solomon Islands

Vanuatu

TIMOR SEA

New Caledonia

CORAL SEA

AUSTRALIA

Great Dividing Range

INDIAN SEA

TASMAN SEA

NEW ZEALAND

Chapter 30

Asia and the Pacific Potpourri

Japan, China, Australia, New Zealand, and, somewhat beyond, Singapore and Thailand—these are the best-known destinations on the far side of the Pacific Rim. But that's just the start. Between the palm-fringed shores of Asia and California float thousands of islands—many quite famous. And beyond that? Well, that's where the public's geographic knowledge really falters. People have heard of Krakatoa volcano, but where is it? In what country is Mt. Everest? And what, for heaven's sake, is a *yurt*?

We omit quite a few Asian countries from this chapter because they're not major tourist destinations. The reasons are many: Warfare in some keeps travelers away; political turmoil is a major deterrent in others; and still others are opening up rapidly, but do not yet warrant their own sections. In addition, some countries, like North Korea and some of the Southeast Asia nations, have governments with questionable human rights records and, therefore, limited tourist appeal. Others in this region are more appealing but are off the beaten path. The most notable: Cambodia, where one of the greatest ruins in the world, the legendary Angkor Wat, is located. Interestingly, there are also countries such as Brunei, which, though having perfectly good relations with most countries, aren't especially interested in encouraging a tourist trade. But keep one important fact in mind: All this can change overnight.

Mongolia

Mongolia's location—sandwiched between China and Russia—combined with its exotic history, makes this nation an intriguingly offbeat destination. Under Genghis Khan, Mongolia was once a world power. Today, the people of this nomadic, fairly primitive culture are more closely tied to Russia than to China.

Southern Mongolia is made up of the **Gobi Desert**; this arid, mountainous region is surprisingly pretty, with much interesting wildlife. The rainier north is where most of the population lives. **Ulan Bator** (nicknamed U.B.), the capital, has many monasteries and quite a few museums. In Mongolia's countryside are some impressive monasteries, many national parks, and, in some places, astonishing mountain scenery. The historic town of **Karakorum** was the capital during the time of Genghis Khan. Those who visit Mongolia do so to experience an adventurous destination well off the beaten tourist path. Oh, and the *yurts*? They're the traditional wooden-framed tents that are transported by nomads as they herd across the countryside.

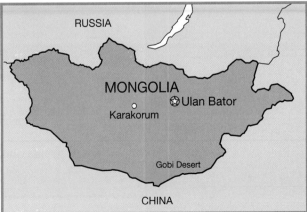

South Korea

Separated from China by only North Korea, South Korea covers the southern strip of the Korean Peninsula; Japan is just across the Sea of Japan on the east, and the Yellow Sea borders South Korea to the west. **Seoul** [SOLE], located in the northwest, is the country's capital. **Incheon International Airport** (ICN), about 30 miles west of Seoul, is the main air gateway. The national carrier, **Korean Air** (KE), **Asiana Airlines** (OZ), and a few North American airlines fly here. Cruise ships occasionally stop at South Korea's largest port, **Busan** (formerly Pusan), on the southeast coast.

Most tourist destinations are toward the north, where the climate is humid. Spring and fall are pleasant in South Korea, with daytime temperatures in the upper 60s and chilly nights; these two seasons tend to be the driest times of the year. Summers are rainy—mid-July to mid-August is a mini-monsoon season—and the highs can soar into the 90s; winters, on the other hand, are cold, with temperatures often plummeting to the 20s or below. The official language is Korean, though English is quite common, especially in business.

Important Places

South Korean tourism, fuelled by visitors who seek shopping bargains and business deals, has reached impressive levels—despite its occasional tensions with North Korea. Seoul, historically surrounded by nine gates, is rich with temples, museums, and palaces. The cultural and shopping opportunities are excellent. Seoul's two most important designated national treasures are the **Namdaemun Gate** (the Great South Gate—destroyed by fire in 2008 but being rebuilt) and the **Dongdaemun Gate** (the Great East Gate). These grand,

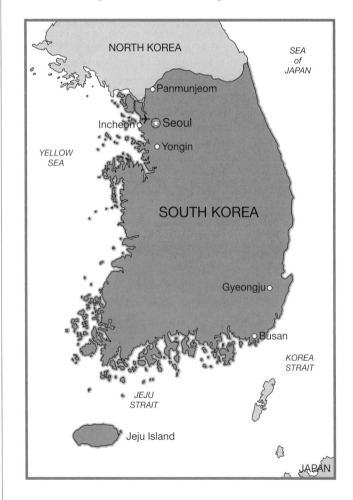

ornate structures are each adjacent to frenetic, popular marketplaces. **Myeong-dong** and **Itaewon** are the city's major tourist shopping areas, but there are many others.

Interesting **day trips** and excursions include:

- **The Korean Folk Village** in **Yongin**, a village museum where ancient life in Korea is re-enacted.
- **Panmunjeom**, in the Demilitarized Zone between the two Koreas, where peace talks occasionally are held. A tense place, with plenty of soldiers stationed on both sides, Panmunjom enables visitors—who must book in advance on an organized tour—to experience one of the world's most important and vexing issues.
- **Namhansanseong Castle**, a spectacular fortress on **Mt. Namhan**.

Other sites in South Korea include:

- **Gyeongju**, the former capital of Korea. Burial mounds, tombs, temples, and a national museum are the attractions here.
- **Jeju Island**, off the southern coast, a resort area famed for its pearl divers. Jeju Island boasts good beaches, major hotels, casinos, and excellent diving. It's reached by air or ferry.

The Demilitarized Zone is the most heavily armed area in the world.

Sales Considerations

South Korea is a convenient extension of a trip to Japan or China. Because of the unfamiliarity of the language, escorted tours are popular. This country will appeal to those who love Asian culture, ancient architecture, and bargain shopping. South Korea offers beaches and skiing for active vacationers. Business travelers should be prepared for the no-nonsense approach of Koreans. Also, keep up on travel advisories. The political situation between North and South Korea fluctuates all the time.

Taiwan

Until the mid-twentieth century, this 240-by-85-mile island was known as Formosa, which in Portuguese means "beautiful." The early settlers from Portugal knew what they were talking about; the island is a glorious one.

For years, Taiwan's rulers claimed to represent the legitimate government of China—all of China. (Taiwan still officially calls itself the Republic of China.) Its airline, for example, continues to be called **China Airlines** (CI)—not to be confused with Mainland China's Air China. Taiwan's other carrier is **EVA Airways** (BR). The country is also serviced by a few North American airlines and several other Asian carriers.

Taiwan is located off the southeast coast of China, slightly northeast of Hong Kong and just north of the Philippines. **Taipei**, its capital and gateway in the north, can be reached via **Chiang Kai-shek International Airport** (TPE). There's also **Kaohsiung International Airport** (KHH) in the southwest, but it's less used. The official language is Mandarin Chinese, but Taiwanese is also widely spoken, as is some Japanese. English is commonly used in business.

Most of Taiwan's tourist destinations are in the north. The weather here is humid; October through December are the nicest months, with temperatures in the mid-70s during the day. January through March is cooler and rainier. The south is drier and warmer, but there's not as much to see. The typhoon season stretches from June to October. Mountain temperatures, of course, are chillier than in the lowlands.

China considers Taiwan to be one of its provinces.

Important Places

All that visitors need to do is gaze at its many shrines or travel through its lush countryside to discover Taiwan's beauty. One of its top destinations is Taipei—a busy, cosmopolitan capital.

There's a wide selection of goods here and many excellent bargains for those who love to shop. The world-class **National Palace Museum** is a must-see. Located just outside Taipei, it has some 700,000 pieces of Chinese art, much of which was brought over from Beijing's Forbidden City when Taiwan's leaders fled the mainland. The classically styled **Martyrs Shrine** is designed after a hall in that same Forbidden City. The **National Taiwan Democracy Memorial Hall** (formerly known as the Chiang Kai-shek Memorial Hall) honors the nation's late general and president; its huge complex features a tower more than 20 stories high. There are many temples to visit in Taipei; the most notable is the historic, 270-year-old **Longshan Temple**. A popular marketplace is nearby.

Among the **day trips** are:

- **Taroko Gorge**, a major destination, featuring an awesome 12-mile drive on its eastern end. It's most commonly reached by a short flight from Taipei southeast to **Hualien**.

- **Yangmingshan** (Grass Mountain) **National Park**, noted for its scenic cherry and azalea trees. The trip here from Taipei passes by the **Beitou Hot Springs**.

- **Yehliu**, reached via an hour's drive to the east through lovely mountains and farmland. Yehliu's strange rocks and wonderful vistas make this a worthwhile half-day excursion.

One major destination far away from the hub of Taipei is **Sun Moon Lake**, created by a dam and offering rich, green, jungle-like scenery. It's Taiwan's number-one tourist destination, with several interesting shrines, temples, and pagodas. Sun Moon Lake is accessed out of **Taichung**, a pretty town two hours away on the southeast coast.

Sales Considerations

Taiwan attracts visitors because of its scenery, graceful Chinese architecture, and bargain shopping. Because the island is so small, it's easy to sample Chinese cuisine and culture without having to tackle the vastness of Mainland China. Some feel Taiwan is a safer destination than China. Taiwan makes a wonderful extension of any trip to Asia—particularly Japan, the Philippines, and South Korea, as well as China. Because of language problems, an escorted tour or a cruise is a good choice.

Taroko Gorge is also called the Marble Gorge
Photo by Justus Ghormley

The Philippines

Comprising 7,107 islands, the Philippines is located off the southeast coast of China in the South China Sea. It stretches from Taiwan in the north to Indonesia in the south. The main island here is **Luzon** in the north, where the capital of **Manila** is located. **Philippine Airlines** (PR), the national airline, services the country, as do several North American and international carriers, and a few cruise lines. Manila (MNL) is the country's gateway; it also serves as a cruise port.

The climate is fairly steady year-round, with highs averaging in the upper 80s, dropping to the mid-70s at night. Winter tends to be a bit cooler and more pleasant; March through May are the hottest months. It's rainiest from June to October (when typhoons are most likely to hit). The official languages are Filipino (based on Tagalog) and English.

Important Places

The Philippines provides historical attractions, scenic sites, popular beach resorts, and good snorkeling and diving. Manila is the political and industrial center of the country. It's a place of contrasts, with millionaire communities near teeming slums. There's excellent

Less than half of the Philippine islands have names; only around 900 are inhabited.

There are 78 languages and over 500 dialects spoken in the Philippines.

shopping here. Visitors can discover Manila's Spanish heritage at **Intramuros**, the old walled city where battle-torn **Fort Santiago** is found. **Corregidor** is an island fortress across **Manila Bay**, with important World War II memorials. Manila has many fine churches. Among the **day trips** from Manila are:

- **Pagsanjan Falls**, which inspires visitors with its canyons, rapids, and craggy rock formations. The two-hour drive east of Manila goes through coconut, sugar, and pineapple plantations.

- **Lake Taal** [TAH-AHL], commonly viewed from **Tagaytay Ridge**, 30 miles south of Manila. Lake Taal, formed by the crater of an extinct volcano, offers a geographic oddity: At its center is an active volcano that, in turn, contains another lake.

  Other destinations in the Philippines include:

- **Baguio**, in the mountains 150 miles north of Manila, the most popular summer resort center of the Philippines. (The climate is cooler here.) Nearby, the **Banaue** [bah-NAH-way] **Rice Terraces** are a fascinating attraction: massive, awesome tiers cut 5,000 feet up a mountainside centuries ago by people using only primitive tools.

- **The Visayas**, a cluster of islands in the middle section of the Philippines. Many old churches dot the Visayas as do beaches and resort developments (especially those at **Cebu**).

Sales Considerations

This tropical island-nation appeals to those who love scenic destinations, relaxing beaches, snorkeling, shopping, history, good value, and a mix of exotic cultures. The Philippines provides good shopping opportunities. Escorted tours are a popular way to get around from island to island. Budget lodging can leave much to be desired and luxury hotels are a relative bargain. The Philippines is close to Taiwan, Vietnam, Indonesia, Malaysia, Thailand, and China, creating potentially longer itineraries. Japan and Australia (though more distant) are also potential add-ons. Asian cruises often call on Manila. So far, political turbulence hasn't severely disrupted tourism in the Philippines, though there's always that possibility. Crime and tourist scams are occasionally a problem here.

Indonesia

Indonesia, with the fourth-largest population in the world, boasts a land area about the size of Alaska and Oregon combined. Yet it stretches 3,000 miles—more than the width of the United States. How can this be? Simple: Indonesia is made up of a spread-out arc of islands (17,508 of them), stretching almost halfway up Peninsular Malaysia on the west and almost to Australia on the east. The largest of its islands, **Sumatra**, lies to the west; **Java**, a densely populated island and the location of the nation's capital, **Jakarta**, is a bit farther east; **Bali** sits at the eastern tip of Java; and the jungles of **Borneo** are to the north. **Soekarno-Hatt International Airport** (CGK) near Jakarta is the gateway into Indonesia and is reached via the national airline, **Garuda Indonesia** (GA).

Most of Indonesia's landmass lies below the equator, so its seasons—limited as they are—are opposite those in North America. The climate tends to be steamy all year. The driest months are June to early November (but it's still humid and there will be rain), with temperatures in the upper 80s. Inland temperatures run slightly cooler. Late November to March is extremely wet; the monsoon season is January and February. Bahasa Indonesia is the official language, though many other dialects and languages are spoken. Many Indonesians speak English.

Indonesia is a mosaic of cultures. It's an ancient land: The prehistoric remains of Java Man were discovered here.

Important Places

- **Bali** features lush jungles, volcanic mountain peaks, exotic Hindu ceremonies, unique national parks, mystical temples, pristine beaches, legendary surfing areas, and a culture that expects almost every one of its people to be a crafts-maker, dancer, painter, or other kind of artist. **Denpasar** (DPS) is the island's main business center—though most tourists stay at the great resorts near the island's southern tip, which features excellent snorkeling, surfing, and diving. Bali is heavily developed; it's no longer the "primitive" tropical place it was a few decades ago. Terrorists have staged several bombings here. Keep up on the current political situation.

- **Yogyakarta** [jog-jah-KAR-tah] (often shortened to "Yogya"), in the center of the island of Java, is a major cultural center. It's known for its batik factories, which are open to tourists. The **Palace of the Sultan** is a complex of elaborate, lavishly designed pavilions. A trip to nearby **Borobudur** [bore-uh-buh-DUR] and its astonishing, spectacular Buddhist temple—built 1,200 years ago and recently restored—is a must. The Hindu **Prambanan Temple complex** is also a major attraction near Yogyakarta.

- **Jakarta**, Indonesia's busy and crowded capital, is located on the west end of Java. It has only a few sites of interest. The **National Museum** has some fine art and historical collections. Jakarta is also a good place for shopping and exotic dining experiences.

- **Surabaya**, in east Java, is an area of many volcanoes. The city has some huge shopping malls and also operates a good zoo with the famed Komodo dragons, huge lizards that were often used in old movies to portray dinosaurs.

- **Sumatra**, a beautiful island with excellent wildlife, is most famous for its Sumatran tigers. Attractions in **Medan** (Sumatra's largest city) include the interesting **Sultan's Palace** and a native village built on stilts.

- **Krakatoa**, an immense volcano, in 1883 produced one of the most famous and ferocious eruptions in recorded history. The explosion was so violent that the entire volcano and most of the island it sat on is now gone. Tour boats visit the site and the small pieces of land that survived. (By the way, there was a movie called *Krakatoa, East of Java*. Krakatoa is actually *west* of Java, but *east* sounded better to Hollywood.)

Sales Considerations

Unless the traveler is going only to Bali, an escorted tour is a great option in Indonesia: Independent travel can be challenging. Indonesia will be popular among those interested in primitive cultures, the religions of the world, water sports, exotic food, shopping, and bargain travel. Cruise ships stop at nearly a dozen different ports. Cruises are also one of the easiest ways to get to see **Komodo Island** and its huge lizards. Parts of Indonesia occasionally suffer from serious political unrest.

Malaysia

Malaysia is divided into two sections: The most populous region lies on the **Malay Peninsula**, bordered by Thailand to the north and Singapore and Indonesia (across the Strait of Malacca) to the south; the more primitive jungle area sits atop the island of Borneo. **Kuala Lumpur** (KUL), the capital and air gateway, is near the west-central coast of Peninsular Malaysia. It's served by the national carrier, **Malaysia Airlines** (MH), as well as several North American and Asian airlines. (Because Singapore is so conveniently close to Malaysia, some travelers prefer to land there instead.) Malaysia is well situated for cruises: **Penang, Port Kelang** (for Kuala Lumpur), and **Malacca** are its main ports.

Malaysia has a hot, tropical climate. Daytime highs average around 90 degrees, with evening lows in the 70s. It's humid all year, though October through January is rainiest, whereas March through June is the most pleasant period. Conditions on the peninsula are

The temple of Borobudur was forgotten for 1,000 years and rediscovered by Sir Stamford Raffles (of Singapore's Raffles Hotel fame).

When Krakatoa exploded in 1883, it created the loudest sound in recorded history. Some believe that an earlier eruption in 535 A.D. and the global climate changes it caused triggered a plague in the Roman Empire, the Dark Ages in Europe, the abandonment of Teotihuacan, and the rise of Islam.

"Peninsular Malaysia" is *not* another term for the "Malay Peninsula." It's the part of Malaysia that's actually on the Malay Peninsula (which also contains parts of Thailand and Burma).

Borneo has more species of plants than the entire continent of Africa does.

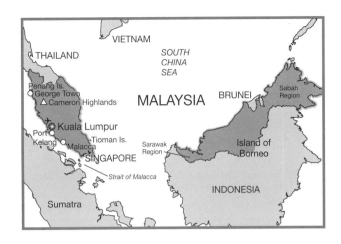

slightly cooler and drier than on the island of Borneo. Malay is the national language, but English is widely spoken, especially in business.

Important Places

A lush country, Malaysia offers beautiful scenery, an austere but intriguing Islamic culture, and some wonderful beaches. Among the most popular destinations are:

- **Kuala Lumpur**, a beautiful city with Moorish architecture. Most notable are the **National Mosque**, the palace-like railroad station, and the twin **Petronas Towers**, two of the world's tallest skyscrapers. The **Central Market** is a busy and entertaining place. Outside the city are the **Batu Caves**, up nearly 300 steps to a Hindu shrine in an exotic grotto, complete with monkeys swinging about. And in the **Genting Highlands** is an upscale resort and recreation area with two very busy casinos.

- **Malacca**, three hours south of Kuala Lumpur. This historic port—Malaysia's oldest city—can be seen as a long day trip from Kuala Lumpur. A multicultured city, it was settled at various times by the Chinese, Portuguese, Dutch, and English. All of these cultures are still in evidence, making Malacca an especially interesting place to visit.

- **Penang Island** is perhaps one of the most interesting and pleasant places to visit in Malaysia. It has great beaches (with windsurfing), intricate temples, historical sites, tropical forests, and architectural gems. Its principal city is **George Town**.

- **The Cameron Highlands**, on the mainland halfway between Penang and Kuala Lumpur. This recreation area offers waterfalls, tea plantations, wonderful weather, and its famous butterflies. The climate here is cooler than that of the lowlands.

- **Tioman**, the principal island amid a group of 64 volcanic islands off the eastern coast. With white coral beaches and crystal-clear waters, these islands are being "rediscovered" for their superb snorkeling opportunities and the summer spectacle of hundreds of turtles that swim to shore to lay their eggs.

Sales Considerations

Malaysia is well located for extending trips to Thailand, Singapore, and Indonesia. It's a country for those who love scenery, beaches, shopping (especially batik and brassworks), and tribal culture. It also offers areas that are ideal for the adventurous. You would be wise to upsell hotels rather than book travelers in unpleasant, basic accommodations. Getting around the country can be bothersome, so tours might be appropriate. And again, Malaysia's proximity to many other nations encourages an expanded trip, often via a cruise.

Kuala Lumpur is commonly called "KL."

The British developed the resorts in the highlands to escape from the heat and humidity of the rest of Malaysia.

The Petronas Towers were the tallest buildings in the world
Image copyright Hu Xiao Fang, 2008. Used under license from Shutterstock.com

Vietnam

For many decades, Vietnam—at war with France and later with the United States—had virtually no tourism. That has changed in a big way. Vietnam has been building a tourism infrastructure and encouraging travelers, especially groups. As a result, many tour operators and cruise lines have positioned Vietnam as an intriguing destination to visit.

Vietnam—a long, thin country that stretches north to south along the Gulf of Tonkin and the South China Sea—can be divided into three regions. The north is where **Hanoi**, Vietnam's capital, is located. It's an unusual amalgam of ancient temples, colonial French homes, interesting museums, and modern skyscrapers. About 100 miles to the southeast is the port of **Haiphong** and nearby **Halong Bay**. Halong Bay is Vietnam's natural wonder, with thousands of small islands, beaches, caves, and grottos. An unusual option: a day or overnight trip in Halong Bay on a Chinese junk.

Vietnam's central region is most famous for **Hue** [hoo-WAY], considered Vietnam's most beautiful city. Once the nation's imperial capital, Hue's most impressive attraction is the **Imperial Citadel**, a huge, moated, partly destroyed complex of structures. Several hours away is **Da Nang**, a port city with many temples and small museums.

Vietnam's southern region is anchored by **Ho Chi Minh City**, more popularly known by its traditional name, **Saigon**. A large, bustling metropolis, Ho Chi Minh City has many French-inspired buildings and more ancient, traditional structures. **Nha Trang**, a developing seaside resort, lies to the city's north.

Most visitors access Vietnam on flights on Asian carriers from Bangkok, or via cruise ships that call on Vietnam's principal ports.

Burma (Myanmar)

Nearly 200,000 monks live in Mandalay, an important Buddhist center.

Sandwiched between India, China, and Thailand, with the Bay of Bengal [ben-GAHL] to the south, Burma—also known as Myanmar [mee-AHN-mahr]—was once a British colony and has retained many vestiges of its colonial past. However, Burma is considered to have one of the most repressive governments in Asia and many tourists to the area avoid the country for philosophical or very practical reasons.

Halong Bay's stone formations have a dream-like quality
Image copyright Holger Mette, 2008. Used under license from Shutterstock.com

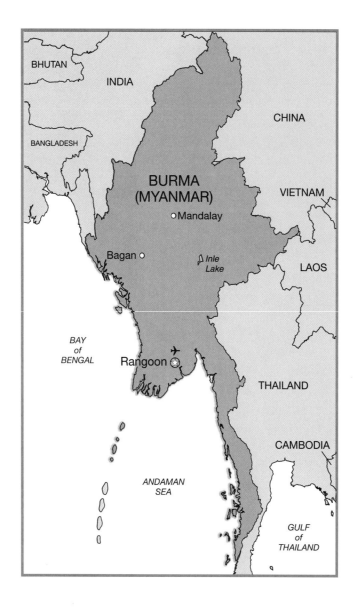

The country does feature several impressive places to visit. **Rangoon** (also called Yangon), the capital city, features an astonishing gold-and-diamond-encrusted, bell-shaped Buddhist shrine, the **Shwedagon Pagoda**. **Mandalay** and **Bagan** [bah-GAHN] (formerly **Pagan**), both former capitals, have many historical attractions and impressive pagodas.

Burma is generally booked as a two- or three-day "extra" on a trip to the more popular destination—adjoining Thailand.

Bhutan

Slightly to the east of Nepal and separated from it only by a thin strip of India, lofty Bhutan [boo-TAHN] is known as the "Land of the Thunder Dragon." A country of unspoiled beauty, it's been open to outside tourists only since 1974 and even now, relatively few tourists visit; the government charges visitors high daily fees and no independent travel is allowed. The awesome Himalaya make Bhutan a major destination for treks and mountain climbing.

Paro (PBH), the gateway to Bhutan, is home to monasteries and museums. The capital of Bhutan, **Thimphu**, is the folk-cultural center, with many ancient structures and good crafts shopping. Parts of Bhutan offer spectacular views of the Himalaya. Not surprisingly, the country offers great trekking opportunities.

The Burmese celebrate New Year's by throwing buckets of water on one another.

A *dzong* is a fortress-monastery.

Nepal

Imagine the most stunning and prodigious mountain range you can. It's likely that you'll be imagining the Himalaya of Nepal. The northern region of this country is perhaps the prime trekking and mountain-climbing destination in the world: This is the land of **Mt. Everest**, the world's tallest peak (29,028 feet). Special permits may be necessary for some of the excursions here, so be sure to check with the Ministry of Tourism. Southern Nepal is merely hilly and, thus, more populous. There has been unrest here, which may worry some travelers, so check for government advisories.

Kathmandu (KTM) is the capital, the main hub for treks, a place of dozens of little architectural, historical, and religious gems. Tourists generally use **Durbar Square** as a hub to visit the city. Near Kathmandu is **Bhaktapur** (also known as Bhadgaon), a cultural arts center. It was built in the twelfth century and has retained many temples, monasteries, and palaces.

Pokhara is the base for treks beginning on the Himalaya's **Annapurna Range**. In the lowlands, **Chitwan National Park** is a popular wildlife preserve, with such rare animals as Royal Bengal tigers and one-horned rhinos. The warm weather and jungle scenery here lend themselves ideally to safaris and rafting excursions. **Tiger Tops** is the area's most famous base camp.

Edmund Hillary and Tenzing Norgay were the first to climb to the top of Mt. Everest.

Tradition states that Buddha was born in Nepal.

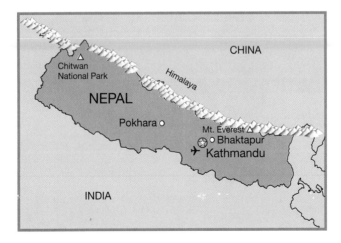

India

India is second only to the United States in the length of its road systems.

The seventh-largest country in the world, India is one-third the size of the United States. It's also the world's second-most populated nation, with over a billion people—more than three times that of the United States. The most populous area of India is the fertile plains around the sacred **Ganges** [GAN-jeez] **River**; this lies below the Himalaya, which anchor the northern border in spectacular fashion. India is a beautiful, mystical land of splendor, exotic culture, and heart-rending poverty. It's located south of China, bordered on the west by the Arabian Sea and on the east by the Bay of Bengal. The island-nation of Sri Lanka (formerly called Ceylon) rests off its southern tip.

New Delhi, the capital, anchors northern India; it's the main gateway, with flights arriving at **Delhi Indira Gandhi International Airport** (DEL). Near the northeast coast is **Kolkata** (formerly Calcutta) (CCU), a major city with a significant port. **Mumbai** (formerly Bombay) (BOM), on the west-central coast, is another important port and a fairly cosmopolitan city. The country is serviced by **Air India** (AI), the national airline, as well as by North American and international carriers.

March through May is a dry and often uncomfortably hot period in India, whereas June through September is the notorious monsoon rain season. It's most comfortable to visit from October to February: The climate in the south ranges from tropical daytime temperatures in the mid-80s to the mid-60s at night. The more mountainous north runs about 25 degrees cooler. The Himalaya, of course, can get quite cold. Of the 22 official languages, Hindi is the national language, though English (an associate official tongue) is common in business and government; more than 1,500 recognized dialects are spoken across India.

Important Places

Where do old cruise ships go when they're decommissioned? They get run aground in India's Alang Beach, where they're taken apart for their valuable metal to be reclaimed.

Many travelers are attracted to India by some of the world's most historical cities and the Himalaya. Among the country's principal destinations is New Delhi, which is actually made up of the old city of Delhi and a more modern development. Its seventeenth-century **Red Fort** was built under order of Shah Jahan, who was responsible for creating the Taj Mahal. New Delhi has many landmark mosques, tombs, and temples. One important memorial—to Mahatma Gandhi—is **Raj Ghat**; it marks the spot where he was cremated.

Two essential **excursions** out of New Delhi are:

- **Agra**, home of the **Taj Mahal**—considered by many to be the world's most beautiful building. This exquisite memorial was built by Shah Jahan for his wife. Most people visit it at sunrise *and* at sunset, because it looks very different in different light conditions. (Also, it's much less crowded at sunrise.) For those who take the time to look beyond the Taj, Agra also has some other fine sights, including the **Agra Fort complex**. From New Delhi, Agra is 30 minutes by plane or about three hours by car.

- **Jaipur**, called the "Pink City" for the color of stone used here. Forts and hills circle the city. **Hawa Mahal** (Palace of the Winds) is in fact no more than a facade with nearly 1,000 windows. The **Amber Fort**—one of Jaipur's principal attractions—impressively overlooks the city. Visitors can ride up to the fort on an elephant.

India's other major destinations are:

- **Varanasi**, also known as Benares. Pilgrims walk down steps (called *ghats*) to cleanse themselves in the holy waters of the Ganges. Each night an impressive "Sacred Light Ceremony" takes place. It's well worth seeing. Varanasi is the center of the Hindu religion in India; many sacred temples grace the city.

- **Kolkata** (Calcutta), the nation's second-largest city. For all its importance, this major port city is painfully squalid. It's not a prime tourist destination, but there are some fine museums, gardens, mansions, markets, and memorials.

- **Chennai** (Madras), on the southeast coast. The first British settlement was here, at **Fort St. George**. The city is also of major Christian and Hindu importance, with temples, palaces, and religious sites. Outside the town are a number of ancient temples.

- **Goa**, a somewhat different sort of Indian destination. Once a Portuguese colony, it's now a tropical beach resort that has a very cosmopolitan feel. The climate is extremely pleasant—even the monsoon season in Goa is relatively mild.

- **Mumbai** (Bombay), the country's business center. Impressive sixth-century cave temples carved into rock can be found on **Elephanta Island**, reached by ferry.

Mumbai is home to the "Bollywood" film industry, which produces more feature films than anywhere else in the world. (The name *Bollywood* is a combination of Bombay and Hollywood.)

The Taj Mahal is almost 400 years old
Photo by Justus Ghormley

- **Ajanta** and **Ellora Caves**; these famous stone carvings lie about 200 miles to the northeast of Mumbai. At Ellora, 34 impressive shrines are cut out of the rock. One cave, filled with carvings, covers twice the area of Athens's Parthenon and took 100 years to complete.
- **Udaipur**, a lovely city where gracefully detailed palaces line a lake.
- **Wildlife reserves**, with some of the rarest creatures in the world. You can book safaris in any number of lush, exciting parks. The most famous: **Kaziranga National Park**. For over 35 years, India has funded "Project Tiger," a conservation program to protect the endangered tiger. Visitors can see these big cats at many sites throughout the country.

Sales Considerations

India is a large country and its culture (and, especially, the poverty) seems challenging to many; as a result, escorted tours (which help buffer tourists) or cruises are excellent options. In addition, you should upsell hotel accommodations, because the alternative can often lead to unpleasant experiences. There's even the possibility of staying in a converted palace. Several luxurious train trips are available. The wildlife here is unique and presents an interesting alternative to the traditional African safari areas. India will also attract religious pilgrims, bargain-seekers, lovers of early culture and history, and those fascinated by philosophy and mysticism. The people of India are very friendly and welcoming to tourists.

One other point: Sri Lanka (an island-nation south of India that has suffered some political turmoil) and the Maldive Islands (coral islands to the southwest that are a common cruise port of call on the way to Africa) are attractive tropical destinations whose tourism industries have shown considerable growth.

Pickled ginger is the most popular pizza topping in India, squid in Japan, and eggs in Australia.

The word *serendipity* comes from the Muslim name for Sri Lanka.

Travel Trivia

Questionable Menu Items

- "Pork with Fresh Garbage" (Vietnam)

- "As for the tripe served you at the Hotel Monopol, you will be singing its praises to your grandchildren as you lie on your deathbed." (Polish tourist brochure)

- "Chopped up cow with a wire through it (shish-ke-bob)." (Athens hotel)

- "Muscles of Marines/Lobster Thermos" (Cairo)

- "Buttered Saucepans and Fried Hormones" (Japan)

- "Sweat from the Trolley" (Europe)

- "Dreaded Veal Cutlet with Potatoes in Cream" (Europe)

- "Fried Friendship" (Nepal)

- "Beef Rashers Beaten Up in the Country Peoples Fashion" (Poland)

- "Cold Shredded Children & Sea Blubber in Spicy Sauce" (China)

- "French Fried Ships" (Cairo)

- "Roasted Duck, Let Loose" (Poland)

- "Teppen Yaki—Before Your Cooked Right Eyes" (Japan)

- "Goose Barnacles" (Spain)

- "Toes with Butter and Jam" (Bali)

NAME _____   **DATE** _____

MAP ACTIVITY

A traveler wants to visit the places listed below. Which number represents each on the map?

Place/Attraction	In Which Country?	Number on Map
A. Mt. Everest	A. _____	A. _____
B. Bali	B. _____	B. _____
C. Elephanta Island	C. _____	C. _____
D. Taipei	D. _____	D. _____
E. The Gobi Desert	E. _____	E. _____
F. The Taj Mahal	F. _____	F. _____
G. Seoul	G. _____	G. _____
H. Kuala Lumpur	H. _____	H. _____
I. Taroko Gorge	I. _____	I. _____
J. Manila	J. _____	J. _____

NAME _____   **DATE** _____

CASE STUDY

Sandra Durant, in her mid-30s, has wanderlust and enjoys going on adventurous trips by herself. This year she has her sights set on about three weeks in Southeast Asia—Malaysia, Indonesia, perhaps the Philippines, and Singapore. Cost is important to her. The flight over is expensive enough and she'll be looking for bargains along the way. But then, she's always felt that roughing it is the best way to see any country.

Circle the answer that best suits their needs.

1 Which of the following services could you recommend?

First-class air tickets   A side trip to Thailand

An escorted safari   Deluxe hotel rooms

Why?

2 Sandra plans to be on the go for most of her trip, but she wants to find one destination in the area where she can stop and spend a bit more time. Where might you suggest?

Tahiti   Fiji

Bali   Bora Bora

Why?

3 Of the following sites, which would *not* be appropriate for you to recommend that Sandra visit?

Borobudur   The Taj Mahal

Batu Caves   Banaue Rice Terraces

Why?

4 Which of the following tips should you suggest?

Lodging may be challenging.   Bring a sweater for the chilly nights.

Convenient transportation is available. There are major trekking opportunities throughout.

Why?

NAME _____ **DATE** _____

CREATIVE ACTIVITY

You work for ACME Cruise Lines, which has decided to inaugurate an 18-day cruise of Asia and the Pacific. The cruise, which will be targeted to culture-seekers, begins in Hong Kong at 7 P.M. Your job: to propose an itinerary that will call on at least four ports (you may end the cruise at any port). List the ports you've chosen, indicate what happens each day, and be prepared to justify your itinerary. Remember that the ship shouldn't cruise a distance between ports that would take longer than three days. The ship is capable of speeds of 20 to 25 mph. Note also that cruise lines usually like to have their ships depart in the early evening and arrive in the early morning so they sail as much as possible at night. (Try to give projected departure and arrival times.) You may have the ship stay at a port for several days or have it merely arrive at a port in the morning and leave that same evening. You may wish to study cruise line brochures to get a few ideas.

Day 1: Embark

Day 2

Day 3

Day 4

Day 5

Day 6

Day 7

Day 8

Day 9

Day 10

Day 11

Day 12

Day 13

Day 14

Day 15

Day 16

Day 17

Day 18

NAME _____ DATE _____

PUTTING IT ALL TOGETHER

The Matching Game

Below is a list of cities, attractions, and so on, some of which we have covered, some of which we haven't. There are all manners of connections among them. With a group of fellow students, you have exactly 10 minutes to come up with as many connections as possible. (Items may be used more than once.) Write your answers below. Note: There are at least 20 possible connections. For example, Yangtze and Li—both are rivers.

Himalaya	Tahiti	Maldives
Lhasa	Katherine	Great Dividing Range
Japan	Queenstown	Yangtze
Wellington	Canberra	Nepal
Noumea	Vietnam	New Caledonia
Li	Coral	Southern
Darwin	Murray	Palace on Wheels
Brunei	Tonga	Alice Springs
Thailand	Overlander	Kuala Lumpur
Beijing	Micronesia	Gold Coast
Taroko	Phuket	Indian Pacific
Blue	Rotorua	Volcano
Chuuk	Shanghai	Western Samoa

Appendix A

Average Length of Stay—Leisure Travelers

The following is a list of major cities and approximately how long the average tourist stays in each (including, perhaps, one day trip) and assuming a leisurely pace. Remember that some visitors may wish to fully explore that city's attractions. Although a city may require only one day to see, a traveler may need two nights' lodging in that city.

City	Number of Days	City	Number of Days	City	Number of Days
Acapulco	3–4	Fairbanks	1–2	Nairobi	1–3
Amsterdam	2–3	Florence	2–4	Nashville	1–2
Anchorage	1–2	Frankfurt	1–2	New Orleans	2–3
Athens	2–3	Geneva	1–2	New York	3–5
Atlanta	1–2	Guadalajara	1–2	Newport, RI	1–2
Atlantic City	1–2			Niagara Falls	1–2
Auckland	1–2	Helsinki	1–2	Nice	2–3
		Hong Kong	2–4		
Baltimore	1–2	Honolulu (Waikiki)	3–5	Orlando	3–5
Banff	1–2	Houston	1–2	Osaka	1–2
Bangkok	2–3			Oslo	1–2
Barcelona	2–3	Istanbul	1–2	Ottawa	1–2
Beijing	3–4	Jerusalem	2–4	Paris	3–5
Berlin	2–3	Kyoto	1–3	Philadelphia	1–2
Boston	2–3			Phoenix	1–2
Brisbane	2–3	Lancaster, PA	1–2	Portland, OR	1–2
Brussels	2–3	Las Vegas	2–3	Puerto Vallarta	2–3
Budapest	1–2	Lima	1–3		
Buenos Aires	1–2	Lisbon	1–3	Quebec City	1–2
Cairo	1–2	London	3–5	Quito	1–2
Calgary	1–2	Los Angeles	3–5	Rio de Janeiro	2–4
Cancun	3–4	Madrid	2–3	Rome	3–4
Chicago	2–3	Marrakech	1–2	Rotorua	1–2
Christchurch	1–2	Mazatlan	2–3	St. Petersburg, Russia	1–2
Copenhagen	2–3	Melbourne	1–2	Salt Lake City	1–2
Cuzco	1–2	Memphis	1–2	Salzburg	1–2
Dallas	1–2	Mexico City	2–3	San Antonio	1–2
Denver	1–2	Miami	2–3	San Diego	2–3
Dublin	1–2	Milan	1–2	San Francisco	2–3
Edinburgh	2–3	Montreal	2–3	Santa Fe	1–2
Edmonton	1–2	Moscow	2–3	Savannah, GA	1–2
		Mumbai (Bombay)	1–3	Seattle	1–2
		Munich	2–3		

City	Number of Days	City	Number of Days	City	Number of Days
Seoul	2–3	Tokyo	2–3	Washington, D.C.	3–5
Stockholm	1–3	Toronto	1–2	Wellington, NZ	1–2
Sydney	2–3	Vancouver	1–2	Williamsburg, VA	1–2
Tampa/Clearwater	2–3	Venice	2–3	Zurich	1–2
Tangier	1–2	Vienna	2–4		

Appendix B

Research Resources

The following resources are available in various formats: print and online.

- *The Weissmann Reports* has plenty of information on virtually every destination in the world, both well-known and obscure. The *Weissmann Reports* gives sample itineraries, food and shopping tips, plus all the basics, too.

- *The World Travel Guide*, an essential research tool, gives enormous detail—including information for business travel—about virtually every nation on earth; its color layout is impressive.

- *The Star Service* analyzes hotels across the world in extreme detail. *The Hotel and Travel Index* (HTI) gives information on thousands of hotels.

Travel guidebook series include the following:

- *Fodor* and *Frommer* are fine all-purpose guides. These publishers also have created separate, more specialized lines of guides.

- *Berlitz Pocket Guides* manage to compress an amazing amount of detail into their compact books.

- *The Lonely Planet* series takes a somewhat counterculture look at places that many other guidebooks neglect.

- *Access* and *Michelin Green Guides* stress history, art, and architecture. Their beautiful graphic presentation makes them especially easy to consult.

- *Insight* and *Eyewitness Guides* also examine the history and culture of a destination, but with the added benefit of high-quality color photographs.

- *The Let's Go, Rough Guide, Time Out*, and *Moon* series treat the particular needs of student, budget, younger, and independent travelers.

- *Tourist Attractions & Events of the World* is a unique compendium of the world's most popular sites. It gives not only useful descriptions but also opening times, admission fees, and addresses.

- *The Destination Specialist* series, created by the Travel Institute, is an admirable group of texts that focus on destinations.

- *The CIA World Factbook*, published by the Central Intelligence Agency, is a little-known print and online resource that contains a wealth of information. In addition to travel information, it gives statistics on a wide variety of topics.

- **Travel trade magazines** and **tourist bureau** materials are often excellent sources of up-to-date information. In addition to search engines, website addresses for most country and many regional tourist bureaus can be found at www.towd.com.

- **Health and political advisories** are regularly issued by the U.S. State Department. You should consult them whenever foreign travel is involved. The website also gives background information and travel tips for each country.

Appendix C

Destination-Related Feature Films

Sometimes the ambience of a place is just around the corner at your neighborhood video store. Below is a selection of films that capture the essence of—or even spoof—their locations. Historical films are, for the most part, excluded. Those rated "R" are indicated accordingly.

Baltimore, MD	*Diner* (R)	North Dakota	*Fargo* (R)	France (Paris)	*French Kiss*
The Catskills, NY	*Dirty Dancing*	Pennsylvania	*Witness* (R)	France (Paris)	*An American in Paris*
California	*Sideways* (R)	Dutch Country		France (Paris)	*Charade*
(Wine Country)		San Francisco, CA	*Bullitt*	France (Paris)	*Gigi*
Hawaii	*Blue Hawaii*	San Francisco, CA	*Vertigo*	France (Riviera)	*To Catch a Thief*
Hawaii	*Hawaii*	St. Louis, MO	*Meet Me in*	Greece (Crete)	*Zorba the Greek*
Hawaii	*Hawaiians*		*St. Louis*	India	*Heat and Dust* (R)
Hollywood, CA	*The Player* (R)	Washington, DC	*All the*	Ireland	*The Quiet Man*
Hollywood, CA	*Sunset Boulevard*		*President's Men*	Ireland	*Ryan's Daughter*
Hollywood, CA	*The Day of the*	Australia and	*Crocodile Dundee*	Italy (Assisi)	*The Assisi Underground*
	Locust (R)	New York City		Italy (Florence)	*A Room with a View*
Las Vegas, NV	*Viva Las Vegas*	Austria	*The Sound of Music*	Italy (Rome)	*La Dolce Vita*
Las Vegas, NV	*Leaving Las Vegas* (R)	Austria (Vienna)	*The Third Man*	Italy (Rome)	*Two Weeks in*
Las Vegas, NV	*Honeymoon in Vegas*	Bermuda	*The Deep*		*Another Town*
Los Angeles, CA	*L.A. Confidential* (R)	Botswana	*The Gods Must Be Crazy*	Italy (Rome)	*Roman Holiday*
Los Angeles, CA	*L.A. Story*	Brazil (Rio)	*City of God* (R)	Italy (Venice)	*Don't Look Now* (R)
Los Angeles, CA	*Chinatown* (R)	Canada	*The Black Robe* (R)	Italy (Venice)	*Summertime*
Los Angeles and	*Annie Hall*	Canada	*Canadian Bacon*	Jamaica	*Dr. No*
New York		Canada	*The Fast Runner* (R)	Japan (Tokyo)	*Lost in Translation* (R)
Miami, FL	*Miami Rhapsody* (R)	China	*Shoes of the Fisherman*	Kenya	*Out of Africa*
Miami, FL	*Miami Blues* (R)	China	*The Last Emperor*	Kenya and Rwanda	*Gorillas in the Mist*
New Orleans, LA	*A Streetcar*	England (London)	*Notting Hill*	Morocco (Casablanca)	*Casablanca*
	Named Desire	Europe	*National Lampoon's*	Scotland	*Braveheart* (R)
New Orleans, LA	*The Big Easy* (R)		*European Vacation*	Wales	*The Englishman Who Went Up a*
New York City	*Manhattan*	France (Paris) and	*A Little Romance*		*Hill But Came Down a Mountain*
New York City	*The Age of Innocence*	Italy (Venice)			
New York City	*On the Town*	France (Paris)	*Paris When It Sizzles*		
New York City	*After Hours* (R)	France (Paris)	*How to Steal a Million*		
New York City	*Cocktail* (R)				
New York City	*The Out of Towners*				

Index